INTERNATIONAL CUISINE

Join us on the web at

www.culinary.delmar.com

INTERNATIONAL CUISINE

Jeremy MacVeigh

DELMAR
CENGAGE Learning™

Australia • Brazil • Japan • Korea • Mexico • Singapore • Spain • United Kingdom • United States

International Cuisine, First Edition
Jeremy MacVeigh

Vice President, Career and Professional
Editorial: Dave Garza

Director of Learning Solutions: Sandy Clark

Acquisitions Editor: James Gish

Managing Editor: Larry Main

Product Manager: Nicole Calisi

Editorial Assistant: Sarah Timm

Vice President, Career and Professional
Marketing: Jennifer McAvey

Marketing Director: Wendy Mapstone

Marketing Manager: Kristin McNary

Marketing Coordinator: Scott Chrysler

Production Director: Wendy Troeger

Production Manager: Stacy Masucci

Senior Content Project Manager: Glenn Castle

Art Director: Bethany Casey

Technology Project Manager: Christopher
Catalina

Production Technology Analyst: Thomas Stover

For product information and technology assistance, contact us at
Professional & Career Group Customer Support, 1-800-648-7450

For permission to use material from this text or product,
submit all requests online at **www.cengage.com/permissions**
Further permissions questions can be e-mailed to
permissionrequest@cengage.com

Library of Congress Control Number: 2008924153

ISBN-13: 978-1418049652

ISBN-10: 1418049654

Delmar
5 Maxwell Drive
Clifton Park, NY 12065-2919
USA

Cengage Learning products are represented in Canada by Nelson Education, Ltd.

For your lifelong learning solutions, visit **www.delmar.cengage.com**

Visit our corporate website at **www.cengage.com.**

Printed in the United States of America
5 X X 10

CONTENTS

PREFACE

INTRODUCTION

International Cuisine was written to supply culinary arts students and enthusiasts with a reference and resource to the cuisines of the world. Chefs today are bombarded with information about foods that come from all over the world, and their understanding of where food products come from and how to use them has never been more important or more challenging. One of the most difficult things for a culinarian, future chef, or food lover to grasp is a sense of the place that a food comes from. All foods can be unraveled into a story that enlightens us about why they are made the way they are or perhaps why certain ingredients must be used for them to taste authentic. The understanding of this story is the biggest hurdle an aspiring chef in today's food industry must undertake. After learning the techniques of how to be a good cook in the kitchen, a chef must acquire the ability to write a themed menu or to pair ingredients when developing new recipes; these tasks are intrinsically linked to the past and to the people and places that created the ingredients. This text is a step in making the link.

WHY I WROTE THIS BOOK

The text was written because of a lack of resources currently available in this specific discipline. I took a position teaching international cuisine; when I looked for textbooks to use to support the learning objectives of the class, I discovered that what was available lacked information about how cuisines differ and how they developed, or the texts just covered a few cuisines or simply provided recipes. I began to write my own outlines because of this lack of information and eventually took on the project of creating this book. This text answers the questions that I had—and does so for 18 different cuisines that span the globe.

To the students reading this text as part of your education, my advice would be to immerse yourself in the culture of that which you strive to inhabit. If the culture you strive to inhabit is the culinary arts, then immerse yourself in it fully by tasting everything you can, absorbing every bit of advice, watching every aspect of what your instructors do and how they act, and being focused on this moment and nothing else. Our trade is one in which success comes from sacrifice. You will be tired, you will feel broken, and you will think that you have pushed yourself too far; but in the end, you will grow, you will be proud, you will earn the respect and admiration of others, and you will realize that you would not have reached the level that you have if you had decided—years earlier—that it was too much or it wasn't coming fast enough or it wasn't fair. By becoming engrossed in what you want to do, your senses will expand and enable you to do things you didn't know you could. I wish each of you the kind of daily satisfaction I have been afforded as part of our proud profession.

ORGANIZATION

The text is organized by geographical region (Europe, Asia, etc.). Within each section are chapters that cover how each cuisine developed, what it is that makes each cuisine different from the rest, important culinary subregions found within each cuisine, recipes common to that cuisine, and terms that are commonly used. In creating this text, we found—from having industry experts review the material—that there was a strong desire to have a text like this published, but that the experts wanted a section on what made each cuisine different from the others. As a result, a section in each chapter discusses the unique components of the cuisine being covered, and I believe the experts were just that—experts—in making this suggestion, as this helps to clarify how and why each cuisine is original. Each chapter includes the following sections:

Introduction

Historic Culinary Influences

Unique Components

Significant Subregions

Recipes

Summary

Review Questions

Common Terms, Foods, and Ingredients

ANCILLARY MATERIALS

For Instructors

Instructor's Manual to Accompany International Cuisine
Each chapter is further supported by an Instructor's Manual.

For Instructors and Students

Online Companion to Accompany International Cuisine
An Online Companion is provided to supply additional resources for the instructor and the students; it includes test bank questions, PowerPoint slides, and additional recipes.

CONCEPTUAL APPROACH

The chapters begin with the Middle East because many of the characteristics of civilization that led to our ability to have distinct cuisines began here. The rest of the chapters in Section I move mainly from east to west across southern Europe, then north through Europe, and end with the Iberian Peninsula. The Iberian Peninsula provides an appropriate transition to northern Africa in Section II, and then to the Americas in Section III, because all of these regions are linked in both history and cuisine. After traveling through Europe, North Africa, and the Americas, Section IV focuses on Asian cuisines. A number of countries are not represented in this text, including all of the sub-Saharan African countries, Australia, and many more. Although it would be great to include these, and others, creating a book that covers the cuisines students are most likely to deal with in the United States was the priority. The hope is that, by opening the door to this subject, students (and others) will be encouraged to step inside the world of global cuisine (and culture) and discover more on their own. The subject is complex and vast, but this book is designed to make it approachable and usable for culinary programs.

THE RECIPES

The recipes chosen for the text are representative of the cuisine of each region and are mostly made using either common ingredients or those that can be obtained by a culinary arts school or at specialty markets. Many of the recipes include accompanying photos of the completed dish, and photos for some of the steps of the more complicated or unique preparations can also be found in the text.

The recipes are in no way a complete representation of the cuisine of the region covered, as each region that has a chapter dedicated to it in this text could easily fill many volumes on its own. The recipes are meant to provide a glimpse into the cuisines by introducing some of the more common, practical, or unique recipes that will help students and others gain an entry into this vast subject. Additional recipes are available from the companion site, and surely many instructors will want to supplement the material presented in this text with recipes that they are more familiar with. All recipes include details about the cooking methods employed in creating them and the expected yield. As with any other recipe, remember that these are guides; variation in products will always necessitate occasional adjustments to compensate for moisture contents, degree of flavor, palate differences, and so forth. One should always use one's senses when cooking.

ABOUT THE AUTHOR

JEREMY MACVEIGH is a chef instructor at the Culinary Arts Campus of the Institute of Technology in Roseville, California, where he has taught classes in international cuisine, nutrition, garde manger, Asian cuisine, and baking and pastry for the last five years. Originally from Needham, Massachusetts, Chef MacVeigh got an early introduction to the life in the culinary field; his first job, at the age of 15, was in a kitchen—and the introduction stuck. As a graduate of the Western Culinary Institute in Portland, Oregon, and with a BS in food science from the University of California at Davis, Chef MacVeigh brings a unique perspective from both the scientific and artistic aspects of the field to this subject. A member of the American Culinary Federation (ACF), Chef MacVeigh has been very active in the Sacramento chapter as a board member of the California Capitol Chefs Association for the last three years, and as a Team Sacramento coach for the student culinary team.

ACKNOWLEDGMENTS

Wow, where to start? First, I wouldn't be the type of person who would try to do something like write this text if it were not for my mom! Setting examples, always being supportive, holding the weight of a family of seven on her shoulders without ever letting any of us know it was hard, and simply the greatest person I have ever known—that is my mom. I know I'm lucky, and now you do too! Thanks, Mom! My siblings also have always been there to lend support and to check in on their little brother over the years, and I am forever grateful to have such great brothers and sisters: Matt, Heather, Shauna, TJ, Mike, and Kathy are the best six siblings I can imagine. I also have those six to thank for a posse of 21 nephews and nieces, all of whom are a true joy to be with.

I also would not be in this position had it not been for all of the professionals I have worked with over the years, instilling in me a deep sense of pride, passion, and respect for our craft. I would like to thank the crew at North Hill in Needham: Chef Frank, Chef Karl, Dr. Ken Gerweck, David Maw, and the rest of the staff, who initiated my sense of being at home in the kitchen when I was 15. Also, special thanks to Steve Feeley, Nick and Angelo Catenza, Peter Keenan, Katherine Bliss, John Bays, Patrick Mulvaney, Rick Mahan, John and Rebecca Lastoskie, Amy Zausch, Andrew Hillman, Pete Treleven, and Steve Kipgen (Kip), for their work ethic and for sharing their knowledge and heart in a way that always made me know I was where I should be.

Many teachers, professors, and friends have left an impression on me or helped keep me headed in a positive direction over the years, and I would like to thank them for doing so. Friends like Russell Blake, Dan Connors, Ted Cosgrove, Ted Olson, Mr. G., and Chris Moore are hard to come by, and I'm forever grateful I did. I had a number of excellent instructors at Sacramento City College, including Ken Naganuma, Sue Roper, and Ramona Fernandez. I also was lucky enough to attend the University of California at Davis and have instructors like Dr. Charles Bamforth and Michael O'Mahony. To all of you, a sincere thanks!

My current colleagues at the Culinary Arts Campus of the Institute of Technology (IT) in Roseville, California, have also been instrumental in providing me with their expertise and support. I would like to thank chefs Don Dickinson, Charlin Wright, Megan Bailey, Rika Mullen, Mark Powell, Robert Mason, Jacob Knutte, Jared Fondrest, and Sandra Colver for sharing their expertise over the years. I also would like to thank Robert Enger, Tamara Marsh, Ashley Weech, Jason Sowa, Margaret Pilgard, Laura Goodson, Todd Lardenoit, Richard Melella, Rick Wood, Jim Haga, and the rest of the staff of the Institute of Technology for their support during my time with the school.

One person at IT has had a particularly big impact on my entry into education, and subsequently this book: Chef Philippe Caillot (I know, I know—he's French!), whose understanding of and passion for the culinary arts have been an inspiration to me (and he has more than once set me straight on French cuisine!). Thanks, Philippe. In addition to the great colleagues I've been privileged to work with I would like to give the sincerest of thanks to all of my former and current students. You've all impacted me in helping me understand culinary arts more than you know (I try not to let on!) and your enthusiasm and passion for our craft is inspirational to all of us instructors. I feel confident about and look forward to the future being in a position to watch the future pass through our doors. What a thrill to see minds and hearts headed in our direction!

I would also like to thank Chef Edward G. Leonard, CMC, for his professional work in directing the production of the food for the photos; Ron Manville, for his expert photography; Patricia Osborn, for her tireless assistance and guidance in writing this text; Chris Downey, for making my rambling legible; and all those at Cengage Learning for their professional work on this project.

Last, but certainly not least, I have had someone at my side supporting me, giving up movie nights together, eating dinner at 11:00 p.m. when I finally get back, and always encouraging me to keep plugging away at this project, and for that I am forever grateful. Anna, you're a constant light in my life, and I hope you never burn out!

Any comments or suggestions about the text will happily be accepted by e-mail at jmacveigh@sbcglobal.net.

Sincerely,
Jeremy MacVeigh

The author and Delmar Learning would especially like to thank the following people for their contributions to making this book a success:

Food Stylist and Recipe Tester
Chef Edward G. Leonard, CMC

Photographer
Ronald Manville

Reviewers

Robert Dahni
Dahni Inc.
El Segundo, CA

Tom Beckman
Chef Instructor
The Cooking and Hospitality Institute of Chicago
Chicago, IL

Bruce Konowalow, CCE
Director of Culinary Arts
Schoolcraft College
Livonia, MI

Joe LaVilla, PhD, CCC
Assistant Academic Director, Culinary Arts
The Art Institute of Phoenix
Phoenix, AZ 85021

Jim Taylor, MBA, CEC, AAC
Chef Instructor
Columbus State Community College
Columbus, OH

Jay Demers
Department Chair
Eastern Maine Community College
Bangor, ME

Jerry Lanuzza, MS Ed, FMP
Department Chair, College of Culinary Arts,
Johnson & Wales University
Charlotte, NC

Master Chef George Karousos
President
International Institute of Culinary Arts
Fall River, MA

SECTION 1

CUISINES OF
EUROPE AND THE MIDDLE EAST

To most Americans, the cuisine of Europe is the most familiar of those covered in this text, because most of the familiar foods of the United States have roots somewhere in Europe. On the other hand, the cuisine of the Middle East is often much less familiar. We have combined these cuisines in this section because much of Europe's cuisine originated in the Middle East. Wheat was first cultivated in the Middle East, and bread is now perhaps the most common food on the tables of European countries. The fermentation of beverages is believed to have been discovered and developed in the Middle East, and beer and wine now appear regularly on the tables of most Europeans. The three most common religions in Europe, along with their dietary restrictions and customs, developed in the Middle East; today, the religions of Christianity, Islam, and Judaism all are represented in Europe (Christianity is the most prevalent, but the others are still significant in some cultures).

One facet that binds the Middle Eastern and European regions together is the importance of wheat in their diets and cultures. Bread has been a basis of European nutrition for centuries, and other wheat-dependent products are common as well. Products like pasta and pastry dough, in particular, are two common and widespread uses of wheat flour. Pastry dough is one of the ingredients that

helps make the cuisine of these regions different from other parts of the world, specifically with regard to the making of desserts. Although sweet foods are eaten in other cultures, the idea of an entire course of sweets—as in the dessert tradition of many European countries—is unique to this region. In other parts of the world, sweets fit into the meal cycle differently and are more typical of what most would think of as a snack. Europe is also unique in that it was, for a period of history, the major power center of the world; as such, its countries held considerable influence over many other parts of the world. The culinary habits of much of Europe have evolved relatively rapidly over the last few centuries, and exploration, colonization, and immigration have all influenced the culture and culinary habits of these populations. During the same period of time in the Middle East, cultural change has been much less dramatic. The preservation of culture has remained a priority for the people of this region, and there have been fewer attempts by Middle Eastern nations to expand into or colonize other regions of the world.

Europe and the Middle East are home to a number of ingredients that are used regularly in other parts of the world, although their origin in this part of the world may not always be recognized. Some ingredients indigenous to Europe and the Middle East include the aforementioned

wheat as well as pine nuts, pistachios, walnuts, artichokes, asparagus, cardoon, cauliflower, caraway, cumin, broccoli, peas, common cabbage, Brussels sprouts, horseradish, watercress, melons, oregano, and mint. Many of these still play important roles in the local cuisine.

Although the cuisines of Europe and the Middle East have evolved over the years, they will forever be connected by their histories. This book begins with a chapter on the Middle East, an appropriate starting point because this region is considered the genesis of many aspects of cuisine (as well as civilization itself). We will travel from east to west, through the southern reaches of the Middle East and Europe, in this section. Then we will move north and east, and finish with one of the southernmost points, the Iberian Peninsula—a natural point from which to move on to African cuisine in our next section.

Although many of these cuisines may be familiar to people in the United States, it is very important for those aspiring to understand today's cuisines of the world to know how these cuisines differ and how they developed into what they are now. The following chapters will reveal many of the aspects that make each of these cuisines unique from one another, as well as how these cuisines have influenced our own in this increasingly global culinary marketplace.

CHAPTER 1

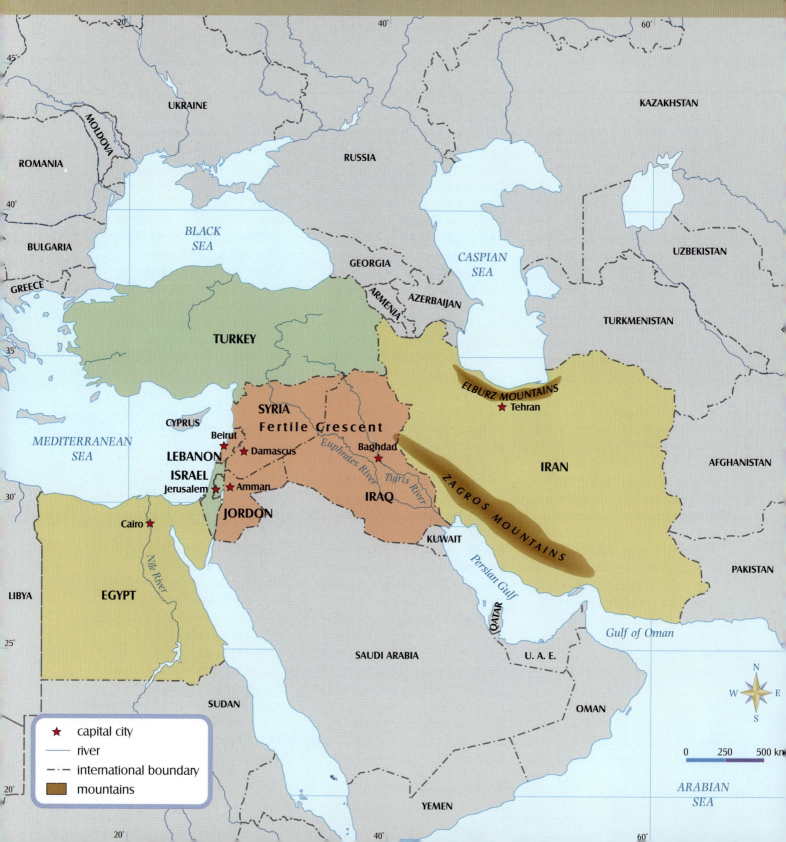

ROMANIA

MOLDOVA

UKRAINE

RUSSIA

KAZAKHSTAN

BULGARIA

BLACK SEA

GEORGIA

CASPIAN SEA

UZBEKISTAN

GREECE

ARMENIA

AZERBAIJAN

TURKMENISTAN

TURKEY

ELBURZ MOUNTAINS

★ Tehran

CYPRUS

SYRIA

Fertile Crescent

MEDITERRANEAN SEA

Beirut ★

★ Damascus

LEBANON

ISRAEL

Baghdad ★

Euphrates River

Tigris River

IRAN

AFGHANISTAN

ZAGROS MOUNTAINS

Jerusalem ★

★ Amman

IRAQ

JORDON

Cairo ★

KUWAIT

Nile River

Persian Gulf

PAKISTAN

QATAR

LIBYA

EGYPT

Gulf of Oman

N
W · E
S

SUDAN

SAUDI ARABIA

U. A. E.

OMAN

★	capital city
---	river
-·-·-	international boundary
▨	mountains

0   250   500 km

ARABIAN SEA

YEMEN

OBJECTIVES

Upon completion of this chapter, you will be able to

- explain what makes the cuisines of the Middle East unique.
- discuss the significance of religion in the cuisines of the Middle East.
- understand common cooking methods used in traditional Middle Eastern cuisines.
- recognize common recipes found in the cuisines of the Middle East.
- produce a variety of recipes common to the Middle East.
- define the terms listed at the conclusion of the chapter.

INTRODUCTION

The cuisines of the Middle East are historic, because they have remained heavily dependent on traditions and methods from early cultures that flourished in this part of the world long ago. These cuisines have, to a large extent, resisted many outward influences while blending components of the dominant cultures within this region over the centuries. Whether it be the Persian (present-day Iran) cuisine that has drifted all the way to Europe, the Ottoman (present-day Turkey) cuisine that has found a home throughout the Mediterranean and beyond, or the spread of Arab traditions throughout North Africa and into Southern Europe, Middle Eastern cuisines have left an indelible mark on most of the world at some point in history, and the qualities that instigated this spread are the same that have preserved it.

This chapter examines the cuisine and culture of this region by focusing on the regions within this large area that have played the most significant role in both the local cuisine and the influences that have spread from it. A number of countries that are usually included in this region are not cited in this chapter simply because there is not enough space to do so. Certainly, entire books can be—and have been—written specifically about the cuisine of the Middle East.

The Middle East has long been a region of turmoil, both politically and religiously. The significance of the religions that exist in this region—Judaism, Islam, and Catholicism are all represented—cannot be overstated in either the context of its historical events or the development of its cuisines. Currently, the dominant religion in the area is Islam, and this faith has much to do with the similarities found in the cuisines of the Islamic nations. All of the countries examined in this chapter are Islamic nations, with the exception of Israel and (to some extent) Lebanon, which has a sizable Christian population. Other factors besides religion certainly are important in the development and uniqueness of the cuisines found here—climate and resources are significant ones, for example—but all evaluations of these cuisines should be viewed within the context of the religious beliefs of the culture as well.

What many may be surprised to learn is that the Middle East is the birthplace of much of what is taken for granted in parts of the Western world today. This chapter will examine some of the contributions the Middle East has made to other cultures, and it will examine some of the most significant influences other cultures have had on this region as well. The culinary variations within this region are also examined, as are some common recipes.

HISTORIC CULINARY INFLUENCES

Throughout history, the Middle Eastern countries have spread their influence in the culinary field during periods of conquest and invasion. The crusaders who descended on this region during the Middle Ages brought some of their own traditions with them, and they stayed in some areas for nearly 200 years. As the crusaders returned to Europe, they brought with them the culinary influences they had experienced during their time in the Middle East. Muslim armies occupied Spain and Sicily for hundreds of years before, throughout, and after the Crusades. Following the expulsion of the Arab armies from Spain, the Spanish exported many culinary techniques and ingredients to the Americas (having been influenced themselves by the Middle Eastern peoples). Throughout these periods, the customs and cuisines of the Middle East spread across much of the world.

Although Middle Eastern cuisines undoubtedly have left their mark on many other countries, the development of these cuisines was also influenced by other cultures. The following section examines the more distinct of these influences, including some that are interregional.

Ancient Greece

Some of the earliest influences on the development of Middle Eastern cuisine came from the Greek incursions into this area during Greece's rise as a civilization. The ingredients that were consumed in the Middle East during this period include cucumbers, melons, leeks, onions, garlic, lentils, fava beans, garbanzo beans, olives, figs, grapes, dates, almonds, and walnuts. The Greeks spread many of these ingredients deeper into the Middle East than their native range, and they took these ingredients back home with them.

Persian and Roman Empires

As the developing empires of the Persians and Romans battled for control of the lands of the Mediterranean, many of the dishes that are now common first developed. The Roman Empire provided expertise in the spread of agriculture; it was the early power in the region after the decline of the Greeks. The Romans are largely credited with providing the structure and experience in irrigation that allowed not only the spread and greater yield of local indigenous produce but also the inclusion of new foods from distant lands in the local crops. This increased productivity and food wealth assisted in the development of more sophisticated cuisines, such as those that evolved with the Persian Empire.

The Persian royalty began a tradition of enormous feasts that included such familiar foods as *polou* and *chelou* (two primary methods of Iranian rice cookery), *dolmas* and *kebabs* (techniques acquired from Turkish nomads), marzipan and stuffed dates, and the use of ingredients such as yogurt, quinces, and honey. This period also saw the development of the sophisticated and artful use of spices and fine rice cookery in early Persian cuisine, which is still a hallmark of the cuisine of Iran to this day. Some of the early spices used by the Persian Empire include cinnamon, cloves, nutmeg, and mace from the Indonesian islands, and cumin, coriander, and fennel from the Mediterranean. The production of some of the finest long-grain rice— along with the precise method of cooking it—has given Persian/Iranian rice cookery much of its lofty reputation.

The Emergence of Islam

Prophet Mohammed of Arabia died in the year 632, and his followers began the spread of the Islamic faith. The Islamic Empire went on to include all of the Middle East, northern Africa, much of western Asia, Spain, Sicily, and parts of Eastern Europe at the height of its power. During this period, many of the ingredients common to the Middle East began to work their way into the cuisines of Europe and Asia. Sugar traveled from India into Europe; rice extended from India into parts of the Middle East that weren't already using it (Iran, Syria, and Iraq grew it already) and into Europe (specifically, Spain). Ingredients that made their way from the conquered lands into the Middle East included dried and salted fish, honey, and hazelnuts from Eastern Europe; cheeses, wine, chestnuts, and saffron from the Mediterranean countries; and spices such as pepper, ginger, cardamom, cinnamon, cloves, nutmeg, and mace, which spread further out from their rooted homes in Persia.

The result of the spread of Islam was not unlike the later discovery of the Americas in the respect that ingredients, recipes, and techniques from conquered lands flowed into and out of the Middle East. Events such as these cause confusion and debate about the origins of many dishes that, over time, are adopted and often renamed in many new locations. From a culinary perspective, everyone won, as is often the case following any period of unrest and invasion since the introduction of new ideas and techniques improves the cuisines for all.

The other culinary significance of this empire was the impact that the dietary guidelines or laws that are part of the Islamic faith have had on the diets of its followers. Similar to the Jewish faith, which also had many followers in the region during this period, Muslims who observed their faith with vigor abstained from eating a number of foods that were common in other Mediterranean cultures at the time. Many Muslims avoided pork, shellfish, and alcohol, which was a notable difference between themselves and the Christians in the region. This influence remains one of the dominant features of Middle Eastern cooking, as most Middle Easterners are Muslim and thus followers of the Islamic dietary edicts.

Ottoman Empire

After the fall of the Islamic Empire, a new empire emerged in the region: the Ottoman Empire. Like the Islamic Empire before it, this empire also stretched into Asia and Europe during its height of power. It left a lasting impression on these lands, and it felt their influence as well.

The Ottoman Empire was based in present-day Turkey and included most of the present-day Middle East, as well as parts of Eastern Europe, northern Africa, and western Asia. This vast empire spread many of its customs and culinary traditions into these lands, and it also brought a number of new ingredients and other culinary aspects into Turkey and beyond.

Some of the Turkish culinary contributions that spread with the Ottoman Empire include the simmering of foods in meat broths, the soup-making tradition, the stuffing of foods (for example, grape leaves), and the honey-soaked pastries for which the Turkish pastry chefs are renowned. These customs became common throughout the Middle East and beyond during this period, and many of the customs of other countries that the Ottomans ruled over flowed into Turkey as well.

During the reign of the Ottoman Empire, the city of Constantinople (present-day Istanbul) developed into a site of grand culinary feasts and banquets. The rulers of the empire and the nobility held well-documented events that included hundreds of dishes and greatly impressed visiting guests from Europe and other countries. Many of the dishes found in the descriptions of these events are enjoyed in countries throughout the Middle East today and are embraced as part of this complex cuisine that so many call their own.

UNIQUE COMPONENTS

The cuisines of the Middle East differ from cuisines that are common in the United States in a variety of ways. These cuisines are ancient and strongly influenced by the history, religion, and cultural identities that unite and divide the populations of the Middle East. The following section highlights some of the distinct components of these cuisines.

Influence of Religious Edict

Religious beliefs in the Middle East have had a dramatic affect—more than in most other places—on the diets of the population. Whether this entails the avoidance of pork, alcohol, or any improperly slaughtered animal for a Muslim; the periods of fasting for a follower of the Jewish faith; or the period of avoidance of meat during the Lenten months for a Christian, religion reigns strongly in this region of the world.

The major religion in this region today is Islam; its followers are known as Muslims. In the Muslim faith, a number of food edicts exist that greatly influence the dietary choices of faithful followers. Followers are required to avoid pork, carnivores, alcohol, birds of prey, improperly slaughtered animals, and blood, unless their life is threatened by such avoidance (such as by starvation or forced feeding). All of these foods are considered *haram* (prohibited) and thus are avoided by strict followers of the faith. On the other hand, Muslims are also encouraged by these edicts to eat other foods that are considered *halal* (permitted), but to eat only for survival and health—self-indulgence is considered haram. Halal foods include all plant foods, cattle, sheep, goats, camel, venison, rabbits, and seafood. Muslims are also highly regarded for their generous hospitality, as it is considered a responsibility not only to welcome a stranger into your home but also to feed that stranger. These edicts are followed by a large part of the population, and in many ways they not only define the cuisine but also are a significant factor in defining the people.

Israel was formed after World War II to provide a homeland to the millions of displaced followers of Judaism, commonly called Jews. Those who are faithful to the Jewish faith also follow a number of edicts with regard to food that play a significant role in their dietary choices. The Jewish faith has many of the same edicts as the Muslim faith, with some notable exceptions. The dietary laws or edicts of Judaism are known as the laws of *kashruth*. These laws are some of the most complex dietary restrictions in the world, and a strict observer follows a custom that ties him or her to religious brethren from thousands of years ago.

The laws of kashruth exclude a number of foods from the diet and associate many foods with particular celebrations and other religious days or periods. The foods that are to be excluded include pork, shellfish, fish without scales, crustaceans, birds of prey, animals that prey on animals or that don't "chew the cud," blood, and improperly slaughtered animals. In addition, milk and meat cannot be eaten together; thus, dairy and meat are not combined. There are also many foods connected with religious holidays, as well as foods that are eaten on the Sabbath (Saturday), that tie followers to their faith in culinary matters.

The avoidance of pork, shellfish, and nonkosher foods is perhaps the most noted and distinct difference from the diets of many Europeans and Americans, but the observance of religious periods throughout the year—and the foods that are associated with those periods—are of equal significance, and diverge from what is commonly practiced in many other parts of the world.

History

This region has made some of the most important contributions to the culinary world. It was here that agriculture is believed to have originated in the eastern world, bread was first produced, beer was first fermented, yogurt was accidentally made, and the three major religions and their dietary restrictions originated. The historic importance of this region to the religions of Islam, Judaism, and Christianity have made this region home to many of the strictest followers of those religions,

and thus to the dietary habits that accompany close adherence to the edicts of these religions.

The history of this region is part of its very core and identity. The people who live here proudly follow the steps of their ancestors and resist the modernization that has occurred in many other parts of the world. There are many examples of foods that are eaten for the observance of religious days or as part of an annual or life ritual, and this history is often visible at the table. This connection with the past is a strong part of both the character and the culinary habits of the inhabitants of this storied region.

Balance of Sweet and Sour

The cuisines of the Middle East often display a skillful art of combining sweet and sour components that balance the acidity of one with the sweetness of another, to allow the aromas of each to be highlighted. This unique combination spread from this part of the world, as the Persian and (later) the Ottoman empires spread across Europe and Asia. Many classic European dishes display these combinations, perhaps as a direct result of the influence of the Middle East.

Some examples of the sweet ingredients commonly used are figs, dried apricots, dried currants, peaches and pears, sugar, *dibs* (reduced grape juice), pomegranate molasses, and other syrups. Some of the sour ingredients common to these cuisines include sumac, pomegranate seeds, dried limes, lime and lemon juice, and *verjuice* (unripe grape juice). Many of these sweet-and-sour components are found in a number of preparations in Middle Eastern cuisine, including in many meat dishes, a characteristic that often helps to identifty foods from this region. These contrasting elements are used with great skill in these cuisines, and the unique combinations can be seen in many dishes—from rice dishes to stews and even desserts.

Baking, Simmering, Stewing, and Fire Roasting

The cooking methods most common to the cuisine of the Middle East include baking, simmering, stewing, and fire roasting. Historically, much of the cooking in the Middle East has been done over an open fire or fire source or in a communal oven, and these methods are employed in the majority of methods from this region.

Today, foods are often cooked in an oven at home, although in many rural parts of the Middle

East, the communal oven is still in use. Bread is included with each meal, and this baking tradition has lent itself to the many slow-simmered stews and braised dishes that can be cooked using the same heat source used to bake the bread.

The outdoor fire pit that was so common to nomadic herdsmen—from whom the ancestors of these areas originated—is still a part of the cuisine today. Many kebabs and fire-roasted eggplant dishes that are common to Middle Eastern cuisine hark back to the days of the Turkish tribes and other nomads that roamed these parts in ancient history.

Wheat and Rice: Grains of Life

Rice and wheat make up the majority of the diet within this region. Wheat is grown extensively throughout the Middle East, and rice is grown in pockets where ample water is found in more localized regions, Iran in particular. Bread is the most common starch used in the Middle East, and it plays an important role in the daily meal patterns of most homes. Flatbreads are used as a utensil in the typical meal, and as such they are part of most meals.

Bread is sacred in the Middle East; a piece of bread dropped on the ground will surely be picked up by the next passerby, who will place it out of harm's way while reciting a prayer. Many varieties of bread are found here, but most of them are yeast-leavened flatbreads that accompany every meal. Wheat is also used in the form of bulgur and couscous in many parts of the Middle East.

Rice has similar importance in the parts of the Middle East where it is the focal point of most meals. In parts of Iran and Turkey, rice is used to make the famous polous, chelous, and *pilafs* that these countries are known for around the world. The preferred rice in these countries is aromatic long-grain rice, which is often replaced with *basmati* when these dishes are made in the United States. The varieties that are grown in the Middle East differ from those available in the United States, as very little of the highest grades of rice in the Middle East ever make it out of the countries in which they are grown (mostly Iran). Some of the highest-prized rice varieties in Iran are *ambar-boo, darbari,* and *sadri,* and these are usually sought out to make polou and chelou dishes.

Spices

The Middle East's position between Asia and Europe has played a significant role not only in the development of this region and its role in many conquests throughout history but also in that it became the route through which spices from the Orient traveled to Europe.

Spices from India, Indonesia, and China all passed through the Middle East in a lucrative trade with European countries that occurred for hundreds of years before being circumvented by the Portuguese (to some degree) when they discovered a sea route around Africa in the late fifteenth century. Prior to this time, and continuing after it at a less feverish pace, the countries of the Middle East were permeated with such spices as cinnamon, nutmeg, cloves, peppercorns, tamarind, ginger, turmeric, and mace, which traveled in large caravans across the region. Not surprisingly, the people of the Middle East became experts on how to use these spices over time, and the incorporation of many spices into the cuisine of the Persian Empire and, later, the Ottoman Empire cemented the use of these spices in the dishes of the Middle East. These spices are mixed with the spices indigenous to the area, which include fennel, coriander, and cumin, resulting in a taste that has long been appreciated by visitors from other countries. The use of these spices, along with the spices of the Americas that were introduced later (chiles and allspice being the most significant), has resulted in many spice blends common to Middle Eastern cooking today.

SIGNIFICANT SUBREGIONS

The Middle East has been home to some of the greatest empires, as well as some of the greatest internal unrest. Although borders have shifted and countries' names have changed, with regard to cuisine the Middle East consists of the following four major regions.

Persia/Iran

Iran is home to one of the most storied and historic of all of the cuisines of the Middle East, because the Persian Empire—which rose to prominence before the modern calendar—developed one of the first great cuisines. This cuisine has had a major impact on the development of the cuisines of all of the other Middle Eastern countries and beyond.

Iran is situated between the Persian Gulf and the Gulf of Oman to the south and the Caspian Sea to the north, with Iraq and Turkey along its western border and Pakistan, Afghanistan, and Turkmenistan along the border to the east. Because of its location between the other Middle Eastern countries, and as the gateway to Asia, Iran has long been a strategic country that has influenced—and been influenced by—these neighbors in all matters.

Iran is a mountainous country; the large Zagros Mountains run along the western border with Turkey and Iraq, and down along the Persian Gulf. Another mountain range called the Elburz Mountains, which ring the shores of the Caspian Sea, dominates the northern portion of the country. The central region of Iran is dominated by a vast semi-arid interior plateau, which is used primarily as pasture for sheep and goats.

The northern section of Iran is the most populated and also the most fertile, with significant production of citrus, pistachios, wheat, sadri rice (similar to basmati), melons, eggplants, and other vegetables. This region has a temperate climate and receives a significant amount of moisture in the mountains, which provides irrigation to the valleys below. In this region, a long tradition of fishing produces some of the world's finest beluga caviar from sturgeon from the Caspian Sea.

The southern section of Iran is considerably more arid and has a warmer climate than the north; production of dates and citrus is more significant in this region. The Persian Gulf and the Gulf of Oman provide a significant amount of seafood, including swordfish, tuna, and shrimp, which are caught in abundance when the stocks are healthy (wars have had a significant effect on fisheries here).

The cooking of Iran in many ways still resembles that of the ancient Persian Empire, with rice dishes such as polou and cholou still adorning tables, accompanied by kebabs and eaten by hand with breads like *lavash* and *barbari*. The tradition of making fine pastries like *baklava* and freezing cordials to make *sharbat* (sherbet) is also a consistent part of Iranian cuisine.

Iranian cuisine has been held in high regard for centuries for the quality of the rice dishes created here; the expertise in baking and pastry, including breads and fine sweetmeats that have spread from Iran into the rest of the Middle East and Greece; the expertise in combining meats with sweet and sour ingredients; and the deft touch in using the many spices that have traveled across this land from Asia on their way to Europe.

Turkey

Turkish cuisine really includes two main cuisines under one roof: the classic Ottoman cuisine that developed with the great Ottoman Empire during the Middle Ages and beyond, and the significantly different Anatolian (central Turkey) and eastern Turkish cuisines, which have greater ties to Arab neighbors. Of these different styles, the Ottoman culinary contributions are clearly more significant in terms of influence over other subregions included in this chapter. The Ottoman Empire once incorporated nearly all of the Middle East and beyond, and during its reign it developed a level of sophistication and a culture of lavish feasts that have rarely been replicated anywhere in the world.

Geographically, Turkey is often referred to as the gateway between the east and the west, as Turkey borders Europe in the west and the Middle East and Asia in the east. Turkey is a large country that separates the Mediterranean Sea and the Black Sea, as well as bordering Greece and Bulgaria in the western part of the country, and Georgia, Armenia, Iran, Iraq, and Syria in the eastern part of the country. The northern, eastern, and southern sections of Turkey are mountainous, whereas the western portion mostly consists of valleys surrounded by the waterways that connect the Black and Mediterranean seas. Turkey is a fertile country, with significant portions of its land used to raise crops of hazelnuts, olives, grapes, figs, sugar beets, wheat, and citrus. With multiple seas on its borders, Turkey is also provided with abundant catches from these waters; swordfish, tuna, turbot, bonito, and anchovies are a few of the prized catches.

The Ottoman Empire began its rise in Turkey in the thirteenth century and continued to rise in prominence and influence during the following centuries. In its grandest years, during the eighteenth century, elaborate banquets were held in the capital of Constantinople (present-day Istanbul). During this time, the court cuisine of the empire included a virtual army of chefs and cooks creating a large variety of specialties that are still common today, as well as in many countries that were encompassed by the empire. Some of the specialties that were made during this period include kebabs, *sherbets*, pilafs, jams, and soups, as well as many types of *halvas*. The Ottoman influence and style includes a penchant for stuffing foods, such as dolmas and stuffed eggplant or peppers, as well as a great tradition of pastries.

On the other hand, the nomadic inhabitants also contributed greatly to the cuisine of the Middle East with their practice of grilling foods over a fire with metal skewers (kebabs) and their production of yogurt. Yogurt is believed to have been discovered and popularized by the nomadic people of eastern Turkey, who also are credited with the introduction of kebabs (the term is Persian, but the method is believed to have been popularized by Turkish tribesmen). The cuisine of the central and eastern portions of Turkey tends to be spicier and more rustic, and it relies heavily on the use of wheat—mainly in the form of bread and bulgur (*burghul*)—lamb, yogurt, and pulses, of which lentils and chickpeas are the most common.

With its contributions from both the Ottoman Empire and some of the nomadic herdsmen, Turkey has had a major influence on the cuisine of not only the Middle East but many other parts of the world as well.

Israel

Israel was created as a homeland for displaced Jews after World War II, and in culinary and cultural terms it is quite different from the other countries of the Middle East. The creation of Israel as a Jewish homeland contrasts its population sharply with that of its neighbors, all of which have a majority population of Muslims. The population of Israel also is made up primarily of immigrants who returned to their native land from all over Europe, the Middle East, Africa, Asia, and the Americas. Both the religious differences and the role of immigrants (and the cuisines that they brought with them) play a significant role in making this cuisine unique from the others in the Middle East.

Two main branches of Judaism have resulted from the periods of Jewish migration out of the Middle East. Because of the significant amount of migration throughout history of followers of the Jewish faith, the Jewish culture developed very differently depending on what part of the world the followers lived in. A general delineation of these groups based on where they lived includes Sephardi Jews and Ashkenazi Jews. The followers who migrated into Eastern Europe, Russia, and the Caucasus are known as Ashkenazi Jews. The other groups, known as Sephardi Jews, are those who once settled in India and other Asian countries, northern Africa, Middle Eastern countries, Spain, and southern Italy. The significant difference between these two groups is that most of the countries in which the Ashkenazi Jews settled were Christian countries that, for the most part, persecuted the Jews when they lived there, whereas the Sephardi Jews lived in mostly Muslim countries (Spain and parts of Italy were once under Arab rule) and were more accepted by the Muslim populations than were their relatives in the Christian world. Because of these differences, the two groups have very divergent cuisines; both groups are represented in present-day Israel in major proportions (the Sephardi Jews are a slight majority).

Ashkenazi Jews have many culinary traditions that mirror the lands they lived in, including *borscht*, *goulash, knishes,* potato *latkes,* and *gefilte.* The Ashkenazi adopted the food customs of the European and Asian countries they immigrated to, making adjustments to some of the foods to follow the dietary edicts of kashruth, such as replacing pork with poultry when making schnitzels. There were (and still are) significant numbers of Jewish immigrants in Germany and Russia, as well as in eastern and central European countries, and those who immigrated to Israel brought the food customs of these countries with them.

In the case of the Sephardi Jews, the culinary customs are much different; these groups have developed primarily alongside Muslim men and women. The Sephardi Jews came from other countries in the Middle East, as well as North Africa and India. Their culinary practices are much like those of the Middle East, with dishes such as *tabbouleh, falafel, hummus, baba ghanoush,* polou, and other classic Middle Eastern dishes serving as mainstays of their diet as well.

The cuisine of Israel is one of constant evolution, because of the influences from these two main groups of Jews and the many countries from which they have come. In many ways, this development mirrors that of the United States, where significant immigrant populations contribute to creativity and an abundance of styles. These groups of immigrants also are coming to learn to understand and appreciate the cultures and specialties of one another, resulting in a cuisine of inclusion that inspires chefs as they form a culinary identity.

The Fertile Crescent and Egypt

The area known as the Fertile Crescent includes the countries of Iraq, Jordon, Syria, and Lebanon. These countries, along with Egypt, have similar culinary customs. The Fertile Crescent is regarded by many as the cradle of civilization, because historical evidence indicates that settled communities with complex social structures began here. Egypt is also a region with an ancient history, and the ancestors of this country played important roles in the development of its early cuisines as well.

The Fertile Crescent is so named because humans are believed to have first cultivated wheat and domesticated sheep here; it may also have been the first region to develop a written language. The methods of using olives to extract oil and grapes to make wine are also believed to have been a part of very early forms of civilization in this region.

Similarly, Egypt is well known as the birthplace of both bread and beer, two techniques that forever changed the course of humankind. Leeks, onions, okra, and fava beans all were indigenous to this region, and their incorporation into the cooking of the ancient Egyptians can still be seen there today.

These regions are steeped in history; without their important developments, much of what we know as food today wouldn't exist. The Fertile Crescent and Egypt share a common religion, Islam, and have many of the same culinary practices as well. In the Fertile Crescent, bread is a part of every meal (usually one of the many styles of Arab flatbreads, and often seasoned with *za'atar*, a spice blend); in Egypt, bread is also a staple and is likely to be flatbread called *battawa* and probably seasoned with fenugreek. Sweets such as halvas (sweetmeats) are common in both regions, as is the use of bulgur (called burghul).

There are some important differences among these regions, as well. In the Fertile Crescent, the use of rice in dishes such as pilafs and lamb in dishes such as *kibbeh* (lamb and bulgur paste), or in making fillings such as *hashwa* (seasoned lamb and rice), is more common. In Egypt, couscous is a very common use of wheat, and pulses such as fava beans (called *fool* or *ful*) and lentils make up a more significant part of the diet.

With regard to climate, this region is now mostly arid desert that relies heavily on irrigation to produce the local crops. The exception to this is the fertile valley in southern Iraq that surrounds the rivers of the Euphrates and Tigris and the region of the Nile River in Egypt. These river valleys produce many of the fruits and vegetables for these countries, including citrus, pomegranates, squashes, beans, olives, grapes, and stone fruits. The more arid regions are turned over to grain crops such as wheat, millet, and barley for raising sheep, as well as the production of dates, which were once (and still are for small groups of nomadic people) a food relied on for sustenance.

These countries have developed what is often referred to as an Arab cuisine that is steeped in history and religious culture. Great respect is given to the generations that came before, and the customs that are passed on from one generation to the next are followed with pride and skill. In this region, the cuisine is considered an important aspect of historic identity.

RECIPES

The following recipes provide an introduction to the cuisines of the Middle East by revealing some of the more common and significant types of food found in this region. Many more recipes could have been included in this section, and further exploration of this cuisine will yield additional recipes that—together with these—make up these storied cuisines.

Baharat MIDDLE EAST
(SPICE BLEND)

As in many other cuisines, spice blends are commonly used in Middle Eastern recipes. This blend provides the typical flavor profile of many Arab dishes and works well for a number of recipes, including the preserved lamb fat recipe in this chapter.

YIELD: 1/3 cup

COOKING METHOD: Dry Toasting of Whole Spices

INGREDIENTS

1 Tbsp	Whole Black Peppercorns
2 tsp	Whole Coriander Seeds
1 Tbsp	Whole Cumin Seeds
1/2 tsp	Whole Cloves
1 tsp	Cardamom, ground
1 tsp	Cinnamon, ground
1 tsp	Nutmeg, ground
2 tsp	Limu, ground (dried Persian lime, also called *loumi*; if unavailable, dried lime zest can be used as a replacement)
1 Tbsp	Paprika

PROCEDURE

1. In a small sauté pan, toast the whole spices over a low flame until the spices become fragrant.
2. Once fragrant, remove them from the heat and allow them to cool at room temperature. Transfer the spices to a spice mill with the other ingredients, and grind to a smooth mixture.
3. Store in a tightly covered container in a cool, dry, and dark place until use.

Za'atar MIDDLE EAST
(MIDDLE EASTERN SPICE BLEND)

INGREDIENTS

3	oz	Sesame Seeds, toasted
2	oz	Shallots, minced
1	tsp	Salt
2	oz	Sumac
4	oz	Extra Virgin Olive Oil
1.5	Tbsp	Fresh Thyme, minced
1.5	Tbsp	Fresh Oregano, minced
2	Tbsp	Fresh Parsley, minced

This spice blend is common throughout the Middle East, where it is used to season flatbread dipped in olive oil and as a seasoning mixture in recipes. This is a wet version in which fresh herbs are used and are emulsified with olive oil, yielding a somewhat different version of the Middle Eastern classic. The traditional za'atar is made by crushing dried herbs between the hands, sifting the resulting powder, and combining it with sumac and crushed sesame seeds to yield a dry and coarse mixture that can be used.

YIELD: 12 ounces

MIXING METHOD: Emulsion Using Mortar and Pestle

PROCEDURE

1. Using a pestle, crush the sesame seeds until they turn into a paste.
2. Add the shallots and salt to the mortar, and continue to grind ingredients until a paste is formed.
3. Add the sumac to the mortar, and slowly grind the sumac into the shallot/sesame paste while slowly drizzling in the extra virgin olive oil.
4. Once all of the olive oil has been incorporated, mix in the minced herbs and grind slightly more to draw out some of the flavors of the herbs into the paste. Store the unused za'atar in a well-sealed container, away from heat and light, when not being used.

Za'atar MIDDLE EAST
(MIDDLE EASTERN SPICE BLEND)

INGREDIENTS

1	oz	Sesame Seeds
1	oz	(by weight!) Dried Oregano
1/2	oz	(by weight!) Dried Thyme
1.5	Tbsp	Sumac, ground
1	Tbsp	Kosher Salt

This version of the popular spice blend is more like the traditional one found in most Middle Eastern homes; it is used to season the flatbread that is common throughout the cuisines.

YIELD: 1 cup

CRUSHING METHOD: Hand Crushing and Sieving

PROCEDURE

1. Preheat oven to 325°F.
2. Place the sesame seeds in the oven, on a baking sheet, and bake for 3 to 4 minutes or until seeds just begin to color. Remove the sesame seeds from the oven, and set them aside to cool.
3. Make sure that the dried herbs being used are good quality and have a nice, strong aroma. If they are old and smell musty or are unidentifiable, discard them and start with newly dried herbs.

(continues)

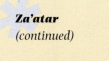

Za'atar
(continued)

4. Crush the herbs using clean, sanitized, and dry hands over a drum sieve or a sifter set over a mixing bowl to catch the sifted/sieved particles.

5. Pick up all of the particles that do not sift through the sieve or sifter and crush again, using your hands, until most or nearly all of the herb pieces have been sieved or sifted.

6. Combine the sumac and salt with the crushed herbs, and add the now-cooled and toasted sesame seeds to the mixture; mix well.

7. Store any unused za'atar in a tightly sealed container in a cool, dry place.

Qawrama   SYRIA, LEBANON, AND IRAQ
(PRESERVED LAMB FAT)

INGREDIENTS

8	oz	Lamb Stew Meat (or trimmings from other cuts)
2	lbs	Lamb Fat (fat taken from racks, trimmed from legs or other fat, can be used to replace the tail fat from the Middle Eastern variety)
1	Tbsp + 1 tsp	Kosher or Sea Salt
1	tsp	Freshly Ground Black Pepper
2	Tbsp	Baharat Spice Blend

Qawrama is a common cooking medium in both vegetable and meat dishes in Arab cuisine, and it provides a unique flavor to dishes. In the Middle East, the species of sheep commonly used are varieties that have very thick and fatty tails—the tails are used to make this fat. A significant amount of salt is used in making this, to assist in preservation, which needs to be taken into consideration when this fat is used. This fat can be used to cook lamb kafta or any of the many meat and dried fruit stews that are common to Middle Eastern cuisine; it provides additional flavor and texture.

YIELD: 1 to 1.5 pounds (depending on rendering and trimmings used)

COOKING METHOD (MEAT TRIMMINGS): Searing

COOKING METHOD (LAMB FAT): Slow Rendering

PROCEDURE

1. Heat a heavy-bottomed pot or pan over a medium-high flame until hot, and add the lamb stew meat or other trimmings to the pan, along with a small amount of the lamb fat. Sear over the heat until the meat pieces are well browned all over.

2. Turn the heat down to a low flame and add the remaining lamb fat. Render the fat very slowly to extract as much liquid fat from the trimmings as possible (this will take at least 2 hours).

3. Once it appears that all of the fat has been rendered, add the salt, black pepper, and baharat, cover the pot or pan, and continue to cook over a very low flame for an additional 2 hours (can also be transferred to an oven set at 200–225°F for this period).

4. Once the mixture has cooked for a total of at least 4 hours (a couple hours longer is fine), remove the pot or pan from the oven or stove, and strain the fat through cheesecloth and into a storage container. Set aside to cool.

5. Once cooled, this fat can be kept covered in a cool, dark place for a least a few months (just check to make sure there is no water in the bottom of the container, which will hasten spoilage).

Dibs Rim'an LEBANON/SYRIA
(POMEGRANATE MOLASSES)

INGREDIENTS

24		Pomegranates, seeds removed and retained
1	qt	Water
12	oz	Sugar
4	oz	Lemon Juice

There are several types of pomegranates in the Middle East, and some of the sour varieties are used to make a thick syrup that is used to season a variety of dishes, including combinations with eggplant and *muhammara*, a seasoned walnut paste that is enjoyed with flatbread in Lebanon.

YIELD: About 3 cups

COOKING METHOD: Slow Simmering/Poaching

PROCEDURE

1. Remove the skin of the pomegranates, and remove the majority of the white membrane that separates the segmented seed sections within the pomegranates.

2. Place all of the seeds into a pot just large enough to hold them, with only a couple of inches above the seeds (to the rim of the pot).

3. Add the remaining ingredients to the pot, and place the pot over a medium flame to bring the mixture to a gentle simmer.

4. Once the mixture reaches a gentle simmer, turn the heat down to a very low flame to very slowly reduce the mixture, pressing occasionally with a slotted spoon or potato masher to force the juice from all of the seeds.

5. Continue to cook over a low flame for 2 hours, and then remove the pot from the stove. Strain the contents through a fine china cap into a smaller pot, pressing all of the seeds to extract as much liquid from them as possible.

6. Once all of the liquid has been captured, return it to the stove and bring it back to a gentle simmer over a medium-low flame. Continue to reduce until the mixture begins to thicken slightly and reaches a temperature of 200°F.

7. Remove from heat once the temperature reaches 200°F, place in sterilized jars, and immediately put on lids.

8. Allow the jars to sit upright for 2 minutes, and then turn them upside down to sterilize them. The pomegranate molasses can be stored at room temperature until opened, at which time it will need to be refrigerated.

Torshi Limu IRAN/PERSIA
(PICKLED LIMES)

INGREDIENTS

4	lbs	Limes (about 20 limes)
1.5	qts	Distilled Vinegar or White Wine Vinegar
8	oz	Kosher Salt

These Persian specialties are a common accompaniment to many common Persian dishes, such as polous and kebabs, and they are pretty easy to make. Use seedless limes, and only make these during drier months of the year to prevent potential spoilage.

YIELD: Two 1-quart Jars (about 3 pounds of finished limes)

(continues)

Torshi Limu
(continued)

PRESERVATION TECHNIQUES: Salting, Air Drying, and Final Preservation in Acidic Vinegar

PROCEDURE

1. Using a grating tool, grate off all of the green zest of the limes by rubbing them against the grater; set the zest aside.

2. Combine the zest from the limes and the vinegar, and transfer this to a couple of mason jars or another suitable storage container; set aside in a refrigerator until the limes are ready (at least a few days).

3. Once all of the limes have had their zest removed, roll the limes in the kosher salt until they are completely covered. Transfer them to a stainless steel or aluminum wire drying rack, and allow them to sit for 20 minutes.

4. After the limes have sat for 20 minutes, roll them again in the salt so that they are liberally covered, and then set the rack either outside in the sun (protected from pests by netting or cheesecloth but still exposed to open air through the cloth) or in a very warm, dry room to allow the limes to dry completely. This may take a number of days (the amount of time needed to cure the limes will depend on the humidity and the temperature of the ambient air). The limes should be dry and hard to the touch.

5. Once the limes are dried out, brush the excess salt from the surface of the limes and pack them into the two 1-quart mason jars or other suitable storage containers that contain the lime-zest–infused vinegar.

Taratoor   MIDDLE EAST
(SESAME SAUCE)

INGREDIENTS

1	oz	Garlic Cloves, minced
1.5	tsp	Salt
14	oz	Tahini Paste
6	oz	Lemon Juice, chilled
12	oz	Cold Water

This versatile sauce is common throughout the Middle East, where it is used as a dip for fried foods, as a seasoning in other recipes, and to accompany fish.

YIELD: 1 quart

MIXING METHOD: Emulsification by Whisking

PROCEDURE

1. Using a mortar and pestle, combine the salt and garlic cloves and turn to a paste by grinding.

2. Transfer the garlic/salt mixture to a mixing bowl and add the tahini paste.

3. Using a whisk, beat in the lemon juice and then slowly beat in the cold water—a small amount at a time—to yield a thick, creamy sauce.

Crushing the garlic with salt for the first step of the Taratoor sauce

Finished Taratoor sauce; note the consistency

Baba Ghanoush   ARAB COUNTRIES
(EGGPLANT PURÉE WITH SESAME AND LEMON)

INGREDIENTS

3	lbs	Eggplant
2	oz	Olive Oil
4	oz	Taratoor sauce (see recipe)
5	oz	Lemon Juice
.5	oz	Garlic Cloves, minced
1	Tbsp	Salt
3	oz	Extra Virgin Olive Oil
		Salt and Taratoor, to taste

This well-known vegetable purée is often served as a starter as part of a *mezze* table and is common in all of the Arab countries of the Middle East, where eggplants are held in high esteem.

YIELD: 3 pounds

COOKING METHOD (INITIAL): Fire Roasting

COOKING METHOD (SECONDARY): Oven Roasting

PROCEDURE

1. Preheat oven to 325°F.
2. Using a sharp paring knife, pierce each of the eggplants 4 or 5 times, in various places on each.
3. Coat the outside of the eggplants with the olive oil (not the extra virgin).
4. Place a metal skewer through each of the eggplants and char all over, over an open flame (you can use burners on the stove or open fire for this step).
5. Place the charred eggplants on a sheet pan, and put them in the preheated oven. Bake for 15 minutes or until eggplant becomes soft throughout.
6. Remove the eggplant from the oven and, once it is cool enough to handle, remove the charred exterior; place the interior on a cutting board, and mince to a pulp.
7. Transfer the pulpy interior to a mixing bowl, and mash in the taratoor sauce, lemon juice, minced garlic, salt, and extra virgin olive to form a purée.
8. Adjust seasoning, if necessary.

Fool Mudammas   EGYPT
(MASHED AND SPICED FAVA BEANS)

INGREDIENTS

1	lb	Dried Small Fava Beans (called *fool misri*), soaked overnight
1	oz	Garlic Cloves
1.5	tsp	Salt
1	tsp	Fresh Dill, minced
1	Tbsp	Fresh Parsley, minced
2	Tbsp	Tahini
2	oz	Lemon Juice
4	oz	Extra Virgin Olive Oil
		Salt, Tahini, and Lemon Juice, to taste

Fool mudammas is a very popular Egyptian breakfast dish that is eaten throughout the Middle East today. The type of fava bean (also called broad bean) that is used to make this has a brown skin and is smaller than the typical dried fava bean found in the United States. Look for smaller fava beans, if possible, and serve with a flatbread and olive oil.

YIELD: 2.25 pounds, or 8 portions (4–5 ounces/portion)

COOKING METHOD: Simmering

PROCEDURE

1. Drain the soaking beans and place them in a small pot; cover with fresh water, by a couple of inches, and bring to a boil over high heat.

(continues)

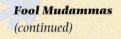

Fool Mudammas
(continued)

2. Once the beans come to a boil, reduce the heat to a gentle simmer and continue to simmer beans until they are tender throughout (the amount of time will depend on the size of the beans).

3. Once the beans are cooked through, drain them and transfer to a mixing bowl; set aside.

4. Using a mortar and pestle, crush the garlic and salt together to form a paste.

5. Once a paste has been formed, mix in the minced herbs and tahini, using a spoon to combine.

6. Mash some of the cooked beans by pressing them with the tines of a fork while also working in the garlic and tahini paste from the previous step.

7. Stir the lemon juice into the beans, and slowly drizzle in the olive oil while mixing to fully incorporate it.

8. Taste the mixture and adjust seasoning, if necessary; serve warm with flatbread.

Three common Middle Eastern preparations, clockwise from upper left: baba ghanoush, tabbouleh, flatbread with no topping, and fool mudammas, and all served on flatbread

Ta'amia or Falafel Egypt
(Spiced Fava Bean Fritter)

Ingredients

2	lbs	Dried, Skinless Fava Beans
1.5	Tbsp	Cumin Seeds, whole
1	Tbsp	Coriander Seeds, whole
2	oz	Garlic Cloves
1	Tbsp	Salt
2	tsp	Baking Powder
12	oz	Yellow Onion, grated and drained
1/2	bunch	Green Onion, minced
1	cup	Packed Parsley Leaves, minced
1	cup	Packed Cilantro Leaves, minced
		Salt, to taste
16	oz	Vegetable Oil (for pan-frying), or as needed

Falafel served with Taratoor sauce

This is an ancient dish that has been popular in Egypt—and now the rest of the Middle East—for centuries. Fava beans have a tough skin on the outside that covers the two segments of the inner beans, and this recipe requires dried beans that have had that part removed prior to drying. These are white-grey in color and may be labeled "split fava" (or "broad") beans. If only the typical brown-skinned variety that still contains the skin is available, it will be necessary to cook the beans for a bit to soften them, and the resulting strained and puréed paste will need to be pushed through a drum sieve to remove the skins.

Yield: Approximately 32 two-ounce Falafels

Preparation Method (Fava Beans): 24-Hour Soaking

Preparation Method (Spices): Dry Toasting

Cooking Method: Panfrying

Procedure

1. Soak the fava beans for a full day in ample cold water (cover by at least 3 inches; they will expand).

2. Drain the fava beans once they have soaked for a full day, and set them on a sheet tray to air-dry slightly while other ingredients are prepared.

3. In a small sauté pan, dry-toast the whole spices over a low flame until they become fragrant. Once cool, grind them in a spice mill or coffee grinder to a powder, and then set aside.

4. Using a mortar and pestle, crush the garlic cloves with the salt to form a paste, and then set aside.

5. Using a food processor, turn the soaked split fava beans, ground spices, garlic salt paste, baking powder, and grated onion into a smooth paste/dough.

6. Mix in the remaining ingredients, and test for seasoning and consistency by frying a small amount in the preheated fryer; taste.

7. Adjust seasoning or consistency (using flour or water), if necessary.

8. Once mixture is ready, divide the paste/dough into approximately 2-oz portions and set aside.

9. Heat 2 oz of the vegetable oil in a sauté pan over a medium-high flame, and pan-fry a few falafel at a time in the hot oil until golden brown on both sides.

10. Drain the fried falafel on paper towels, and serve while still hot.

11. Continue with steps 9 and 10 using the remaining oil and portioned fritter paste until all of the falafel has been cooked.

NOTE: *These are often coated in sesame seeds and may be served with hummus bi tahini (see recipe in Chapter 2, "Greek Cuisine") or Taratoor sauce. These are commonly made using cooked chickpeas (or garbanzo beans) in place of the fava beans as well.*

Tabbouleh LEBANON/PALESTINE
(BULGUR AND HERB SALAD)

INGREDIENTS

1	lb	Bulgur, Fine or Medium (size will dictate soaking time)
2	cups	Parsley Leaves, packed (about 2.5–3 bunches) and then minced
1.5	cups	Mint Leaves, packed (about 2 bunches) and then minced
1/2	cup	Green Onions, minced
8	oz	Ripe Tomato, seeds removed and diced small
1	tsp	Salt
1/4	tsp	Freshly Ground Black Pepper
3	oz	Lemon Juice
5	oz	Extra Virgin Olive Oil
		Salt, Pepper, Lemon Juice, and Olive Oil, to taste

This well-known salad utilizes the abundant and very common fresh herbs that are used in the fertile Mediterranean region of the Middle East. Bulgur, wheat that is cooked, dried, and then cracked to varying sizes, is also a common ingredient in this part of the Middle East.

YIELD: 2.25 pounds, or 9–10 portions (approximately 4 ounces each)

METHOD (BULGUR): Rehydration

PROCEDURE

1. Soak the bulgur in cool water until the grains are soft and hydrated (usually less than 10 minutes for medium grain bulgur; be sure to get bulgur and not cracked wheat, which has not been precooked and would need to be cooked if using in place of bulgur).
2. Drain the grains once they are hydrated, and set aside.
3. Place the minced herbs, green onion, and tomato in a mixing bowl; add the hydrated bulgur, and toss to combine well.
4. Add the salt and pepper to the bowl; while mixing with a spoon, add in the lemon juice to distribute well.
5. Add in the extra virgin olive oil while mixing.
6. Taste and adjust seasoning, if necessary.
7. Serve the tabbouleh over whole romaine leaves, or cut up the romaine lettuce and use it as a bed for presentation.

NOTE: *Tabbouleh is traditionally served with Arab flatbread.*

Kibbeh LEBANON AND SYRIA
(POUNDED LAMB AND WHEAT)

INGREDIENTS

For the Lamb Mixture

2	lbs	Very Lean Lamb (such as loin)
7	oz	Bulgur Wheat, fine or medium
3	cups	Very Cold Water
1	tsp	Freshly Ground Black Pepper
1	tsp	Allspice, ground
1/4	tsp	Cinnamon, ground
1/4	tsp	Cayenne Pepper, ground
2	tsp	Salt
3	oz	Extra Virgin Olive Oil
		Salt and Freshly Ground Black Pepper, to taste

This is considered one of the best dishes throughout much of the Middle East, and it is prized for its quality of ingredients—much as the similar steak tartare is prized in European cuisine. This is traditionally made by pounding together the meat and the soaked bulgur wheat to produce a paste that is then seasoned and served with traditional Arab flatbread. However, because this is an impractical procedure for most kitchens, the following recipe calls for freshly ground lamb instead of pounded lamb. If the traditional texture is desired (it has a pastier texture due to the pounding versus grinding), it can be achieved by pounding the lamb and soaked bulgur using a large mortar and pestle. Because this is an uncooked recipe that uses meat, it is very important to buy high-quality meat from a respected purveyor and follow strict sanitary guidelines throughout.

NOTE: *Be sure to wash and sanitize all equipment and hands when making this dish.*

YIELD: 8 portions (5 ounces/portion)

SPECIAL METHOD: Fine Sanitary Grinding of Raw Meat

(continues)

Kibbeh
(continued)

For Serving

2	Tbsp	Minced Parsley
1	Tbsp	Minced Fresh Mint
2	oz	Extra Virgin Olive Oil

PROCEDURE

1. Ensure that all equipment is cleaned and sanitized, and then place grinder parts into a freezer (for at least an hour) and allow them to get very cold.

2. Go over the lamb to see if there is any significant fat or connective tissue that can be removed, and do so if necessary (this may mean you will need to get more lamb if some is discarded or removed).

3. In a bowl large enough to hold the bulgur and water, combine the two and allow the bulgur to soak for 15 minutes. Remove and strain through cheesecloth, and squeeze out any excess water; set aside the soaked bulgur.

4. Cut the lamb into strips that will fit into the food grinder; grind through the medium plate, catching all of the ground lamb in a bowl set over ice to keep it very cold.

5. Run the ground lamb through the grinder again, this time using a fine plate to yield a very finely ground lean lamb. Once done, cover the ground lamb and set it in the refrigerator until called for next.

6. Using a mortar and pestle, grind together the soaked bulgur, spices, and salt to form a paste.

7. Transfer the spice and bulgur paste to the ground lamb and, using clean and sanitized hands, mix the two together very well.

8. While mixing the lamb/bulgur mixture, slowly drizzle the 3 oz of extra virgin olive oil into the mixture, to incorporate and emulsify into the meat and wheat mixture.

9. Taste the mixture for seasoning and adjust, if necessary, with salt and pepper.

10. To serve, place 5 oz of the kibbeh on a serving plate (it is often formed into a smooth mound but could be shaped however the chef prefers), and garnish/season with the minced parsley and mint.

11. Drizzle a little of the extra virgin olive oil over each portion, and serve immediately.

NOTE: *Kibbeh is traditionally served with Arab flatbread, which can be made for this, or pita bread can be used as an adequate substitute.*

Etli Biber Dolmasi   TURKEY

(STUFFED GREEN PEPPERS)

INGREDIENTS

10		Green Bell Peppers
24	oz	Ground Lamb
2	cups	Rice, long grain (uncooked)
3	oz	Extra Virgin Olive Oil
10	oz	Yellow Onion, diced small
1	oz	Garlic Cloves, minced
1	cup	Packed Parsley, minced (about 1/2 bunch)
3	Tbsp	Oregano, minced (about 1/4 bunch)
6	oz	Tomato Paste
1	Tbsp	Cumin, ground
1/4	tsp	Cayenne Pepper
2	tsp	Salt
1/2	tsp	Freshly Ground Black Pepper
1	qt	Water

Turkish cuisine is well known for its stuffed dishes, including this one.

YIELD: 10 portions; one stuffed pepper/portion (about 10–12 ounces each)

COOKING METHOD: Baking

PROCEDURE

1. Preheat oven to 350°F.
2. Clean the peppers in fresh running water, taking care to clean the area by the stem.
3. Cut the tops off of the peppers, removing approximately 1/2 inch from the top, and set aside.
4. Remove the seeds and inner membrane of the pepper: use a paring knife to cut away the flaps of membrane coming from each of the pepper segments, and pull them out.
5. In a mixing bowl, combine the ground lamb, rice, olive oil, onion, garlic, parsley, oregano, tomato paste, cumin, cayenne, salt, and pepper, and mix thoroughly to combine. Stuff the mixture into the cavity at the bottom of the green peppers, dividing it evenly among all of the peppers.
6. Place the stuffed peppers into a baking dish (that the peppers fit into snugly), and then add the water to the dish.
7. Cover the pan, place it in the preheated oven, and bake for 50 minutes.
8. Remove the pan from the oven and check to see if the rice is cooked. If so, remove. If not, return to oven and cook for a few more minutes.

Imam bayildy (stuffed eggplant) on left; etli biber dolmasi (stuffed pepper) on right

Imam Bayildy   TURKEY

(EGGPLANT STUFFED WITH TOMATO)

INGREDIENTS

For Prepping the Eggplant

2	lbs	Japanese Eggplant (the elongated eggplants are best for this; if unavailable, use smaller eggplants if possible), split lengthwise in half, with bottom side of each half peeled (leaving 1/2 inch of skin on each half, all the way around the cut portion of the eggplant)
1	Tbsp	Salt

For Making the Filling

2	oz	Olive Oil
8	oz	Yellow Onion, diced small
1	oz	Garlic Cloves, minced
12	oz	Tomato Concassée
1	Tbsp	Tomato Paste
2	Tbsp	Parsley, minced
1	oz	Fresh Lemon Juice
1/2	tsp	Lemon Zest, minced
1/2	tsp	Salt
1/8	tsp	Black Pepper
		Salt and Black Pepper, to taste

For Sautéing, Stuffing, and Roasting the Eggplant

4	oz	Olive Oil (may need more or less, depending on how much is absorbed by eggplant; be sure the pan(s) are hot before adding the eggplant to avoid sogginess)
		Eggplant (see above)
		Stuffing (see above)
4	oz	Extra Virgin Olive Oil
		Salt and Pepper, to taste

This is a very well-known vegetable dish from Turkey whose name means "the imam fainted," an apparent reference to an imam (Islamic scholar) who was overcome by the quality of this creation.

YIELD: 12 portions at 4–5 ounces/portion (1/2 stuffed eggplant/portion)

COOKING METHOD (FILLING): Sweating/Sautéing

COOKING METHOD (EGGPLANT): Sautéing; Finished by Roasting

PROCEDURE

For Prepping the Eggplant

1. After the eggplants have been split in half lengthwise, and the bottom portion of each half has been peeled (this will allow the bottom to caramelize while being roasted), scoop a well into each half using a spoon or melon baller.

2. Once the eggplants have all been cleaned, sprinkle the salt over all of the eggplant pieces and rub it into the flesh to distribute it evenly.

3. Allow the eggplants to sit for 30 minutes before proceeding to next step.

4. Rinse the salted eggplants and pat them dry, or allow them to air dry; set aside.

For Making the Filling

1. In a sauté pan large enough to hold all the filling ingredients, add the olive oil, onions, and garlic. Heat over a low flame to sweat the aromatics until they are tender and translucent (this should take about 10 minutes).

2. Once the onions and garlic are very tender, add the tomato concassée and turn up the heat to a medium-high flame. Cook for 2 minutes, to drive off some of the moisture in the tomatoes.

3. Add the tomato paste to the pan, remove from heat, and stir well to combine.

4. Add the parsley, lemon juice, lemon zest, and salt to the pan, and stir well to combine.

5. Taste the filling and adjust seasoning with salt and black pepper, if necessary.

6. Set the filling aside.

For Sautéing, Stuffing, and Roasting the Eggplant

1. Preheat oven to 375°F.

2. In a large sauté pan(s), heat the olive oil over a medium-high flame. Once hot, sauté the eggplant halves on both sides to caramelize to a light golden-brown (you may need to add more olive oil to the pan as you go, to ensure they color evenly).

3. Once the eggplants have been sautéed, remove them from the pan and place the stuffing inside the cavity of each half, distributing it evenly among all of the eggplant halves.

(continues)

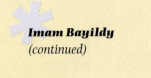

Imam Bayildy
(continued)

4. Return the eggplants to the sauté pan(s), and drizzle the extra virgin olive oil evenly over the surface of the stuffed eggplants.

5. Cover the pan(s) with a tight-fitting lid, or cover tightly with foil, and place in the preheated oven; bake for 30 minutes.

6. Check the eggplants to see if they are very tender throughout and nicely colored on the bottom (remember the peeled part!). If so, remove them—they are ready to serve. If not, return them to the oven and continue to cook until done.

Sis Kebabi TURKEY

(SKEWERED GRILLED LAMB)

INGREDIENTS

3	lbs	Leg of Lamb, boneless and cut into 1.5-inch cubes
1	lb	Yellow Onion, chopped
2	oz	Garlic Cloves, chopped
1	Tbsp	Salt
1	Tbsp	Freshly Ground Black Pepper
5	oz	Olive Oil

This Turkish specialty is believed to have been invented by the nomadic tribes that would cook their meat over a fire while traveling. There are many varieties of sis kebabi throughout Turkey and the Middle East (and beyond); this preparation method has found fans all over the globe.

YIELD: 3 pounds, or 8 portions (6 ounces/portion)

PREPARATION METHOD: Marinating

COOKING METHOD: Grilling

PROCEDURE

1. Remove any significant connective tissue from the pieces of lamb; cover the lamb and set it aside in the refrigerator.

2. In a food processor, add the onions, garlic, salt, and pepper. With the processor running, slowly drizzle in the olive oil to make a smooth purée of the vegetables.

3. Transfer the contents of the food processor to the container with the lamb, and mix well to combine and coat all of the lamb pieces with the marinade.

4. Allow the lamb to marinate in the mixture for at least 2 hours before cooking the lamb (overnight is even better).

5. Once the lamb has had time to marinate, pierce the lamb pieces using skewers; thread on as many pieces as will fit on the grill. (In Turkey, metal skewers are used. Metal skewers are far better for grilling than wooden ones, commonly found in the United States, which often burn. If possible, use metal. If not possible, soak the wooden ones to help prevent them from burning.)

6. Once all of the lamb has been skewered, grill the skewers over the hottest part of the grill to desired doneness. It is easier to cook them longer in the oven, if desired, than it is to cook them more on the grill, which should be quite hot to sear the meat well.

NOTE: *Sis kebabi is traditionally eaten with flatbread and other accompaniments combined with the bread and meat. Some of the common accompaniments include salads of cucumber, onion, and mint; yogurt-based sauces; grilled vegetables; and seasoned, shaved onions.*

Grilled sis kebabi (skewered and grilled lamb) served over grilled vegetables and pilavli (rice pilaf) and topped with cucumbers coated in yogurt sauce

Pilav TURKEY
(RICE PILAF WITH CURRANTS AND PINE NUTS)

INGREDIENTS

3	oz	Vegetable Oil
10	oz	Onions, minced
4	oz	Pine Nuts
1	tsp	Allspice, ground
1	tsp	Cinnamon, ground
1/2	tsp	Freshly Ground Black Pepper
4	cups	Basmati Rice, rinsed until clear
3	oz	Currants (raisins can be substituted if currants are unavailable)
6	cups	Hot Chicken Stock
2	tsp	Salt
3	oz	Whole Salted Butter, cut into 4 or 5 pieces
		Salt and Pepper, to taste

The Turkish method of cooking rice has long been followed in many other parts of the world, and it is a common component of classic culinary preparations in cooking schools across the United States. The rice pilaf found in professional cooking texts is based on this method, in which rice grains are coated in fat and fried slightly before being combined with hot stock and cooked covered. This recipe includes some of the seasonings that are commonly used in Turkey to make a classic pilav.

YIELD: 2 quarts cooked rice, or 10 portions (5–6 ounces/portion)

COOKING METHOD: Pilaf Method for Rice

PROCEDURE

1. Preheat oven to 325°F (this can also be prepared on the stovetop, if desired, although the oven is usually more consistent).

2. In a pot large enough to hold all ingredients, heat the vegetable oil over a medium-low flame until hot; add the minced onion.

3. Sweat the onions over the low flame until they become translucent and soft. Lower the heat and continue to cook for an additional 5 minutes (covered) to soften onions further.

4. Once the onions are very soft, remove the cover and add the pine nuts, turning the heat up to a medium-high flame.

5. Fry the onions and pine nuts together in the oil until the pine nuts begin to color slightly (stir to prevent the pine nuts from burning).

6. Once the pine nuts have begun to color slightly, add the spices and the basmati rice, and stir all of the ingredients well with a wooden spoon. Continue to cook for a couple of minutes, stirring all along.

7. Add the currants and hot stock to the pot. Cover the pot with a very tight-fitting lid, or with foil and a tight-fitting lid if necessary (it is important not to lose moisture at this point so the rice can cook properly).

8. Place the covered pot into the preheated oven, or continue to cook on the stove over a low flame, for 20 minutes.

9. Once the rice has cooked, remove it from the oven and uncover to check that rice is cooked through (if it is not, return it to the oven; check to see if it has absorbed all of the water first).

10. Add whole butter pieces to the cooked rice, and stir to mix in and melt.

11. Adjust seasoning of rice, if necessary, and serve.

❋ Chelou PERSIA/IRAN

(CRUSTED RICE IN STYLE OF PERSIA)

INGREDIENTS

1	lb	Basmati Rice (jasmine makes a good substitute if basmati is not available)
1.5	gal	Water (for the cooking step, not rinsing or soaking)
1/4	cup	Salt
1	ea	Egg Yolk
1.5	oz	Salted Butter
2	oz	Water
		Salt, to taste

This common preparation for rice—a traditional method used in Iran and other parts of the Middle East—results in crust-layered rice that provides both texture and flavor to the finished product. This method of cooking rice is unique to this region (specifically Iran) and contrasts with the Turkish technique of cooking rice, which is commonly taught in culinary schools as rice pilaf. The traditional varietals of rice used in Iran—ambar-boo and darbari—are difficult to find in the United States but are aromatic long-grain varietals like basmati and jasmine.

YIELD: 2.5 lbs cooked rice, or 10 portions (4 ounces/portion)

COOKING METHOD (RICE): Boiling in Ample Water

COOKING METHOD (FINAL CHELOU): Chelou Method (Baking or Cooking on Stovetop to Form a Crust)

PROCEDURE

1. Preheat oven to 350°F.
2. Rinse the rice in a pot of clean, cold water, rubbing the grains with your fingers to help to release some of the surface starch.
3. Change the water a couple times while repeating step 2 to ensure that the rice is well rinsed.
4. In the same pot—using fresh, cold water again—soak the rice for an hour, and then drain well in a colander.
5. In a 2-gallon or larger pot, bring water and salt to a boil over high heat. Add the rinsed and drained rice to the pot, and stir the water with a spoon to ensure that the rice grains are not clumped together.
6. Once the pot of water returns to a boil, stir it occasionally to prevent grains from sticking. Test the grains every minute or so until the rice is cooked through (this should take about 3 to 5 minutes after water boils).
7. Strain the cooked rice into a china cap, and rinse briefly under room-temperature water to cool rice and remove excess starch.

NOTE: *At this point, you have made traditional plain rice in the Persian style, which can then be used—following the next steps—to make chelou, or it can be mixed with other cooked ingredients and baked to make a polou-style Persian dish.*

8. In a small mixing bowl, combine 1 cup of the cooked rice and the egg yolk. Mix thoroughly, and place at the bottom of a smooth-bottomed pot, spreading it out over the bottom surface of the pot (pots with pitting or scratches will make it more difficult to remove the crust after baking).
9. Cover the rice mixed with egg yolk with the remaining rice. Cover with a tight-fitting lid and/or aluminum foil, and place the pot in the preheated oven. Bake, covered, for 10 to 12 minutes.
10. Combine the salted butter and water in a saucepan, and heat over a medium flame until hot. Pour this mixture over the top of the cooking rice after it has been in the oven for 10 to 12 minutes.

(continues)

Chelou
(continued)

11. After adding the butter and water mixture to the rice, re-cover the pan and return it to the oven. Continue to bake for an additional 25 minutes, undisturbed, and then remove the rice from the oven. Allow it to sit at room temperature for 15 minutes before proceeding to the next step.

12. After the rice has rested, uncover the rice and turn out the portion that is not sticking to the bottom into a holding pan. Check for seasoning, and adjust as necessary.

13. Remove the browned crust on the bottom of the pan by working the sides off of the pan; be gentle to yield the whole section in one piece, and serve the rice with the browned crust on top. (This is typically served family or buffet style.)

Cooking the chelou (Persian rice) in ample water

Topping the egg-mixed cooked rice with the plain cooked rice when making chelou (Persian rice)

Finished baked chelou; note the crusted portion on the plate from the egg-mixed rice at the bottom

SUMMARY

The Middle East is the site of the birthplace of civilization and some of the world's major religions, and the cuisines of this region are closely linked to this history. In those areas where the population is mostly of the Islamic faith, dietary practices are primarily consistent with the religious edicts of Islam; the cuisine of Israel mirrors the Jewish edicts as well. The Persian and Ottoman empires were major culinary influences on the cuisine of much of this area, and many traditional foods from these periods are still common today. The cuisine of the Middle East is based on a diet of grains, mostly in the form of breads and rice, supported by meats (typically lamb or goat) and vegetables. Flatbread, often eaten with highly spiced foods, plays a significant role in the daily diet and eating practices of much of the population. The spice trade between Europe and Asia was once controlled by the inhabitants of the Middle East, and the use of spices in the local cuisine is still a major component of the cuisine. The cuisine of the Middle East differs from others in the use of spices, the role of religion in the daily dietary habits, the use of sweet-and-sour components in all facets of the cooking, and the role of flatbreads as not only nourishment but also a tool.

REVIEW QUESTIONS

1. What are the foods that are considered halal (permitted) and haram (prohibited) according to the dietary edicts of Islam?

2. From what part of the world do Ashkenazi Jews and Sephardi Jews come, and how is that important to the cuisine of Israel?

3. What were two empires that had a significant influence on the cuisine of the Middle East? Name one dish that can be traced to each.

COMMON TERMS, FOODS, AND INGREDIENTS

The following will assist in the understanding and recognition of the foods and techniques used in the cuisines of the Middle East.

✳ Arabic-Speaking Countries

Ingredients and Foods

alya – Rendered lamb fat taken from the tail

baharat – Spice blend (many versions)

baklava – Pastry made of layers of thin sheets of buttered dough, coated with ground nuts and seasonings, and then baked. It is then coated with a sweet syrup that usually contains honey, lemon, and rose or orange water. The origin of this well-known pastry is not clear; it has a long history in Iran, Turkey, Greece, and the Arab countries in the Middle East.

battawa – Egyptian flatbread, typically highly seasoned with fenugreek

burghul – Bulgur wheat

dibs – Concentrated grape juice

dibs rim'an – Pomegranate syrup (often called pomegranate molasses)

falafel – Seasoned fava bean or chickpea puree that is deep fried; common in Arab-influenced Middle Eastern countries

fool akhdar – Fresh fava beans

fool misri – Small, dried brown fava beans

fool mudammas – Mashed and spiced fava beans

haba – Large, dried split fava beans

halvas – Sweet, dense cakes seasoned with various ingredients and eaten as a snack or dessert. These are made from cooking thickened, sweetened mixtures and then pouring them to let them set before cutting into smaller pieces; called halawah or halawa in some parts of the Middle East.

hashwa – Lamb and rice

kharouf – Lamb

kibbeh – Pounded lamb and burghul, seasoned with spices, olive oil, and often onions; served raw or used to make a number of cooked dishes from the raw form, including fried balls stuffed with various ingredients

laban – Yogurt

muhammara – Seasoned walnut paste common in Lebanon

qawrama – Preserved lamb fat

ta'amia – Spiced fava bean or chickpea fritters (also called falafel)

tabbouleh – Salad of chopped herbs and bulgur, seasoned with lemon juice and olive oil

tahini – Sesame seed paste

taratoor – Sauce made from tahini seasoned with lemon juice and garlic

za'atar – Spice blend commonly eaten with Arab bread and olive oil; made from sumac, sesame seeds, oregano, and thyme

Food Customs

halal – Foods that are permitted to be eaten according to the laws of Islam

haram – Foods that are prohibited according to the laws of Islam

✳ Israel

Ingredients and Foods

borscht – Beet soup brought from Eastern Europe and Russia

dfina – One-pot stew (to be eaten on the Sabbath) common to the Sephardi Jews

falafel – Seasoned fava bean or chickpea purée that is deep fried; common in Arab-influenced Middle Eastern countries

gefilte fish – Poached fish forcemeat or dumpling common to the cooking of Ashkenazi Jews

goulash – Spiced stew of Eastern European heritage common among Israeli populations whose families once lived in this region

hummus – Chickpea purée seasoned with tahini, lemon juice, and garlic

knish – Thin pancake filled with savory foods (typically fish or cheese), from Russian influence

latkes – Thin potato pancakes, popular during the holiday of Chanukah

matzoh – Unleavened bread eaten during Passover

zhug – Spiced relish used for seasoning; made with garlic, cumin, fenugreek, chiles, and coriander

Food Customs

kashruth – Jewish dietary laws or edicts that govern acceptable foods, unacceptable foods, or combinations of foods to be followed by those of the Jewish faith

kosher – Designation given to foods that have been deemed "fit for use" according to the laws or edicts of kashruth

pareve – Foods that are considered neutral under the guidelines of kashruth and thus can be eaten with either dairy products or meat. These foods are considered to be inherently kosher and thus fit for consumption.

Pesach – Passover; during this holy period, followers are to avoid all leavened products (thus, the importance of matzoh)

✳ Turkey

baba ghanoush – Puréed eggplant seasoned with garlic, olive oil, and lemon juice. This is a common appetizer served with bread.

borek – Small, stuffed savory pastries in the shape of a cigar, made from phyllo-type doughs; typically filled with cheese and often other ingredients

chorba – Soup

dolmas – Stuffed foods; a typical dolma is grape leaves stuffed with seasoned rice and lamb

etli beber dolmasi – Stuffed green peppers

imam bayaldi – Eggplant stuffed with tomato

kebabs – Skewered and grilled meats; versions range from simple marinated lamb pieces to kofte or other seasoned ground meats

kofte – Ground and seasoned meat shaped into a ball; these may be added to stews or soups, or skewered and grilled to make a kebab

manti – Oval-shaped pasta with an open pouch, filled with various stuffing (usually ground lamb) and poached in broth

mezze – A number of flavorful foods served prior to a meal or sometimes as a meal. This style of eating is similar to the tapas style in Spain (see Chapter 10, "Iberian Cuisine"), in which several foods are eaten in small quantities.

pilav – Rice cooked first in fat, along with onions, and then finished with liquid

sherbet – Same meaning as English name (which comes from the Turkish name); believed to have been incorporated into the cuisine from the influence of Persian cuisine on the Ottoman Empire

sis kebabi – Skewered and grilled meats, typically lamb or mutton

Persia/Iran

Ingredients and Foods

ambar-boo – Amber-scented, long-grain rice that is very highly prized and comes from the northern region of Iran

barbari – Persian flatbread

chelou – Persian style of cooking rice, in which a portion of cooked rice is mixed with eggs or sometimes yogurt, placed on the bottom of a pan and covered with more cooked rice, and then baked along with clarified butter to yield a crusted bottom, which is served on top of or along with the finished rice dish

darbari – Prized long-grain rice from Iran

donbeh – Rendered fat of fat-tailed sheep used as cooking fat, traditionally in Persian cuisine

lavash – Thin, yeast-leavened bread cooked on the inside wall of a clay or earthenware oven and traditionally used to scoop food when eating limu omani – dried limes (also called *loumi*)

polou – Any of a number of Persian rice dishes that are served with other ingredients

sadri – Long-grain rice from Iran that is very similar to basmati from India (may actually be basmati variety brought to Iran from India long ago)

sharbat – Sherbet; frozen fruit juices; these have been enjoyed in the Middle East for centuries, with the tradition thought to have originated in the northern mountainous region of present-day Iran

torshi limu – Pickled limes

torshis – Pickled vegetables

Other Terms

basmati – Aromatic long-grain rice from India, often used to replace aromatic rice of Iranian cuisine

verjuice – Juice of unripened grapes

CHAPTER 2

THE FORMER
YUGOSLAV REPUBLIC
OF MACEDONIA

BULGARIA

RHODOPE MOUNTAINS

*BLACK
SEA*

ALBANIA

THRACE

Northern Greece

Axios River

*SEA OF
MARMARA*

G R E E C E

EPIRUS

THESSALY

Western and Central Greece

PINDUS MOUNTAINS

SPORADES
ISLANDS

*AEGEAN
SEA*

TURKEY

IONIAN
ISLANDS

ATTICA
★ Athens

*IONIAN
SEA*

THE
PELOPONNESE

CYCLADES

DODECANESE ISLANDS

SEA OF CRETE

CRETE

★	capital city
——	river
——	region boundary
——	sub-region boundary
—·—·	international boundary
▨	mountains

N
W · E
S

0   50   100

MEDITERRANEAN SEA

OBJECTIVES

Upon completion of this chapter, you will be able to

- discuss the importance of the sea in Greek cuisine.
- discuss the importance of olives, bread, and cheese in the Greek diet.
- recognize the influences that make Greek cuisine a crossroads of sorts in Europe.
- recognize some of the common recipes of Greek cuisine.
- prepare a variety of Greek foods.
- define the terms listed at the conclusion of this chapter.

INTRODUCTION

The foods of Greece are not as familiar to most Americans as some of the other European cuisines, but they will surely become more popular as people come to discover the fresh, bright flavors so common to this Mediterranean cuisine. Some might call Greece the birthplace of cuisine, because the first book on cooking and eating good food was written here (*Gastronomia,* written by Archestratus in the fifth century BC). In fact, many of the items that are used frequently in other cuisines actually originated in Greece. The French mother sauce béchamel, versatile mayonnaise, and the classic fishermen stew bouillabaisse all can be traced back to Greece. Even the tall white hat that chefs wear has Greek heritage—cooks in Greece wore white hats to distinguish themselves from monks who wore black hats in monasteries. Greek cuisine is certainly not limited to *moussaka, baklava,* and the generic Greek salads that are commonly served in the United States. Greek cuisine is far more complex, including a seemingly endless variation of seafood preparations, plenty of fresh vegetables, stuffed pies, and many types of bread.

Contemporary Greek cuisine has developed from proudly held traditions and techniques, as well as numerous outside influences during periods of takeover by foreign invaders. Greece has been occupied by several cultures over the centuries, including Romans (modern-day Italy), Ottoman Turks (modern-day Middle East), Venetians (modern-day Italy), and the English; all of these influences have resulted in the nuances of modern-day Greek cuisine. Although these historic powers may have held sway over Greeks at one time in history, Greek cuisine exists as it does today because of steadfast adherence to the ancient traditions, including the culinary practices of the ancient Greeks.

The ancient Greek ingredients included grapes, figs, honey, garlic, onions, wheat, barley, yellow lentils, kid (young goat), lamb, cheese, Mediterranean fish, shellfish, octopus, and squid, and these ingredients are still the cornerstones of Greek cuisine today. Of course, Greece, like any other country, has added many other ingredients from other cultures over the years, and these have been incorporated into the modern-day cuisine.

HISTORIC CULINARY INFLUENCES

The following periods and countries have had a significant impact on the development of Greek cuisine as it is known today.

Ancient Greece

Greece has a very volatile history that has greatly influenced the culinary landscape of the country. Ancient Greeks populated the areas of Southern Italy, Turkey, and North Africa, bringing back ingredients from those cultures and taking olives, grapes, and pulses with them. As mentioned in the introduction, the ancient Greeks had a sophisticated cuisine that included many of the ingredients that remain part of the core of the cuisine today. The dependence on the sea for food, the use of olives and their oils, the reliance on wheat as a storable source of food, and an understanding of the local plants for yielding vegetables and edible greens were all part of the ancient Greek way of life.

Alexander the Great and Roman Rule

Under the rule of Alexander the Great, Greece's borders grew to include India, resulting in the inclusion of such ingredients as rice and spices such as cinnamon, nutmeg, and saffron. This period was followed by Roman rule, during which time the vast Roman Empire added many new ingredients to the Greek diet, including foods from the Middle East, such as eggplant, caviar, citrus, melon, and cane sugar. The Middle Eastern influence also provided the understanding of the distillation process, which enabled the Greeks to make what has since become a national drink: *ouzo*.

Ottoman Empire

During the period of rule by the Ottoman Turks, Greeks incorporated beans, spinach, rice, yogurt, and coffee into their culinary repertoire. The Turkish practice of skewering meat and grilling or roasting it also was adopted at this time, resulting in the emergence of *souvlakia*. The Turks also introduced small portions and bite-size dishes, which developed into the still-popular *meze* tradition found in Greece today.

Italian and English Influences

Crete was ruled by Italian people for hundreds of years after the thirteenth century and thus had a large impact on the cuisine of that area of Greece. Ingredients from the Americas were introduced, such as squashes, tomatoes, corn, and peppers, as well as the pastas of Italian culture. Britain also had a period of influence, stemming from the British protectorate period of the Ionian Islands. Some culinary influences from Britain include roasted meats, mustard, and brewing.

UNIQUE COMPONENTS

Greek cuisine is unique largely because of its geographical location and because of the great history of this proud country. Greece is located in the Mediterranean (literally—there are approximately 2,000 Greek islands in the sea), and this climate has greatly impacted the products grown and enjoyed here. Because Greece is a peninsula that extends into the sea, it is located between the very Western-influenced area of Italy and the shores of the Eastern-influenced Middle East, making Greece a natural go-between for these cultures. The Greek Empire is also credited with providing the philosophical foundation that much of the Western world embraced, including some of the foundations used today in professional kitchens, and the people of Greece are fiercely proud of this rich history.

Island Cuisine

Greece's nearly 2,000 islands include many that have been inhabited for centuries by people who live a seafaring life, resulting in a cuisine of determination. The Greek islands often provide a limited supply of both local produce and water, due to their location in the arid part of the Mediterranean. As a result, the Greek islanders have utilized what does grow here to the fullest extent, and they have turned to the sea or to the nearby mainland to make up for what they lack.

The interaction between the islanders and the surrounding countries has influenced not only the island cuisine but also the cuisine of Greece as a whole, even though much of the population of Greece does not live on the islands. The islanders often make trips to the mainland, and mainlanders visit the many islands as well, so that culinary customs are shared by both.

The emphasis on utilization of local and seasonal products in the cuisine of the islands has resulted in a great variety of foods being made from a relatively small amount of common island products. Because the islands are mostly arid land, the plants that can tolerate low water conditions are some of the more common; these include grapes, *garbanzo beans*, fava beans, rosemary, fennel, olives, figs, and a number of legumes and grains. These ingredients are common components of the local cuisines and often are combined with cheese and goat or lamb meat, traditionally making up the predominant part of the islanders' diet. The traditional parts of the cuisine of the islands may not always be as apparent as they once were, but the heart of this cuisine still exists for those who want to find it, and its influence has left its permanent mark on Greek cuisine.

East Meets West

Greece is located in between the eastern reaches of the Western world and the western reaches of the Eastern world, and many of the influences of both converge here. Although the Balkan area borders the western part of Greece, much of the Balkans are considerably north of the country. The boot part of Italy stretches toward Greece in the Mediterranean Sea. Greece is also a neighbor of Turkey, and only the sea separates Greece from the shores of the Middle East and Egypt. Because of this location, and the historical periods of domination by both European powers and the Turkish Ottomans, Greece has unique combinations of traditional indigenous foods and foods from Europe and the Middle East.

During the rule of the Ottoman Empire in Greece (from the fifteenth century until 1821, for most of Greece), many foods were introduced to the Greek kitchen and became part of Greek traditions. Many of the Ottoman influences can be traced back to the Persian Empire (present-day Iran), because the Ottomans included the people of this region as well. The use of *phyllo* dough can be traced to this period of influence, as the Ottomans produced thin dough in the same manner as later Greek cooks would. Phyllo is used extensively in Greek cuisine to make recipes ranging from *spanakopita* (savory pies wrapped in phyllo) to baklava (layered phyllo brushed with butter and then layered with nuts in honey syrup). The Greeks inherited a penchant for stuffing vegetables and other dishes, such as dolmas (stuffed grape leaves) and boreks (Turkish stuffed phyllo turnovers), during this period as well.

Prior to the rule of the Ottomans in Greece, the Venetians had conquered Greece in 1204 and influenced the Greeks during this and later periods of Greek history. The most obvious influence from Italy is the profusion of pasta that is common in Greek cuisine, but many stews and fish dishes were also introduced to the Greeks from Italy as well. Some of the common pastas that are found in the cuisine include *flomaria* (either thin like a string or slightly flattened like linguini), *hilopittes* (egg noodles, either long and thin or square), and *kritharakia* (rice-shaped pasta commonly called orzo in the United States).

This blending of Eastern and Western culinary methods and customs is part of what makes Greek cuisine unique and often so attractive to a wide audience. The combination of its traditional foods and some of the newer original dishes makes Greek cuisine one of the most interesting to study and sample.

Olives, Cheese, and Bread

Few things remain constant throughout nearly all parts of Greece, but one is the regular inclusion of olives or olive oil, cheeses, and breads in the daily Greek diet. There are many varieties of each of these three commodities found throughout the regions of Greece, with local variations often being one of the distinguishing components of an area. In the case of olives, a number of varieties are common—either brined and eaten or pressed for their oils to be used in cooking and seasoning. Some of the most common olive types include *amfissa, kalamata, elies neratzates, halkidika, maonias,* and *thassos throumba.*

Greek cheeses are typically made from goat's milk, sheep's milk, or a combination of the two, with cow's milk being much less common. Greece has an arid climate in which cows do not thrive, but goats and sheep do. Many versions of these cheeses are salted or brined and yield very flavorful varieties that provide a distinct flavor to many dishes, making them immediately identifiable as Greek. Some of the most common types are *anthotiro, feta, graviera, haloumi, kasseri, kefalotyri, ladotiri, manouri,* and *mitzithra.*

Bread is also a major part of the traditional Greek diet. Many types of bread have religious connections and are included in the feasts of celebrations that occur throughout the year. Greek breads often vary in shape.

SIGNIFICANT SUBREGIONS

Greek has a diverse cuisine that varies depending on what area of Greece one is looking at, and the following guide gives an overview of what some of those variations are.

Northern Greece

This region includes the city of Macedonia to the west and the province of Thrace to the east, and it has a milder climate than much of the rest of Greece. Northern Greek cuisine is characterized by heartier fare than much of the rest of the country, and it is known for its many preserved items as well as the spices commonly used in many of the dishes. Many of the Greeks in this region come from families that were expelled from present-day Turkey; thus, Turkish cuisine has had a significant influence here, including the use of spices such as cinnamon, allspice, and cloves.

Western and Central Greece

This region includes the mountains of the Epirus section in the west as well as the fertile plains of Thessaly. Attica lies to the south and contains the famous Greek capital of Athens. These areas cover a dramatic range of Greek cuisine and culture—from the ranches of the plains and the honey and wild-game–producing mountains to the city life of Athens, where much of the cuisine of Greece comes together.

The Peloponnese

The Peloponnese is virtually an island but for the thin stretch of land connecting it to Attica and mainland Greece. This region consists of vast coastal and inland plains and mountain ranges that provide Greece with much of its vegetables and fruits, such as kalamata olives, figs, grapes, citrus, eggplant, wheat, garlic, and artichokes, as well as cheese and pork. The coastal regions also yield significant catches of octopus and bonito tuna, which are used for various dishes.

The Islands

Greece contains nearly 2,000 islands, of which about 200 are inhabited. The islands are mostly rugged lands that do not support a large variety of agriculture but do provide access to a rich sea. Separating the islands regionally would result in the Ionian Islands to the west in the Ionian Sea, the large island of Crete to the south, the Dodecanese Islands off the coast of Turkey in the east, and the Aegean and Sporades Islands to the north in the Aegean Sea. All of these regions are known for particular specialties, including the pasta dishes of Corfu in the Ionian, the chickpea fritters found in the Dodecanese, the sea urchin of the northern Aegean, and the squid cooked with olive and fennel from Crete. A few things are constants among all of the islands: there is an abundance of fisheries; the dry, rough terrain of most areas is ideal for the growth of olives and many grapes; and many areas are dependent on the mainland for much of their basic food (as the mainland eagerly awaits the catch from the sea). This setup has historically driven the people of this region to the sea not only for seafood but also as a means of accessing necessities on the mainland.

RECIPES

The following recipes provide an introduction to Greek cuisine and the methods used in making Greek meals.

Yogurt

(SOURED MILK)

INGREDIENTS

2	qts	Whole Milk (sheep's milk, or cow's milk if sheep's milk is not available)
4	oz	Plain Yogurt with active culture (or substitute 2 oz buttermilk)

Yogurt is a common ingredient in Greek cuisine and is still made in many homes throughout Greece, although most now purchase it from the store. Yogurt can be made continuously, using some of each batch to start the next batch, assuming that everything is handled properly. It is very important to follow all the rules of sanitation when making yogurt—contamination can give undesirable bacteria the opportunity to grow.

NOTE: *This recipe depends on the proper sanitation of all equipment and on clean handling practices. Extra care must be used to guard against contamination at any point during this process!*

YIELD: 2 quarts

SPECIAL METHOD: Sanitary Fermentation

(continues)

PROCEDURE

Yogurt
(continued)

1. Heat milk in small pot to 180°F and hold at temperature for 4 minutes.

2. Let milk cool to 85°F before adding plain yogurt, and stir thoroughly to mix.

3. Transfer milk/yogurt mixture to sanitized glass jar or ceramic pot (be sure to thoroughly clean and sanitize fermentation vessel), and cover with clean cloth secured with a rubber band or another tie to keep cloth from contacting the mixture inside.

4. Place the fermentation vessel with the yogurt starter in area approximately 70°F, and allow fermentation without disturbing for 1 day.

5. Check for fermentation progress of mixture by checking consistency of mixture. It should thicken to yogurt consistency; if not thickened, give mixture another day and check again. If still not thickened, discard. (Making yogurt is a controlled fermentation done by inoculating the milk mixture with lactobacillus bacteria—from yogurt—which sour and preserve the milk by producing lactic acid. Lack of thickening is an indication that acidity is not being achieved, and the cautious response is to discard the milk with unknown bacterial growth.)

6. Save some of the thickened yogurt to use as a starter for the next batch of yogurt.

Tzatziki

(YOGURT, CUCUMBER, AND MINT CONDIMENT)

INGREDIENTS

12	oz	Fresh Yogurt, strained (hang in cheesecloth or strain in coffee filter to remove excess moisture)
8	oz	Cucumber, peeled, seeded, grated, and squeezed of excess moisture
.5	oz	Garlic Cloves, minced
1	Tbsp	Minced Fresh Mint
1	fl oz	Extra Virgin Olive Oil
		Salt and Pepper, to taste

This is a very common condiment that is served with lamb and other grilled foods.

YIELD: 1 pint

METHOD: Mixing

PROCEDURE

1. After draining yogurt in cheesecloth, wring slightly to remove additional liquid and transfer to mixing bowl.

2. Add squeezed cucumber, garlic, and mint, and mix while slowly whisking in olive oil.

3. Season with salt and pepper.

Hummus bi Tahini

(CHICKPEA AND SESAME SPREAD/DIP)

INGREDIENTS

For Soaking Chickpeas (soaked overnight)

9	oz (1.5 cups)	Dried Chickpeas (garbanzo beans)
3	cups	Water

For Cooking Chickpeas

1	Tbsp	Olive Oil
4		Garlic Cloves, minced
2	oz	White Onion, minced
		Soaked Chickpeas (see above), water drained and discarded
4	cups	Water
2	Bay	Leaves
2	tsp	Salt

For Puréeing the Hummus

		Chickpea Mixture (see above), excess water drained off
5	oz	Tahini
3	fl oz	Lemon Juice
5	fl oz	Extra Virgin Olive Oil
		Salt and Pepper, to taste

The Arab influence on Greek cuisine is found in the popularity of this dish, which is common throughout the Middle East.

YIELD: 2.5 cups

COOKING METHOD (CHICKPEAS): Simmering

METHOD (FINISHING): Puréeing

PROCEDURE

1. One day in advance, soak chickpeas in water to rehydrate.
2. Drain excess water from soaked chickpeas prior to next step.
3. In small pot, sweat garlic and onions in 1 Tbsp olive oil until translucent.
4. Add drained chickpeas, water, bay leaves, and salt to pot; bring to a simmer.
5. Simmer chickpeas until chickpeas become completely soft, adding water if necessary to keep chickpeas submerged.
6. Once chickpeas are tender, strain off excess moisture and transfer to food processor.
7. Add tahini and lemon juice to food processor and, with processor running slowly, add in olive oil to form a smooth paste.
8. Season mixture with salt and pepper.

Hummus bi tahini with slices of accompanying flatbread on left

Avgolemono

(LEMON SAUCE)

INGREDIENTS

3		Egg Whites
3		Egg Yolks
2		Lemons, juiced
1.5	cup	Stock, warm (130–140°F)

This classic Greek sauce is commonly served with fish or used to thicken soups, which is why it is sometimes referred to as a soup. Care must be taken to make this properly, for the eggs can get too hot and curdle.

YIELD: 2 cups

METHOD (EGG WHITES): Whipping to Create Foam

METHOD FOR FINISHING: Whisking

PROCEDURE

1. Beat the egg whites to stiff peaks with a wire whip.
2. Beat the egg yolks and add them to the beaten whites.
3. Combine the lemon juice and stock, and add to the egg mixture while stirring constantly.

First step in making avgolemono (lemon sauce): whipping the egg yolks and egg whites separately before combining

Beating the stock and lemon juice into the egg mixture to finish the avgolemono

Horta

(WILD GREENS)

INGREDIENTS

6	bunches	Arugula (can substitute dandelion or radish greens)
2	bunches	Sorrel
3	Tbsp	Extra Virgin Olive Oil
2	Tbsp	Fresh Lemon Juice
		Salt and Black Pepper, to taste

Wild greens are very common in Greece, where they would be collected (more commonly cultivated now, as elsewhere) to make salads or dishes such as this one.

YIELD: 8 portions (approximately 2 ounces each)

COOKING METHOD: Boiling

PROCEDURE

1. Heat a pot of salted water over a high flame until it reaches the boiling point.
2. Quickly blanch the greens in the salted water until just wilted, and remove from water with a strainer.
3. After greens have cooled to room temperature, season with olive oil, lemon juice, salt, and pepper; serve.

✳ Pita Bread

(POCKETED FLATBREAD)

INGREDIENTS

1.5	oz	Active Dry Yeast
1	tsp	Sugar
1	cup	Water, warm
2	lbs + dusting	Bread Flour
2.5	tsp	Salt
1	cup	Water
3	oz	Unsalted Butter, melted
		Cornmeal, as needed

Rolling the pita dough pieces prior to second proofing

Rolled pita dough in proof box after second proofing; note that the dough doesn't rise significantly during second proofing

Baked pita; note that the dough should "puff" from intense heat and just color (pita in lower right corner is slightly overdone, whereas the others are perfect)

Bread is a mainstay of Greek cuisine, and this is an example of their expertise in utilizing the characteristics of bread to make a unique product. The pocket is formed in the pita from the rapid expansion of trapped CO_2 and steam from being proofed (allowed to sit at optimal temperature and humidity for yeast growth) twice and then placed in a very hot oven. Pita is actually another example of the Middle Eastern influence on Greek cuisine, as they introduced the process of making flatbreads to the Greeks.

YIELD: 10 pitas

MIXING METHOD: Straight Dough

COOKING METHOD: Baking at Very High Heat

PROCEDURE

1. Preheat proofbox to 90°F.

2. Bloom yeast in first cup of warm water with sugar added.

3. Sift flour into mixing bowl; add salt and mix thoroughly.

4. Add bloomed yeast and water to mixing bowl, and mix to combine.

5. Using a dough hook attachment, add remaining water and melted butter to mixing bowl to form a smooth dough (if dough sticks to the bowl, add more flour until it no longer sticks).

6. Mix on low speed until dough has become smooth and can be stretched into a thin, transparent sheet without tearing.

7. Place dough in a lightly oiled pan and allow it to proof until double in volume (approximately 1 hour).

8. Remove dough from proofbox, punch dough down, and turn to makeup area.

9. Divide dough into 10 pieces and roll out dough into circles on a lightly floured surface; place rolled circles onto a sheet pan. Once completed, place the sheet pan back into the proofbox and preheat oven to 500°F.

10. Remove dough from proofbox after 10 minutes and let it rest on the table for 10 more, covered in a clean cloth.

11. Place the sheets on bottom rack of oven for 3 to 4 minutes, or until dough has puffed up. At this point, check the bottom of the pita and see if it is still moist and doughy, or if it is drier and set. If it is drier and set, the pita is done and the next step is unnecessary.

12. Turn oven down to 450°F and move the sheet pan to the middle of the oven to finish baking (about another 4 to 5 minutes).

Fava Santorinis
(YELLOW SPLIT PEA PURÉE)

INGREDIENTS

2	oz	Extra Virgin Olive Oil
1		Small Yellow Onion, minced
8	oz	Dried Yellow Split Pea
2	cups	Water
1/2	tsp	Dried Oregano
1		Bay Leaf
4	oz	Lemon, juiced
4	oz	Extra Virgin Olive Oil
		Salt and Black Pepper, to taste

This spread makes an excellent appetizer served with pita or other flat-breads and is a common part of a meze table.

YIELD: 3 cups

COOKING METHOD: Simmering

PROCEDURE

1. In a small saucepot, heat the olive oil and sweat the onions until translucent.
2. Add the split peas, water, oregano, and bay leaf, and simmer until the split peas are completely soft and mushy. Add more water during this process, if necessary.
3. Transfer mixture to food processor or use a handheld blender to purée mixture to smooth paste, adding lemon juice as it is being puréed.
4. Finish with extra virgin olive oil.
5. Season to taste with salt, black pepper, and more olive oil, if desired.

Patates Psites
(LEMON POTATOES)

INGREDIENTS

2.25	lbs	Yukon Gold Potatoes, peeled and cut into inch wedges
2	oz	Olive Oil (preferably extra virgin)
1	Tbsp	Dried Oregano (or substitute 2 Tbsp fresh, minced oregano)
1/2	tsp	Salt (more or less, to taste)
		Juice and Zest of 2 Lemons
		Water, as needed
2	oz	Olive Oil (preferably extra virgin)

These potatoes are cooked in a unique manner: they are roasted while partially covered in a flavored liquid. By cooking them in this manner, the potatoes absorb the flavorful liquid and crisp as the liquid evaporates.

YIELD: 8 servings (approximately 5 ounces each)

COOKING METHOD: Roasting

PROCEDURE

1. Preheat oven to 400°F.
2. Toss the potatoes, 2 oz olive oil, oregano, salt, lemon juice, and zest together in a mixing bowl to coat potatoes with mixture.
3. Place potatoes in a pan that will hold them snugly in a single layer.
4. Add water to just cover potatoes.
5. Bake in oven until the water has evaporated.
6. Remove pan from oven and drizzle remaining olive oil over the potatoes. Return to oven, baking until potatoes turn golden brown.

Briami
(Summer Vegetable Casserole)

INGREDIENTS

8	oz	Zucchini, halved and sliced on bias
8	oz	Waxy Potatoes, cut into 1/2-inch wedges
8	oz	Eggplant, diced large (3/4 inch square)
8	oz	Tomatoes, concassée
12	oz	Yellow Onion, diced large
6	oz	Green Bell Pepper, diced large
1/4	bunch	Italian Parsley, minced
1/2	tsp	Dried Oregano
1/4	tsp	Dried Thyme
1/4	tsp	Salt
1/4	tsp	Black Pepper
4	oz	Extra Virgin Olive Oil
4	oz	Water
8	oz	Feta Cheese, crumbled

Greek cuisine includes many recipes that use fresh vegetables; in this example, the vegetables are used to make a casserole that is topped with one of Greece's most well-known cheeses.

YIELD: 10 portions (approximately 4 ounces each)

COOKING METHOD (INITIAL): Baking

COOKING METHOD (TO FINISH): Broiling

PROCEDURE

1. Preheat oven to 350°F.
2. Combine all ingredients except for water and feta cheese, and toss to mix thoroughly.
3. Place mixture into 1/2 sheet pan, add water, and place uncovered in the oven for 1 1/2 hours. Check periodically to ensure that water has not completely evaporated.
4. Once potatoes become tender, take them out of the oven and distribute the cheese over the vegetables. Place them under the broiler to melt and color cheese.

Keftedes
(Lamb Meatballs)

INGREDIENTS

1	slice	White bread
2	oz	Water
1	lb	Ground Lamb
5	oz	Yellow Onion, minced
1/2	tsp	Oregano, dried
1	tsp	Mint, fresh and minced
1	Tbsp	Flat-Leaf Parsley, fresh and minced
1/2	tsp	Salt
1		Large Egg, beaten
1	oz	Flour (more, if needed to coat)
3	oz	Olive Oil
1		Lemon, cut into wedges or halves for squeezing

Yet another example of the Middle Eastern influence in the cuisine of Greece, these seasoned meatballs are believed to have evolved from Middle Eastern preparations of pounded lamb. These are often made small and served as part of a meze table, as this recipe intends.

YIELD: Approximately twenty 1-ounce meatballs

COOKING METHOD: Panfrying

PROCEDURE

1. Combine white bread and water in a bowl, and allow it to soak for 5 minutes.
2. With hands, squeeze out excess moisture from bread and place it in a mixing bowl.
3. Add all other ingredients except flour, olive oil, and lemon to mixing bowl with bread, and mix thoroughly with hands to make a smooth mixture.
4. Make small meatballs with mixture by rolling it in your hands, and set aside.
5. Heat sauté pan with olive oil. Coat each meatball with flour, taking care to pat off any excess flour. Panfry the meatballs in the heated olive oil.
6. Squeeze fresh lemon juice over the meatballs before serving.

Souvlakia

(SKEWERED AND GRILLED LAMB)

INGREDIENTS

2		Lemons, zested and juiced
6	oz	Olive Oil
.5	oz	Garlic Cloves, minced
1	Tbsp	Minced Fresh Oregano
1/2	tsp	Salt
1/2	tsp	Freshly Ground Black Pepper
2	lbs	Leg of Lamb, cut into 1-inch cubes
1.5	lbs	Green Peppers, cut into 32 squares
1	lb	Yellow Squash, cut into 32 slices
1.5	lbs	Pearl Onions, peeled (should be about 32 onions)
16		12-inch Metal Skewers (if these are unavailable, use wooden skewers that have been soaked in water for 1 hour)

This is a popular preparation for lamb and is often served with pita bread and tzatziki so that the grilled lamb pieces can be wrapped in bread and eaten out of hand. This also makes a nice entrée when served with lemon potatoes and yogurt sauce (see the accompanying photo).

YIELD: 16 skewers (approximately 4 ounces each)

COOKING METHOD: Grilling

PROCEDURE

1. Combine lemon juice, zest, garlic, oregano, salt, and pepper in mixing bowl, and mix thoroughly.

2. Using the metal skewers (or soaked skewers), place the lamb and vegetables onto the skewers. Take care to place 2 of each vegetable and approximately 3 pieces of lamb on each skewer.

3. Pour the marinade from step 1 over the skewers, and make sure to rub marinade into the surface of all of the individual skewers.

4. Grill the skewered lamb and vegetables to desired doneness.

Souvlakia (lamb skewers) plated with tzatziki sauce (yogurt/cucumber sauce) and patates psites (lemon potatoes)

Moussaka
(Eggplant Casserole with Lamb)

INGREDIENTS

For Preparing Eggplant

| 5 | lbs | Eggplant, sliced 1/2-inch thick |
| 1 | Tbsp | Salt |

For Preparing Béchamel Sauce

2	fl oz	Clarified Butter
2.5	oz	Flour
5	cups	Whole Milk
		Pinch of Nutmeg
2		Egg Yolks
1/4	tsp	Salt

For Preparing Meat Sauce

1	oz	Olive Oil
12	oz	Yellow Onion, minced
1	oz	Garlic Cloves, minced
1.5	lbs	Lamb, ground (can substitute beef, if desired)
8	fl oz	Dry White Wine
16	oz	(2 cups) Canned Diced Tomatoes with Juice
2	Tbsp	Tomato Paste
2	Tbsp	Flat-Leaf Parsley, minced
		Salt and Pepper, to taste

For Panfrying Eggplant

| 1 | cup | Olive Oil |
| | | Eggplant (see above), rinsed of salt and dried |

For Assembly of Moussaka

1	Tbsp	Olive Oil
		Eggplant (see above)
		Meat Sauce (see above)
		Béchamel (see above)
2	oz	(1/2 cup) Dried Bread Crumbs
10	oz	(2 cups) Grated Kefalotyri Cheese (substitute pecorino or parmesan, if necessary)

This well-known Greek casserole consists of layers of eggplant and meat (or meat sauce), topped with béchamel sauce that browns as the casserole is baked.

YIELD: 10 portions (approximately 8 ounces each)

COOKING METHOD (BÉCHAMEL AND MEAT SAUCE): Simmering

COOKING METHOD (EGGPLANT): Panfrying

COOKING METHOD (FINAL CASSEROLE): Baking

PROCEDURE

For Preparing Eggplant

1. Preheat oven to 350°F.
2. Sprinkle 1 Tbsp of salt over the slices of eggplant, and spread eggplant out on sheet pan. Allow it to sit for 15 minutes (this draws out excess water and reduces the bitterness of the eggplant) before rinsing eggplant with cold water and patting it dry with a clean paper towel.

For Preparing Béchamel Sauce

1. Add clarified butter to a small pot over a medium flame, and add in flour to make white roux.
2. Remove roux from heat and add in milk, whisking to ensure the complete distribution of the roux throughout the milk.
3. Bring mixture to a light simmer and reduce heat; allow mixture to cook over low flame for 30 minutes. (Take care to control the heat, and stir often to prevent scorching.)
4. Remove béchamel sauce from heat, and allow it to cool for 10 minutes before adding nutmeg, egg yolks, and salt.

For Preparing Meat Sauce

1. Heat olive oil in a medium pot; add onion and garlic, and sweat until translucent.
2. Add ground lamb to the pot and turn up heat to sauté the lamb/onion mixture.
3. Once the lamb has begun to color (be careful not to burn it), deglaze with white wine.
4. Reduce white wine by half, and then add tomato and tomato paste. Turn down the heat to cook slowly.
5. Simmer slowly for 40 minutes (adding water, if necessary); remove from heat and season with parsley and salt.

For Panfrying Eggplant

1. Add 1 oz of olive oil to a sauté pan, and then add just enough slices of rinsed and dried eggplant slices to cover the bottom of the pan. Sauté eggplant on both sides in hot olive oil; cook until golden brown before removing from pan. Continue this process until all of the eggplant has been sautéed, adding more olive oil as needed.

(continues)

Moussaka
(continued)

For Assembling the Moussaka

1. Add 1 Tbsp of olive oil to the bottom of a hotel pan, and spread to coat bottom of pan.

2. Place panfried eggplant in one even layer, one slice thick, on top of the greased pan. Spread a thin layer of the meat sauce mixture over the eggplant, and continue to layer until all of the eggplant and meat sauce have been distributed.

3. Cover this mixture with the béchamel sauce, and spread with moistened metal spatula to make even.

4. Sprinkle bread crumbs and cheese over the top of this mixture, and place the hotel pan in the preheated 350°F oven.

5. Bake the casserole for 25 minutes, checking it after 20 minutes. If it is browned on top, remove and serve (if not, return it to the oven and bake until it browns).

Casseroles of briami (top) and moussaka (bottom right)

Panfried Mullet with Citrus Sauce

INGREDIENTS

2		Lemons, zested and juiced
1		Orange, zested and juiced
2	fl oz	Extra Virgin Olive Oil
1	Tbsp	Fresh Oregano, minced
1	tsp	Black Pepper, freshly ground
4	lbs	Red Mullet Fillet (substitute other lean whitefish if this is unavailable), cut into 20 pieces
3	oz	Flour, seasoned (for dredging)
2	fl oz	Olive Oil
12	fl oz	Dry White Wine
3		Oranges, rinds removed and cut into 1/4-inch wheels
1		Lemon, rind removed and cut into 1/4-inch wheel
3	oz	Extra Virgin Olive Oil
1	Tbsp	Fresh Parsley, minced
1/2	tsp	Salt

Fish is a major part of the Greek diet, and mullet is one of the more commonly enjoyed Mediterranean varieties. The abundance of citrus in Greece makes for frequent pairings of citrus and fish, as in this recipe.

YIELD: 10 portions (approximately 7 ounces each)

COOKING METHOD: Panfrying

PROCEDURE

1. Combine the lemon juice, lemon zest, orange juice, orange zest, extra virgin olive oil, oregano, and black pepper in a mixing bowl, and mix thoroughly.

2. Cover fish with this marinade. Cover fish with plastic and allow it to marinate in refrigerator for 2 to 4 hours.

3. Remove fish from marinade, letting excess drain off; dredge in seasoned flour.

4. Panfry lightly floured fish in sauté pan with pure olive oil, taking care to color both sides of the fish without burning the bottom of the pan.

5. Deglaze pan with white wine, and add orange and lemon wheels to pan.

6. Let wine and citrus mixture reduce slightly before finishing with extra virgin olive oil.

7. Season with salt and add parsley.

Baklava

(LAYERED CRISP DOUGH WITH CRUSHED NUTS SOAKED IN SPICED HONEY SYRUP)

INGREDIENTS

For Making the Syrup

12	oz	Honey
18	oz	Sugar
2		Cinnamon Sticks
4		Whole Cloves
2		Whole Lemons, squeezed (Whole Lemon cut in half and added)
1.5	cups	Water

For Assembling the Pastry

5	oz	Pistachios, whole
4	oz	Almonds, whole

This classic Eastern-influenced sweet reveals the link between Greece and its neighbors to the east. Many cultures claim to have invented baklava, and much evidence points to the Middle East as its place of origin. Although Greece might not have been its birthplace, the Greeks certainly have embraced and mastered the methods of making some of the finest baklava around.

YIELD: Approximately 20 pieces (3 ounces each)

COOKING METHOD: Baking

PROCEDURE

For Making the Syrup

1. Combine all ingredients in a small saucepan; simmer gently for 30 minutes or until syrupy in consistency.

2. Strain syrup while still hot to remove cinnamon stick, cloves, and lemon.

(continues)

Baklava

(continued)

1	tsp	Cinnamon
3	oz	Plain Dry Bread Crumbs
4	oz	Sugar
10	oz	Unsalted Butter, melted
1	lb	Phyllo Dough, commercially prepared
		Syrup (see above)

For Assembling the Pastry

1. Preheat oven to 300°F.

2. Place almonds and pistachios on baking sheet; bake for 8 to 10 minutes, or until nuts just begin to color slightly, before removing from oven to cool. Reset oven to 350°F.

3. After nuts have cooled, crush them coarsely using either a mortar and pestle or a rolling pin.

4. Combine crushed nuts with cinnamon, bread crumbs, and sugar; mix thoroughly.

5. To assemble the baklava, first brush a shallow baking dish (approximately the same size as the phyllo sheets) with butter. Add 2 sheets of buttered phyllo dough to the bottom of the dish, and sprinkle a thin layer of nut/bread crumb mixture onto the sheets.

6. Place another buttered phyllo sheet on top of the nut/bread crumb mixture, and then top that sheet with a thin layer of nut/bread crumb mixture; continue this layering until you have either reached the top of your pan or you have added 10 layers, finishing with a layer of phyllo dough with no nut mixture on top of it.

7. Sprinkle or spray the surface of the phyllo dough with some water to moisten it, and cut into a diamond-shaped pattern by cutting straight lines the length of the narrow part of the dish, approximately 2 inches apart, followed by cutting lines at 45° angles to the straight lines (also approximately 2 inches apart).

8. Cover the prepared baklava with a sheet of aluminum foil, if baking in a convection oven (the phyllo will be blown off if this is not done).

9. Place baklava into preheated 350°F oven; bake for 30 to 40 minutes, or until the surface is golden brown.

10. Remove baklava from the oven and allow it to cool completely.

11. Reheat syrup in a small saucepan for a thinner consistency, and pour evenly over the surface of the baked, cooled baklava.

12. Slice the baklava using the diamond pattern on the surface to serve.

Baklava drizzled with honey reduction

SUMMARY

Greek cuisine is one of the world's true ancient cuisines, and the location of Greece between countries of both European and Middle Eastern culture has greatly influenced its development. The Greeks formed one of the earliest empires, and part of the glory of this empire was found in the kitchens, where the beginning of a refined cuisine was evident. Greek cuisine is typical of the Mediterranean, in that olives, olive oil, grapes, and citrus all thrive, and in the dependence on bread as a main food. However, it differs dramatically from other European cuisines of the Mediterranean in the prevalence of lamb and goat as typical meats, and in its Middle Eastern-influenced dishes. Fresh vegetables and wild greens are a major part of the Greek diet. Combining lamb, many types of seafood, and the constant presence of bread, cheese, and olives, the Greek diet reflects a blending of both Eastern and Western influences.

REVIEW QUESTIONS

1. What two divergent cultures have influenced the cuisine of Greece?

2. How has Greece's geographical location influenced the development of its cuisine?

3. What type of milk is most commonly used to make the Greek cheeses?

4. Besides cheese, what are the main sources of protein in the Greek diet?

COMMON TERMS, FOODS, AND INGREDIENTS

✳ Ingredients and Foods

amfissa – Brine-cured, rounder black olive

anthotiro – Sheep's or goat's milk cheese made from whey; it is typically soft, with characteristics similar to ricotta

avgolemono – Lemon sauce common in Greek cuisine; also the name of a soup prepared in the same manner

baklava – Pastry made from layering and buttering phyllo dough with nuts, spices, and sugar, and then topping with a flavored honey syrup after baking

briami – Baked, seasoned vegetable mixture topped with feta cheese

elies neratzates – Olives cured and then steeped in bitter orange juice

fava santorinis – Yellow split pea purée

feta – The best known of the Greek cheeses, made from either sheep's or goat's milk; it is typically stored in brine

flomaria – Type of Greek pasta that is either long and thin as a string or slightly flattened

garbanzo beans – Another name for chickpeas

graviera – Hard cheese made from cow's milk, similar in texture and flavor to Swiss cheese

halkidika – Brine-cured, large green olive

haloumi – Firm sheep's or goat's milk cheese with a very high protein content, which allows it to hold its shape when heated and enables it to be grilled

hilopittes – Greek egg noodle pasta that is typically long and thin or cut square

horta – Wild greens

hourmades – Dried, wrinkled black olives from the Aegean Islands off of the coast of Turkey

hummus bi tahini – Cooked and puréed chickpeas seasoned with olive oil, garlic, lemon juice, and tahini

kalamata – Brine-cured, elongated black olive

kasseri – Semi-hard sheep's milk cheese

kefalograviera – Hard-grating cheese, typically made from the milk of goats, sheep, or a combination of the two

kefalotyri – Salty, tangy hard cheese made from sheep's or goat's milk

keftedes – Seasoned lamb meatballs

kritharakia – Greek pasta shaped like a rice grain that traditionally were made from barley but now are often made from wheat; commonly called orzo in the United States

ladotiri – Hard cheese matured in oil

louza – Cured pork loin made by salting and washing the loins followed by a spice rub and air drying; some types are also soaked in wine and given a spice rub before being smoked over burning grape vines

manouri – Mild, soft sheep's milk cheese

maonias – Brine-cured black olive

meze – Small snacks or bite-size portions of food, typically served with alcohol

mitzithra – Semi-soft sheep's milk cheese with crumbly texture, made from whey

moussaka – Baked dish made from layered eggplant with white sauce, meat sauce, and cheese

orzo – Italian name for kritharakia, rice-shaped pasta

ouzo – Anise-flavored distilled beverage

patates psites – Roasted potatoes with lemon and oregano

phyllo – Thin dough common to both Greek and Middle Eastern cuisines; the literal translation is "leaf," as this dough is compared to thin leaves

pita – Flatbread baked at very high temperatures, which causes it to puff and have a pocket in the center (also spelled "pitta")

psari – Fish

psarolia – Cured fish found on some of the islands; fish is salted and sundried for preservation. This is used in making some fish keftedes (chopped fish patties).

roka – Arugula

souvlakia – Skewered and grilled lamb

spanakopita – Savory pies wrapped in phyllo and typically baked

tahini – Sesame seed paste

thassos throumba – Salt-cured black olive

tzatziki – Yogurt cucumber sauce seasoned with garlic

zoupes – Wrinkled, black, salt-cured olives found on the Dodecanese Islands

CHAPTER 3

NORWAY

NORTH SEA

BALTIC SEA

SWEDEN

ESTONIA

LATVIA

RUSSIA

DENMARK

LITHUANIA

BELARUS

NETH.

POLAND
★ Warsaw

BELGIUM

GERMANY

UKRAINE

LUX.

★ Prague
CZECH REPUBLIC

SLOVAKIA

CARPATHIAN MOUNTAINS

MOLDOVA

FRANCE

Danube River

AUSTRIA

★ Bratislava

Danube River

★ Budapest

Tisza River

HUNGARY

ROMANIA

LIECH.

SWITZERLAND

SLOVENIA
★
Ljubljana ★ Zagreb

CROATIA

BOSNIA-
HERZEGOVINA

★ Belgrade

TRANSYLVANIAN ALPS

Danube River

★ Bucharest

Sarajevo ★

YUGOSLAVIA
(SERBIA
MONTENEGRO)

Danube River

DINARIC ALPS

Balkan Peninsula

BULGARIA

BLACK SEA

ADRIATIC SEA

ITALY

★ Skopje

MACEDONIA

Tirana ★

ALBANIA

GREECE

TURKEY

N
W   E
S

0   100   200 km

★ capital city

─── river

─·─·─ international boundary

▓▓ mountains

MEDITERRANEAN SEA

MALTA

Eastern European Cuisine

OBJECTIVES

Upon completion of this chapter, you will be able to

- explain what makes the cuisine of Eastern Europe unique.
- explain the similarities that Eastern European cuisine shares with cuisines of surrounding areas.
- discuss how wars, redrawn borders, and ethnic migrations have made country-specific cuisines in this region obscure.
- understand the common cooking methods employed in Eastern European cuisine.
- recognize some examples of Eastern European recipes.
- produce a variety of recipes common to Eastern European cuisine.
- define the terms listed at the conclusion of the chapter.

INTRODUCTION

Eastern Europe is a land that has been torn, redrawn, and torn again; this section of Europe has long been one of overlapping cultures and ethnicities that have had relatively little time over the course of history to develop a "home" of their own. The major ethnic groups of this region include Slavic peoples, who are thought to be indigenous to the area of Poland; Turkish peoples, who are believed mostly to be descendents of Ottoman peoples; Romani peoples (often called *gypsies* in the United States), who are believed to have migrated to this region from northern India 1,000 years ago; the Magyars, who are believed to have migrated from southwestern Asia into present-day Hungary; Albanian peoples from the area of present-day Albania; and Ashkenazi Jewish peoples, who migrated here following their persecution in the Middle East. Smaller populations of Germanic, Greek, and Tartaric peoples also are found in this region. The Slavic peoples, who compose a major population of the region, can be further divided into Serbian, Croatian, Bulgarian, Polish, and Czech, among other nationalities. Clearly this is a complex and diverse region, one that is partially defined by this complex mix of ethnicities. As such, the cuisines of this section are also varied. Because many of these groups have been persecuted and ruled by outside forces at some point in history, it should not be a surprise that their culinary traditions have been retained proudly; often, the ethnicity of a person is a better indicator of their typical diet than the country in which he or she resides. This should be kept in mind as you read this chapter, because the border drawings and forced migrations that are a part of the history of this region often do not coincide with the heritage of someone living within a country's border.

Eastern Europe covers a vast area and includes many different climatic and agricultural regions. On the northern end of this region lie the vast plains of Poland, which stretch from the Baltic Sea to the Carpathian Mountains on Poland's southern borders. The plains are seasonal, with a temperate climate suited to producing many of the agricultural products found in other northern European countries, such as potatoes, cabbage, parsnips, cucumbers, and beets. Heading south from Poland, the terrain becomes more hilly and mountainous, and the climate becomes warmer, with the exception of the highlands in Romania and the Balkans. In the southernmost section of Eastern Europe, the countries of Albania, Montenegro, Bosnia, Herzegovina, Croatia, and Slovenia all lie on the Mediterranean Sea. On the eastern borders of this region are the former Soviet republics of Belarus and Ukraine in the north; the Black Sea, Turkey, and Greece border the southern sections. To the west, the bordering countries are Germany in the north, Austria, and Italy in the south.

The following chapter examines this large and complex region and provides an overview of some of the most important aspects of what makes this cuisine both unique and familiar.

HISTORIC CULINARY INFLUENCES

Historically, Eastern Europe has been the site of numerous conflicts, redrawn borders, and shifting ethnic cultures. The overlapping of cultures throughout the history of this region makes descriptions of the influences complicated and often difficult to follow; however, some cultures have had a more profound effect than others on the culinary traditions of this region, and those will be the focus of this section.

Greek Empire

Much of Eastern Europe came under the influence of the Greek Empire during the height of its power. Some of the Greek practices that spread into the southern part of the region, include the production and use of olive oil, the inclusion of olives in cooking, the process of bread making (which the Greeks learned from the Egyptians), and advances in cultivating techniques. These early influences helped to put in place the conditions that would encourage the creation of civilizations in years to come.

Roman Empire

The Roman Empire spread into the southern portion of Eastern Europe shortly before the beginning of the new calendar and remained a dominant influence throughout the fourth century. The biggest contribution to the area of food was the Roman expertise in organization. One of the lasting influences of the Roman Empire—wherever they ruled—was their formation of irrigation and agricultural improvements, which meant more foods, more variety, and the relative leisure that comes with these. As these improvements became part of Eastern European cultures, the culinary impact was an increase in available products and often the possibility of making "gourmet" products. Prior to these improvements, survival had been the primary culinary goal.

Magyars from Asia

The ancestors of much of the population of present-day Hungary were known as the Magyars, a group that migrated west in the ninth century to this area from Asia during the height of power of the Byzantine Empire. These people traditionally cooked rich stews over a fire in a large kettle, and this cooking method and dish was known as *gulyas*—a name and method that remain to this day. Although many stews are no longer cooked in large kettles over a fire, the fundamental aspects of slow cooking in a liquid to yield a highly flavored stew remain a part of Hungarian cooking today. The later addition of paprika from the Ottoman Turks, and onions from Italy (following a marriage of Hungarian and Italian royalty), resulted in what are commonly known as gulyas today. The heavy use of paprika in stews is characteristic not only of Hungarian cuisine but also of many of the neighboring countries to which Hungarians lent their influence.

Another tradition of the Magyars is that of air drying foods. This method is seen not only in the production of paprika from the chiles used to make the spice but also in their tradition of making *tarhonya*, the dried pasta-like dough that has been a part of their culture for centuries.

Turks from the Ottoman Empire

The influence that the Ottoman Empire had throughout Eastern Europe was significant, because much of this land was ruled by the Ottomans during the height of their power. The most heavily influenced area was the Balkan region, which was ruled over for more than 500 years, as recently as the twentieth century. The Turkish influence can be seen in foods like stuffed vegetables, yogurt-based sauces, and skewered and grilled meats; the use of phyllo dough (also called *pita* in some Balkan areas); the cookery and use of rice; and the inclusion of honey-soaked sweets and sweet-thickened nuts and grains, such as *halva* (sesame dried fruit and honey bars) and *baklava* (layered phyllo, nuts, and honey). These influences have given a strong character to the cuisine of Eastern Europe, especially in the more southern areas, where Turkish rule was longer and more consistent. In the Balkan region, lamb and mutton are very common meats, often served with rice dishes cooked in the Persian fashion that the Turks called pilaf or pilav. These typically are served with either a yogurt-based sauce or a sheep's milk cheese.

The Ottoman Turks had one of the most dominant influences on Eastern Europe, introducing many techniques and refinements to the native cuisine that provide much of the richness of this cuisine today.

Italy

Throughout history, the inhabitants of present-day Italy have influences this part of the world—first during the reign of the Roman Empire and later, during the Renaissance period (sixteenth century), by the nobility of the great regions of Italy. In Hungary, the wedding of King Matthias to Beatrice, the Italian daughter of the king of Naples, brought the same influx of Italian culinary foundations and methods to Hungary as Catherine de' Medici brought to France. Onions, garlic, stuffed meats, and an array of sauces were introduced to Hungary and spread to other areas from there. In Poland during the sixteenth century, King Sigismund married an Italian, Bona Sforza from Milan, who brought with her chefs from Italy and thus introduced the methods of Renaissance Italy to Poland. In some of the Eastern European regions closer to Italy, the Italian influence is evident in the use of pastas and gnocchi, and in many of the dessert preparations.

Considering Italy's artistic output during the critical development period of the Renaissance, the culinary influence that radiated out of Italy during this time cannot be overstated. Similar to the way French cuisine would further refine the culinary arts in the years to come, much of the groundwork throughout Europe was laid by the Italian chefs of this time, often in a quest to impress the royalty of another land.

Austrian Habsburg Empire and Austro-Hungarian Empire

The Habsburg Empire of the Middle Ages introduced many German traditions to the areas that came under their control during the height of their rule. Foods such as sauerkraut, dumplings, and sausages were brought to the more eastern portion of Europe as this empire battled the Ottoman Empire and others for control of lands. Dishes like leberknödel (liver dumplings) and speckknödeln (bacon dumplings), and the techniques for making sausages, spread along with the Habsburg influence. The Austrian and German influence from this period of rule is felt mostly in the northern areas of the region covered in this chapter, although the influences are certainly seen in the southern areas as well. This empire was one of the dominant forces in the region at the same time as the Ottoman Empire, which was pushing its rule up from the south, and these two empires provided the most significant influences seen in this region today.

In addition to the German influence, the culture that developed in Vienna at this time also had an effect. Vienna was the power center during the fifteenth and sixteenth centuries, and the royalty of the Habsburgs—centered in Vienna—drew interest from all over Europe, which resulted in one of history's richest culinary centers. The well-known *Wiener schnitzel* (breaded and panfried veal cutlet, fashioned from Italian examples) and *sachertorte* (chocolate torte developed in Vienna) were two foods that entered the scene first in Vienna and eventually entered the Eastern European realm. The pastry arts that developed in Vienna during this period introduced many methods and foods into Eastern European kitchens. The very popular *strudel* (thin dough wrapped around various fillings and baked in loaf form) that is made throughout much of the northern area of Eastern Europe as well as Germany is believed to be a Viennese interpretation of the thin dough popular throughout the Middle East and Turkish Empire, commonly called phyllo. Rolled-in doughs, such as croissants and danishes, were also popularized in this region at this time and eventually made their way to many other areas of Eastern Europe as well. The Viennese also popularized coffee and the tradition of coffee drinking (with accompanying pastries) that is still common in many parts of Eastern Europe. The Viennese may have picked up the methods for making and drinking coffee from the Turks of the Ottoman Empire, but it was the

Viennese who popularized the typical café combination of coffee and European pastries that remains a popular trend today. The grandeur of the Austrian Empire was most visible in Vienna, and the culinary scene of this city was the center of imported influences and innovation that spread into the neighboring countries, leaving a mark of sophistication and a blend of Western and Eastern culinary influences.

UNIQUE COMPONENTS

The cuisines of Eastern Europe possess a complex set of influential factors, because this region lies in or on the border of the gray area that separates Europe and Asia. Much of the uniqueness of the cuisines from this area is connected to the diversity that makes Eastern Europe difficult to define.

Ethnic and Culinary Diversity

The region covered in this chapter is home to over 60 ethnic groups, all of which contribute to the local cuisines. The majority of the people in this region are of Slavic heritage, but the diversity within this population reflects the complexities of the ethnic make-up of this area. The major Slavic populations are located in Poland in the north, Romania in the east, and the Baltic region in the south. Although history has further splintered these groups into Croatians, Serbs, Slovenes, and so forth, many of their traditions have survived these divisions. Other significant ethnic groups include the Magyars in Hungary; the Roma people residing mostly in Romania (a minority in this country); the Germanic people in the northern areas; the Sephardic Jews, who are also mostly in northern areas; the Russians in former republics of the Soviet Union; and Turks and Greeks, mostly in the Balkans. In addition to ethnic diversity, there is religious as well, with Orthodox Christians, Catholics, Jews, and Muslims all represented in this region.

Most of these groups remain segregated wherever they live; thus, the cuisines can be quite different from one area to the next, depending on which ethnicities are dominant in each place. One historical fact that is always helpful to remember when considering the cuisine of this region is that Eastern European borders have been drawn and redrawn numerous times throughout history, and often not in the interest of particular ethnic groups. As a result of this history of unrest and political posturing, many ethnic groups have been mixed, deported, and forcibly relocated, or in many cases have become part of a country not their own. One impact of this is that local cuisine slowly becomes less noticeably ethnic, as the exposure to varied foods and ingredients diversifies it and makes it more inclusive. This is clearly a rule in Eastern Europe, where Turkish, Germanic, French, Slavic, and Russian foods often share the table with the more ethnic dishes of people not from the previously mentioned cultures.

From the Mediterranean to a Northern Tundra Cuisine

Because the area covered in this chapter is so large—and thus the climates, resulting markets, and ultimately the cuisines are very different—it is important to differentiate between these to understand this region. The northern part of Eastern Europe is a land of longer winters, shorter growing seasons, and thus a cuisine of limited resources. Comparing the cuisine of Poland to the cuisine of Bulgaria or other Mediterranean countries is like comparing the cuisine of Germany to that of Spain; although there are connections that tie some of these areas to one another culturally, it is important to acknowledge their major differences.

The cuisine in the north is composed largely of heartier dishes, with stews, soups, and a heavy reliance on grain products providing the sustenance needed in this harsher climate. Butter, sour cream, sausages, and preserved vegetables are part of the fabric of the cuisine of the north. In contrast to the northern cuisine, the southern section of this region features a cuisine that is very similar to other Mediterranean foods, with a heavier emphasis on fresh vegetables, herbs, and the use of olive oil as a cooking fat. The cheeses of the southern cuisines are often made from goat's milk and sheep's milk, and yogurt is a common dairy product, in contrast to the butter and sour cream that are common in the north.

As with cuisines from other parts of the world, location is often one of the most significant factors in what is found on tables across Eastern Europe. This factor is significant in this region, in particular, because the area covered includes such a wide variety of climates and historical influences. In general, the cuisine of the northern portion of the area covered in this chapter reveals the significant influences of the Asiatic tribes, to whom many of the people of this region can trace their heritage, mixed with the European powers that once ruled much of this land. The cuisine of the north is one of hearty foods often stewed or simmered and served with rich sauces, sour cream, and butter. In the southern sections, many of the people also trace their heritage to Asiatic tribes that migrated to these regions, but in this case they have been more significantly influenced by the eastern cuisine because of their history of rule by the Ottoman Turks. Combine the differences in influences between north and south and the difference in climate between these areas, and a clearer picture begins to emerge of these cuisines. However, keep in mind the many ethnicities that are found in both the north and south that make the picture more complex and simultaneously more interesting.

SIGNIFICANT SUBREGIONS

The eastern part of Europe has a storied history that has witnessed the clashing of many cultures, invasions of sovereign lands, and redrawing of borders following horrible wars. This turbulent history has resulted in unrest and shifting borders that have placed a strain on the people who live here. Ethnic lines often don't follow the pattern of drawn borders, and, as such, there are numerous examples of cultures that exist across borders, living in lands controlled by a different culture. This historical shifting and tension are part of the fabric of Eastern European culture, and the cuisine is not immune to the strain. It is helpful to consider the historical context that each of these subregions has endured when considering how the cuisine has evolved in each area.

Poland

Poland is located in the northern part of Europe; the northern border is the Baltic Sea and Russia, the eastern border is the former Soviet republics of Belarus and the Ukraine, the southern border is Slovakia and the Czech Republic, and the western border is Germany. Like many other countries discussed in this chapter, Poland has been overrun, ruled, partitioned, and even shifted in location, only becoming an independent country again with the fall of the Soviet Union. Most Poles are Slavic in heritage, and there are clear similarities in the cuisine of the Poles to other Slavic peoples, although other cuisines have been incorporated into the Polish repertoire as well.

Poland contains a vast agricultural basin throughout much of the heartland of the country, which is broken by mountainous terrain along the southern borders. The land is productive, and many crops typical of this northern geographic location are grown in abundance and included in the local cuisine. Typical food crops include wheat, rye, buckwheat, barley, cabbage, potatoes, beets, kohlrabi, and mushrooms; all make regular appearances on the Polish table.

Poland is a country pulled between Western Europe and Russia, both of which have at one time ruled this area. In terms of culinary influences, Poland has strong links to both western European cuisine, specifically German and Czech influences, and Russian cuisine. From the western influences, the fondness for all things related to the pig is evident in the many varieties of *kielbasa* (Polish sausage) that are found in the markets or included in the foods made in home kitchens. *Sauerkraut* (fermented and preserved cabbage) is also a regular component of the diet and is often used as a filling for stuffed items such as a *golabki* (stuffed cabbage) or *pierogi* (filled pasta); eaten as an accompaniment to savory dishes or included in the cooking of main dishes, such as the layered and much-loved *bigos* (layered stew with meats, sausage, and sauerkraut) that is often referenced as a classic Polish dish. The Polish also have a sweet tooth for many of the desserts from Austria and the Czech Republic; strudels, tortes, and *serniks* (cheesecakes) all are common, as well as the much-enjoyed *mazurkas* (flat cakes topped with various ingredients).

Many Russian foods are also common; *kasza* (cooked grains) is a regular part of the diet, as are many *zupa* (soups) similar to those found in Russian cuisine, such as the beet soup called *borscht* in Russia and *barszcz* in Poland. The fondness for sour flavors is reminiscent of many Russian foods, as is the use of sour cream.

Polish cuisine is a rich and varied cuisine that has drawn from some of the best of its regional neighbors and also maintained many ethnic traditions through periods of struggle and persecution. The Polish character of perseverance is illuminated not only in the country's history but also in the cuisine that has stood the test of time.

Romania

Romania is located in the eastern portion of Europe, bordering the Ukraine to the north, the Black Sea to the east, Bulgaria to the south, and Hungary to the west. This country is home to a mostly Slavic population that has experienced many periods of foreign rule. Romania was ruled by the Romans, the Ottoman Turks, the Austro-Hungarian Empire, and finally the Soviet Russians before it acquired independence with the collapse of the Soviet Union. Today, Romania is a democratic country made up of mostly ethnic Slavic peoples—primarily devout members of the Eastern Orthodox Church—with smaller populations of Hungarian, Roma, and other ethnic groups represented as well. The greatest influences on the local cuisine come from the Slavic heritage, blended with traditional foods and dishes introduced by the cultures that ruled this land at one time.

Traditional Slavic foods are part of the cuisine of Romania, with bread, filled pastries, stuffed cabbage dishes, soups (especially sour soups called *ciorbas*), and stews serving as frequent components. In addition to these Slavic foods are many examples of external influence on the cuisine, with dishes from Turkey, Greece, and Russia to the east and Hungary, Austria, and Germany to the west contributing to these inclusions.

Hungary

Hungary is located in the heart of Eastern Europe and is bordered by Romania to the east, Slovakia to the north, the Czech Republic to the west, and Croatia and Serbia to the south. Hungary is different from some of the other subregions covered in this chapter in that the majority of the population is not of Slavic descent. The main ethnic makeup is from a group called the Magyars, who migrated to this land about 1,000 years ago. Where these people migrated from is unclear (there are a number of theories, ranging from just east of the Ural Mountains to northern China), but what is clear is that they brought distinct culinary traditions with them that remain a significant part of this culture today.

One tradition that has remained from their distant history is the cooking of foods in large kettles to yield a rich stew called *gulyas* (often mistranslated as "goulash" in the United States). This traditional cooking method still exists today, although most often in smaller batches and not necessarily over a fire as in the past. A number of styles fall under this method, depending on how much liquid is used in the making of the dish and what ingredients are included. The most common variants of these dishes include *pörkölt*, which are typically thicker gulyas with less liquid, and meats cut into cubes; *paprikas*, which are heavily spiced with paprika and often contain sour cream; and *tokány*, a less seasoned version in which meats are cut into strips rather than cubes. One of the most unique parts of Hungarian cuisine is the tradition of sweet noodle dishes called *melek tészták*. These may be as simple as cooked buttered noodles tossed with cinnamon, sugar, and nuts, or they may be more like ravioli, with a sweet cheese or jam filling, such as the plum jam-filled *barátfüle* (eaten either as dessert or to finish a lighter meal). Many other savory examples of stuffed pastas exist in the cuisine, and these are called *derelye* (filled pasta).

One of the dominant components of Hungarian cuisine is the use of chili powders called *paprika*, of which there are many variations ranging from sweet blends to mildly spicy and smoky to spicy. The chili pepper has come to replace or complement other traditional seasonings since the introduction of the chili from the Americas via the Turks of the Ottoman Empire, who acquired it from trade with the Spanish. Paprika is added to many dishes besides the previously described gulyas, such as the well-known sauce base called *lesco*, which consists of slowly cooked onions, green peppers, and tomatoes seasoned with paprika (and often eaten as a salad).

Like Poland, Hungary has experienced many periods of foreign rule, and evidence of these periods is clear in the cuisine as well. There are numerous examples of influence from Western countries; Hungary was under the control of both the Habsburgs and the Austrians prior to the formation of the Austro-Hungarian alliance. As a result, many recognizable German and Viennese dishes were introduced, including *rétes* (strudels), *tortáks* (tortes), *tésztáks* (dumplings), and the use of *káposzta* (cabbage or sauerkraut). Periods of influence from Italy and France also left their mark on the cuisine, as stuffed meat dishes and many of the sauces common to Hungarian cuisine reveal. There are also many examples of eastern influences, including the stuffing of vegetables and the use of various spices, which are attributed to the period of rule by the Ottoman Empire.

Hungarian cuisine is one of the more varied cuisines found throughout the sub-regions in this chapter and also one of the more unique. With their tradition of drying foods and slow-cooking stews and soups, along with their uses of seasoning, Hungarians have developed a highly respected cuisine despite being subjected to many periods of suffering at the hands of others.

Balkan Peninsula

This region includes the countries of Slovenia, Croatia, Albania, Bosnia-Herzegovina, Yugoslavia, Macedonia, Bulgaria, and Romania, all of which are located east of Italy and south of Hungary. This area was once a part of the Ottoman Empire, from the fifteenth to the twentieth century; the main difference between the Balkan region and the rest of the Eastern European regions covered in this chapter is the depth of the Ottoman influence from this period of rule. The Ottoman Turks that ruled parts of Europe during the height of their empire held this part of Europe for much longer than other areas. Thus, their influence is more deeply rooted here. Much of this region was also under Communist control after the end of World War II, although this period had less of an impact on the cuisines of this region. One of the other distinguishing features of the Balkan region is the diversity of peoples, religions, and languages that exist and commingle here.

The Turkish and Greek tradition of *meze* (small plates or dishes) is common throughout this region, and many examples of the foods that might be found in these other countries are found here as well. Common dishes on a meze table include olives, *hummus*, roasted peppers, eggplant purée, and marinated vegetables. Another Turkish influence is the regular use of yogurt as a sauce, drink, and ingredient in many dishes. *Bulghur* (cooked and cracked wheat) is also commonly used in this region, as are other starchy foods such as lentils and chickpeas. There is significant use of vegetables and fruits throughout this region, because the Mediterranean climate supports the growth of citrus, fava beans, eggplant, olives, and grapes, as well as a variety of nuts and seeds. Meat is scarcer in the eastern portion of the subregion, and what meat is eaten is usually lamb—although other types (pork, beef, and veal) are more common as you move closer to Italy. Cheeses are enjoyed throughout this region, and most are made from sheep's or goat's milk because these animals are more common here.

Brinza cheese is similar to Greek feta cheese, and *kanach* is a mold-ripened cheese with a pronounced flavor.

Other Turkish and Greek influences are also evident in stuffed foods such as *sarmas* (stuffed grape leaves), boreks or *boeregs* (stuffed phyllo with savory fillings), and *pitas* (another type of filled, thin phyllo-like dough that may be sweet or savory), as well as rice preparations such as *pilav* (this name is used to describe a wide variety of rice and meat dishes of the region). This decidedly eastern-leaning cuisine undoubtedly connects this region to the Middle Eastern-influenced Turkish and Greek cuisines, but there are numerous examples of foods from Italy and other western European countries that appear regularly as well.

As one moves closer to Italy, the Italian influence becomes more evident as *gnocchi* (small dumplings), pasta, and *polenta* all become more common. These varied influences make the cuisine of the Balkan region one of the most interesting and complex in all of Europe.

RECIPES

The following recipes provide an introduction to the cuisines of Eastern Europe. This is a complex region with many influences and a rich culinary history; further exploration is encouraged.

Ogórki Kiszone POLAND
(BRINE-PICKLED CUCUMBERS)

INGREDIENTS

1	lb	Pickling Cucumbers, washed
1.5	Tbsp	Mustard Seeds
2		Horseradish Leaves, cut into strips
1/2	oz	Garlic Cloves, chopped
1	Tbsp	Fresh Dill, minced
1	tsp	Dill Seeds
1.5	oz	Kosher Salt (do not use iodized salt, the iodine will cause discoloration of pickles)
1	qt	Purified Water (can use bottled water, if desired)
1	qt	Pickling Jar (such as Mason or Kerr) with sealing lid

As with other neighboring northern European countries, Poland has a long tradition of preserved foods, and one of the highly prized items of the Polish cupboard is the brined cucumber. In order to make these correctly, they should be allowed to ferment at a low temperature (use the warmest part of a refrigerator, if necessary) to produce the characteristic flavor from a slow lactic acid production. A couple of steps need to be followed carefully in order to yield a good quality product and prevent spoilage. One important step is to carefully measure the ingredients, and another is not to overtighten the lids and cause the produced carbon dioxide to dissolve, which will in turn cause the pickled cucumbers to become mushy rather than crisp. (The temperature of fermentation is important as well.)

NOTE: *Because this is a fermentation process, strict sanitary procedures should be followed at all times!*

YIELD: 1 pound

PRESERVATION METHOD: Brine Fermentation

(continues)

Ogórki Kiszone
(continued)

PROCEDURE

1. Place the cucumbers and all of the seasonings, except for the salt and water, into the pickling jar (pack the cucumbers so that they fill nearly all of the space, and put the last one in horizontally to hold the others down, keeping them from coming out of the brine).

2. In a small saucepan, dissolve the salt in the water over a low flame, and then set it aside to cool to room temperature (you must let it cool so that natural bacteria are not killed by hot water).

3. Once the saltwater solution has cooled to room temperature, pour brine over the cucumbers until they are completely covered (some of the brine will probably leak out as you put on the lid, so carry out the next step over a sink).

4. Put the lid on the jar, tightening just a half a turn or so once the lid grasps the grooves in the jar. The lid should be noticeably loose, so that developing carbon dioxide can escape from the jar. Remember that this is one of the critical steps in making the pickles well; traditionally, pickles would be made in large wooden barrels and held down under the brine, with the top of the barrel exposed to the air, so the carbon dioxide could escape. We are making a small batch, so the air must be allowed to escape by leaving the jar loose initially.

5. Once the jar is fitted properly, place it in a cool place to allow fermentation to occur naturally (the ideal temperature is 50–55°F).

6. Allow fermentation to take place in the loose-fitted jar at this temperature for 4 weeks. Next, tighten the lid of the jar and place the pickles to the refrigerator until ready to use.

Gedünstetes Kraut   POLAND AND CZECH REPUBLIC
(BRAISED CABBAGE)

INGREDIENTS
For Salting the Cabbage

4 lbs Green Cabbage, cored and sliced 1/4 inch thick

2 Tbsp Salt

Cabbage is a common ingredient throughout much of the northern portions of Eastern Europe, and this preparation utilizes this vegetable for a dish to be served with an entrée (such as a roast).

YIELD: 15 portions (4–5 ounces/portion)

PREPARATION METHOD: Salting Cabbage

COOKING METHOD: Braising (vegetable braise; no browning of the vegetable)

(continues)

Gedünstetes Kraut

(continued)

For Braising the Cabbage

4	oz	Lard or Rendered Bacon Fat
		Salted, Rinsed Cabbage
		(see above)
1/4	cup	Sugar
2	oz	White Wine Vinegar
1	Tbsp	Caraway Seeds
1	tsp	Salt
1/2	tsp	Black Pepper, freshly ground
3	cups	Chicken or Vegetable Stock
		Salt and Pepper, to taste

PROCEDURE

For Salting the Cabbage

1. In a large mixing bowl, combine the sliced cabbage and salt, and work the two together with hands to assure that the salt is distributed throughout the cabbage mixture.

2. Place the cabbage into a colander; allow it to sit for at least 30 minutes to allow the salt time to draw out moisture and soften the cabbage.

   Once the cabbage has sat for 30 minutes or more, rinse the cabbage with cool water to wash off excess salt, and then squeeze out as much moisture from the cabbage as possible. The cabbage is now ready for the next step.

For Braising the Cabbage

1. In a heavy-bottomed pot or pan large enough to hold all of the ingredients, melt the lard or bacon fat over a medium-low flame.

2. Once the fat is melted, add the rinsed and squeezed cabbage and the remaining ingredients (except the stock), and sweat the ingredients in the fat over a medium-low flame for 10 minutes. Stir often to prevent any browning on the bottom of the pan (lower the heat if any browning is seen during this process).

3. Once the cabbage and other ingredients have been sweated for 10 minutes, add the stock to the pan and bring the mixture to a simmer over a medium-high flame.

4. Once the mixture comes to a simmer, reduce the heat to a low flame, cover the pot/pan with foil and a tight-fitting lid, and allow the mixture to cook covered on the stove for 30 minutes.

5. Uncover the pot/pan and taste the mixture for seasoning. Adjust, if necessary, and serve.

Salted cabbage draining into mixing bowl for gedünstetes kraut (braised cabbage)

Braising the previously salted, rinsed, and drained cabbage for gedünstetes kraut

Lescó   HUNGARY

(STEWED PEPPERS AND TOMATOES WITH PAPRIKA)

INGREDIENTS

4	oz	Bacon
8	oz	Yellow Onion, diced small
1.5	lbs	Green Bell Peppers, stem removed, seeded, and sliced
10	oz	Paprika Sausage, diced medium (can substitute other mild chili-flavored sausage, if paprika sausage is unavailable)
2	lbs	Tomatoes, concasséed
1.5	Tbsp	Paprika
1.5	tsp	Salt

The use of paprika in Hungarian cooking is extensive, and this is but one more example of how it can be used (along with other products of the Americas) to produce a dish with a Hungarian flavor. It is common to include a paprika sausage in this recipe although it can be made without meat as well.

YIELD: 4.25 lbs, or 15 portions (4 ounces/portion)

COOKING METHOD: Stewing

PROCEDURE

1. In a large sauté pan, render the bacon over low heat until all of the fat has been melted out (about 10–15 minutes).

2. Once the bacon has been rendered, add the onion and green peppers to the pan and turn the heat up to a medium-low flame. Sweat the onions and peppers in the bacon fat until they are very tender (about 10–15 minutes)

3. Once the vegetables are very tender, turn the heat up to a medium flame and add the paprika sausage. Cook over medium heat until pan just begins to color from the heat, and then add the tomatoes, paprika, and salt.

4. Cover the pan and cook all of the ingredients together in the pan over a low flame for another 10–15 minutes before uncovering and serving.

Finished lesco (stewed peppers and tomatoes)

Töltött Káposzta Hungary
(Stuffed Cabbage)

Ingredients
For Making the Filling

1	oz	Lard
3	oz	Bacon, diced small
10	oz	Yellow Onion, minced
1	oz	Garlic Cloves, minced
3	Tbsp	Sweet Paprika
1	tsp	Black Pepper, freshly ground
1	Tbsp	Salt
1	cup	Long Grain Rice
1.5	lbs	Ground Lean Pork
1	Tbsp	Fresh Marjoram, minced (or substitute 1 tsp dried)
2		Eggs, beaten

For Blanching the Cabbage

2	lbs	Savoy Cabbage, cored and whole leaves separated (you need at least 20 large leaves)
1	gallon	Water
3	Tbsp	Salt
		Ice Bath (for shocking)

For Braising the Stuffed Cabbage

4	oz	Bacon, diced small
1	Tbsp	Paprika
2	lbs	Sauerkraut (see Chapter 7, "German Cuisine," if making in-house)
8	oz	Yellow Onion, grated
2	cups	Chicken or Vegetable Stock
		Stuffed Cabbages (see above)
2	cups	Sour Cream
		Salt and Black Pepper, to taste

The Turkish tradition of stuffing foods is common in much of Eastern Europe because it was once a part of the Ottoman Empire; this recipe is one example of this culinary influence. This particular dish includes influences from many cultures: sauerkraut from the Asian Tartars via Germany, paprika from the Americas via Spain, and the method—as mentioned—is Turkish.

Yield: 20 stuffed cabbages (4–5 ounces each); 2–3 ounces sauerkraut sauce

Cooking Method (Cabbage Leaves): Blanched in Boiling Water

Cooking Method (Stuffed Cabbage): Braising

Procedure

For Making the Filling

1. Heat the lard in a large sauté pan over a medium-low flame, until the pan gets hot, and then add the bacon to render the fat out.

2. Once the fat has been rendered from the bacon (this should take at least 5 minutes, if done properly), add the onion and garlic to the pan and sweat them in the fat until both are translucent and soft (about 5 minutes over medium-low flame).

3. Once the onions and garlic are tender, add the paprika, black pepper, salt, and rice. Stir to coat the rice with the fat; remove from heat, transfer to a mixing bowl, and allow the mixture to cool completely.

4. Once the mixture has cooled completely, add the ground pork, marjoram, and eggs. Mix the stuffing very well to combine, and then set this mixture aside until the cabbage is prepared for stuffing.

For Blanching the Cabbage

1. Bring the water and salt to a boil over a high flame. Once boiling, add the Savoy cabbage leaves to the boiling water, one at a time, and blanch until just tender. Shock them immediately in the ice bath once tender.

2. Repeat the first step with the remaining cabbage leaves until all are blanched, and then remove the cabbage leaves from the ice bath and pat them dry with a paper towel before using for filling.

3. Once the cabbage leaves have been patted dry, place about 3 ounces of the filling made in the previous section in the center of the cabbage leaves, and roll the stuffing into the leaves by first folding the sides of the cabbage leaves over the stuffing and then rolling the leaves up to completely encase the stuffing.

(continues)

Töltött Káposzta
(continued)

Finished töltött káposzta (stuffed cabbage), with cabbage being rolled in background

For Braising the Stuffed Cabbage

1. Preheat oven to 325°F.

2. Using a heavy-bottomed sauté pan that is large enough to hold all of the stuffed cabbages (if you do not have a pan large enough to hold all of them, split this part of the recipe and carry out the following steps in two or more pans), place the pan over a medium-low flame to heat it.

3. Once the pan is hot, add the diced bacon and heat over the low flame until the fat has been rendered and the bacon is crisp and browned (8–10 minutes).

4. Once the bacon has been rendered, add the paprika, sauerkraut, grated onion, and chicken stock to the pan.

5. Place the stuffed cabbages on top of the sauerkraut, and cover the pan tightly—first with first foil and then with a tight-fitting lid. Place into the preheated oven and bake for 45 minutes.

6. Once the stuffed cabbages have been cooked covered for 45 minutes, remove them from the oven and check to see if they are done, either by using a thermometer (the cabbages should be at least 165°F in the center) or by feeling to make sure they are solid throughout. If they are not finished, return them to the oven, still covered, to cook until done.

7. Once the stuffed cabbages are cooked through, remove them from the pan and set them into a holding pan on a steam table or another holding area, and return the pan with the sauerkraut to the stove.

8. Temper the sour cream into the sauerkraut mixture, and then simmer it gently before adjusting the seasoning of the sauerkraut/sour cream sauce, if necessary. Serve the stuffed cabbage with the sauce.

Bográs Gulyás   HUNGARY
("KETTLE" BEEF STEW)

INGREDIENTS

2	oz	Lard
10	oz	Yellow Onion, diced small
1	oz	Garlic Cloves, minced
1.5	lbs	Green Peppers, seeded and diced medium
1/3	cup	Hungarian Paprika (sweet paprika)
1	tsp	Ground Caraway

The food called goulash in the United States is a variation of the Hungarian gulyás, which developed from a tradition of kettle cooking in Hungary. This version uses beef, but pork is also very common in Hungary and could be used in this recipe as well. One of the notable differences in this stewing method is that the meat is not colored, which yields a less strongly flavored broth, but the copious use of paprika provides both flavor and color to the resulting stew.

YIELD: 20 portions (8 ounces/portion)

COOKING METHOD: Stewing without Browning Meat

(continues)

Bográs Gulyás
(continued)

1 tsp	Freshly Ground Black Pepper
1 Tbsp	Salt
3 lbs	Beef Stew Meat, cut into 1.5-inch cubes, with heavy fat and connective tissue removed
2 lbs	Diced Tomato (concasséed, if fresh; diced and peeled, if canned)
1 qt	Chicken Stock
1 qt	Beef Stock
1.5 lbs	Boiling Potatoes, diced large (Red Bliss, Yukon Gold, or other suitable varietals)
1 Tbsp	Fresh Marjoram or Oregano, minced
	Salt and Pepper, to taste

PROCEDURE

1. Add the lard to a heavy-bottomed pot large enough to hold all of the ingredients, and place the pot over a medium flame.

2. Once the oil has gotten hot, add the diced onion, minced garlic, and diced green peppers. Sweat the vegetables in the lard for 10–15 minutes, or until they become very tender and the onions are translucent.

3. Once the vegetables are tender, add the paprika, caraway, black pepper, and salt, and turn the heat up to a medium-high flame. Cook, while stirring constantly, until the spices become very fragrant but do not caramelize.

4. Once the spices have become fragrant, add the stew meat, the tomatoes, and the stocks to the pot, and turn the heat up to a high flame to bring the mixture to a simmer.

5. Once the stew reaches a simmer, turn the heat down to maintain a very gentle poaching temperature. Cover the pot with a tight-fitting lid, and check the contents every 10 minutes or so to make sure the pot doesn't overheat. Cook covered for 1 hour.

6. Once the stew has cooked for an hour, uncover it and add the potatoes and marjoram to the pot. Re-cover and cook for another 45 minutes, at the same temperature as before.

7. Once the stew has cooked for 45 minutes with the potatoes, remove it from heat and taste it for seasoning. Add salt and pepper, if necessary, and serve.

Finished bográs gulyás (beef goulash) served with a bowl of spaetzel (see recipe in Chapter 7, "German Cuisine")

Wiener Schnitzel VIENNA

(BREADED VEAL CUTLET)

INGREDIENTS

For Breading the Veal

2	lbs	Veal Top Round, trimmed and sliced into 1/4-inch cutlets
		Salt and Black Pepper, to taste
16	oz	All-Purpose (A.P.) Flour
1.5	tsp	Salt
1/2	tsp	Freshly Ground Black Pepper
6		Eggs
4	oz	Milk
1.5	lb	Fine Dry Bread Crumbs

For Panfrying and Serving the Veal Cutlets

		Breaded Veal Cutlets (see above)
4	oz	Clarified Butter, melted
4	oz	Lard, melted
4		Lemons, wedged in eighths

This well-known dish was once a regular on the Viennese table; although still fairly common and prized, it harks back to the glory days of the Austro-Hungarian Empire. Meat is central to the diet of most Austrians, and this is but one example of the many different preparations to satisfy that demand. Although Austria is not included in this chapter, this dish is commonly found in the northern and central regions covered here. Today it is often made with pork instead of veal.

YIELD: 16 portions (5 ounces/portion)

COOKING METHOD: Panfrying

PROCEDURE

For Breading the Veal

1. Pound the veal cutlets with a meat mallet between two sheets of plastic wrap until they are approximately half as thick as they were to begin with.

2. Season the veal cutlets with salt and pepper, and portion the veal into 4 oz portions if a 16-portion yield is desired.

3. Once the veal has been pounded, seasoned, and portioned, it can be breaded for panfrying using the three-stage breading station. The first station to set up is the flour station. Combine the A.P. flour, salt, and freshly ground black pepper in a container wide enough to easily fit the veal cutlets; mix well to combine.

4. For the second station, whisk together the eggs and milk in a mixing bowl, and place the mixture in a suitable container for easy dipping of the cutlets.

5. For the third and last breading station, the fine (make sure they are fine and not coarse—passing them through a sifter is a good idea), dry bread crumbs placed in a suitable container.

6. Once the breading station has been set up, the breading process can begin. Take care to ensure that one hand is always used for the wet ingredients and one hand for the dry ingredients, to prevent excessive waste of product (from breading your hand instead of the veal) and to make the process as efficient as possible.

7. Bread all of the veal cutlets using the three-stage method (flour, then egg wash, then bread crumbs), making sure to just coat the surface of the cutlets with each of the stages. Remove excess flour and breading by tapping the veal against the inside of the container and allowing the excess egg wash to drain off before placing it into the bread crumb mixture. Place the cutlets onto a sheet pan or another suitable pan lined with parchment paper (be sure to keep the portions separate to ensure control of the product).

8. Once all of the veal cutlets have been breaded using this method, place them covered in a refrigerator and allow them to chill for at least 30 minutes before proceeding to the next stage.

(continues)

Wiener Schnitzel
(continued)

For Panfrying and Serving the Veal Cutlets

1. Combine the melted clarified butter and lard.

2. Heat a large sauté pan over a medium flame, and add a few ounces or more of the lard/clarified mixture (should form a coating across the entire pan).

3. Once the fat mixture is hot, add only as many veal cutlets as the pan can handle without cooling (the amount will be determined by the size of the pan), and panfry the cutlets on both sides until they turn a light golden brown (do not let them turn a deep golden brown, or the meat will be dry and overcooked). Remove them from the pan.

4. Repeat steps 2 and 3 until all of the cutlets are cooked, adding more fat as needed to keep the bottom of the pan coated.

5. As soon as the cutlets come out of the pan, they should be served with the lemon garnish for best results.

Wiener schnitzel (veal cutlet) served with lemon

Guiveciu De Ciuperci   ROMANIA
(BRAISED MUSHROOMS IN SOUR CREAM SAUCE)

INGREDIENTS

6	oz	Bacon
3	oz	Shallots, minced
2	lbs	Mushrooms, sliced (wild mushrooms work well in this recipe)
2	Tbsp	Fresh Parsley, minced
1	tsp	Salt
1/4	tsp	Freshly Ground Black Pepper
1	Tbsp	A.P. Flour
10	oz	Sour Cream
1	Tbsp	Fresh Parsley, minced
		Salt and Black Pepper, to taste

Stews, soups, and ragouts are typical foods found on the Romanian table, because these mostly Slavic people have a strong connection to their past. A dish such as this would traditionally be served with mămăligă (next recipe), the polenta-like dish made from coarse cornmeal, which is a staple in Romanian cuisine.

YIELD: 2.75 lbs, or 10 portions (4–5 ounces/portion)

COOKING METHOD: Braising

PROCEDURE

1. Place a sauté pan large enough to hold all of the ingredients over a medium-low flame to heat.

2. Once the pan gets hot, add the bacon and slowly render it to yield lightly crisped and browned bacon with little remaining fat.

3. Once the bacon has rendered, add the shallots to the pan and continue to cook over the medium-low flame until the shallots become translucent and soft.

4. Once the shallots have been cooked, add the mushrooms, parsley, salt, and black pepper to the pan. Turn the heat up to a high flame and brown the mushrooms in the fat from the bacon, making sure to toss the all of the ingredients to ensure even cooking.

5. Once the mushrooms have colored, reduce the heat to a low flame and remove the pan from heat to allow it to cool before proceeding to step 7.

6. In a small mixing bowl, combine the A.P. flour and the sour cream, and whisk together to combine completely.

7. Once the pan with the mushrooms has cooled, temper the sour cream mixture into the pan. Slowly heat up the mixture, and add parsley.

8. Adjust seasoning, if necessary, and serve. (This dish would typically be served with mămăligă; see the following recipe.)

Bowl of mămăligă (cornmeal porridge) topped with guiveciu de ciuperci (braised mushrooms)

Mămăligă ROMANIA

(CORNMEAL PORRIDGE)

INGREDIENTS

1	qt + 3 cups Water
1	Tbsp Salt
2	cups Coarse Stone-Ground Yellow Cornmeal
4	oz Unsalted Butter, cut into 6 smaller pieces
	Salt, to taste

Bread is a common part of the Romanian diet, but this porridge runs a very close second to bread with regard to importance and reverence in this country's cuisine. It is believed that corn was introduced by the Turks during the periods of Ottoman influence in this region; the Turks traded for the products of the Americas with the Spanish and other colonial powers. Mămăligă can be eaten as is, but it is eaten most commonly with stews, ragouts, and other dishes that provide a sauce.

YIELD: 2 quarts, or 16 portions (4–5 ounces/portion)

COOKING METHOD: Boiling

PROCEDURE

1. Put the water and salt in a heavy-bottomed pot large enough to hold all of the ingredients, and place over a high flame on the stove to bring the water to a boil.

2. As soon as the water reaches a boil, begin simultaneously adding the cornmeal and stirring with a wooden spoon or whisk (if using a whisk and an aluminum pot, do not scrape the bottom or the color will be altered; it is best to use a wooden spoon with an aluminum pot) until all of the cornmeal has been added.

3. Continue to stir until the mixture becomes very thick (this will happen quickly, so pay attention), and then turn the heat down to a very low flame.

4. Cook over the very low flame for 5 minutes, and then begin to melt the butter into the mixture by adding the pieces one at a time, while stirring simultaneously, until all of the butter has been incorporated.

5. Take the mămăligă off of the heat and adjust seasoning with salt, if necessary.

NOTE: *Mămăligă is often cooled and then cut into desired shapes and sizes to be used in a variety of ways in Romanian cuisine. It might be coated in cornmeal and pan-fried in butter to be served with bacon for breakfast, topped with a feta-like cheese called* brânză, *dusted with powdered sugar and served with jam as a dessert, or eaten as made in this recipe with stews, ragout, or other sauced dished (like the mushroom recipe included in this chapter).*

SUMMARY

Eastern European cuisine is a mixture of a number of ethnic cuisines that have developed in this region over years of strife and political turmoil. The majority of the countries covered in this chapter are home to an ethnically diverse Slavic population, whereas Magyars, Romanians, Jews, Turks, and Germanic peoples exist in smaller numbers as well. All of these cultures lend different culinary traditions to the cuisines found in pockets throughout the region. This region experienced centuries of invasion from European and Middle Eastern powers that often exerted control and left the populations with mixed ethnicities—and redrawn borders—as well as the culinary traditions of the invaders. Many of the culinary traditions that are found in this region have origins in other countries, including Germany, Austria, Greece, Turkey, and Russia. Some traditional foods occur as well, primarily from the Slavic and Magyar (Hungarian) peoples.

REVIEW QUESTIONS

1. What are some of the major ethnic groups that are represented in this chapter?

2. What other cultures have influenced the cuisine of Eastern Europe?

3. Which section of Eastern Europe has been heavily influenced by Turkish and Greek cuisines? Which part has been influenced by Austria and Germany?

COMMON TERMS, FOODS, AND INGREDIENTS

The following terms are helpful in understanding some of the foods used in the cuisines of Eastern Europe, as well as in identifying some of the common dishes and ingredients that might be found on a menu.

❋ Ingredients and Foods

Poland

babka – Rich yeast cake with almonds and raisins, traditionally eaten for Easter celebration

barszcz – Beet soup

bigos – Dish of sauerkraut and various meats and sausage stewed with onions, often mushrooms, and sometimes prunes to yield a highly flavored stew

gedünstetes kraut – Braised cabbage

golabki – Stuffed cabbage rolls filled with various items, ranging from grains and mushrooms to seasoned meat mixtures and sauerkraut, and typically served with sour cream

kasza – Groats made from various grains

kielbasa – Polish pork sausage that is lightly smoked and found both fresh and dried

koldamer – Cow's milk cheese with small holes and excellent melting qualities

mazurkas – Flat cakes topped with various ingredients

ogórki kiszone – Brine-pickled cucumbers

pierogi – Stuffed noodle dough, similar to ravioli (Italy) or variniki (Ukraine), and typically filled with sauerkraut,

potato mixture, mushrooms, cheese, or a combination of these

sauerkraut – Well-known fermented cabbage of German cuisine; also common in Polish cuisine

sernik – Cheesecake

Romania

ardalena – Made from the milk of water buffalos, this cheese is highly prized for its flavor and its excellent grating and cooking properties

brânză – Rich and salty brine-cured sheep's milk cheese found in various stages of maturity and used in a variety of ways

buninca – Rich pudding set with eggs that may contain meat or vegetables

caltaboşi – Type of sausage made with pork and liver

ciorbă – Tangy soup

clătite – Thin pancake or crepe

găluşcă – Dumpling

guiveciu de ciuperci – Braised mushrooms in sour cream sauce

mămăligă – Polenta

musaca – Eggplant dish of Greek/Turkish influence (called *moussaka* in Greece; see Chapter 2, "Greek Cuisine")

pilaf – Rice cooked in pilaf style from Turkish influence

plăcinte – Savory pies

sarmale – Stuffed vegetables, common in Romanian cuisine

telemea – Sheep's milk cheese that is brine-cured much like feta. This cheese is used mostly in salads, or it is eaten along with other ingredients, such as olives, or by itself as a snack.

zacuscă – Spreads made from eggplant, roasted peppers, and spices; served with bread (sometimes made with beans instead of eggplant, and may include other ingredients such as tomato and onion)

Hungary

balaton – Firm cow's milk cheese with small holes and mild flavor. This cheese is loaf shaped and used in a variety of manners, from a table cheese to inclusion in recipes as a melting cheese.

barátfüle – Pasta filled with plum jam

bográs gulyás – Beef gulyas (stew)

derelye – Filled pasta

fogas – Fish found only in Lake Balaton in Hungary, and a relative of the salmon; these have white flesh and are very flavorful *gulyas* – Goulash, stews/soups of meats and vegetables cooked in heavily spiced broth (typically spiced with paprika)

halászlé – Fish stew spiced with sweet and spicy paprikas

káposzta – Cabbage or sauerkraut

lesco – Either a sauce or a salad made from slowly stewed onions, green peppers, and tomatoes (and often spiced with paprika)

liptauer – A blended cheese made from a mixture of sheep's and cow's milk, with a distinct flavor that combines very well with the spiciness of Hungarian food

meleg tészták – Hot, sweet noodle dishes

palacsinta – Thin pancake

paprikas – Name for chiles. Also refers to stews made with meats or poultry in rich paprika-based sauce; similar to goulash (gulyas) but thicker and cooked with sour cream to yield thick, rich stew

pörkölt – Thick, spiced stew made in similar style as goulash (gulyas) but with less liquid

rétes – Hungarian name for strudels

tarhonya – "Egg barley" made from forming dough with flour and eggs and rubbing between hands to produce little balls of pasta, which are then dried and stored to be used to cook and accompany dishes. This method is an ancient Magyar tradition that has been performed for centuries, much like the tradition of making couscous in North Africa.

tészták – Dumplings

tokány – Another stew variant that resembles goulash (gulyas), but the meats used in this preparation are cut into strips, and fewer onions and seasonings are used

töltött káposzta – Stuffed cabbage filled with seasoned ground pork and rice

tortáks – Tortes

The Balkans (Many of the following are common throughout the Balkans; items labeled A [Armenia] and C [Croatia] are names specific to those areas)

bakalar (C) – Salt cod

baklava – Layered phyllo, nut, and honey sweet of Middle Eastern origin (introduced by the Ottomans)

basterma (A) – Dried, spiced beef

boereg (A) – Stuffed pastry; these are found throughout Turkish- and Greek-influenced areas under various names that are often phonetically similar to the term *borek*

brinza (A) – Brine-cured sheep's cheese from Armenia, similar to feta cheese found in Greece

bulghur – Cooked and cracked wheat common in the Balkan region

bukek (C) – Croatian name for borek (see *boereg*)

dolmas (A) – Stuffed vegetables

gnocchi – Small dumpling of Italian heritage found in the Balkan region

halva – Middle Eastern sweet bar made by cooking sesame seeds with honey and dried fruits or nuts (introduced by the Ottomans)

hummus – Chickpea purée seasoned with lemon, olive oil, garlic, and often tahini (sesame seed purée)

kanach (A) – Sheep's cheese ripened with mold from Armenia, similar in method and characteristics to Roquefort (see Chapter 5, "French Cuisine")

kashkavel – Sheep's milk cheese common throughout the Balkans, with versatility as a table cheese or even on the grill (it can withstand heat without melting)

meze – Appetizer foods served in style similar to Spanish tapas

pilav – Rice dished cooked in Ottoman (Turkish) style

pita – Name given to phyllo dough in Balkan area

polenta – Italian cornmeal porridge common in the Balkan region

sarma (C) – Stuffed sauerkraut, typically filled with rice and seasoned ground meat (usually beef, veal, or pork)

tahini – Sesame seed purée

titvash (A) – Home-cured pickles

Other Terms

sachertorte – Chocolate torte from Vienna

strudel – Thin pastry wrapped around various fillings and baked

Wiener schnitzel – Breaded and panfried veal cutlet

CHAPTER 4

SWITZERLAND

AUSTRIA

HUNGRY

TRENTINO/ALTO ADIGE

A L P S

Bolzano

FRIULI-VENEZIA GIULIA

SLOVENIA

Trent

Aosta

VAL D' AOSTA

LOMBARDIA

VENETO

Trieste

CROATIA

FRANCE

Milan

Venice

Po River

Turin

Po River

Po Valley

Asti

PIEMONTE

Piacenza

Parma

BOSNIA-HERZEGOVINA

Reggio
nell'Emilia

Modena

LIGURIA

Genoa

Bologna

EMILIA-ROMAGNA

I T A L Y

Pesaro

LIGURIAN
SEA

Lucca

Pisa

Livorno

Florence

Ancona

A P E N N I N E S   M O U N T A I N S

TUSCANY

MARCHE

ADRIATIC
SEA

Ascoli Piceno

UMBRIA

CORSICA
(FRANCE)

L'Aquila

Pescara

ABRUZZI

★ Rome

LAZIO-ROME

MOLISE

Campobasso

Foggia

Bari

CAMPANIA

PUGLIA

Naples

Salerno

Potenza

Taranto

BASILICATA

SARDINIA

CALABRIA

IONIAN
SEA

Palermo

Legend

- • towns and cities
- ★ capital city
- —— river
- —— region boundary
- —— sub-region boundary
- ─·─·─ international boundary
- ▨ mountains

N
W   E
S

SICILIA

0   50   100 km

Italian Cuisine

OBJECTIVES

Upon completion of this chapter, you will be able to

- discuss the importance of regionalism in Italian cuisine.
- discuss the major influences in Italian cuisine.
- discuss why certain Italian foods are common in the United States and others are not.
- discuss the differences between northern and southern Italian cuisine.
- recognize some of the regional products and recipes that identify the regions of Italy.
- prepare a selection of Italian recipes.
- define the terms listed at the conclusion of this chapter.

INTRODUCTION

Italian cuisine has always been considered one of the main influences of the new American cuisine developing in the United States; although it certainly is a major influence, many people don't realize that only a fraction of the true Italian cuisine has made its way across the ocean. Italian cuisine is incredibly diverse for a country only slightly larger than New England in landmass. Much of this diversity can be attributed to the fact that Italy was a collection of independent nation-states as recently as 1861, and these regions all have storied histories and local traditions. Within each of these former states, which now make up the regions of Italy, fierce culinary traditions have developed—and each area is distinctly proud of the products and dishes that are unique to it. Many of the culinary traditions of Italy are grounded in the family kitchen, and it is perhaps because of this that Italian cuisine is as complex as it is. One constant remains, however, wherever you look in Italy: a robust love of cooking and an appreciation for the finer things in cuisine. This approach to eating and cooking developed differently in every region of Italy, resulting in one of the most varied and complicated national cuisines in the world.

For most of us, the thought of Italian cuisine conjures images of lasagna or spaghetti with tomato sauce, but this is only a tiny fraction of the many types of pasta that are commonly eaten throughout the country, not to mention all the other types of dishes that have nothing to do with pasta. Much of the traditional American perception of Italian cuisine can be attributed to the fact that most Italian immigrants to the United States were from southern Italy—Naples and Sicily, in particular. Southern Italians have long relied on dried pasta as a main component of their cuisine, and it is also here that the widely imitated pizza originated. Yet, as one moves north in Italy or examines the cuisine with a closer eye, the diversity and regional differences of the cuisine become increasingly apparent.

For this reason, Italian cuisine may be the most difficult to attempt to describe; the range of variations is perhaps more complex here than in any other country.

Prior to the 1860s, the area that we now know as Italy comprised many distinct, smaller, autonomous nations, and each had a complex culinary history. Part of this history often involved periods of invasion or rule by other cultures. These periods in history greatly influenced the development of the regional cuisine. One thing that ties all of these regions together, however, is their focus on local products within the regional cuisine. Italian regional products are some of the world's best, and the artisan products produced in each region are part of the definition of the local cuisine. Unlike the classic system of French cuisine, in which there is tremendous respect and discipline for what was learned and taught by the classical chefs (such as Careme and Escoffier), Italians have a greater affinity for staying closer to home. Whether it is the recipe that has been passed from one generation to the next for ragù alla Bolognese, or a pasta shape that has been a long-standing tradition in a village, Italians tend to follow family traditions or their own footsteps when it comes to cooking. Italian cuisine is dominated by home-made cooking, with less focus on "dining" than some other cuisines. This home cooking is often laborious and requires knowledge that is passed from one generation to the next. This local and family-based development of culinary culture plays a large role in why Italian cuisine is so regional.

Italian cuisine is one of the world's most celebrated; with regional autonomy driving a creative and proud tradition of local cuisines, it is not surprising that this cuisine has found an audience in the United States and other places throughout the world.

HISTORIC CULINARY INFLUENCES

Italy is a dynamic country that has experienced many outside influences on its native culture and cuisine throughout history; just as important, Italians have had significant influences on other cuisines as well. The Italian peninsula is situated in the Mediterranean Sea between the Iberian peninsula and the Balkan peninsula, and as such has served as a natural location for trade over the centuries. Present-day Italy was once the home of the great Roman Empire, which spread its influence across southern Europe, northern Africa, and into the Middle East, and the cultures of these areas left their imprint on the Italian cuisine as well. After the decline of the Roman Empire, a number of other cultures ruled parts of Italy and influenced the development of the cuisine in certain regions. The following guide takes a closer look at some of the more significant influences on the development of the cuisine of Italy.

Ancient Greeks

The ancient Greeks were known for their appreciation of the arts, and many culinary traditions developed by the Romans in present-day Italy are credited to the influence of the Greeks on Roman life. During the height of the Greek Empire (600 BC–200 BC), the Greeks settled many colonies for trading purposes, many of which developed into some of today's cities, including Naples and Reggio. The Greeks also settled Sicily and brought with them an appreciation for many of the ingredients that now are main elements of the Sicilian table, including grapes, olives, citrus, and several preparations of the local seafood. In time, the Greek influence in Sicily and other trading ports spread throughout mainland Italy and became entwined with the local cuisine as it developed with the Roman Empire.

Roman Rule

At its peak, the Roman Empire included most of central and southern Europe, much of the Middle East, and part of Northern Africa. This rule brought the cultures of the conquered lands into Roman homes. As the Romans traveled to these lands, and the products from these lands came back to Roman homes, new ingredients became incorporated into the cooking of the homeland. At this period in history, the cuisine would not be recognizable as Italian because most of the population subsisted on minimal foods while the rich feasted on elaborate meals that were heavily spiced, a practice that contrasts with most of the cuisine of Italy today. The important contributions during this period were more about the foods that were brought into the realm of cooking, including the many spices from the East that made their way into the cuisine.

Moorish Rule

In AD 827, Moorish Arabs conquered Sicily and ruled the island for 200 years, along with parts of southern Italy and Sardinia, and they brought with them an understanding of distillation (for example, *Marsala* [fortified wine] and *grappa* [distilled wine product]) and freezing techniques (for example, *gelato* [frozen flavored milk], *sorbeto* [frozen flavored juice], and *granite* [slushy flavored ice]). Some of the ingredients that the Arabs brought to Italy were spinach, pine nuts, eggplant, coffee, bitter oranges, spinach, rice, sugar, almonds, *marzapan* (almond paste), and spices, and many of these ingredients would become regular components of Sicilian as well as Italian cuisine in the years that followed.

The Arab rule of Sicily and other parts of Italy is often noted as the influence that brought about many of the sweet preparations that are found in Italian and in particular Sicilian cuisines. The use of sugar in making sweet preparations is largely believed to have started after the Arabs introduced this commodity to Sicily, and Sicily is where some of the most well-known pastries are made, including *cannolis* (fried pastry stuffed with sweetened cheese and other ingredients) and *cassatas* (rich cakes with dried fruit and marzipan topping) as well as numerous frozen desserts.

Normans

The inhabitants of western Europe (Scandinavia, England, and part of France) invaded southern Italy in AD 1000 and fought for control of the land, during which time *baccalà* (salt cod) was introduced to the Italians. Salt cod was particularly attractive to many because it was relatively inexpensive at the time, and there was no need to use it right away since it was well preserved. For these reasons, salt cod is found in a number of classic Italian recipes.

Spanish

Spain fought with France for many years for influence in the Mediterranean and also ruled Sicily from AD 1550 to AD 1714, during which time many of the New World ingredients were introduced to the peninsula, including chiles, chocolate, tomatoes, corn, potatoes, and beans (but not fava or garbanzo, which were common throughout the Mediterranean). Corn was quickly adopted in the northern parts of Italy, but it took much longer for some of the other ingredients from the Americas to obtain general acceptance in Italy, because some were thought to be poisonous. These ingredients would eventually revolutionize the cuisine of Italy, and many have become synonymous with Italian cuisine. One can hardly imagine Italian food without tomatoes, beans, or polenta now that we know this country's cuisine as we do.

French

The French have had a long history of rule over areas of Italy, such as the former area of Savoy in northwestern Italy, or cross-cultural influences. The marriage of Catherine de' Medici to the eventual king of France is but one example of why culinary traditions and ideas flowed so freely between the two countries. The northwestern regions of Italy reveal the most significant influence from France, with many examples of the grandiose classical French cuisine seen in these areas. Refined sauces, roasted meats, stewed meats and vegetables, puréed soups, and the prevalence of cheese all reveal this connection.

Austrian

The northern part of Italy that borders Austria was under Austrian control in 1713, and this period resulted in a significant similarity between the cuisines of northern Italy and Austria—one needs only to look at the *crauti* (sauerkraut), *strudel*, and *goulash* found in the north for proof. The northern reaches of Italy have long been a region of cross-cultural trade, and ideas and techniques flowed between the bordering regions of northern Italy and their neighbors.

UNIQUE COMPONENTS

Italian cuisine is world renowned and often easily identified by other cultures. With a long history of a high regard for eating and producing fine products, Italy is perhaps one of the most difficult countries to pinpoint what makes the cuisine so unique. A couple of aspects stand out, as regionalism is quite apparent in the cuisine of Italy, and the reverence and culture that support the artisan products from these region set Italy apart from other cuisines.

Regional Autonomy

As mentioned in the opening of this chapter, Italy only became a nation relatively recently; prior to 1861, Italy was made up of separate city-states that were (and are) proud, autonomous regions and cultures. This regional character is very evident in traditions, customs, and—of course—food. The culinary traditions of many of Italy's regions are a part of the character of the people who live there, and clear distinctions can be made in the cuisines of different parts of Italy. Today, Italy has twenty regions, each of which has its own traditional recipes and local products that are not likely to be found in other regions. This centrality of place in the cuisine is stronger in Italy than in other parts of the world; it offers literally thousands of products and recipes that are made or produced locally. Although similar themes are seen in other countries, such as France, the extent of this regional and even subregional character in the cuisine is most significant in Italy.

Regionalism of Italian products is one reason for this distinction, because many products have been made in specific areas of the country for many decades and are part of the character of the local cuisine. The following section on the artisan culture explores this facet in more detail.

Artisan Culture

Italian culture has prized the skills of artisans for generations, and this appreciation has led to a culture that produces many products of very high quality. Whether it is *fontina* (rich cow's milk cheese) from the Alpine north, *Gorgonzola* (rich, blue-veined cow's milk cheese) from Lombardy, or *Parmesan* (grana-style aged cow's milk cheese) from the Emilia-Romagna region, the focus on producing the highest quality product for generations has led to a tremendous variety of some of the world's best products. Many of the artisan products that are produced in Italy are regional specialties that could not be replicated elsewhere because of climatic conditions that make that region ideal for each product. In the case of Gorgonzola, the combination of natural mold spores, humidity, and temperature enabled this cheese to evolve into the prized rounds we know today. Although these conditions now can be controlled to produce Gorgonzola-like cheeses in other parts of the world, it is only in Lombardy, where the cows feed on the diet that they have for centuries, that the cheese is produced naturally under these conditions.

Italy has for many years maintained a regulatory system, which is set up specifically to control the authenticity of products from specific regions. This quality-control system designates high-quality items using a label indicating that they were produced in a specific region and under specific guidelines. Products that meet these requirements are given the label of Denominazione di Origine Controllata, or DOC, which is a guarantee of the product's origin of

production as well as the ingredients and processes used to make the specific product. Italy has hundreds of products with this designation, and these products can only be produced in specific areas; for example, if a pork producer made a cured leg in the style of a prosciutto di Parma outside of the region designated with the DOC for this food, the producer would not be able to legally label it as such, regardless of the quality of the product. This system protects the value and authenticity of these products and is one of the major differences between many European products (as there are similar systems in other European countries) and those found in the United States (there are some systems like this in the United States, but they are not government driven and regulated, with the exception of the wine industry).

Italy is a major producer of cheeses, cured hams, fresh and preserved sausages, wines, vinegars, olive oil, and, of course, pasta, many examples of which are evident in the following section covering the regions of Italy. Many of these products are of the highest quality, and they make up the backbone of Italy's regional dishes and culinary traditions.

Pasta

The great variety of pasta that exists in Italian cuisine highlights the importance that this form of wheat has had on the country's cuisine. The credit for inventing pasta has often gone to the Chinese, with Marco Polo said to have been exposed to noodles and the ideas of pasta making on his travels to China, and to have then brought that idea back to Italy. However, there is ample evidence that pasta was being made in Italy prior to Marco Polo's fateful trip. Whatever its origin, pasta has long been a major component of Italian cuisine as well as a window into the diversity of the country.

Much is made of the difference between the cuisines of northern and southern Italy, where the north is the land of wealth and Italian foods unfamiliar to most Americans, while the south is the land of the familiar *pizza, spaghetti,* and tomato sauces people envision when asked about Italian cuisine. This general dichotomy is also true, to an extent, when it comes to pasta; the north is the Italian locale where one can find many varieties of fresh egg pasta dishes, whereas the south is where one can find dried, eggless pastas. Yet, the story goes much deeper in the case of pasta, and this is only the first of many possible divisions of pasta and pasta dishes: shape, size, length, and stuffed or un-stuffed are major factors as well.

The variety of pastas found in Italy is so numerous, it is difficult to say how many kinds exist—some estimate the number to be close to 2,000. A more helpful way of grasping this diversity is by looking at pasta types in relation to their use. Pasta finds its way into Italian cuisine in every course, with the exception of the antipasto ("not pasta") course (and probably only because of the name!). The following guide introduces the varieties of pasta, but keep in mind that much more could be written on this detailed subject.

dry pastas – Dried pastas are a part of southern Italian cuisine; this part of Italy experienced a large growth in the manufacturing of dried pastas in the eighteenth and nineteenth centuries. Dried pasta was much cheaper to make than fresh pasta, and it contains no egg.

soup pastas – Soup pastas are used in all varieties or soups, from simple light broths to heavier thick soups, with the pasta selected typically from smallest for light broths to somewhat larger for thicker soups. Some examples of this group include:

acini di pepe – One of the smallest pastas; resembles peppercorns and is typically used in light broths

conchigliette – Small, seashell-shaped pasta that is well suited for broth-based soups containing small vegetables or legumes

risi – Pasta shaped like a grain of rice

tubetti – Short, tube-shaped pasta used in thicker soups such as thick minestrones

ribbon pastas – Ribbon pastas are typically meant to be served tossed with a simple sauce that clings well to the noodles. Some examples of ribbon pastas include:

capellini – Very thin ribbon pasta best used with broth-based or sieved sauces that cling to this delicate pasta

fettuccine – thicker ribbon pasta, meant to be used with thicker, cream-based sauces or other sauces of similar consistency

linguine – Medium-thickness ribbon pasta meant to be used with butter or olive oil sauces or with pesto sauce

spaghetti – Smaller ribbon pasta used traditionally with lighter tomato sauces and olive oil-based sauces

trenette – Thin ribbon pasta, similar to linguini from the Liguria region; this is the traditional pasta to serve with Liguria pesto sauce

tubular pastas – Tubular pastas have the advantage of holding sauces (and potentially other foods) inside a tube; these grew in popularity after the invention of cast dies that were used to extract this dried form of eggless pasta. Some examples of tubular pastas include:

bucatini – Long, thin tubular pasta traditionally used with sauces containing pancetta

candele – Long and large tubular pastas that are traditional for meat sauces

penne rigate – Short, ridged tubular pasta shapes that are meant to cling to olive oil-based sauces. Penne are cut on a bias and thus have a quill shape.

rigatoni – Much like penne, rigatoni are ridged and short tubular pasta shapes that are cut square on the ends; these are meant for meat-based sauces and are also used in baked pasta dishes

shaped pastas – Not only are pastas created in small sizes for soups, in lengths for simple sauces, and in tubular shapes for thicker or oil-based sauces, they are also shaped either to imitate something else or to help hold specific sauces or foods. Some examples of shaped dried include:

conchiglioni – Very large, shell-shaped pastas meant to be cooked and then stuffed and baked

fusilli – Corkscrew-shaped pastas that are meant to hold meat-based sauces inside the curls of the pasta

orecchiette – Pasta shaped like little ears; meant to be cooked with thicker, vegetable-based sauces

fresh pastas – Fresh pastas are made with egg as well as wheat and water. These yield a more delicate product, as they do not have the strength that dried, eggless pastas have. Fresh pastas can also be flavored and will deliver flavor better than would a dried pasta made without egg (dried, eggless pastas are often colored and said to be flavored, but the most notable part is the color).

A number of the same shapes are made with fresh pastas, but a few possibilities exist when making fresh pastas that are not as feasible with dried pastas, such as stuffing them with fresh meats and cheeses. The following lists introduce stuffed and ribbon fresh pastas.

stuffed fresh pastas – Stuffed fresh pastas are common in a number of regions of Italy and vary less with regard to how they will hold sauces than with what they are filled or their desired size and appearance. Some common stuffed fresh pastas are:

agnolotti – Stuffed pastas formed by folding a circular piece of dough in half over a small amount of stuffing. These typically include cheese and/or vegetable fillings.

anolini – Half-moon–shaped stuffed pasta from the Emilia-Romagna region; traditionally served in a broth

cannelloni – Large, tube-shaped pastas that typically include thick meat fillings and are baked after being smothered with sauce and sometimes cheese. These are made by cutting rectangles of pasta sheets, piping the filling along the entire center of the length, and then rolling the pasta sheets around the filling—ending up with a filled pasta "log."

cappelletti – Pasta shaped like a kerchief that is made by filling a 2-inch square piece of dough, folding the dough in half to cover the filling by putting the points of opposite corners together to form a triangle, and then pulling the two other ends together to cover the filled section of the dough. These are typically filled with meat or cheese.

caramelle – Filled pastas that are shaped like a wrapped candy and traditionally would be filled with a sweet filling, such as pumpkin or winter squash. These are made by filling lengths of rectangular pasta with intermittent small amounts of the sweet filling, cutting in between the fillings, and rolling the filling with the pasta (leaving approximately ¾ of an inch of unfilled dough on each end of the filled sections). The free ends are then twisted like a candy wrapper, and the resulting filled pastas are often cooked and served with a light butter sauce.

mezzaluna – Small, half-moon–shaped, filled pastas that are typically served with a cream sauce and may have a wide variety of fillings, including meats, cheeses, and vegetables. These are made just like agnolotti, only the circular pieces of dough are smaller and there is less filling.

ravioli – These are made by laying double sheets of pasta, one on top of the other, with fillings placed in between the two sheets. Ravioli are often made using forms that cut the dough with fluted edges, and they are cut into squares to maximize yield.

tortellini – Small, triangular-shaped stuffed pasta that has its thin edges folded back and sealed to yield a shape resembling a hat and typically filled with cheese (these are also made dried)

ribbon fresh pastas – Like dried pastas, there are many versions of ribbon-shaped fresh pastas, and once again many of the differences have to do with the thickness of the lengths of pasta that are made. Many of the dried forms of pasta are mimicked with fresh pasta, but fresh egg pasta is not as sturdy as dried eggless pasta, and applications of the pasta should be considered before deciding which shape to use, and whether the pasta should he fresh or dried. Some common ribbon fresh pastas are:

maccheroni alla chittara – Fresh ribbon pasta made by pressing a sheet of pasta through a metal stringed tool (called a chittara) that resembles the stringed section of a guitar and slices the sheet into strips of width determined by the amount of space between the metal strings

pappardelle – Thick pasta ribbons, approximately ¾–1 inch in width, which traditionally have fluted edges. Pappardelle is typically served with thick and hearty sauces that this larger pasta can support.

pizzoccheri – Pasta made from buckwheat that has the appearance of a whole-grain pasta product (in that it is brown in color). This is a specialty of the Lombardy area and is traditionally served with potatoes and cabbage and topped with cheese.

lasagna – This well-known variety is made in both fresh and dried forms and is one of the largest sheet pastas and ribbon pastas made. Lasagna typically is layered with sauces and other ingredients to make the familiar baked casserole recipes that are common in the United States as well as Italy.

tagliatelle – Fresh ribbon pasta traditionally made in the Emilia-Romagna region and served with Bolognese sauce

NOTE: *When determining how much pasta to make for a given amount of people, note that one pound of dried pasta will yield between 2.5 and 2.75 pounds of cooked pasta, whereas one pound of fresh pasta will yield between 1.5 and 1.75 pounds of cooked pasta. In addition, fresh pasta cooks in a fraction of the time that it takes to cook dried pasta. When cooking fresh pasta, it is best to stay with the pasta and not walk away—just a minute or two too long often results in ruined pasta.*

Salumi and Cheeses

Many of the artisan products made in Italy are the backbone of the local cuisines, and the meat products (salumi) products and cheeses are certainly two of the most notable and exceptional. The variety within just these two types of products is astonishing, and both of these processes of preserving the yields from animals are highly regarded in Italian culture.

Cheeses

Some of the most important cheeses produced in Italy include:

Asiago – A high-fat cow's milk cheese from the Veneto region that is aged (to sharpen the flavor) and formed in large wheels

bel paese – A rich cow's milk cheese made to imitate the French Port Salut; this cheese is from the Lombardy region

burrata – Soft cow's milk cheese made in a laborious process that includes stuffing cooked curd and cream into strings of cheese to form a balloon-shaped cheese that is traditionally wrapped in leeks and develops a unique flavor with a creamy texture. This is a very perishable cheese that only lasts a day or so.

caciocavallo – A semisoft cow's milk cheese common in southern Italy, versatile in its use depending on its age. When young, it is eaten as a table cheese; after aging for months, it will be used as a grating cheese.

caciotta – Cheese that may be made with cow's, ewe's, or goat's milk, or a mixture of milks. It is a small, flat cheese that weighs less than 2 pounds and is very common in central Italy.

canestrato – Uncooked hard ripened ewe's milk cheese

castelmagno – A very highly regarded semisoft cow's milk cheese from the Piedmont region, which, when mature, develops a blue-veined mold

casumarzu – Essentially a pecorino that has had maggots added to it during its maturation, to impart a particular flavor to the cheese

fontina – Rich cow's milk cheese from the Val D'Aosta region, with excellent melting qualities and flavor

Gorgonzola – Famous blue-veined cow's milk cheese from the outskirts of Milan. This is a rich cheese with piquant flavor due to the growth of mold that forms naturally within the cheese as it ages in caves.

grana – Term for hard, aged cheeses with granular textures, such as Parmesan. Also the name of some of the lesser-known cheeses made in the same style as Parmesan, such as grana padano from the Po Valley regions of northern Italy.

mascarpone – A very rich cream cheese made originally in the Lombardy region

montasio – Semisoft or ripened hard cheese with small holes and sweet-to-piquant flavor, depending on its age

mozzarella – Originally the name of a fresh, soft cheese made from water buffalo's milk with a mild taste and excellent melting quality. This was a common cheese of southern Italy used in many familiar dishes, such as pizza and caprese. This name is now used to describe not only the original cheese but also the semisoft cow's milk cheese made in a similar manner as the original that also has good melting properties.

Parmesan – Famous sharp, dry aged cow's milk cheese from the Emilia-Romagna region of Italy. The large wheels go through a long maturation process (18 months to 2 years) to produce this fine grana-style cheese. This is the most well-known cheese of Italy, with the **parmigiano-reggiano** being one of the most highly regarded.

pecorino – A sheep's milk cheese usually aged and used as a grating cheese; when served young and softer, it is called pecorino da tavola. There are many versions of this cheese in Italy, which vary depending on which region they are made in. Some of the more highly regarded versions include **pecorino romano,** originally made outside the city of Rome, and **fiore sardo** from Sardinia.

provatura – Soft buffalo's milk cheese that is shaped in small balls and eaten fresh

provolone – Cows milk cheese with creamy texture; excellent for melting

ragusano – Made in Sicily, this is a used as a table cheese when younger and then grated when it has matured and dried further. It is a sweeter cheese when young that develops a sharpness from aging.

ricotta – Mostly made in southern Italy, this cheese is made from whey that remains from other cheese making (*ricotto* means "twice cooked"). Most ricotta is used as a fresh cheese, although in the marches it is salted and preserved between aromatic leaves, and it is also made into *ricotta salada* (a salted, preserved ricotta).

scamorza – Pear-shaped cow's milk curd cheese with mild flavor; these are sometimes smoked to yield a slightly colored rind and light, smoky flavor

tomini – A goat's milk cheese that is preserved in pepper; a specialty of the Piedmont region

Salumi

Some of the most common salumi products from Italy include:

Salame (Dry-Cured and Aged Encased Forcemeats)

boudin – A type of blood sausage found in the Aosta Valley (as well as France) that is made from pig's blood and a mixture of boiled potatoes and bacon

cacciatorino – Hunter's salami; salami made of half pork and half beef with pork fat, black pepper, garlic, and other spices that are aged for at least a month. This traditionally was made to be taken and eaten on trips (hence, the term *hunter*).

fegatino – This type of salami from the Marche region is made from pork leg, and liver replaces the usual pork fat

finocchiona – Anise-flavored salami made of finely ground pork and pork fat seasoned with fennel seeds

salame di milano – Salami from the Lombardy area consisting of equal parts pork, beef, and pork fat

salame di varza – Traditional salami from the Lombardy area made with coarsely ground lean pork, pork fat, and seasoned with white wine

salame napolentano – Salami flavored with chili peppers made from dried ground peperoncino (chiles), lean pork, and pork fat. This salami has a distinctive red hue from chiles and is quite thin.

ventricina – Pork salami from the Puglia region flavored with peperoncino, fennel, and orange zest

Salami Cotti (Cooked and Cured Meats)

bresaola – Meat made from beef that has been salted and spiced and wrapped in netting prior to being dry aged

capocolla – Cured pork shoulder seasoned with either hot or sweet peppers (sold as hot or sweet capocolla)

coppa – Also known as *capocollo*, this a pork neck that is marinated in stages with wine, salt, and seasoning, and then is encased before being aged

coppa al ginepro – A specialty type of coppa that is rubbed with juniper berries during the aging process to impart its special flavor

culatello – Cured rump of pork; this is a specialty of the Parma area of Emilia-Romagna

fegatino – Pork liver sausage from Marche

mocette – Traditionally made from ibex meat (but no longer made from ibex because they are threatened), this is now made from goat or chamois meat. Mocette is a specialty of the Aosta Valley in northern Italy, and it is made by brining the meat prior to its being hung to air-dry and age.

mortadella – Made from very finely ground beef and/or pork and pork fat, and seasoned with pepper, coriander, pistachios, and wine, this meat is packed into either a pig's or cow's bladder and cooked very slowly. Mortadella typically also has pieces of lard mixed into the forcemeat and is perishable, so it is kept in a cooler.

pancetta – This common product is often found in the United States, as it is very versatile and can be used in sauces or on its own after being rendered. Pancetta is the cured belly from pork, which is then rolled to yield something that looks quite different from bacon (bacon is also smoked, but pancetta is just cured), even though it is made from the same cut.

pancetta steccata – An uncommon but interesting specialty of the Aosta Valley, pancetta steccata is a type of pancetta (cured pork belly) that is sewn to itself and pressed between two pieces of juniper wood for two months for its dry aging

prosciutto – Made from salted and aged pork legs, this Italian specialty has gained particular attention in the United States. The pork legs are salted for a period of about 2 weeks and then dry-aged in well-ventilated areas after the exposed cut surface has been sealed with pork fat. The aging process for the fine prosciuttos made in the Parma area and in the San Daniele area of Fruili takes at least a year.

soppressa – Made from pork shoulder or legs, this is made in much the same way as the coppa, but it is aged longer (because it is larger). This meat is a specialty of the Veneto area.

speck – Made with pork leg that has been cured and marinated with spices and juniper berries prior to being smoked over burning juniper wood, this specialty is produced in the northern Adige area.

SIGNIFICANT SUBREGIONS

Italian cuisine is often misunderstood in the United States because of the lack of understanding about the importance of regional cuisine in Italy. Much of the Italian cuisine that is commonly served in the United States comes from immigrants of southern Italy, where pasta, bread, garlic, tomato sauces, and the like are a big part of the regional cuisines. Only recently have the cuisines of the northern regions started to make appearances in restaurants and books. However, even this inclusion does not satisfy the true diversity and cultural significance of the 20 Italian regions. It is important to realize that Italy is made up of these 20 distinct regions that all have a storied history, revere their local customs and traditions, and rely on the local ingredients to make what are often very different regional dishes.

To understand Italian cuisine, therefore, it is essential to know which "Italian" you are referencing—Sicilian Italian? Tuscan Italian? Italian from Milan? These regions are distinct, and the foods that are made in each can be dramatically different. The following guide covers some of the important distinctions between the regions as well as what products and ingredients are used in the local cuisines. Definitions of the cheeses, pasta, and salumi that are mentioned in this section can be found in the "Unique Components" section of the chapter; all other definitions are found at the conclusion of the chapter. The following guide is organized from west to east and then north to south.

Val D'Aosta

This region includes the northwestern part of Italy, which borders France and includes the major cities Aosta and Turin. With its proximity to France, this region includes some culinary traditions that resemble French traditions and recipes. The region was once part of a kingdom called Savoy that included part of France. Dominated geographically by its location within the Alps, Val D'Aosta has an alpine climate that has contributed to a heartier, more simplistic cuisine than much of the non-alpine regions of Italy.

Some of the common ingredients from this area are *funghi* (mushrooms), *castagne* (chestnut), *granoturco* (corn), *manzo* (young ox), and *fagiano* (pheasant). Some of the products that are produced in the Valley of Aosta include fontina, which may be found in local *fonduta* (melted cheese dip) as a means of using the scraps of cheese left from cutting. The cured meats and sausages from this region are also well known and include pancetta steccata, coppa al ginapro, and mocette. This region has produced a number of local specialties, including *zuppa di pane* (bread soup), *carbonade* (sauce with pancetta and egg), *montebianco* (sweetened chestnut purée), and *polenta cunsa* (polenta layered with cheese and mushrooms).

Piemonte (Piedmont)

This region is located to the east of the Aosta Valley and is also situated within the Alps, as well as in a large valley called Po Valley. As with the Val d'Aosta, this region—including the cities of Turin and Asti—has some cultural and culinary connections with areas that are now part of France. The Piedmont area includes the foothills of the Alps, which are rich in game and truffles, as well as the Po Valley, where much of the quality rices are grown that are used to make the famous risotto. Piemonte's climate is very hot in the summer and very cold in the winter.

Some of the ingredients that are common to this region include *nocciola* (hazelnuts), *tartufi* (truffles), *manzo*, *arborio*, and *carnaroli* (short-grain rices). Some of the recipes and products common to this region include tomini, *bagna caôda* (olive oil, garlic, and anchovy dip), castelmagno, *bollito misto* (mixed boiled meats), *salsa verde* (parsley caper sauce), *risotto* (creamy rice preparation), *grissini* (bread sticks), and *zabaglione* (sweetened foamed egg yolks).

Lombardia

This region of Italy occupies the center of the most northern section of Italy, with its northern neighbor of Switzerland bordering its northern reaches. Milan and the Po Valley make up the southern portion of this region, and the city of Milan plays a large role in the cuisine and other segments of this area's lifestyle. Milan is a city of business and, as such, has grown culturally in a way that puts more emphasis on time for work and less on time for culinary endeavors compared to many other areas of Italy. Nonetheless, there are many recipes and products that hail from this industrious area. This region is the birthplace of such well-known recipes as *risotto alla Milanese* (risotto with saffron), pannetone (rich cake with dried fruit), osso bucco (braised veal shank), and tortelli de zucca (pasta stuffed with squash), as well as the producer of bresaola, Gorgonzola, bel paese, Asiago, and mascarpone. Some of the ingredients that are common in this region's cuisine include *asparagi* (asparagus), *vitello* (veal), *maiale* (pork), *oca* (goose), *trota* (trout), *burro* (butter), and *zucca* (squash).

Trentino/Alto Adige

This region is further east than Piemonte and also dominated geographically by its mountainous terrain; it includes the cities of Trent and Bolzano. Although the two areas of Trentino and Alto Adige have some distinct differences, both have significant influences from earlier times and have only relatively recently become influenced significantly by their southern countrymen. Alto Adige did not become part of Italy until 1918, and it has very strong historical and cultural links to Austria that are easily seen in its cuisine, including the commonplace uses of rye and potatoes. In contrast, Trentino maintains strong influences from the Venetians, which is clear in the cuisine as well as in the abundant use of corn. The Trentino area has a very harsh climate and isn't well known for its cuisine, having been home to a poorer population that required simpler fare. Some of the ingredients that are common to the cuisines of this region include *patatas* (potatoes), *cipolle* (onions), *granoturco* (corn), *mela* (apple), *cavolo* (cabbage), *maiale*, and *strutto* (pork fat). Products and recipes that are common to this region include *gnocchi di patata* (potato dumpling), *strudel* (thin pastry filled with various ingredients), *crauti* (sauerkraut), *polenta*, Asiago, speck, and *canederli*.

Veneto

This region includes the most eastern portion of the Po Valley that stretches toward the Adriatic Sea. Veneto includes the famous city of Venice, which was once the major trading port of Europe and controlled the trade of *caffe* (coffee), *sale* (salt), *spezie* (spice), and sugar. Venice was a very wealthy city that held elaborate feasts and celebrations, and it was here that the first use of the fork is purported to have occurred. There was some influence on the region from periods of Austrian rule, including the use of *crauti* (sauerkraut). The coastal area of this region is well known for seafood, whereas the cuisine of the inland area

utilizes the large array of vegetables and grains that are produced there.

Some of the common ingredients of this region include granoturco, *riso* (rice), *radicchio*, *fagioli* (beans), asparagi, zucca, cavolo, patatas, pesce, and burro. The region's significant products and recipes include *pasta e fagioli* (pasta and beans), *risi e bisi* (rice and peas), *carpaccio* (thinly sliced raw beef with garnishes), polenta, and *tiramisu* (layered sponge fingers with mascarpone cream).

Friuli-Venezia Giulia

This region is at the most northeastern part of Italy and borders Austria to its north, Slovenia to its east, and the Adriatic Sea to its south. Like the other northern regions of Italy, this area is dominated geographically by the alpine mountains to the north. It also has been significantly influenced by its northern neighbors, including Austria, Hungary, Slovenia, and Croatia. This area includes Trieste, an important seaport to the region that has a long history as a trading port, resulting in local incorporation of ingredients from other countries, such as poppy seeds, paprika, caraway, and horseradish.

When it comes to ingredients used in this area, the most important is polenta, which is a main component of the local cuisine. Other common ingredients include fagioli, patatas, cavolo, funghi, maiale, and *capriolo* (venison). Some of the specialty products and recipes of the area include the fine-cured prosciutto di San Daniele, *grappa* (distilled beverage), montasio, Asiago (now mostly made in Lombardy), *jota* (bean and barley stew), and *frico* (cheese fritters).

Liguria

This region is bordered by Piedmont to the north and by Emilia-Romagna and Tuscany to the east, and includes the major city of Genoa. Liguria borders the Ligurian Sea (part of the Mediterranean) on its western and southern reaches, and lies within a valley before the foothills of the mountains to the east. The mild climate of this coastal area makes for a very fertile region, which results in a bounty from the gardens. Some of the common ingredients of the area include *sultanas* (golden raisins), *coniglio* (rabbit), *basilica* (basil), *pinoli* (pine nuts), *noce* (walnut), *oliva* (olive), and *pesce* (fish). Some of the common dishes and recipes of this region include *pesto alla Genovese*, *vincigrassi* (baked, layered pasta), *salsa di noci* (walnut sauce), trenette, *gnocchi* (small dumplings), *buridda* (fish soup), *ciuppin* (fish stew), *torta pasqualina* (chard- and cheese-filled savory pie), ravioli, and *focaccia* (flatbread with olive oil).

Emilia-Romagna

The western and northern portion of this region includes the southern part of the fertile Po Valley, while the southern portion is dominated by the Apennines Mountains that run through the heart of Italy. The eastern section of this region ends with the Adriatic Sea. One of Italy's most famous "gourmet" regions, Emilia-Romagna has been renowned for the products made here by Italians since the Middle Ages. Some of the major cities include Parma, Bologna, Reggio, Modena, and Piacenza, and each contributes to the richness of the cuisine of the region. Women are famous for their ability to make the local types of egg pasta, and the pork products from this region have no parallel. This region has developed around the foods that are produced here, and they play a large role in the cuisine as well.

Some of the ingredients common to this region include mela, maiale, *latte* (milk), *sogliola* (sole), *anguilla* (eel), *pomodoro* (tomato), *uva* (grapes), *origano* (oregano), and other *erbe aromatiche* (aromatic herbs). Some of the common products and recipes of this region include Parmesan cheese, prosciutto, cutatello, mortadella, *aceto balsamico* (aged wine vinegar), cotechino, *brodetto* (fish soup), anolini, tortellini, tagliatelle, and lasagna.

Tuscany/Umbria

Lying south of Emilia-Romagna and bordering the Arcipelago Sea in the west, the Ligurian Sea in the east, and north of the capital, Tuscana is one of the richest culinary regions of Italy. With a cuisine undeniably based on local, seasonal ingredients that accompany the holy trinity of wine, olive oil, and bread, Tuscans revere uncomplicated, familiar foods prepared perfectly. This region is home to the cities of Pisa, Livorno, Lucca, and Firenze (Florence), and historically was a poorer region that made the best out of its local products. Although the region is no longer a poor one, the Tuscan appreciation for utilizing ingredients persists. One Tuscan tradition relating to the frugal past that still persists today is the lack of salt in the local bread. Tuscan bread is made with no or very little salt, a tradition that began centuries ago with the implementation of a salt tax to which the bakers responded by leaving the salt out. The custom was to eat this bread with highly flavored spread or the famous local olive oil.

This region is a significant producer of *olio d'oliva* (olive oil), *cavolo nero* (Tuscan cabbage), pecorino, *salvia* (sage), pinoli, fagioli, *spinaci* (spinach), *finocchio* (fennel), and *baccelli* (fresh fava beans). Some of the significant products and recipes from this region include *panzenella* (bread and tomato salad), *crostini* (toasted bread with topping), *papperdelle alla cacciatore* (thick pasta with sausage), *arista alla fiorentina* (roast pork), *pisella alla fiorentina* (peas with pancetta), *buccellato* (Tuscan cake), and *castagnaccio* (chestnut flatbread).

Marche

This region lies between the Apennines Mountains and the Adriatic Sea in central Italy and includes the cities of Pesaro, Ancona, and Ascoli Piceno. This lesser-known region of Italy boasts fine seafood from the shores of the Adriatic and plentiful vegetables and meats in the valley leading to the hills of the Apennines. The region includes many specialties that have one interesting connection—they are all stuffed! Whether it is stuffed olives, stuffed rabbit, stuffed pasta, or stuffed whole piglet, there is clearly a penchant for stuffing here.

Some of the ingredients common to this region include maiale, *congilio* (rabbit), *quaglie* (quail), cavolfiore (cauliflower), finocchio, tartufo, funghi, and numerous other verdure and pesce (vegetables and fish). Some of the recipes and products from this region include ricotta salada, pecorino, coppa, fegatino, *porchetta* (roasted and stuffed pig), *coniglio in porchetta* (roasted and stuffed rabbit), brodetto, and *olive all'ascolana* (stuffed olives).

Lazio-Rome

This region is located in the middle of the western coast of Italy and is bordered by Tuscany and Umbria to the north, Abruzzi to the east, and Campania to the south. It is also home to the capital of Italy, Rome. The ancient capital of Rome dominates this region, which once supplied the great empire with much of the needed ingredients for the local cuisine. The cuisine of this region also has been influenced by the other areas of Italy, because it was the hub of the developing country ("all roads lead to Rome"). Even with the outside influence, there is still distinction in the local use of offal, greens, and other fresh vegetables, as well as in their use of matured pork fat to create the local cuisine.

Ingredients commonly used in this region include *abbacchio* (baby lamb), *vitello* (veal), *carciofi* (globe artichoke), *cardo* (cardoon), *peperone* (bell peppers), *rucola* (arugula), and *puntarelle* (chicory). Some of the significant products and recipes from this region include pecorino romano, ricotta, *strutto* (rendered pork fat), *gnocchi di semolina* (small, hard wheat dumplings), *spaghetti alla carbonara* (thin pasta with egg, bacon, and cheese sauce), *spaghetti all puttanesca* (thin pasta with spicy tomato sauce), and *saltimbocca* (sautéed meat with prosciutto and sage).

Abruzzi/Molise/Puglia (Apulia)

These regions make up the southeastern border of Italy running along the back of the southern portion of "the boot." They are bordered by the Adriatic Sea to the east and Lazio, Campania, and Basilicata to the west, and they include the cities of Pescara, L'Aquila, Campobasso, Foggia, Bari, and Taranto. The regions of Abruzzi and Molise are mostly mountainous, and the cuisine is simpler due to the herding livelihoods. These regions are known as the birthplace of an instrument called a *chitarra,* which was used to make the strips of sheet pasta, such as fettuccini, by pressing the sheets through the wires that lined this rectangular instrument. The region of Apulia, in contrast to Abruzzi and Molise, is mostly flat and a very productive farming area. This region produces much of the wheat used to make the pasta so common in southern Italy, grapes, and olives, as well as many of the pulses and vegetables that are used in the local cuisine (and distributed to the rest of the country). Not surprisingly, the cuisine of the Apulia region is based on the local produce.

Some of the ingredients that are commonly used in the local cuisine of these regions include *peperoncini* (chili peppers), peperone, *lenticchia* (lentils), patatas, *piselli* (peas), *catalogna* (Italian dandelion), *puntarelle*, *cime di rapa* (turnip greens), *polipetti* (small octopus), and *agnello* (lamb). Some of the products and recipes that are of particular interest from these regions include ventricina, capocollo, scamorza, *incapriata* (puréed fava beans and boiled chicory), maccheroni alla chitarra, and *tarantella* (cured tuna "sausage").

Campania/Basilicata

These regions are bordered by Apulia and Molise to the east and the Mediterranean and Calabria to the west and south. Campania and Basilicata include the cities of Naples, Salerno, and Potenza. These regions are home to many of the specialties known by Americans, because many of the Italian immigrants traveled to the United States from here (particularly from the area of Naples).

The ingredients that define the cuisine of these regions include agnello, maiale, *capretto* (young goat), patates, pomodoros, peperone, peperoncino, and *melanzana* (eggplant). Some of the significant recipes and products from this region include mozzarella, burrata, provolone, caciocavallo, *pizza* (baked thin dough with tomato and cheese topping), *calzone* (baked stuffed dough), *caprese* (water buffalo cheese and tomato salad), spaghetti alla puttanesca, and *Parmigiana di melanzane* (eggplant Parmesan).

Calabria

This region makes up the toe of "the boot" of Italy and is bordered by Basilicata to the north; otherwise, it is surrounded by the Mediterranean. As with other southern Italian regions, the cuisine from Calabria has roots in poorer times, but it definitely doesn't lack in flavor or complexity. Calabria has been both plagued and graced with a history of invasion very similar to that of Sicily. Although many cultures brought pain and hardship to the region over the course of history, they also brought ingredients and techniques that are fundamental to the cuisine of the region today. The region has experienced periods of control or strong influence by Greeks, Arabs, Normans, Spanish, and French; all have contributed to the current cuisine.

Because of the cultural influence from nearby countries, a wide variety of ingredients are common in the local cuisine, including peperone, peperoncino, melanzana, citron, *fico* (figs), pomodoro, fagioli, oliva, sultanas, *nocciola* (hazelnuts), *mandorla* (almonds), *pesce spada* (swordfish), *acciuga* (anchovies), *sarda* (sardines), and *tonno* (tuna). Some of the specialty products and recipes of the area include scamorza, provolone, mozzarella, caciocavallo, capocollo, *insalata di mare* (seafood salad), and *cannelloni* (filled and baked pasta sheets).

Sardinia

The island of Sardinia lies off the western coast of Italy, parallel to Lazio and Campania. Because of location in the heart of the Mediterranean, it has been the target of invasions throughout history. Sardinia has seen periods of rule by Arabs and Romans, as well as interference by Austria and the former region of Savoy, to name a few examples, all of which have left their impact on the island's people and culinary habits. Part of the effect of the constant harassment from outsiders has been the population's reliance on the land more than the sea for products of survival. The invaders would occupy the ports, and thus the population became accustomed to relying on the land for their food. Seafood is a significant part of the cuisine of Sardinia, but it is agricultural and meat products that make up its heart. Of particular importance are cheeses (particularly from sheep's milk), bread, and meat.

Some of the ingredients that are commonly used in Sardinian dishes are maiale, agnello, capretto, peperoncini, pomodoro, *zafferano* (saffron), fagioli, *grano* (wheat), *ceci* (chickpeas), *cappero* (capers), and finocchio. Some of the products and recipes of particular interest from this region include pecorino sardo, ricotta, *porceddu* (spit-roasted piglet), *pane carasau* (thin, crisp bread), *malloreddus* (saffron-flavored dumplings), *bottarga* (grey mullet roe), and *favata* (pork and bean stew).

Sicilia

The island of Sicily is located at the "foot" of the mainland in the Mediterranean Sea and stretches toward the coast of northeastern Africa (Tunisia). The island has a 10,000-year history filled with invasions and perseverance, and has significant culinary influences from Greek and Arab periods of rule that are still clearly evident in the current cuisine. Sicily is an autonomous region, exercising greater regional freedom, and Sicilians are known for their proud individuality. The climate is arid and hot on most of the island, greatly influencing the types of foods produced there.

Sicily's major crops include oliva, *arancia* (oranges), uvas, grano, *noco* (walnuts), and mandorla, while the fisherman provide *pesce spada* (swordfish), tonno, *sepia* (cuttlefish), *cernia* (grouper), *sarago* (sea bream), and *dentice* (dentex). Some of the recipes and products from this region include ragusano, ricotta, *cassata* (rich cake with marzipan topping), canestrato, *caponata* (sweet and sour eggplant), *gelato* (sweetened iced milk), *peperonata* (stewed peppers, tomatoes, and onions), *scaloppine al Marsala* (thinly sliced meat sautéed with Marsala wine), *pasta reale* (marzipan shaped like fruits), and *arancini* (fried, filled rice balls).

RECIPES

The following recipes provide a glimpse into the complex world of Italian cuisine. Obviously, this is far from a complete representation of what Italian cuisine has to offer; most books on Italian cuisine focus on particular regions because of the enormity of options. The recipes included here give a feel for the variety and quality that make up Italian cuisine.

Gnocchi VENETO
(POTATO DUMPLING)

INGREDIENTS

6	lb	Russet Potatoes
1	lb + 6 oz	All-Purpose (A.P.) Flour
1/4	cup	Rosemary, minced (optional)
3	Tbsp	Salt
6	oz	Butter, melted
1/4	cup	Sage Leaves, packed (about 1 average bunch)

Gnocchi is the term given to any small dumpling that is common throughout northern Italy. Many varieties exist, but this recipe is perhaps the most well known. Some other types include gnocchi di zucca, which is made from a variety of squash/pumpkin in Lombardy; gnocchi di riso, which is made from leftover rice in Reggio-Emilia; and gnocchi di polenta, which is made from leftover polenta in the northernmost part of the country.

YIELD: 15 portions (5 ounces/portion)

MIXING METHOD: Hand Kneading

COOKING METHOD: Boiling

PROCEDURE

1. Preheat oven to 300°F, and bring two pots of salted water to a boil.
2. Bring large pot of salted water to a boil and add potatoes; cook until potatoes are tender throughout (do not allow the potatoes to disintegrate while cooking from being overcooked).

(continues)

Gnocchi
(continued)

Rolling gnocchi (potato dumplings) between gnocchi paddles (note that a spoon can also be used to make similar ridges in dough that will provide the same function of holding clinging sauces)

3. Strain potatoes in a colander and allow to cool slightly before peeling them (the potatoes can be peeled first, in which case they will be more moist and require slightly longer in the oven).

4. Put the potatoes on a sheet pan, and place them in the oven for 5 minutes to dry slightly.

5. Pass potatoes through a food mill into a mixing bowl, and season with salt and rosemary (if desired).

6. Slowly add the flour to the potatoes while kneading the resulting dough with your free hand, using your knuckles to work the flour into the center while you knead.

7. Continue adding flour and kneading until the dough loses its sticky nature and develops some structure. At this point, stop kneading or adding flour, and turn the dough to the bench.

8. Once on the bench, break the dough into approximately eight pieces and work with each one individually, rolling each into a cylinder approximately the thickness of a penny.

9. Once the dough has been rolled into cylinders, cut each cylinder into 3/4-inch lengths and make the characteristic indentations, using a gnocchi paddle, fork, or grater.

10. In the second pot of boiling salted water, cook the gnocchi until they float (2 minutes), and then remove them with a slotted spoon.

11. Once the gnocchi have drained, toss with melted butter and sage; serve.

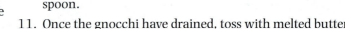

Finished gnocchi with sage

Pesto LIGURIA
(BASIL, GARLIC, AND OLIVE OIL PASTE)

INGREDIENTS

1	oz	Pine Nuts
1	pint	Basil Leaves, packed (about 2 typical bunches)
.5	oz	Garlic Cloves
1/8	tsp	Coarse Sea Salt
1.5	oz	Parmesan Cheese, grated (about 1/4 cup)
1/3	cup	Extra Virgin Olive Oil (milder variety is best, not peppery)

This classic Genoa herb paste is made with the young basil leaves of the local variety of basil, which are not pungent like much of the basil that is sold in the United States. Try to find smaller leaves, which are milder and yield a more authentic version.

YIELD: Approximately 1 cup

MIXING METHOD: Crushing in Mortar and Pestle

PROCEDURE

1. Preheat oven to 325°F. Place the pine nuts in a small pan and bake them until they just begin to turn golden (about 5–8 minutes). Remove them from the oven and set aside to cool.

2. (The traditional method of making pesto is in a mortar and pestle, which will yield a smoother-textured pesto than that made in a food processor. Directions for both will be given here.) For the mortar and pestle version, place the cooled pine nuts, basil leaves, garlic, and salt into the mortar, and grind to a paste with the pestle. Once ground to a paste, add the cheese and mix. Slowly add the olive oil to the paste, mixing it with a wooden spoon or the pestle to form the finished pesto.

3. For the food processor version, add the cooled pine nuts, basil, garlic, salt, and Parmesan cheese to the food processor, and then pulse to purée the ingredients together. Once ground, add the olive oil in a slow, steady stream to the purée, while the processor is running, to form the finished pesto.

Polenta al Burro FRIULI/VENEZIA GIULIA
(BOILED COARSE CORNMEAL WITH BUTTER)

INGREDIENTS

1	cup	Polenta
3	cups	Water
2	Tbsp	Butter, salted
		Salt, to taste

This simple dish is very versatile, because the polenta can have cheese added to it and be baked or it can be topped with sauces.

YIELD: 6 portions (1/2 cup/portion)

COOKING METHOD: Boiling

PROCEDURE

1. In a saucepan, bring water to a boil over high heat.

2. Once boiling, add the polenta to the water, slowly stirring the whole time, until all of the polenta is added.

3. Cook over high heat until the mixture thickens to a pudding-like consistency. Immediately reduce the heat to a very low flame and continue to cook for 20 minutes, stirring frequently until polenta becomes crusted on pan and pulls away from this crust.

4. Add butter to polenta, and season with salt to taste. At this point, polenta can be used as is or cooled and cut after cooling.

Polenta al burro (coarse cornmeal with butter) topped with basil pesto (herb/garlic paste) and shaved Parmesan cheese

Pasta Fresca NORTHERN ITALY
(FRESH EGG PASTA)

INGREDIENTS

2	lbs	A.P. Flour
8		Eggs, large
1	tsp	Salt

This is the typical egg pasta that is more common in northern Italy. The southern Italian counterpart is typically dried, does not contain egg, and is usually cut into circular shapes (via extrusion machines). Most pasta in Italy is dried, which is made with hard durum semolina wheat and water; this was a more economical way of producing pasta and common over much of southern Italy.

YIELD: 3 pounds

MIXING METHOD: Hand Kneading

PROCEDURE

1. Mix the flour and salt thoroughly and place on work surface in a cone-shaped mound.
2. Beat the eggs together in a bowl.
3. Make a small well in the center of the flour and add the eggs.
4. Work the eggs into the flour using a fork or fingers until half the flour has been absorbed.
5. Begin to knead the dough with hands to continue to incorporate more flour until all of the flour has been absorbed and a stiff dough is achieved.
6. Continue to knead the dough for an additional 10 minutes to develop the gluten properly.
7. Cover the dough with a damp, clean cloth and allow it to rest for 30 minutes prior to rolling it out to make desired shape of pasta.
8. To make sfoglia, cut the dough into approximately 6-ounce pieces to work individually through a pasta machine. Each piece will make one sheet approximately 2 feet long.
9. To properly develop the dough for the sfoglia, flatten each dough piece by hand or with a rolling pin until it is 1/2 inch thick, and then pass that piece through the pasta machine at the largest setting (open the widest).
10. Once passed through the machine, the dough should be folded in thirds or the proper thickness to fit back into the machine when turned 90°, and then passed through the machine again.
11. Repeat the preceding step once more; the dough should have loosened considerable and be ready to roll into a thin sheet by passing it through successively smaller settings to form the finished sfoglia.
12. Once the dough has been rolled out to desired width, it can be cut to desired thicknesses (fettuccini, linguini, etc.) or used as sheets to make other types of pasta (ravioli, tortellini, agnolotti, etc.).

Pasta types: sfoglia (rolled sheet, on left), pappardelle (center top), fettuccini (center bottom), and ravioli (on right)

Ragu alla Bolognese EMILIA-ROMAGNA

(TOMATO AND MEAT SAUCE IN THE STYLE OF BOLOGNA)

INGREDIENTS

1	oz	Extra Virgin Olive Oil
10	oz	Pancetta, diced small (or ground)
2	lbs	Veal, ground
1	lb	Yellow Onions, diced small
5	oz	Carrots, minced
5	oz	Celery, minced
12	oz	Dry White Wine
1	qt	Tomato Purée
5	cups	Tomato Concassée (or canned diced tomato)
2	Tbsp	Tomato Paste
1	Tbsp	Fresh Oregano, minced
2	cups	Veal Stock
2	oz	Extra Virgin Olive Oil
		Salt and Black Pepper

This famous meat sauce from the Emilia-Romagna region of Italy is often used to sauce the egg pastas of the area or to make lasagna alla Bolognese.

YIELD: 3 quarts

COOKING METHOD: Stewing

PROCEDURE

1. In a 6–8-quart heavy-bottomed pot, heat 1 oz of olive oil over a medium-high flame until the oil ripples, and then add pancetta.

2. Sauté pancetta in olive oil until fully rendered and browned; add the ground veal to the pan, turning the heat up to caramelize it.

3. Once the veal has been caramelized, add onions, carrots, and celery, and reduce heat to a medium flame to slowly sweat the vegetables until tender and translucent.

4. Once vegetables are tender, deglaze the pan with the white wine, making sure to scrape the pan with a wooden spoon to dissolve particles.

5. Add the tomato product, oregano, and veal stock, and bring to simmer.

6. Reduce heat and allow sauce to simmer lightly for at least 1 hour.

7. Finish with extra virgin olive oil, and season with salt and pepper.

Pizza Margherita CAMPAGNA

(PIZZA WITH TOMATO, BASIL, AND MOZZARELLA)

INGREDIENTS

For the Dough

1	oz	Fresh Compressed Yeast
1/2	cup	Water, lukewarm
2	Tbsp	A.P. Flour
4	cups	A.P. Flour
1/2	tsp	Salt
		Water, as needed

For the Topping

		A.P. Flour, as needed for dusting

The first pizza Margherita was invented in 1889 by Raffaele Esposito as a tribute to the queen of Italy, Margherita di Savoia.

YIELD: Two 12-inch pizzas

MIXING METHOD: Kneading

COOKING METHOD: Baking

PROCEDURE

Preheat oven that will be used to make the pizza.

For the Dough

1. Combine the fresh yeast, warm water, and 2 Tbsp of flour in a small container; cover and allow to bloom (this step ensures that the yeast is active).

(continues)

Pizza Margherita
(continued)

2	cups	Ripe Tomatoes, peeled, seeded, and chopped
1	Tbsp	Basil, fresh chopped
1	oz	Extra Virgin Olive Oil
		Salt, to taste
12	oz	Mozzarella Cheese, grated
2	Tbsp	Extra Virgin Olive Oil
16		Basil Leaves (about 1/4 bunch)

The yeast mixture should foam a bit and have distinct yeasty aroma. If it does not, discard and start with new yeast that does.

2. Sift the salt and 4 cups of flour together and put on a workbench (for making by hand) or in a small mixer. Add the yeast mixture to the center of the flour/salt mixture.

3. If working from the bench, knead in the yeast mixture and begin to add water to the dough, while kneading, until you form a smooth dough that doesn't stick to the bench but forms a solid ball.

4. If using a mixer, use the dough hook and turn to low speed; add water until dough forms a smooth unit without sticking to the bowl.

5. Using the bench method, continually knead the dough by flattening and folding it over, using your palms to stretch the dough until in loosens and becomes elastic (this may take some time, depending on your wrist strength and vigor).

6. Using the mixing bowl method, continue to mix on low speed until dough becomes soft and elastic (time will depend on mixer used).

7. Once the dough has developed, either put it in a proofbox or cover it with a damp, clean towel and keep it in a warm place (80–90°F) until it has doubled in volume.

For Assembling the Pizza

1. Once the dough has doubled in volume, it can be removed from the proofbox or uncovered and turned to the bench, where it can be punched down and divided into two pieces (use dusting flour to keep dough from sticking to bench).

Baked pizza Margherita

2. Using your fingertips, work the dough into a disk by flattening the dough and spreading it until each piece is 12 inches in diameter. (Note: The dough should be thicker around the edges than in the center.)

3. Combine the tomato, 1 Tbsp of basil, and 1 oz of extra virgin olive oil in a small bowl, and season with salt.

4. Spread the tomato and basil mixture evenly over the dough, leaving 1 inch of the edge uncovered.

5. Top the tomato mixture with the grated mozzarella cheese.

6. Drizzle 1 Tbsp of extra virgin olive oil over the top of each pizza.

7. Place the pizzas into the preheated oven (or pizza oven) and bake until edges brown and cheese begins to caramelize (time will vary greatly depending on the oven used; wood-fired ovens may take 5 minutes, whereas conventional ovens may take 15–20 minutes).

*Carpaccio

(Raw Shaved Beef)

Ingredients

12	oz	Beef Tenderloin, trimmed of connective tissue

Accompaniments

1	Recipe	Salsa per Carpaccio
4	oz	Parmesan, shaved
3	oz	Mushrooms, slivered
2	oz	Shallots, shaved

This is a relatively new addition to the Italian culinary repertoire, having been introduced in the 1960s in Venice. Traditionally served with a spiced mayonnaise, carpaccio is often made with the sauce that follows this recipe.

Yield: 8 portions (1.5oz/portion) + garnishes

Special Method: Freezing and Slicing on a Machine

Procedure

1. Wrap trimmed tenderloin very tightly in plastic wrap, and place in the freezer.

2. Once tenderloin has frozen (or frozen through 3/4, at least), remove it from the freezer, unwrap it, and slice on a meat slicer—as thin as possible without it falling apart. As it is being sliced, the meat should be put on a plate or platter right away, because it will defrost and be difficult to handle almost instantly.

3. Drizzle with sauce, and garnish with Parmesan, mushrooms, and shallots.

Carpaccio (shaved beef) topped with salsa per carpaccio (carpaccio sauce), shaved Parmesan cheese, and mushrooms

Salsa per Carpaccio
(CARPACCIO SAUCE)

INGREDIENTS

1	Small Shallot, minced (about 1 Tbsp)
2 Tbsp	Cornichon, minced
2 Tbsp	Capers, minced
2	Anchovy Fillets, minced
2 oz	Red Wine Vinegar
5 fl oz	Extra Virgin Olive Oil
1/4 bunch	Parsley, minced (about 1/4 cup)
	Black Pepper, freshly ground, to taste

Carpaccio is often served with garnishes of olive oil, capers, shaved Parmesan, minced onions, and sliced mushrooms. This sauce is also used as a traditional accompaniment.

YIELD: 8 servings (1.25 ounces each)

MIXING METHOD: Grinding in Mortar and Pestle

PROCEDURE

1. Combine shallots, cornichons, capers, anchovy, and vinegar in a mortar and pestle (or food processor, if not available), and grind to a paste while slowly adding the olive oil.
2. Mix in the parsley, and season with black pepper.

Insalata di Arance   SICILY
(ORANGE AND FENNEL SALAD WITH ROSEMARY)

INGREDIENTS

For the Vinaigrette

3 oz	White Wine Vinegar
5 oz	Olive Oil, pure
4 oz	Extra Virgin Olive Oil
4 tsp	Fresh Rosemary, minced
	Zest from 5 oranges
	Salt and Black Pepper

For the Salad

3	Fennel Bulbs, shaved
1	Large Onion, shaved
	Vinaigrette (see above)
10	Oranges, peeled and sliced in 1/4-inch rounds, or cut into segments

Sicily is well known for its citrus, which were introduced to the island during a period of Arab control. This recipe highlights the fruit in a light salad.

YIELD: 10 portions (6 ounces/portion)

MIXING METHOD: Non-Emulsified Vinaigrette

PROCEDURE

1. To make the vinaigrette, combine all of the ingredients in a mixing bowl and mix thoroughly before seasoning to taste with salt and fresh black pepper.
2. For the salad, both the fennel and onion should be shaved very fine using a mandoline or slicer, and then combined with the vinaigrette and allowed to sit for at least 1 hour.
3. Once the fennel and onion have marinated, the salad is ready to be assembled by peeling the oranges and cutting them into desired shapes (rounds or wedges).
4. The oranges can then be arranged on the plate and topped with the fennel/onion mixture, making sure to coat the oranges with some of the vinaigrette.

Insalata di arance (orange and fennel salad)

Bagna Caôda PIEDMONT
(HOT ANCHOVY GARLIC OIL DIP)

INGREDIENTS

4	oz	Butter, salted
14	oz	Extra Virgin Olive Oil
3	oz	Anchovy Fillets
2	oz	Garlic Cloves, minced
		Salt, to taste

Commonly used as a sauce to accompany fresh vegetables from the Piedmont area, this would usually be kept warm in an earthenware pot over a small flame.

YIELD: 10 portions (2 ounces/portion)

COOKING METHOD: (Anchovies and Garlic): Poaching/Steeping

PROCEDURE

1. In a small saucepan, heat butter and oil over a very low flame until butter is fully melted.
2. Add anchovies to the butter/oil mixture and continue to cook over very low flame until anchovies begin to disintegrate (about 40 minutes).
3. Add minced garlic to pan, and continue to cook for another 5 minutes to completely soften garlic.
4. Serve warm with raw or blanched vegetables.

Cacciucco TUSCANY
(FISHERMAN'S SEAFOOD STEW, FROM LIVORNO)

INGREDIENTS

2	lbs	Black Mussels
1	lb	Hard-Shell Clams
1	lb	Calamari, cleaned and cut into rings
.5	lb	Shrimp, 26/30 shell-on
1	lb	Lean White Fish Fillet (sea bass, cod, haddock, mullet, or other appropriate fish)
1	oz	Extra Virgin Olive Oil
1	oz	Garlic Cloves, minced
1	lb	Onion, sliced thin
2	cups	White Wine, dry
1.5	tsp	Red Pepper Flakes
6	cups	Tomato Purée
2	oz	Extra Virgin Olive Oil
		Salt and Pepper, to taste
16		thick slices of quality bread

One of the many fisherman's stews of Italy, this recipe utilizes some of the seafood products commonly available in the United States.

YIELD: 8 portions (1.5 cups/portion)

COOKING METHOD: Stewing

PROCEDURE

1. Clean the shellfish by scrubbing it under cold running water and removing beards of mussels.
2. Cut the fillets of white fish into 1-inch cubes.

(continues)

Cacciucco (fisherman's stew)

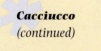

Cacciucco
(continued)

3. In a heavy saucepan that is large enough to hold all of the seafood and vegetables, heat 1 oz of extra virgin olive oil over a low flame, and then add the sliced onions to sweat in the oil.

4. Slowly sweat the onions until they become translucent, and then add the garlic and turn the heat up to a high flame. Cook garlic quickly with fat.

5. As soon as the garlic becomes aromatic and translucent, add the white wine and the red pepper flakes, and stir to combine well.

6. Allow the wine to reduce by 50%, and then add in the tomato purée. Turn heat down to a low simmer, and simmer mixture for 20 minutes.

7. Add the seafood to this mixture, according to the amount of time that each will take to cook (add the fish first, then the clams, shrimp, calamari, and mussels).

8. Once all of the seafood has cooked, stir in the extra virgin olive oil and season to taste with salt and pepper.

9. Serve with slices of bread.

Risotto alla Milanese LOMBARDY
(STEWED SHORT-GRAIN RICE IN THE STYLE OF MILAN)

INGREDIENTS

1	oz	Butter, unsalted
12	oz	Yellow Onion, minced
1	lb	Rice, Arborio (or other suitable short-grain rice)
5	cups	(approximately) White Stock (Chicken or Veal), held hot
1	tsp	Saffron
4	oz	Parmesan, grated
2	oz	Butter, salted
		Salt and White Pepper, to taste

This famous dish is the classic accompaniment to osso bucco.

YIELD: 10 portions (5 ounces/portion)

SPECIAL COOKING METHOD: Risotto Method

PROCEDURE

1. Add the saffron to the hot stock to infuse the stock with the saffron.

2. In a sauté pan or heavy-bottomed saucepan, melt the unsalted butter over a medium flame and add the minced onion. Sweat in the fat until onions are translucent.

3. Add the rice and continue to cook over lower flame for a few minutes, stirring to coat the rice completely with the fat.

4. Add the saffron-infused stock to the rice in small increments (add a cup for the first addition, and then reduce the amount added to 1/2 cup after that), stirring the rice all the while to draw the surface starch from the rice into the stock.

5. Continue with the stock additions and stirring until the rice is cooked al dente. (More stock may be needed, depending on how high the heat on the stove is.)

6. Once the rice is al dente, remove from heat and stir in the grated Parmesan and salted butter.

7. Season to taste with salt and ground white pepper.

Gremolata   LOMBARDY

(PARSLEY, GARLIC, AND LEMON SEASONING)

INGREDIENTS

1	bunch	Italian Parsley (Flat-Leaf Parsley), stems removed
2		Lemons, zested and zest minced (lemons can be juiced for other applications)
.5	oz	Garlic Cloves, minced

This combination is the traditional seasoning for osso bucco.

YIELD: 1/2 cup

PROCEDURE

1. Finely mince all of the ingredients, and mix thoroughly.

Osso Bucco alla Milanese   LOMBARDY

(BRAISED VEAL SHANK IN STYLE OF MILAN)

INGREDIENTS

8		Veal Shanks, cut 1–1.5 inches thick
		Salt and Pepper, to taste
1/2	cup	A.P. Flour
2	oz	Olive Oil
10	oz	Yellow Onions, minced
5	oz	Celery, minced
5	oz	Carrots, minced
1	oz	Garlic Cloves, minced
12	oz	White Wine
1.5	qt	Veal Stock
3	lbs	Tomatoes, concasséed
4		Bay Leaves
1	tsp	Fresh Thyme, minced
1	tsp	Fresh Oregano, minced

These braised veal shanks become very tender from the long braising method and are prized for the marrow that comes with each cut.

YIELD: 8 portions (1 veal shank/portion)

COOKING METHOD: Braising

PROCEDURE

1. Preheat the oven to 300°F.

2. Season the veal shanks with salt and pepper, then coat lightly with flour to cover entire surface.

3. In a heavy-bottomed sauté pan, heat olive oil over a medium-high flame. Once pan is hot, add the veal shanks to sauté on both sides, coloring the shanks deep golden brown.

4. Remove the shanks from the pan. Add minced onion, carrots, celery, and garlic to the pan, and lower heat to sweat the vegetables in the remaining oil until vegetables are translucent.

5. Deglaze the pan with the white wine, making sure to scrape all of the particles off the bottom of the pan while reducing the wine by 50%.

6. Add the veal stock, and return the veal shanks to the pan. Adjust heat as needed to return to a simmer.

7. Once the veal shanks are brought to a simmer, add tomatoes, bay leaves, thyme, and oregano; cover with snug lid and place in oven for approximately 1.5 to 2 hours, depending on thickness of shanks. (Check to see that the meat will fall off the bone to indicate that it is cooked properly.)

8. Serve topped with gremolata and with risotto alla Milanese.

Osso bucco (braised veal shank) in center, served surrounded by risotto alla Milanese (risotto in style of Milan) and topped with gremolata (lemon/parsley/garlic seasoning)

Lombo di Maiale Ripieno   TUSCANY
(SALUMI STUFFED PORK LOIN)

INGREDIENTS

For Making the Forcemeat

8	oz	Veal Stew Meat, ground coarse
2	oz	Prosciutto, ground coarse
3	oz	Pancetta, ground coarse
2	oz	Parmesan Cheese, grated
1		Whole Egg
5	cloves	Garlic, minced
1/4	tsp	Salt
1/4	tsp	Black Pepper, freshly ground
6	oz	Heavy Cream

For Stuffing and Tying the Roast

6–7	lb	Boneless Pork Loin, fabricated into one 3/4-inch–thick flat sheet
		Salt and Pepper
		Forcemeat (see above)
		Butcher's Twine

For Roasting the Pork Loin

		Stuffed Loin (see above)
2	oz	Olive Oil
1	Tbsp	Fresh Rosemary, minced
		Salt and Black Pepper

Tuscany is well known for the roast porks that are commonly found in restaurants and homes. This recipe is an example of the utilization of Italian products to make an excellent stuffed pork loin that also presents very well.

YIELD: 16 portions (7 ounces/portion)

MIXING METHOD (FORCEMEAT FILLING): Emulsification via Food Processor

COOKING METHOD (STUFFED PORK): Roasting

COOKING METHOD (VEGETABLES FOR SAUCE): Roasting

SAUCE FOR ROAST PORK: Enriched Puréed Vegetable

PROCEDURE

For Making the Forcemeat Filling

1. Place the ground veal, prosciutto, pancetta, Parmesan cheese, egg, garlic, salt, and pepper in a food processor. With the processor running, slowly add the cream to make a thick emulsion.

2. Transfer the forcemeat to a chilled container, and place in the refrigerator until the pork loin has been fabricated and is ready to be stuffed.

For Stuffing and Tying the Pork Loin

1. Fabricate the whole boneless pork loin by laying it on a cutting board with the fat side facing up.

2. Make a cut the length of the pork loin on the clean meat side—the part of the loin that was against the chin bone of the bone-in loin (consult your instructor or text if you are not sure what part of the loin this is), approximately 3/4 of an inch or an inch above the cutting board.

3. Continue to cut horizontally into the loin, keeping the portion of the loin under the knife approximately 3/4 inch thick until you are

(continues)

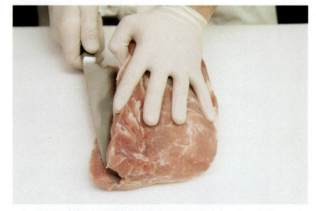

Fabricating the pork loin for making the lombo di maiale ripieno (Note: Start approximately an inch from top of loin, with loin turned upside down—fat side down—to start cutting it)

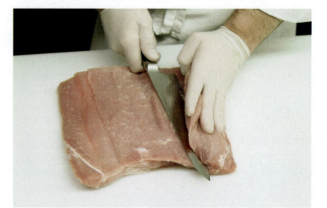

Finishing fabrication of loin; loin has been made into a flat sheet that can be filled with forcemeat

Lombo di Maiale Ripieno
(continued)

For Roasting Vegetables for the Sauce

1	lb	Yellow Onion, quartered
1.5	lbs	Tomatoes, peeled and halved
1	oz	Garlic Cloves, whole
2	oz	Extra Virgin Olive Oil
1	tsp	Fresh Rosemary, minced
1/8	tsp	Salt
		Foil

For Making the Pan Sauce

6	oz	Dry White Wine
3	cups	Beef Stock
		Roasted Vegetables (see above)
2	oz	Beef Glaze
1.5	oz	Extra Virgin Olive Oil
		Salt and Freshly Ground Black Pepper, to taste

approximately 3/4 of an inch to an inch from the other side of the loin (this entire cut will be about 3 to 4 inches in length along the entire length of the loin).

4. Once this cut is completed, lay out the remaining part of the loin and do the same thing: cut approximately 3/4 of an inch horizontally above the cutting board, along the length of the loin. This will yield a wider "sheet" of the loin.

5. Continue cutting until the entire loin is 3/4 inch thick and opened like a sheet.

6. Once the loin is fabricated in this manner, season the exposed portion of the loin with salt and pepper, and then spread the forcemeat evenly over the surface of the loin, leaving a inch or so of space on the ends of the loin.

7. Once the forcemeat has been spread over the loin, roll the loin tightly in the opposite direction from which it was fabricated to return it to the shape and look of the original loin (it will be a little larger from being stuffed, but otherwise it will look the same).

8. Once the loin has been rolled, secure the loin by trussing with butcher's twine, tying every 1 to 2 inches along the length of the loin to ensure that the stuffing remains inside and the loin retains its shape during cooking.

For Roasting the Loin

(**NOTE:** *The vegetables can be roasted for the sauce at the same time—or before—but in a separate oven.*)

1. Preheat the oven to 400°F.

2. Place the loin in a large roasting pan (the loin can be cut in half if it is too large for your roasting pan), and rub the outside of the loin with the olive oil before seasoning it with the rosemary, salt, and pepper.

3. Place the stuffed loin in the preheated oven and roast for 20 minutes, or until the exterior turns golden brown.

4. Once the exterior is golden brown, turn the oven down to 300°F and finish cooking at the lower temperature until the interior temperature of the loin reaches 145°F; this will take approximately 30 to 35 minutes more, depending on the size of the loin (be sure to move the thermometer back and forth once the temperature settles

(continues)

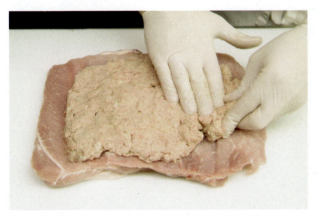

Spreading the forcemeat over the fabricated pork loin when making the lombo di maiale ripieno

The stuffed, tied, and seasoned pork loin ready to be roasted for lombo di maiale ripieno

Lombo di Maiale Ripieno
(continued)

to ensure that the reading is accurate—if the temperature drops, you were not in the coolest part of the meat and need to allow the temperature to settle again).

5. Once the loin reaches this temperature, remove it from the oven and place it on a cutting board for carving. C it with foil and allow it to sit for 15 minutes before carving for service.

For Roasting Vegetables for the Sauce

1. Preheat the oven to 325°F.

2. Combine the quartered onions, peeled tomatoes, garlic cloves, olive oil, rosemary, and salt in a mixing bowl, and mix well to coat all of the vegetables with the oil.

3. Once the ingredients have been mixed, transfer them to a large piece of aluminum foil and wrap them, bringing the open part of the foil together above the vegetables. Place foil-wrapped vegetables on a sheet pan and place in the preheated oven.

4. Roast in the oven for 1 hour or until the vegetables are very soft, and then remove them from the oven and set aside to cool.

5. Once the vegetables have cooled enough to handle, place them in a blender and purée until smooth. Add water, if necessary, to achieve smooth consistency.

For Making the Pan Sauce

1. In a large sauté pan, combine the white wine, beef stock, and puréed and roasted vegetables, and place over a medium flame to bring mixture to a simmer.

2. Once the mixture comes to a simmer, add the glaze and, if necessary, reduce until the mixture becomes thick enough to coat the back of a spoon.

3. Once consistency is achieved, swirl in the extra virgin olive oil to the gently simmering sauce to form a smoother sauce.

4. Season the sauce with salt and pepper, if necessary, and serve under the slices of the loin.

Lombo di maiale ripieno over roasted vegetable sauce (on left) and asparagi alla parmigiana (on right)

Scaloppine al Limone LOMBARDY

(Sautéed Veal with Lemon Sauce)

INGREDIENTS

1	oz	Clarified Butter
1	lb	Veal, Eye of the Round (or other cut for scaloppine), cut into eight 2-oz medallions and pounded thin (1/4 inch) with a mallet
		Salt and White Pepper
2		Lemons (140 count)
6	Tbsp	Butter, whole salted

A very quick recipe to make that preserves the tenderness of the veal.

YIELD: 4 portions (5 ounces/portion)

COOKING METHOD: Sautéing

PROCEDURE

1. In a sauté pan, heat half of the clarified butter over a high flame until pan is very hot.

2. Season the scaloppine with salt and white pepper.

3. Using just a couple of the scaloppine at a time, sauté on both sides until golden brown and then remove from pan.

4. Continue to follow steps 2 and 3, adding more of the clarified butter as necessary, until all of the veal has been sautéed. (Be careful not to burn the bottom of the pan, as this will become part of the sauce.)

5. Deglaze the pan with the juice of the lemons, and reduce the heat to a lower setting to simmer.

6. Add about 10 small pieces of butter, one at a time, to form an emulsified lemon butter sauce.

Bollito Misto PIEDMONT

(Mixed Boiled Meats)

INGREDIENTS

1		Beef Tongue (about 2 lbs)
2	lbs	Cotechino (substitute a fresh pork sausage, if this is unavailable)
1.5	gallons	White Stock
2	Tbsp	Black Peppercorns
6		Bay Leaves
3		Cloves, whole
1	Tbsp	Coarse Salt
3	lbs	Beef Brisket
2	lbs	Pork Butt
1		Large Chicken (4-lb Hen, if available)
2	lbs	Leeks, halved and cleaned
1	lb	Carrots, peeled and cut into half-inch pieces
2	lbs	Red Potatoes, quartered

This classic Piedmont dish traditionally would be served with salsa verde (called *bagnet verd* in the local dialect) and made—as here—with veal and calf's head as well as other meats.

YIELD: 20 portions (10 ounces/portion) of meat and vegetables

COOKING METHOD: Boiling

PROCEDURE

1. Clean all of the meats (not necessary for tongue or sausage) to be cooked by removing any excess fat from their surface.

2. Fill a pot (large enough to hold the tongue) with salted water, and bring to a boil.

3. Add the tongue to the pot, and reduce heat to simmer the tongue until it is tender (approximately 2 to 2.5 hours). Once the tongue is done, allow it to cool and then peel off the tough skin that covers it by piercing the tip with a knife and pulling it back to the base. The tongue can be added to the main pot when the vegetables are added.

4. In a pot that will fit the cotechino, bring another pot of salted water to a boil and add the sausage, which should have been pricked with a knife to allow grease to escape; reduce heat to slowly simmer the sausage until it is cooked (approximately 1.5 hours, if using cotechino; less if using smaller sausages).

(continues)

Bollito Misto
(continued)

5. Once both the tongue and sausage are cooked, their resulting broths can be discarded and the meats added to the by-now simmering main pot of vegetables.

6. For the main pot, add the white stock to a pot large enough to hold all of the meats and vegetables, and turn flame to high heat.

7. Wrap the seasoning in cheesecloth, and add it to the heating stock.

8. Once the stock has come to a boil, add the beef brisket and pork butt, and reduce the heat to simmer the meats in the stock for 1.5 hours.

9. Add the chicken to the simmering meats after 1.5 hours, and continue to cook for an additional 30 minutes.

10. Add the vegetables to the pot after the chicken has cooked for 30 minutes, and continue to cook for an additional 45 minutes; remove the pot from heat.

11. Check for doneness of all of the items in the pot (if the sausage and tongue have not been added to the pot by this time, add them here). If any of the items are not yet tender, return them to the broth and simmer until they are.

12. Once all of the items are tender, they can be sliced and served with salsa verde (Italian, not Mexican!).

Salsa Verde   LOMBARDY

(GREEN SAUCE)

INGREDIENTS

4	bunches	Flat-Leaf Parsley, stems removed
6		Anchovy Fillets, minced
2		Garlic Cloves
1.5	Tbsp	Capers, drained
1	fl oz	White Wine Vinegar
1/4	tsp	Salt
1		Egg Yolk
3.5	fl oz	Extra Virgin Olive Oil
		Salt and Black Pepper, to taste

This sauce is the traditional accompaniment to the classic bollito misto. Bollito misto is simply a combination of boiled meats and sausage that may be served with the vegetables they are cooked with.

YIELD: 1.5 cups

MIXING METHOD: Grinding to a Paste with Mortar and Pestle

PROCEDURE

1. Using a mortar and pestle, food processor, or other appropriate vessel, work the first 6 ingredients to a paste.

2. Add the egg yolk to the paste produced from step 1, and incorporate completely.

3. Slowly add the olive oil to the mixture, mixing the entire to time to create an emulsion.

4. Season to taste with salt and pepper.

Bollito misto (mixed boiled meats) served with salsa verde (green sauce in sauce boat; top right)

Asparagi alla Parmigiana Emilia-Romagna

(Asparagus, Parma Style)

INGREDIENTS

2	lbs	Asparagus, bottoms trimmed and stems peeled
2	oz	Butter, whole salted
		Black Pepper, freshly ground
4	oz	Parmesan Cheese, grated fine

This simple preparation for asparagus highlights the excellent flavor of the classic grana-style cheese from Parma.

YIELD: 8 portions (4 ounces/portion)

BLANCHING METHOD: Steaming

COOKING METHOD: Broiling

PROCEDURE

1. Preheat the oven to 450°F.

2. Blanch the asparagus in a steamer for 1 minute or until asparagus just starts to soften in the stem without losing its color. (Steaming time may vary, depending on the thickness of the asparagus spears.)

3. Toss the steamed asparagus with the whole butter to melt it, and season with freshly ground black pepper.

4. Place the asparagus onto a half-sheet pan or another shallow pan that will hold them in a single layer.

5. Cover the asparagus with the grated Parmesan cheese and place in the preheated oven for 3 to 4 minutes, or until the cheese has melted and crisped on top of the asparagus.

Crema Limoncina Sicily

(Lemon Cream)

INGREDIENTS

5		Egg Yolks (save the whites)
1.5	cups	Sugar, granulated
1/2	cup	Lemon Juice
1	Tbsp	Lemon Zest
6		Egg Whites
1/2	tsp	Lemon Juice
1/2	cup	Confectioner's Sugar

This Sicilian dessert sauce is a great accompaniment to pastries or eaten on its own.

YIELD: 1 quart

COOKING METHOD: Tempering over a Double Boiler

PROCEDURE

1. Place a small saucepan filled with 2 inches of water on the stove, and turn on high heat to bring to a simmer.

2. Combine the egg yolks, sugar, lemon juice, and lemon zest in a stainless steel bowl, and mix thoroughly.

3. Place the bowl over the simmering water, lowering the heat on the stove to maintain very light steam under the bowl; whisk the sweetened egg yolk/lemon mixture over heat until they lighten in color and thicken (same principle as first step in making hollandaise sauce).

4. Once the mixture has thickened, remove it from heat and continue to stir to cool mixture over an ice bath.

(continues)

Crema Limoncina
(continued)

5. Add the egg whites and lemon juice to a mixing bowl, and beat with a wire whip until soft peaks are formed.

6. Add the confectioner's sugar to the egg white foam while continuing to beat to form a glossy foam with stiff peaks.

7. Fold the meringue into the sweet egg yolk/lemon mixture before it cools completely, but not before it has cooled to the touch.

8. Refrigerate for at least 2 hours before serving.

Tiramisu VENETO
(MASCARPONE AND COFFEE TRIFLE)

INGREDIENTS

4		Egg Yolks
2	oz	Fine Sugar (Caster or Baker's)
1	oz	Marsala
.75	lb	Mascarpone Cheese
1	oz	Rum
.75	cup	Heavy Cream
1/2	tsp	Vanilla
1	Tbsp	Confectioner's Sugar
2		Egg Whites
Pinch		Cream of Tartar
1	Tbsp	Fine Sugar
1.5	cups	Espresso
1	oz	Brandy
8	dozen	Lady Fingers
3	oz	Chocolate, grated

The actual origins of this very popular dessert are debated throughout Italy, because a number of regions claim to have invented it. One thing is for sure: the name translates to "pick me up," and this recipe will do just that.

YIELD: One 2-inch half hotel pan

COOKING METHOD: Tempering over Double Boiler

PROCEDURE

1. Prepare a double boiler.

2. Place the egg yolks, fine sugar, and Marsala into a stainless steel bowl, and whisk while heating over double boiler until mixture thickens and increases in volume (this mixture is called zabaglione). Once thickened, remove from heat and allow it to cool before proceeding.

3. Add the mascarpone and rum to the cooled zabaglione, and whisk to combine well.

4. In a stainless steel bowl, combine the heavy cream, confectioner's sugar, and vanilla; whisk mixture to form stiff peaks.

5. In a separate bowl, whisk egg whites and cream of tartar until soft peaks are formed. Then add fine sugar to make a stiff meringue.

6. Fold in the whipped cream and egg white mixture to the mascarpone/zabaglione mixture.

7. To assemble, the mixture is alternately piped between layers of the ladyfinger cookies, which are quickly rolled through the espresso and brandy mixture in a half hotel pan.

8. Once all of the ladyfingers have been used to make the layers, an additional layer of the mascarpone/zabaglione mixture is placed on top, and the whole dish is topped with grated chocolate.

Tiramisu

SUMMARY

Italy as a country is relatively new to the world, but the cuisine that hails from this land is ancient and one of the world's most recognizable and respected. Italian cuisine is not really a cuisine at all, but more accurately a collection of cuisines; the regional character of local cuisines is stronger in Italy than anywhere else in the world. The regional cuisines of Italy have developed over centuries, dating back to Roman times and including many elements of the cultures that have influences the cuisine over time (including the Romans, Moors, Spanish, and French). The one characteristic that is constant throughout the country is the appreciation of the highest quality foods and food products, including cheeses, oils, vinegars, wines, preserved meats, and pastas, which form the backbone of this diverse cuisine. The diversity of Italian ingredients and regional dishes speaks of the regional pride as well as the Italian penchant for creating new dishes or improving on classics.

REVIEW QUESTIONS

1. What is the general distinction between the pasta found in northern Italy and the pasta found in southern Italy?

2. What does it mean for a product to be labeled Denominazione di Origine Controllata (DOC), and why is it a significant component of the cuisine of Italy?

3. Why is the cuisine of Italy very different, depending on what part of the country one is in?

4. From what area of Italy did most Italian immigrants come to the United States? How has this shaped the perception of Italian cuisine in the United States?

COMMON TERMS, FOODS, AND INGREDIENTS

As Italian cuisine includes seemingly endless variations—from the regional differences to the pure depth of development—it is helpful to become more familiar with the ingredients and terms used in this complex cuisine. The following guide provides a start to becoming more acquainted with the many terms used in Italian cuisine.

NOTE: *For lists of pastas, cheeses, and salumi, see the "Unique Components" section in this chapter.*

❋ *Grains and Other Starchy Staples*

arborio – Short-grain rice commonly used to make risotto

carnaroli – Prized short-grain rice used to make risotto

farro – Type of wheat variety that is typically cooked and eaten as whole grain

grano – Wheat

granoturco – Name given to corn (translates to "Turkish grain") that, when introduced to Italy in the sixteenth century, was thought to have come from Turkey (it actually came from the Americas)

lenticcha – Lentils

polenta – Coarse ground, dried corn used to make a porridge-like dish common throughout northern Italy

riso – Rice

❋ *Vegetables and Seasonings*

aglio – Garlic

asparagi – Asparagus

baccelli – Fresh fava beans

basilico – Basil

capperi – Capers

carciofi – Globe artichokes

cardi – Cardoons

castagne – Chestnuts

catalogna – Type of chicory sometimes called Italian dandelion

cavolfiore – Cauliflower

cavolo – Cabbage

cavolo nero – Tuscan cabbage

cime di rapa – Turnip greens

cipolle – Onion

erbe aromatiche – Aromatic herbs

fagioli – Beans

finocchiella – Fennel seeds

finocchio – Fennel

funghi – Mushrooms

granoturco – Corn

melanzana – Eggplant

oliva – Olive

origano – Oregano

patate – Potato

peperone – Bell peppers

peperoncini – Chili peppers

piselli – Peas

pomodoro – Tomatoes

puntarelle – Chicory

radicchio – Lettuce with red leaves and a slightly bitter taste; common in northern Italy as one of three species: the round radicchio *variegato* (most common in the United States), the elongated radicchio *trevisano*, and the white-based radicchio *di chioggia*

rucola – Arugula

sale – Salt

salvia – Sage

specie – Spice

spinaci – Spinach

tartufi – Truffles

verdure – Vegetables

zucca – Gourd squash

✳ Fruits and Nuts

arancia – Orange

castagne – Chestnut

citron – Citrus fruit

fico – Fig

limone – Lemon

mandorla – Almond

mela – Apple

nocciola – Hazelnut

noce – Walnut

pinoli – Pine nut

sultanas – Golden raisins

uva – Grape

✳ Meats/Poultry

abbacchio – Young lamb

agnello – Lamb

capretto – Young goat

capriolo – Venison

coniglio – Rabbit

fagiano – Pheasant

lingua – Tongue (from veal or pork)

maiale – Pork

manzo – Young ox

oca – Goose

quaglie – Quail

rete – Caul fat (from pork)

uova – Eggs

vitello – Veal

vitellone – Beef slaughtered between 14 and 16 months of age

✳ Fish/Shellfish

acciuga – Anchovy

anguilla – Eel

baccala – Dried salted cod

branzino – Sea bass

calamari – Squid

cernia – Grouper

cozza – Mussels

dentice – Delicate Mediterranean fish; sometimes called "dentex" in the United States

pesce – fish

pesce spada – Swordfish

polipetti – Small octopus

polpo – Octopus

rana pescatrice – Monkfish

sarago – Sea bream

sarda or sardina – Sardine

scampi – Saltwater crustacean resembling small lobsters with claws (not a type of shrimp, which is often incorrectly called *scampi*)

seppia – Cuttlefish

sogliola – Sole

stoccafisso – Dried cod

tonno – Tuna

trota – Trout

vongola – Clam

✳ Oils and Vinegars

aceto balsamico – Balsamic vinegar, made from aging red wine vinegar in oak casks to yield rich and dark vinegar

burro – Butter

grasso – Fat; general term for fat and oils

olio d'oliva – Olive oil

strutto – Rendered pork fat

✳ Sauces

carbonara – Cooked with sauce made from cured pork jowl or pancetta, eggs, and Parmesan cheese; popular way of cooking pasta, for example, spaghetti alla carbonara

pesto – Blend of basil, garlic, pine nuts, Parmesan cheese, and olive oil; traditionally made using a mortar and pestle *puttanesca* – Tomato sauce with black olives, capers, anchovies, and garlic

ragu – Tomato meat sauce

ragu alla Bolognese – Traditional meat sauce of Bologna that is served with fresh pasta from the region (Emilia-Romagna)

salsa di noci – Walnut sauce

salsa per carpaccio – Sauce to be served with carpaccio (thin sliced beef) made from an emulsification of capers, cornichons, and anchovies with vinegar and oil

salsa verde – Green sauce made from parsley, extra virgin olive oil, and good quality vinegar; often has bread, capers, garlic, onion, and anchovy added to it. This sauce hails from the Lombardy region.

Cooking Methods

abbrustolito – Cooked over an open flame

affogato – Poached

affumicato – Smoked

ai ferri – Grilled or barbecued

al dente – "To the tooth"; denoting the degree to which something is cooked

al forno – Baked

al vapore – Steamed

alla graticola – Broiled; usually refers to seafood cooked in this way

alla griglia – Grilled

allo spiedo – Broiled on a spit; usually refers to meats

arrosto – Roasted

bollito – Boiled

brasato – Braised

cartoccio – Baked wrapped in parchment or foil

farcito – Stuffed

fogolar – Open hearth

fritto – Fried

ripieno – Stuffed

Prepared Foods and Drinks

arancini – Fried rice balls filled with various filling

arrista alla fiorentina – Tuscan/Florentine roasted pork with rosemary and garlic

asparagi alla parmigiano – Asparagus topped with Parmesan cheese and broiled

bagna caôda or bagna cauda – Sauce of olive oil, butter, garlic, and anchovies gently melted together; often served with raw vegetables to dip in the sauce

bollito misto – Mixed boiled meats typically containing sausages, tongue, beef, veal, chicken, and calf's head, combined with vegetables to make a very rich and flavorful meal, traditionally found in the Piedmont area

bottarga – Dried, compressed roe of the grey mullet eaten as an antipasto with olive oil and lemon

brodetto – Fish soup common throughout the Adriatic Sea region

buccellato – Tuscan cake flavored with grappa, anise, citrus peel, and raisins; probably originated in Sicily

burrida – Ligurian fish soup made with cuttlefish or squid, shrimp, and other fish stewed with onions, mushrooms, tomatoes, anchovies, wine, pine nuts, and extra virgin olive oil

cacciucco – Fishermen's stew of Livorno (in Tuscany region)

caffe – Coffee

calzone – Stuffed dough filled with various fillings and baked; this is essentially a pizza that has been folded to enclose the topping before being baked

canederli – Dumplings

cannelloni – Thick pasta typically filled with meat ragu and topped with either cheese or béchamel sauce

cannoli – Fried pastry dough filled with sweetened ricotta cheese and other ingredients

caponata – Eggplant cooked in sweet-and-sour sauce from Sicily

caprese – Fresh tomato and water buffalo mozzarella (called fresh mozzarella in the United States) salad topped with basil and extra virgin olive oil

carpaccio – Thinly sliced beef topped with sliced mushrooms and traditionally served with a sauce made from parsley, capers, anchovies, olive oil, and vinegar

cassata – Sweet, rich cake made with dried fruit and almond paste

castagnoccio – Flatbread made from chestnut flour

ciuppin – Ligurian fish stew with tomatoes, garlic, and white wine; the cioppino of San Francisco is a version of this stew

coniglio in porchetta – Rabbit cooked in manner of Tuscan roast pig (see *porchetta*)

crauti – Fermented cabbage (sauerkraut)

crema al limone – Lemon cream used in sweet preparations

crostini – Sliced and toasted bread topped with various ingredients

favata – Pork and bean stew with fennel and cabbage of Sardinia

fegatini – Chicken liver spread often served with crostini *focaccia* – Yeast-leavened bread made in Liguria; flattened like a pizza (but usually square) and topped with olive oil, salt, and sometimes onions or olives

fonduta – Melted cheese dip

frico – Cheese fritter

gelato – Frozen sweetened and often flavored milk; similar to ice cream but traditionally lighter and with less air incorporated during the freezing process

gnocchi – Small dumplings made from a variety of different ingredients including potatoes (gnocchi di patate), corn (gnocchi di polenta), and wheat (gnocchi di semolina)

goulash – Spiced stew of Hungarian origin common in northeastern Italy as a result of Austrian influence in the area

granita – Slushy sweetened and flavored ice

grappa – Distilled grape pomace made from the remnants after grapes have been processed for wine

grassini – Thin breadsticks, which originated in Turin, served as a snack all over Italy

gremolata – Mixture of lemon zest, garlic, and parsley used to season foods

incapriata – Vegetable dish of puréed dried fava beans and boiled chicory, served together with olive oil

insalata – Salad

insalata di arance – Orange salad

insalata di mare – Seafood salad

jota – Bean and barley stew

lombo di maiale ripieno – Roasted pork loin stuffed with salumi

malloreddus – Small gnocchi made from semolina and colored and flavored with saffron

Marsala – Fortified wine produced in Sicily

marzapane – Almond paste made from almond, sugar and eggs; called "marzipan" in the United States

montebianco – Chestnuts cooked in milk and puréed and seasoned with sugar, vanilla, rum, and cocoa, and then topped with whipped cream

olive alla ascolana – Olives stuffed with seasoned meat and cheese

osso bucco – Braised veal shanks

pane carasau – Thin, crisp bread of Sardinia

panforte – Christmas fruit and spice cake

pannetone – Rich cake from Milan with golden raisins and citrus peels

panzenella – Bread and tomato salad common in central Italy

papperdelle alla cacciatore – Thick, fresh ribbon pasta with sausage

Parmesan di melazane – Fried eggplant layered with tomato sauce and cheese, and then baked; called "eggplant Parmesan" in the United States

pasta e fagioli – Pasta and beans made with cannellini beans, pasta, and typically a tomato-based sauce

pasta fresca – Fresh egg pasta

pasta reale – Marzipan paste shaped and colored like fruit; a Sicilian specialty

peperonata – Stewed onion, tomatoes, and peppers with olive oil

pesto alla Genovese – Paste made from basil, garlic, pine nuts, Parmesan, and pecorino cheeses and olive oil

pisella alla fiorentina – Florentine-style spring peas with pancetta

pizza – Flat dough topped with tomato sauce and cheese and various other toppings and then baked

pizza margarita – Pizza with fresh tomato, basil, and mozzarella cheese

polenta – Coarse-ground dried corn

polenta burro – Polenta with butter

polenta cunsa – Polenta layered with cheese and mushrooms

porceddu – Spit-roasted piglet cooked over juniper and olive wood; a specialty of Sardinia

porchetta – Small pig roasted in a wood-fired oven and typically stuffed with peppers, garlic, rosemary, and fennel

risi e bisi – Rice and peas

risotto – Short-grain rice cooked while adding liquid slowly and stirring, which results in a creamy rice dish

risotto alla Milanese – Risotto cooked with saffron to yield creamy, yellow/orange rice

saltimbocca – Thin pieces of veal, chicken, or pork sautéed and topped with prosciutto and sage; typically made with a Marsala sauce

scaloppini al limone – Sautéed thin slices of meat or poultry in lemon sauce

scaloppini alla Marsala – Thin slices of meat or poultry sautéed and cooked with Marsala wine sauce

schiacciata – Tuscan yeast-leavened bread rolled flat and seasoned with salt and olive oil (often rosemary and sage, as well); similar to focaccia of Liguria

sorbeto – Frozen and sweetened mixtures made without dairy

spaghetti alla carbonara – Thin ribbon pasta with carbonara sauce (see *carbonara*) *spaghetti alla puttanesca* – Thin ribbon pasta with puttanesca sauce (see *puttanesca*)

strudel – Filled pastry made from paper-thin sheets of dough that are filled with various fillings before being baked; this technique is the result of Austrian influences in northeastern Italy

tarantello – Fish "sausage" made from cured and spiced tuna belly packed into casing

tiramisu – Espresso-soaked sponge cake (ladyfingers) layered with sweetened mascarpone cream and topped with shaved chocolate or powdered cocoa; literally, "pick me up"

torta pasqualina – Easter pie made with layered dough filled with sliced artichokes, swiss chard, cheese, and eggs

tortelli de zucca – Pasta filled with zucca squash (similar to pumpkin) found in Piedmont region

vincigrassi – Liguria baked pasta with prosciutto, mushrooms, and sweetbreads

zabaglione – Rich dessert sauce made from whipping egg yolks, sugar, and Marsala wine together over a double boiler until it gets thick and frothy

zuppa di pane – Bread soup flavored with meat broth and garlic, and often topped with cheese

CHAPTER 5

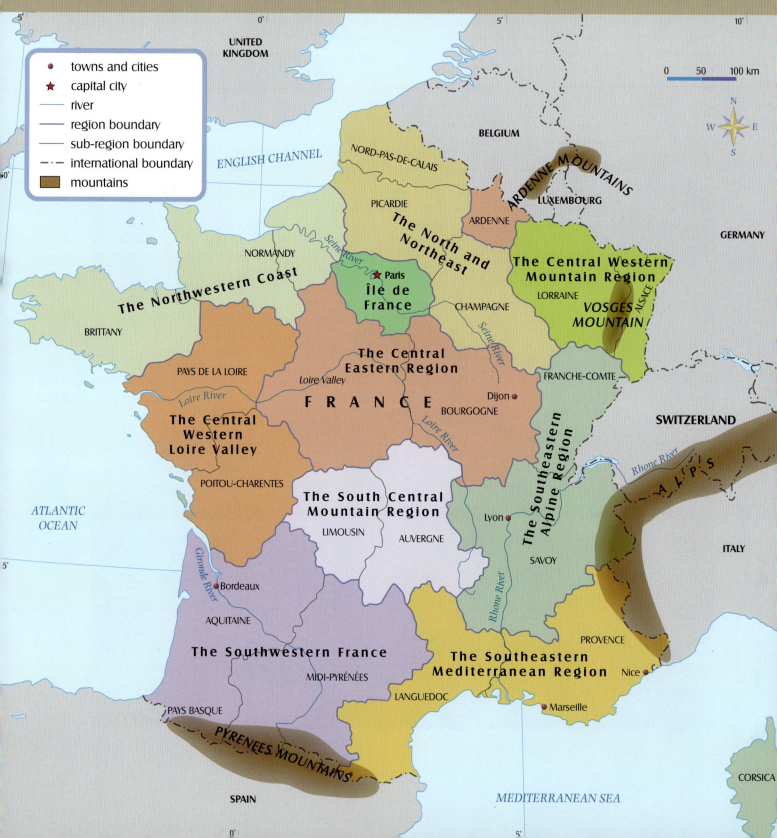

UNITED KINGDOM

BELGIUM

LUXEMBOURG

GERMANY

0   50   100 km

N
W   E
S

ENGLISH CHANNEL

NORD-PAS-DE-CALAIS

PICARDIE

ARDENNE MOUNTAINS

ARDENNE

The North and Northeast

The Central Western Mountain Region

NORMANDY

Seine River

★ Paris
Île de France

CHAMPAGNE

LORRAINE

ALSACE

VOSGES MOUNTAIN

The Northwestern Coast

Seine River

BRITTANY

FRANCHE-COMTE

PAYS DE LA LOIRE

Loire Valley

The Central Eastern Region

F R A N C E

Dijon

BOURGOGNE

SWITZERLAND

Loire River

The Central Western Loire Valley

Loire River

Lyon

The Southeastern Alpine Region

A L P S

Rhone River

POITOU-CHARENTES

The South Central Mountain Region

ITALY

ATLANTIC OCEAN

LIMOUSIN

AUVERGNE

SAVOY

Gironde River

Rhone River

Bordeaux

AQUITAINE

PROVENCE

The Southwestern France

MIDI-PYRÉNÉES

The Southeastern Mediterranean Region

Nice

LANGUEDOC

PAYS BASQUE

Marseille

PYRENEES MOUNTAINS

CORSICA

SPAIN

MEDITERRANEAN SEA

French Cuisine

OBJECTIVES

Upon completion of this chapter, you will be able to

- explain what makes the cuisine of France unique.
- discuss the importance of French cuisine in the training of professional chefs today.
- discuss some of the significant chefs who have played an important role in the development of French cuisine.
- recognize the common cooking methods employed in French cuisine.
- recognize some examples of French recipes.
- produce a variety of recipes common to French cuisine.
- define the terms listed at the conclusion of the chapter.

INTRODUCTION

Of all the cuisines covered in this text, none has the aura or lofty reputation of French cuisine. Why is that? The answer to that question is not simple, although it can be summed up with a simple explanation: because the French have held cuisine to the highest standard in recent history, and culinary professionals in France are some of the most dedicated and appreciated professionals in the world.

France is blessed with an advantageous geographical location when it comes to all things related to food products. France is bordered by the Atlantic Ocean to the west, the English Channel to the north, and the Mediterranean Sea to the southeast, all of which contribute different treasures from their waters. France also has a varied climate and fertile countryside throughout the different regions that enables the production of a large variety of land products and animals. When combined with the high arability of the land (33%) and the national attitude toward quality foods, the conditions for providing people with great cuisine are in place.

As we will see, much of what is thought of as French cuisine has in fact developed relatively recently. The reverence for the best available product, and the handling and cooking of that product to yield a dish that highlights its intrinsic qualities, is a philosophy that has developed in stages—mostly since the French Revolution in the eighteenth century, although the traditions that led up to that point were equally important.

French cuisine is often looked upon as the trendsetter, the epitome of the best, with the best ingredients paired with the best talent and the best palette yielding masterpieces of human ingenuity that drive chefs worldwide to try to match or trump this great cuisine. The following chapter is an introduction to French cuisine and looks at some of the factors that enabled this cuisine to develop as it has. Much could be written about French cuisine, and much has been. After you review the information in this chapter, a deeper look into French cuisine will only provide a better understanding and appreciation for this country's contribution to the culinary arts.

HISTORIC CULINARY INFLUENCES

French cuisine is one of the few cuisines that appear to have left more of an imprint on other cuisines than the other way around. Yet, even with this distinction, French cuisine has experienced a number of influences—from both inside and outside the country—on the development of what is thought of as French cuisine today. As with most cuisines throughout the world, what was eaten in the home of a peasant 300 years ago or served at the royal table 300 years ago is quite different from what currently is cooked in homes and found on the tables of fine dining establishments. One of the differences in the cuisine of France, compared with most others, is that the cuisine of the nobility in many ways became the cuisine of the public. How that evolution occurred in France is perhaps a glimpse into many of the changes that currently are occurring in other parts of the world. The following guide is not meant to be an exhaustive recount of the development of French cuisine—that subject can easily fill multiple volumes—but a general introduction of some of the particularly important periods and influences that have contributed to the development of this highly esteemed cuisine.

The Roman Empire

The groundwork for what is known as French cuisine today was laid by the Romans during the height of the Roman Empire in the second century AD. It was the Romans who introduced vineyards and thus wines into France, as well as olives into southern France, where this tree would eventually become the source of the local cooking fat as olive oil production became commonplace. The Romans were well known for their organizational skills and for developing irrigation systems to allow greater productivity from the lands, and their influence in this area is largely responsible for the rate of development that was to occur in the coming decades. The Roman influence is felt throughout France, particularly in the central heartland, where vineyards and irrigation systems paved the way for the current agricultural systems. The most Roman-influenced areas of France are in the south, particularly the area of Provence and—even more so—Corsica,

the French island that lies in the Mediterranean, where olives are a main food and the frequent use of citrus, bread, and cheese is still evident today.

Italian Imports and Catherine de' Medici (1519–1589)

Italian culinary methods and traditions have long been imported into the French repertoire, just as the opposite has occurred between these two close neighbors. The sixteenth century witnessed cuisine refinement and a focus on the arts centered in Italy during the Renaissance, and set the stage for the development of French cuisine as we know it today. Although the cuisine that began to come into fashion in the royal courts of Italy and France would not be recognized today as typical French fare, the basis for current French cuisine was set in motion. The idea that eating should be a formal affair; the importance placed on the presentation of the food; and the seeds for a more standard methodology and focus on techniques were all being introduced at this time.

The wedding of Catherine de' Medici and the eventual king of France, Henri II, proved to be a monumental occasion for the gastronomy of French cuisine. Catherine brought with her a number of her Italian chefs, as well as the dining etiquette and palate of Renaissance Italy at the time. At this time, Italy was the jewel of the arts, and royalty who traveled to Italy from France would regularly come back smitten with their Italian dining experiences. Dining manners were drastically different from the voracious feasts that were common in France, and food was less altered in the kitchen; a greater focus was placed on the preservation of quality products. A number of these qualities were imported to France from these visits to Italy by French nobles, and in a more direct manner by the arrival of Catherine de' Medici at the royal table, along with her cooks.

Catherine's troop of chefs and cooks brought with them their repertoire of Italian soups, sauces, and desserts, all of which would make their way relatively quickly into the cuisine of France. The near army of 50 chefs, waiters, and household help that came with her to France introduced a cuisine that was simpler, less heavily spiced, and that placed a focus on highly flavored ingredients instead of heavy sauces that masked other foods. The method of whipping cream to make *mousse* and *mousseline* arrived with these cooks. the use of *aspics* in cold food preparations was introduced, as well as some important new ingredients like *truffles* and artichokes. The different types of foods and the emphasis on their presentation began to reflect the Italian influence, as in foods such as *quenelles* (shaped dumpling), which are thought to be an adaptation of the many Italian dumplings. Prior to this period, sauces were thickened using bread or bread purées; only after the Italians introduced the use of *roux* (a thickening agent made of cooked flour and butter) did it become a part of French cuisine. All of these contributions encouraged a more refined cuisine that was not one of the focuses of early French cuisine but would certainly become a dominant feature over the next decades and centuries.

Perhaps one of the greatest contributions that can be credited to Catherine de' Medici herself was her influence on table etiquette and the inclusion of women at the table. Prior to her arrival in France, women were not allowed to dine with men in the royal arena. Catherine de' Medici not only expected to be included at the table, she also expected those dining with her to act with dignity and grace; her presence forced others to be more reserved when eating. In France, this was the start of dining as it is known today, where a level of good manners is expected and the food is meant to stimulate the appetite visually as well as in taste. This period of history was followed by decades of other small developments with regard to the dining habits of royalty, which consequently influenced the eating habits and customs of the nobility. As the expectations of how one was to act when dining spread throughout the ranks of those who attended these events, the simple ideas of keeping oneself clean during eating, of using utensils to pick up food, and of keeping conversation polite and respectful spread as well. This seemingly obvious development set the stage for a change in public attitude regarding how one should act and enjoy food in the coming years.

François Pierre de La Varenne

La Varenne was a significant contributor to the development of French cuisine; in 1652, he published one of the first books to greatly influence the formation the new French cuisine that had begun to emerge following the import of Italian chefs. The book, titled *Le Cuisinier François*, was of particular importance because it did not include the heavily spiced foods that previously had been part of the cuisine and instead focused on many Italian-inspired dishes, as well as

others that focused more on the particular ingredients and less on overbearing sauces that masked flavors. La Varenne had trained with some of the Italian chefs who had traveled to France with another Italian bride—a cousin of Catherine de' Medici named Marie de' Medici—and surely was influenced by these Florentine chefs. One of the now-classic French recipes credited to La Varenne is the wonderful use of mushrooms in making *duxelles* (a sauce of mushrooms and shallots flavored with herbs).

The French Revolution and the Evolution of the French Restaurant

The French Revolution of 1789 set the stage for many changes in the cuisine of France. First, the revolution meant that all of the chefs who had worked for royalty prior to the revolution needed to find new employment; many found work opening or running restaurants in various parts of France, mostly Paris. Once the country began to get on its feet again economically, the revolution also created a new middle class that could afford (and now had access to) the restaurants where the great chefs worked. The result was a newly appreciative audience and proprietorship that together grew a new sector of the French economy. The development of the French restaurant and the subsequent development of the national palate were major factors in the evolution of French cuisine from one of extremes—the royalty and nobles who held elaborate buffets while the peasants lived mainly on bread and provincial soups and stews—to a new, more moderate cuisine available to a much wider audience. This new cuisine combined the elements of the royalty's refinement and skill with the frugality of the masses to yield a more realistic cuisine that highlighted the possibilities a professional chef could achieve.

The growth of the restaurant also enabled the development of other culinary aspects, because of the difference in logistics between feeding the masses and cooking at home. Now, more complicated foods could be introduced to the public—a kitchen staff can toil with techniques that require time and attention, which a typical household cook often would not do. Products from other provinces could be purchased because of the buying power inherent to mass buying, and the flow of ingredients from one area to another increased significantly. This sales opportunity also gave rise to a support system for craft purveyors, who could now sell their products to more than just the local nobility, again helping to make fine products available to the general public. All of these things combined to create the conditions in which the French people were connected to the best their country had to offer. The evolution of the French public's dining habits, paired with the evolution of professional chefs focusing their attention on a newly appreciative audience, began a marriage that enabled a new philosophy of eating to develop throughout much of the country.

Marie-Antoine Carême (1783–1833)

The name Marie-Antoine Carême perhaps is familiar to most readers by now (it should be, anyway!), and for good reason. Carême had a major influence on the development of French cuisine in a way that—looking back on his work—seems quite ironic. Carême worked to reduce the "fluff" and unnecessary embellishments that were common in the French banquets of his day. He also was a master of planning arrangements; he knew how to balance foods as well as their proper presentation and serving order. The irony in this, from today's perspective, is that the cuisine Carême helped create seems greatly overdone—or fluffier—when compared with modern culinary offerings. However, his cuisine actually was significantly more reserved than what was created just prior to his time. The period between Catherine de' Medici and Carême was one in which each banquet was expected to be more elaborate and grand than the previous one. In classic French cooking of the late 1700s and early 1800s, most banquets and feasts were overwhelming and, by today's standards, grossly overdone affairs. Three hundred different dishes might be served, and these would be presented all at once in an elaborate display that included *gross pieces* (or "grand pieces") that might feature huge replicas of wild animals or other inedible creations as part of the display.

Carême believed that this was all too much, and his contribution was to make smaller presentations using only edible products that focused on achieving a balance between the presentation and types of food that were offered. He felt that the guest was overwhelmed when presented with a ghastly display that served no purpose—just excess. His presentations were smaller (perhaps including only 100 items!), and the presentations were planned around what foods would go well with one another, how the textures would be balanced, and so forth. This was a major first step for French cuisine on its road to refinement. Carême also

worked to classify parts of the cuisine at this time, including four "mother sauces" from which other sauces could be derived. Three of the four mother sauces that Carême categorized are still used and taught to this day (a fifth, tomato sauce, was added later, following the introduction of the tomato to Europe from the Americas; additionally, Escoffier later replaced allemande, the fourth mother sauce from Careme that was later dropped in favor of egg emulsion sauces by Escoffier with hollandaise as an emulsion sauce).

Carême went on to become a celebrated chef in the royal courts of not only France but England and Russia as well, and his influence on the other chefs of this period helped steer French cuisine in the direction of quality and well–thought-out combinations rather than quantity and excess. Carême also wrote a number of volumes, not only on cooking but also on the organizational aspect of running a kitchen, the guidelines for proper food service, and how to correctly set up buffet presentations. His contribution to the culinary arts was tremendous, and his "edible creation" was the inspiration for the modern wedding cake—an influence that has spread well beyond France.

Georges Auguste Escoffier

The king of chefs and the chef of kings, as he has been fondly remembered, Auguste Escoffier had a similar effect on the development of French cuisine. Escoffier is considered the father of *haute cuisine* (high cuisine) that developed in the fine hotels during his career. The haute cuisine (now referred to as classical French cuisine) included many courses of small-portioned highly flavored foods, extensive wine cellars, and professional service staff. Even though Carême had been successful in reducing the showmanship of the court cuisine in France during the height of his influence, Escoffier still felt that the garnishing and the number of dishes served—as well as the way they were served—needed to change. He did away with most garnishes to ensure that the focus was on the food itself, and he embraced what was at the time a new system of presenting food, one item at a time in courses. Prior to this period in French dining, foods were presented all at once, or many different dishes were served simultaneously. This old system often resulted in foods getting cold before people could eat them, thus affecting the quality of the dishes. The new system was borrowed from Russia (and is called "Russian service" to this day) and utilized the system most familiar to us today: plating and delivering the food for each course as it is ordered.

In addition to adopting this type of service, which enabled a dramatic improvement in product quality, Escoffier also developed and implemented a new organizational system within the kitchen called the *"brigade system."* This system revolutionized the professional kitchen by creating stations for the cooks and integrating the foods that were being cooked within these stations. Therefore, a dish that at one time was cooked entirely by the meat cook was now cooked by the *saucier*, who made the sauce for the meat; the *rôtisseur*, who grilled the meat; and the *légumier*, who prepared the vegetables. All prepared the dish simultaneously, and worked together in concert to plate the food. This system not only was more efficient than previous methods, it also enabled operations that served large numbers of people to create better-quality food.

Escoffier's talents in organization were put to use by a gentleman named César Ritz, who organized what would be the beginning of a worldwide chain of luxury hotels. Ritz and Escoffier worked together to create fine-dining hotels that eventually became known as the Ritz Carlton chain. As if Escoffier's legacy of further refining French cuisine and developing organizational blueprints that would be followed for decades to come weren't enough, he also wrote texts on French cuisine, including *Le Guide Culinaire*, which is considered a classic reference.

Fernand Point (1897–1955): Restaurant de la Pyramide

The father of *nouvelle* cuisine, Fernand Point didn't change the culinary traditions of France by making proclamations about cuisine, by writing books about how to cook, or by moving to Paris and influencing the elite; he did it by sticking to some basic principles and teaching those principles to young, aspiring chefs. Fernand Point believed that the quality of the product was of utmost importance, and that anything that detracted from that which it inherently possessed was wrong. Simply put, he was a perfectionist who was happy to deliver his best to anyone who visited his restaurant, La Pyramide. His greatest contribution turned out to be his open sharing of how to cook the best ingredients and retain their quality to those who trained under his watch, including Paul Bocuse, Raymond Thuilier, Alain Chapel, Jean and Pierre Troisgros, and Louis Outhier, all of whom went on to become Michelin three-star chefs themselves! Fernand had instilled in each of these

eventual chefs the importance of knowing purveyors, the value of perhaps paying more for the best product, how to correctly store and maintain that product, and what methods were best for cooking the product to highlight its character. All of these aspects may seem like common sense, but in reality they are often the first thing that a cook forgets. Forget the flair, the elaborate presentations, and the complex combinations of ingredients. Instead, start with the best raw product, treat it properly, and only then consider other aspects. This approach to cooking began the newest chapter not only of French cuisine but also of what most consider the height of the culinary arts.

Although Fernand Point is generally credited with the grassroots development of nouvelle cuisine in France, the term was actually coined by a couple of food critics named Henri Gault and Christian Millau. Their ten commandments of nouvelle cuisine fairly well sum up the ideals (although some apprentices may well disagree with a couple of them); they are as follows:

1. Thou shalt not overcook.
2. Thou shalt use fresh, quality produce.
3. Thou shalt lighten the menu.
4. Thou shalt not be systematically modernistic.
5. Thou shalt nonetheless seek out what new techniques can bring you.
6. Thou shalt avoid marinades, the hanging of game, fermentations, etc.
7. Thou shalt eliminate brown and white sauces.
8. Thou shalt not ignore dietetics.
9. Thou shalt not cheat on thy presentations.
10. Thou shalt be inventive.

Although these are not the ideas of Fernand Point himself, they do include a few of his guiding principles: the use of the best-quality products, the focus on not disturbing the intrinsic quality of each ingredient, and respect for the classic while simultaneously looking to create new ideas and dishes that honor the methods but not necessarily the recipes. This approach has enabled French cuisine to reach the heights that it has in the last 100 years. France's record of producing great chefs is clearly connected to this model of thinking, with an almost instinctive feel for food preparation yielded from this focus on quality and respect. This model of learning and professional development—based on beginning with a solid foundation of classic techniques before attempting the creative side of culinary arts—is a model that most culinary programs try to emulate today.

UNIQUE COMPONENTS

French cuisine is indeed unique. When food lovers are asked to name the most highly regarded cuisine in the world, French is the most common response. French cuisine is taught by culinary programs all over the United States, and with good reason; the organization and refinement of the techniques are in a class by themselves. Learning to cook and to develop the skills that enable someone to become a chef requires a solid understanding of cooking methods, their appropriate application, and systems for organizing a menu and a kitchen. All of these aspects make French cuisine an appropriate choice for culinary programs. The following section examines some of the components that make this so.

The Audience

The French populace is without a doubt the most educated culinary group in the world. For many growing up in France means growing up knowing food, learning where it comes from, viewing craft food sources as a way of life, and being proud of what is produced locally that contributes to the national cuisine. The impact of this on the culinary conscience of the national character is profound. Food is the pride of France, and the public contributes to this by supporting the networks behind the artisan products that make the cuisine what it is.

The Chefs

Escoffier, Carême, Point: these are just the tip of the iceberg when it comes to groundbreaking chefs in France, where being a chef has been a highly skilled position for many years. Only relatively recently have U.S. chefs been viewed as skilled professionals, and the change in opportunities and influx of aspiring chefs are obvious effects of the change in public attitude regarding chefs in America. In France, chefs have been held in high esteem for centuries, and thus the idea of becoming a chef is considered an honor for many French people.

Clearly, pioneers like Carême, Escoffier, and Point paved the way for others to follow them and carry on the traditions that these fathers of French cuisine established. The list of great French chefs seems to grow by the day, but there is a common thread among virtually all who have achieved their fame in France—a respect for the profession and a commitment to excellence that is very rare in any field today. Most, if not all, of the famous French chefs toiled in the kitchens themselves for many years prior to becoming well known, a point often made by those who criticize "TV chefs" of modern society. The idea of earning one's place in the kitchen is encouraged by the brigade system, which rewards loyalty, dedication, and skill. This is not a trade of talkers or a position that someone can obtain by "faking" his or her way into a spot. Lack of skill, technical know-how, and the ability to handle pressure will be exposed quickly in someone who is not prepared. As a result, the cream rise to the top, and in doing so gain a great sense of self-respect and appreciation for the effort that it takes—something that creates a bond between fellow chefs similar to what is seen among elite athletes.

The chefs in France have contributed to the development of this cuisine by holding themselves to a high standard. Today, a chef who can say that she or he learned from any of the classically trained masters of years past is assumed to possess the discipline and rigor to assure the quality of the product as well as the skill in the kitchen to allow the diner to experience the best that the food has to offer. French chefs simply demand the highest-quality products, which results in a support system for craft farmers, fishermen, mushroom foragers, cheese makers, *charcuterie* experts, ranchers, and others who provide these products. The guests who frequent French restaurants can taste the difference, and thus support the creation of similar establishments, which further supports the growers; this cycle is the engine of French gastronomy. As with all economics, the rule of supply and demand is at work here. The demand for quality forces the supply of the product, a wonderful system in which the skill and knowledge of the most dedicated professionals drive the quality and standards ever higher, and the public adores them for it. In France more than anywhere else, a nation's habits and customs are intricately wound with the cuisine.

Refinement

Not just forcemeat, but a finely sieved one that is formed into a masterpiece inside a rich pastry shell and layered with other ingredients to create a shaped piece of art . . . not just a flavorful broth or soup, but one that has been made almost perfectly clear and garnished with a specific combination of vegetables all cut exactly the same . . . not just a flavorful liver from a well-raised duck or goose, but one that has been specially fattened on a specific diet. These are but a few examples of how French cuisine works to make a product or a dish better. This is not a lazy cuisine by any account, as French chefs are notorious for their insistence on not cutting corners, to ensure that the end product is as good as it can be.

This sort of perfectionism is instilled in the population by parents who show their children how to choose the best melon, and by habits that revolve around getting products at their freshest—such as knowing exactly when the bakers will be finishing their bread so it can be picked up warm. This same approach is taken in restaurant kitchens and culinary schools throughout France, where these habits of quality and high expectations—which are part of growing up in France—are raised to another level. Apprentices learn about cooking by first learning how to determine a fish's freshness by looking at its gills, what size lobster will have the best tenderness and flavor, or how to properly open an oyster to leave all of the liquor behind but no shell pieces. We have all at some point had to make the decision whether or not to use a product that isn't ideal, and it is at moments like these that high standards are set. If the best quality is demanded, the overall attention to this aspect of cooking is elevated and reflected in the end product. This attitude is undoubtedly applied the world over, but it is often part of the fabric of the character of French culinary professionals to a notably higher degree.

Why do they take these painstaking measures to ensure everything is at its best? Because there is a consumer who will notice whether they do or don't, and because they were raised with this expectation from a young age. This philosophy is part of the pride of being French and is instilled in each successive generation, ensuring that the cycle continues. With this history and mentality firmly in place, the future of French (or any other country's, for that matter) cuisine is unlimited.

Organization

Whereas French cuisine often inspires wonderment from visitors at the skills of the chefs, at the appreciation that the populace has for the foods that they

create, and at the attention given to the littlest details that make the cuisine what it is, it is the organization of French cuisine that impresses the cook or uninitiated chef. French cuisine has been thought out like an elaborate war plan, including the best position of each person, the most efficient way to produce multiple items by making a hierarchical plan in the production of sauces and other basic preparations, and the assurance that all members of the staff know how this system works and what their roles are. These are very basic principles of military operations, and they are also the basis of the modern French kitchen. There is a leader who isn't called a general, but rather a chef, and he or she directs the next in command (*sous chefs*) in ensuring that assignments are carried out exactly as he or she has directed. There is no discussion about how it will be done—it will be done as directed, or the cook will need to find work somewhere else. Although this practice was used by chefs in other parts of the world and even by other French chefs, Escoffier implemented it in a way that left little doubt about his belief in the efficiency and durability of this type of system. Escoffier was clearly affected by the time he served in the French military, and he adopted the same philosophy in the kitchen.

The organization of French cuisine doesn't stop with how the kitchen is set up; it is the basis for much of the cooking as well. Any culinary student can rattle off the mother sauces if he or she has studied in a French-based system, and will know that the mother sauces are used to make small sauces or intermediary sauces that then can be transformed into small sauces. The logical and pyramid-shaped organizational structure of French cuisine enables much greater efficiency in kitchens that produce many items, and it provides a system that can be taught to the staff so that everyone will know each layer of a final product—a vastly more versatile and trainable system than one in which each end product takes a completely different path to its creation. Using this system, one can say to an apprentice "I need a white stock" and feel confident that, if that person has been properly trained, the results will be the same regardless of who trained the apprentice or where he or she is from. The same cannot be said for many cuisines, where the background of a given person might be the biggest factor in what they do. In France, everyone is trained to do exactly the same thing. Only when one masters the fundamentals does the chance to alter menu plans and combinations of food come into play.

People are often turned off by this type of mentality, but consider the problems for staff and customers if each person in the kitchen feels that she or he can alter a recipe or method because of her or his personal preference for a dish. The result is food that is inconsistent and a kitchen that can't control its product, two of the leading reasons for failures of food service establishments the world over. Consistency breeds confidence and is the hallmark of any successful kitchen, and the French have an advantage in their ability to maintain this high standard.

The French Trinity: Bread, Cheese, and Charcuterie

As much as the refinement of the ballroom banquets and court cuisine are associated with France, the backbone of the country's everyday fare is the breads, cheeses, and charcuterie. These are the foundation upon which the cuisine is built. They are enjoyed on a daily basis by the masses, and they are made with such care and regional reverence that a tremendous variety exists among just these three types of foods. Simply add wine, and you have the foundation of many of the great products that have made France so well known.

More than 400 types of cheeses can be found in this country, which is smaller than California; the great regions of wine produce hundreds of well-known labels; and the bread and charcuterie products that are found throughout the country are almost as varied. Simply review the section of this chapter that discusses the different regions, and it should become apparent how important cheese and charcuterie are to the general population (bread and wine are equally important, and could fill volumes all on their own).

The Restaurant

In 1765, a Frenchman by the name of Monsieur Boulanger opened what most consider the first restaurant in the Western world, and this was to become one aspect of French cuisine that set it apart from others. Although the restaurant certainly didn't become a French monopoly, it did find deeper roots in France and a system that supported the idea of a restaurant better than elsewhere. The French Revolution of 1789 occurred not long after the fateful opening of this first restaurant, and this led to conditions that would prove perfect for the rapid expansion of this new type of establishment. With its

removal of royalty and the expulsion of nobles who employed the great French chefs of the day, the revolution changed the lives of those who made their living preparing glorious feasts and serving the finest food. The great French chefs of the day were out of work, and it doesn't take much of an imagination to understand that they saw this new type of establishment, which was gaining popularity, as an opportunity to find work and provide their services to a new clientele, the public.

Prior to the opening of the first restaurant, there were places where one could eat and sleep, and there were places where one could get a cup of coffee, but there were no establishments that focused solely on public eating and offered a list of food choices from which someone could choose. The term *restaurant* actually translates best to "restorative," as this name was originally used to describe rich meat-based broths or bouillons that were thought to enliven a weary traveler. The use of this term in the naming of the eating establishment as we know it today was not an accident; this was precisely the goal of the first restaurants, to provide a restorative place to someone who traveled to the city and didn't have a home to go to for nourishment. In the decades that followed, the infrastructure and public support for this system grew, and the "restorative" turned into something else entirely. The restaurant became a place to visit *instead* of going home, because the food prepared by professional chefs for the restaurant was the best available anywhere.

Why is this significant? Once again, the groundwork was laid for what would become a vehicle to connect the creative professional chef and the increasingly discerning public palate that are integral parts of modern French cuisine.

SIGNIFICANT SUBREGIONS

France is blessed with many geographical features that provide a bounty of ingredients with which to work. Two major bodies of water surround the French shores, with the northern and eastern portion bordering the Atlantic Ocean and the protected English Channel and the southeastern portion bordering the Mediterranean Sea. Mountain ranges also separate the borders with other countries: the Alps run along the eastern portion of France that borders Italy and Switzerland, and the Pyrenees run along the southern border with Spain. In the central portion of the country are many streams and rivers, including the Rhône River, the Loire River, the Seine River, and the Gironde River, all of which provide many of the means for the rich agricultural lands that help support the regions in their culinary endeavors.

French regions are confusing and complex for a variety of reasons. First, the names of old provinces (historic regions that include ethnic and cultural histories) and the 21 newer administrative regions that are subdivided into departments (newly drawn maps that separate the regions in a different manner than the historic regions) often result in cultural groups existing in two regions that were once one. In addition, certain regions are very well known for either the wine they produce (such as Bordeaux) or the food that is named after the area (such as Dijon), and these names are often neither the historic province nor the new regions or departments. For example, Bordeaux, which many people from the United States know because of the fine wines produced here, is now a part of the region called Aguitaine, which was once part of the historic area called Guyenne, neither of which is a commonly known name in the United States. In many culinary texts, dishes may be described by names that include references to a historic area, such as Savoy or Gascony. In order to try to keep the confusion to a minimum, this section will describe the areas in terms of their geographical location.

The North and Northeast: Nord-Pas-De-Calais, Picardie, and Champagne

The northern portion of France is most well known for the sparkling wines produced here called *champagne*, and the food from this region may surprise those who assume that the grandeur and sophistication associated with Champagne are not displayed in the local cuisine. This area is one of the agricultural regions of France that supplies many of the foods used throughout the rest of the country. Fields of *blé* (wheat), *pommes de terre* (potatoes), *betterave* (beets), and *chou* (cabbage) are all part of the landscape of this fertile but cold region. The cuisine of this region is more reserved and simple than that of the fine restaurants in nearby Paris that uncork the crisp bottles of champagne produced here. This is not to say that the cuisine does not contribute to the national character, for it certainly does, but it does so with dishes of simpler game forcemeats such as *pâtés* (fine forcemeats), *chaudiere* (the ancestor to New

England clam chowder) and dishes cooked *á la carbonnade* (with beer, mustard, and onions). The forests of the Ardenne Mountains are home to wild mushrooms, game, and *truite* (trout), which are all found in the local cuisine.

A local taste for sweets and pastries is also notable here, as a number of pastries and confections are common in this region as well. One will find *gaufres* (waffles) sweet breads such as *pain d'espices* (ginger spiced bread), *raffolait* (thick, caramelized milk) served with pancakes, as well as the use of *massepain* (marzipan), or almond paste, in local pastries.

The Northwestern Coast: Normandy and Brittany

The Normandy region is well known in the United States as the landing place of the Allied forces in World War II, but not so much for the great dairy products, apples, and seafood that were also made famous here. Viking explorers settled this part of France in the ninth century, and their heritage as sailors has been maintained since.

Normandy is in the northwestern part of France, lying on the coast of the English Channel, and thus has a far more docile coastline than its south and western neighboring region of Brittany. The English Channel is fertile fishing ground that the Normans have historically enjoyed, landing significant catches of *merlu* (hake), *plie* (plaice), *saint-pierre* (john dory), dover sole, and an abundance of *fruit de mer* (shellfish). The combination of the local seafood and the local dairy products is a common one in the Norman kitchen, as the local *buerre* (butter) and *crème* (cream) are both sought-after commodities throughout the country. The colder climate of this northern region probably contributed to the development of the many orchards here that not only supply great *pommes* (apples) but also the locally made *cidre* (cider) and cider distillate known as *calvados*. This region is also where a number of the prized cheeses originated, with Camembert, Neufchâtel, livarot, and gournay being some of the most notable. Normandy and Brittany are also well known for the *crêpe* (thin pancake) used in many sweet preparations and the *galette* (buckwheat pancake) used in savory variants.

Brittany is surrounded by the sea and filled with the brisk saltwater air that seems to invade all things Breton. The lamb from this region is even called *agneau pre-salé* (presalted lamb), as the meat from the animals grazing in the salt marshes is thought to be more flavorful. This region lies on the Atlantic coast and is subject to harsh winds from the Atlantic as well as fierce storms that make fishing off this coast a dangerous profession. Oddly, this region that borders Normandy also was settled by immigrants, but in this case it happened in the fifth century and it was the Celts who were fleeing their British Isle homes as Anglo-Saxons invaded there. This connection with the Celts is evident in the cuisine of the region, seen in the commonality of stews and porridge in the daily fare as well as the crepe, which—although it may not at first appear related to Celtic foods—is quite similar to the many drop-batter foods found in Celtic Ireland, Wales, and Scotland. The prized *kig ha farz* (beef and salt pork stew) of Brittany also reminds one of the stews in Ireland, but with the clever addition of simmering the porridge inside the stew to yield a flavorful dumpling-like starch to serve with the stew.

The cuisine of Brittany is often overlooked when examining the French regions, but the products of Brittany certainly are not. This is the land of the *huitre* (oyster), *homard* (lobster), *coquille Saint Jacques* (scallop), *palourde* (clam), and *moules* (mussels), all of which are highly prized throughout France and elsewhere. These regions also produce excellent vegetables, including *artichaut* (artichokes), *choufleur* (cauliflower), *petit pois* (peas), and *pommes de terre* (potatoes), as well as much sought-after sea salt called *guérande*.

Île de France: Paris

Paris is first and foremost a city, and thus has no real connection with the local land and what is produced—except if that local land is considered to be France herself, in which case Paris is the most complex of all regions. In reality, Paris, like any other major metropolitan city, draws from other regions to get both inspiration and product. Because of the business opportunities in the city, chefs from all parts of France often are lured there, and each brings the traditions of his or her region along. Because most residents of Paris can trace their roots to someplace else, a support web for regional cuisines exists in the city as well. Paris is often a leader in innovative foods, as this mixture of styles and product encourages experimentation, and the local chefs certainly have the skill and imagination to deliver to those who are interested in new ideas.

The Central Western Loire Valley: Pays de la Loire and Poitou-Charentes

The Loire River is a major waterway that provides the vast Loire Valley with the water needed to produce crops from this region, which in many cases are sent out to other parts of France. In the case of the *champignon de Paris* (button mushrooms), the flow of ingredients even made it into the name of the product; at one time, the supply of button mushrooms to Paris mainly came from the caves of this region—hence, the name. Other products that come from this region include *asperges*, *poireau* (leeks), *carottes* (carrots), *mâche* (corn lettuce), and other lettuces. The fertile region that surrounds the Loire River is home to vineyards producing famous white wines, orchards of *prunes* (plums) and *poires* (pears), and the river itself, which yields excellent freshwater fish such as *saumon* (salmon), *brochet* (pike), and *anguille* (eel). In addition to the excellent fish and produce from the valley, the *bœuf* (beef) and *agneau* (lamb) from this region are also highly prized and utilized to the fullest extent.

The Central Eastern Region: Ardenne, Bourgogne, and Lyon

When people think of the rich and flavorful foods of French cuisine, they are often thinking of dishes from this region. The rich sauces based on the local wine, the buttery pastries that are found in bakeries, the choicest cuts of beef, the chicken and rabbit dishes such as *coq au vin* (cockerel stewed with red wine), and the well-known *escargot* (snails with garlic butter) are all found here. Found within this region are some of the finest products in France, including the *poulet* (chicken) de Bresse, the largest *gros Bourgogne* (snails), the most prized beef in all of France from Charollais, the mustard everyone has heard of called *Dijon*, and not only some of the best wines found in the world but also a delicious liqueur made from black currants called *crème de cassis*. Many of these products are *en ragoût* (stewed) or cooked in one of the many *rotisseries* (rotating ovens or spits) that are common here.

Burgundy has long been a region of nobles, dating back centuries when this was the center of a powerful kingdom of France, and the grandeur of these times is still felt in the local cuisine. A dish cooked *à la bourguignonne* is cooked with a red wine sauce and *lardons* (bacon), *champignons* (mushrooms), and *oignons* (small onions), whereas one *served* with a red wine sauce is described as *en meurette;* examples of these combinations abound in the local cooking.

Other notable local products include *Pernod* (an anise-flavored liquor), *marc* (a brandy-like distillate made from leftover skins of grapes), *epoisses* (fine-textured and strong cheeses made by washing the exteriors with marc), *chèvre* (goat's milk cheese), *morille* (morel), and other wild mushrooms, as well as many quality nut oils pressed from the nut orchard yields that are used in salads and for dressings and other applications. Local charcuterie includes the well-known *rosette de Lyon*, similar to the Italian salami; *sabodets* (strong pork sausage), which includes hog's head and skin as part of the filling; and *andouillettes de mâcon*, a smoked sausage made from the lining of the intestines and stomach. With this rich land and its great products, it is no wonder this region has become one of France's most celebrated.

The Central Western Mountain Region: Alsace and Lorraine

This region borders Germany to the east and shares many common ingredients and foods with its German neighbors; this is particularly true of the cuisine of Alsace. Alsace was part of Germany prior to World War I, and the locals eat a similar fare that commonly includes *porc* (pork), *chou* (cabbage), *pommes de terre* (potatoes), and *nouilles* (noodles) in the typical foods. There are a number of dishes based on *choucroute* (sauerkraut), some that combine it with pork, and others with different types of *saucisson* (sausages)— and this is just one part of the quality charcuterie from Alsace. The fertile area of the Alsatian plains produces many fruits that are used to make the local *schnapps* (fruit distillate), a number of which are used in the local sweet and savory preparations.

The people and the food of Alsace have more in common with Germany than with other parts of France; Lorraine, on the other hand, is a region with historic and cultural ties to the rest of France. Alsace and Lorraine are not only separated by their different cultural aspects but also by the Vosges Mountain range, which separates the more mountainous Lorraine from the fertile valleys of Alsace. Although the cuisine of Lorraine utilizes many of the same ingredients as those found in Alsatian cuisine, the types of dishes made with them are more synonymous with France than Germany. The well-known *quiche Lorraine*, with its rich pastry crust and creamy custard does include *lardons* (bacon), is a favorite of German cookery, but this savory tart highlights the pastry arts that are a notable part of French cooking. Lorraine is also well known for its sweets and liqueurs, some of which find their way into the cuisine of Paris. *Madeleines* (small, lemon-flavored cakes in the shape of elongated scallops) and *macaroons* (almond-flavored meringue) are two of the pastry connections to this area that are found in Parisian shops, while local *kirch* (cherry brandy) is used to add a unique taste to other sweet creations.

The Southeastern Alpine Region: Franche-Comte and Savoy

This region is dominated by the Alps, which provide a natural border between this part of France and both Switzerland and Italy. This alpine country is also known for the great dairy products that come from the local cattle grazing in the hills. A number of well-known cheeses hail from this region, including *tomme de Savoie*, a mild, excellent slicing cheese, and *comté*, which is similar to Swiss cheese but aged to yield a rich flavor. This mountainous terrain also supports fruit and nut orchards, with *noix* (walnut) orchards common to this region; their oil and nuts are used in salads, stuffing, and desserts. The clear streams from the melting Alpine water supports some of the best *truite* (trout) in the country, and the Rhone River that cuts through the valley provides *brochet* (pike), both of which are prepared locally in a variety of ways— ranging from cooked in local wines or used to make more refined preparations such as *quenelles*. This is also a traditional charcuterie area and a number of fine products are produced here, including excellent air-dried cured and smoked *jambon* (ham) and *bresi* (beef), as well as a type of smoked sausage called *saucisse de Morteau*. A couple of components from the Americas are also very common in this region: corn and potatoes both are used extensively. The inclusion of these ingredients is also a hint at some of the influences on this region, including both Italian and Spanish.

Parts of this region were at one time part of the House of Savoy, a kingdom that was a dominant force over a section of northern Italy. Some of the local dishes have similarities with the cuisines of both Northern Italy and Switzerland, and the focus on dairy is a notable component. Some common dishes from this region include *matafans*, cornmeal pancakes often wrapped around foods; *gratins* of all sorts, in which the surfaces of the foods are browned from intense heat; and *raclette*, a dish of melted cheese served with potatoes.

The South Central Mountain Region: Auvergne and Limousin

The south central region of France is one of the more rural areas and boasts a hearty cuisine based on fine local ingredients. This hilly and mountainous area is yet another region blessed with quality products, producing some of the best charcuterie from excellent local porc, prized *lentilles vertes du puy* (lentils), and earthy *châtaignes* (chestnuts) often used in stuffing for a roasted *oie* (goose), which also yields the prized *foie gras* (fattened liver) sought throughout the country. The region also is a significant producer of nuts and fruits, as well as *miel* (honey) from the bees that help maintain the orchards. The mountains of this region are not as dramatic as the Alps that lie to the east, and they yield wonderful products allowed by the less severe terrain. Some notable products from this region include *Cantal, Saint-Nectaire,* and *Bleu d'Auvergne,* all fine cow's milk cheeses that take advantage of the rich milk that the local cows produce. As mentioned earlier, this is also charcuterie country, and numerous examples are found here of excellent saucisson and other force-meat preparations such as *galantines* (boned poultry or other meat that is stuffed and rolled before being cooked and served cold), and *pâtés* (seasoned smooth forcemeat served hot or cold). This is also the region in which *clafouti*, a baked custard often made with cherries, is believed to have originated. Other common local specialties include *aligot*, a rich, creamy dish made from potatoes cooked with whey and garlic, and dishes that are now commonly referred to as à la limousine, which denotes that they are served with braised red cabbage and chestnuts. The hearty cuisine of this region excels in both satisfying and highlighting the qualities of the excellent local products.

The Southeastern Mediterranean Region: Provence and Languedoc

The south of France is gastronomically and climatically different from most of the rest of the country, in that the warming effect of the Mediterranean Sea promotes a garden of plants on which the local cuisine is based. Herbs like rosemary, thyme, basil, oregano, sage, and lavender grow profusely and are used extensively in this cuisine. Along with olive oil and garlic, these ingredients are part of the distinct flavor of this land of the sun. This region is considerably warmer than most of the country, and thus foods that require this climate—such as figs, melons, citrus, and olives—are grown in abundance and make their way into the local cuisine.

The history of this region has had an important effect on the cuisine as well. Provence is not only close to Italy geographically, but parts of Provence were at one time parts of former Italian states. The major city of Nice was once part of the Italian region of Savoy, and it wasn't until 1860 that the area became a permanent part of France. There are many similarities between the cuisine of Provence and that of the nearby Liguria region of Italy. Pasta, polenta, and gnocchi are significant parts of the cuisine in Provence, and other common preparations—such as *pistou* (herb paste made with basil) and *aioli* (emulsion made from olive oil and garlic)—clearly reveal further similarities between these regions. This isn't to say they are the same, as there are many aspects of the cuisine of Provence that are unique. Some of the most well-known Provençal dishes include *pissaladière*, an onion, caper, and anchovy-topped dough; *bouillabaisse,* a fisherman's stew with the yields of the Mediterranean scented and colored by saffron; *ratatouille,* a stewed vegetable dish highlighting the local produce; and *tapenade,* a paste made from olives, capers, garlic, and olive oil that is served with crusty bread as a starter.

Southwestern Region: Aquitaine, Midi-Pyrénées, and Pays Basque

The Southwestern region is a one of rich history, equally rich culture, and some of the most well-known and sought-after French products. This region is home to foie gras truffles, *Roquefort* cheese (blue-veined sheep's milk cheese), and Bordeaux wines, as well as the traditions of making duck legs cooked and preserve in their own *confit* (fat); *cassoulet* (rich bean, sausage, and meat stews); and *croustade* (open pastries wrapped around sweetened apples or pears). This area also is well known for its highly flavored products and dishes. The more northern part is the most famous wine growing location in France (although some might argue for Burgundy or Champagne), and the dishes that are made in the style of this region are often referred to as *à la bordelaise*, indicating that they are served with a wine sauce enriched with shallots, thyme, and stock. The fat from the ducks and geese raised to yield their famous livers is prized here as well; confit is made by using the rendered fat to cook the tougher parts of the birds until tender, and then packing the meat in the fat to preserve and mature it for later use. Many of the products found in this region are particularly rich and, as such, so is the food. The area of Perigord is known for its heavily scented truffles, and they are often cooked locally with scrambled eggs or used to make more elaborate foods such as *pâté de foie gras*, a very flavorful, smooth forcemeat that includes fattened goose or duck liver. Another local charcuterie product of note is a garlicky sausage called *louquenkas*, which is often a component in the popular meat and bean stew called *cassoulet*.

The southwestern border with Spain is home to the Pyrenees Mountains and the people known as Basques, whose culture is deeply rooted in culinary traditions. The Basque people have lived in this area as long as history has been recorded here, and they are considered instinctive cooks known for their use of chiles, tomatoes, and peppers, all New World products introduced by the Spanish. The Basque have a tradition as fishermen, and a number of fish dishes are part of their cuisine and include the use of *morue* (salt cod), which has been used extensively as a reliable source of protein in this community since its introduction by the Scandinavian traders. The Basque are also known for their excellent *jambon de Bayonne* (hams) and *ardi gasna* (sheep's milk cheeses) that are also common ingredients in the local cooking.

RECIPES

The following recipes provide an introduction to some of the aspects of French cuisine that have contributed to its worldwide reputation. Professional cooking texts are also a good reference for French cuisine, because traditional culinary texts in the United States use French cuisine as a model to teach students the art of culinary production—and with good reason.

Huiles de Cèpes SOUTHWEST FRANCE
(CÈPE-INFUSED OIL)

INGREDIENTS

1	oz	Dried Cèpes (often called porcini)
1	Tbsp	Fresh Thyme Leaves, minced
1		Garlic Clove, smashed
2		Bay Leaves
1/4	tsp	Black Peppercorns, crushed
1	pint	Good Quality Olive Oil

Highly flavored oils are prized in many French dishes, including dressings for salads or to be served with cold foods. Many of the flavored oils come from nuts, such as walnuts, pistachios, and so forth, and still others are made from infusions (such as this one). An oil such as this can be used to make a flavorful dressing for a chèvre salad, for example, or even a dressing to be served with the terrine recipe that follows later in the chapter.

YIELD: 1 pint

SPECIAL METHOD: Infusion of Oil

PROCEDURE

1. Place all ingredients except olive oil into a dry, clean container that will just hold all of the ingredients and has a tight-fitting lid (ideally the container will not allow light to pass through—use brown glass, for example), and pour olive oil over the ingredients.

2. Place container in a cool, dark place and allow to infuse for 2 weeks before using.

Crème Frâiche NORMANDY
(CLOTTED/FERMENTED CREAM)

INGREDIENTS

30	oz	Heavy Cream
2	oz	Buttermilk (or crème frâiche)

This process has been done for centuries to make a product with an extended shelf life and a notable character from the natural fermentation that takes place. It is not a foolproof practice that is sure to always yield wholesome results. Care must be taken *not* to contaminate during any step of this process. (**Note:** Instructors need to supervise from beginning to end when making this recipe.) There is another way of making this recipe that yields slightly different but more assured results: follow the steps for making yogurt in Chapter 2, "Greek Cuisine," but use cream instead of milk.

YIELD: 1 quart

SPECIAL METHOD: Lactic Acid Fermentation

PROCEDURE

1. Combine heavy cream and buttermilk in sanitized container, and mix together with sanitized whisk.
2. Cover container with plastic wrap and set aside at room temperature (70–75°F) and allow culture to sour the cream. This usually will take approximately 24 hours; higher ambient temperatures speed the process up slightly, and lower ambient temperatures slow the process down.
3. Once the cream has thickened (to the consistency of yogurt), place it in the refrigerator. If the cream has not thickened after 36 hours, discard and start again, making sure the buttermilk is fresh.
4. If crème frâiche will be used regularly, some should be reserved to start the next batch.

Sauce Mignonette BRITTANY
(SHALLOT AND PEPPER-INFUSED VINEGAR)

INGREDIENTS

8	oz	Red Wine Vinegar
3	oz	Shallots, minced very fine
1	Tbsp	Freshly Ground Pepper
		Salt, to taste

This classic infused vinegar is likely to be served with fresh oysters eaten on the half shell along with fresh lemon.

YIELD: 11 ounces (enough for 3 dozen oysters)

SPECIAL METHOD: Infusion of Vinegar

PROCEDURE

1. Combine all ingredients in a mixing bowl or storage container, and mix thoroughly; allow at least 1 hour of infusion prior to use.
2. Serve with freshly shucked oysters; oysters are often served on rock salt to allow them to be transported without losing the liquor that they contain (*liquor* is the term commonly used to describe the liquid inside a live shellfish—it is very flavorful and typically prized and retained).

Salade de Chicorée et Pomme de Terre The North

(Belgian Endive and Potato Salad)

Ingredients

For Steaming (or Boiling) the Potatoes and Eggs

2	lbs	Red Bliss Potatoes, preferably new (small) potatoes
5		Large Eggs
		Ice Bath

For Making the Vinaigrette Dressing

1	oz	Shallot, minced
1	tsp	Salt
2	Tbsp	Dijon Mustard
2	oz	Champagne Vinegar
6	oz	Vegetable Oil (can substitute olive oil)
1/2	bunch	Chives, minced
1/4	tsp	Freshly Ground Black Pepper
		Salt and Pepper, to taste

For Assembling the Salad

5		Belgian Endives
2	qt	Water
3	oz	Lemon Juice
		Cooked Potatoes and Eggs (see above)
12	oz	Cherry Tomatoes, halved
1/2	bunch	Chives

The region of France north of Paris is influenced by the Flemish country of Belgium and is also a region that relies on the hardy vegetables of the earth. Potatoes, beets, cabbage, and that great Flemish invention of underground lettuce—known as Belgian endive in the United States (and confusingly called chicorée in France)—all play significant roles in the cuisine of this region, and a few are incorporated into this recipe as well.

Yield: 10 salads (6–7 ounces/portion)

Cooking Method (Potatoes and Eggs): Steaming or Boiling

Mixing Method (Dressing): Emulsifying Vinaigrette

Procedure

For Steaming (or Boiling) the Potatoes and Eggs

1. Preheat a steamer or, if unavailable, place a large pot of water on the stove and bring to a boil. Add 2 Tbsp of salt per gallon of water.

2. Once the steamer or boiling water is prepared, add the potatoes to a perforated pan (if using a steamer) and cook until tender throughout (the length of time will depend on the size of the potatoes; new potatoes should take approximately 15–20 minutes).

3. Once the potatoes are done, remove them from the steamer/water and set them on a sheet pan inside a refrigerator to allow them to cool.

4. Add the eggs to the perforated pan and steam for 12 minutes, and then immediately place them into the ice bath to cool.

5. Once the eggs are cool, peel them and set them aside.

For Making the Vinaigrette Dressing

1. Place the minced shallot, salt, mustard, and vinegar in a small mixing bowl and—using a whisk—slowly whisk in the oil to form an emulsified dressing.

2. Add the minced chives and freshly ground black pepper, and whisk to combine.

3. Adjust seasoning, as necessary, with salt and pepper.

For Assembling the Salad

1. To prepare the Belgian endive, take 2 heads and remove all of the leaves by pulling them from the stem. Immediately add them to a container with 2 qts of water and 3 oz of lemon juice.

2. Remove the leaves and set them in a colander; cover with a clean towel dampened with the lemon water (do not discard the water and lemon juice).

3. For the other 3 Belgian endives, cut off the end of each endive, split it in half, and remove any remaining core at the base by wedging it out with a chef's knife.

(continues)

Salade de Chicorée et Pomme de Terre
(continued)

4. Cut each of the halves in half again, and then cut the quarters into 1/2-inch sections. Immediately add them to the lemon water.

5. To prepare the potatoes, cut each into large diced cubes (if using larger potatoes) or quarter them (if using the small new potatoes) and then set aside.

6. To prepare the eggs, slice each into 6 pieces by cutting in half with a wet, clean, and sharp knife, and then cutting each half into thirds; set aside.

7. To finish preparing the cut Belgian endive, remove it from the lemon water and place it in a salad spinner. Spin to dry the cut endive and set aside.

8. To assemble the salads, place the cut Belgian endive in a mixing bowl, along with the cherry halves and the cut potatoes, and toss with half of the dressing.

9. On each plate, place three whole Belgian endive leaves in a triangle pattern near the center of the plate.

10. Place about 5 oz of the dressed salad mixture in the center of the plate, covering the broken ends of the Belgian endive.

11. Place three egg wedges in between each of the Belgian endive leaves, and drizzle a little of the dressing over each of the egg pieces.

12. Garnish each plate with a couple of spears of chives, and serve at once.

Salade de chicorée et pomme de terre (Belgian endive and potato salad)

Galettes au Jambon, au Fromage et a l'Oeuf Brittany

(Buckwheat Pancakes with Ham, Cheese, and Egg)

Ingredients

For Making the Galette Batter

10	oz	Buckwheat Flour
10	oz	All-Purpose (A.P.) Flour
2	tsp	Salt
12	oz	Milk
16	oz	Water (more or less may be needed)
4	oz	Melted Butter

For Cooking and Filling the Galettes

2	oz	Vegetable Oil
		Galette Batter (see above)
6	oz	Butter
12		Eggs
12	oz	Gruyère Cheese, grated
18	oz	Ham, sliced very thin

Breton cuisine is more simple and understated than much of the rest of the country's cuisine. Many of the best products from this region are shipped off to Paris to be served in the finest restaurants, while those who toil for them enjoy a more rustic cuisine at home. Galettes and crêpes are two similar canvases made to be enjoyed with some of the local fare.

Yield: Twelve 9-inch galettes (approximately 8 ounces/galette)

Mixing Method (Galette Batter): Batter Method—Wet to Dry

Cooking Method (Gallette): Griddling

Procedure

For Making the Galette Batter

1. Sift the flours into a bowl large enough to comfortably hold all of the ingredients, and add the salt to the bowl. Mix to combine, and then make a well in the center of the flour.

2. Using a wooden spoon, add half of the milk to the well in the flour and stir to combine it with the flour. Make a stiff dough/paste with no lumps (add more milk, if needed), and set this dough/paste aside for 20 minutes to rest.

3. Transfer the dough/paste to a mixer and, using a paddle attachment, gradually add the remaining milk to the dough, with the machine running on a low speed.

4. Once all of the milk has been incorporated into the dough, add enough water to the dough— again with the machine running—to make a batter the thickness of crêpe batter or a thin pancake batter.

5. Once the batter is the right consistency, add the melted butter; mix just until it disappears.

6. Set the batter aside until you are ready to cook the galettes.

For Cooking and Filling the Galettes

1. Preheat a 9-inch crêpe pan or griddle to 375°F (if using a crêpe pan, you will need to adjust the flame to hold this temperature, which is determined by testing the batter and noting the behavior of the oil).

2. Once the griddle is hot, wipe it with the vegetable oil using a clean cloth or towel.

3. Once the griddle is prepared, pour 4 oz of the galette batter onto the griddle and immediately spread it into a thin circle using a wooden rake or other tool.

4. Cook the galette until just browned on the bottom, and then quickly turn it over using a spatula.

(continues)

Galettes au jambon, au fromage et a l'oeuf (ham, cheese, and egg galette)

Galettes au Jambon, au Fromage et a l'Oeuf
(continued)

5. As soon as it is turned over, place a 1/2-oz pat of butter on the galette and break one egg over one end of the galette, spreading it out; top the egg with 1 oz of the grated Gruyère cheese and 1.5 oz of the thinly sliced ham.

6. Cook the galette until the egg white begins to cook from the heat conducting through the galette.

7. Once the egg begins to cook, fold the half that the egg is not on, and flip. Cook for an additional minute, and then remove the galette from the griddle and serve.

8. Repeat steps 2–7 with the remaining galette batter and prepared fillings to make 12 total galettes (if using a large griddle, multiple galettes can be made at the same time, space permitting).

Soupe de Poissons PROVENCE
(FISH SOUP)

INGREDIENTS

For Cleaning the Fish

2 lbs   Fish Bones, from lean fish such as halibut, sole, or cod (make sure it is fresh!)

6 lbs   Whole Fish (preferable bony Mediterranean fish such as whiting, eel, or gurnard; if these are not available, use other whole lean fish such as those mentioned above or rock cod, snapper, etc. Again, the fish needs to be fresh!)

Although bouillabaisse gets all the press and inclusion on U.S. menus, a more common fish soup found regularly in the Mediterranean coastal area of Provence is this simple yet great recipe, which uses some of the smaller and less desirable of the Mediterranean fish. As with all things seafood, the quality of this stew is dependent on the quality of the fish, so be sure to use fresh bones and whole fish. Remember check the gills and the eyes to determine freshness.

YIELD: 3 gallons, or 48 portions (8 ounces/portion)

COOKING METHOD: Simmering

SPECIAL METHODS: Immersion Blending and Straining through a China Cap

PROCEDURE

For Cleaning the Fish

1. If the fish are not already gutted, do so first, making sure to cut through the membrane at the back of each fish's gut against the backbone that covers the blood line; rinse and rub the blood line out. (The fish may be gutted but the blood line still may need to be cleaned out.)

2. If the fish are not scaled, scale the fish as well.

3. Remove the gills of the fish by cutting the narrow section in the bottom of each fish's neck between the two gill openings and then cutting the gills off from each side, where they attach to the inside of the head (you should be able to get them both out in one piece, if this is done correctly).

4. Rinse the fish off well under cold running water, cut the fish into smaller pieces (if they will not fit into the pot you intend to use), and set the fish in the refrigerator until you are ready to start the soup.

Soupe de poissons (fish soup) served with bread and rouille sauce

(continues)

Soupe de Poissons
(continued)

For Making the Soup

2	oz	Olive Oil
1	lb	White Part of Leeks, diced medium, about two average bunches
1	lb	Yellow Onions, diced medium
8	oz	Carrots, diced medium
2	oz	Garlic Cloves, crushed
2	lbs	Tomatoes, concasséed
1	oz	Tomato Paste
1/4	cup	Parsley, minced (about 1/2 bunch)
16	oz	Dry White Wine
		Cleaned Fish (see above)
2	gallons	Water
1/2	tsp	Freshly Ground Black Pepper
2	Tbsp	Salt
		Salt, to taste

(handwritten annotations: .5, 4, 4, 2, .5, 8, .5, 2 Tbs, 4, 1/2, 64 oz, 1/8, .5)

For Making the Soup

1. Over a medium flame, heat a pot that is large enough to hold all of the ingredients, and add the olive oil.
2. Once the oil gets hot, add the leeks, onions, and carrots, and sweat the aromatic vegetables in the oil until they are tender and the onions become translucent (about 15 minutes).
3. Once the vegetables are tender, add the garlic and tomato concassée, and continue to cook for an additional 5 minutes, watching the heat to make sure that there is no coloring.
4. After cooking the garlic and tomatoes for 5 minutes, add the tomato paste and parsley, and deglaze the pan with the white wine.
5. Add the fish to the pot at this time, and cook for a couple minutes over a high flame before adding the water, pepper, and salt; bring the mixture to a simmer.
6. Once the soup reaches a simmer, adjust heat so that it doesn't boil, and allow the soup to simmer for approximately 40 minutes or until the fish are completely tender and falling apart (length of time will depend on size and type of fish used).
7. Once the fish are completely tender, place an immersion blender in the pot and purée everything together (the bones, too!). If an immersion blender is not available, the soup can be puréed in a food processor in batches—be careful when doing this, however, because it is hot!
8. Once the soup has been puréed until relatively smooth, strain the soup through a China cap to remove all of the remaining particles.
9. Taste the soup and adjust with salt, if necessary.
10. Serve the soup with croutons and, if desired, aioli or rouille.

Mousseline de Saumon aux Poireau ÎLE DE FRANCE
(SALMON MOUSSELINE WITH BRANDIED SHRIMP AND WALNUT CRUST OVER CREAMED LEEKS)

INGREDIENTS

For Making the Mousseline

.75	lb	Salmon Fillet pieces, kept cold (scrap pieces work well)
2		Egg Whites, cold
8	oz	Heavy Cream, cold
1/2	tsp	Salt

For Folding In

4	oz	Shrimp, peeled and deveined and cut into 1/4-inch pieces

The Île de France is the region in which Paris is located, and it is in Paris that many of the components of French cuisine come together to make some of the more refined and celebrated dishes. This recipe is an example of the utilization of some of the excellent products of France, with salmon and shrimp from the Atlantic, walnuts from southern France, leeks from the Loire Valley, cream from Normandy, and brandy from any of the wine regions coming together to make a wonderful appetizer.

YIELD: 1.75 lbs mousseline (about 8 portions at 3 ounces each)

MIXING METHOD (FORCEMEAT): Mousseline Emulsification Method

COOKING METHOD FOR SAUSAGE (INITIAL METHOD): Poaching

COOKING METHOD (CREAMED LEEKS): Quick Braising

COOKING METHOD FOR SAUSAGE (FINAL METHOD): Sautéing

(continues)

Mousseline de Saumon aux Poireau
(continued)

2 oz	Brandy (can use Cognac, if preferred)
	Pinch Salt
1 tsp	Chives, minced
1/4 tsp	Tarragon, minced

For Poaching the Sausage

	Plastic Wrap
	Water

For the Walnut Crust

3/4 cup	Walnuts
1/4 cup	Bread Crumbs
1/4 tsp	Tarragon, minced
	Salt, to taste

For the Creamed Leeks

1 oz	Olive Oil
3	Leeks, cleaned, green section removed, and cut julienne
1 cup	Heavy Cream
	Salt and Freshly Ground Black Pepper, to taste

For Sautéing the Sausage

1 oz	Olive Oil
	Salmon Sausage (see above)
	Walnut Breading (see above)
2 oz	Olive Oil

Mousseline de saumon aux poireau
(salmon mousseline over creamed leeks)

PROCEDURE

For Making the Mousseline

1. Add the cold salmon fillet and egg whites to a food processor, and pulse to begin puréeing the fish.

2. As the fish is being puréed, add the cold heavy cream with the salt added to it in a slow steady stream to form an emulsion.

3. Remove this paste from the processor and press it through a fine mesh strainer or drum sieve to yield a smooth paste.

4. In a small sauté pan, sauté the shrimp and deglaze with the brandy. Set aside to cool, and season with salt.

5. Transfer the paste to a mixing bowl and fold in the sautéed shrimp and remaining ingredients for the mousseline. Test this mixture for seasoning by cooking a small amount in poaching liquid.

6. To cook the forcemeat, bring a pot of water to poaching temperature over a medium-low flame on the stove.

7. Place 3 oz of the forcemeat on a sheet of plastic wrap, and wrap and roll to form a sausage shape. Secure the ends of the plastic wrap with small strips of plastic wrap, and tie off to ensure that no water will get inside the sausage.

8. Place the wrapped forcemeat in the poaching water, and cook until the interior temperature of the forcemeat reaches 145°F. Remove the forcemeat from the water and set aside to cool.

For the Walnut Crust

1. Combine the walnuts, bread crumbs, tarragon, and salt in a food processor, and process until the mixture forms fine crumbs. Set aside for sautéing.

For the Creamed Leeks

1. Add the olive oil to a sauté pan and heat over a medium flame until hot; add the leeks.

2. Sauté the leeks until they begin to wilt, and then add the heavy cream, Simmer until the cream becomes slightly thick.

3. Season the mixture with salt and freshly ground black pepper, and set aside.

For Sautéing the Sausage

1. Bread the salmon sausages by rolling them in a small amount of olive oil and then rolling them in the bread crumbs.

2. Using a sauté pan set over a medium-low flame, sauté the sausages in a small amount of olive oil until they turn golden brown all over.

3. Remove the sausages and cut in them half on a bias; serve over a bed of the creamed leeks.

Confit de Canard SOUTHWEST

(CURED DUCK LEGS COOKED AND PRESERVED IN DUCK FAT)

INGREDIENTS

For Curing Mixture

1	cup	Kosher Salt
1	Tbsp	Black Peppercorns, crushed
1	Tbsp	Chopped Fresh Tarragon (optional)
2	Tbsp	Fresh Thyme, chopped
1/2	cup	Italian Parsley, chopped (about 1/2 bunch)

For Making the Confit

8	lbs	Duck Legs, trimmed of excess fat
3	qts	Rendered Duck Fat (this can be bought or rendered from fat removed from legs and whole ducks; however, you won't have enough from the 8 lbs of legs above)

Duck confit is one of the French creations that simply has to be tried to be appreciated. Once again, a less than desirable part of a product—when understood and handled properly—produces a product of great quality. Confit can obviously be eaten on its own but is also often used in other preparations to give a richness and a salty, meaty taste to other dishes, including the southwest classic cassoulet.

YIELD: 6 lbs (approximately half if just using meat)

SPECIAL METHOD: Curing Duck Legs

COOKING METHOD: Slow "Poaching" in Rendered Fat

PROCEDURE

For Curing Mixture

1. Using a spice blender, grind all of the curing mixture ingredients together until all herbs are thoroughly ground into salt.

2. Remove any sections of excess fat from the duck legs (this can be rendered over very low heat to yield some of the duck fat required). Usually, this fat will be found on the underside of the legs and on the edges of the skin. You don't want the fat layer to be thicker than 1/4 inch.

3. Weigh the duck legs and then rub the curing mixture into them at a ratio of 1 oz of curing mixture per 1 lb of duck legs (you will have some of the curing salt left over).

4. Cover the salted duck legs and allow them to cure for 1 day before proceeding to the next step.

For Making the Confit

1. Preheat an oven to 190°F (this may be below the dial of some ovens, in which case turn it to the lowest setting, place an oven thermometer inside, and adjust to ensure that it is at 190°F).

2. Remove the salted duck legs and rinse under cool water to remove the excess salt. Pat completely dry with a clean towel.

3. Place the duck legs in a pan in which they fit snugly, with a couple inches of room above the legs, and then melt (if not warm already) and add the rendered duck fat.

4. Place the duck into the preheated oven and bake for 8 hours (the duck meat on the legs should be falling off of the bones; if it is not, return to the oven and continue). This step is often done overnight so that an oven is not tied up during service. However, it is very important to be comfortable with the safety and control of your oven prior to leaving it on overnight.

5. Once completely tender, the duck can be removed from the oven and stored, packed so that the fat completely covers the legs. It will last for a couple weeks or more.

Curing the duck legs (in mixing bowl), and finished confit de canard (preserved duck) packed in duck fat (note: the duck would be completely covered for long storage)

Sauté de Ris de Veau   CENTRAL EASTERN REGION

(SAUTÉED VEAL SWEETBREADS)

INGREDIENTS

For Soaking the Sweetbreads (should be soaked overnight)

3	lbs	Veal Sweetbreads
1.5	qts	water
1.5	oz	Salt

For Blanching the Sweetbreads

		Sweetbreads (see above), drained and rinsed
2	qts	Veal Stock, cold

For Sautéing the Sweetbreads

		Sweetbreads (see above), cleaned, cooled, and pressed
1	cup	Flour
1	tsp	salt
1.5	oz	Clarified Butter
4	oz	Bacon, medium diced
4	oz	Shallots, minced
2	oz	Carrots, minced
2	oz	Celery, minced
4	oz	Mushrooms, sliced
2	oz	Marsala Wine

Veal is prized in France not only for its tender and mild cuts that marry well with the many sauces of the French repertoire but also for the enlarged thymus gland of these younger animals, called the sweetbreads. When properly prepared, sweetbreads have great flavor and texture, and this recipe highlights these qualities by combining them with a typical French pan butter sauce.

YIELD: 15 portions (4 ounces/portion)

SPECIAL METHOD: Soaking Sweetbreads in Brine

COOKING METHOD SWEETBREADS (INITIAL): Blanching in Stock

SPECIAL METHOD SWEETBREADS: Pressing

COOKING METHOD SWEETBREADS (FINAL): Sautéing

PROCEDURE

For Soaking the Sweetbreads

1. Combine the sweetbreads, water, and salt in a nonreactive container, and place in the refrigerator overnight.

For Blanching the Sweetbreads

1. Drain the soaking water from the sweetbreads and set the sweetbreads into a small pot or pan, which will just hold the sweetbreads and cold veal stock for the blanching.
2. Bring the cold veal stock with the sweetbreads in it to a simmer over a medium-high flame, and simmer for 5 minutes.
3. Remove the sweetbreads from the blanching liquid and set aside to cool.
4. Once the sweetbreads are cool, trim the connective tissue from the surface of the sweetbreads (do not trim into the sweetbreads, which would result in their coming apart in pieces).
5. Place pieces of plastic wrap inside a 2-inch hotel pan, and put the trimmed sweetbreads in the pan.
6. Place another piece of plastic wrap over the sweetbreads, and place another 2-inch hotel pan on top of the sweetbreads. Put one or two #10 cans in the top hotel pan to weight down and compress the sweetbreads.
7. Place sweetbreads into the refrigerator, and leave overnight to compress.

For Sautéing the Sweetbreads

1. Remove the sweetbreads from the refrigerator, and take them out of the hotel pan. Slice into 1-inch pieces by cutting on a bias.
2. Combine the flour with the salt and mix thoroughly.
3. Heat a large sauté pan over medium-high heat and add half of the clarified butter.
4. Flour the sweetbreads lightly with the flour/salt mixture (tap against the side of the pan to ensure no excess flour), and sauté half in the large sauté pan, cooking until golden brown on each side. Remove the sweetbreads from the pan and place in a container set to hold briefly.

(continues)

Sauté de ris de veau (sautéed veal sweetbreads)

Sauté de Ris de Veau
(continued)

4 oz	Red Wine
24 fl oz	Veal Stock
6 oz	Whole Butter, salted, softened, and cut into 10 pieces
	Salt and Black Pepper, to taste

5. Continue to flour and sauté the remaining sweetbreads, using the additional clarified butter as needed until all of the sweetbread slices have been sautéed and removed from the pan (there should be some nice fronds on the bottom of the pan from this process—carefully control the heat so you don't burn any!).

6. Once all of the sweetbreads have been sautéed, add the diced bacon to the sauté pan; lower the heat to a medium flame to slowly render and brown bacon.

7. Once the bacon is rendered and crisp, add the minced shallots, carrots, and celery, and sweat the vegetables over a medium-low flame until all are tender.

8. Add the mushrooms and turn up the heat; sauté all ingredients together until they begin to caramelize.

9. Deglaze the pan with the marsala and red wine, using a wooden spoon to dissolve all of the fronds left on the bottom of the pan.

10. Once alcohol has reduced au sec (until almost dry), add the veal stock and reduce by half.

11. Once the veal stock has reduced by half, begin to finish with the whole butter pieces until a thickened sauce remains.

12. Return the sweetbreads to the pan to coat with sauce and to reheat slightly before serving.

Duxelles CENTRAL EASTERN REGION
(GROUND SEASONED MUSHROOM AND SHALLOT PASTE)

INGREDIENTS

2 oz	Butter, salted
2 oz	Shallots, minced
1/2 oz	Garlic Cloves, minced
1.5 lbs	Mushrooms (trimmings, stems, or whole), ground
1 tsp	Fresh Thyme Leaves, minced
1/2 tsp	Salt
1 tsp	Parsley, minced
1/2 tsp	Fresh Thyme Leaves, minced
	Salt, to taste

This recipe is a great example of the ingenuity of chefs who—rather than throw out the stems of mushrooms—turned them into a product that adds value to any food. A *duxelle* is a simple preparation and is very versatile in the kitchen.

YIELD: Approximately 1 pound or 1 pint

COOKING METHOD: Slow Sweating

PROCEDURE

1. Melt the butter over a medium-low flame in a sauté pan large enough to hold all of the ingredients, and add the shallots and garlic; gently sweat them until tender and translucent.

2. Add the ground mushrooms, the first tsp of minced thyme, and salt, and continue to cook over a medium-low flame to drive out most of the moisture in the mushrooms (this will take about 45 minutes if done properly—you do not want to color the pan). The finished duxelles should have a thick paste consistency.

3. Once reduced to a thick paste consistency, remove the pan from the heat and allow the mixture to cool before adding the parsley and remaining thyme.

4. Season duxelles to taste with salt, if needed.

Terrine de Ris de Veau aux Champignon

(VEAL MOUSSELINE WITH MUSHROOM PURÉE AND SWEETBREADS)

INGREDIENTS

For Preparing the Sweetbreads (this will need to be started 2 days in advance)

12	oz	Veal Sweetbreads
1	qt	Water
1	Tbsp	Salt
1	qt	Brown Stock
1	tsp	Salt

For Molding the Sweetbreads into a Circle

Cleaned Sweetbreads (see above)
Plastic Wrap
Water for Poaching

For Making the Mousseline

1	lb	Lean Veal, ground and chilled
2		Large Eggs Whites, chilled
6	oz	Mushroom Duxelle (see recipe)
6	oz	Crème Fraîche, chilled
1.5	tsp	Salt
2	tsp	Fresh Parsley, minced
1	tsp	Fresh Thyme, minced
1/2	tsp	Fresh Tarragon, minced
6	oz	Crème Fraîche, chilled and whipped to soft peaks
		Salt, to taste

For Blanching the Leek Greens and Spinach

6	oz	Leek Green Tops, no discolored ends or ripped sections (you will need approximately 2 typical bunches of leeks to yield this amount)
4	oz	Mature Spinach Leaves, veins removed (you will need to use the larger mature leaves and not baby spinach)
2	quarts	Water
1	Tbsp	Salt
		Ice Bath (for shocking)

Charcuterie is one of the disciplines of French cuisine that sets it apart from many others. There are seemingly endless variations of recipes that utilize and represent classic French foods. Whether you make a *terrine*, *galantine*, *ballotine*, or sausage, the opportunity to showcase skill and ingenuity is equally possible. This recipe uses some French classics to make a beautiful and delicious terrine and, at the same time, should impress upon anyone making it the complexity and skill of many French dishes.

YIELD: 1 terrine, which should yield approximately 12 portions (3–4 ounces/portion)

COOKING METHOD (SWEETBREADS): Poaching

MIXING METHOD (MOUSSELINE): Emulsification from Puréeing and Incorporation of Air from Whipping and Folding

COOKING METHOD (LEEKS AND SPINACH): Boiling/Blanching

COOKING METHOD (TERRINE): Baking in a Bain Marie

COOKING METHOD (MUSHROOMS): Reduction

MIXING METHOD (DRESSING): Emulsification from Blending

PROCEDURE

For Preparing the Sweetbreads

1. Combine the sweetbreads with water and salt in a nonreactive container; cover with plastic wrap and set in a refrigerator to soak overnight (this will draw out impurities from the sweetbreads).

2. After the sweetbreads have soaked overnight, discard the soaking water and rinse the sweetbreads under clean, cold water; set aside.

3. Place the brown stock and salt in a small pot and bring to a boil over high heat. Once boiling, lower the heat to poaching temperature.

4. Poach the sweetbreads for 5 minutes in the brown stock, and then remove and set aside to cool.

5. Once the sweetbreads have cooled enough to handle, use a sharp paring knife or boning knife to remove the thin membrane covering the sweetbreads.

6. Once the sweetbreads have been cleaned of the membrane, place the sweetbreads on a large sheet of plastic wrap and roll them tightly in the wrap to yield a cylinder slightly shorter in length than the terrine mold that will be used to cook and form the eventual terrine.

7. After tightly wrapping the sweetbreads with plastic, roll the sweetbreads on the counter while holding the ends of the plastic to seal the sweetbreads inside, and then tie the ends of the plastic with butcher's twine or more plastic wrap.

8. Using a pot large enough to hold the plastic-wrapped sweetbreads, fill it with enough water to comfortably poach the sweetbreads and place it over a high flame to bring the water to the poaching temperature (160–170°F).

(continues)

Terrine de Ris de Veau aux Champignon
(continued)

For Assembling and Cooking the Terrine (have all components set up prior to this step)

	Prepped and Formed Sweetbreads (see above)
	Prepared Veal Mousseline (see above)
	Blanched Leeks and Spinach (see above)
1	Terrine Mold

For Making the Dressing

.5	oz	Dried Cepes (also called Porcini) Mushrooms
1	cup	Brown Stock
2	oz	Shallots, chopped
2		Garlic Cloves, minced
3	oz	Sherry Vinegar
1	tsp	Dijon Mustard
1	tsp	Fresh Thyme
10	oz	Extra Virgin Olive Oil
		Salt and Pepper, to taste

For Plating the Terrine

		Cooked and Cooled Terrine (see above)
		Mushroom Vinaigrette (see above)
1	bunch	Chives, picked into 3-inch lengths

Laying the wrapped sweatbreads on a layer of the veal mousseline in terrine previously lined with blanched leeks (for the terrine de ris de veau aux champignon)

9. Once the water has reached the proper temperature, place the plastic-wrapped sweetbreads in the water and poach until they are just cooked through (150°F in the center), which should take about 10 to 12 minutes in the preheated water if the roll is 1.5 inches in diameter.

10. Once the sweetbreads are cooked, remove them from the water and set them in a refrigerator to cool completely before using inside the terrine.

For Making the Mousseline

1. Prechill the body and blade of a food processor by submerging them in ice water for 30 minutes before starting this procedure. (It is important to keep your forcemeat cold to form a stable emulsion—being careful not to overprocess your forcemeat also helps, so keep that in mind in the following steps!)

2. Place the lean veal, egg whites, and mushroom duxelle into the chilled food processor and, with the processor running slowly, pour the crème frâiche (in a small stream) into the puréeing meat to form a smooth emulsion. Stop the machine as soon as you have the crème frâiche incorporated.

3. Remove the mousseline from the food processor and transfer to a mixing bowl. Fold in the salt, minced herbs, and whipped crème friache.

4. Remove 1 oz of the forcemeat and poach—wrapped tightly in plastic—until it is cooked through (about 3 minutes). Remove it, allow to cool, and taste to determine if more salt needs to be added.

5. Cover the mixing bowl with plastic film, and place it in the refrigerator until you are ready to assemble the terrine.

For Blanching the Leek Greens and Spinach

1. Place a small pot on the stove and add the water and salt. Bring to a boil over a high flame.

2. Check the leeks to ensure that there are no degrading parts or discoloration, and then make a cut along the length of the leek greens to open each one up into a wider piece (like a small sheet).

3. Rinse the prepped leeks under warm water to remove any dirt, and then rinse the spinach leaves in warm water to clean as well.

4. Blanch each piece of leek in the boiling water until all are just tender but still retain their bright green color.

5. Shock the leeks in the ice bath as soon as they are removed from the boiling water, and set them aside to air-dry slightly before use.

6. Once the leeks have all been blanched and dried, rub the top of each leek section individually, which should separate the leek into two sections (each leek "leaf" is actually shaped like a flattened tube). These sections can then be pulled apart lengthwise to make two thinner pieces, one slightly longer than the other.

7. Repeat the same blanching procedure with spinach leaves, quickly blanching to wilt and soften, and then shock in the ice bath (these are not pulled into two pieces).

(continues)

*
Terrine de Ris de Veau aux Champignon
(continued)

For Assembling and Cooking the Terrine

1. Preheat the oven to 300°F and locate a pot to hold the water that will be used to cook the terrine in a water bath.

2. Place the pot on the stove and add a few gallons of water to it. Bring water to a boil to have it ready for the water bath.

3. Line the terrine mold with one unbroken sheet of plastic wrap, being careful to press the plastic wrap into the corners of the mold and pull the plastic wrap taut to prevent wrinkles as much as possible.

4. Place the mousseline inside the terrine mold, filling it a third of the way up with the mousseline and then stopping.

5. Remove the sweetbreads from the plastic so they can be wrapped in the spinach leaves.

6. On a clean, sanitized workspace, wrap the sweetbreads with the blanched spinach leaves, making sure to overlap the spinach leaves slightly to cover all parts of the sweetbreads.

7. Place the spinach-wrapped sweetbreads in the center of the terrine, and press down gently to secure them in the mousseline (already inside the terrine).

8. Add the remaining mousseline to the terrine (it can be piped in using a pastry bag, if desired), filling the mold and covering the spinach-wrapped sweetbreads completely.

9. Once all of the mousseline is added, use an offset spatula dipped in warm water to spread the mousseline flat.

10. Once the mousseline has been flattened, cover the top of the terrine with the extra plastic wrap that is hanging over the sides, and place the lid on the terrine.

11. Place the pan for holding the water and the terrine in the preheated oven, and put the terrine inside the pan.

12. Add enough of the preheated hot water (from step 2) to the holding pan so that the water level rises to just below the lid of the terrine.

13. Bake the terrine until the center internal temperature of the terrine reaches 140°F (this will take approximately 30 to 40 minutes, if water was preheated; the best way to monitor the temperature is to insert a digital probe in the center of the terrine that is connected to a programmable monitor with an alarm outside of the oven). Remove both the terrine and the water bath, and allow to cool for 15 minutes before removing the terrine from the water bath.

14. Place the terrine in a refrigerator to cool completely before moving to the next step (this will allow the terrine to set).

15. Once the terrine has cooled, remove it from the mold carefully and wrap the terrine with the blanched and separated leeks, overlapping each leek as it is laid—one after the other—along the length of the terrine (it is helpful to return the terrine to the mold after doing this to help form the leeks tightly to the terrine).

For Making the Dressing

1. Soak the cepes in the brown stock for at least an hour (longer is even better), and then strain the liquid into another container, discarding the last 1 oz or so (there is often some sand or dirt in the dried mushrooms).

(continues)

Terrine de Ris de Veau aux Champignon
(continued)

2. Place the retained mushroom/stock mixture in a small pot, along with the shallots and the garlic, and heat over a medium-low flame to bring to a gentle poach.

3. Slowly poach the mixture together until almost all of the water is gone (this should take approximately 40 minutes—remember that it's a gentle poach); all of the mushrooms and other ingredients should be very tender.

4. Once everything is tender and the liquid has nearly evaporated, remove it from the heat and add the sherry vinegar. Allow the mixture to cool completely (if you need it sooner, set it on an ice bath).

5. Place the cooled mushroom/sherry vinegar mixture into a blender, and add the mustard and fresh thyme.

6. With the blender running, add the extra virgin olive oil in a slow, steady stream to form an emulsion.

7. Season to taste with salt and pepper.

For Plating the Terrine

1. Remove the terrine from the mold and place it on a clean and sanitary cutting board.

2. Cut the terrine (mark it first for portion sizes by scoring the surface with a ruler) using a very sharp knife, and more of a sawing motion than a cutting motion, which will enable you to cut through the spinach and sweetbreads without deforming the mold.

3. Put about 1–1.5 oz of the dressing on the plate.

4. Place one slice of the terrine on top of the dressing, and garnish the plate by placing few pieces of the chives on the outside of the plate; serve.

Finished terrine de ris de veau aux champignon (veal mousseline terrine with sweatbreads and mushrooms) with mushroom vinaigrette

Poulet Sautée a la Normande   NORMANDY

(SAUTÉED CHICKEN BREAST WITH CAMEMBERT AND CALVADOS CREAM SAUCE)

INGREDIENTS

10		Chicken Breast Supremes from Fryer Chicken (about 6–7 oz each; also called airline breasts in the United States), wing bone frenched, skin on
1/2	tsp	Salt
1/4	tsp	Freshly Ground Black Pepper
3	oz	Clarified Butter
10	oz	Camembert Cheese, cut into 1/4-inch lengths
4	oz	Shallots, minced
8	oz	Calvados (Apple Brandy can be used as a substitute, if this is unavailable)
2	oz	Chicken Glaze (substitute 2 cups of chicken stock reduced to 2 oz, if this is unavailable)
20	oz	Heavy Cream
		Salt and Pepper, to taste

Poulet sautée a la Normande (sautéed chicken in the style of Normandy), served with baby carrots and a quenelle of mashed potatoes

Sautéed poultry, meat, and vegetable dishes are some of the preparations at which the French have excelled, and numerous examples could be given. In this example, some of the fine French products of the Normandy region come together to yield a rich and harmonious dish that displays the great dairy products and apple distillate of this region.

YIELD: 10 portions (approximately 8 ounces/portion)

COOKING METHOD: Sautéing Followed by Roasting to Finish the Chicken in the Oven

PROCEDURE

1. Preheat oven to 350°F.

2. Season the frenched chicken breasts with salt and pepper, and set aside.

3. Using two large sauté pans that can each hold 5 chicken breasts comfortably for sautéing (they should not be crowded in the pan or the recipe will need to be done in stages), add half of the clarified butter to each of the pans and heat over a medium-high flame until the butter is very hot. Place 5 of the seasoned chicken breasts into the pan, skin side down, and sauté until they become golden brown before turning over to do the same to the other side. Adjust heat as necessary to ensure that the pans do not become burnt during this process (the pans will be used to make the sauce).

4. As soon as the chicken breasts have been seared on both sides and colored well, remove them from the pan and set them skin side up on a 1/2 sheet pan or other suitable pan for roasting.

5. Place the chicken breasts in the preheated oven and roast them for 5 minutes before removing them and placing 1 oz of Camembert cheese on top of each breast. Set them aside as the sauce is made.

6. Using the same pans you used to sauté the chicken breasts, discard any excess fat remaining in the pan, except for a tablespoon or so, and return the pans to the stove over a high flame to reheat them.

7. Once the pans start to get hot, add the minced shallots and sauté them briefly until they just begin to color.

8. As soon as the shallots begin to color, add the calvados to the pan (be careful—the alcohol will flambé!). As soon as the flames die down, add the glaze and the cream to the pan while simultaneously scrubbing the bottom of the pan to dissolve the fronds left from the chicken into the sauce.

9. Once the cream sauce starts to simmer, turn down the heat so that the sauce very gently simmers and place the pan with the chicken breast and the cheese back in the oven.

10. Roast the chicken in the oven for an additional 2 to 3 minutes to finish cooking the breast and melt the cheese. Remove it from the oven once again.

11. Finish the sauce by reducing it to nappe (coats the back of a spoon) consistency, and then check to see if the sauce needs seasoning before serving the sauce along with the chicken.

Gnocchi à la Parisienne   Île de France
(Dumpling Made from Pastry)

INGREDIENTS

For Making the Pâté à Choux

12	oz	Water
1	Tbsp	Salt
6	oz	Unsalted Butter
8	oz	A.P. Flour
1	oz	Dijon Mustard
5	oz	Comté Cheese, shredded fine
6		Eggs
2	Tbsp	Fresh Chives, minced
2	tsp	Fresh Tarragon, minced

For Simmering the Gnocchi

3	gallons	Water
1/4	cup	Salt

For Sautéing the Gnocchi

8	oz	Unsalted Butter
		Cooled Gnocchi (see above)
2	Tbsp	Fresh Chives, minced
		Salt and Freshly Ground Black Pepper, to taste

One example of a French adaptation of an Italian specialty is this version of gnocchi, which is made with pâté à choux, which is piped out of a pastry bag into boiling water to make the classic-shaped dumpling. These dumplings are richer than the traditional potato version of Italian heritage, but they have similar versatility in applications and are excellent simply sautéed in butter, as in this recipe.

YIELD: 10 portions (6–7 ounces/portion)

SPECIAL METHOD: Pâté à Choux Dough Method

COOKING METHOD FOR GNOCCHI (INITIAL): Boiling

COOKING METHOD FOR GNOCCHI (FINAL): Sautéing

PROCEDURE

For Making the Pâté à Choux

1. Place the water, salt, and unsalted butter in a small pot, and place over a high flame; bring mixture to a boil.

2. As soon as the mixture reaches a boil, carefully pour in the flour and, using a wooden spoon, begin stirring immediately. Lower the heat to a medium-low flame. (The mixture will thicken almost immediately and must be stirred constantly to prevent it from sticking and coloring against the pan.)

3. Continue to cook over a low flame—while stirring—until the dough pulls away from the pan and a film of dough develops on the inside of the pan (this will take approximately 5 minutes, so be patient!). The dough will stop sticking to the pan and pull away before the film develops, so don't stop when the dough stops sticking to the sides.

4. Once the dough has been cooked properly in the pan, transfer the dough to an electric mixer bowl. Add the mustard and grated cheese while mixing the dough on a low speed.

5. After the mustard and cheese have been incorporated into the dough, add the eggs one at a time with the mixer running at low speed, and allow the dough to fully incorporate each egg before adding another.

6. Add the minced fresh herbs once all of the eggs have been incorporated, and mix on low to combine; shut off the mixer.

7. Transfer the dough to a pastry bag (or bags) with a large round pastry tip, and put aside to rest while water for cooking is set up.

For Simmering the Gnocchi

1. Make sure everything is in place for removing the gnocchi, and put them on a sheet pan to cool.

2. Place a large pot filled with 3 gallons of water on the stove, and add the salt to it. Heat over a high flame to bring the water to a simmer (the water should be approximately 180°F to cook the gnocchi—a rolling boil will not enable you to determine whether the gnocchi are done, and too low of a temperature will result in soft gnocchi).

Process of cutting pâté à choux as it is piped out of a pastry bag into boiling water to cook gnocchi à la parisienne (dumpling made from pastry)

(continues)

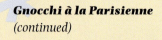

Gnocchi à la Parisienne
(continued)

3. Once the water comes up to temperature, adjust the flame to maintain the heat as the gnocchi are cooked. Using the pastry bag, pipe just enough gnocchi to lightly coat the bottom of the pot by squeezing the bag with one hand while cutting the protruding dough (after about an inch of dough comes out) with a knife held in the other hand. As you do this, move the bag around the pot so that the dropping gnocchi do not fall on top of one another (otherwise, they will stick), and stop as soon as you have about 20 in the pot or when you have been cutting and dropping them into the water for about 1 minute—whichever comes first (speed is a virtue in this business!). You will need to do these in batches to cook them all (you can also get multiple pots of water going to do this faster).

4. Once a batch of gnocchi is dropped, wait until the gnocchi rise to the surface (this is why you don't want the water boiling: you wouldn't be able to tell when this happens). They will sink when first dropped in the water; when they rise, they need to cook for about another minute, and then they can be scooped out using a strainer, drained quickly, and placed on a sheet pan to cool.

5. Continue to cook all of the gnocchi dough as described in steps 3 and 4. When all are done, set the sheet pan in a cooler to cool the gnocchi completely before using them (they can also be frozen at this stage by patting them dry, laying them in single layers, and wrapping them tightly with plastic wrap before freezing).

For Sautéing the Gnocchi

1. This step will need to be done in batches, as a typical sauté pan will not be able to accommodate this much gnocchi. Four batches should be sufficient if you use larger sauté pans (14 to 16 inches); if you use 10-inch sauté pans, do this in eight batches.

2. Be sure to check that the gnocchi are dry after cooling. If not, pat them dry with a clean towel (they can also be lightly coated with olive oil, if needed—if they are at all wet, they will stick to the sauté pan and the results will not be good).

3. Add 2 oz of the butter to the large sauté pan, and place over a medium-high flame to melt the butter.

4. As soon as the butter has melted, add the gnocchi to the pan and keep the pan in constant motion as the butter heats—this will prevent the gnocchi from sticking (unless they are wet!).

5. As the pan heats up, the gnocchi will begin to brown; continual motion will allow you to lightly brown them all over.

6. As soon as they are colored, remove the pan from the heat and add some of the minced chives; season with salt and pepper.

7. Turn out the gnocchi to the serving dish, and serve at once.

8. Repeat steps 3 through 7 with the remaining gnocchi to finish.

✳ Purée de Céleri-Rave The North
(Celery Root Purée)

INGREDIENTS

2	lbs	Celery Root, trimmed of outer tough skin and diced large (you will need about 3 lbs of celery root to yield this amount)
10	oz	Russet Potato, diced large
8	oz	Yellow Onion, sliced thin
1	qt	Water
2	cups	Chicken Stock
1	Tbsp	Salt
8	oz	Cream
		Salt and Pepper, to taste

The use of many vegetables not common to the United States as accompaniments is one of the distinguishing aspects of French cuisine. Vegetables are used in season and are selected with consideration for their harmony with what they are served. This recipe is an example of using a vegetable to provide texture and a rich yet mild flavor that would complement grilled meat or panfried fish quite nicely.

YIELD: 3 pounds, or 12 portions (4 ounces/portion)

COOKING METHOD: Simmering

PROCEDURE

1. Place the cleaned and cut celery root into a pot large enough to hold all of the ingredients, along with the potato and the onion.
2. Cover the celery root and the potato and onion mixture with the water and chicken stock, add the salt, and place the pot over a high flame; bring mixture to a boil.
3. Once the mixture reaches a boil, turn the heat down and simmer the mixture until the celery root and potatoes are completely tender (this will take about 25 minutes).
4. Strain the mixture, and reserve the cooking liquid by capturing the resulting broth in a container below the strainer; allow the mixture to drain for a couple of minutes to get rid of excess water.
5. Pass the mixture through a food mill and into a mixing bowl.
6. Heat the cream in a small sauté pan over a medium flame until it just begins to steam, and then remove it from the heat.
7. After puréeing the celery root mixture, add the heated cream to the celery root purée, stirring with a whisk to incorporate it fully.
8. If mixture is too thick, add some of the reserved cooking liquid.
9. Season to taste with salt and pepper, and then serve.

✳ Artichauts de Blanc Northwest
(Artichoke Bottoms Cooked to Remain White)

INGREDIENTS

1.5	gallons	Water
3	oz	Flour
6	oz	Lemon Juice
3	Tbsp	Salt
10		Large Artichokes

Artichokes are a common vegetable throughout France—when in season—and the French have taken a special interest in learning how to cook them to retain their best qualities. Cooking in a *blanc* is performed to preserve the white or near-white color of a vegetable, which yields the most presentable results possible. This recipe will yield beautiful artichoke bottoms that can be used in a wide variety of applications and will also help you develop finer knife skills—trimming artichokes requires both hand strength and finesse.

YIELD: 10

COOKING METHOD: Cooking in a Blanc

(continues)

Artichauts de Blanc
(continued)

PROCEDURE

1. To prepare the blanc for cooking the artichokes, whisk 2 cups of water into the flour, and then transfer the flour water to a pot large enough to hold everything.

2. Whisk the remaining water into the flour water, add the lemon juice and the salt, and place the pot over a high flame; bring to simmer.

3. To trim the artichokes, first cut off the top third of each using a sharp chef's knife or strong/stiff bread knife, removing a large part of each of the petals as you do so.

4. Cut approximately half an inch off the bottom of each stem, and discard it.

5. Next, remove the outermost layer of the petals (now the harder work begins!).

6. Using a strong paring knife, trim away the petals of the artichoke until you reach the solid bottom and begin to expose the choke.

7. Trim the stem—using either a peeler or the paring knife—down to the whiter portion of the stem.

8. Once the stem has been trimmed, all of the petals have been trimmed, and the choke is exposed, clean the artichoke bottoms.

9. Add the cleaned artichokes to the simmering pot, and place another pot or lid on top; cook until the artichoke bottoms are tender throughout (start checking them after about 15–20 minutes).

10. Once the artichokes are tender throughout, remove them from the blanc. When the blanc has cooled to room temperature, the artichokes can be returned to it and held for an hour or so, if needed.

Trimmed artichokes for artichauts de blanc

Clafouti aux Myrtilles CENTRAL FRANCE (LIMOUSIN)
(BLUEBERRY CLAFOUTI CUSTARD)

INGREDIENTS

For Making the Pâté Sucrée via the Creaming Method

6	oz	Granulated Sugar
14	oz	Unsalted Butter, at room temperature
1		Egg
1	tsp	Vanilla Extract
1	lb	Bread Flour (you can substitute A.P., if this is unavailable; regardless of which kind you use, you will need a little extra for rolling out the completed dough)
1.5	lbs	Uncooked Beans (for blind baking the crust)

For Making the Custard Batter

1	oz	Flour
12	oz	Granulated Sugar
6		Eggs
8	oz	Heavy Cream
12	oz	Whole Milk

For Filling and Final Baking of the Clafoutis

1 lb 4 oz	Blueberries (ideally, fresh blueberries; if using frozen ones, defrost them first and drain off any excess water)

A clafouti is a custard in which whole pieces of fruit are set, sometimes in a pastry shell (as in this recipe). The most common clafouti is made with fresh cherries, and this recipe could be easily adapted to include cherries in place of blueberries. The dough used in this recipe, called *pâté sucrée,* is commonly used in French cuisine to line tarts and other liquid-filled pastries.

YIELD: Two 9-inch clafoutis, or approximately 16 portions (4–5 ounces/portion)

MIXING METHOD (DOUGH): Creaming

COOKING METHOD (CUSTARD BASE): Tempering

PRECOOKING METHOD: Blind Baking of Crust

FINAL COOKING METHOD: Baking Liquid-Filled Crust

PROCEDURE

For Making the Pâté Sucrée via the Creaming Method

1. Using the paddle attachment, cream the butter and sugar together in a mixing bowl until completely combined.

2. Add the egg and vanilla extract to the mixing bowl—while it is running—and allow the machine to incorporate them fully before proceeding to the next step.

3. Add the flour in batches (approximately 1/4 pound at a time), allowing the flour to become incorporated into the dough before adding more.

4. Once all of the flour has been incorporated, slop the machine and remove the dough. Wrap it in plastic wrap and place it in a refrigerator, to allow the dough to rest for at least 20 minutes before rolling it out for the crust.

For Making the Custard Batter

1. Combine the flour, sugar, and eggs in a mixing bowl; whisk to combine well, and then set aside.

2. In a small pot, add the heavy cream and milk, and bring this mixture to just below a boil. As soon as it just below boiling, remove it from the heat to prevent it from boiling over.

3. Slowly temper in the dairy mixture to the egg/sugar/flour mixture by whisk, making sure to whisk constantly.

4. Set the custard mixture aside while the crust is blind baked.

For Blind Baking the Crust

1. Preheat the oven to 350°F, and prepare two 9-inch, 2-piece tart pans by spraying the insides and bottoms with pan spray.

2. Remove the chilled and rested dough from the refrigerator, and place it on the workbench along with some extra flour for flouring the bench.

(continues)

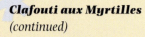

Clafouti aux Myrtilles
(continued)

3. Divide the dough into two pieces and roll each out into 1/4-inch-thick circles, making sure to flour underneath the dough as you do this so it doesn't stick to the bench (you will want to have long, thin spatulas on hand to slide under the dough circles and turn them as they are being rolled out).

4. Once the dough is rolled out carefully, roll one piece onto a large rolling pin and then unroll it over the assembled tart pan.

5. Once the dough is over the tart pan, carefully lift up the outer edges of the dough and tuck it into all of the corners of the tart pan, leaving the excess hanging over the edge.

6. Once the dough has been tucked into all of the corners, take the rolling pin and roll it over the top of the tart pan; this will cut the dough right at the edge of the tart pan and make for a clean edge.

7. Repeat steps 4–6 with the second piece of dough and the second tart pan.

8. Place parchment paper on top of each tart dough, and fill the tart pans with uncooked beans; place in the preheated oven and bake for 15 minutes, or until tart dough has just set.

9. Remove the tart doughs from the oven and set aside to cool.

For Filling and Final Baking of the Clafoutis

1. Lower the oven temperature to 325°F.

2. Remove the beans and parchment paper from the tart pans (the beans can be saved for blind baking in the future).

3. Spread the blueberries evenly over the two tarts, place the tarts on a sheet pan, and finish the final work close to the oven.

4. Carefully pour the custard mix into the tart pans, up to 1/4 inch from the top (do not fill them more, or they will boil over), and place them in the preheated oven. Bake for 30 minutes, or until the custard sets.

5. Once the custard sets, remove the clafoutis from the oven and set them on a cooling rack to cool completely before removing from the tart pans.

6. Once the clafoutis have cooled, remove them from the pans by pressing on the bottom ring of each pan (if the dough appears to stick anywhere on the top, use a paring knife to separate the sticking point from the pan—this may happen if the custard boils over and gets in between the crust and the pan).

7. To remove each clafouti from the bottom piece of its pan, a long metal spatula can be inserted underneath to slide it off and onto a cutting board or cardboard cake circle.

8. To yield portions described at the beginning of the recipe, cut each clafouti into 8 pieces.

Clafouti aux myrtilles (blueberry clafouti)

Raffalait THE NORTH
(PRESERVED AND CARAMELIZED MILK)

INGREDIENTS

2	qts	Whole Milk
1.5	lbs	Sugar
1/8	tsp	Baking Soda
1	tsp	Vanilla Extract or 1 Vanilla Bean

The northern part of France has a decidedly sweet tooth, and a number of preparations for pastries and other sweet dishes appear regularly in the local cuisine. One of the most common sweets in this region is the local *gaufres,* which typically are eaten with cream and sugar. This recipe is often served with pancakes, resulting in another example of the wonderful combination of dairy and sugar.

YIELD: 2 quarts

COOKING METHOD: Gentle Simmering

PROCEDURE

1. In a heavy-bottomed pot that is large enough to hold all of the ingredients, add the milk and place it over a medium-high flame to bring it to a boil (be around to ensure that it doesn't boil over as it comes close to a boil).

2. Once the milk comes to a near boil, add the sugar and the baking soda; whisk well to combine, and melt the sugar in the milk for a few minutes.

3. Once the mixture again begins to come to a boil, turn the heat down and gently simmer the mixture, stirring occasionally at first and more constantly as it begins to thicken (it will take approximately 30–40 minutes to do so).

4. Once the mixture begins to thicken, continue to cook it over the lower flame and stir until it begins to caramelize and turn golden brown.

5. Upon caramelizing, remove it from the heat and allow it to cool completely.

6. Add the vanilla extract, and the mixture is ready to be used.

SUMMARY

French cuisine is thought by many to be the pinnacle of world cuisines, and this reputation has been earned by a history of great chefs, a public passion for the best, and a drive for organization and continuity that enabled it all. France has a strong tradition of great chefs who have laid the foundation for the cuisine of today, with much of the early chefs' efforts focused on the organization of operations and the regimented training of later chefs, who shifted the focus to the quality of the foods and their presentations. The stage was set by the advent of the restaurant in France, followed by the French Revolution; the resulting receptive audience has since become part of the character of France, where good food and high quality are proud components of the national spirit.

REVIEW QUESTIONS

1. What was the significance of the wedding of Catherine de' Medici and King Henry II of France in the development of French cuisine?

2. How did the evolution of the restaurant in France connect to the development of the country's cuisines?

3. In which part of France would sauerkraut and sausage typically be found on a menu?

4. In which area(s) of France is butter the normal fat used for cooking, and in which is it olive oil?

COMMON TERMS, FOODS, AND INGREDIENTS

The following terms are commonly used in French cuisine and are an important component in understanding the naming of dishes and the deciphering of menus.

✳ Ingredients and Products

agneau – Lamb

anguille – Eel

artichaut – Artichoke

asperges – Asparagus

betterave – Beet

blé – Wheat

bœuf – Beef

brochet – Pike

buerre – Butter

calvados – Apple brandy from Normandy region

carotte – Carrot

champignon – General term for mushroom

champignon de Paris – Button mushroom

Charollais – Breed of cattle prized for flavorful and tender meat

châtaigne – Chestnut

chou – Cabbage

choufleur – Cauliflower

cidre – Fermented juice of pears or apples

coquille Saint Jacques – Scallop

crème – Cream

crème de cassis – Liqueur made from black currants

Dijon – City in central France in which wine mustard is produced under the same name

endive – Belgian endive

foie gras (de canard, de oie) – Fattened liver (of duck, of goose)

fruit de mer – "Fruits of the sea"; seafood

gros Bourgogne – Large snails from the Burgundy region

guérande – Prized sea salt from Brittany's coast

homard – Lobster

huitre – Oyster

jambon – Smoked ham

kirch – Cherry brandy

lardons – Bacon

lentilles vertes du Puy – Prized green lentils from the south central region

mâche – Corn lettuce or lamb's lettuce

marc – Type of distillate made from the fermentation of leftover skins or grapes from wine making

massepain – Almond paste (marzipan)

merlu – Hake

miel – Honey

morille – Morel

morue – Salt cod

moule – Mussel

noix – Walnut

nouilles – Noodles

oie – Goose

oignons – Onions

palourde – Clam

Pernod – Anise-flavored liqueur

petit pois – English pea

plie – Plaice; fish in the flounder family caught in the English Channel

poire – Pear

poireau – Leek

pomme – Apple

pomme de terre – Potato

porc – Pork

poulet – Chicken

prune – Plum

Saint-Pierre – John Dory

saumon – Salmon

schnapps – Fruit distillate

truffle – Name of tuber-shaped aromatic fungus prized in France; also called *truffle* in the United States

truite – Trout

✳ Preparations and Methods

aioli – Emulsion made from garlic and olive oil, often with the addition of eggs (much like mayonnaise)

aligot – Mashed potatoes flavored with cheese and garlic; from the south central mountain region

artichauts de blanc – Artichokes cooked to remain white (cooked in a blanc)

au sec – Nearly dry; a term used to describe the amount of reduction in a liquid just before the pan dries

blanc – Method of cooking or blanching white vegetables in water to which an acid and flour have been added; preserves the color of the vegetables

bouillabaisse – Fisherman's stew from the southern Mediterranean region, colored and flavored with saffron

(à la) bordelaise – made in the style of Bordeaux; most often means that a dish includes a wine sauce that has been flavored with shallots, thyme, and stock or marrow

(à la) bourguignonne – In the style of Burgundy, typically denoting that a dish is cooked with red wine and includes mushrooms, onions, and bacon

(à la) cabonnade – Term describing a dish cooked with beer, onions, and often mustard; from the north

cassoulet – Dish of stewed beans and various meats; from the southwest region

Champagne – Name of region and of sparkling wine from same region in northern France

chaudiere – Rustic fisherman's stew from northern part of the country

choucroute – Sauerkraut; fermented (soured) cabbage

clafouti – Baked custard typically made with cherries; from the south central mountain region

clafouti aux myrtilles – Clafouti with blueberries

confit – General term used to describe a preserve; most often used to describe duck, goose, or pork cooked and preserved in their own fat

confit de canard – Duck legs cooked and preserved in their own fat

consommé – Clarified flavorful stocks garnished with various ingredients and cuts

coq au vin – Cockerel stewed in red wine

crème fraîche – Clotted, soured cream

crêpe – Thin, delicate pancake, often used in sweet preparations by wrapping these around fillings or layering with other ingredients

croustade – Rustic pastry wrapped around various sweet fillings; from southwestern region. Also a term that describes an edible container used to hold other foods.

duxelle – Ground mushrooms and shallots cooked in butter and finished with herbs (and sometimes cream)

escargot – Broiled snails stuffed with garlic and herb butter

fondue – Melted; term is used to describe melted cheese used for dipping other ingredients

galette – Round, thin cake or savory pancake

galettes au jambon, au fromage et a l'oeuf – Buckwheat pancakes filled with ham, eggs, and cheese

gaufres – Waffles

gratin – Browned crust formed on top of foods from intense heat from above or a very hot oven

gross pieces – Name given to elaborate decorations used in classical French banquet or court cuisine; rarely created today

huiles de cepes – Oil infused with cepes (wild mushrooms)

kig ha farz – Breton stew made with beef, salt pork, potatoes, onions, garlic, and leeks, stewed with a sack of buckwheat porridge and eaten together when finished

(à la) limousine – In the style of Limousin; typically denotes that a dish is served with braised red cabbage and chestnuts

macaroon – Meringue flavored with almond

madeleine – Scalloped, shell-shaped cake with lemon flavor

matafans – Cornmeal pancake

meringue – Stiffly whipped egg white and sugar

(en) meurette – Dish served in the style of Burgundy; that is, served with red wine sauce

mousse – Light and air-filled food made from folding in whipped cream and/or egg whites

mousseline de saumon aux poireau – Salmon mousseline with creamed leeks

nappe – Term that describes the proper consistency of a sauce so that it will coat the food it is intended to be served with yet be thin enough to flow naturally; often described as the thickness required to coat and cling to the back of a spoon

pain d'espices – Ginger-spiced bread from the north

pissaladière – Flatbread topped with onions, capers, and anchovies; from the southern Mediterranean region

pistou – Paste made of basil, garlic, and olive oil; from the southern Mediterranean region

poulet sauté a la normande – Sautéed chicken in the style of Normandy

quenelle – Dumpling; typically formed into three-sided shape using two spoons

quiche – Pastry shell with savory custard filling

quiche Lorraine – Quiche made with bacon

raclette – Dish of boiled potatoes with melted raclette cheese

raffolait – Thickened, caramelized milk

ragoût – Stewed

ratatouille – Stewed vegetable recipe from the southern Mediterranean region; made with zucchini, tomatoes, eggplant, onions, peppers, and garlic

rôti – Roast

rotisserie – Rotating oven or spit oven

rôtisseur – Grill or rotisserie cook in the brigade system

roux – Equal parts by weight clarified butter and flour (though often slightly more flour), cooked to varying degrees and used as a thickener

sauce mignonette – Vinegar infused with coarse black pepper and shallots, used as an accompaniment to oysters on the half shell

sauté – To cook quickly in a hot pan with little fat

sauté de ris de veau – Sautéed veal sweetbreads (thymus glands)

tapenade – Paste made of olives, capers, garlic, and olive oil; from the southern Mediterranean region

terrine – Rectangular-shaped mold used to pack and serve cold preparations

terrine de ris de veau aux champignon – Veal terrine with sweetbreads and mushrooms

✳ Charcuterie and Cheeses

andouillettes de mâcon – Small, smoked pork sausage from Burgundy region

ardi gasna – Basque name for sheep's milk cheeses

aspic – Gelatin set consommé and used to glaze cold charcuterie products

ballotine – Boned, stuffed, and rolled poultry, often served hot

Bleu d'Auvergne – Rich, creamy, and pungent blue-veined cheese from the south central mountain region

bresi – Cured and smoked beef

Camembert – Name of rich cow's milk cheese produced originally in village of same name in Normandy

Cantal – Cow's milk cheese found in varying stages of maturity (and thus with a stronger taste in longer-aged selections) from the southern central mountains

charcuterie – General term for foods made from forcemeats and other preservation techniques, such as sausages, pâtés, ballotines, galantines, mousselines, and terrines (see specific listings)

chèvre – Goat cheese

Comté – Excellent melting cheese from the Jura region; made from cow's milk and formed into very large wheels, often used in making fondue

epoisses – Strong cheeses from Burgundy region; both rich and salty

galantine – Boned, stuffed, or rolled poultry (typically) cooked and then chilled and served cold with aspic glaze

gournay – Soft, rich cow's milk cheese from Normandy region used to make Boursin cheese when blended with various herbs and spices

jambon de Bayonne – Prized hams of Basque area in southwest region

livarot – Strong, ripened cow's milk cheese from Normandy

louquenkas – Garlic-flavored sausage from the southwest region

mousseline – Lightened preparation from addition of whipped heavy cream or egg whites; term commonly used to describe forcemeats with cream that provides the fat for the emulsion

Neufchâtel – Creamy cow's milk cheese from Normandy region; typically heart shaped

pâté – Potted meat; typically made with smooth forcemeat with a significant portion of fat incorporated into the preserve, making this a rich and flavorful food

pâté de foie gras – Potted forcemeat made with fattened goose or duck liver

Roquefort – Strong blue-veined sheep's milk cheese produced in southern France

rosette de Lyon – Salami-like forcemeat from Lyon in the central eastern region

sabodet – Strong pork sausage made from the head and skin of the pig and typically served hot

Saint-Nectaire – Rich, semihard cow's milk cheese from the south central mountain region

saucisse de Morteau – Smoked plump pork sausage

saucisson – Sausage

tomme de Savoie – Mild, excellent melting cow's milk cheese from the Savoy region

✳ Cuisine Culture and French Chefs

apprenti – Cook apprentice in brigade system

boucher – Butcher in brigade system

boulanger – Baker in brigade system

brigade system – Kitchen organizational system created by Escoffier; designed after a military system in which the chef is the general, and organized in a way to make the staff as efficient as possible

Carême, Marie-Antoine – Famous French chef credited with developing mother sauces, inventing the wedding cake, and refining the cuisine of his day

chef de cuisine – Kitchen chef in the brigade system who would oversee the daily operation of the staff and food production

chef de partie – Senior chef in the brigade system

communard – Cook who prepared the food for the staff in brigade system

entremetier – Entrée cook in the brigade system

Escoffier, Georges Auguste – Famous French chef credited with developing the brigade system for organizing a large kitchen operation and with refining the cuisine of his day

garde manger – Pantry supervisor in the brigade system

haute cuisine – High cuisine or grand cuisine that developed in the French hotels and is now referred to as classical French cuisine

La Varenne, François Pierre – Author of the book *Le Cuisinier François* that has been identified as one of the turning points in the development of French cuisine

légumier – Cook responsible for cooking the vegetables in the brigade system

nouvelle – Young; this term has been used to describe the emergence of a lighter cooking style that focused more on quality ingredients and less on heavy sauces. This style has grown in popularity within the last century in France and beyond.

pâtissier – Pastry cook in the brigade system

Point, Fernand – Chef with a philosophy of not wavering from using the very best products, handling them the best way, and cooking them to highlight their qualities, not to mask them. He also trained a number of other chefs who have themselves gone on to become highly regarded.

poissonnier – Fish cook in the brigade system

potager – Soup cook in the brigade system

restaurant – Translates as "restorative"; this was originally a place to eat a simple bite that would provide the fuel needed to get home for the real food. It evolved into what we know it as today: a place to go to enjoy some of the best food, made by professionals.

rôtisseur – Grill or rotisserie cook in the brigade system

saucier – Cook responsible for making the sauces in the brigade system

sous chef de cuisine – Deputy kitchen chef who is in charge of the kitchen in the brigade system when the chef de cuisine is not present

CHAPTER 6

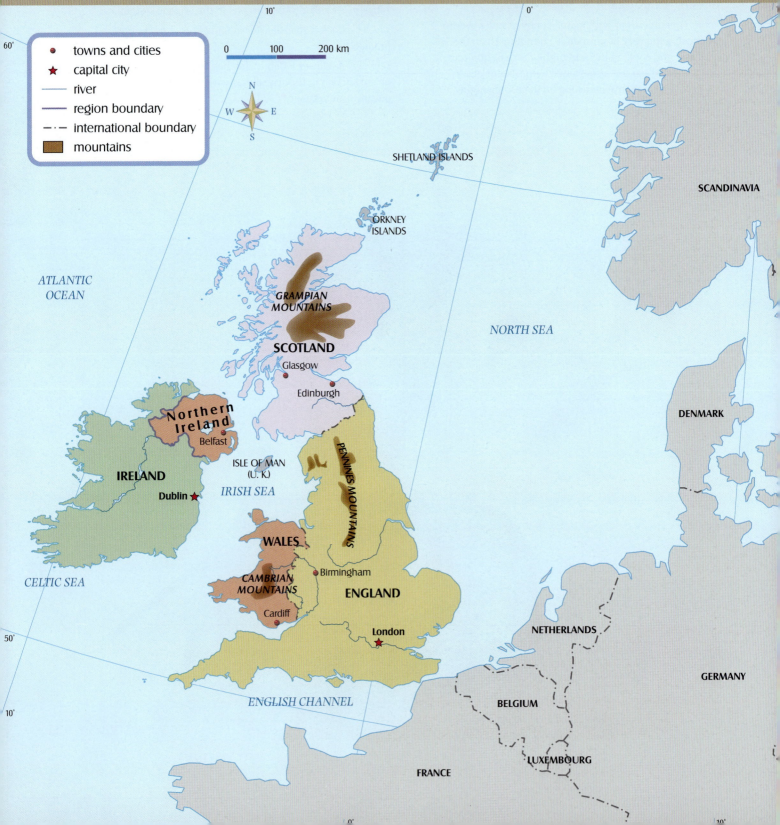

Legend:
- towns and cities
- ★ capital city
- river
- region boundary
- international boundary
- mountains

0   100   200 km

N
W   E
S

ATLANTIC OCEAN

SHETLAND ISLANDS

SCANDINAVIA

ORKNEY ISLANDS

GRAMPIAN MOUNTAINS

SCOTLAND

Glasgow

Edinburgh

NORTH SEA

DENMARK

Northern Ireland

Belfast

IRELAND

Dublin ★

ISLE OF MAN (U. K.)

IRISH SEA

PENNINES MOUNTAINS

CELTIC SEA

WALES

CAMBRIAN MOUNTAINS

Cardiff

Birmingham

ENGLAND

London ★

NETHERLANDS

GERMANY

BELGIUM

ENGLISH CHANNEL

LUXEMBOURG

FRANCE

Cuisines of the British Isles

OBJECTIVES

Upon completion of this chapter, you will be able to

- explain what makes the cuisines of the British Isles unique.
- discuss the common cooking methods used in these traditional cuisines.
- recognize the common recipes found in British, Irish, and Scottish cuisines.
- produce a variety of recipes common to the British Isles.
- define the terms listed at the conclusion of the chapter.

INTRODUCTION

The cuisines of Britain, Ireland, Scotland, and Wales provide the basis for a cooking style that reminds people of the purpose of food, comfort, and nourishment. The countries that make up the British Isles have storied histories and have followed very different paths. Britain became one of the greatest empires and colonized countries all over the world, including neighboring Ireland, Scotland, and Wales. This history of colonization has played a significant role in the development of modern British cuisine, whereas in Ireland, and to a lesser extent in Scotland and Wales, the cuisine developed predominately as a peasant/poor cuisine that focused mostly on survival and much less on indulging or celebrating. Although these countries have followed different paths to their present-day cuisines, many aspects tie all of them together—and indeed, several of the classic dishes are found in all of the countries. The following chapter examines these cuisines and the components that make them unique.

HISTORIC CULINARY INFLUENCES

The British Isles have been conquered by many nations and also have been the conqueror in more recent times. Both of these aspects have played significant roles in the development of the cuisines of these countries, and the historical influences are examined in the following section.

Ancient Ancestors

The inhabitants of the British Isles subsisted off of the land, as most prehistoric cultures did, relying on oatmeal porridge, flatbreads, and whatever wild game, vegetables, and fruits could be gathered or hunted. Some of the foods known to have been part of the diet at this time included wild boar, hare, duck, pigeon, salmon, trout, eels, apples, and hazelnuts. The original inhabitants of these islands were either overrun or assimilated by the first invading group, who are referred to collectively as the Celts; their lineage is still significant in Ireland, Scotland, Wales, and the Cornish area of England. The Celts resisted invading other peoples over the centuries, and thus they were pushed into the more remote areas of the British Isles. The Celts are known to have employed a method of boiling foods in large cauldrons by adding stones from a fire. The cuisine that developed following the Celts' arrival still remains in much of the spirit of the region's cuisine today, as seen in its reliance on the immediate land and other simple methods.

Ancient Romans

In AD 43, during the height of the Roman Empire, its reign extended into the British Isles; the Romans then ruled the region for 350 years. During this period of rule, the native Britons learned a great deal from their Roman conquerors and were introduced to many new ingredients that became part of their regular diet.

The Romans introduced numerous fruit trees, grapes, and thus vinegar and wines, as well as many new herbs including marjoram, thyme, and sage. The pungent sauce very common in Roman cuisine at the time, called garam (made from salted and fermented fish), was also introduced to the Britons, and it was used to flavor (some would say to mask) meats and poultry. Romans also are believed to have introduced the process of making more complex cheeses to the natives, one component of the cuisines of this region that is highly regarded to this day.

Invading Germanic Tribes

Germanic tribes from mainland Europe began to invade the British Isles in the fourth century and eventually became a dominant force on British soil as the Roman Empire faded. The two main tribes were the Angles and the Saxons, which is where the term *Anglo-Saxon*—used to describe descendents of these people—comes from. The Anglo-Saxons were an aggressive people, and they quickly pushed the native populations of present-day Great Britain into the northern mountains that make up present-day Scotland and the western mountains that make up present-day Wales.

The Anglo-Saxons introduced wheat breads, beer making, and additional processes in cheese making and techniques in butter making that would become part of the character of the cuisine of this region.

Viking Raiders

The Vikings descended upon the British Isles in the late eighth century, and through military superiority conquered many of the lands they raided for the next 300 years. The Vikings generally looked for goods to take back home and did not establish major popula-

tions in the lands they invaded. They did, however, expose the people they raided to the goods that they brought with them. Thus, the natives learned about the production of salted and dried cod, herring, and smoked salmon. The Viking raiders also introduced some of their preservation techniques to the native peoples and imported a number of the berries and preserves from Scandinavia to the isles, and these techniques—as well as the preservation of fish from salting, drying, and smoking—are still common in the British Isles today.

Normans

In AD 1066, a Norman general called William the Conqueror (also called William the Bastard—depending on one's point of view, I guess!) invaded England and proceeded to take control of much of the country. The Normans, who lived in neighboring France and were originally from Scandinavia, were an organized and settled people who brought these traits to England. They ruled present-day England and introduced a system of ownership and stewardship of the lands they conquered. The Normans are believed to have introduced peas to the British Isles, which were adopted by cuisines throughout the region. They also ate in courses rather than all at once, and brought this custom—as well as the techniques of making pastries and custards—to the British Isles, two techniques that were widely adopted across the land.

The Norman system of land organization is considered by many to be the beginning of the class-based system that would later prevent many laypeople from being able to live off of local products. Because this developed into a system of lords and nobles ruling the arable land, and peasants living on this land but outlawed from "stealing" animals and other food products, the gap between available, nourishing foods for those who ruled and those who were ruled widened dramatically. This perhaps stunted the development of these regional cuisines, as the majority of the population simply tried to survive off of the few products they could get (generally, this consisted of bread, beer, oats, barley, occasionally cheese, and later the potato).

British Colonies

With the rise of the British Empire and its colonization of different part of the world, the stage was set for the introduction of many new techniques and foods. The most important British colonies, in terms of their influence on the development of the national cuisine, were those in the Americas and India. From the Americas, the British were introduced to turkey, beans, and eventually potatoes and tomatoes from the Spanish colonies.

From India, the British brought back many spices, as well as the many Indian servants/slaves who produced the *curries*, rices, and breads common to India. The island nation of present-day Sri Lanka also became a major tea-growing area, as is India, and both supplied the British with a vast array of teas that became very fashionable and eventually led to tea being served as its own course, with scones, cookies, and other small bites. Additionally, cabbage from China was introduced via British trade in the region, and this vegetable gained wide acceptance on the isles; it was added to soups and potatoes, and combined with other items in boiled meat dishes.

Britain has been greatly influenced by the cultures of the native people in the many colonies that the country has controlled at one time or another. These influences also spread into the other nations of the British Isles, as interactions and close proximity exposed the Scottish, Irish, and Welsh to these ingredients and foods as well.

The Irish Potato from the Americas

There is much debate about how the potato got into Ireland, but one thing is for sure: its arrival changed the course of Irish history and its culinary traditions. Prior to the arrival of the potato, the Irish subsisted on a diet of oats (as porridge), breads, cheese, and whatever meats might be available. After the arrival of the potato (from South America, probably through Spain) in the seventeenth century, this new crop quickly became the center of the Irish diet. Within 50 years, the potato was being eaten by the masses for breakfast, lunch, and dinner. The average consumption of potatoes per person in Ireland at this point in history was almost 8 lbs/day, a seemingly huge amount of potatoes, and sometimes the sole source of energy. Not surprisingly, this reliance led to one of the greatest famines in history in 1845, when the worst crop failure in Irish history occurred (following a few years of very poor crops); as a result, 1 million people starved to death, and another 2 million immigrated to the United States between 1842 and 1847.

The potato is still very much a part of Irish cuisine, and it is used in an astonishing number of ways in their traditional cooking. The potato is also a common ingredient throughout all of the United Kingdom, and the importance of its introduction to the cuisines of the other countries is significant as well.

UNIQUE COMPONENTS

The cuisines of the British Isles are distinctive among the world's cuisines because of the techniques used as a foundation for the cooking and the population's attitudes toward food. There are some clear connections with the northern European countries, such as the baking tradition and preservation techniques, as well as with the former foe across the channel (France), with many of the sauces and spices coming from the French Normans, but these imports are interspersed with traditional foods that have been a part of British Isles cooking for many centuries. The following section examines some of the more important aspects that make these cuisines unique.

Hearth Boiling, Griddling, and Baking

The historic cooking methods of the cuisines of the British Isles are boiling, griddling, and hearth baking, all traditionally done over a fire burning in *hearths* that were found in nearly all homes across the Isles. While most cooking is no longer cooked over a fire in people's homes, this tradition is the basis for many of the techniques and recipes that make up the backbone of the cuisines of this area. Whether the prepared dish is Irish stew, soda bread, drop scones, roast beef, boiled corned beef and cabbage, or the many English puddings and pies, these methods are employed to make these classics as well as many others.

Throughout the British Isles, the hearth was used not only to heat the home but also to do all of the cooking, and the instruments used to cook revolved around the heat from the burning turf in the hearth. Burning dried turf from the countryside provided the fuel for these fireplaces, and the hearth became a favorite part of the home for many.

The boiling tradition goes back in history to when the inhabitants of these islands would fill large wooden troughs with water and add rocks from a fire to boil their meats and game. Once the invention of iron works came into common use, this turned into a large three-legged pot called a *bastible* that was held over a fire to bake breads and pies, while *griddles* were used to cook flatbreads, pancakes, and drop scones, and to sear bacon or ham. Meats were often hung over the fire and turned to roast, or placed in a pan covered by an upside-down pot (put in the embers to make rustic ovens). These traditions lasted for many centuries, and, although modern equipment enables other methods of preparation that are more practical, these recipes and traditional methods continue to this day.

Breakfast

One of the starkest differences between many other European cuisines and the cuisines of this area is the substantial breakfast that is commonplace in the British Isles. All of the countries in the United Kingdom, as well as Ireland, have a traditional breakfast. In Ireland, it is the *Irish Fry,* and in the U.K. it is the British *Fry Up,* two famous courses that still constitute a traditional meal in these countries. Although it is less common for people to eat the substantial breakfast of the past, it is still eaten occasionally as part of everyday life and is enjoyed by tourists and vacationers on a more regular basis. The main components of both versions are eggs, bacon or ham, and other foods as the person desires, such as sausage, fried tomatoes, *black pudding* (blood pudding), or fry bread, to name a few. The tradition of eating a substantial breakfast began in the eighteenth century and was a popular and common component of the diet well into the twentieth century, when its role in heart disease became known; this began the decline of its popularity (much like in the United States).

The American tradition of eggs, sausage, bacon, and potatoes can be traced back to the British, Irish, and Scotch immigrants who made up a significant part of the U.S. population in the eighteenth and nineteenth centuries.

Royalty, Classes, and Wars

The ruling classes of the United Kingdom and, to a lesser extent, Ireland long had a very different existence than the common folk. The privileged few not only had access to more prized products and a greater variety than people of more modest means—a situation that is common to all countries—but the gap in choices and health throughout the period of rapid culinary development (the sixteenth to nineteenth centuries) between the rich and working class was dramatic. While the royalty and privileged within the British Empire feasted on a variety of meats, fish, rich pudding, cheeses, and imported goods, the field workers who made up the vast majority of the populace subsisted on little more than hard flatbreads, ale (beer), and *porridge* (oatmeal gruel). Much of the population was undernourished and certainly not concerned with finer foods as much as filling foods and foods that provided nourishment. As a result, the development of a cuisine for the masses was practically nonexistent for most of the population. At the same time, the ruling royalty, nobles, and lords of these countries held great feasts, which is where many

of the traditional recipes and foods come from. The nonelite of these countries associated many of the foods of the royalty with excess and selfishness, and the typical modest diet of the common man and woman was considered more proper by many.

The timing of World War I and World War II was such that, just as the general population was gaining access to more variety and better quality foods, particularly around the time of the Second World War, the British Isles had to start rationing and faced widespread food shortages. Because these are island countries that obtain some of their goods from outside countries, the rationing and shortages from the Second World War not only were severe but lasted well into the 1950s, after the war ended. The rationing from this period had a significant stunting effect on the development of the cuisines of all of the United Kingdom, as well as Ireland.

The combination of a social distaste for privileged excess and war rationing had a lasting impact on the views of food for many in these countries. Simple and nourishing food was considered desirable, and a culture of culinary excellence was neither sought nor was it revered by the majority of the population during these periods. As a result of these attitudes regarding food, a large part of the populations of these countries developed simple, economical, and conservative food tastes. This encouraged a tradition of foods based on grains and products that were readily available, a tradition that is still evident in the cuisines today.

This approach to cuisine and cooking has changed during the last couple of decades, as the culinary arts receive increased attention and traditional foods are prepared with pride. Many of the foods that were regarded as food of the common folk are now being combined with the foods that were regarded as items of the upper class to create a cuisine that embodies the spirit of the whole culture.

Colonial Impact

Great Britain was one of the great empires during the period of discovery, from the sixteenth century through the nineteenth century, and the empire's colonies impacted the culture and the cuisine at home. The British Empire invaded, conquered, and colonized the eastern seaboard of North America and all of Canada, many islands of the Caribbean, parts of India and Southeast Asia, much of southern and eastern Africa, Australia, New Zealand, and many islands in the South Pacific. With this vast source of resources, as well as numerous instances of soldiers and aristocrats traveling to these lands and returning home with stories, foods, and indentured servants, it is no wonder that the cuisine in Britain was impacted. Some of the most important contributions from these lands included many of the indigenous products of the Americas, such as potatoes, tomatoes, and turkey, as well as many items from Asia, with curries, tea, sugar and spices being some of the most significant. The British Empire ruled India from 1858 until 1947, and during this time many ingredients and food customs were imported to Britain, where they became part of the British culinary repertoire. The curry that most are used to in the United States is as much of a British influence as an Indian one: the British sought to import some of the foods that they enjoyed from India, and a generic spice blend became known to the English as curry. In fact, in India spice blends are far more complex and varied, and the term *curry* didn't mean a spice blend at all but rather a type of preparation that included a spicy sauce. The English use of the term has stuck not only here and in the British Isles but also, to some extent, in India, where the term is sometimes used to indicate the spice blends as well as the preparation from which the term derived. The imported curry—as well as the tea, sugar, and spices of Asia and the ingredients from the Americas—all transformed the cuisine of the British Isles as these became common components.

The popularity of these foods and the later introduction of other European nations' products made present-day England a country of mixed cuisines. Ethnic restaurants are very common in England, and to a lesser extend Ireland and Scotland, and they have assumed the identity of native cuisine, with Indian and Italian cuisine becoming common home-cooked foods along with the traditional British and Irish fare.

SIGNIFICANT SUBREGIONS

The British Isles can be divided into many regions, depending on the degree to which analysis of the products is desired. For the purpose of this text, the regions have been divided based on the different nations that make up the British Isles. The nations are predominantly confined to two large islands that lie of the coast of mainland Europe, a short distance from France. The larger of the two islands is Great Britain and contains Scotland in the north, England in the center and south, and Wales in the west. The smaller and more westerly island is Ireland, which consists of Northern Ireland—a part of the United Kingdom—and the independent country of Ireland, which is called Eire by the native Irish. The regions are discussed from east to west and then from north to south.

Scotland

The northern part of the largest island of the British Isles is the nation of Scotland, one of four nation-states that make up the United Kingdom. This section of the United Kingdom is a land of mountains and rough terrain that has provided shelter to the natives from many invading peoples over the years. These mountains also contain high plains that are commonly used for grazing sheep, while the lower eastern coastal areas are dedicated to crops. Scotland has strong culinary influences from Scandinavia (from the period of Viking invasions and settlement) and France, from historic periods of alliances with the French against England as well as the royalty connection from Marie de Guise Lorraine of France, who married James V of Scotland. These influences are evident in the prevalence of cured and smoked foods, which reveals the influence of the Scandinavian countries, as well as in many of the methods (including pastries and soups) as well as much culinary terminology from France.

Scotland is well known for a number of products and recipes that range from the well-regarded Scottish smoked salmon, *finnan haddock, kippers,* and *Arbroath smokies* to the often joked-about *haggis.* Scotland is also where scones and marmalade originated, and it was a significant contributor to the development of the royal high tea.

Scotland has a long tradition of fishing, as it is surrounded by the North Atlantic and North Sea on three sides and also is home to much of the game still found in Great Britain. Both of these components are a big part of traditional Scottish cuisine; seafood and game dishes often serve as classic foods.

England

England is the largest of the nation-states in the United Kingdom and is located on the island of Great Britain. England has the richest agricultural land on Great Britain and has a long history of dairy production; it also produces much of the produce for the country. England is bordered by Scotland to the north, Wales to the southwest, and Ireland across the Irish Sea on its western shores, while the English Channel and North Sea separate the eastern shores from mainland Europe. England is mostly lowlands and rolling hills, with a fertile eastern section dedicated to most of the country's crops. The central and southern sections are significant dairy production areas, and the northern, more mountainous section is used for sheep grazing. This dairy culture has produced a number of well-known and regarded cheeses, among them *Stilton, cheddar, double Gloucester,* and *Cotswold.* As with the other countries of the British Isles, the climate is mild for their location in the north, from the warming effect of the Gulf Stream, but it is still regularly cool and damp.

England is mainly the product of a couple of conquering cultures, with the Anglo-Saxons and Normans playing significant roles in the development of the country. These cultures influenced the creation of a country driven to succeed in the world through its conquests of other lands and people. This focus on ruling and land acquisition set the stage both for a relative neglect of the development of a national cuisine and for the introduction of new cuisines from conquered lands. While the focus of the majority of the population may have been on outward expansion, the culinary scene at home developed a number of unique dishes and components.

One of the traditional English meals is roast rib of beef, which is traditionally served with *Yorkshire pudding* and horseradish sauce; this dish is made elsewhere, but not with the same reputation and accompaniments as the English roast beef. The English also developed a number of *pasties* (savory-filled pastries) and pies that are essentially pastry-wrapped meat, seafood-filled dishes, or thick, savory fillings cooked inside a pastry shell (pie).

England has long been the dominant political, military, and financial center of the United Kingdom, and this has played a role in the development of the cuisine local to this region. The colonization of India brought curries and *masala* to England, and these remain common dishes in England today, as does the incorporation of Indian spices into the traditional cuisine. Other colonies also brought new ingredients and techniques to England; even the very English *fish and chips* is thought to have made its way into English cuisine from the Americas; the fried potatoes via the Belgians (through Spanish rule of Belgium); and the method of preparing fish via the Sephardic Jews (from their period of living in Spain and Portugal).

Ireland

Ireland actually comprises two countries: the northern portion is known as Northern Ireland, which is part of the United Kingdom, and the larger, southern portion is the independent country of Ireland, known as the Republic of Ireland. The central section of Ireland is lowland that is dotted with peat bogs and contains a significant amount of the country's crops. The outer portions of the island are mountainous and covered with many green pastures that are home to flocks of sheep and herds of cattle. Ireland has long been appreciated for the fine-quality meats that come from this land, in particular the areas closer to the sea where the sheep feed on the flavorful grass growing in the mist of the salty ocean. Ireland has a long tradition of families farming small plots by their homes, and this is still common today.

Because the Irish have have been able to resist many of the invading cultures over time, several traditional dishes and recipes have been retained over the centuries (Ireland was under the control of the English for many years, but mainly in the northern cities that now constitute Northern Ireland).

Traditional Irish cooking was done on or around a fire, using the methods of simmering, boiling, baking, spit roasting, or cooking in a bastible; these methods are still the foundations of much of the cooking today.

Many of the culinary customs of the Celtic ancestors can be seen in the recipes that have remained, including the use of oats, barley, lamb, fish, *sloke* (seaweed), bacon, and dairy in much of the cuisine. Of all of the items introduced to the Irish diet and their culinary customs, none has had a more dramatic or tragic impact as the potato. The potato quickly became a central component of the Irish diet—to the point of overreliance—following its introduction to Ireland in the 1600s, which eventually led to the great potato famine of the mid-1800s and the resulting mass starvation and emigration. The potato is still a major part of the Irish diet, and the Irish have maintained many methods and customs that revolve around its production and consumption from the period of heavy reliance on the potato for sustenance.

Some of the traditional uses for the potato include *colcannon* (mashed potato with either kale or cabbage), *boxty* (cake made from grated potato), *champ* (potatoes and spring onions), and potato breads. Another common recipe is the Irish breakfast, or *Irish Fry;* the breakfast may also be accompanied by one of the many types of soda breads common in Ireland, such as the fried wedges known as *farls.* Stews and soups are also common dishes in the cuisine, with *Irish stew* being the most well known.

Wales

Wales makes up a small portion of the island of Great Britain and is located on the western portion of the island. Wales has a large amount of mountainous terrain and, like Scotland and Ireland, has a significant portion of its land dedicated to herding sheep. The

Welsh were one of the groups of Celtic tribes (the other was the Scottish) that were pushed out of England when the Anglo-Saxons arrived. Many ties and similarities exist between the customs in Wales and in Scotland and Ireland because of this Celtic connection. For example, the *crempogs* (type of pancake) found in Wales resemble the drop scones of Scotland, and the *bara brith* (fruit bread) of Wales is called *barmbrack* in Ireland.

Wales also has an excellent reputation for local fish, lamb, and cheese. The most well known of the Welsh cheeses is *Caerphilly*, which may be eaten with bread or used to make a variety of dishes, including Welsh rarebit (cheese sauce served over toast). The local lamb is one of the traditional meats of the Welsh diet and cuisine, and it is commonly used in making stews and pasties. The locally caught salmon, shellfish, and trout are used to make soups and savory pies, and herring is often pickled (or "soused"). Another Welsh specialty is called *laverbread* and it is made from local seaweed that is dried and boiled and usually mixed or eaten with oatmeal. This type of preparation is also found in Ireland and Scotland, where it is called *sloke*, although it is more common in Wales.

RECIPES

The following recipes provide an introduction to the cooking and cuisines of the British Isles.

Bacstai Gridille NORTHERN IRELAND
(BOXTY BREAD)

INGREDIENTS

1 lb	Russet Potatoes, peeled
1 lb	Cooked Mashed Potatoes
1.5 tsp	Salt
5 oz	All-Purpose (A.P.) Flour + more for griddling

Wedges of bacstai gridille (Irish boxty bread) served with piped butter

Boxty is a name given to dishes that call for grated raw potato, the most common of which is often simply a griddled pancake of grated potatoes. In this version, dough is made and then cooked on the griddle to yield a type of bread that is eaten fresh with butter or later panfried in bacon fat to be eaten with breakfast.

YIELD: 12 (3 ounces/boxty)

COOKING METHOD: Dry Griddling

PROCEDURE

1. Preheat griddle to 350°F.
2. Grate the peeled russet potatoes into a bowl with 2 cups of water in it.
3. Remove the grated potatoes from the water (do not discard the water) and combine them with the cooked mashed potatoes in another mixing bowl; mix to combine.
4. Add the salt to the potato mixture.
5. The potato/water mixture should have potato starch settling on the bottom of the bowl. If the water is relatively clear and the bottom can be seen, pour off the water and add the starch to the potato mixture. If the water is still very cloudy, let it settle for a few minutes longer.
6. Gradually add the flour to the potato mixture, a few tablespoons at a time, and knead to work it in (do not knead a lot—just enough to incorporate the flour) until the mixture becomes smooth dough.
7. Divide the dough into 2 pieces, and roll out the 2 pieces into circles about 1/4 inch thick.
8. Cut each circles into 6 wedges, and cook on the griddle (on both sides) until they brown slightly, adding a small amount of flour to the griddle to keep them from sticking.
9. Once done, they can be served immediately with sweet cream butter, or they can be saved to be panfried for breakfast.

Drop Scones   SCOTLAND

INGREDIENTS

1	lb	Flour
1	tsp	Baking Powder
3	oz	Sugar
1/2	tsp	Salt
2	Tbsp	Light Corn Syrup
8	oz	Buttermilk
2		Large Eggs
		Pan Spray, as needed

Another quick bread common to the islands are these drop scones, which are found in throughout the British Isles, particularly in Scotland. These drop scones are part of the light foods that accompany tea.

YIELD: Approximately sixteen 2-ounce scones

MIXING METHOD: Muffin Method

COOKING METHOD: Griddling

PROCEDURE

1. Preheat the griddle to 350°F.
2. Combine the flour and baking powder, and mix well in a mixing bowl.
3. In a mixing bowl, using a paddle attachment or a whisk, combine the remaining ingredients (except pan spray) and mix well.
4. Add the flour mixture to the wet mixture and mix just enough to combine.
5. Drop approximately 2 oz of the batter on greased (with pan spray), preheated griddle, and cook until golden brown on the bottom. Turn over and cook until golden on the second side and cooked through.

NOTE: *These are traditionally served warm with butter and/or marmalade or jam.*

Drop scones with
Dundee marmalade
and piped butter

Dundee Marmalade SCOTLAND

INGREDIENTS

1	lb	Seville Oranges
1	lb	Lemons (preferably Meyer lemons)
5	cups	Water
2	lbs	Sugar

The legend of this marmalade is that a Spanish ship docked in the harbor of Dundee during a fierce storm, and the ship was loaded with Seville oranges (a bitter variety) that were then bought by a local merchant who discovered he couldn't sell them fresh (because they were bitter). Thus, his wife ingeniously made marmalade out of them.

YIELD: 2 pounds

COOKING METHOD: Boiling/Reducing

PROCEDURE

1. Wash the oranges and lemons thoroughly to remove any dirt or impurities.
2. Combine the whole oranges, lemons, and water in a pot, and bring to a boil over high heat.
3. Once they reach a boil, turn the heat down and simmer the fruit for 1 hour, or until they are completely soft when pierced with a knife (if necessary, add more water during this process so they are covered).
4. Remove the fruit and place them in a holding pan to cool, retaining the liquid used to boil them.
5. Once the fruit are cool, slice them into 1/4-inch-thick pieces with a sharp knife and remove any seeds.
6. Chop the sliced fruit coarsely.
7. Add the chopped fruit back to the boiling liquid, and bring to a boil again over high heat.
8. Add the sugar to the pot once it comes to a boil, and continue to boil over high heat until the mixture reaches 220°F (use a candy thermometer).
9. Once this temperature is reached, remove from heat and pour this fruit/syrup mixture into freshly sterilized mason jars; cover at once.
10. Allow mixture to cool at room temperature for an hour or two, and then the jars can be stored in the refrigerator indefinitely.

Oatcakes IRELAND

INGREDIENTS

8	oz	Raw Rolled Oats
1.5	oz	Sugar
2.5	oz	A.P. Flour + dusting flour
1/2	tsp	Baking Powder
		Pinch Salt
4	oz	Unsalted Butter

Oatcakes were one of the traditional foods that the Irish cooked over a fire in a griddle. These are still popular today, and are found in Scotland and Wales as well.

YIELD: 12 small oakcakes (1 ounce each)

COOKING METHOD: Baking

PROCEDURE

1. Preheat oven to 350°F.
2. In a mixing bowl, combine the rolled oats, sugar, flour, baking powder, and pinch of salt; mix thoroughly to combine.

(continues)

Oatcakes
(continued)

3. In a saucepan, melt the butter over a low flame and mix in the dry ingredients to form a dough once it is melted.

4. Transfer the mixture to a bench and, using some additional flour for dusting the bench, roll out the dough into a 1/4-inch-thick sheet.

5. Using circular cutters, cut out small cakes from the dough sheet.

6. Bake in preheated oven for approximately 15 minutes, or until the cakes become lightly golden.

7. Remove from the oven and allow cakes to cool on cooling rack (if storing).

Brotchán Foltchep   IRELAND

(LEEK AND OATMEAL SOUP)

INGREDIENTS

3	oz	Butter, clarified
5	oz	Raw Rolled Oats
1	qt	Vegetable Stock
12	oz	Leeks, cleaned and sliced thin across their width
1	tsp	Salt
1/4	tsp	Black Pepper
2	cups	Milk
		Salt and Pepper, to taste
1/4	cup	Parsley, minced

Oatmeal has been a part of the cuisine of Ireland since before recorded history of the peoples there, and this soup is representative of what was available to the ancient Irish. Irish cuisine has always relied on hearty warming foods that help fight the chill of this cold and wet country.

YIELD: Approximately 1.75 quarts

COOKING METHOD: Simmering

PROCEDURE

1. In a pot large enough to hold all of the ingredients, add the butter and heat over a low flame.

2. Once hot, add the oats and gently fry them in the butter, stirring constantly with a wooden spoon until oats become golden brown.

3. Once the oats have been toasted well, stir in the vegetable stock and add the leeks, salt, and pepper to the pot.

4. Bring this mixture to a gentle simmer over a medium flame; simmer for 45 minutes, or until leeks are tender.

5. Once the leeks are tender, temper in the milk and adjust seasoning, if necessary; garnish with minced parsley.

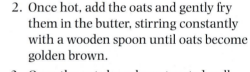

Bowl of brotchán foltchep (leek and oatmeal soup)

Welsh Rarebit ENGLAND AND WALES

(TOAST WITH CHEESE/BEER SAUCE)

INGREDIENTS

20	fl oz	Brown Ale
1	Tbsp	English Mustard
3	Tbsp	Worcestershire Sauce
4	oz	Unsalted Butter
4	oz	A.P. Flour
40	fl oz	Milk
1.5	lbs	Cheddar Cheese, grated
		Salt and Black Pepper, to taste
6		Egg Yolks
15		slices of Pullman Bread, toasted and cut in quarters to yield 4 triangles each
		Worcestershire Sauce, to taste
2	Tbsp	Parsley, minced

There are many humorous explanations for the name of this southern UK classic. One explanation is that it was originally called Welsh rabbit—because rabbit was substituted for other meat by the poor, and the Welsh were often too poor to even afford rabbit but would instead eat cheese—while another explains the use of the name *rarebit* because it would be a "rare bit" for a Welshman to have cheese to make this. Either way, a Welshman may not be amused, but this dish reveals the simplicity and dependence on dairy of many of the early U.K. recipes.

YIELD: 12 portions (5 ounces/portion)

COOKING METHOD (SAUCE): Simmering and Thickening with Roux

COOKING METHOD (FINAL RAREBIT): Broiling

PROCEDURE

1. Preheat broiler/salamander or oven on broiler setting.

2. In a small saucepan, combine the brown ale, English mustard, and Worcestershire sauce, and slowly reduce over a medium-low flame until this mixture thickens (reduce by about 75%).

3. In another saucepan, make a white roux with the butter and flour, and set aside to cool.

4. In a separate pot, carefully bring the milk to a simmer over a medium flame, and then whisk it into the cooled roux.

5. Bring the milk/roux mixture to a gentle simmer over a medium flame and, once reached, lower the heat to thicken the mixture.

6. Cook this mixture over a low flame for 20 minutes; add water if it gets too thick, and be sure to stir regularly to prevent scorching the bottom.

7. Once the mixture has been cooked for 20 minutes, remove it from the heat and melt in the grated cheese, whisking to make a smooth sauce.

8. Add the beer, mustard, and Worcestershire sauce reduction to the cheese sauce, and whisk to combine.

9. Season the sauce with salt and pepper, if necessary.

10. While still whisking, mix in the egg yolks to yield a thick, smooth cheese sauce.

11. Place 4 triangles (one piece of toast) in each of 12 ovenproof casseroles (oval casseroles are traditionally used).

Welsh rarebit (toast with cheese/beer sauce) shown with tomato slices

Potted Shrimp and Haddock   Scotland

INGREDIENTS

1	lb	Very Small Shrimp (size 60 +)
1	oz	Butter, clarified
3	cups	Water, boiling
1	lb	Haddock Fillet (you can substitute cod, if haddock is unavailable)
1/2	lb	Butter
2	oz	Butter, softened
3		Anchovy Fillets
		Pinch Cayenne Pepper
		Salt and Black Pepper, to taste

Potted meats and fish have a long tradition in the British Isles, where they are commonly eaten with bread or toast. The tradition of potting foods is associated with the travels of the sailors and their need to take foods on long journeys. This would be a common sight on a tea table or served for a light lunch or snack.

YIELD: 2 pounds

COOKING METHOD (SHRIMP): Steeping

COOKING METHOD (HADDOCK): Poaching

MIXING METHOD: Mortar and Pestle

PROCEDURE

1. In a small pot, combine shrimp and butter and sear over high heat until shrimp turn red; remove from heat.

2. In a separate pot, bring water to a boil and pour it over the seared shrimp. Allow the shrimp to sit and steep in the pot for 1–2 minutes to cook.

3. Remove the shrimp from the liquid and peel them, setting the meat aside for later and returning the shells to the water in which they were steeped.

4. Return the pot with shells and water to the stove, and set over a low flame to bring liquid to poaching temperature.

5. Wrap the haddock fillet in cheesecloth and tie with butcher's twine to contain it. Place it in the poaching liquid with the shrimp shells, and poach until haddock is cooked (about 4–5 minutes for smaller fillets—thickness will determine the length of time required).

6. Remove the haddock and set it aside to cool.

7. While the haddock cools slightly, add the 1/2 lb of butter to the pot of water and shrimp shells, and turn up heat to reduce the liquid to make shrimp butter.

8. Place the poached haddock into a mortar, and crush it (using a pestle)—along with the 2 oz of softened butter and the anchovies—into a paste. Add the pinch of cayenne pepper.

9. Chop the poached shrimp meat, and mix it into the pounded fish paste.

10. Taste the mixture and adjust seasoning with salt and pepper, if needed; transfer to a storage pot/jar, with room above for the shrimp butter.

11. Once the liquid has been reduced from the shrimp shell/water/butter mixture, strain the butter through a cheesecloth on top of the potted fish and shrimp.

12. This mixture can be stored covered in the refrigerator for weeks, if sealed well. Serve with toast.

Potted shrimp and haddock in small jar with tea sandwiches, topped with some of the potted shrimp and haddock

Mint Sauce ENGLAND

INGREDIENTS

3	oz	Water
1	oz	Sugar
1	cup	Mint Leaves, finely minced (about 1/2 bunch)
4	oz	White Wine Vinegar

A traditional accompaniment to roasted lamb, this sauce is simple and makes a great meal with lamb and roasted new potatoes.

YIELD: 1 cup

COOKING METHOD: Boiling and Infusing

PROCEDURE

1. Bring water and sugar to a boil to dissolve sugar.
2. Set aside to cool until the mixture is just warm to the touch.
3. Add the sugar water to the mint and vinegar, stir well, and set aside for at least 30 minutes before using to allow flavors to infuse.

Roast Rib of Beef ENGLAND

INGREDIENTS

1		Beef Rib, bone-in (about 16 lbs)
1/4	cup	Salt
1	Tbsp	Freshly Ground Black Pepper

The English have a long history of roasting meats and have certainly mastered the art of roasting a great rib, especially using the method described in this recipe. This roast would traditionally be served on Sunday with roasted potatoes, Yorkshire pudding, and horseradish sauce.

YIELD: 15 portions (10 ounces/portion)

COOKING METHOD: Roasting

PROCEDURE

1. Preheat the oven to 425°F.
2. Rub the spice mixture all over the roast, and place the beef rib in a heavy roasting pan.
3. Place the rib in the preheated oven and roast for 20 minutes, or until brown crust begins to develop on outside of the rib (you do not want a deep brown or well-developed crust at this point, as the oven will take some time to cool to the next temperature).
4. Once the crust has begun to form, turn the oven down to 275°F; after another 20 minutes, check the roast again to see if there is good coloring all over the surface of the meat (if there is not, the oven will need to be turned up to 350°F to achieve the nice crust and fully develop the flavor, and then turned back down to 275°F). If the coloring is good, continue to roast until the internal temperature—taken in the center of the rib—reaches 120° (this will yield a rare rib roast).
5. Remove the roast from the oven and place it in another roasting pan; cover it with aluminum foil to hold until carving.
6. After the roast has rested at least 20 minutes, it can be sliced.
7. With the roast standing on end, slice horizontally to the bone and then vertically down to cut off each portion.

NOTE: *Reserve the fat from the roasting pan to use for the Yorkshire pudding (see following recipe).*

Yorkshire Pudding ENGLAND

INGREDIENTS

4	fl oz	Whole Milk
4		Eggs, beaten
1	tsp	Salt
10	oz	A.P. Flour
12	fl oz	Whole Milk
2	fl oz	Beef Dripping from Roast Beef (see recipe, this chapter)

This is the traditional accompaniment to the English roast rib of beef.

YIELD: 12 portions (3 ounces/portion)

COOKING METHOD: Baking

PROCEDURE

1. Preheat the oven to 400°F.
2. In a mixing bowl, mix together the 4 oz of whole milk, eggs, and salt, and beat with a whisk until the mixture becomes frothy.
3. Slowly add the flour to the egg/milk mixture, beating constantly (if mixture gets too thick when you add flour, add a little of the remaining milk).
4. Once all of the flour is incorporated, slowly add the remaining milk to form a smooth batter the consistency of a thin pancake batter.
5. In a heavy roasting pan (12 inches × 20 inches × 3 inches deep), or another relatively shallow, heavy pan with a similar total volume (this recipe can be scaled to fit different pans, but pan depth, volume, and ability to hold heat well are all important for good results), add the beef pan drippings (make sure they are predominantly fat) and heat the pan over a high flame until the drippings sputter from the heat.
6. Pour the prepared batter into the greased and hot pan, and place in the preheated oven; bake for 15 minutes.
7. Reduce the heat to 370°F after 15 minutes of cooking, and continue to cook until the pudding rises above the top of the pan and becomes crisp and browned.
8. Remove the pudding from the oven and serve immediately with the now properly rested rib roast.

NOTE: *This recipe is best prepared when the rib starts to measure about 110° (see roast rib recipe) so that the batter is ready to go right when the roast comes out of the oven (the oven will have to be turned up to 400°F right after it is removed). The beef fat drippings can be drawn off of the pan shortly before the roast is actually done.*

Roast rib of beef served with Yorkshire pudding and horseradish sauce

Horseradish Sauce   ENGLAND

INGREDIENTS

5	oz	Prepared Horseradish
1	oz	White Wine Vinegar
1	oz	Worcestershire Sauce
2	tsp	Sugar
1/2	tsp	Dry Mustard
1	tsp	Salt
1/4	tsp	White Pepper
10	oz	Heavy Cream

This is the traditional accompaniment to the common roast beef of England.

YIELD: 2 cups

MIXING METHOD (CREAM): Whipping to Soft Peaks

MIXING METHOD (FINAL SAUCE): Folding

PROCEDURE

1. Place the prepared horseradish in a couple layers of cheesecloth, and wring out excess moisture.

2. Transfer the dried horseradish to a mixing bowl and combine with the white wine vinegar, Worcestershire sauce, sugar, dry mustard, salt and white pepper; mix thoroughly with a whisk to combine.

3. In a separate bowl, whisk the heavy cream until soft peaks are formed.

4. Fold the horseradish/spice mixture into the whipped heavy cream, and taste; adjust seasoning, if necessary.

Brandy Snaps   ENGLAND

INGREDIENTS

8	oz	Unsalted Butter
4	oz	Confectioners' Sugar
1/4	cup	Light Corn Syrup
1	Tbsp	Molasses
5	oz	A.P. Flour
1	tsp	Ginger, dried powder
2	oz	Brandy
1	Tbsp	Lemon Zest, minced

These cookies are a common sight at the tea table in England and are often served with sweetened whipped cream.

YIELD: About twenty-five 3-inch cookies

COOKING METHOD: Baking

PROCEDURE

1. Preheat the oven to 350°F.

2. In a small pot, melt the butter and add the confectioners' sugar, corn syrup, and molasses; mix well to combine over a low flame until the sugar has dissolved into the butter.

3. Mix the flour and ginger together in a mixing bowl.

4. Using a wooden spoon, stir in the flour/ginger mixture to the syrup, and then add the brandy and lemon zest, mixing well to combine until smooth.

5. Once mixture is smooth, place about a tablespoon of this batter/dough onto a silicone baking mat (you can also cook it directly on a well-buttered sheet pan to prevent sticking), spacing the drops

(continues)

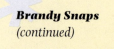

Brandy Snaps
(continued)

apart by at least 4 inches (they will spread into thin circles). Bake in preheated oven until cookies spread and bake to a golden color, and then remove from the oven.

6. When the cookies are done baking, they can be shaped into rolls or curls before they cool and set. If this is desired, the cookies will need to be shaped as soon as they have cooled enough to hold a shape but before they cool enough to harden. This requires being ready to shape them, and working quickly once they are the right temperature, before they set.

Placing a small amount of brandy snap batter on a silicone baking mat; note the amount of space between each to allow for spreading during cooking

Baked brandy snaps with some rolled brandy snaps in front of the sheet pan

Grabhar Biabhóg IRELAND
(RHUBARB CRUMBLE)

INGREDIENTS

For the Rhubarb Filling

2	lbs	Rhubarb, peeled and cut into 1/2-inch sections
10	oz	Sugar
		Unsalted Butter, as needed

For the Crumble Topping

1	lb	A.P. Flour
8	oz	Unsalted Butter
6	oz	Rolled Oats
7	oz	Brown Sugar

Fruit crumbles are a common dessert in Ireland and are particularly good at the height of the fruit's season. This style can be made with many other fruits substituted for the rhubarb.

YIELD: Two 9-inch crumbles (in pie dish)

COOKING METHOD: Baking

PROCEDURE

For the Rhubarb Filling

1. Combine the rhubarb and sugar in a mixing bowl, and mix well to combine.
2. Rub the inside of two 9-inch pie pans with the butter to coat the walls and bottom (other suitable baking dishes can be used as well).
3. Pour the rhubarb mixture into the pie pans.

For the Crumble Topping

1. In a mixing bowl, add the flour and butter; cut in the butter until it resembles peas throughout the flour.
2. Stir the brown sugar and oats into the flour/butter mixture to combine.
3. Sprinkle this mixture over the top of the rhubarb in the pie pans.
4. Transfer to a 350°F oven, and bake until the top turns a golden color; remove.

NOTE: *This is traditionally served with cream or whipped cream.*

Grabhar biabhóg (rhubarb crumble) in bowl, along with the baked pan of crumble

SUMMARY

The British Isles, lying off the western coast of mainland Europe, is home to cuisines influenced by the cultures that have settled this area over the centuries, as well as influences from cultures that the British once controlled. The early inhabitants of the British Isles were the Celts, who traditionally cooked over fires or by boiling foods in water. Later invasions and settlements in this area resulted in the introduction of products and methods such as cheese making, sauces, smoked foods, preserves, and pastries. One of the unique components of these cuisines is the importance and substance of their breakfasts compared to those of other European countries.

REVIEW QUESTIONS

1. Which culture introduced cheese making to the British Isles?

2. What were the traditional cooking methods of the Celts that are still used today in much of the cooking of the British Isles?

3. How does the first meal of the day in the British Isles make its cuisines unique among those of Europe?

COMMON TERMS, FOODS, AND INGREDIENTS

The following terms are common products and methods used in the cooking of traditional British, Irish, Scottish, and Welsh cuisine. Many of the foods listed under particular countries are common throughout the United Kingdom and Ireland.

General Terms and Cooking Equipment

bastible – Heavy iron pot with three legs used to bake and roast foods over a fire

griddle – Flat cast-iron cooking surface used to make the many examples of quick drop breads and seared foods found in the cuisines of the British Isles

hearth – Low fireplace found in homes throughout the British Isles, used for heating the home and for cooking

porridge – Made by cooking oatmeal with milk or water and added seasonings to yield a thick, cooked starch

Scotland

Arbroath smokies – Small haddock that are cleaned, salted, and then tied into pairs by the tail and smoked over a fire of oak or silver birch chips

Cullen skink – Chowder made of finnan haddock

finnan haddock – Cured and smoked haddock made in Findon; this is well known and sought after all over the world

haggis – Traditional boiled meat "pudding" made from filling the stomach lining of a sheep with seasoned and ground offal and suet bound with oatmeal

kippers – Smoked herring

spelding – Wind-dried and cured whiting

sqonn – Gaelic name for dropped-batter breads; now known as scones

England

black pudding – Made from pig's blood and pork fat, this is a common accompaniment to the English breakfast

bubble and squeak – Dish of leftover roast beef cooked with cabbage and onions; today, this dish commonly incorporates leftover cooked mashed potatoes as well

cheddar – Semifirm cow's milk cheese with varying levels of sharp flavor, depending on the amount of aging

Cornish pasty – Pastry filled with meat, vegetables, and sometimes sweets that was traditionally taken to work for a carry-out meal

Cotswold – Type of Gloucester cheese made from cow's milk with a sharp flavor and a semifirm texture; usually flavored with chives and colored orange/yellow

curries – Generic name used to describe Indian-influenced spice dishes that contain some of the typical Indian spice blends commonly referred to as curry by the British (although not by the Indians; in India, a *kaari* is the name of a vegetable dish in Southern India that contains spices and coconut milk)

double Gloucester – Whole milk cheese from the Gloucester area of England with a creamy texture and a full flavor

fish and chips – Battered and fried fish (usually cod or other lean whitefish) and fried potatoes

Fry Up – Name of traditional breakfast throughout much of the U.K.; this would typically consist of eggs and bacon, which may be accompanied by many other items, such as sausages, ham, blood sausage, bubble and squeak, tomatoes, fry bread, and mushrooms

masala – Name of Indian-inspired dish of meat (often chicken) cooked in a spiced tomato/yogurt sauce and usually served with rice *pasties* – Pastry filled with savory ingredients and baked; a traditional preparation thought to have originated in Cornwall, one of the Celtic regions of the United Kingdom

shepherd's pie – A dish consisting of minced, cooked mutton or lamb and onions covered with mashed potatoes and baked until golden

Stilton – Blue-veined cow's milk cheese prized for its creamy texture and rich flavor

Yorkshire pudding – Savory pudding made from a batter and cooked in the drippings of a roast beef, for which it is the traditional accompaniment

☀ *Ireland*

barmbrack – Spice and fruit bread commonly eaten on Halloween

bastible – Heavy iron pot with three legs used to bake and roast foods over a fire

boxty – Potato griddle cake made from grated potatoes cooked on a flat iron pan

champ – Mashed potatoes and spring onions

colcannon – Dish of mashed potatoes with cabbage or kale

farls – Individual soda breads that are traditionally eaten with Irish Fry or sliced in half to hold eggs, bacon, or sausage between the layers (think of a breakfast sandwich—these are the originals). Also a name given to foods that are cut into wedges; for example, potato farls would be wedged cuts of potato.

fool – Mixture of sweetened fruit and cream

Irish Fry – Traditional breakfast; this would usually consist of bacon, sausage, black pudding, eggs, and potato cakes or farls

Irish stew – Stew made traditionally by layering lamb or mutton with vegetables (now often with potatoes) and then covered with water and cooked over a fire in a bastible for a couple hours, or until everything is very tender

sloke – Type of seaweed used in traditional Celtic cuisine

☀ *Wales*

bara brith – Spiced fruit bread

Caerphilly – Well-known Welsh cow's milk cheese with moist texture and mild flavor; this cheese is used in cooking and often eaten with bread

cawl – Welsh stew made from lamb and leeks

crempogs – Buttermilk pancakes

laverbread – A dish made of cooked laver, a type of seaweed, which is rolled in oats and panfried

pasties – Savory pastries filled with meat or seafood and eaten out of hand

pie – Often refers to a savory-filled pastry crust (as in the other countries of the British Isles)

Welsh rarebit – A dish of cheese sauce served over or with toast; also called Welsh rabbit

CHAPTER 7

SCANDINAVIA (DENMARK)

BALTIC SEA

NORTH SEA

Legend
- towns and cities
- ★ capital city
- —— river
- —— region boundary
- —— sub-region boundary
- —·—·— international boundary
- forests
- mountains

SCHLESWIG-HOLSTEIN

MECKLENBURG-VORPOMMERN

Hamburg

Bremen

LOWER SAXONY

Northern Germany

BRANDENBERG

★ Berlin

Frankfurt

POLAND

NETHERLANDS

Rhine River

Münster

G E R M A N Y

WESTPHALIA

SAXONY-ANHALT

Elbe River

SAXON

Düsseldorf

Cologne

NORTH RHINE

Central Germany

THURINGIA

BELGIUM

HESSE

LUXEMBOURG

RHINELAND-PALATINATE

CZECH REPUBLIC

SAARLAND

West and Southwestern Germany—The Rhineland

Southeastern Germany—Bavaria

BOHEMIAN FOREST

FRANCE

Rhine River

BAVARIA

BLACK FOREST

BADEN-WURTTEMBERG

Munich

N W E S

0   50   100 km

AUSTRIA

B A V A R I A N   A L P S

German Cuisine

OBJECTIVES

Upon completion of this chapter, you will be able to

- explain what makes German cuisine unique.
- identify the common cooking methods used in traditional German cuisine.
- recognize with the common recipes found in German cuisine.
- produce a variety of German recipes.
- define the terms listed at the conclusion of the chapter.

INTRODUCTION

German cuisine does not have the fine reputation that many of the other European cuisines enjoy, because it is often perceived as a heavy, simple cuisine. However, German culinary traditions have contributed many components that are basic foundations of today's culinary repertoire. One must remember a couple of important things when considering the cuisines of Germany. Most of Germany has a cold climate, and this has played a significant role in the development and traditions of the national cuisine (as will be explored in greater detail in this chapter). In addition, Germany has been a united country for less than 100 years, in total, and it has been home to many destructive wars throughout history. These factors contribute to the national character of the people as well as the cuisine.

Although German cuisine may be more simple and have contributed less to the culinary archives than the cuisine of some of the local European neighbors, one must recognize the absolute comfort the native German culinary customs provide as well as the many areas that Germany's masters have brought to new heights, including the production from fine German gebäck-chefs (pastry chefs); these chefs produce excellent *kuchen* (savory and drier cakes), *tortes* (sweet and moister cakes and tarts), and distinct *brots* (breads), while the savory chefs have produced a seemingly endless variety of *wursts* (sausages). German chefs have also created great dishes from methods believed to have been introduced to them by foreigners, including *sauerkraut* (fermented cabbage dishes) and *spätzle* (type of small pasta), which is believed to have been introduced to the Germans by either the Romans or other Italians.

For many Americans, German cuisine is perhaps more familiar than they realize because of the significant number of German-inspired traditions that are found in the United States but go unnoticed. Whether it be the tradition of meat and potatoes as a standard, the appreciation for sausages, the common combination of sweet and savory, or an affinity for stews and roasted meats, many parts of the United States have strong ties to this European country.

HISTORIC CULINARY INFLUENCES

Germany is yet another European country with a history of conquests and invasions that have played significant roles in the culture, and thus the food traditions, of the local people. Germany is a relatively new country; German cuisine is strongly influenced by other countries and cultures, but the common thread of an appreciation for comfort foods (especially filled plates of meats and, later, potatoes) has been evident in the people of this great country, whether it was known as Germany or not. The following guide examines some of the more influential of those exchanges in regard to culinary traditions.

Early Beginnings

The early inhabitants of present-day Germany are often referred to as the Germanic tribes, and little is known about their culinary traditions except for accounts from Roman writers who commented on their rustic living conditions. What is known is that they subsisted on a diet of mostly grains that were grown in the area, including millet, oats, barley, rye, as well as dairy products such as milk, cheese, and cream, combined with whatever could be gathered or caught. Some of the items common to the area for gathering or hunting included berries, honey, boar, herring, salmon, venison, hare, and eel. In many ways, some of these traditional components are still common today; herring, salmon, bread, pork, game, rye, and barley play crucial roles in the typical German diet.

The Roman Empire

During the height of the Roman Empire, its reach spread into present-day southern Germany, resulting in significant amounts of culinary changes and influences to the German diet. The Romans introduced grapes, almonds, meat, and vegetable preservation techniques, such as sausage making and curing, and spices from the east such as ginger, cinnamon, cloves, and nutmeg. The Romans also introduced the cooking technique of hanging kettles over an open fire to simmer foods; thus, there was an increase in the production of soups and stews. Charlemagne, the French leader of the Roman Empire from the late eighth to early ninth century, introduced the use of fresh herbs and gardens in the everyday fare of people's diets. During the Renaissance period in the sixteenth century, German cuisine became more sophisticated, and the improved agricultural and farming practices allowed more of the population to enjoy the refined cuisine that was developing because of the influence of the Mediterranean Romans. It was also through the Romans that the Christian faith was introduced to and adopted by the local people, and this would prove to be a major influence on Germany's cuisine development. Fast days, celebratory days, and the introduction of monasteries would all become major facets of the culture's cuisine.

Mongolian Tartars

The Tartar horsemen from Mongolia in Asia had contact with Germans dating back to more than 1,000 years ago, and they passed on some culinary traditions that have since become a regular component in the cuisine of Germany. The Tartars taught the Germans about the technique of fermenting cabbage to preserve it (they had learned this from the Chinese), and thus began the sauerkraut tradition in Germany. The Tartars also introduced a technique in which they carved off pieces of raw meat, which eventually evolved to become a common dish in Germany known as *rindsfleisch tartare* (steak tartar).

Northern Neighbors

Many of the cooking techniques common to German cuisine are similar to those of its northern neighbors, with the Scandinavian countries in the west and Poland (as well as the more southerly Slavic countries) to the east lending much influence. The use of preserves and the technique of salting fish are consistent with the methods of the Nordic countries in the northern Atlantic, and the prevalence of stews and soups show a clear connection with the eastern countries that border northern and central Germany. In addition, there are numerous examples of foods in the German culinary repertoire that rose to popularity during the Austro-Hungarian Empire, especially pastries and breaded and panfried cutlets.

Prussia and Frederick the Great

Without a doubt, the greatest culinary influence of Frederick the Great of Prussia was the role he played in getting the German peasants to embrace the potato. By AD 1744, when Frederick's quest to help quell hunger in Germany by utilizing this productive crop began to succeed, potatoes had been in Germany (coming from South America) for almost 200 years. Today it seems hard to imagine the reluctance of the

German people to include the potato in their cuisine, as it has since become a cornerstone of German dishes. Potatoes are used for dumplings, in soups and stews, and to make warm and cold salads, and the frequency of their appearance at the table highlights their importance to the German diet. Before the introduction of the potato to Germany, famine was a regular part of this society; although one cannot say that the potato in and of itself removed this condition, it did reduce it significantly—and the German people adore it because of this. In the southern part of the country, the potato is also used to make *schnapps*, and this beverage is a common part of the cuisine of this region.

Frederick the Great also felt an affinity for the refinement of French cuisine, and he brought many French chefs to Germany. Frederick enjoyed the cuisine of the courts in France and imported the dining traditions at this time to the German region, including the addition of coffee, tea, and chocolate drinks to the dining scene as well as the use of silverware as a custom. The cuisine that the French chefs produced had an additional influence that is still seen in Germany today, mostly in the southern part of the country.

French Chefs

In the late eighteenth and early nineteenth centuries, there were an increasing number of imported French chefs in Germany, which played a role in the perception that French culinary techniques and customs were the best and should be imitated. These chefs were brought to the royal courts of the German nobility to create foods that the nobles had enjoyed in France; thus, these foods and techniques were introduced into the German repertoire. During this period, many French dishes and ingredients became more common in Germany, including many classic French sauces, the technique of poaching, soufflés, more refined charcuterie, and ingredients such as fine herbs, foie gras, and baby vegetables. Some of these influences stayed with the Germans, but many were briefly accepted, as the traditional customs and recipes passed on to the next century. The influences from the French are most evident in the regions that border France.

English Breakfast

Kaiser Wilhelm II's rule of Germany from 1888 to 1918 introduced yet another facet to the German diet,

because his mother was the daughter of Queen Victoria of England. As a result of his upbringing in an English-influenced household, he was accustomed to the typical English breakfast and introduced this heavier meal to the German nobility and royal court (and, thus, eventually to the public). Although this influence did not become a countrywide tradition for the morning meal—most Germans still start their day with buttered bread—it is common to see the eggs, sausages, and potatoes served in certain parts of the country.

UNIQUE COMPONENTS

German cuisine is unique in the importance it places on preserved foods as well as its affinity for products derived from pork. As with all of the regional/national cuisines, German cuisine is the result of numerous factors, but some aspects stand out when compared to other cuisines of the world. Some of the most important distinctions are as follows.

Preservation

One unique aspect of German culinary traditions is the use of preserved products in their food. Whether it is sauerkraut, the many smoked, cured, or cooked wursts or *schwein* (pork), *bier* (beer; preserved grain), brot (bread; preserved grain), or *pökelfische* (pickled herring; preserved fish), German cuisine relies like few others on preserved foods. The cuisine of Germany often revolves around these products because they can be utilized throughout the year, and the variations within these preserves are numerous—for example, wurst varieties include *bratwurst* (raw); *rohwurst* (cured, smoked, and ready to eat); *bruhwurst* (smoked, scalded, and eaten hot); and *kochwurst* (cooked, smoked varieties). The ability of German chefs to create some of the world's best products from preserved goods is one of the most impressive aspects of this cuisine.

Germany's location in the northern part of Europe is certainly a factor in this dependence, as growing seasons are shorter and long winters necessitate products that can be relied on throughout the year.

Prevalence of Rich Foods

The German diet is one of the richest in the world and includes many thick sauces, preserves, meat, dairy, and pork products. There is a comforting, filling quality to this food that provides a distinct back-bone to the cuisine that is undeniable. The common methods of cooking, including foods that are *geschmort* (braised), *gesotten* (simmered), *eintopf* (stewed), *pfannengerichte* (panfried), and *geräuchert* (smoked), only serve to heighten the richness of the food. The cuisine throughout much of the country utilizes butter, sour cream, and pork fat or bacon in many of the dishes. In historic times, the typical German ate little more than bread, beer, grains, and what little could be found in the wild at any given time. The foods commonly associated with Germany today were often considered special meals for most, as the products used to make them were not regularly available. This historic lack of significant foods in a region of long, cold winters likely played a major role in the eventual prevalence of richer foods, once they did become available to the masses, which didn't truly happen until after World War II.

Historically, such rich products were available in limited quantities in a country that has experienced significant periods of war and internal conflict. Following World War II, Germany experienced a boom that resulted in these foods being made available to more of the population, and this in turn raised concerns about the nutritive aspects of the traditional rich foods. In recent years, the cuisine has begun to change in response to health concerns, but the traditional foods still play a major role in the national diet.

Sweet/Sour and Savory/ Sweet Combinations

Germans have a taste for combining sweet and sour components and savory and sweet components in their cooking that is evident in many of the classic German dishes. Sugar was not used in significant quantities prior to the seventeenth century in Germany, so these combinations mostly included fruits and savory foods. The many orchards and vineyards of southern Germany provide the fruits that are utilized in the recipes with a sweet element.

Some dishes that highlight the sweet-and-sour combination include *sauerbraten* (vinegar marinated roast with raisins), *rotkohl mit äpfeln* (red cabbage with apples), and many of the *kartoffelsalat* (potato salad), *suppe* (soup), and sauerkraut recipes. Some common examples of sweetness added to savory products are the combination of *kartoffelpuffer* (potato pancakes)

and *apfelmus* (applesauce) or cooked meats with dried fruits, which is a common combination.

Simple, Straightforward Quality

German cuisine is not as complex or refined as other European cuisines, such as French or Italian, but it has a distinct and straightforward quality to it. There is an appreciation in Germany for reserve and working for one's keep that aligns well with a cuisine that is uncomplicated and familiar. This does not mean that Germans prefer bland or poorly made food—quite the opposite—but rather that the food be unpretentious and provide warmth, sustenance, and familiarity in this often cold land. Traditionally, less emphasis has been placed on retaining the visual qualities of foods, and more emphasis placed on the taste. Although the many stewed or braised dishes, dumplings, sausages, or soups might not draw the attention that a sautéed dish in France or stuffed roast in Italy might, the taste of any of these will easily rival what is made by southern European neighbors, and this is often one of the first things that foreigners note when they visit Germany. This simple food is also prepared with great skill, and its quality is revealed as soon as one sits at the table and samples all that the German kitchen has to offer.

Limited Products

German cuisine relies on a limited number of products that are available throughout the country and utilized extensively. The most closely associated protein source in German cuisine is the ever-common pork (schwein), which is used in thousands of ways, including as the major source for sausages as well as an ingredient in stews or simply roasted. Pork is highly prized and common in traditional German cooking, as hundreds of varieties of sausages are found throughout the country; many of the favored German meals include pork as a major component. Other common meats include *kalb* (veal), game (including *hasen,* or hare), and *wildbret* (venison). For vegetables, you'll find *krauts* (cabbages), *kartoffels* (potatoes), and *zwiebels* (onions) used frequently, and for fruits, *apfel* (apples), *birnen* (pears), and *beeren* (berries) are some of the most common.

Using a limited number of ingredients, German chefs have invented a vast repertoire of traditional recipes. In Germany alone, there are said to be over

1,500 varieties of sausages, hundreds of varieties of bread, several uses of sauerkraut, and many applications of the potato, thus proving that limited ingredients don't necessarily equal limited recipes.

The threads that tie these unique aspects together are climate (Germany is a cold country and historically had to preserve much of its summer bounty); history (Germany has experienced significant periods of food shortages); and human nature (a rich diet of comforting food is a natural human response to living in a colder part of the world). All of these factors have influenced the development of the national and regional cuisines of Germany and have provided us with these great contributions to the culinary collection.

The simplicity of German cuisine has changed a bit in recent years, as more people become interested in other cuisines and in refined culinary artistry. In many parts of the world, foreign cuisines are becoming increasingly popular with adventurous diners, and many examples exist in Germany of restaurants that specialize in foreign cuisines. However, there always seems to be a strong appreciation for the culinary roots that German cuisine calls its own, and invariably the Germans return to their roots at the kitchen table.

SIGNIFICANT SUBREGIONS

Germany does not have the significant regional differences that some other European countries have, such as Italy and France, but many regional traditions do exist, and significantly different foods and ingredients are available in different parts of the country. Regional German cuisine has been influenced by the countries that border the region, the most significant being the French in the southwest, the Scandinavians in the north, and the Eastern Europeans in the east (considered part of the central region in this section). The following guide examines some of the more important variations.

Northern Germany

The northern section of Germany is made up of lowland plains that comprise a less fertile sandy area—with the exception of the eastern part, which is a rich agricultural area. This region is covered with rivers and lakes and borders both the North Sea and the Baltic Sea. Not surprisingly, this area's local cuisine includes more fish than the southern part of Germany. There are many examples of fine preparations that include fish throughout this region, including many that utilize cream sauces—such as herring served with a crab-flavored cream sauce, and horseradish-flavored cream sauces served with carp and other freshwater fish. This region is well known for the prolific use of potatoes and the many fine dishes that utilize trout, pike, and herring from the local waters. Bacon is a favorite cooking fat in this region, and pork in general is a common ingredient; but it is the prevalence of eggs, cream, and butter in the cuisine of this region that often distinguishes it from the others. Northern Germany shares many similarities and influences with its northern Scandinavian neighbors, including the use of salt-cured fish, the extensive pickling of foods, the sweet yeast doughs used to make *wienerbrot* (Danish pastries), and the prevalence of hearty soups and stews. Some of the specialties of this region include dishes with *hering* (herring), *forelle* (trout), and *stockfische* (salt cod), as well as the significant use of *speck* (bacon), *kartoffels* (potatoes), and *saure crème* (sour cream).

This section includes the regions of Mecklenburg, Schleswig-Holstein, Brandenburg, Lower Saxony, and Saxony-Anhalt, as well as the city-states of Bremen, Hamburg, and Berlin. This region is bordered by Denmark to the north, Poland to the east, and the Netherlands to the west.

Central Germany

The central region of Germany lies at the beginning of the highlands that lead into the more elevated southern portion of the country. This is a region of hills and valleys and some mountain ranges, and it is known for its fine hams and hearty fare. Some of this region's specialty products include *pumpernickel*, a dense rye bread that takes two days to make; *skinken*, the local name for the famous hams; *klöss*, light dumplings commonly served with meats and gravy or in soups; and numerous casseroles or one-pot meals called *eintopf*. This region is often thought of as the dividing line between the north, where potatoes are popular, and the south, where dumplings and noodles are the main starches. The eastern portion of this region also exposes influences from the Eastern European countries, as the use of caraway, paprika, dried mushrooms, and sour cream are quite common here. In the western portion of the region, it is more common to see prized hams, dry pumpernickel, and *steinhäger* (gin) at the table. Throughout the central region, one will find many examples of wursts, sauerkraut, and pork preparations included in the local cuisine.

This area includes the regions of Westphalia, Hesse, Thuringia, and Saxony, as well as the cities of Münster, Frankfurt, and Cologne. The major country bordering this region is the Czech Republic, along the eastern portion of Saxony.

West and Southwestern Germany: The Rhineland

This region includes the major German river the Rhine, which runs through the heart of the hills. It also includes the area of Baden-Wurttemberg—which is often referred to by its old name, Swabia—and the Black Forest. Western Germany has the hottest summers in the country and also is a prime producer of some of the best produce. It is famous both for its wine industry and for the Black Forest. Some of the specialty products and recipes from this area include the white *spargel* (asparagus) of Baden, various types of spätzle (tiny dumplings) and sauerbraten (braised beef with sour/sweet sauce), and *Schwarzwälder Kirschtorte* (Black Forest cake). The cuisine in this region tends to be a little lighter than the cuisine of the north, central, and southeastern sections of Germany; salads and vegetable-based dishes are more common here. There is also a significant amount of influence in this region from neighboring France and Switzerland.

Many foods found in the countries that border Germany are also found on the German side; tarts filled with bacon, onions, and cream cheese are common, as is the use of juniper to flavor foods and the love of *schnapps* (distillates made from fruit or grain) as an aperitif. *Nudeln* (noodles) are quite common throughout this region—as one of the distinguishing features of Swabian cuisine, in particular—and they are often mixed with bacon or ham and sour cream, used in clear soups, and used to make sweet preparations. In addition, one can easily find *maultaschen* (filled pasta), which are often filled with ground-meat mixtures or herbs and sometimes formed like Italian ravioli or rolled (like a strudel). The maultaschen are typically eaten in two stages: the first fresh batch is eaten with a broth, and the next day's batch is eaten with onions fried in butter.

This region includes the areas of North Rhine-Westphalia, Rhineland-Palatinate, Saarland, and Baden-Wurttemberg, as well as the cities of Cologne and Düsseldorf. Belgium and France border this region to the west, and Switzerland borders it to the south.

Southeastern Germany: Bavaria

This region is home to the Bavarian Alps and has always been well known for the many fine beers that are produced here. Southeastern Germany includes many lush upper meadows and fields that yield grain crops as well as significant beet and potato crops. This is a colder region than the nearby Rhineland, because much of it is located at higher elevations. Not surprisingly, the food found here tends to be heavy, as in the north and central regions. There are also significant influences on the cuisine of this region from neighboring Austria, including dumplings and many veal-based dishes. However, the pig reigns supreme here—not only is pork featured in many styles, but all parts of the pig are utilized. There is a particular affinity and skill for preparing the *innereien* (organ meats, innards, etc.) in this region. Some local specialties include wursts, *schweinshaxen* (braised pork knuckles) and *wammerl* (pickled pork belly). Kraut (cabbage) is made in numerous ways here, and the forest produces many types of *pilze* (mushrooms) while the field bees produce much *honig* (honey). When most people think of German cuisine, they most likely think of the foods typically found in Bavaria; it is here that you are most likely to see plates of sausages, sauerkraut, and dumplings, accompanied by a large glass of beer.

This area comprises one large region, Bavaria, and includes the major city of Munich. This region is bordered by Austria and the Czech Republic to the south and east, respectively.

RECIPES

The following recipes provide an introduction to German cuisine. Some of the recipes require strict sanitary practices in order to ensure that the products do not become contaminated. Pay careful attention to the directions in these recipes; if the proper equipment is not available, it is best not to attempt those that require special consideration.

Rindsfleisch Tartare EASTERN AND SOUTHERN GERMANY

(RAW GROUND BEEF WITH GARNISHES)

INGREDIENTS

1	lb	Beef Tenderloin, trimmed of all fat and connective tissue and ground very fine (you may need to pass it through fine grinding plates a couple of times)

Garnishes

4		Egg Yolks
1/4	cup	Capers
1/2	cup	Yellow Onions, minced
1/4	cup	Parsley, minced finely
1/4	cup	Anchovy Fillets, chopped finely
		Freshly Ground Black Pepper, to taste
		Salt, to taste
8	slices	Dark Pumpernickel
4	oz	Butter

This traditional dish is a common holiday meal—as the use of finer cuts of meat usually is. The dish should be made as close to serving time as possible, and strict sanitary practices must be followed during the grinding procedure to ensure that the meat can safely be eaten raw. This is another example of a Tartar-influenced dish (see sauerkraut).

YIELD: 4 portions (5 ounces/portion) + bread

SPECIAL METHOD: Grinding raw meat that will not be cooked before serving (you must follow strict sanitation guidelines to ensure that food is sanitary)

PROCEDURE

1. The meat should be served shortly after grinding, as it will discolor in a short period of time when exposed to air. Strict sanitation guidelines should be followed to ensure that the meat is not contaminated from other sources after grinding; keep the ground beef in the container in which it was ground to prevent chances of cross-contamination, and keep it covered until plating.

2. On a serving platter or individual plates, arrange the freshly ground beef into four servings.

3. Make a well in the center of the beef, and place an egg yolk in it.

4. Serve with each of the garnishes arranged around the beef, or in separate dishes along with the beef.

5. If desired, spread butter on the pumpernickel prior to serving.

Beefsteak tartare served with raw egg in the center of ground meat, with capers leading to pumpernickel bread, onions, and anchovies in center of plate

Heringsstippe   Northern Germany
(Herring and Apple Salad)

Northern Germany borders both the Baltic Sea and the North Sea and has historically used herring in a great variety of dishes. This salad is a common example of one of the herring and sour cream combinations found in German cuisine.

Yield: 10 portions (7–8 ounces/portion)

Preparation Method (Herring): Leaching Salt

Method (Salad): Assembling Composed Salad

Ingredients

For Soaking the Herring

1.5	lbs	Preserved Matjes Herring Fillets
2	cups	Buttermilk

For Making the Dressing

10	oz	Sour Cream
1	oz	Lemon Juice
1	Tbsp	Sugar
3	oz	Sour Pickle, diced small
1	Tbsp	Spicy Mustard
1	Tbsp	Fresh Dill, minced
3	oz	Red Onion, minced
1	lb	Tart Apples (such as Granny Smith), peeled and diced medium
1/2	tsp	Salt
		Black Pepper and Salt, to taste

For Assembling the Salad

4	oz	Red Onion, shaved paper-thin
1	lb	Yukon Gold Potatoes, cooked, cooled, peeled, and cut 1/4 inch thick
		Dressing (see above)
		Herring fillets (see above), drained and rinsed
		Fresh Dill and Lemon for Garnish

Procedure

For Soaking the Herring

(**NOTE:** *This part should be done the night before making the salad.*)

1. Cover the herring fillets with the buttermilk in a nonreactive container and place in the refrigerator to sit overnight (or for at least 8 hours).
2. Once it has sat for long enough, remove the herring fillets from the buttermilk and rinse them carefully with cold water. Set aside for assembly.

For Making the Dressing

1. Combine all ingredients in a mixing bowl, and mix well to combine.
2. Test the seasoning and adjust, if necessary.

For Assembling the Salad

1. Toss the shaved onions and potatoes with 3/4 of the dressing in a mixing bowl, and place about 5 oz of the dressed potato/onion mixture on the salad plate.
2. On top of the dressed mixture on the plate, place a 2–3-ounce piece of herring fillet; drizzle some of the dressing over the fillet.
3. Garnish with lemon and dill, and serve.

Heringsstippe (herring and apple salad) served with lemon wedges

Kartoffelpfannkuchen THE RHINELAND (SOUTHWESTERN GERMANY)
(POTATO PANCAKE)

INGREDIENTS

2.25	lbs	Russet Potatoes, grated
10	oz	Yellow Onions, minced or grated
1	tsp	Salt
3		Whole Large Eggs, beaten
3	Tbsp	All-Purpose (A.P.) Flour
1	tsp	Salt
6	oz	Lard (or other fat) for panfrying
		Salt and Pepper, to taste

Potato pancakes are a common sight in western Germany, and they are often eaten with applesauce, jams, or other sweets, or taken with coffee. These thin potato "cakes" are now commonly used in savory dishes in many cuisines, as a base for pairing with other items.

YIELD: 10 (3 ounces/pancake)

COOKING METHOD: Panfrying

PROCEDURE

1. In a mixing bowl, combine the grated potato, onion, and 1 tsp of salt. Using clean hands or wearing latex gloves, squeeze out as much moisture as possible.

2. Return the squeezed ingredients to the mixing bowl, and add the beaten eggs, flour, and remaining salt to the mixture; mix thoroughly to yield a thick batter-like mixture.

3. Add enough of the lard (or other fat) to panfrying depth in a heavy skillet, and heat over a medium flame until fat is hot enough to panfry.

4. Place desired amount (3 oz will make a cake about 4–5 inches in diameter) of the potato mixture onto the pan, and carefully flatten it to a thickness of 1/4 inch.

5. Panfry on both sides until crisped and golden brown/yellow, and then remove from the pan.

6. Season with salt and pepper to desired taste, and either serve right away or set on a sheet pan to be reheated at a later time.

7. Repeat steps 4 through 6 with the remaining batter, adding more fat as necessary to panfry all of the batter.

(**NOTE:** *These can be panfried in advance and then reheated in the pan with a small amount of fat for serving (many people say they taste better this way!).*

Kartoffelpfannkuchen (potato pancake) topped with raspberry jam and served with coffee

Frankfurter Grüne Sosse FRANKFURT (CENTRAL GERMANY)
(GREEN SAUCE IN THE STYLE OF FRANKFURT)

INGREDIENTS

2	Tbsp	Chives, minced
1	Tbsp	Parsley, minced
1	Tbsp	Dill, minced
1	Tbsp	Tarragon, minced
2	tsp	Sorrel, minced
2	tsp	Chervil, minced
12	oz	Sour Cream
5	oz	Yellow Onion, chopped
4	oz	Mayonnaise
1	tsp	Salt
1		Hard-Boiled Egg, minced
		Salt, to taste

This herb sauce is used as a base for light meals when served with hard-boiled eggs or boiled red potatoes, or as a condiment when served with boiled beef or brisket. Traditionally, this sauce is made with seven herbs selected from the following: borage, sorrel, dill, cress, chervil, chives, parsley, tarragon, and burnet. Any of these can be substituted in this recipe, if desired.

YIELD: 3 cups

MIXING METHOD: Puréeing

PROCEDURE

1. Combine all of the chopped fresh herbs in a mixing bowl, and mix well.
2. Remove half of the fresh herb mixture and combine with the sour cream, chopped onion, mayonnaise, and salt in a food processor; process until smooth and well blended.
3. Remove from the food processor and fold in the remaining chopped herbs and chopped hard-boiled egg. Adjust seasoning with salt and pepper, if necessary (it should be very flavorful, as it usually will accompany blander foods).

Niederrheinische Leberwurst LOWER RHINELAND (SOUTHWESTERN GERMANY)
(LOWER RHINELAND-STYLE COUNTRY LIVER SAUSAGE)

INGREDIENTS

For Base Proteins and Fats

1.5	lbs	Calf's Liver, ground fine
8	oz	Pork Back Fat, ground fine
1.5	lbs	Pork Liver, ground coarse
1	lb	Fresh Bacon (unsmoked; you can also use salt pork), minced or diced small

For Binder

10	oz	Country Bread, soaked in veal stock until softened (about 5 minutes)

For Seasonings

2	Tbsp	Salt
1/4	tsp	White Pepper
6	oz	Yellow Onion, grated (can also be ground with bread in grinder)

This is a country-style liverwurst common to the lower Rhineland region of southern Germany. It is more coarse than most liverwurst eaten today, but it has a great flavor and can be encased and smoked or cooked in a sterilized mason jar.

YIELD: 5.5 pounds

COOKING METHOD: Smoking or Pressure Cooking

PROCEDURE

For Base Proteins and Fats

1. Place metal grinding parts in an ice-water bath to keep very cold until ready to proceed, and ensure that all areas are kept very clean and sanitary.
2. Grind the calf's liver through a small grinding plate twice, keeping it very cold before and in between grindings; set ground liver aside when done, and keep cold.
3. Grind the pork back fat through the same grinder plate once, and add it to the ground calf's liver.
4. Remove the fine plate and replace it with a slightly larger plate. Grind the pork liver once through the larger plate, and add it to the ground calf's liver and ground pork fat.

(continues)

5. Mince or dice the fresh bacon into small pieces, and then mix it into the other ground livers and fats.

For Combining the Binder

1. Run the soaked bread through the grinder directly into the other ground ingredients.
2. Add the seasoning to the mixing bowl with the other ingredients, and mix thoroughly with cleaned and sanitized hands or fresh latex gloves.

For Cooking the Liverwurst

Follow one of the next two preparations methods depending on desired results and equipment available

For Encasing and Smoking

1. Encase the forcemeat using a sausage stuffer, and tie off both ends of the casing.
2. Place the encased liverwurst in a heat-controlled smoker, and smoke at desired temperature until the liverwurst becomes firm to the touch (the temperature must be at least 180°F to maintain sanitary conditions—the higher the temperature, the less smoky the final flavor will be).

For the Mason Jars

1. Ensure that the mason jars are cleaned and sanitized before starting this method.
2. Fill the jars 3/4 of the way to the top and secure the lid.
3. Place in the pressure cooker and cook for 1 hour, and then allow to cool (if a pressure cooker is not available, this can be done in a water bath for 2 hours, with the jars covered, or in a steamer for 1.5 hours).

Niederrheinische Leberwurst

(continued)

1.5 tsp	Fresh Thyme, minced (or substitute 1/2 tsp dried)
2 tsp	Fresh Marjoram, minced (or substitute 1/2 tsp dried)

For Encasing and Smoking

	Hog Casing (thickness will determine length needed), cleaned

For Mason Jars

14 1-cup	Mason Jars and lids, cleaned and sanitized

Schwäbischer Kartoffelsalat   SWABIA (SOUTHEASTERN GERMANY)
(SWABIAN STYLE POTATO SALAD)

Potato salads come in many variations in Germany; this one is common in the south and includes Dijon mustard and fine herbs (parsley, tarragon, and chervil)—a reminder that France is not far away.

YIELD: 12 servings (5–6 ounces/serving)

COOKING METHOD: Steaming

PROCEDURE

1. Preheat steamer to cook potatoes or, if steamer unit is not available, set up a stovetop steaming unit and bring water to a boil to steam.
2. Rinse and scrub the potatoes clean, and place them into the steamer or steamer setup; cook until they are tender throughout (the amount of time this will take will vary, depending on the thickness of the potatoes—for a 2-inch-thick potato, this will take approximately 25 minutes in a steamer).
3. Once the potatoes are cooked, remove them from the steamer and set them aside to cool slightly (you will want to work with them

INGREDIENTS

3 lbs	Red Bliss Potatoes (these would be made with the Mäuschen variety in Germany; Red Bliss makes a good substitute in the United States)
2 oz	Red Wine Vinegar
6 oz	Olive Oil
4 oz	Veal Stock
8 oz	Yellow Onion, grated fine
1 oz	Dijon Mustard
1 oz	Sugar
2 tsp	Fresh Parsley, chopped fine
1 tsp	Fresh Tarragon, chopped fine
1 tsp	Chervil, chopped fine

(continues)

Schwäbischer Kartoffelsalat
(continued)

1 tsp   Salt
        Freshly Ground Black Pepper,
        to taste
        Additional Salt, as needed

when they are still warm but not hot, and the potatoes can be peeled or the skins left on depending on preference).

4. While the potatoes are cooling, combine all of the other ingredients in a mixing bowl and mix until combined very well.

5. Once the potatoes have cooled to slightly warmer than room temperature, slice them 1/4 inch thick, taking care not to break them apart too much.

6. Combine the sliced potatoes with the dressing, and move the potatoes around gently to allow them to be coated in the dressing but not broken.

7. Allow this mixture to sit and cool for at least 45 minutes before mixing the dressing in more and then serving.

✳ Kartoffelsalat mit Speck NORTHERN GERMANY
(WARM POTATO SALAD WITH BACON)

INGREDIENTS

For Boiling the Potatoes

2.5 gallons   Water
  4 Tbsp   Salt
  8 lbs   Red Bliss Potatoes

For Sautéing Bacon and Onions

 12 oz   Bacon, sliced into 1/2-inch
         squares
  1 lb   Yellow Onion, sliced thin

For Marinating Potato Salad

  3 oz   Sugar
  1 Tbsp   Salt

This "salad" is really more of a side dish and would often be held warm on the stove to be served with the main meat dish in many northern German homes.

YIELD: 15 portions (8 ounces/portion)

COOKING METHOD (POTATOES): Boiling in "Jackets" (with skins)

COOKING METHOD (BACON): Rendering/Sautéing

COOKING METHOD (ONIONS): Sweating and Sautéing

PROCEDURE

For Boiling the Potatoes

1. In a large pot, combine water, salt, and potatoes, and bring to a boil over high heat.

2. Cook potatoes until they are tender throughout, checking with a knife or skewer for resistance.

3. Once cooked, drain the potatoes through a colander and set onto a sheet pan to cool slightly before cutting.

For Sautéing Bacon and Onions

1. In a large sauté pan, render the bacon over a medium-low flame to slowly crisp and render out as much fat as possible—this should take at least 15 minutes.

2. Once the bacon has been rendered, add the sliced onions and sweat them in the bacon fat until they become very soft and translucent.

3. Once the onions are translucent, turn the heat up and continue to cook until the onions just begin to color; remove them from the heat and set aside to cool.

A bowl of kartoffelsalat mit speck (warm German potato salad; back left) and a bowl of sauerkraut with sausages (front)

(continues)

Kartoffelsalat mit Speck
(continued)

6	oz	White Wine Vinegar
6	oz	Salad Oil
1.5	tsp	ground Black Pepper
		Bacon and Onions (see above)
		Cooked Potatoes (see above), cooled and sliced 1/4 inch thick

For Marinating Potato Salad

1. In a mixing bowl, combine the sugar, salt, white wine vinegar, and black pepper; mix thoroughly with a whisk.
2. Add the cooked bacon and onions to the dressing once it has cooled to room temperature.
3. Slice the potatoes when they are still warm and add them to the dressing, mixing thoroughly.
4. Heat the entire potato salad to at least 165°F and then hold hot for service. (This salad improves in taste if it is stored for a day or two before use, in which case it would be cooled and stored covered before being reheated for service.)

Linsensuppe NORTHERN GERMANY
(LENTIL SOUP)

INGREDIENTS

For the Broth

3	oz	Bacon
2	oz	Shallots, minced
5	oz	Leeks, diced small
5	oz	Yellow Onion, diced small
4	oz	Carrot, diced small
4	oz	Celery, diced small
3	qts	Chicken Stock (vegetable stock can be used as well)
3	Bay	Leaves
2	tsp	Salt
2	Tbsp	Parsley
		Salt and Ground White Pepper, to taste

For the Lentils

2	qts	Water
2	tsp	Salt
12	oz	Brown Lentils

Germany is well known for the many great soups it produces, and this recipe is typical of some that are found in the northern part of the country.

YIELD: 1 gallon

COOKING METHOD: Simmering

PROCEDURE

For the Broth

1. In a small pot over a medium-low flame, render the bacon until no visible fat remains and it turns brown and crisp.
2. Once the bacon has been rendered, add the shallots, leeks, onions, carrots, and celery; sweat over a medium-low flame until all of the vegetables are tender and the onions are translucent.
3. Add the chicken stock, bay leaves, and salt, and bring the mixture to a simmer over a high flame. Reduce the heat to gently simmer the broth.
4. Once the lentils are cooked and ready to add (see the following section), the parsley will be added with the cooked lentils.

For the Lentils

1. In another small pot, add the salt and water and bring to a boil.
2. Once the water comes to a boil, add the lentils and reduce the heat to simmer the lentils until they are tender and cooked throughout (this should take about 12–15 minutes).
3. Once the lentils are cooked, strain them from the liquid; if you are serving the soup right away, the lentils can be added along with the parsley, and the soup can be adjusted for seasoning as needed.
4. If the soup is going to be served later, set the lentils and parsley aside, adjust the seasoning of the soup as needed, and add the lentils and parsley just before serving.

Sauerkraut GERMANY ✗

(SOURED/PICKLED CABBAGE)

INGREDIENTS

For the Fermentation

10	lbs	Green Cabbage, shredded very thin—use a deli slicer or mandoline, if necessary (**Note:** The cabbage must be weighed after it is sliced so the correct amount of salt is added)
4	oz	Salt

For Braising the Sauerkraut

8	oz	Bacon cut in 1/2-inch squares
1	lb	Large Yellow Onion, sliced thin
1	oz	Garlic Cloves, minced
1	cup	White Wine
3	cups	Chicken Stock
5		Juniper Berries
3		Bay Leaves
1	tsp	Caraway Seeds
		Rinsed Fermented Sauerkraut (see above)
		Black Pepper and Salt (**Note:** The kraut was salted and probably won't need more)

First step in making sauerkraut: pressing the salted cabbage down so it is covered by the released liquid to begin fermentation

This ingredient is found in many German recipes, from soups to stuffed pastries, or it is served as an accompaniment to meat. The process of making sauerkraut was taught to the Germans by the Tartars, horsemen from northern Asia who traveled and hunted/traded. The Tartars learnt the method of fermenting and preserving cabbage from the Chinese and then passed this technique on to the Germans, who have been preserving cabbage in this way for centuries.

YIELD: 8.5 pounds (this yield can vary depending on water loss during the fermentation process)

SPECIAL PREPARATION: Fermentation (all sanitation principles must be adhered to!)

COOKING METHOD: Braising

NOTE: *This recipe involves a fermentation process and, as such, the rules of sanitation are very important. Close attention must be paid to ensure that no cross-contamination occurs during this process.*

PROCEDURE

For the Fermentation

(**NOTE:** *This step may take almost 2 weeks, depending on ambient temperature.*)

1. In a very large mixing bowl (this may need to be done in batches), combine the thinly shredded cabbage and the salt (remember: the ratio is 10 lbs of prepared cabbage to 4 oz salt) and rub the cabbage together with *very clean hands* to distribute it and begin drawing the liquid from the cabbage.

2. Once the cabbage and salt have been mixed together, place the mixture in a *sanitized* 5-gallon plastic bucket, and push it down to compact it.

3. Place a small, *sanitized* bowl or plate on top of the cabbage, and place a *sanitized* nonreactive container on top of that bowl or plate filled with *sanitized* heavy objects (at least 5 lbs) to push the cabbage down even further in the container. The salt will draw water—and with it natural sugar—from the cabbage, which will then be fermented by lactic acid bacteria (the salt ensures that it is just lactic acid bacteria) that are naturally present everywhere; the cabbage will sour or pickle in the resulting acidic liquid it is forced into by weight.

4. Cover the container with plastic wrap and label it clearly, so that everyone is aware that it is meant to be out of the refrigerator.

5. Place the bucket in a warm area and allow it to ferment until the cabbage turns from the light green color of fresh cabbage to a dull grey/green color, which indicates that the liquid the cabbage is in has a pH below 4.5 (in which case, the cabbage is preserved). Note that the cabbage needs to be under the liquid the whole time; if some part of the cabbage is not covered by liquid, it will mold and

(continues)

Sauerkraut
(continued)

Fermented cabbage in mixing bowl next to fermentation vessel; note the difference in color between fermented cabbage and fresh cabbage

need to be discarded—this usually occurs as a result of not slicing the cabbage thin enough or not placing enough weight on it.

6. Once the cabbage has fermented, remove it from the bucket and strain it through a colander (it will have a noticeably sour aroma, which is normal).

7. Rinse the cabbage with cool running water to rid it of excess salt and fermentation liquid.

For Braising the Sauerkraut

1. Heat a heavy-bottomed pot or braising pan over a medium-low flame until hot, and then add the bacon; slowly render until bacon is crisp and most of the fat has been rendered out of it (this should take 15 minutes or more).

2. Once the bacon is rendered, add the onions and sweat until translucent before adding the garlic; continue to cook for 2–3 minutes.

3. At this point, the remaining ingredients (except pepper and salt) can be added, including the fermented cabbage. Then cover the pot with a tight-fitting lid, or aluminum foil and a lid, and set the pot over a low flame and allow to cook for at least 1.5 hours, checking periodically to ensure that the liquid has not evaporated entirely (if it is drying up, more chicken stock or water can be added).

4. Once the sauerkraut has gently simmered for at least 1.5 hours, it can be checked for seasoning and served.

Spätzle SWABIA (SOUTHEASTERN GERMANY)
(TINY DUMPLINGS)

INGREDIENTS

2	lbs	A.P. Flour, sifted
1	Tbsp	Salt
5		Large Eggs, beaten
1	cup	Cold Water + extra reserved (another 1/2 cup)

These pasta-like dumplings are commonly served with rouladen or other dishes, along with a rich gravy that can be mixed with the spätzle. They are also eaten as a starch often tossed with butter or topped with cheese and melted in a broiler. The origin of the term spätzle is often debated, as some believe it is derived from the German word for "little sparrows" (because they resemble sparrows); others believe it is derived from the Italian term *spezzato*, which means "pieces cut into strips" (accurately describing how they are made). Traditionally, these are made by pressing small lengths of the dough off of a wooden paddle and into boiling water, which results in longer lengths than described in this recipe.

YIELD: 4 pounds

MIXING METHOD: Pasta Dough/Spätzle Method

COOKING METHOD: Boiling

PROCEDURE

1. Preheat a roasting pan or large braising pan, filled to within 2 inches of the top, with water over a couple of burners on the stove; bring the water to a boil.

2. In the bowl of an electric mixer, combine the sifted flour and salt; mix briefly with a paddle attachment.

(continues)

Spätzle
(continued)

3. Combine the beaten eggs and the cup of cold water, and add them to the mixing bowl. Mix on low speed with the paddle attachment until a dough is formed.

4. Once the liquid has been absorbed, check the consistency of the dough, which should be sticky and not holding its shape. If the dough is stiff, add more water—a couple of tablespoons at a time—until this consistency is achieved.

5. Once the proper consistency is achieved, beat the dough in the mixer on a slightly higher speed until it becomes bubbly and elastic.

6. Once developed properly, remove from the mixer and test a bit of the dough by dropping a small amount into the now boiling water from step 1. Taste this for seasoning and adjust the batter/dough with salt, if necessary.

7. To cook the spätzle, place a perforated 2-inch hotel pan over the boiling water and gather the following mise en place together:

   Plastic bench scraper: to push the dough through the perforations on the pan

   Strainer: to remove the spätzle from the boiling water

   Large container with ice water: to chill the spätzle if it won't be eaten immediately

8. Once all of the mise en place are gathered, cook the spätzle by pouring a couple of cups of the batter/dough onto the perforated pan and pressing the dough against the pan with the bench scraper to force the dough through the holes (you will end up with small balls and squiggles of dough in the water).

9. Once the dough pieces rise to the surface, they are cooked and can be removed by lifting them out with the strainer and placing them in the ice water (if not eaten right away).

10. To reheat the spätzle, they can be either steamed very briefly or dropped into boiling water again very briefly. It is best to coat them with some oil after cooking so that they do not stick together.

(**NOTE:** *For variations of spätzle, add chopped fresh herbs such as dill, parsley, or chives to the dough, or add any other flavoring (like you would to flavor pasta).*

Spätzle dough (for tiny dumplings); note the sticky texture and consistency of the properly made dough

Pressing the spätzle dough through a perforated hotel pan into boiling water to cook the dumplings

Shocking the cooked spätzle in an ice-water bath to prevent overcooking; note the floating spätzle in the pot that are being removed (when they float, they are done)

Kartoffelknödel SOUTHERN GERMANY
(POTATO DUMPLING)

INGREDIENTS

For Cooking the Potato

1.5	qts	Boiling Water
2	tsp	Salt
1	small	Russet Potato (about 8 oz)

For Making the Dumplings

2	qts	Stock (you can use beef or chicken stock, or water if neither of those is available), simmering gently
2	lbs	Russet Potatoes, grated
8	oz	Milk, very hot
		Cooked Potato (see above), grated
2		Large Eggs, beaten
1	Tbsp	Fresh Parsley, minced
1/4	tsp	Nutmeg
1	Tbsp	Salt
1/2	tsp	Freshly Ground Black Pepper
10	oz	Flour
		Salt and Pepper, to taste

For Sautéing the Bread Crumbs

2	oz	Whole Butter
1/2	cup	Bread Crumbs

Dumplings are a very common accompaniment to many main dishes, such as roasts or braises that have a sauce with them. This version uses potatoes, but many others use ingredients such as bacon, apples, meat, liver, or sauerkraut as well.

YIELD: 3 pounds dumpling batter, or approximately 25 dumplings (2 ounces/dumpling)

COOKING METHOD (POTATO): Boiling

COOKING METHOD (DUMPLING): Simmering

COOKING METHOD (BREAD CRUMBS): Sautéing

PROCEDURE

For Cooking the Potato

1. Bring the water, potato, and salt to a boil over a high flame in a small pot.

2. Once the potato is tender, strain off the water and set the potato aside to cool.

3. Once the potato is cool, peel off the skin and grate the potato into a bowl.

For Making the Dumplings

1. Preheat stock on the stove by bringing it to a gentle simmer in a small pot.

2. Grate the raw russets into a mixing bowl (add cold water to the bowl to prevent them from discoloring).

3. Once the potatoes have been grated, drain off the water and squeeze out the excess moisture from the potatoes; transfer them to a clean, dry mixing bowl.

4. Pour the very hot milk over the grated and squeezed potatoes; allow them to sit until the milk cools to room temperature.

5. Once the milk has cooled, add the grated cooked potato, beaten eggs, parsley, nutmeg, salt, and pepper to the bowl; mix ingredients well.

6. Add the flour to this mixture, and mix as little as possible to yield sticky dough (the amount of flour added may vary depending on how much moisture is in the potatoes—start with less and test the dough until desired consistency is achieved).

7. Once the dough has been made, test it for consistency and seasoning by cooking a small ball in the simmering stock. (If the dough is too wet, the dumplings will come apart in the simmering stock. If the dough is too stiff, the dumplings will be very dense.) Adjust the dough with flour or milk as needed.

8. Form the dumplings by rolling approximately 2 oz of the dumpling batter in clean, wet hands to form a ball (keep a container of water

(continues)

Kartoffelknödel
(continued)

at your side so that you can keep your hands wet as you form them).

9. Once the dough consistency and flavor are correct, cook the dumplings by simmering to desired size in the stock.

10. As the dumplings are cooking (they will take about 15 minutes to cook in the stock if they are the size of a golf ball), place them in a hotel pan and hold warm until all are done.

For Sautéing the Bread Crumbs

1. Heat a small sauté pan over a medium-low flame, and add the butter to melt it.

2. Once the butter is melted, add the bread crumbs to the pan and carefully sauté them until they are brown and crisp.

3. Pour this bread crumb/butter mixture over the cooked dumplings, and serve.

Rotkohl Mit Äpfeln THURINGIA (CENTRAL GERMANY)

(BRAISED RED CABBAGE WITH APPLES)

INGREDIENTS

4	lbs	Red Cabbage, shredded
10	oz	Red Wine Vinegar
2	oz	Sugar
1	Tbsp	Salt
2	oz	Bacon, diced small
1.5	lbs	Gala Apples (or Macintosh), peeled, cored, and cut into thin slices
1	lb	Yellow Onion, sliced thin
3		Bay Leaves
1/8	tsp	Cloves, ground
2	qts	Water
4	oz	Red Wine
		Salt, to taste

This dish is a traditional accompaniment to rouladen and provides a nice sweet-and-sour balance to the savory meat rolls.

YIELD: 5 pounds, or approximately 15 portions (5 ounces/portion)

COOKING METHOD: Braising

PROCEDURE

1. Combine shredded cabbage, vinegar, sugar, and salt in a mixing bowl; mix thoroughly, cover, and set aside.

2. In a pot large enough to hold all of the ingredients, render the bacon over a medium-low flame until all of the fat has been melted out and the bacon has browned.

3. Once bacon has browned, add the sliced apples and onions and cook over medium heat until apples and onions become soft and slightly browned.

4. Add the remaining ingredients and bring the entire mixture to a simmer over medium-high heat.

5. Once the mixture has reached a simmer, cover and lower heat to gently simmer until all of the liquid has been absorbed or evaporated (about 1.5 to 2 hours).

6. Once the cabbage has absorbed the remaining liquid, check the seasoning and serve.

Pichelsteiner Eintopf GERMANY
(MEAT AND VEGETABLE STEW)

INGREDIENTS

2	lbs	Beef Stew Meat, cut into 1-inch cubes
2	lbs	Pork Butt, trimmed of significant fat and cut into 1-inch cubes
1.5	lbs	Waxy Potatoes, diced large (use Red Bliss or Yukon Gold, if available)
1	lb	Boiling Onions, peeled and halved through the root
8	oz	Carrots, peeled and diced large
1		Celery Root, trimmed of other skin and diced large
8	oz	Leek Whites, split, cleaned very well, and cut into 1-inch lengths
1		Savoy Cabbage, split through root into 8 pieces
1.5	Tbsp	Salt
1/4	tsp	White Pepper
5		Bay Leaves
2	gal	Flavorful Brown Stock
		Salt and Pepper, to taste

This national dish showcases the typical hearty German fare of meat, potatoes, and vegetables. Unpretentious and simple, when made with a good stock and other ingredients, this is a great stew.

YIELD: 12 portions (10 ounces/portion)

COOKING METHOD: Stewing

PROCEDURE

1. Place all of the trimmed and cut meats and vegetables into a heavy-bottomed pot large enough to hold the meats, vegetables, and stock.

2. Add the salt, pepper, and bay leaves to the meats and vegetables; mix well.

3. Add the stock to the pot with all of the vegetables and meats, and bring the entire mixture to a simmer over a high flame on the stove.

4. Once the mixture has reached a simmer, lower the heat so that the liquid barely bubbles and place a tight-fitting lid over the pot (use foil, if necessary, to seal the pot very well so that liquid does not escape).

5. Cook the stew covered for 1.5 hours, and then uncover to check the doneness of the meat. If it is tender, move on to the next step; if it is still tough, cover tightly again and return it to the stove.

6. Once the meat in the stew is tender, remove it from the stove and check the seasoning; serve.

Rindsrouladen GERMANY
(ROLLED BEEF STUFFED WITH PICKLES AND BACON)

INGREDIENTS

For Making the Rouladen

12		Bacon Slices, cut an inch longer than the pounded meat pieces
10	oz	Yellow Onion, sliced thin
12	4-oz	Beef Top Rounds (3 lbs total), pounded to 1/4 inch thick
2	Tbsp	Spicy Prepared Mustard (such as Dijon)
3		Sour Pickles (such as dill or cornichon), split into four pieces
		Freshly Ground Black Pepper, to taste
		Flour, as needed
24		toothpicks (or butcher's twine)

This dish is popular all over Germany and is a common sight on German menus in the United States as well. The combination of spicy mustard and sour pickles makes these beef rolls jump in the mouth.

YIELD: 12 servings (5 ounces/serving) + sauce

COOKING METHOD: Braising

PROCEDURE

For Making the Rouladen

1. In a sauté pan over a medium flame, render the pieces of bacon until the majority of the fat has been melted (but is not completely gone) and the bacon is crisp (this should take about 3–4 minutes, turning as needed). Remove the bacon pieces and set aside.

2. Once all of the bacon pieces have been cooked, pour off the excess fat from the pan, leaving approximately 2 Tbsp in the pan, and add the sliced onions; cook over a medium-low flame until they are tender and translucent.

(continues)

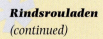

Rindsrouladen
(continued)

For the Sauce

2	oz	Clarified Butter
		Rouladen (see above)
8	oz	Yellow Onions, minced
4	oz	Carrots, minced
4	oz	Celery, minced
2	oz	Shallots, minced
1	qt	Veal Stock
2	oz	Sour Pickle Juice
1	oz	Spicy Prepared Mustard
1	oz	Tomato Purée
		Salt and Black Pepper, to taste
		Cornstarch Slurry, as needed

Rindsrouladen (rolled stuffed beef) served with spätzle and rotkohl mit äpfeln (braised red cabbage with apples)

3. Place the pounded beef pieces on a clean board and coat each piece with approximately 1/2 tsp of the mustard.

4. Place one piece of partially cooked bacon, one wedge of sour pickle, and a small amount of the cooked onions on each of the beef rolls.

5. Season each piece with some freshly ground black pepper, and roll up tightly.

6. Dredge each of the rolled beef pieces in flour, and then secure the open ends of the rouladen with a couple of toothpicks or tie them with butcher's twine.

For Cooking the Rouladen and Making the Sauce

1. Preheat the oven to 300°F.

2. In a heavy-bottomed large sauté pan, heat the clarified butter over a medium-high flame until it is rippling and hot.

3. Add just enough of the rouladen to the pan so that the pan will remain hot, and brown them well on all sides; remove from the pan and set aside.

4. Repeat step 2 until all of the rouladen have been well browned in the pan, taking care not to allow the pan to get so hot that the bottom gets burned (you are going to make a sauce in this pan!).

5. Once all of the rouladen have been well browned, turn the heat down to a medium-low flame and add the onions, carrots, celery, and shallots; sweat them until they are all tender and translucent.

6. Once the vegetables are tender, add the veal stock, pickle juice, prepared mustard, and tomato purée, and return the browned beef rouladen to the pan.

7. Cover the pan tightly with foil and a tight-fitting lid, and place it in the preheated oven; cook for 75 minutes.

8. Once it has finished cooking in the oven, remove the pan and carefully remove the lid (watch out for the steam!). Move the rouladen to a holding pan while the sauce is finished.

9. Pour the contents of the pan into a blender and blend until smooth; if there is little liquid left, add more veal stock to bring it to a sauce consistency.

10. Return the sauce to the pan and adjust consistency with slurry (if it's too thin); season with salt and pepper to taste.

11. Combine the sauce with the rouladen, and serve.

Rheinischer Sauerbraten   THE RHINELAND (SOUTHWESTERN GERMANY)
(MARINATED BEEF ROAST WITH SWEET-AND-SOUR SAUCE)

INGREDIENTS

For Making the Marinade

1.5	cups	Red Wine
1.5	cups	Red Wine Vinegar
6	cups	Water
1	lb	Yellow Onion, sliced thin
1	tsp	Black Peppercorns, crushed
2	tsp	Juniper Berries, crushed
5		Bay Leaves
1	Tbsp	Salt
6	lb	Beef Top or Bottom Round, fat trimmed to 1/4 inch

For Braising the Marinated Beef

2	oz	Lard
		Marinated Beef (see above), removed from marinade (strained and saved) and patted dry
8	oz	Yellow Onion, diced small
6	oz	Carrots, diced small
4	oz	Celery, diced small
2	oz	Flour
2	cups	Veal Stock, cool
4	cups	Reserved Marinade, cool
4	oz	Raisins
8	oz	Sour Cream
		Salt, to taste

Rheinischer sauerbraten (marinated beef roast with sweet-and-sour sauce) served with braised red cabbage and spätzle (tiny dumplings)

There are several versions of sauerbraten in Germany, and all are made from marinated beef that is braised in a sour marinade. The version found in the lower Rhineland of western Germany is a bit different than some of the others, in that it uses wine as well as vinegar in the marinade, along with raisins to provide sweetness that counteracts the sourness of the marinade. This would traditionally be thickened using gingerbread (you can omit the roux from this recipe and thicken with gingerbread instead, for a more traditional version) and served with potato dumplings and red cabbage.

YIELD: 12 portions (6–7 ounces/portion) + sauce

COOKING METHOD: Braising

PROCEDURE

For Making the Marinate

1. Combine the red wine, red wine vinegar, water, onion, spices, bay leaves, and salt in a small pot, and bring mixture to a boil over a high flame.
2. Once the mixture has come to a boil, remove from the heat and allow it to cool to room temperature.
3. Place the marinade in a sanitized container just large enough to hold the beef roast and marinade (about 6 qts), and add both the beef and the marinade; cover, label, and place in refrigerator for 3 days, turning the meat occasionally.

For Braising the Marinated Beef

1. Preheat the oven to 325°F.
2. Remove the beef from the marinade, straining the marinade through a chamois or cheesecloth and reserving the liquid.
3. Pat the moisture from the surface of the beef, and set it aside.
4. Heat a large sauté pan or a small braising pan over a medium-high flame, and add the lard.
5. Once the lard has gotten hot, add the beef round to the pan and sear on all sides until the roast has developed a deep brown color (be careful not to burn the fronds in the pan, as they will provide much of the flavor).
6. Once the beef has been seared, remove it from the pan and set it aside.
7. Add the small diced onions, carrots, and celery to the pan with the remaining fat; lower the flame slightly to sweat the vegetables until they are tender.
8. Turn the heat up on the pan, and allow the vegetables to brown slightly before adding the flour to make a blond roux.
9. Once the roux has colored, add the cool veal stock and marinade, stirring vigorously with a whisk as you do so to avoid any lumps.
10. Add the raisins and then the beef roast; cover with foil and a tight-fitting lid, and place in the preheated oven. Roast for 2–3 hours, or until the beef becomes very tender.

(continues)

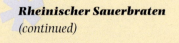

Rheinischer Sauerbraten
(continued)

11. Once the beef is very tender, remove it from the oven and place the beef on a cutting board; allow it to cool before slicing.

12. Strain the resulting sauce from the pan through a sieve, and press some of the vegetables through the sieve along with the sauce.

13. Return the sauce to the stove and adjust the consistency via reduction or thinning using the remaining reserved marinade (if you are adding the marinade, make sure to bring the mixture back to a boil, ensuring that the raw marinade has been sanitized by cooking it).

14. Once consistency has been adjusted, temper in the sour cream; adjust seasoning, if necessary.

15. Slice the roast into 1/4-inch slices, and serve with sauce.

Lebkuchen   BAVARIA (SOUTHEASTERN GERMANY)
(GINGERBREAD)

INGREDIENTS

18	oz	Honey
8	oz	Brown Sugar
2	tsp	Lemon Zest
2		Large Eggs, beaten
2	lbs	Whole Wheat Flour
10	oz	Almond Flour
2	Tbsp	Baking Powder
1	Tbsp	Cinnamon, ground
1	tsp	Ginger, ground
1/2	tsp	Nutmeg, ground
1/2	tsp	Cloves, ground

After merchant traders introduced spices from the east to German ports, the use of these spices in particular areas became quite common. One of the uses that persists today is in making gingerbread. Nuremberg was the center of many baking guilds and is also the largest producer of lebkuchen.

YIELD: Half sheet pan

MIXING METHOD: Hand Kneading

COOKING METHOD: Baking

PROCEDURE

1. Preheat the oven to 325°F.

2. Combine the honey, brown sugar, and lemon zest in a small pot, and gently heat to infuse all of the flavors and melt the brown sugar (heat over a very low flame for 10 minutes); once done, set aside to cool.

3. Once the honey mixture has cooled to room temp or slightly warmer, add the beaten egg and stir very well.

4. Sift together the whole wheat flour, almond flour, baking powder, and spices, and transfer to a mixing bowl with a paddle attachment.

5. Add the honey/egg mixture to the sifted ingredients and mix, just until a dough is formed.

6. Turn the dough out onto a lightly floured, clean workbench, and knead the dough until it becomes smooth and not sticky.

7. Wrap the dough in plastic wrap and place it in the refrigerator to rest for 1 hour.

8. Once the dough has rested, remove it from the refrigerator and turn it out onto the workbench; roll out to a piece that will fit into a half sheet pan (18 × 13).

9. Transfer the rolled dough onto a half sheet pan lined with a sheet of parchment paper and sprayed with pan spray; bake it in the preheated oven until done (this should take about 15–20 minutes), or until the bread springs back from the touch.

10. Remove from the oven and, if desired, coat with sugar icing.

Bayerische Crème BAVARIA (SOUTHEASTERN GERMANY)
(BAVARIAN CREAM)

INGREDIENTS

7	oz	Sugar
6		Large Eggs, yolks only
1		Vanilla Bean, split (substitute 2 tsp vanilla extract, if bean is unavailable)
12	oz	Whole Milk
1	Tbsp	Gelatin, bloomed in 3 Tbsp water
8	oz	Heavy Cream
2	tsp	Sugar (vanilla sugar, if available)

This well-known dessert component is often served with sugar-coated fruits or flavored with fruit brandies such as kirchwasser (cherry brandy). It was actually invented in France—in a Paris café that was a regular spot for Bavarian nobility—but it has since become a common component of German cuisine.

YIELD: 4 cups, or approximately 6 servings

COOKING METHOD: Careful Simmering/Thickening

MIXING METHOD (CREAM): Whipping to Stiff Peaks

MIXING METHOD (CREAM TO CUSTARD): Folding

PROCEDURE

1. In a small mixing bowl, combine the sugar and egg yolks; mix to combine.

2. Put the milk in a small pot, and scrape the tiny seeds and pulp out of the vanilla bean with the back of a chef's knife. Add both the pulp and the 2 pod halves to the milk, and heat the milk to just under simmering over a medium-low flame.

3. Remove the pod pieces from the milk and temper the milk into the egg yolk/sugar mixture, mixing constantly while adding.

4. Add the bloomed gelatin to the egg and milk mixture, and place the contents of the mixing bowl in a small pot. Return the pot to the medium-low flame, and, while constantly stirring, heat the mixture until it thickens.

5. Once the custard thickens, remove it from the heat and allow it to cool to room temperature on an ice bath (don't allow it to get too cool, or you will have a very difficult time folding in the whipped cream).

6. Combine the heavy cream and sugar in a mixing bowl, and beat with a wire whisk or in an electric mixer with a whip attachment until stiff peaks are just achieved (do not go past the early stiff peaks, or folding will be much more difficult).

7. Fold the whipped cream into the custard mix, taking care not to overmix and lose the volume attained by whipping the cream.

8. Place the Bavarian cream in the refrigerator for at least 2 hours before serving.

Bowl of bayerische crème (Bavarian cream) served with fruit and lebkuchen (gingerbread)

SUMMARY

German cuisine emphasizes substance over style and relies on the utilization and creation of foods that keep people warm in this cold land. German cuisine is based on foods that can be preserved, as this is a northern country with a relatively short growing season. Some of the common preserved items include cabbage preserved as sauerkraut, beets preserved by pickling, meats preserved in the making of sausages and by smoking, and grains preserved in the making of beer and bread.

Pork products, potatoes, beets, bread, and beer are some of the main components of the German diet, and a large variety of foods are created with just this limited group of ingredients. The cuisine of Germany has a comforting and inviting quality that varies by region, with local specialties combined with the typical ingredients common throughout the country.

REVIEW QUESTIONS

1. How does preservation play a significant role in the cuisine of Germany? Give some examples of preserved foods that are common in the typical diet.

2. How did Frederick the Great play a significant role in the development of the German cuisine?

3. How does the climate of Germany affect the types of foods that are typically eaten?

COMMON TERMS, FOODS, AND INGREDIENTS

The following German terms are some of the most commonly used and important in German cuisine.

✳ Ingredients and Prepared Foods

apfel – Apple

apfelmus – Applesauce

apfelstrudel – Apple strudel (apple-filled thin pastry)

bayerische crème – Bavarian cream, a thickened vanilla-flavored custard mixture often served with fruits or flavored with liqueurs

beeren – Berries

bier – Beer

birnen – Pears

birnen, boden, und speck – Hamburg dish of pears, beans, and bacon

brot – Bread

eintopf – Stews or casseroles with a variety of ingredients to make a one-pot meal; also a term used to indicate the stewing method

fisch – Fish

fleisch – Meat

forelle – Trout

Frankfurter grüne sosse – Green sauce in the style of Frankfurt; this sauce is made by crushing fresh herbs and mixing them with mayonnaise and sour cream to yield a highly flavored sauce that is served with potatoes or other bland foods

hackepeter – Chopped raw pork, highly seasoned and served on a roll

hasen – Hare

hering – Herring

heringsstippe – Herring and apple salad

Himmel und Erde – "Heaven and Earth"; dish of mashed potatoes and cooked apples topped with panfried blood sausage and sautéed onion rings

honig – Honey

innerrien – Innards/offal from animals

kalb – Veal

kalbsrolle – Stuffed rolled veal breast

kartoffelklösse – Name for potato dumpling in northern Germany

kartoffelknödel – Name for potato dumpling in southern Germany

kartoffelpfannkuchen – Potato pancake; also called kartoffelpuffer

kartoffelpuffer – Potato pancake; also called kartoffelpfannkuchen

kartoffels – Potatoes, also called erdapfel (earth apple) in southern Germany

kartoffelsalat – Potato salad

kartoffelsalat mit speck – Potato salad with bacon

klöss – Dumpling (more common name in northern Germany)

knödel – Dumpling (more common name in southern Germany)

kraut – Cabbage

kuchen – Cake

lebkuchen – Gingerbread

linsensuppe – Lentil soup

maultaschen – Filled pasta of the Swabian region of Germany that is formed like ravioli or rolled like strudel

niederrheinische leberwurst – Country-style liver sausage from lower Rhineland region of Germany

nudeln – Noodle

pfannengerichte – Panfried

pichelsteiner eintopf – Meat and vegetable stew common throughout Germany

pilze – Mushrooms

pökelfische – Pickled herring

pumpernickel – Bread made from rye from the Westphalia region of Germany

rheinischer sauerbraten – Marinated and braised beef in the style of the Rhineland. The meat is marinated in wine and vinegar and then braised and served with the sour sauce, to which raisins have been added for sweetness.

rindsfleisch – Beef

rindsfleisch tartare – Steak tartare

rindsrouladen – Rolled and stuffed beef cutlet cooked with gravy

rotkohl mit äpfeln – Braised red cabbage and apples

rouladen – Rolled stuffed meat, usually filled with bacon and mustard or sauerkraut

sauerbraten – Marinated and braised sour beef

sauerkraut – Fermented and soured cabbage

saure crème – Sour cream

schnapps – Distillate of fruit or grain common in southern Germany; often made from the fruit of the local orchards

schwäbischer kartoffelsalat – Swabian-style potato salad; this salad includes mustard and herbs, indicative of the French influence in the region

Schwarzwälder Kirschtorte – Black Forest cake

schwein – Pork

schweinshaxen – Braised pork knuckles

skinken – Ham from central Germany

spargel – Asparagus

spätzle – "Little sparrows"; name given to tiny dumplings of Swabia; name also could have derived from the Italian *spezzato*, which means "pieces cut into strips," an accurate description of the traditional way of making spätzle

speck – Cured and smoked pork belly (very similar to bacon)

steinhäger – Juniper berry–flavored distillate from Steinhägen; similar to gin in the United States

stockfische – Salt cod

strudel – Flaky pastry with various fillings, such as apples or cheese

suppe – Soup

tortes – Sweet, moist cakes and tarts

wammerl – Pickled pork belly

wienerbrot – Literal translation is Vienna bread, but these are known as Danish pastries in the United States

wildbret – Venison

wurst – Sausage

zwiebels – Onions

✳ Cooking Methods and Equipment

binden – To thicken a soup or sauce with a starch

blanchieren – To blanch in boiling water

braten – To braise

dämpfen – To steam (sometimes called *dünsten*)

dünsten (or pochieren) – To poach (also may mean to steam, depending on usage)

eintopf – Stewing

gebäck – Chef

geräuchert – Smoked

geschmort – Braised; also called *braten*

gesotten – Simmered

kneten – To knead

marinieren – To marinate

panieren – To coat with bread crumbs or another starch

pfannen – Pan

schwenken – To sauté

töpfe – Pot

überkrusten – To brown the top surface of a dish using a broiler or salamander (often called *gratin* in the United States)

unterheben – To fold in an ingredient to another base

CHAPTER 8

Map legend:
- towns and cities
- capital city
- river
- international boundary
- mountains

0   100   200 km

N
W   E
S

ARCTIC OCEAN

ICELAND

NORWEGIAN SEA

KJOLEN MOUNTAINS

SWEDEN

FINLAND

S C A N D I N A V I A

JOTUNHEIM MOUNTAINS

NORWAY

Helsinki

Bergen

Oslo

Stockholm

ESTONIA

RUSS

NORTH SEA

LATVIA

BALTIC
SEA

DENMARK

LITHUANIA

Copenhagen

KALININGRAD
(RUSSIA)

IRELAND

U. K.

BELARUS

ATLANTIC
OCEAN

NETHERLANDS

POLAND

BELGIUM

GERMANY

UKRAINE

FRANCE

LUXEMBOURG

CZECH

70°   20°   10°   0°   10°   20°   30°   40°

60°

50°

0°   10°   20°

Scandinavian Cuisine

OBJECTIVES

Upon completion of this chapter, you will be able to

- explain what makes Scandinavian cuisine unique.
- identify the common cooking methods used in traditional Scandinavian cuisine.
- recognize the common recipes found in Scandinavian cuisine.
- produce a variety of Scandinavian recipes.
- define the terms listed at the conclusion of the chapter.

INTRODUCTION

The northernmost countries of Europe have long been known for the mariner Vikings (general name for Scandinavian seamen) who sailed from their shores, and not so much for the foods and culinary traditions that spread from these cold countries. Although the countries of Finland, Sweden, Norway, and Denmark (Iceland is often included with these countries, as well, when referring to Scandinavia) may not be the culinary hubs that their southern European neighbors are, they do have a culinary repertoire that is underappreciated—perhaps purposely so. The Scandinavian nature has long been to explore and appreciate other lands but not so much to gloat about the merits of their own culinary heritage. Perhaps they wanted to keep it to themselves. Whatever the reason, the cuisine from this northern region will surely become more common and indeed more popular as more people become familiar with it.

Scandinavia makes up the northernmost part of Europe and lies in a region of cold but fertile seas, long winters, and short summers. It is often said that this northern land only has those two seasons, and the difficulties associated with living in a cold climate certainly play a significant role in Scandinavia's culinary traditions. Most of the cooking in Scandinavia is based around the stove or fire; many foods are baked or roasted inside the stove, or panfried, stewed, or sautéed on top of the stove. The challenges of the climate have also resulted in the development of many preserved foods as part of the diet. Salting, smoking, pickling, and drying all play important roles in the cuisine and in sustaining life through the winter months.

Scandinavia is a region of natural beauty and purity, and these characteristics reveal themselves in the native cuisine. Like many other part of the world today, customs and ingredients from other places are becoming more common here, but the Scandinavians still treasure the traditions that have sustained them through the centuries—and for that we should all be thankful.

HISTORIC CULINARY INFLUENCES

Scandinavia has a storied history of conquest and conquers that dates back many centuries. Much of the impetus for the early Vikings to explore came directly from their culinary predicament: how could they survive in a land where the sun sets for long stretches of time and food supplies dwindle? Scandinavia is a land of contrasts—the summer yields incredible bounties from the land and sea, but the winter is long and cruel—and the inhabitants of these lands had to learn how to survive under these circumstances. Because of the bounty of the summer months, these lands were subject to invasion from some of their neighbors, and the Scandinavians sought out comforts from other lands as well. These influences will be explored in the following section.

Early Vikings

Because the Vikings were one of the main inhabitants of today's Scandinavian countries, their traditions and culinary habits are still found in a great deal of Scandinavian cooking. They relied on the many available ingredients to make an uncomplicated and efficient cuisine, which enabled them to get through the difficult winters of these northern lands.

Some of the ingredients used in these early times included meats such as *fårkött* (mutton), *renkött* (reindeer), *gås* (goose), *skogshare* (arctic hare), and *anka* (duck); fish such as *lax* (salmon), *sill* (herring), and *torsk* (cod); fruits such as *hjortron* (cloudberry) and *lingon* (lingonberry); vegetables such as *rödbeta* (beet), *kål* (cabbage), and *lök* (onion); and staple grains of *korn* (barley), *råg* (rye), and *havre* (oats). These foods were prepared simply and freshly, and the techniques that were used to preserve them first began to expose the inventiveness of these people.

Very early on, the Vikings learned about preservation techniques that could extend their harvests through the winter, in good years, and allow them to survive the cold, dark winters. Some of the preservation techniques that they employed included salt curing, air-drying, pickling, and fermenting. These techniques would not only make it easier for the people to survive but would also become part of the very fabric of life, and they are still very common here, even though they are no longer necessary for survival.

European Traders

With the Vikings roaming the seas and looking for goods to help ease life back home, trade between other European countries and the Norsemen became increasingly common. The Vikings traveled in many directions and with varying intentions. Many of the Vikings from Denmark and Norway raided ships and port towns along the western part of Europe, while the Swedish Vikings often traveled far to the east, reaching Baghdad and Greece, and were often looking to trade their goods. It was through these exchanges that salt cod and herring became staples in many European countries, including such southern countries as Spain, Portugal, and Italy. Both of these preserved fishes could be stored in the warmer and more humid Mediterranean, whereas many of the local ingredients could not. While the northern fish flowed south, southern goods and customs flowed north, and the Scandinavians were introduced to many items found in southern Europe, such as capers, spinach, wine, and grapes. Many spices also began to be introduced into Scandinavian cooking at this time as the use of spices in the cooking of Southern European countries was adapted by the sailors who visited these countries. It is not known when Scandinavians transported dill (same name Scandinavia), *senap* (mustard), or *fänkål* (fennel) from the Mediterranean region but it is clear that these spices all were adopted eagerly into the cuisine of Scandinavia.

Swedish East Indian Company

The formation of the Swedish East Indian Company in 1731 began a period of trade that introduced a number of new ingredients into the kitchens of Scandinavia. This company was formed to trade wood and steel from Sweden for goods from China and India mainly, as much success in this trade was seen by the Swedes from both the Dutch and the English of this time period. Tea from China was one of the major trade goods as were spices from India, including the spice blends so commonly associated with Indian cuisine. *Garam Masala* (Indian "warm" spice blend) and *curry* (the generic name for spice blends in India) both are commonly found in Scandinavian cooking, and the spices used to make these blends—such as peppercorns, ginger, cardamom, and cloves—are also common components of the cuisine. During this period of trade the import of sugar increased greatly and became more common in the household of the Scandinavians, providing the ingredient needed or what would become a constant in the Scandinavian diet as sweet pastries were adopted to go along with the new hot drinks of coffee and tea.

Frederick the Great of Prussia and the Potato

Frederick the Great, who ruled the land of Prussia (present-day Germany and Poland) from the late eighteenth century through the beginning of the nineteenth century, forced the peasants of these countries to plant potatoes, which had been introduced to Europe from South America. The peasants were reluctant to plant or eat the potatoes initially, because they viewed them as dirty—tubers were thought to be closer to the devil. Frederick's orders to have the armies ensure that potatoes were part of the crop planting to help protect against famine resulted in the slow acceptance of the potato in these regions. Swedish soldiers who served in the Prussian army at this time brought the potatoes back to Sweden, and eventually the other Scandinavian countries, and they began to be accepted there as well. In 1771–1772, a horrible crop failure of the staple grains occurred, and the importance of the potato was recognized from then on. By the early 1800s, potatoes had become a component of every family's diet—and still are to this day.

The French Connection

In the eighteenth century, French chefs—who commanded great respect at the time for their home cuisine—began to be imported to serve royalty and aristocrats in the Scandinavian countries. The French chefs produced mostly classic French cuisine, and many of their techniques and recipes flowed into the Scandinavian cuisine during this period; for example, the use of roux, béchamel, meringues, and many soups became common elements in Scandinavian cuisine. The importation of French chefs did not last for a long period of time, because many of the Scandinavian foods came more into fashion in the years to come, but the impact was already made with regard to several techniques. The most notable of the French influences that has remained a part of the cuisine of Scandinavia is the techniques and diverse use of sauces and soup making. With the introduction of the process of making roux and béchamel, the Scandinavians developed a varied repertoire of sauces that are still found in many of the traditional preparations. Soups are a major part of the typical diet as well, and many examples of fish, vegetable, and starch-based soups can be found.

Russia and the Karelians

An area of present-day Russia was once part of Finland and home to a group of people known as the Karelians, who have cultural ties to the western Russian Karelians. After World War II, Finland ceded a section of its country to Russia as part of the agreement to end hostilities. Amazingly, all of the Karelians in the ceded land decided to pack up and move into the remaining territory of Finland rather than stay and be subject to rule by Russia. The rest of the country of Finland absorbed all 400,000 Karelians into their homes until they could get back on their feet. The Karelian people brought with them their culinary traditions and methods, which mirror many of those found in Russia. Some of the influences include *piirakkas* (filled savory pasties or pies), *borsch* (beet soup), *blinis* (thin pancakes with sweet or savory fillings), caviar, and stroganoff (hearty stew with sour cream).

UNIQUE COMPONENTS

The geographic position of the Scandinavian countries plays a significant role in the cuisine that developed there. This is cold country, where the winters are long and the growing seasons short, both of which impact yearly planning and selection. This is also a country of seafaring traditions and dependence—Scandinavians have always turned to the sea for sustenance. All of these elements play a part in this unique and efficient cuisine.

Summer Bounty

These northern countries are home to an annual ritual of the summer harvest like few other places in the world. The summer means long days of light, and it also means the retreating snow will yield many products that are used throughout the year. In the woods and marshes, berries reveal themselves in huge numbers. In the ocean, the herring runs are a source of huge catches (Norway has one of the largest fishing fleets in the world), and cod is plentiful as well. In the seemingly endless number of streams and rivers, salmon spawn and *kräftor* (crawfish) are found, providing two other main elements of this northern diet. During the warmer summer days and ample sunlight, the crops grow and the cows calve, producing some of the best milk in the world. This cycle of bounty is seen every year in this northern land, and every year the Scandinavians are hard at work during this time because they know the winter is always right around the corner.

An important point of consideration regarding this bounty is the relative lack of farming that is possible in these countries. With the exception of Denmark, most of the land in Scandinavia is very difficult to farm, and thus the emphasis for food is on collecting and hunting, historically making the summer bounty a period of great importance to the livelihood of the peoples of this region. The irony of this bounty is that much of it needs to be preserved; many of the products that are available throughout the summer months are preserved in one manner or another to provide for the upcoming winters. Although this is not as necessary today as it was in the past, with transportation enabling products from other parts of the world to be brought in, this preservation culture is still a common fabric of the Scandinavian lifestyle.

Survival Techniques

The long and dark winters of these northern countries necessitated that they use whatever techniques possible to survive the difficult season. The early settlers of this region learned quickly that they could dry food to preserve it; in time, they also learned to smoke, pickle, and salt foods as well. These preservation methods were once a necessity to survive and, although they are in many ways no longer such a necessity (in some ways they still are—they help to utilize large harvests of fish before they spoil or to prevent a market from collapsing from too much product during harvest), they are still practiced and revered in this region. When it comes to drying, many of the breads of this region traditionally were baked and then dried to allow them to last through the winter—this is why many varieties have a hole in the middle, which was used to hang them as they dried in the rafters. Pickling is used to make the pickled beets and herring that are very common throughout Scandinavia, and curing is used to preserve fish and meat. Were it not for the understanding and use of these methods, Scandinavians surely would have struggled to survive in their challenging climate; their admiration for these products is evident in their continued use, despite more modern conveniences.

Coffee and Sweets

Scandinavians have long enjoyed coffee and pastries as a snack and for formal occasions, midmorning meals, afternoon get-togethers, or virtually any other reason. Scandinavia has some of the highest coffee consumption in the world and, as part of this custom, produces many types of breads, pastries, and cookies to accompany the coffee for all occasions. These range from the well-known *wienerbrød* (Danish filled and unfilled pastries, simply called Danishes in the United States) to coffee cakes, sweet breads, and sugar cookies such as *pepperkakor* (gingersnaps) and *krumkaker* (delicate cone-shaped cookies).

Because of the Scandinavians' preservation skills and the surplus that would often result, these countries have a long tradition of trading with other nations. Dried cod from Scandinavia was an important commercial product that provided the Scandinavians with products from many other countries in southern Europe and beyond. Coffee and sugar also were brought in from trade frequently, as were spices (such as ginger and cinnamon, which were used commonly used in the pastries) and other food commodities.

Preservation Techniques

The preservations techniques of curing and pickling have been practiced in Scandinavia for centuries. *Stokkfisk* (dried cod), *inlagd sill* (pickled herring), *roget sill* (smoked herring), and *gravlax* (salt-cured salmon) were likely invented here (gravlax, which literally translates to "grave salmon," originally was buried and fermented, a technique similar to the predecessor of modern sushi; this technique may have made its way from China to Scandinavia via the Mongols). Their popularity spread to the rest of Europe from here. Once vinegar was introduced to the Scandinavians, the pickling of vegetables and fish came very common and remains so today. Many of these preserved products are used in recipes; as a result, Scandinavians eat a significant amount of savory foods that would be considered salty or quite sour to the typical American palate. The Scandinavian contributions to the culinary arts have had an impact throughout the world, as salt cod in particular came to be depended on for many ranging from the Iberian Peninsula to the Caribbean, and other areas because it provided an economical protein source that could be stored for significant lengths of time. The traditions of preserving foods by means of smoking, salting, and air-drying spread beyond the countries of Scandinavia and helped to ensure a food supply to people in faraway lands.

Seafood

Scandinavians have an affinity for, and much experience in, living off of the seas and streams. All of the countries in this region have extensive coastlines and thousands of lakes and streams. *Lax*, *sill*, and *torsk* all play significant roles in the cuisines of these countries, as do many other species from the local waters. In Finland, the crayfish are loved and looked forward to each summer, while in Denmark the eels and lobsters are eagerly awaited. In both Norway and Sweden, the annual salmon runs are anticipated, as is fishing season for trout in the streams, and the Norwegians have a love affair with the local mussels and oysters from their shores. All of these countries include herring as part of their regular diet and appreciate the lasting quality of salt cod (or air-dried salt cod) treated with lye, called *lutefisk*. Another constant in the cuisines of Scandinavia is forcemeats made from fish—and often formed into balls—which are poached and served with soups and fish entrees. Fishing has long been a major trade of the Scandinavian people, dating back to the time of the Vikings; the fishing tradition and industry are still major components of the cuisine of this region today.

SIGNIFICANT SUBREGIONS

Scandinavia covers a vast area that—not surprisingly—includes many different culinary traditions and a range of ingredient availability. The following guide explores these different regions by examining the countries that make up Scandinavia (**Note:** Iceland, which lies some 600 miles off the eastern coast of Norway, is often included in this region, but it is not included in this text so that we can focus on the larger influences). The countries are listed from east to west and then from north to south.

Finland

The easternmost portion of Scandinavia is the country of Finland, which borders Russia to the east and the Baltic Sea and Sweden to the west. Finland is a country of forests and waterways; the arable land is found on the coasts, and this is where the majority of the population resides. With limited land for raising crops, most of the suitable land is committed to such foods as potatoes, beets, onions, cauliflower, and grains. The dense forests also yield a significant amount of wild mushrooms, berries, and game, while the thousands of streams, lakes, and the Baltic Sea yield the many varieties of fish and shellfish. Some of the common varieties of fish include the Baltic herring, trout, burbot, and a small relative of salmon called *muikku*. From these products, the Finns produce many dishes that show their relation to the other Scandinavian countries as well as their historic connection with neighboring Russia. This country has deservedly acquired a reputation for producing hearty

and honest cuisine that makes the most of what nature provides.

Throughout history, Finland has been a country of perseverance. Once ruled by the Swedes for 600 years, and ruled by the Russians for 100 years, the Finns have steadfastly held onto their traditions—many even packed up all their belongings and moved after part of Finland was ceded at the end of World War II. The northernmost portion of the country is known as Lapland and is home to the Sámi people, who have lived in the arctic country for centuries, largely off of the reindeer that roam these lands. Baking in brick ovens has long been a tradition in Finland, and one main component of the Finnish diet is *ruisleip* (a sour rye bread), which is made frequently in eastern Finland (and has a soft texture); in western Finland, it is traditionally made twice a year and hung through a hole in its center to dry out for storage (this is why it is usually made with a hole in the center). Other foods include crayfish boiled with dill and eaten on buttered toast, many types of *piirakkas* (filled pasties) and *pashas* (cheesecakes), and several stews and casseroles that warm the body in this cold land. The Finn's tradition of game hunting and living off of the land is still evident in many menus, with the common inclusion of game meats and birds as selections.

Another way Finnish people stay warm is by taking a sauna, which is a weekly tradition in Finland. It is also used to cure and smoke meats, the most common of which is a leg of lamb.

Sweden

Sweden is the most populated of the Scandinavian countries. It lies just north of Denmark across the Baltic Sea and borders Norway to the west. Sweden has a milder climate in the southern sections than much of Finland or Norway, but its northern reaches are bitter cold. The Swedes are some of the most advanced peoples in northern Europe, in terms of economic health and technological advancement, and as a result have access to more options than some of their neighbors.

When most people think of Swedish cuisine, the *smörgåsbord* comes to mind: a table full of choices, from cold to hot, including herring preparations, a variety of open-faced sandwiches, meatballs, and omelets. Although this can still be found in Sweden, the smörgåsbord is mostly a thing of the (royal court) past, as the gorging and expense of this tradition are not as common as they once were. Many of the components of the smörgåsbord tables are still found on menus in

Sweden or are made in household kitchens. For example, *Janssons frestelse* (Jansson's temptation), *sillsallad* (herring salad), inlagd sill (pickled herring), gravlax (cured salmon), and *köttbullar* (Swedish meatballs) are all still regular parts of the typical Swedish diet. In addition to the prepared foods found on the smörgåsbord a number of cheeses and sausages are also common. Some cheeses that are likely to be served include *sveciaost* (semifirm cow's milk cheese), *västerbottenost* (prized hard cow's milk cheese from Vasterbotten), and *hushållsost* (slightly sour, mild cow's milk cheese) while sausages such as *falukorv* (lightly smoked, boiled, smooth sausage made from beef or veal and pork), *herrgårdskorv* (rich pork sausage), and *spiekekorv* (salami-like fermented dried sausage) are all likely to be found as part of the presentation.

Swedes, like their Scandinavian neighbors in Norway and Denmark, are likely to be found eating non-Swedish foods these days. With the focus on health and the increased availability of products from other parts of the world, foreign foods like pizza and sushi have made their way into the typical diet. Yet, even with these considerations, Swedes still crave and turn to their traditional foods on a regular basis. Whether it be the smörgåsbord components, *ärtsoppa* (yellow split pea soup) warming the cold winters, *korv* (Swedish sausage) from a market stand, or even the very strong-smelling *surströmming* (soured Baltic herring), the Swedish affinity for these items is as deep as the typical American craving for the occasional burger and fries.

Norway

Norway, the westernmost portion of Scandinavia, is a country of mountains, streams, and ocean access. The Norwegian fishing fleet is the largest in all of Europe, and this industry is second only to oil and gas in Norway, providing employment to a large sector of the community. As a result of this tradition and the limited amount of agricultural areas, fish has always played a significant role in the Norwegian diet. Some of the species eaten most frequently are *torsk, lax,* and *sild,* as well as trout from the many streams that descend from the mountains. Much of the catch from the Norwegian fishing fleet is preserved either by air-drying it, as with *stockfisk* (air-dried cod); by drying it in the crisp, cold artic air of the Norwegian west coast on large wooden racks (called *hjell*); or by salting and then drying it, as is the case with *klippfisk* (salt cod). The Norwegian diet is similar in many ways to that of Sweden, as these two countries not only share a border but also were once united as a country only a little over 100 years ago.

Lefse (potato flatbread) is a common component of many Norwegians diets and is used to wrap other ingredients, much as a flour tortilla is used in Mexican cuisine. Also common are *fiskesuppe* (fish soup), *fiskefarse* (fish forcemeat), and *fiskepudding* (fish pudding), all of which might be served with *rekesaus* (shrimp sauce) and indicate this country's connection to the sea. Hunting wild game is a popular Norwegian activity, and one frequently comes across game at the table such as venison, elk, hare, and other species that are found in the mountains of the Norwegian interior.

Denmark

Denmark is the only Scandinavian country that is directly connected to mainland Europe; the others are connected to Russia (Iceland is not connected to either, because it is located hundreds of miles off the cost of Norway). Denmark is connected to northern Germany and shares many traits with its southern neighbors. Like the Germans, the Danish have a special affinity for pork and potatoes and also have a long tradition of fine baking (their pastries are world renown). Denmark is also a country of pastures and produces some of the world's best dairy products. Not surprisingly, these dairy products are common in their cuisine, from their appreciation of cheeses to their use of butter and cream in cooking. The Danish diet has long been one of the richest in Scandinavia.

Some of the cheeses from Denmark are *Tybo* (a nutty cow's milk cheese often flavored with caraway), *Danbo, Havarti,* and *Samso* (often called the "cheddar of Denmark"), to name just a few.

Sharing in the traditions of its northern neighbors, the Danish are also well known for their elaborate cold tables—in particular, for their *smørrebrød* ("buttered bread" by translation, but this name also includes additions to the top of the buttered bread). The many toppings (called the *pålæg*) for the buttered bread might include roasted pork or beef, pickled herring, liver pâté, pickled beets, smoked salmon, any of the many Danish cheeses, and so on. These open-faced sandwiches are typically served on the well-known Danish *rugbrød* (rye bread).

The Danish bakers are not as well known for their bread as they are for their pastries, as a Danish in the United States refers to a sweet pastry rolled with cinnamon, filled with jam, and so forth. The baking tradition in Denmark goes back a long way, but it was the period when the Danes would *not* bake that led to their strong reputation. In the late 1800s, the Danish bakers went on strike, and, in the meantime, Viennese bakers were hired to make the breads and sweets. These Viennese bakers made a rolled-in dough, which layers butter and dough, and this product gained instant popularity with the Danish people. Once the Danish bakers returned, they recognized this product's popularity and imitated it; eventually they perfected it and broadened the scope of products made with it. In Denmark, this is known as wienerbrød (Vienna bread), and the popularity of this style spread all over Europe and into the United States as well, where it is known as a danish.

RECIPES

The following recipes provide a glimpse into the culinary repertoire of Scandinavians. As with many other cultures today, these countries have seen a fair amount of change in their diets as the focus on nutrition grows and the availability of foreign foods becomes easier. Many of the heavier foods that are traditional to this region are being eaten less, but they still make up a major part of the general diet.

✳ **Lefse** NORWAY
(POTATO FLATBREAD)

INGREDIENTS

2	gal	Water
1	Tbsp	Salt
4	lbs	Russet Potatoes, peeled
5	oz	Butter, melted
6	oz	Heavy Cream
1	Tbsp	Salt
2	Tbsp	Sugar
1	lb	All-Purpose (A.P.) Flour + flour for dusting

Cooking lefse on the griddle

Flatbreads have been a part of the baking tradition in Scandinavia for many years, and lefse is a very popular version found in Norway. When these flatbreads originally were made, they would be prepared in large quantities because they keep very well when stored in a cool, dry place or the freezer (there are many freezers in Scandinavia—better known as "outside"!).

YIELD: 40 (approximately 2 ounces/lefse)

COOKING METHOD (POTATOES): Boiling

COOKING METHOD (LEFSE DOUGH): Dry Griddling

PROCEDURE

1. Preheat the oven to 300°F.

2. Combine water and 1 Tbsp salt in a pot, and bring to a boil over a high flame on the stove.

3. Cut potatoes into quarters and place them in boiling water; cook until potatoes are tender throughout when pierced with a knife.

4. Drain the potatoes; allow them to steam off and then transfer them to a pan. Place them in the preheated oven for 5 minutes to dry further.

5. Once potatoes have dried in the oven, run them through a food mill and combine with butter, heavy cream, salt, and sugar.

6. Transfer this mixture to a mixing bowl, and allow it to cool to room temperature.

7. Preheat a griddle to 400°F.

8. Once the potato mixture has cooled, work flour into it by adding 4 oz of the flour at a time—for first 12 oz of flour—and then add the remaining flour as needed to yield a dry (not sticky) and smooth dough (you may not need all of the flour).

9. Once the dough has been formed, divide it into about 40 pieces, each the size of a racquetball (about 2 oz).

10. On a floured bench, roll out the dough pieces to the thickness of 1/8 inch (about the thickness of a tortilla). This would traditionally be done using a grooved rolling pin that makes very thin rolling easier.

(continues)

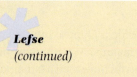

Lefse
(continued)

11. Cook the dough pieces on the preheated, ungreased griddle until they turn golden on the first side (about 2 minutes); carefully turn them over and briefly cook the pieces on the other side before removing them (the lefse should be flexible and still slightly soft).

NOTE: *Lefse are commonly eaten spread with butter or sprinkled with cinnamon and sugar.*

Rågsiktlimpör   SWEDEN
(SWEDISH RYE SPICE BREAD)

INGREDIENTS

1	oz	Fresh Compressed Yeast
4	oz	Warm Water
1	Tbsp	Sugar
2	tsp	Caraway Seeds
1	tsp	Fennel Seeds
8	oz	Molasses
1	qt	Milk
6	oz	Vegetable Oil
1	Tbsp	Salt
5	oz	Raw Rolled Oats
12	oz	Light Rye Flour
3.5	lbs	Bread Flour (you might need more than this, so have more on hand)
3	oz	Bread Flour (for a different step)
		Pan Spray, as needed

Rye breads are very common throughout Scandinavia, because rye is one of the grains that grow well in these northern lands (the others are barley, buckwheat, and oats). Bread such as this is used for making open-faced sandwiches—as is the tradition in Denmark—or is simply buttered and eaten with a meal.

YIELD: 4 loaves (1.5–1.75 pounds/loaf)

COOKING METHOD: Baking

PROCEDURE

1. Combine fresh compressed yeast, warm water, and sugar in a small mixing bowl; mix to combine, cover with foil, and set aside to allow yeast to bloom for 10 minutes (mixture should foam slightly and have a distinct yeast smell).

2. Add the caraway and fennel seeds to a small, dry sauté pan, and place over a low flame on the stove. Toast the whole spices in the pan for a few minutes, until the aroma of the spices becomes noticeable, and then remove pan from the heat and allow it to cool.

3. Transfer the cooled spices to a spice grinder, and grind until the spices are turned to a powder.

4. Add the ground spices to the bloomed yeast, and transfer to a mixing bowl large enough to mix all of the dough (if only smaller bowls are available, mix and divide the yeast spice mixture before transferring to mixing bowls).

5. Add the molasses, milk, vegetable oil, and salt; mix into the yeast mixture, using a dough hook.

6. Add rolled oats, rye flour, and 3/4 of the bread flour; turn the mixer on, at slow speed, to incorporate the flour into the liquids and start to form a dough.

7. The dough should be sticky and soft; add some of the remaining flour in small batches to form a smooth, stiff dough that does not stick to the bowl.

8. Develop the dough with the dough hook by mixing at slow speed until the dough can be spread into an almost transparent sheet, without tearing, when stretched thin.

9. Once the dough is properly developed, transfer it to a mixing bowl and cover it with plastic wrap (with a couple of holes cut into it); place in the refrigerator and cool overnight to retard and relax the dough.

(continues)

Rågsiktlimpör
(continued)

10. Preheat proofbox and oven to 370°F.

11. Remove the dough from the refrigerator and allow it to warm at room temperature for an hour.

12. One the dough has warmed, transfer it to a mixer with a dough hook. Add the additional 3 oz of flour and develop in mixer for 2–3 minutes, or until dough becomes smooth, and then turn it out to a workbench.

13. Divide the dough into three even pieces; work on the bench to form loaves out of dough pieces, and place them in greased loaf pans.

14. Put the loaf pans in the preheated proof box, and allow the dough to double in volume (about 60–75 minutes).

15. Place the proofed bread dough in the preheated oven and bake until the bread is done (consult with instructor, if necessary).

16. Remove bread from the oven and allow it to cool.

Gravlax SWEDEN
(CURED SALMON FILLET)

INGREDIENTS

2	2-lb (4 lbs total) Salmon Fillets, center cut with pin bones removed
3/4 cup	Sugar, granulated
3/4 cup	Kosher Salt
2.5 Tbsp	White Peppercorns, cracked
2 Bunches	Fresh Dill, 1 bunch minced and 1 bunch left whole

Gravlax (cured salmon fillet) served on a potato pancake (see recipe in Chapter 7, "German Cuisine") with gravlaxsås (mustard dill sauce)

This Swedish specialty has been prized all over the world for many years and is at once very simple yet elegant and resourceful. Cured foods have been a means of sustenance across all of Scandinavia for many years; this is but one example of this technique.

YIELD: 3 pounds

PRESERVATION METHOD: Salt and Sugar Curing

PROCEDURE

1. In a small mixing bowl, combine the sugar, salt, crushed peppercorns, and 1 bunch of minced dill, and set aside.

2. Place a sheet of plastic wrap in a full 2-inch hotel pan so that it covers the bottom.

3. Cut a sheet of cheesecloth 3 times the length of the salmon fillet, and lay one length of it in the pan; the bottom third of the cheesecloth should be in the center of the hotel pan, with the rest hanging over the edge.

4. Place a salmon fillet in the center of the cheesecloth, with the skin side down, and coat the cut fillet with about half of the sugar/salt/dill mixture (it will seem like way too much, but keep going).

5. Once that is coated, place the second fillet on a cutting board and coat the cut fillet side with half of the remaining sugar/salt/dill mixture; set aside.

6. With one fillet laid skin side down on the cheesecloth, place the dill fronds across the top of the fillet, and then place the other fillet skin side up on top of the first (thus, both cut sides of the salmon fillets are sandwiching the dill).

7. Cover the fillets with the remaining mixture of sugar/salt/dill.

(continues)

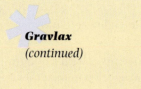

Gravlax
(continued)

8. Place the two fillets—one on top of the other—on the bottom third of the cheesecloth, and fold over the cheesecloth to wrap around the salmon pieces; tuck any excess under the fillets.

9. Secure the cheesecloth with butcher's twine by tying the wrapping as if making a roast.

10. Once the salmon is wrapped and secured, place it in the center of the plastic-wrapped hotel pan and sprinkle the curing mixture that has fallen off of the fillets during the wrapping process back on the wrapped salmon.

11. Place a sheet of plastic wrap on top of the salmon, and place another hotel pan on top of the first. Put a couple of #10 cans on the top pan to weigh down the salmon fillets.

12. Allow the salmon to cure for 2 days before removing it from the refrigerator; rinse and dry the fillets, and slice them very thin for gravlax.

Gravlaxsås   SWEDEN
(MUSTARD/DILL SAUCE FOR GRAVLAX)

INGREDIENTS

2	Tbsp	Honey
2	Tbsp	Dijon Mustard
1	Tbsp	Sugar
1.5	oz	White Wine Vinegar
12	oz	Canola Oil
3/4	cup	Dill, chopped (about 1 good-sized bunch)
		Salt and Black Pepper, to taste

This sauce is the traditional accompaniment to gravlax in Sweden.

YIELD: 1 cup

MIXING METHOD: Emulsification

PROCEDURE

1. In a blender or by hand in a mixing bowl, add all ingredients except canola oil, dill, salt, and pepper.

2. With the blender running slowly (or, if you are using a mixing bowl, while constantly whipping), add the canola oil in a steady stream to make a smooth emulsification.

3. Remove the sauce from the blender and mix in chopped dill.

4. Season to taste with salt and pepper.

Janssons Frestelse   SWEDEN
(JANSSON'S TEMPTATION)

INGREDIENTS

1	oz	Clarified Butter
1	lb	Yellow Onion, sliced thin
2	lbs	Russet Potatoes, cut julienne
5	oz	Swedish Anchovies, wiped of excess salt (these are available in cans; if you can't locate any, substitute Mediterranean canned)

The origin of this dish's name is subject to much debate, but what isn't debated is that it has long been a favorite of the Swedes. This is a common late-night snack and is often eaten upon returning from a night on the town. It is also sure to be found on the smörgåsbord table.

YIELD: 12 portions (5 ounces/portion)

COOKING METHOD (ONIONS): Sautéing/Sweating

COOKING METHOD (POTATO CASSEROLE): Baking

(continues)

Janssons Frestelse
(continued)

1.5	tsp	Salt
1/4	tsp	White Pepper
12	oz	Heavy Cream
3	oz	Whole Butter, salted

Janssons frestelse (Jansson's temptation)

PROCEDURE

1. Preheat the oven to 375°F.
2. Melt the clarified butter in a sauté pan and add the sliced onions; cook over a medium-low flame until onions are tender and translucent—but not colored—and set aside when done.
3. Combine the cut potatoes with the salt and white pepper, and toss to season.
4. Place a layer of the potatoes 1/4 inch thick in a casserole dish that will hold all of the ingredients at a depth of 1 inch (you can also use sauté pans, if necessary).
5. Combine the sautéed onions and anchovies; place half of this mixture on top of the first layer of potatoes.
6. Repeat steps 4 and 5 once more, and then place the remaining potatoes on top of the final layer of the onions and anchovies.
7. Heat the cream in a small saucepan to just under a simmer, and pour it over the potatoes.
8. Cut the butter into 6–8 pieces and place them, evenly spaced, over the surface of the casserole. Put the casserole in the preheated oven.
9. Bake for 35–45 minutes, or until potatoes become crisp and the liquid has mostly evaporated.

NOTE: *This is commonly served with pickles or green salad, or with gravlax and capers.*

Piirakka FINLAND
(KARELIAN RICE PASTRY)

INGREDIENTS

For Making the Pastry

12	oz	Water
2	tsp	Salt
2	oz	Unsalted Butter, melted
12	oz	A.P. Flour + more for dusting
8	oz	Light Rye Flour (you may need more or less, depending on the strength of the A.P. flour)

The Karelian people have a number of culinary traditions with links to Russia and even further back to Mongolia. The piirakkas found in Finland may have a variety of fillings, such as meat, fish, or rice. Some are cooked (as this recipe is) by panfrying in butter, and others are cooked on a dry griddle or pan. In this recipe, the filled pastry is similar to many found in Russian cuisine, and the rice indicates a link to the Mongols.

YIELD: 20 (4 ounces/each)

MIXING METHOD (PASTRY DOUGH): Straight Dough Method

COOKING METHOD (RICE): Pilaf Method (traditionally, the rice would be boiled)

COOKING METHOD (PASTRIES): Panfrying

(continues)

Piirakka
(continued)

For Making the Rice Filling

1	oz	Butter, clarified
4	oz	Yellow Onion, minced
1.5	cups	Long-Grain Rice
18	oz	Water, boiling
1	tsp	Salt
1	oz	Lemon Juice
1/8	tsp	White Pepper
1	Tbsp	Parsley, minced
1		Hard Boiled Egg, minced
2	oz	Whole Butter
		Salt, to taste

For Cooking the Piirakka

6	oz	Clarified Butter

PROCEDURE

For Making the Pastry

1. In a mixer with a dough hook, combine the water, salt, melted butter, A.P. flour, and half of the rye flour; mix on low speed to form a loose dough/batter.

2. Add more rye flour—a couple of tablespoons at a time—until the dough no longer sticks to the sides of the mixing bowl.

3. Once the dough is the proper consistency, develop it for a few minutes in the mixer until it becomes smooth and elastic.

4. Remove the dough from the mixer and wrap it in plastic wrap; let the dough rest in the refrigerator for 30 minutes before rolling out to fill it.

For Making the Rice Filling

1. Preheat the oven to 350°F.

2. In a small pot (2 qts), melt the clarified butter and add the minced onions; sweat over a medium-low flame until the onions are tender and translucent.

3. Add the rice and continue to cook over the medium-low flame, while stirring with a wooden spoon, for a few minutes—until rice begins to turn translucent and shiny.

4. Add the boiling water, salt, lemon juice, and white pepper. Cover the pot tightly with foil, put a lid on the pot, and transfer it to the preheated oven.

5. Bake rice in the preheated oven for 18–20 minutes, and then remove it (the rice should be fully cooked and have absorbed all of the moisture by this point; if it hasn't, return it to the oven to finish cooking—and have your thermostat checked).

6. Once the rice is done, uncover it and add the parsley and the minced hard-boiled egg. Melt in the whole butter.

7. Season the rice to taste with salt, if needed.

For Cooking the Piirakkas

1. Remove the dough from the refrigerator and divide it into 20 pieces on a lightly floured surface.

2. Roll out the dough pieces into 1/8-inch-thick circles.

3. Place a couple (or a few) tablespoons of the filling in the center of the circle of dough, and fold in half to encase the filling.

4. Seal the dough where the top and bottom meet by pressing a fork through the two layers, all the way around the pastry.

5. To cook the piirakkas, panfry them in the clarified butter over a medium flame until they turn golden on both sides.

6. Serve warm or hot as a snack or as an accompaniment to a soup or salad.

Inlagd Sill SWEDEN (ALSO MADE IN OTHER SCANDINAVIAN COUNTRIES)
(PICKLED HERRING)

INGREDIENTS

4	lbs	Herring, fresh (about 6 fish; see alternative method following the procedure if fresh fish is not available)
2	qts	Cold Water
5	oz	Sugar
1	tsp	Allspice Ground
1.5	Tbsp	Allspice Berries, crushed
1	tsp	Crushed Black Peppercorns
4	Bay	Leaves
4	cups	White Wine Vinegar
1	lb	Red Onion, peeled and sliced 1/8 inch thick
6	oz	Carrots, peeled and sliced 1/8 inch thick

This food is a very common sight on Scandinavian tables and is used to make many of the herring recipes found throughout all of the Scandinavian countries. Dishes such as herring salad (sill sallad) and roasted beet salad are very common.

YIELD: 2.5 to 3 pounds

PRESERVATION METHOD: Pickling

SPECIAL CONTAINERS: 2-qt Sanitary Mason Jars

PROCEDURE

1. To prepare the herring, remove the heads behind the gills, eviscerate the fish, and put into clean container with 2 qts of cold water; allow herring to sit overnight.

2. After it sits overnight, remove the herring from the cold water and fillet by following the backbone along the length of the fish with a small and very sharp knife.

3. Remove the rib bones by angling the knife in same direction and carefully slicing them off.

4. Remove top and bottom fins (leave skin on).

5. Once the fillets have been removed, cut them into 1-inch-wide strips and set aside.

6. In a mixing bowl, combine the sugar, ground allspice, allspice berries, black peppercorns, bay leaves, and vinegar; mix to combine (if the sugar does not dissolve in the mixture, heat it slightly on a stove to dissolve, and then cool before using).

7. Alternate the herring, sliced onions, and carrots in layers in the mason jar (the traditional way of doing this is to rub the herring, skin side out, on the outside of the jar so the whole jar shines from the fish). Be sure to pack the ingredients closely so that they end up covered.

8. As the layers are being put in, add a little of the pickling mixture so that the spices are distributed throughout the jar.

9. Once all of the herring and vegetables have been added, add enough of the pickling mixture to completely cover the fish and vegetables.

10. Place the lid on the jar and secure it; set the jar in the refrigerator and allow it to pickle for at least 5 days before using (this serving will last for 5–6 months, with the fish becoming softer and more pronounced in flavor over time).

NOTE: *If fresh herring is not available, this can be made using canned herring with the following adjustments.*

1. Replace 1/2 of the vinegar with water.

2. Increase the sugar from 5 oz to 8 oz.

3. This will last only a week or so and can be used within a few hours.

Syltede Rødbeder   DENMARK (ALSO FOUND IN OTHER SCANDINAVIAN COUNTRIES)

(PICKLED BEETS)

INGREDIENTS

For Roasting the Beets

4	lbs	Beets

For Pickling the Beets

5		Bay Leaves
5		Allspice Berries, crushed
8	oz	Horseradish, peeled and diced small
8	oz	Yellow Onion, sliced thin
2	qts	Water
1	cup	Sugar
3		White Peppercorns, crushed
1/2	cup	White Wine Vinegar
		Peeled Roasted Beets (see above)

Beets are one of the root vegetables that are commonly found in all of Scandinavia, and one of the preservation techniques used to extend the shelf life of beets includes pickling them (as in this recipe). These beets are commonly used in making salads or open sandwiches, or they are simply eaten on their own.

YIELD: 3 pounds

COOKING METHOD (BEETS): Roasting

PRESERVATION METHOD: Pickling

PROCEDURE

For Roasting the Beets

1. Preheat the oven to 325°F.

2. Wash the beets under warm water and remove the long, tapered root end if it is still attached (the leaves should be removed as well, if they are attached).

3. Transfer the beets to a sheet pan and place in the oven; roast until the beets become tender when pierced with a knife (this will take as long as 2 hours, depending on the size of the beets—pierce one before putting it in the oven so you know how dense they are before cooking).

4. Once the beets are done, set them aside to cool. Once they are cool, peel them using a sharp paring knife (and latex gloves, so your hands don't get stained).

For Pickling the Beets

1. Combine the bay leaves, allspice, horseradish, onion, water, sugar, and peppercorns in a pot, and bring mixture to a boil over a high flame.

2. Once the mixture reaches a boil, remove it from the heat and cool it completely in an ice bath.

3. Once the mixture has cooled, add the vinegar and the peeled and roasted beets; store in the refrigerator.

4. Allow the beets to pickle in this solution for at least 2 days before using.

Lax Med Potatis   NORWAY/SWEDEN
(DILLED SALMON AND POTATO SALAD)

INGREDIENTS

For Poaching the Salmon

2	qts	Water
12	oz	White Wine
2		Lemons (zest them first and reserve zest for salad, and then squeeze juice into poaching liquid and add the whole lemon)
2		Bay Leaves
1	tsp	Black Peppercorns
2	bunches	Fresh Dill Stems (from dill used in salad)
3	lbs	Salmon Fillets

For Parboiling the Potatoes

1.5	gal	Water
2	Tbsp	Salt
5	lb	Red Bliss Potatoes

For Making the Dressing

2	cups	Mayonnaise
2	cups	Yogurt
1.5	bunches	Fresh Dill, chopped (stems should have been removed in the poaching step)
1	tsp	Freshly Ground Black Pepper
2	Tbsp	Lemon Zest, minced

The Atlantic salmon found in the Norwegian Sea and running through the rivers of Norway and Sweden have long been prized for their rich and clean taste. With the introduction of the South American potato to this region—after Frederick the Great of Prussia forced people to grow them, and their popularity spread north—dishes like this one began to marry the new tuber with ancient staples, such as salmon and dill.

YIELD: 20 entrée salads (8 ounces/salad)

COOKING METHOD (SALMON): Poaching

COOKING METHOD (POTATOES): Boiling

SALAD ASSEMBLY: Composed

PROCEDURE

For Poaching the Salmon

1. In a small pot or fish poacher, combine the water, white wine, lemon juice, and lemons; place over a medium flame to begin to heat the poaching liquid.

2. Using a length of cheesecloth, wrap the bay leaves, peppercorns, and dill stems, and add them to the poaching liquid.

3. Once the poaching liquid has come to a simmer, turn the heat down to yield a gentle poaching temperature (165–180°F).

4. Add the salmon fillet to the poaching liquid and poach until the salmon is just cooked throughout, which can be determined by attempting to separate the fillet along its segmentation lines (these will separate when done, or reveal the uncooked center if not yet done). If the salmon fillet has sections of significantly different thicknesses, cut the thick sections to yield a more uniform piece that will cook in the same amount of time).

5. Once the salmon has cooked through, remove it from the poaching liquid and allow it to cool completely.

For Parboiling the Potatoes

1. Place the water, salt, and potatoes in a 2.5-gallon or larger pot, and set over a high flame on the stove to bring mixture to a boil.

2. Boil potatoes until they become tender throughout (check them with a knife or skewer for resistance).

3. Once they are cooked, strain the potatoes through a colander. When the excess water has drained off, place them on a sheet pan and allow them to cool completely.

Lax med potatis (dilled salmon and potato salad) served in a lettuce cup, with some of the salad served on individual potato rounds

(continues)

*
Lax Med Potatis
(continued)

3	Garlic Cloves, minced
1.5 lbs	(or about 4) Cucumbers, peeled, seeded, and diced small
2 bunches	Green Onions, minced
10	Large Eggs, hard-boiled and chopped
	Salt and Black Pepper, to taste

For Assembling the Salad

	Cooked Potatoes (see above)
	Dressing (see above)
	Poached Salmon (see above)
3	Butter Lettuce Heads, cleaned and spun dry
.5 bunch	Fresh Dill

For Making the Dressing

1. Combine all ingredients into a large mixing bowl and mix thoroughly.
2. Check the seasoning of the dressing and add more salt and pepper, if necessary. (Remember that this is going to be the seasoning for the salad, so it should be very flavorful.)
3. Add the cooled potatoes to the completed salad dressing and mix thoroughly, taking care not to break up the potatoes (this step can be done up to a day ahead of time).

For Assembling the Salad

1. Place a couple of leaves of butter lettuce at the base of each service plate.
2. In a mixing bowl, add the desired amount of potato salad with dressing, and add a couple ounces of the poached salmon; gently mix to coat the salmon with the dressing (alternatively, you can reserve some of the dressing prior to dressing the potatoes, and dress the salmon separately from the potatoes for a different presentation).
3. Place the dressed salad on top of the butter leaves, and garnish with sprigs of fresh dill.

*
Köttbullar SWEDEN
(SWEDISH MEATBALLS)

INGREDIENTS
For Making the Meatball Mixture

1.5	lbs	Beef Chuck, lean and cut into 1-inch strips
1.5	lbs	Veal Stew Meat or Veal Clod, cut into 1-inch strips
1.5	lbs	Pork Butt, trimmed of excess fat and cut into 1-inch strips
1	lb	Red Onion, chopped
4		Eggs, beaten
3/4	cup	Heavy Cream
1/4	cup	Vegetable Oil
2.5	Tbsp	Salt
1	tsp	Black Pepper
4	oz	Honey
2	cups	Bread Crumbs, dry and ground fine
		Salt and Black Pepper, to taste

These meatballs can be served as an appetizer without sauce or, as this recipe is written, as an entrée. Swedish meatballs are typically served with mashed potatoes, lingonberry preserves, and pickled cucumbers. In Norway, these are called *frikadeller*.

YIELD: 20 portions (6 ounces/portion, or about 3 meatballs + sauce)

COOKING METHOD: Sautéing

PROCEDURE

For Making the Meatball Mixture

(**NOTE:** *This can be done a day ahead of time, or at least an hour ahead, to allow the ingredients to marinate.*)

1. Sanitize and chill medium and fine grinding plates, blade, and housing for meat grinder.
2. Pass the strips of beef, veal, and pork through the grinder using a medium plate; collect the meat in a stainless steel mixing bowl sitting on ice.
3. Add the onion to the meat mixture and mix well.
4. Disassemble the grinder and replace the medium plate with a finer plate; reassemble the grinder and pass the mixture through the finer plate, again collecting the meat in a mixing bowl sitting on ice.

(continues)

Köttbullar
(continued)

For Sautéing the Meatballs

6 oz   Clarified Butter

For Making the Pan Cream Sauce

3 cups Chicken Stock
4 cups Heavy Cream
        Salt, to taste

Köttbullar (Swedish meatballs) served with mashed potatoes, smörgåsgurka (pickled cucumbers), and lingonberry preserve

5. In a separate bowl, combine the eggs, heavy cream, and vegetable oil; whisk to combine, and then set aside.

6. Add the salt, black pepper, and bread crumbs to the meat and onion mixture, and mix to combine.

7. Pour the egg/cream/oil mixture into the meat mixture; using freshly cleaned and sanitized hands or latex gloves, stir the mixture very well for a couple of minutes to distribute everything evenly.

8. Sample the mixture by panfrying a small amount in a little clarified butter. Adjust seasoning with salt and black pepper, if necessary.

9. Once seasoning is adjusted, set the mixture in the refrigerator and allow it to sit for at least an hour (ideally, it should sit for a day).

For Sautéing the Meatballs

1. Form the meatballs by measuring them to 1.5–1.75 oz each and rolling them in the palm of your hands (sanitized or wearing latex gloves); set aside formed meatballs on a sheet pan.

2. Heat a small amount of the clarified butter in a sauté pan over a medium flame until it is rippling and hot.

3. Add a few of the meatballs to the pan (don't add too many at a time, or the pan will cool too much!) and sauté, turning the meatballs as they caramelize in order to brown as much of the surface of the meatballs as possible (watch the pan closely—you do not want to burn anything in the bottom of the pan, because you will use the pan later to prepare a sauce).

4. As the meatballs are done, set them aside—in another pan—and continue, or use more sauté pans (and divide the sauce ingredients accordingly).

For Making the Pan Cream Sauce

1. Once all of the meatballs have been sautéed, pour the excess grease from the pans and deglaze with chicken stock, scraping the pans with a wooden spoon. Reduce the chicken stock by three quarters.

2. Once the chicken stock has been reduced, temper in the cream; when it has come to a simmer and reduced slightly itself (and thus has become thick enough to coat the meatballs in consistency), season the sauce with salt and serve with the meatballs. (If the meatballs did not cook throughout when sautéing, finish cooking them in the sauce.)

Smörgåsgurka   SWEDEN
(QUICK PICKLED CUCUMBERS)

INGREDIENTS

For Making the Pickling Solution

3	cups	Water
2	cups	Sugar
2		Bay Leaves
4		Allspice Berries
1	cup	White Wine Vinegar

For Salting and Pickling the Cucumbers

2		English Cucumbers, seeded and sliced paper-thin (can be sliced lengthwise or into smaller pieces, depending on preference and desired presentation)
2	Tbsp	Kosher Salt

A traditional accompaniment to Swedish meatballs, these pickled cucumber are easy to make and can refresh the palate when served with heavy foods.

YIELD: 3 cups

PREPARATION METHOD: Salting Vegetable to Remove Moisture

PRESERVATION METHOD: Pickling

PROCEDURE

For Making the Pickling Solution

1. Combine all of the ingredients (except the white wine vinegar) in a small pot, and bring to a simmer. Remove the pot from heat and allow it to cool to room temperature.
2. Once the mixture has cooled to room temperature, add the vinegar to the solution and set it aside until the cucumbers are ready to be added to the mixture.

For Salting and Pickling the Cucumbers

1. After slicing the cucumbers, spread them out on a sheet pan and sprinkle the salt over them evenly.
2. Allow the salted cucumber slices to sit for 10 minutes, and then transfer them to a colander; rinse under cold water, allowing them to sit in the colander for a few minutes after rinsing to allow the excess water to run off.
3. Once the cucumbers have sat for a few minutes, press them gently with a clean towel (while still in the colander) to remove any trapped moisture between the slices, and then transfer them to a storage container.
4. Add the cooled pickling mixture to the cucumbers, and allow the cucumbers to pickle for at least 30 minutes before use.

Karjalanpaisti   FINLAND
(KARELIAN STEW)

INGREDIENTS

1.5	lbs	Beef Stew Meat
1.5	lbs	Pork Shoulder, diced large
1.5	lbs	Lamb Stew Meat
2	lbs	Yellow Onion, diced large
1	Tbsp + 1 tsp	Salt

This traditional Karelian stew is very simple to make and yields very good flavor from its mixture of meats. These were traditionally made in communal ovens using the heat left over after baking bread for the community. The stew would slowly cook in these ovens for hours as the embers died.

YIELD: 15 portions (10 ounces/portion)

COOKING METHOD: Stewing

(continues)

Karjalanpaisti
(continued)

1 Tbsp Allspice Berries, crushed
3 qts Beef Stock or Water Salt and Black Pepper, to taste

PROCEDURE

1. Preheat the oven to 325°F.

2. In a mixing bowl, combine the meats, onion, salt, and allspice berries, and mix thoroughly.

3. Transfer the mixture to a pot that will hold all of the ingredients.

4. Pour the stock into the pot with the other ingredients, and place the pot in the preheated oven to bake uncovered for 1 hour.

5. Cover the pot with a tight-fitting lid and/or aluminum foil, and bake for an additional 2–3 hours, or until the meat is very tender.

6. Remove the pot from the oven and check to ensure that the meat is very tender.

7. Adjust seasoning with salt and pepper, and serve.

NOTE: *This dish is usually served with mashed potatoes and lingonberry preserves.*

Mørbrad med Svedsker og Aebler DENMARK

(PORK LOIN STUFFED WITH PRUNES AND APPLES)

INGREDIENTS

For Making the Stuffing

8	oz	Pitted Prunes, dried and cut into quarters or diced medium
5	oz	Aquavit (substitute vodka, if this is unavailable)
6	oz	White Wine, dry
2	Tbsp	Butter
3	oz	Shallots
8	oz	Tart Apples (such as Granny Smith), diced medium
1/4	tsp	Salt
		Black Pepper, to taste
1/4	cup	Heavy Cream

For Stuffing and Roasting the Loin

4	lbs	Pork Loin, center cut
1	tsp	Salt
1/4	tsp	Freshly Ground Black Pepper Stuffing (see above)

Denmark is a rich agricultural country, and one of its prized commodities is the pig. The Danes are particularly fond of pork in their cuisine.

YIELD: 12 portions (6–7 ounces/portion)
COOKING METHOD (STUFFING): Braising
COOKING METHOD (PORK LOIN): Roasting

PROCEDURE

For Making the Stuffing

1. Combine the prunes, aquavit, and white wine; allow the prunes to hydrate and marinate in the mixture for at least 30 minutes (this can be done up to a day in advance by leaving the mixture in the refrigerator).

2. In a medium-size sauté pan, heat the butter over a medium-low flame and add the shallots; sweat them in the butter until they are translucent and tender.

3. Add the apples, and turn the heat up to sauté them in the butter until they are soft and begin to caramelize.

4. Once the apples begin to caramelize, deglaze the pan with the aquavit and wine that the prunes have not absorbed, adding the prunes to the pan as well.

5. Add the 1/4 tsp of salt to this mixture, and season to taste with the freshly ground black pepper.

6. Once the liquid in the pan has been reduced until it is almost dry (*au sec*), add the heavy cream and continue to cook until the entire mixture is thick.

7. Remove the mixture from the heat and set aside to cool.

(continues)

Mørbrad med
Svedsker og Aebler
(continued)

For Stuffing and Roasting the Loin

1. Preheat the oven to 375°F.

2. To stuff the loin, make an incision in the center of the cut end of the loin with a long, thin knife; open a cavity the length of the loin. (This can also be done using a cleaned knife steel or a boning knife.) The opening should be a couple of inches in diameter, to allow room for enough stuffing to be placed in the loin. The opening should also extend the entire length of the loin—it may be necessary to enter the loin from both ends, if the knives used are not long enough. The loin can also be cut into shorter lengths, if necessary.

3. Once the loin has been opened, place the cooled stuffing mixture in a large pastry bag with a large, open tip (or without a tip, if the stuffing pieces are too big to fit through one).

4. Place the end of the pastry bag inside the cut end of the pork loin, and pipe the filling into the loin. If necessary, pipe the filling into both ends of the loin to ensure that a sufficient amount is inserted. The loin will get thicker and firmer where the stuffing is piped in.

5. Once the loin has been stuffed, secure the ends of it with butcher's twine and season the exterior of the loin with the tsp of salt and 1/4 tsp of black pepper. Place the loin in an appropriate pan for roasting.

6. Put the stuffed loin in the preheated oven and bake until well browned on the exterior.

7. Once the loin is sufficiently colored, if it has not yet reached 155°F turn the oven down to 300°F to finish cooking until it reaches 155°F, and then remove the roasted loin.

8. Allow the loin to rest for 15 minutes, covered in aluminum foil, to allow the juices to settle and for the roast to finish carryover cooking.

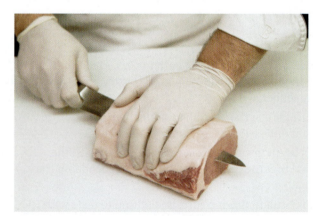

Mørbrad med svedsker og aebler (stuffed pork loin); preparing the pork loin using a long, thin knife to create a pocket for stuffing

Stuffing the pork with the prune/apple stuffing using a pastry bag

Smørdampete Nypoteter NORWAY

(BUTTER-STEAMED NEW POTATOES)

INGREDIENTS

4	oz	Water
4	lbs	New Potatoes (waxy variety and very small, usually about an inch wide), cleaned and dry
8	oz	Unsalted Butter, melted and held warm
1	Tbsp	Kosher Salt (or other coarse salt)
1/4	tsp	White Pepper
1/4	cup	Fresh Dill (about 1 large bunch), minced
1	Tbsp	Fresh Parsley, minced

These tiny and tender new potatoes are a sign of the growing season and are prized for their delicious taste and texture. This recipe provides a common Norwegian method for preparing these potatoes, which often are served with fish or meat dishes, such as the preceding pork recipe.

YIELD: 12 portions (5 ounces/portion)

COOKING METHOD: Oven Steaming

PROCEDURE

1. Preheat the oven to 300°F.

2. Place the water in the bottom of a hotel pan and set aside.

3. In a mixing bowl, combine the new potatoes, warm butter, salt, and white pepper; toss to coat the potatoes with seasonings.

4. Transfer the potatoes and seasonings (be sure to transfer all of the melted butter, as well) to the hotel pan, and cover the pan first with plastic wrap and then with aluminum foil to completely seal it. (**Note:** The plastic wrap will not melt onto the potatoes, but it *will* melt onto the lip of the hotel pan, so be sure to remove any melted plastic wrap stuck to the pan before it is used for anything else.)

5. Place a hotel pan lid (or another suitable lid) on top of the hotel pan. Put the pan in the preheated oven and bake for 45 minutes.

6. Remove the pan from the oven, and carefully lift up one corner of the plastic and foil that are covering the pan; check to see if the potatoes are tender throughout. If they are, proceed to the next step. If they're not, cover them and return to the oven to finish.

7. Once the potatoes are tender throughout, remove the foil and plastic wrap, and return the potatoes to the oven for 5 minutes.

8. Remove the potatoes from the oven and allow them to cool slightly (5 minutes).

9. Add the freshly minced dill and parsley; serve.

Mørbrad med svedsker og aebler (prune- and apple-stuffed pork loin served with smør-dampete nypoteter (butter-steamed new potatoes)

SUMMARY

Scandinavia is a region in northern Europe that includes the countries of Norway, Sweden, Finland, and Denmark. The cuisine of this region is known for its many seafood preparations as well as for the quality of foods created from the various preserved ingredients found here. The Vikings once called Scandinavia home, and their history as a seafaring people greatly impacted the cuisine of this region—many products were developed that could survive at sea, that came from the sea, or that were influenced by places where the Vikings traveled. Because this land is located in the far north, the growing season is quite short, and thus the bounty of the summer is traditionally preserved by pickling, drying, smoking, and curing the foods. These preserves are the backbone of the cuisine, and much of the seafood, berries, and vegetables from the area are used after preservation. The result is a cuisine that utilizes its products and tends toward richness to warm the inhabitants of this cold land.

REVIEW QUESTIONS

1. How did the Viking history of traveling to overseas lands affect the development of the Scandinavian cuisine?

2. What is significant about the summer bounty in Scandinavia in relation to the foods that are used throughout the year?

3. What are some of the most common ingredients in Scandinavian cuisine that come from the sea? List some of the preserves made from these ingredients.

COMMON TERMS, FOODS, AND INGREDIENTS

The following terms include many that are commonly used in kitchens outside of Scandinavia, as well as some of the more common ingredients and dishes found in these countries.

✳ Finland

blinis – Small, thin pancakes that are eaten with either sweet or savory fillings

borsch – Beet soup

karjalanpaisti – Karelian stew

muikku – Tiny relative of the salmon, usually cooked whole because its bones disintegrate during cooking

pasha – Cheesecake

piirakka – Pasties or savory filled pies

ruisleip – Sour rye bread

stroganoff – Meat stew that is thickened and flavored with sour cream

✳ Sweden

anka – Duck

äppelkaka – Applecake

ärtsoppa – Yellow split pea soup; a common part of the winter diet in Sweden

curry – Generic name for spice blends of Indian origin used in the cuisine of Sweden and other Scandinavian countries

dill – Herb; has same name in the United States

falukorv – Smooth boiled sausage made with a mixture of beef or veal with pork; these are lightly smoked for a milder flavor

fänkål – Fennel

fårkött – Mutton

garam masala – "Warm" spice blend of India common in Scandinavian cooking

gås – Goose

gravlax – Salmon fillet cured in a salt/sugar/dill mixture. The name *gravlax* ("grave salmon") comes from the ancient method of preparing this, in which the salmon would be buried and allowed to ferment.

gravlaxsås – Sauce to accompany gravlax, typically made with mustard and dill

havre – Oats

herrgårdskorv – Rich smoked pork sausage

hjortron – Cloudberry

hushållsost – Semihard cow's milk cheese with good melting qualities and a mild, somewhat sour taste

inlagd sill – Pickled herring

Janssons frestelse – Jansson's temptation; a dish of herring, potatoes, and onions that are cooked with cream and butter and commonly served either as part of a smörgåsbord or as a late-night snack

kål – Cabbage

korn – Barley

korv – Swedish sausage; made with potatoes and ground meats

köttbullar – Swedish meatballs

kräftor – Crayfish

lax – Salmon

lax med potatis – Salmon and potato salad

lingon – Lingonberry

lök – Onion

pepperkakor – Crispy, thin gingersnaps

råg – Rye

rågsiktlimpör – Spiced rye bread

renkött – Reindeer

rödbeta – Beet

roget sill – Smoked herring

senap – Mustard

sill – Herring

sillsallad – Herring salad with sour cream dressing

skogshare – Arctic hare

smörgåsbord – Elaborate table of cold and hot items that is eaten buffet style and was common to Sweden and other parts of Scandinavia; this is still found on a limited basis at specialty restaurants

smörgåsgurka – Sweet pickled cucumbers

spiekekorv – Slightly sour fermented and dried pork sausage similar to a salami

surströmming – Soured Baltic herring; this spread is made by fermenting the Baltic herring until it has become quite soft and pungent. It is considered a delicacy in Sweden.

sveciaost – Semifirm cow's milk cheese with irregular holes, a creamy texture, and a light yellow color

Västerbottenost – Highly prized hard aged cow's milk cheese from Västerbotten with a granular texture; aged for a minimum of one year

Norway

fiskefarse – Fish forcemeat, often shaped like a meatball and poached

fiskepudding – Similar to fish forcemeat, but it might be a little softer and formed in a casserole

fiskesuppe – Fish soup; many varieties are common in Norway, including several that are similar to chowders

hjell – Special drying racks common in western Norway to make the air-dried cod called stockfisk or tørrfisk

klippfisk – Salted and air-dried cod (unlike stockfisk, which is just air dried)

krumkake – Delicate cone-shaped cookie, typically cooked on what looks like a waffle iron but makes a thin cookie also called krumkager

lefse – Potato and flour flatbread commonly often used to wrap other ingredients to eat

lutefisk – Air-dried cod treated with lye and rehydrated to form a sort of fish paste; this has long been a part of the Scandinavian diet

rekesaus – Shrimp sauce commonly served with fish or fish forcemeats

smørdampete nypoteter – Buttered new potatoes

stokkfisk – Air-dried cod; also called tørrfisk (differs from klippfisk in not being salted)

tørrfisk – Air-dried cod; also called stokkfisk

torsk – Cod

Denmark

brød – Bread

Danbo – Nutty-flavored semisoft cow's milk cheese that is a very common household cheese in Denmark

Havarti – Semisoft cow's milk cheese with a buttery-sweet taste; may or may not be flavored with ingredients such as dill or caraway seeds

konditori – Bakeries

mørbrad med svedsker og aebler – Pork loin stuffed with prunes and apples

pålæg – Sandwich toppings for the open-face sandwiches that are common in Denmark

rugbrød – Rye bread

Samso – Often called the "cheddar of Denmark," this is a ripened cow's milk cheese that improves and sharpens with age

smørrebrød – Butter and bread sandwich served open-faced with various ingredients

syltede rødbeder – Pickled beets

Tybo – Similar to the Samso cheese that it is modeled after, this variety is often flavored with caraway seeds

wienerbrød – Vienna bread; the name given to Danish pastries and the method of layering butter between sheets of dough. This food came to Denmark from Viennese pastry chefs/bakers who worked in the country during a bakers' strike in the 1800s. This product was much loved, and Danish bakers are said to have improved on the Viennese techniques over the years.

CHAPTER 9

ARCTIC OCEAN

ARCTIC OCEAN

75°

SIBERIA

Central Asian Russia

North Asian Russia

RUSSIA

SCANDINAVIA

Inland Northern European Russia

BERING SEA

St. Petersburg

60°

ESTONIA

Volga River

LATVIA

★ Moscow

LITHUANIA

Baltic Russia

BELARUS

POLAND

UKRAINE

CAUCASUS MOUNTAIN RANGE

KAZAKHSTAN

45°

SURAMI MOUNTAIN

MONGOLIA

BLACK SEA

UZBEKISTAN

GEORGIA

KYRGYZSTAN

NORTH KOREA

SEA OF JAPAN

ARMENIA AZERBAIJAN

TURKEY

TURKMENISTAN

TAJIKISTAN

SOUTH KOREA

CHINA

JAPAN

IRAQ

IRAN

AFGHANISTAN

PACIFIC OCEAN

30°

LIBYA

EGYPT

SAUDI ARABIA

PAKISTAN

NEPAL

BHUTAN

TAIWAN

INDIA

15°

CHAD

SUDAN

YEMEN

OMAN

MYANMAR

THAILAND

VIETNAM

PHILIPPINES

CENTRAL AFRICAN REPUBLIC

ETHIOPIA

CAMBODIA

0°

DEMOCRATIC REPUBLIC OF CONGO

KENYA

SOMALIA

Georgia and Southern European Russian Regions

MALAYSIA

SINGAPORE

INDONESIA

PAPUA NEW GUINEA

0 50 100 km

TANZANIA

ANGOLA

15°

ZAMBIA

MADAGASCAR

INDIAN OCEAN

AMIBIA

BOTSWANA

AUSTRALIA

30°

SOUTH AFRICA

●	towns and cities
★	capital city
——	river
——	region boundary
-·-·-	international boundary
▨	mountains

NEW ZEALAND

Russian Cuisine

OBJECTIVES

Upon completion of this chapter, you will be able to

- explain what makes the cuisines of the Russian Federation unique.
- discuss the importance of the Orthodox Church in the dietary habits of the Russian community.
- recognize the common recipes found in the cuisines of the Russian Federation.
- produce a variety of recipes common to Russia.
- define the terms listed at the conclusion of the chapter.

INTRODUCTION

The Russian Federation encompasses a massive area, diverse cultures, and many climates; as a result of this diversity, it is not surprising that the cuisines found here also vary widely, although a number of themes are common throughout. The typical Russian is a master of survival, extremely hospitable, enjoys the warming effects of the many soups eaten around the country, and adheres to the customs of the Eastern Orthodox Church. The cuisines found within the borders of this massive country range from Slavic-influenced soups, to East Asian–influenced grilled meats, Persian-influenced rice preparations, French-influenced classical Russian dishes, and Siberian reindeer. This complexity is one of the endearing aspects of this great land's cuisine, and thorough exploration of it could fill volumes of books.

The Russian Federation is the latest configuration of this storied country, which traces its roots back to mostly Asian ancestors. The collapse of the Union of Soviet Socialist Republics, or the USSR, in the early 1990s resulted in a number of former Soviet areas becoming independent countries. However, political borders are but one factor in defining a cultural group, and the Russian Federation is a prime example of newly drawn political boundaries that both exclude and include groups that are culturally a part of Russia or one of its former republics.

The Russian Federation is home to a dizzying array of ethnic groups, including Nordic peoples originally from the area of present-day Scandinavia, Slavic peoples formerly of Eastern Europe, Turkish peoples from Asia, nomadic Siberian tribes, Korean immigrants, Persian peoples originally from the Middle East, Mongolian peoples from Mongolia, and more. Because of this tremendous ethnic diversity, it is difficult to generalize about Russia's culinary culture as a whole. The regionalism of culinary customs is important to the Russian Federation, but that doesn't clear up the confusion; many ethnic groups were relocated as a result of Soviet communism, which installed ethnic groups far from home as part of a plan to improve the economy. This ethnic diversity simply necessitates that one interested in understanding

Russian cuisine remember that authentic Russian cuisine is not just Slavic or Persian or Turkish, but rather all of these—and more—at once.

Geographically, the Russian Federation reaches from the Baltic Sea and the border of Finland in Scandinavia, east to the Pacific Ocean, just miles from both Alaska and Japan. This area covers a significant portion of northern Europe and virtually all of northern Asia. The dividing line within Russia, marking where Europe ends and Asia begins, is generally considered the Ural Mountains that run north and south in the western portion of the country. The vast majority of the Russian Federation territory is in Asia, although a large part of the population lives within the European portion. If you happen to be in one of the republics of eastern Russia, you may eat a meal that contains yogurt, pilaf, and kebabs. If, on the other hand, you are in the Baltic region, the meal might consist of pickled herring, butter, and rye bread. These seemingly unrelated foods are actually part of the same country's cuisine, because this country is a diverse ethnic landscape that stretches from the heart of Europe to the edge of Japan.

Russian cuisine is not very well known in the United States, because the Cold War years prevented both sides from learning more about each other's culture. Now that the Cold War is history, Americans are starting to learn more about the many dumplings, fabulous soups, caviar grades, hearty breads, rice preparations, sauces, stuffed pastas, and pickled foods that are just the beginning of what will surely be another cuisine of significant interest.

HISTORIC CULINARY INFLUENCES

Russia is a huge country, and many cultures have at some point in history made their impact felt in some part of this region. When reviewing the following guide, keep in mind the particular regions on which influences were felt, as they often remained in those areas and did not spread throughout the Federation. The influence of the Ottoman Empire, for example, was felt in the Caspian regions and the former Republic of Kazakhstan, but there is little evidence of this influence in the Siberian or Baltic regions, as these were outside the range of influence. Russia is also a complex ethnic mix, which can further cloud the picture of a national—or even regional—cuisine. The following guide provides an overview of some of the more important influences on the development of the varied Russian cuisines. The chapters on the cuisines of the Middle East, Germany, China, France, and Scandinavia are all good references for the cuisine of Russia as well.

Scythians from Asia

Some of the earliest inhabitants of present-day Russia came from Asia about 3,000 years ago and brought with them their customs and culinary techniques. The Scythians were nomads who subsisted on a diet of horsemeat, milk, and fermented milk products, as well as gathered foods and grain products. These nomadic tribes ruled southern Asiatic Russia for 300 years, from the seventh century BC, and taught the Slavs how to make leavened breads and *koumiss* (fermented mare's milk). It was also during the rule of the Scythians that many of the complex trading routes, including the well-known Silk Road (the name given to the trading routes from China to Europe), were developed, enabling many products and techniques to travel from China and India westward and from Europe and the Middle East eastward and northward, respectively. This time period still holds some mysteries regarding food development, but it is clear that many ideas traveled with the more obvious movement of ingredients.

Slavs

The Slavic language and culture—a major feature of the Russian Federation—derived from a culture that developed in Eastern Europe and western Asia and relocated throughout the eastern portion of Europe after crossing the Ural Mountains when nomadic Turkish peoples pushed them west. Some of the foods eaten by the ancient Slavic peoples in this region included grains—with rye, oats, and, to a lesser extent, barley regularly found in the diet in the form of gruel, crude breads, or porridges. They also harvested root vegetables such as turnips, carrots, radishes, beets, and onions, and gathered wild berries, currants, mushrooms, apples, and—in some parts—cherries. In addition, the Slavic peoples hunted wild game such as hare, boar, and venison, and fresh and saltwater fish.

In time, these people developed a number of food customs that are still significant parts of the Russian diet today, including *pirog* and other baked, filled savory pastries; many of the traditional soups, such as *ukha* (fish soup) and *shchi* (cabbage soup); and the addition of dairy products such as *smetana* (sour cream) and *tvorog* (fresh cheese) to traditional recipes (the use of fermented or soured dairy is thought to have been introduced to the developing Slavic peoples by the Tartars).

The Persian Empire

The rise of the Persian Empire, centered in present-day Iran, proved to be an influential period for Russia in the development of a more refined court cuisine. As the Persian Empire extended its reach into areas of present-day Russia, the local people were exposed to a cuisine that prized presentation, more formal service, and complex cooking techniques. This exposure left its mark even after the Persian Empire faded, as the leaders and wealthy landowners of the influenced areas emulated some of the practices that the Persians had shown them.

The Persian Empire reached into the southern areas of European Russia, as well as some of the regions of South Asian Russia, between the eighth and tenth centuries. Persian melons and nuts were brought into the Caucus area of southern Russia during this time and are now common components of the cuisines in this region, including Georgian cuisine. Some of the Persian customs that are evident today in the southern European and Asian sections of Russia include the tradition of making elaborate rice dishes such as *palov*, which resembles the Persian polou or Turkish pilaf, as well as varieties of flatbread such as *non*, which resembles the Indian naan—itself a Persian-influenced flatbread—and the many lamb dishes that are also eaten here.

Scandinavian Traders

Some of the early inhabitants of the areas of the Russian Federation came from the present-day Scandinavian countries, and it is from these people that the name *Russia* is derived, as they were known as the Rus. These same Scandinavians also introduced their techniques for curing and smoking fish and meats, as well as pickling and brining, to these western areas of the present-day Russian Federation and the former states of the USSR. Perhaps one of the greatest contributions to Russian cuisine from the Scandinavians was the introduction of their smörgåsbord (appetizer table), which in time evolved into the Russian tradition of *zakuski*, simply another version of the Scandinavian beginning to a meal. This tradition was introduced to the nobility of Russia and spread to the other classes; it is now a part of most festive occasions in many parts of Russia.

Additionally in the eighth through tenth centuries, traders in the Baltic region brought spices to the inland areas of the Baltic states—the introduction of ginger and cardamom occurring during this time period.

Mongols and Tartars

Russia was dominated for more than 300 years (from the thirteenth century until 1552), first by Mongols and then by Tartars. These nomadic peoples introduced a number of processes and foods to the mostly Slavic diet of that time period. The now common use of smetana and other fermented dairy products is attributed to the introduction of products like these by the Tartars, and the Mongols introduced their tradition of making noodles, called *lapsha* in Russia.

Genghis Khan brought his Mongol army into Russia in the early thirteenth century and stormed across the nation, taking control of much of the present-day Russian Federation. Along with the Mongols came their culinary techniques of making yogurt, eating raw meat and boiled meats. The Mongols and Tartars, both of Eastern-Asian descent, had learned a number of techniques from the Chinese, and these were probably introduced to the Russians through this contact as well. Some of the Chinese techniques that are thought to have been introduced at this time include the making of stuffed pastas and steaming dumplings, and the use of Eastern spices.

The Tartars were primarily Turkish peoples who traveled and overthrew many areas in order to arm themselves with supplies. The Tartars controlled much of the eastern portion of the present-day Russian Federation; although they left a great deal of destruction in their wake, they also introduced new methods to the populations they impacted. The old Silk Road was reopened, with the Tartars in command of the Russian frontier, and ingredients began to flow into Russia from Asia again (the introduction of saffron and cinnamon is believed to have occurred during this time period). The Tartars also are thought to have introduced the native Russians to the process of fermenting cabbage to yield *kvashinaya kapusta* (sauerkraut) around this time.

Peter the Great and Westernization

Peter the Great had a dramatic effect on the development of Russian cuisine; because of his extensive travels in Europe, and having attended banquets for heads of state, he became almost obsessed with the refinement and other qualities of the cuisines he experienced—French cuisine, in particular. With the ascension of Peter the Great to the crown in the late seventeenth century, Russia's path was dramatically altered in a culinary sense. Peter felt that the etiquette he was exposed to in Europe and the focus on the enjoyment of each dish were traits that he must instill in the Russian aristocracy. As a result, he began to import food and chefs from Europe to create these presentations. Soon, many other wealthy Russians were importing European chefs, and the upper class started a period in Russian culture in which customs from southern Europe became the fashion. This focus was primarily on the customs and foods of France.

Marie-Antoine Carême, the famous French chef, became the personal chef to Alexander I, the Russian czar, during his visits to France. Carême introduced many of the classic French techniques into the Russian repertoire, and he created new dishes for the royalty.

Incorporation of French Culinary Techniques

In the eighteenth century, as a result of Peter the Great's efforts to westernize Russia, French culinary practices became the desired standard for nearly all elite Russians. Many cutlets now common to Russian cuisine developed from this period of influence; in the nineteenth century, the French technique of using pounded pieces of quality chicken breast meat (*côtelettes de volailles*) led Russian chefs to apply familiar techniques to their foods, resulting in dishes such as *koteleti po Kievski* (chicken Kiev), *kotlety Pozharsky* (chicken Pozharsky), and *teliatina po-Orlovski* (veal Prince Orlov). Many other techniques common to France at the time also became part of the Russian repertoire, including the making of mousses, composed salads, vinaigrettes, consommés, and other light soups. Carême himself introduced one recipe that is still strongly connected to this period in history: his charlotte russe (Bavarian cream set inside a mold lined with ladyfingers) is often associated with (and is commonly found in) Russia. However, several charlottes found in Russian cuisine are more similar to traditional charlottes, featuring layers of cake filled with fruit and a sweetened cream mixture. Although this association with Carême and Russian cuisine may be misguided, this period in history did introduce Russia to the techniques and foods common to France.

The French classification system of sauces also became popular during this period in Russian cuisine, and more refined sauces and dishes began to appear, mainly among the wealthy. Although many of the dishes that developed during this period still exist as classic Russian recipes, these influences became simply another layer in the complex development of Russian cuisine.

Korean Immigrants

Throughout periods of history, significant numbers of Koreans have immigrated into Russia and brought along their techniques and a penchant for highly spiced foods. Although the Korean population in Russia isn't as large as many other ethnic groups, the Koreans who have come here have made an impact on the Russian diet by their presence in the local markets and their farming abilities. The Koreans sell their excess produce and many of the same foods they enjoyed in Korea at markets to support their families, and these are enjoyed by many Russians; a number of them (as well as some new adaptations) have even become Russian favorites. Some of the Korean-inspired foods now popular in Russia include gochujang (chili paste), spiced pickled carrots, and other spiced pickled vegetables.

UNIQUE COMPONENTS

The cuisines of the Russian Federation are becoming better known in the United States but are still relatively uncommon compared to many other cuisines of Europe and Asia. Most of the Russian Federation experiences long, cold winters, which certainly influences the types of foods found here. Historically, many of the foods have been prepared by slow cooking on the large stoves that also heated the homes. Religion is also an important factor in making this cuisine unique and identifiable Russian cuisine is quite varied; this country covers a vast area, and its variety surely will be enjoyed by all who take the time to learn more about the cuisine of this part of the world.

Orthodox Christians

One of the central components of Russia's national identity in the present-day Russian Federation is faith. More than three-quarters of the population in this area are members of the Orthodox Church, part of the eastern branch of Christianity. Although the period of Communist rule by the USSR officially promoted no religion, many of the traditions of the Orthodox Church survived these years, and a great deal of the traditional foods—and fast and feast days—were never abandoned.

The Orthodox Church has more fast days than any other branch of Christianity: about 220 per year for most followers. The fasting days occur every Wednesday and Friday, as well as during the entire period of Lent, which can last as long as 49 days. The fasts differ in their dietary restrictions, but in general they require abstaining from eating meat, dairy, and often fish, and abstaining from drinking alcohol. During these periods, the diet consists mainly of grains, typically in the form of bread or *kasha* (groats—broken and cooked grains), fruits, mushrooms, and vegetables—for example, *borscht* (beet soup), which is a common dish that uses beets.

The fast periods typically are followed by feast days to celebrate the end of the fasting period, and these feasts often have traditional foods associated with them. The longest fasting period, Lent, is broken at midnight on Easter Sunday to celebrate the rising of Jesus Christ. The foods typical of the Easter celebration include painted eggs, *kulich* (a type of bread), *paskha* (a rich cheese spread), and lamb.

The link between most Russians and the Orthodox Church is strong, and the religion's impact on the culinary habits of its followers is certainly one of the unique components of Russian cuisine.

Climate

The Russian Federation covers many of the northern parts of Eastern Europe and most of northern Asia, all areas of long winters and short growing seasons. As a necessity, the people who inhabited these regions developed systems and methods to sustain them through the long winters by preserving and storing much of what they could grow, forage, or hunt during the warmer months. As a result of this tradition, the cuisine of the Russian Federation includes numerous examples of foods that utilize preservation methods (or foods that have already been preserved).

Some of the most common methods of preservation in Russia include the use of brines or cures to preserve the foods, as in *kvashinaya kapusta* (sauerkraut—salted and fermented cabbage), *solionye ogurtsy* (brined cucumbers), and *kolbasa* (cured sausage). Many foods are also smoked, or frozen in the arctic cold to be preserved as well. The Siberian dumplings called *pel'meni*, for example, use the cold air to freeze; they typically are made in large batches and cooked as needed. *Vetchina* (smoked pork) is an example of a smoked product.

The climate is also an obvious factor in the abundance of root vegetables and grains, which are the backbone of the Russian diet, as these crops grow successfully in these conditions. Bread is commonly eaten throughout the country, and hearty vegetable crops such as potatoes, beets, turnips, and cabbage are regular components in many recipes. Because of its cold surroundings, Russian food is often hearty and includes a number of rich components—such as sour cream and butter—that provide the desired warming and filling effect often craved in these climatic conditions. Just as the foods of the southern Mediterranean are typically lighter and fresher, the foods of northern climates are typically heavier and often contain preserved products. (Keep in mind, however, that Russia is very large, and this generalization about the cuisine is not accurate for the entire country—particularly the southern sections in the Caspian area, where the climate is much milder and the foods tend to be much lighter.)

Ethnicity

One of the defining characteristics of Russian cuisine is the many ethnic foods that contribute to it. As mentioned in the opening of this chapter, it is difficult to generalize about the cuisine of Russia because of its many contributing ethnic groups; instead, it is best to think of this cuisine in the same ways we often regard the cuisine of the United States. Simply put, the correct explanation depends on whom you ask and where you are! Ask a Georgian descendent what Russian cuisine is, and you are likely to hear about the walnut sauces, *toné* baked breads, or sweet *khalvas* that are all common to this cuisine and inspired by the native Caucasus region; on the other hand, ask a Russian from the Baltic region, and you'll more likely hear about the tradition of the zakuski table, as well as herring dishes and cured and pickled foods.

Russia is a nation of diversity, and this diversity is one of the greatest strengths of the culinary character found here. You will find *manti* (lamb-stuffed steamed dumplings) and palov (the Persian-inspired rice dishes) in the restaurants of the Baltic region, and pel'meni (the Siberian stuffed dumplings) in Moscow or the Caucasus. Although these foods may be far from their place of origin, they are still embraced and enjoyed by all Russians.

One notable component of Russian history that has affected the cuisine is communist rule, and the policies during the communist rule that encouraged the migration of populations within the former Soviet Union. Many ethnic groups were moved during the Soviet period, for various social reasons; as a result, the cuisines of these populations have been introduced into regions with little history of these ethnic groups. Prior to this policy, and the resulting movement of many ethnic groups from one region of Russia to another, the different areas of Russia had significantly fewer minority populations—thus, food traditions often remained static for many decades. As a result of these new ethnic groups being introduced, their foods spread to other parts of the former Soviet Union. Now, foods once found in former Soviet republics—including the Baltic region and eastern Russia—are eaten in western Russia, and vice versa.

Stewed, Simmered, and Slow Roasted

It wasn't until the nineteenth century that smaller wood-burning and coal-burning stoves were introduced to Russia; prior to this time, the cooking device used in most homes was a large, square, wood-fired clay or stone oven, called a *pleeta*, which is still common in many rural parts of Russia. The fires would be allowed to die down in the pleeta before the spent embers and ashes were swept out, and pots were set inside this large earthenware vessel, which held a tremendous amount of heat. Because the cooking was done using this retained heat, large batches of foods were most often stewed, simmered, or slow roasted; thus, many classic Russian preparations use these techniques. Although newer ranges are more common today, particularly in the cities, the tradition of slow-cooked foods still permeates the Russian Federation cuisine.

SIGNIFICANT SUBREGIONS

Russia and the republics cover a huge area that extends from the Baltic Sea in the west to the Pacific Ocean in the east, and from the Artic Circle in the north to the Caspian Sea and the borders of the Mediterranean countries in the south. This huge land mass makes up more than one-eighth of all the land on Earth and, as such, provides for tremendous variety in climates,

ethnicities, and cultures. The following guide will help to clarify some of this variation by looking at the major culinary contributors within this area. These regions are organized from east to west and north to south.

North Asian Russia: Siberia

Siberia is a region of extreme winters and very short summers; vast forests and herds of reindeer are part of the landscape; and nomadic Chukchi (native Siberians) still live off the frozen tundra, as they have for centuries. Although it is not suited for the development of large cites and cultural centers, Siberia has managed to influence some of the Russian culinary traditions.

The famous pel'meni of this northern region highlights the ingenuity and culinary wisdom of the Siberian peoples. These stuffed dumplings are made in bulk after a slaughter and kept outside in the freezing cold to be used as needed. Pel'meni are best when cooked after being frozen, as the texture of the dough is better and they are much less likely to stick to each other. Clearly, these were created exactly where they should have been. The Siberian region is also home to vast forests that yield many of the wild berries and mushrooms now an integral part of Russian cuisine. This is also the origin of much of the game that was once a significant part of the royal cuisine, during the eighteenth and nineteenth centuries, and is still prized by Russians today.

Central Asian Russia

The Central Asian region of Russia is home to many ethnic groups and has been significantly influenced by the Middle East and other parts of Asia, such as India/Pakistan, Mongolia, and China. This region has many similarities with the former republics that lie just to its south, the largest of which is Kazakhstan. This region has also been a strategic one in term of the trade routes between Asia, Europe, and the Middle East, as part of the Silk Road historically came though this area. This region is largely made up of semiarid steppes, which were easy to navigate and less protected than the other routes west. Another distinguishing feature of this region is the significant number of people of the Islamic faith (Muslim); most Russians in other areas are Orthodox Christians.

This region was invaded by nomadic peoples of Mongolian or Tartar descent, and many of the culinary traditions that exist here (some of which were originally Chinese) were clearly brought from them, including the common use of yogurt, lamb, and steamed dumplings such as manti. Lamb is the dominant meat of this region, and large flocks are still raised here today. Examples of lamb dishes influenced by the nomadic Tartars include *chebureki* (lamb-filled pastries) and *shashlyk* (skewered lamb kebab).

In addition, this area was once controlled by the Ottoman Turks, and many of the foods still common here were introduced during that period—including the Persian-inspired rice dishes that the Ottomans adopted, called *palov* (the Ottomans called it *pilaf*), as well as many stuffed vegetable dishes and eggplants. The Persian influence on the Ottomans can be seen here, not only in the palov but also in the making of flatbreads such as non (probably named after Indian naan, which is thought to have been inspired by the Persians as well) and the common use of nuts in savory and sweet preparations.

Inland Northern European Russia

The inland area of Russia west of the Ural Mountains is home to Moscow, the capital of Russia, as well as the heart of the Slavic communities that have been a central component of the country's development. This region is home to the great Volga River, which historically has provided the locals with large amounts of freshwater fish, including the well-known sturgeon that supplies the *ikra* (caviar) so often identified with Russian cuisine (although much of the catch that produces the best caviar comes from the more southerly Caspian Sea).

Soups reign supreme in this region, and shchi (cabbage or sauerkraut soup), ukha (fish soup), and borscht (beet soup) are but a few examples of the many vegetable-based soups that might be found in kitchens here. Bread is the central source of food here, as it is in the rest of Russia, and the varieties of breads to be found are matched only by the variations of pirog (filled savory pastry) available. The use of dairy products rounds out this hearty diet, with smetana (sour cream), *maslo* (butter), and tvorog (fresh cheese) being some of the more commonly added components.

Georgia and Southern European Russian Regions

Although it is no longer a republic of the Soviet Union, the region of Georgia is firmly attached to the Russian cuisine. Many of the dishes now common in Russia and proudly identified as Russian have their origins here. Georgia is a small region that is situated in between the Caspian and Black seas, and between the southern Caucasus and Surami mountain ranges. The regions of Russia that border this nation include many similarities to Georgia, with regard to cuisine, and are included in this section as a result.

The people of Georgia have a long tradition of highly evolved cuisine and have been blessed with a fertile climate and terrain that provide its chefs with many high-quality products not typically associated with (or often even possible in) nearly all of the rest of the territories. These foods include figs, nuts, grapes, olives, citrus, and stone fruits. This region is well known for its highly flavored foods that often contain flavorful sauces, such as *tkemali* (sour plum sauce), *bazha* (walnut sauce), and *ajika* (hot pepper paste); many fragrant herbs and spices, such as *kinza* (coriander the spice and cilantro the herb), *shaffron* (marigold petals—different from saffron), *rebani* (opal basil), *niakbouri* (dill), *tsitseli* (chiles and chili powders), and the difficult to describe *utskho suneli*, which is not found in the United States but is said to have a fragrance reminiscent of fenugreek.

Some of the foods that are commonly found in Russian cuisine that reign from this region include *satsivi* (turkey with walnut sauce), *tabaka* (pressed *tsitsila*, or chicken), which is traditionally served with tkemali sauce or one of the many walnut sauces, and *kotmis garo* (grilled chicken with walnut and garlic sauce).

Baltic Russia

The Baltic region of Russia has many of the same traditions, foods, and customs as its Scandinavian neighbors. This region is home to the major seaport of St. Petersburg, which has been a hub of fishing fleets for many years, bringing in much of the Baltic catch of *silyotka* (herring) and *syomga* (Atlantic salmon) that is used to make the foods for zakuski, such as pickled or salted herring and smoked salmon. This region is important to the country, not only because it provides a significant portion of the seafood catch but also because it is home to fertile coastal plains that produce many dairy products as well. The use of maslo, smetana, and tvorog are all common in this region.

The tradition of starting a meal with a wide selection of foods, which is reminiscent of the Swedish smörgåsbord, hails from the days of Catherine the Great and the period when the Russian capital was located in St. Petersburg. This is also where trade was established with the Nordic nations of Scandinavia, and many of their customs were common here— not only because of trade but also because many Scandinavians settled in this part of Russia.

RECIPES

The following recipes provide an introduction to the cuisines of the Russian Federation by revealing some of the more common and significant dishes found in this region. There are obviously many other recipes that can be explored to help provide a deeper understanding of the cuisine of this area.

Filled Dumplings   RUSSIAN FEDERATION

INGREDIENTS

1	lb	All-Purpose (A.P.) Flour
1	tsp	Salt
3		Egg Yolks (save the whites for sealing the dumplings)
2	oz	Vegetable Oil (you can also use olive oil, if desired)
		Water, as needed (you will need approximately 4 oz)

Filled dumplings highlight both the variation and continuity of the cuisines of the Russian Federation all at once. Many varieties and sizes of dumplings appear throughout the region, and each provides some information about the local cuisine and traditions while relying on a common principle and technique. Whether they are manti, vareniki, or another style, all dumplings typically are made with egg noodle dough and often highlight some of the region's other components in their fillings. Variations of these stuffed dumplings were once a distinct component of the zakuski tables that Russian royalty and elite enjoyed during the eighteenth and nineteenth centuries, when Russian cuisine started to become more refined. All of the following dumplings can be made with the noodle dough recipe provided here.

YIELD: 1.5 pounds egg noodle dough

MIXING METHOD: Food Processor or Electric Mixer with Dough Hook

PROCEDURE

(**NOTE:** *Dough can be made in a food processor or mixing bowl.*)

1. Sift the flour into a mixing bowl; add salt, and mix to combine.

2. If making in a food processor, add the egg yolks, oil, and 4 oz of water to the food processor, and then add the flour mixture on top of the liquids; pulse mixture until a smooth dough is formed (you may need to adjust the dough by adding either flour or water, depending on the composition of the flour). If making in a mixing bowl with the dough hook attachment, add the dry ingredients first, and then the egg yolks, oil, and water as needed, as the machine is running on low speed to form a smooth dough.

3. If using the food processor, it often is necessary to remove the dough from the machine and work it briefly by hand, kneading the dough on a workbench to yield a smooth dough. The mixing bowl method should yield a smooth dough by allowing the machine to knead it for a couple minutes.

4. Once the dough is smooth, remove it from the machine and wrap it with plastic wrap; allow it to rest on the bench for 20–30 minutes before proceeding to make the filled dumpling.

Vareniki UKRAINE
(STUFFED NOODLES)

INGREDIENTS

For Making the Filling

1	lb	Red Bliss Potatoes (or other waxy variety)
2	oz	Unsalted Butter
5	oz	Yellow Onions, minced
.5	oz	Garlic Cloves, minced
1/2	tsp	Freshly Ground Black Pepper
1.5	tsp	Salt
4	oz	Grated Mild Cheese (such as Cheddar or Monterey Jack)

For Stuffing and Cooking the Dumplings

1/2		Egg Noodle Recipe (see above)
1	cup	A.P. Flour
		Egg Whites (leftover from dough recipe)
		Stuffing (see above)
3	gallons	Water
3	Tbsp	Salt
2	oz	Salted Butter

Stuffed noodles are common throughout much of the Russian Federation and the former states of the USSR, and this version is but one example of the filled noodles that can be found in the Ukraine. This version utilizes a potato and onion filling, but other versions use such fillings as sauerkraut, cheese, ground meats, and sweet varieties.

YIELD: 25–30 filled dumplings (1.5 ounces/dumpling)

COOKING METHOD: Boiling

PROCEDURE

For Making the Filling

1. Place a pot holding 1.5 qts of water and 1 Tbsp salt on the stove over a high flame, and bring to a boil.

2. Once the water reaches a boil, add the potatoes and boil until tender throughout; remove potatoes from heat, and strain. Set them aside to cool.

3. Once the potatoes are cool enough to handle, peel them and mash them using a fork.

4. In a sauté pan, heat the butter over a medium-low flame; add the minced onion and garlic once hot.

5. Sweat the onions and garlic in the butter until they are very tender and translucent.

6. Once the onions are very tender, add the potatoes, black pepper, and salt to the pan; mix well.

7. Remove the potato mixture from the heat, and set aside to cool.

8. Once the potato mixture is cool, mix in the grated cheese and check the mixture for seasoning. Adjust with salt and/or pepper, if necessary.

For Stuffing and Cooking the Dumplings

1. Place a large pot on the stove and fill it with the 3 gallons of water and the salt; place it over a high flame to bring the mixture to a boil.

2. Using a rolling pin and extra flour to prevent the dough from sticking, roll out 1/2 of the dough for the dumplings to 1/16 inch (very thin).

3. Using a circular pastry cutter about 3 inches in diameter, cut the dough sheet into circles, and then ball up all of the scrap and combine it with the other 1/2 of the dough.

4. Using a pastry brush, lightly brush the outside 1/8 inch of each of the circles with the leftover egg whites from making the egg noodle dough (add a little water to the egg whites to thin and stretch them, if needed).

5. Once all of the dough circles have been brushed, place a couple of teaspoons of filling in the center of each dough piece.

(continues)

Vareniki
(continued)

6. Fold over each piece of dough to yield a half-moon–shaped dumpling, and then press the edges where the dough comes together with the tines of a fork (be sure to press firmly and seal them well all the way around).

7. Repeat steps 2 to 6 with the remaining dough (but omit adding the scrap to remaining dough), and then proceed to the next step.

8. Once all of the dough has been rolled and stuffed, the dumplings can be cooked in the boiling salted water (if the water level has dropped too much by the time you are ready to cook the dumplings, refill it to the original amount and let it return to a boil before cooking).

9. Place 10 (or more, depending on space) dumplings into the boiling water, and stir gently with a wooden spoon to prevent them from sticking to one another; turn the heat down to prevent them from breaking due to rapid boil.

10. Continue to cook the dumplings in the boiling water for 2 minutes, and then remove them with a strainer and add more dumplings to the boiling water. Repeat these steps until all of the dumplings have been cooked.

11. Place the cooked dumplings in a pan with the melted butter, and toss gently to coat; serve.

The plate on the right shows the filled pasta types prior to being closed (from top to bottom: vareniki, pel'meni, and manti). The finished stuffed doughs are also shown.

Manti UZBEKISTAN AND KAZAKHSTAN
(STUFFED DUMPLINGS)

INGREDIENTS

For Making the Filling

12	oz	Lamb Stew Meat or Trim (connective tissue and heavy fat removed)
5	oz	Yellow Onions, minced
1		Garlic Clove, minced
1/2	tsp	Fennel Seed, ground
1/2	tsp	Coriander Seed, ground
1/2	tsp	Freshly Ground Black Pepper
1.5	tsp	Salt
1/4	cup	Packed Cilantro, minced (about 1/2 bunch)
1	oz	Lemon Juice

For Stuffing and Cooking the Dumplings

1/2		Egg Noodle Recipe (see above)
1	cup	A.P. Flour, for dusting
		Lamb Filling (see above)
		Small Container of Cold Water (for dipping fingers)
2	qts	Water (in bottom of steamer setup)
		Tsatsiki (optional sauce for serving; see Chapter 2, "Greek Cuisine," for recipe)

This version of the stuffed dumpling is typical of the Muslim and Middle Eastern–influenced areas of some of the nations that were once part of the USSR; they can still be found in areas with populations from these former republics. The Chinese influence is evident in these dumplings as well, as they are steamed in multileveled steamers—similar to how Chinese dumplings are made—only these have a lamb filling instead of pork, which is often used in Chinese dumplings. They are sometimes cooked like ravioli or other stuffed pasta, being boiled with water instead of steaming.

YIELD: 12 to 15 dumplings (2–3 ounces/dumpling)

COOKING METHOD: Steaming

PROCEDURE

For Making the Filling

1. Using a sharp, heavy knife, chop all of the cleaned lamb meat until it is finely minced (do not use a food processor, or the meat will become pasty and dense; a grinder can be used, but the results will be inferior to hand chopping).

2. In a mixing bowl, combine the chopped lamb, onions, garlic, spices, salt, cilantro, and lemon juice; mix well.

3. Cook a small amount of the lamb mixture in a small pan to check for seasoning; adjust, if necessary.

For Stuffing and Cooking the Dumplings

1. Preheat the steamer by putting water in the bottom section and placing it on the stove while you fill the dumplings (you can also use a commercial steamer for this).

2. Using the A.P. flour to prevent sticking, roll out the egg noodle dough to a thickness of approximately 1/16 inch (very thin).

3. Using a 4-inch circular dough cutter (or a template to be cut with a knife), cut out circles from the rolled-out dough.

4. Place a couple of tablespoons of filling in the center of each dough piece.

5. Pull the dough up the sides of each dumpling. Dip your free hand in the cold water and moisten the dough at the top. Pinch the dough together at the top to seal the dumplings (they should look like small, tied beanbags with the filling held tightly in the rounded bottom section).

6. Continue to fill each of the dough pieces as described in steps 4 and 5 until all of the filling and/or dough pieces are used up.

7. Spray the perforated steamer tray(s) with pan spray to help prevent the dumplings from sticking.

8. Place the filled dumplings in the steamer tray(s), making sure that they do not touch each other—they will stick, if they do.

(continues)

Manti
(continued)

9. Place the filled steamer trays onto the steamer setup (or in the commercial steamer); steam for 8–10 minutes, or until the filling is completely cooked.

10. Remove the dumplings from the steamer and serve (the tsatsiki recipe from the Chapter 2 is very similar to the yogurt/garlic sauce that is traditionally served with these).

Pel'meni SIBERIA
(MEAT-FILLED DUMPLINGS)

INGREDIENTS

For Making the Filling

6	oz	Lean Beef (such as top round, tenderloin, or lean trim), diced large
6	oz	Lean Pork (such as tenderloin or loin), diced large
3	oz	Beef Suet or Veal Suet
4	oz	Yellow Onion, chopped
1/2	tsp	Freshly Ground Black Pepper
1.5	tsp	Salt
3	oz	Ice-Cold Water

For Filling, Cooking, and Serving the Dumplings

2	qts	Veal Stock
1/2		Egg Noodle Recipe (see above)
1	cup	A.P. Flour
		Egg Whites (leftover from dough recipe)
		Meat Filling (see above)
4	oz	Sour Cream
1	Tbsp	Fresh Dill, minced
1/4	tsp	Salt

These Siberian dumplings are still very common in Russia today, although they are less commonly prepared in the manner that made them both popular and sensible. In Siberia, where freezers are not a necessity, pel'meni would be made in batches of hundreds to utilize a slaughter (usually of a horse) and would simply be set in a bag outside, where they would freeze and then be used as needed. The traditional pel'meni were made from horsemeat, but this recipe calls for beef and pork instead.

YIELD: 40–45 dumplings (under 1 ounce/dumpling)

COOKING METHOD: Poaching/Simmering in Broth

PROCEDURE

For Making the Filling

1. Set grinding equipment into an ice bath to get very cold (and be sure that all equipment is clean and sanitary prior to setting it in the ice bath).

2. Once the equipment is chilled properly, set up the grinder and grind the beef and pork using a medium plate.

3. Once the beef and pork have been ground once, add the beef suet and chopped onions to the mixture, change the grinder plate to a fine plate, and pass meat mixture through the grinder again.

4. Transfer the meat mixture to a mixing bowl and, using a paddle attachment, mix the spices into the meat mixture.

5. With the mixer running at low speed, slowly add the ice-cold water to form a light, smooth mixture.

6. Cook a small amount of the meat mixture in a little veal broth to taste for seasoning; adjust, if necessary.

For Stuffing, Cooking, and Serving the Dumplings

1. Using the A.P. flour to prevent sticking, roll out 1/2 of the egg noodle dough to a thickness of approximately 1/16 inch (very thin).

2. Cut dough into 2-inch strips, and then cut each strip into 2-inch squares.

3. Brush the outer edge of each square with some of the egg white using a pastry brush (add a little water to the egg white, if needed, to make it thinner).

(continues)

Pel'meni
(continued)

4. Place a teaspoon of the meat mixture in the center of each square, and then fold the dough over from one corner to the other, making a triangle. Be careful to prevent trapping air as you do this by gently pressing the dough against the meat filling when you fold it over.

5. Seal each of the dough pieces shut by either pinching the overlapping dough edges together between your fingers or using the tines of a fork to do so.

6. Repeat steps 3 to 6 to complete all of the pel'meni.

7. Place the pel'meni pieces on a sheet pan(s), cover them with plastic wrap, and place them in a freezer (the prepared pel'meni can be kept in the freezer for weeks if covered well or put into sealed freezer bags once frozen).

8. Once you are ready to cook the pel'meni, proceed to the next step.

9. Place the veal stock on the stove and bring it to poaching temperature over a medium-low flame.

10. Combine the sour cream, dill, and salt in a mixing bowl, and set aside.

11. Gently place 5 to 6 pel'meni at a time into the poaching stock to cook, turning the heat up slightly as you do so to bring the stock to a gentle simmer (do not boil, or the pel'meni will break apart).

12. Once the pel'meni rise to the surface, allow them to cook for an additional minute and then remove them from the stock. Serve them in a bowl with a couple ounces of the veal stock and topped with a small dollop of the sour cream/dill mixture.

NOTE: *These also could be served with vinegar and freshly ground black pepper, as they traditionally were eaten this way.*

Bliny
(THIN BUCKWHEAT PANCAKES)

INGREDIENTS

For the Sponge

3	cups	Whole Milk, warmed to 100°F (do this over a low flame or in a microwave oven, and be sure to stir the milk well before adding yeast, or the yeast could be killed by hot spots in the milk).
2	tsp	Sugar
2	oz	Fresh Compressed Yeast
10	oz	Buckwheat Flour (if this is unavailable, use A.P. flour)

Bliny have a long tradition in Moscow and other Russian cities, where they often are eaten as a symbol of the coming of spring; the round shape and glistening melted butter are said to be symbolic of the bright shining sun. This classic dish is traditionally served with peas and kasha or eaten with melted butter and sour cream or caviar.

YIELD: Approximately 2 dozen 6-inch pancakes

COOKING METHOD: Griddling

PROCEDURE

For Making the Sponge

1. In a mixing bowl, combine the warmed milk, sugar, and yeast; set aside, covered with a clean cloth, for 5 minutes to ensure that the yeast is active (it should foam slightly and have a yeasty aroma).

2. Once yeast is determined to be active, add the buckwheat flour and whisk together the ingredients until smooth.

(continues)

✳

Bliny
(continued)

For Making the Batter and Cooking

2	oz	Unsalted Butter, melted
10	oz	A.P. Flour
1	tsp	Sugar
20	fl oz	Whole Milk
5		Egg Yolks (save the whites)
1	tsp	Salt
5		Egg Whites
4	oz	Clarified Butter

For Serving the Bliny

Salted Butter (softened), to taste

3. Set this sponge aside to ferment for 1–1.5 hours, or until the sponge begins to fall back on itself.

For Making the Batter and Cooking

1. To the sponge you have already prepared, add the melted butter, A.P. flour, and sugar; beat with a whisk (or using a mixing bowl with a whisk attachment) to form smooth dough/batter.

2. Set this mixture aside, covered with a damp, clean cloth, until it has doubled in volume.

3. Once the dough has doubled in volume, heat the milk in a saucepan until it is just about to boil, and then remove it from the heat. Beat it into the dough, followed by the egg yolks and salt, to form a smooth batter.

4. In a separate (clean) bowl, whip the egg whites until they form soft peaks, and fold them into the bliny batter. At this point, you are ready to start cooking the bliny.

5. Heat a nonstick crêpe pan over a medium flame until it is hot, and add 1/2 teaspoon of the clarified butter to the pan.

6. Once the oil is hot, add a 2-oz ladle of the bliny batter to the pan, tilting the pan to allow the batter to completely coat the bottom in a thin layer before cooking.

7. Allow the batter time to cook on one side (about 1 minute or so), and then flip it to the other side and cook for another 30 seconds to finish.

8. Remove the bliny from the crêpe pan; keep covered with a clean table linen or foil with holes poked in it until serving.

9. Repeat steps 6 to 9 until all of the bliny are cooked.

10. Serve at once with desired accompaniments (melted butter and sour cream are common, as are caviar, smoked fish, and pickled fish—such as herring).

Bliny (buckwheat pancakes) served with caviar and sour cream

Marinovannye Griby
(MARINATED MUSHROOMS)

INGREDIENTS

2	cups	White Wine Vinegar (or distilled vinegar, if this unavailable)
1.5	cups	Water
5		Bay Leaves, broken
5		Whole Cloves
1	tsp	Black Peppercorns, crushed
1	Tbsp	Sugar
1	oz	Salt
.5	oz	Garlic Cloves, slivered
2	oz	Olive Oil
2	lbs	Small Mushrooms, brushed of any debris or dirt (don't wash them: they will absorb some of the water and dilute your marinade)

Mushrooms are one of the distinguishing ingredients of Russian cuisine, because the vast forests of the Russian Federation yield a tremendous quality and quantity of mushrooms that are incorporated into many of the traditional foods. One of the common uses of the bounty is in making preserved mushrooms, as in this recipe, so they can be enjoyed for weeks after they begin sprouting up. Mushrooms also have traditionally been eaten as a substitute for meat during the many fast days of the Russian Orthodox Christian faith.

YIELD: 2.5 pounds

PRESERVATION METHOD: Marinating/Pickling

PROCEDURE

1. In a pot, combine the vinegar, water, spices, sugar, and salt; bring this mixture to a simmer over a medium flame.
2. Once the mixture simmers, remove it from the heat and add the garlic slivers to the mixture; set it aside to cool.
3. Place the mushrooms in a sealable jar into which they pack tightly (use a couple, if necessary, but make sure they fill it almost completely and are packed in snugly).
4. Carefully pour in the marinade mixture to completely cover the mushrooms, leaving a small space so the oil will fit.
5. Pour the olive oil on top of the marinade, and then seal the jar.
6. Place the jar in the refrigerator and allow the mushrooms to marinate for a week before opening and using (a couple of weeks is even better).

Kasha
(BUCKWHEAT GROATS)

INGREDIENTS

2	cups	Buckwheat Groats, coarse (also may be called kasha)
2		Eggs, beaten
5	cups	Boiling Water
1	Tbsp	Salt
2	oz	Butter, unsalted
8	oz	Yellow Onion, minced
1	lb	Mushrooms, chopped fine
4	oz	Butter, Unsalted

Buckwheat was introduced into the Russian diet by trade with the Byzantine Empire in the tenth century, and it has been a main ingredient ever since. One of the uses of buckwheat is to make kasha, often served to accompany meals and—in lean times—eaten with bread to sustain the poor and less fortunate. This version includes the typical pre-toasting of the groats, and the addition of egg and mushrooms.

YIELD: 1.5 quarts cooked kasha, or approximately 12 portions (4–5 ounces/portion)

COOKING METHOD (BUCKWHEAT): Simmering

COOKING METHOD (MUSHROOMS): Sautéing

(continues)

Kasha
(continued)

PROCEDURE

1. In a 2.5-qt pot, combine the buckwheat groats and the beaten egg; mix well with a fork.

2. Place the pot over a medium-low flame and toast the grains while stirring, until the buckwheat becomes slightly fragrant and the liquid is gone from the egg (stir the whole time so the buckwheat doesn't color; this step takes about 5 minutes).

3. Add the boiling water and salt to the buckwheat, and stir to combine; cover with a tight-fitting lid and cook over a low flame until the buckwheat is tender (about 20 minutes).

4. In a separate sauté pan, heat the 2 oz of butter over a medium-low flame, and sweat the onions until they are translucent.

5. Once the onions are translucent, add the mushrooms and turn the heat up; sauté the mushrooms over a medium flame until the moisture is gone.

6. Transfer the onion and mushroom mixture to the pot of buckwheat and stir in along with the remaining butter to combine well.

7. Check the seasoning of the finished kasha and adjust with salt, if necessary.

Borscht
(BEET SOUP)

INGREDIENTS

For Roasting the Beets

4	lbs	Beets, scrubbed clean (but not peeled)

For Making the Soup by Broth Soup Method

2	oz	Unsalted Butter
1	oz	Garlic Cloves, minced
12	oz	Yellow Onion, minced
2		Celery Roots (about 1.5 lbs), peeled and grated coarse
2		Parsnips (about .75 lbs), peeled and grated coarse
1	gallon	Veal or Beef Stock
1	oz	Sugar
4	oz	Red Wine Vinegar
2	Tbsp	Salt
		Roasted Beets (see above), peeled and grated coarse
1	lb	Red Bliss Potatoes, peeled and diced medium

When people are asked to name a Russian recipe, the most common response is borscht. Borsht is one of many hearty soups common to Russian Federation cuisine (shchi, a cabbage-based soup, is probably the second most common). These soups take advantage of the hearty root vegetables and cabbage that grow in the shorter growing seasons of the Russian plains.

YIELD: 2 gallons, or 32 servings (8 ounces/serving)

COOKING METHOD (BEETS): Roasting

COOKING METHOD (SOUP): Clear Broth Soup Method

PROCEDURE

For Roasting the Beets

1. Preheat the oven to 325°F.

2. Scrub the beets clean under cool running water, put them on a sheet pan, and place them in the preheated oven.

3. Check the beets for doneness by piercing them with a knife or skewer (the beets will take about 1 hour and 15 minutes at this temperature, if they are the usual 10–12 oz size; smaller beets will take considerably less time, and larger ones will take more. It is always best to start checking them early, so that they do not overcook).

(continues)

Borscht
(continued)

1	lb	Green Cabbage, shredded fine
1.5	lbs	Boiled Beef Brisket, fully cooked (if not cooked, this can be simmered in the veal or beef stock until very tender, and then the broth can be strained through cheesecloth to remove impurities; at this point, it can be used in the soup)
1/4	cup	Italian Parsley, minced (about 1 bunch)
		Salt, to taste
2	cups	Sour Cream

4. Once the beets are cooked, remove them from the oven and set them aside to cool.

5. Once the beets have cooled enough to handle, peel them with a paring knife and grate them on a coarse grater to be used in the soup.

For Making the Soup by Broth Soup Method

(**NOTE:** *The soup won't be clear, but it is not thickened with any starches or puréed*).

1. In a pot large enough to hold all of the ingredients, heat the pot and butter over a medium-low flame until the butter is hot.

2. Add the minced garlic and onions to the pot and cook, stirring occasionally, until the onions and garlic are tender and translucent (about 5–8 minutes).

3. Once the onions and garlic are tender and translucent, add the grated celery root and parsnips; continue to cook over a medium-low flame for another 4–5 minutes, while stirring.

4. Add the veal stock, sugar, red wine vinegar, salt, and grated beets, and bring this mixture to a gentle simmer over a high flame.

5. Once a simmer is reached, turn the heat down to a very low flame, cover the pot, and allow the vegetables to simmer gently for at least 1–1.5 hours (the longer, the better).

6. If the liquid level has changed much during the gentle simmering process, add more stock or water as needed.

7. Add the Red Bliss potatoes, cabbage, and beef brisket, and gently simmer over a low flame; uncover for an additional 40 minutes, and then remove from heat.

8. Add the minced parsley and check the seasoning of the soup; add salt, if necessary.

9. Serve the borscht with a dollop of sour cream on top.

Borscht (beet soup) served with sour cream

Kotlety Po Kievski

(CHICKEN KIEV; BREADED CHICKEN CUTLET WITH BUTTER STUFFING)

INGREDIENTS

For Making the Compound Butter

10	oz	Salted Butter, room temperature
1	oz	Lemon Juice
.5	oz	Garlic Cloves, minced
2	Tbsp	Chives, minced
1	Tbsp	Parsley, minced
1/2	tsp	Freshly Ground Black Pepper
1/4	tsp	Salt

For Stuffing and Breading the Chicken

10	6-oz	Boneless, Skinless Chicken Breasts
		Compound Butter (see above)
2	cups	A.P. Flour
5		Large Eggs, beaten
4	oz	Whole Milk
1	qt	Seasoned Bread Crumbs

For Panfrying the Chicken

		Vegetable Oil, as needed

The influence of the French on the cuisine of Russia—particularly the Baltic area of European Russia—is evident in many recipes that require sautéing or panfrying, methods that were imported from France; this recipe is one example of this influence. This dish of the classic Russian court cuisine is traditionally served with peas and kasha.

YIELD: 10 portions (7 ounces/portion)

COOKING METHOD: Panfrying

PROCEDURE

For Making the Compound Butter

1. Using a small mixer with a paddle attachment, combine the butter, lemon juice, garlic cloves, minced herbs, pepper, and salt; mix on low speed until all of the ingredients are combined well.

2. Remove the butter from the bowl and place it in a small pastry bag; pipe out the compound butter in 10 equal-size strips, about 1.5 inches long, on a small pan lined with parchment paper.

3. Cover the pan with plastic wrap, and set the butter in the refrigerator to firm up while you gather the other ingredients.

For Stuffing, Breading, and Panfrying the Chicken

1. Preheat the oven to 325°F.

2. Place plastic wrap over the chicken breasts, and pound them with a mallet to an even 1/4-inch thickness (don't pound so hard that you break through the breast meat completely—just hard enough to separate the muscle fibers on the surface and stretch the chicken).

3. Place one compound butter strip (see above) in the bottom third of each chicken breast, and tightly roll the breast around the butter.

4. Bread the stuffed and rolled chicken breasts using this three-step procedure: first coat the chicken in the flour, then in the egg wash (beaten eggs and milk, combined), and finally in the seasoned bread crumbs (remember to use one hand for dry ingredients and one hand for wet ingredients!).

5. Once all of the chicken breasts have been breaded, set them in the refrigerator; they will be ready for panfrying in 15 minutes (it is a good idea to let the breading firm up prior to panfrying, as this will help the breading stay adhered to the chicken; note that the breaded chicken can be kept in the refrigerator for a day or two, if needed).

6. In a small to medium-sized sauté pan, heat enough oil to coat the bottom of the pan at a depth of approximately 1/8 inch; place over a medium high-flame to heat the oil.

7. Once the oil is hot, panfry the breaded chicken until the outside is golden brown all over, and place the chicken breasts in a baking pan (1/2 sheet pan) as they are done.

(continues)

Kotlety Po Kievski
(continued)

8. Once all of the chicken breasts have been panfried, transfer them to the preheated oven and bake until the chicken is just cooked through (this should take about 5 minutes, if you are using 6-oz chicken breasts that have been pounded properly).

9. Serve at once.

Breading the kotlety po Kievski (chicken cutlet with butter stuffing) in the last two stages of the breading station (egg wash followed by bread crumbs)

Panfrying the kotlety po Kievski

Kotlety Pozharsky
(BREADED CHICKEN CUTLET)

INGREDIENTS

For Making the Ground Chicken Mixture

4	oz	Whole Wheat Bread, crust removed and, if not sliced, sliced into 1/2-inch-thick pieces
4	oz	Heavy Cream
2	lbs	Chicken Breast Pieces (these will be ground, so they don't have to be whole breasts)
1	lb	Veal Stew Meat
10	oz	Yellow Onion, chopped
2	oz	Salted Butter, softened
4		Egg Yolks (save two of the whites for use later in this recipe)
1/2	tsp	Black Pepper
2	tsp	Salt
2		Egg Whites

This dish is named after a tavern that served a version of this recipe. The very famous Russian czar Alexander I is said to have visited this tavern, after sampling this particular dish, he had it put on the menu at the royal palace.

YIELD: Approximately 18 cutlets (4 ounces/cutlet)

COOKING METHOD: Panfrying

PROCEDURE

For Making the Ground Chicken Mixture

1. Place all of the components of the meat grinder in ice water to chill completely (you will need both a medium and a fine plate), making sure that everything is clean and sanitized prior to placing it in the ice bath.

2. In a small bowl, combine the bread slices and cream; set aside.

3. Assemble the grinder; while it is still very cold, grind the chicken and veal stew meat through a medium plate and into a mixing bowl set over an ice bath.

4. As soon as all of the chicken and veal are ground, add the onions and butter to the mixture, change the plate on the grinder to a fine plate, and pass the meat and onion mixture through the grinder again.

5. Add the cream-soaked bread pieces, egg yolks, salt, and pepper to the meat mixture; using clean and sanitized hands, work the mixture together with your fingers to yield a smooth mixture.

(continues)

Kotlety Pozharsky
(continued)

For Breading and Panfrying the Cutlets

6		Large Eggs, beaten
4	oz	Whole Milk
1	qt	Dried Bread Crumbs
10	oz	Clarified Butter

6. In a separate bowl, whip the egg whites to form soft peaks.

7. Fold the whipped egg whites into the ground meat mixture.

For Breading and Panfrying the Cutlets

1. Before forming the chicken, fill a container with cold water, and wash and sanitize your hands.

2. Cover two sheet pans with plastic wrap and set them next to your work area.

3. Take approximately 4 oz (about 1/2 cup) of the meat mixture in your hands and form it into an oval shape; immediately set it on a plastic-wrap–lined sheet pan.

4. Continue forming the ground meat mixture until all of it has been used (you should end up with approximately 18 formed pieces).

5. Cover the cutlets with plastic wrap, and set the sheet pans in the refrigerator; allow the mixture to firm up for 1 hour before breading (this makes the cutlets a lot easier to handle).

Kotlety Pozharsky topped with kasha (buckwheat groats), and served with mushroom sour cream sauce, Brussels sprouts and baby carrots

6. Once the cutlets have set, remove them from the refrigerator and place them in a work area with a breading station set up as follows: combine the eggs with the milk in one bowl, and place that mixture before a bowl containing bread crumbs.

7. Bread each of the cutlets by dipping them first into the egg mixture, and then into the bread crumbs (use the wet hand/dry hand technique to avoid wasting product and having to stop to clean your hands before finishing).

8. Once all of the cutlets are breaded, set a large sauté pan on the stove, over a medium flame; add half of the clarified butter to the heated pan.

9. Place 5 or so of the chicken cutlets in the heated pan, and panfry the cutlets until they are golden brown. Remove these and continue with the others, only adding as many cutlets as the pan can handle. Add more clarified butter as needed.

10. Once all of the chicken cutlets have been panfried until golden brown, place them all on a sheet pan and into the preheated oven for about 3–4 minutes, or until they are cooked throughout (their juices should run clear when poked with a skewer).

11. Serve the cutlets at once (these are often served with a mushroom sauce; see next recipe).

Mushroom Sour Cream Sauce (to Accompany Kotlety Pozharsky)

INGREDIENTS

2	oz	Butter
8	oz	Yellow Onion, diced small
2	lbs	Mushrooms
1	tsp	Salt
1/2	tsp	Freshly Ground Black Pepper
2	cups	Chicken Stock
2	cups	Heavy Cream
2	cups	Sour Cream
		Salt and Pepper, to taste

YIELD: 2 quarts, or approximately 18 portions (3.5 ounces/portion)

COOKING METHOD (ONIONS AND MUSHROOMS): Sweating in Butter

COOKING METHOD (FINAL): Gently Simmering

PROCEDURE

1. Heat a large sauté pan over a medium flame. Once the pan is hot, add the butter and onions; sweat/sauté the onions until they just begin to color.

2. Once the onions begin to color, add the mushrooms, salt, and pepper to the pan; continue to cook over a medium flame until the mushrooms lose much of their moisture and begin to color.

3. Once the mushrooms begin to color in the pan, add the chicken stock and the heavy cream; bring to a gentle simmer.

4. Continue to simmer the mixture until it begins to thicken slightly.

5. Once the mixture begins to thicken slightly, remove the pan from heat and add the sour cream by stirring in small amounts at a time.

6. Once all of the sour cream has been added, return the pan to a low flame and slowly heat the sauce to desired temperature before checking for seasoning. At this point, it is ready to be used.

Bef Stroganov

(BEEF STROGANOFF)

INGREDIENTS

For Making the Sauce

4	oz	Clarified Butter
1	lb	Yellow Onions, diced small
4	oz	A.P. Flour
2.25	qts	Brown Beef or Veal Stock (cold, or at least cool)
1/4	cup	Strong Prepared Mustard (such as Dijon)
3/4	cup	Tomato Purée
1/2	tsp	Freshly Ground Black Pepper
2	tsp	Salt
1	cup	Sour Cream

This well-known Russian classic got its name from the famous Russian Pavel Stroganov, who was a well-connected gourmand in early twentieth-century St. Petersburg. The recipe is thought to have come from a common dish in his family, and its name was given in honor of Pavel, because he popularized the dish publicly.

YIELD: 15 portions (7 ounces/portion)

COOKING METHOD (SAUCE): Stewing/Simmering

COOKING METHOD (BEEF): Sautéing

PROCEDURE

For Making the Sauce

1. In a pot large enough to hold all of the ingredients for the sauce, heat the clarified butter over a medium-low flame; once the butter is hot, add onions.

2. Sweat the onions in the butter until they are translucent and softened; add the flour and stir well, while continuing to cook, to make a brown roux (adjust consistency of the roux, if necessary, with additional flour).

(continues)

Bef Stroganov
(continued)

For Sautéing the Beef

2 oz	Clarified Butter
5 lbs	Tender Cut of Beef (such as tenderloin or tri-tip—a good and more economical choice is beef tenderloin tips), trimmed of excess fat and any connective tissue and cut into strips approximately 1/2 inch wide and 3 inches long, seasoned with salt and pepper

Bef Stroganov (beef in sour cream sauce) served with thick-cut fried potatoes

3. Once a brown roux is achieved, add the cold stock—while mixing vigorously with a wooden spoon or wire whisk—until the roux has been dissolved into the stock (be sure to scrape the sides of the pot to dissolve the roux).

4. Add the mustard, tomato purée, salt, and pepper to the sauce.

5. Turn the heat up to a high flame and bring the sauce to a simmer, stirring as it heats to prevent lumping and scorching on the bottom of the pot.

6. Once the mixture reaches a simmer and begins to thicken, turn the heat down to a low flame to simmer gently.

7. Gently stew/simmer the sauce for at least 45 minutes, to cook out the starch of the roux and develop flavor.

8. Cook the meat prior to finishing the sauce in the next step (see following section).

9. After the meat has been cooked (by following the directions outlined next), use a whisk to mix the sour cream into the simmering sauce.

10. Taste the sauce for seasoning; adjust, if necessary, with salt and pepper.

For Sautéing the Beef

1. In a large sauté pan, heat the clarified butter over medium-high heat until the butter is hot; add just enough strips of the seasoned meat to cover half of the bottom of the pan.

2. Sauté the beef strips until they are browned, and then remove them from the pan and set them aside in another container (this should result in medium-rare pieces of meat. If you desire that they cook more, they can be simmered in the sauce; if you desire that they cook less, they can be cut thicker when preparing the ingredients).

3. Repeat step 2 until all of the beef strips have been sautéed.

4. Once all of the strips have been sautéed, finish the sauce as outlined in step 9 of the "For Making the Sauce" directions.

5. Once the sauce is finished, the beef can be combined with the sauce and served.

NOTE: *Beef Stroganoff is traditionally served with thick-cut fried potatoes.*

Medivnik   EUROPEAN RUSSIA
(HONEY WALNUT CAKE)

INGREDIENTS

6		Egg Yolks (save egg whites for use later in this recipe)
12	oz	Granulated Sugar
12	oz	Vegetable Oil
14	oz	Honey
4	oz	Warm Water
2	Tbsp	Espresso Powder (if this is not available, substitute liquid espresso for 2 oz of the water)
2	lbs	Flour
1	Tbsp	Baking Powder
2	tsp	Baking Soda
2	tsp	Cinnamon, ground
1	tsp	Cardamom, ground
1/4	tsp	Cloves, ground
2	Tbsp	Orange Zest, minced
6		Egg Whites
1	cup	Walnut Pieces

Medivnik (honey walnut cake)

This classic Ukrainian cake—which is common throughout European Russia today—combines some of the spices that were introduced to Russia from Asia, via the Silk Road and Scandinavian sea traders, with the original sweetener for much of Europe: honey.

YIELD: Two 9-inch springform pans

MIXING METHOD: Foaming Cake Batter

COOKING METHOD: Baking

PROCEDURE

1. Preheat the oven to 350°F.
2. In a mixer with a wipe attachment, combine the egg yolks and sugar; whip on high speed until the mixture becomes a thick, light yellow color and ribbons are formed when pulling the wipe out of the mixture.
3. In a separate bowl, combine the vegetable oil, honey, warm water, and espresso powder.
4. Slowly pour the oil/honey mixture into the egg yolk and sugar mixture, with the whip running at medium speed, until all of it is incorporated.
5. In another bowl, sift together all of the dry ingredients (flour, leavening agents, and seasonings—not the zest).
6. Add the dry ingredients to the mixing bowl that contains the wet ingredients, and mix until just smooth.
7. Remove the batter from the mixer, and mix in the orange zest and walnut pieces.
8. Using another mixer or a clean mixing bowl, beat the egg whites with a whisk until they just form stiff peaks.
9. Fold half of the egg whites into the cake batter using a plastic spatula; once incorporated, fold in the second half.
10. Prepare the 2 springform pans by making a parchment circle for the bottoms and spraying the sides with pan spray; close each spring to seal.
11. Divide the batter between the two springform pans, and place them in the preheated oven; bake for 30 minutes.
12. After 30 minutes, turn the oven down to 325°F, and continue to bake until the cake is done (this will take approximately another hour or more). Check cake for doneness by inserting a skewer to see if it comes out dry and clean.
13. Once cooked, allow the cake to cool on a cooling rack before attempting to remove each piece from the springform pan.

NOTE: *This cake improves in flavor if it sits for a day or so before being eaten.*

SUMMARY

Most of the territory that makes up the very large country of Russia lies in the cold northern reaches of Europe and Asia, resulting in a predominantly cold-weather cuisine. Thus, much of the food is rich and warming and relies on the limited ingredients that can be produced in this climate. Russian cuisine is strongly influenced by its neighbors as well as by the different ethnic populations that reside within its borders. The majority of the population, including a large amount of Slavic and Scandinavian peoples, lives in the European part of the country; the more eastern areas of Russia are home to mostly ethnic Tartars; Turkish peoples are the majority in the center of the country and parts of the south; and the northernmost areas are inhabited by Chukchi, ancient nomadic peoples. The cuisine of each of these areas is quite different, as each ethnic group brings its own culinary traditions. One distinct difference is that, in the more populated European section, most people are Orthodox Christians, which greatly influences their diet. In much of the Asian section, however, many people are followers of the Islamic faith, and this impacts their diet in a very different way. Russian food is characterized by many types of soups, stews, breads, braised foods, and simply prepared grains in the northern sections of the country, and by many grilled meats, rice dishes, stuffed vegetables, and flatbreads in the southern sections.

REVIEW QUESTIONS

1. How does the faith of the Orthodox Christians in Russia influence their eating customs?
2. How has the climate of much of Russia influenced the cuisine?
3. What are the major ethnic groups that are found in Russia, and in which parts of Russia are they found?

COMMON TERMS, FOODS, AND INGREDIENTS

The following terms are phonetic translations of some of the more common ingredients, foods, and equipment used in Russian cooking. These terms are common to the cuisine of Russia and will assist in the understanding and recognition of the foods and techniques used here. Most of the terms are phonetic (translated from sound), and thus you may find alternative spellings in other sources.

✳ Caviar

beluga – Considered the best of the sturgeon caviars, this comes from the largest species of the Caspian sturgeon and features larger (usually black, but sometimes lighter in color, ranging to gray) eggs

ikra – Russian term for caviar

malossol – Lightly salted; the most prized caviars are this type, where the eggs are fresher from not being salted as heavily as some lower grades. Beluga, osetra, and sevruga all can be found in this form.

osetra – Smaller sturgeon (and smaller caviar) than the prized beluga

sevruga – Smallest of the sturgeon; this yields the smallest caviar

sterlet – Rare golden-colored sturgeon caviar

✳ Common Ingredients and Tools

agooryets – Cucumbers

avyos – Oats

chai – Tea

chiryeshnya – Cherry

griby – Mushroom

iablaka – Apple

ichmyen – Barley

kazi – Dried horsemeat sausage

kinza – Coriander or cilantro

kizil – Tart cherry found in the Caucus area of Russia

koumiss – Fermented mare's milk common in the northern Asian portion of Russia

kurdiuk – Fat-tailed sheep of central Asia, prized for the cooking fat yielded from their tails

look – Onion

maslo – Butter

niakbouri – Dill

pleeta – Traditional Russian furnace/stove used to both heat the home and cook the food

rebani – Opal basil

rideeska – Radish

ryepa – Turnip

samovar – Tea kettle used to make tea on the stove and keep it hot

shaffron – False saffron made from marigold flower petals

silyotka – Herring

smetana – Sour cream

svyokla – Beets

syomga – Atlantic salmon

tikooschii – Currants

tkemali – Type of tart plum used in Georgian cuisine, especially for making sauces

toné – Earthenware lined fire pit used to cook breads on in Georgia

tsitseli – Chiles

tsitsila – Chicken

tvorog – Fresh cheese similar to cottage cheese

utskho suneli – Spice used in Georgian cuisine that is similar to fenugreek

yagada – Berry

zayats – Hare

✳ Common Recipes

ajika – Fiery red chili sauce from Georgia region

bazha – Walnut sauce from Georgia region

belyashi – Tartar dish of fried dough with minced meat and onion filling

bitki – Highly seasoned small meatballs common on a zakuski table

blinchiki – Thin, pancake-like crepe served as dessert

bliny – Buckwheat pancake or crepe

borscht – Beet soup

bublichki – Bread in the form of a ring

charlotte russe – Dessert made of sweetened and congealed mousse inside a ring of ladyfinger cookies

chebureki – Fried pastry with mutton or lamb and onion filling; of Crimean Tartar origin

garo – Walnut and garlic sauce with coriander; from the Georgia region

kasha – Cooked grains, often simply boiled and served with butter

khalvas – Middle Eastern–inspired sweets traditionally made from sesame paste (called *halvas* in the Middle East)

kolbasa – Cured and often smoked pork sausage (similar to Polish kielbasa)

kotlety – Ground meat patty

kotlety pozharsky – Breaded chicken cutlets

koteleti po Kievski – Chicken Kiev; a classic preparation of chicken that is stuffed with a seasoned butter and then breaded before being panfried

kotmis garo – Grilled chicken with walnut/garlic sauce; from Georgia

kulich – Traditional Russian Easter bread

kvashinaya kapusta – Fermented cabbage (sauerkraut)

lapsha – Noodles

manti – Filled steamed dumpling, or a dumpling baked in a tomato broth, typically filled with spiced ground lamb mixture; from Central Asia

marinovannye griby – Marinated mushrooms

medivnik – Honey walnut cake

non – Flatbread (see *naan* in Chapter 15, "Indian Cuisine")

palov – Rice dish that originated from the influence of the Persian and Ottoman empires in parts of Russia and former states in the Central Asian region

pashtet – Similar to a pâté, cooked meat is seasoned, pushed through a sieve, and encrusted in a pastry before being baked and cooled; served cold

paskha – Cheese spread shaped like a pyramid and eaten as part of the Easter celebration

pel'meni – Noodle dumpling from Siberia, typically filled with a mixture of ground meats

pirog – Savory pie

pirozhki – Stuffed yeast dough with savory filling; usually fried or baked

rassol'nik – Soup made with sorrel, brined cucumber, and various other vegetables and topped with chopped kidney

salat oliv'ye – Salad made with potatoes, peas, carrots, onions, pickles, and chicken, bound with mayonnaise

satsivi – Turkey with walnut sauce

shashlyk – Sis kebab (Russian name for Turkish skewered and grilled meats)

shchi – Cabbage soup

solionye ogurtsy – Brined cucumbers

tabaka – Roasted, butterflied, and pressed chicken from Georgia

teliatina po-Orlovski – Veal prince Orlov; a French-influenced preparation of mushroom purée layered between veal loin slices, topped with a béchamel sauce, and then browned under the broiler

tkemali – Georgian plum sauce served with tabaka

ukha – Fish soup, typically made with freshwater fish

vareniki – Ukrainian stuffed noodles filled with various mixtures that include sauerkraut, cheese, and potatoes, or sweet fillings such as cherries. Savory versions are typically served with sour cream, and sweet versions are served with confectioners' sugar or crème fraiche.

vetchina – Smoked pork, ham, or other cut

vinegret – Salad of potatoes, pickled cucumbers, beets, carrots, and onions, dressed with an oil and vinegar dressing

zakuski – Small bites; appetizers set out to be eaten prior to the beginning of a meal

zalivnoe – Jellied meats, poultry, or fish

zharkoe – Stew made from slow-simmered roasted meats with potatoes and other vegetables

CHAPTER 10

BAY OF BISCAY

FRANCE

Northern Atlantic and Basque Country

ASTURIAS

CANTABRIA

CORDILLERA CANTABRICA MOUNTAIN RANGE

BASQUE

PYRENEES MOUNTAINS

GALICIA

NAVARRE

Northeastern Spain– Calalonia and Aragon

ATLANTIC OCEAN

LA RIOJA

CASTILE LEON

Douro River

Ebro River

CATALONIA

Barcelona

Porto

Douro River

CENTRAL PLATEAU

ARAGON

Northern Portugal

MADRID

Madrid

IBERICO MOUNTAIN RANGE

BALEARIC SEA

PORTUGAL

Central Spain/Madrid and Extremadura

Tagus River

VALENCIA

BALEARIC ISLANDS

Tagus River

SPAIN

EXTREMADURA

Valencia

Valencia and the Levante

Lisbon

LA MANCHA

MORENA MOUNTAINS

Southern Portugal

Guadalquivir River

MURCIA

Southern Spain

Seville

BETICOS MOUNTAIN RANGE

ANDALUSIA

MEDITERRANEAN SEA

Jerez

N W E S

0   50   100 km

●	towns and cities
★	capital city
—	river
—	sub-region boundary
—	region boundary
–·–	international boundary
▦	mountains

CANARY ISLANDS

ALGERIA

MOROCCO

OBJECTIVES

Upon completion of this chapter, you will be able to

- explain the importance of the "discovery" of the Americas and the role that Spain and Portugal played in this significant period in history.
- list some of the ingredients that are integral to modern Iberian cuisine that are indigenous to the Americas.
- recognize some of the recipes and ingredients common to the different regions that make up Spain and Portugal.
- produce some of the recipes from this region.
- define the terms listed at the conclusion of this chapter.

INTRODUCTION

The Iberian Peninsula stretches south from the Pyrenees Mountains in the south of France to just five miles short of northern Africa at the gate to the Mediterranean Sea and the Atlantic Ocean. This area has a diverse landscape and climate, ranging from the colder and wet northern reaches, the mostly hot and arid plains of the Estremadura, the hot summers and mild winters along the Mediterranean, to the fertile shores of the flat Levante. Because of its location at what was at one point thought to be the western edge of the world, this area has been a center of exploration for centuries.

Historically, this area has experienced turbulent periods as explorers and conquering peoples have swept through the land repeatedly, either to spread their culture or to find routes to riches. When these cultures occupied the area, they often brought with them the products on which they relied and new techniques that became incorporated into the local customs.

This significant strategic location has played a role in the development of Spain and Portugal as countries, and in the cuisine that helps define those who call the peninsula home. In more recent times, the people of this peninsula expanded their borders through exploration and exploitation, further developing the cuisine as new products made their way here.

Spanish cuisine is similar to other Mediterranean cuisines in the use of olive oil as the main fat for cooking, the importance of bread in the daily diet, and the production and consumption of wines; however, it differs in significant ways as well. Many of the traditions in the country have links to the religious struggles that have marked this land. After the expulsion of the Moors in the late fifteenth century, the rise of Catholicism and the resulting inquisition and expulsion of all non-Christians resulted in a significant emphasis on the consumption of pork and pork products. This tradition persists today, with pork finding its way into many of the national and regional dishes. The development of the cuisine has been based on common foods eaten by the general population, and thus it is not as refined as some of the neighboring cuisines. The most common cooking methods throughout Spain are boiling or simmering, although regional specialties exist.

The cuisine of Portugal shares some similarities with Spain but also has some distinct differences. Both countries feature extensive use of pork products and ingredients from the New World, but cilantro is used regularly in Portugal and almost not at all in Spain. Another difference is the way rice is used in the two countries: in Spain it is usually cooked with other ingredients, such as with paella, whereas in Portugal it is usually prepared plain, to accompany other foods (as in the Orient). Similar to Spain, the most common cooking methods throughout Portugal are boiling and simmering. The following chapter explores these and other aspects of these well-regarded cuisines.

HISTORIC CULINARY INFLUENCES

The Iberian Peninsula is located in one of the more strategic locales in the world—it is home to one-half of the gate to the Mediterranean Sea in its southernmost portions, and it provides access to the Atlantic Ocean as well. As a result of this location, the peoples of this land have been subject to repeated invasions by other cultures that have left their imprint on the cuisine. Additionally, both Spain and Portugal were initiators of the westerly expansion to the New World and thus received significant influences from the ingredients and techniques that resulted from the exploration of the Americas. During these countries' height of power, they also had colonies in many parts of the world, which further influenced the cuisines back home.

Original Inhabitants

Not a lot is known about the original inhabitants of the Iberian Peninsula, because this area has been inhabited since far before written history. The ethnic groups known to have inhabited this area include Celtic and Basque peoples, both of which are still represented in the region today: Basque peoples live in the northern portion of Spain along the border with France (and also in France), and the Celtic peoples blended with those living on the peninsula prior to their arrival. The Basque peoples have a long history as herders and fishermen, and the products of this labor have been a part of their cuisine for many

centuries. The Celtic tradition of cooking porridges, stews, and boiled meats is also evident in the cuisine of the people of the Iberian Peninsula.

Ancient Influences

Centuries ago, Phoenician traders traveled across the Mediterranean and the Atlantic, bringing with them some of the products of their culture in what is now the Middle East. Their major contribution to the Iberian Peninsula was the *uvas* (grapes) that eventually were used to make fine wines, sherry, and Madeira in this region. Greeks also traveled the Mediterranean during the height of the great Greek civilization, and they introduced *aceituna* (olives), *trigo* (wheat), and the practice of using *miel* (honey) to sweeten foods.

Moorish Rule

From the eighth century until the fifteenth century in Spain and the twelfth century in Portugal, most of the Iberian Peninsula was ruled by the Moors. *Moor* was a name given to a number of different groups of people from the present-day Middle East or northern Africa, all of whom were Muslim. These cultures brought many of their advanced techniques for cultivating crops to this area, as well as many of the ingredients upon which they relied. Some of the products they introduced to the peninsula during this time were *naranjas* (oranges), *limónes* (lemons), *arroz* (rice), *almendras* (almonds), *berenjena* (eggplant), *espinaca* (spinach), *azúcar* (sugar), and *azafrán* (saffron).

Spanish and Portuguese Exploration and Colonization

In 1492, the same year that Spain expelled the Moors from their homeland, Christopher Columbus landed in the Caribbean under the Spanish flag; his search for a route for the spice trade yielded more than expected. Portuguese explorers were landing in the Americas and India, and navigating around the tip of Africa, during the same period of history, which resulted in Europe's exposure to previously unknown ingredients as well as greater access to the spices of the Orient. Spain went on to colonize Mexico, parts of the present-day United States, Puerto Rico, Cuba, and much of South America, while the Portuguese colonized Brazil and set up a seaport in Goa on the western coast of India. As a result of these explorations and eventual colonization of many parts of the world, many new ingredients were introduced and incorporated into Spanish and Portuguese cuisine.

Without a doubt, the "discovery" of the Americas made one of the most influential impressions on the development of modern Spanish and Portuguese food. With new ingredients available, such as *tomates* (tomatoes), *pimentón* (chili powder), *pimientos* (chili peppers), chocolate, *papas* (potatoes), and *frijoles* (beans), the cuisines of Spain and Portugal would be forever changed.

UNIQUE COMPONENTS

Iberian cuisine is both unique and historical; many important parts of the cuisine are entwined with important historical events that have involved Spain and Portugal. The following section examines some of the important aspects that make this cuisine unique.

Tapas

The Spanish influence on the cuisine of the Iberian Peninsula is felt in the many *tapas* (small plates of individual items served with drinks) bars of Spain, as well as in the similar dishes found in Portugal. A number of theories exist about how the tapas tradition began in Spain, the most common of which cites the introduction of small bites of food—such as olives or chorizo—placed on plates to keep flies out of drinks in bars. Regardless of how the tapas tradition got started, it is now part of the fabric of life in Spain, where it is typical for people to visit a tapas bar before going to eat a meal at a restaurant.

Not only have tapas become virtually a separate course in Spain, a whole segment of the culinary scene is dedicated to creating small dishes that work well for tapas. Because these items are not meant to be filling and typically are made to be eaten out of hand, the result is an array of dishes that highlights simplicity and quality of methods and ingredients. Many of the common tapas dishes are simply preserved foods such as *jamón serrano* (cured ham), aceitunas, or cheeses (such as *Manchego*). Many other tapas styles and dishes exist, such as slices of *tortilla Española* (potato and egg "cake"), *pinchitos* (skewered and grilled items), *croquetas* (breaded and fried thick bechamel with seasonings), and *montaditos* (foods placed on slices of bread or crostini). All of these foods are simple to finish and plate, and they rely on good quality products to produce good tapas. Every region of Spain includes its own specialties in terms of the tapas that are found there, and these local specialties often are offered with some of the types mentioned here to add variety and flavor to this great cuisine.

Exploration/Colonization

Both Spain and Portugal were major players in the period of exploration and colonization of other parts of the world that occurred from the fifteenth century onward. The impact of this history on the cuisines of the Iberian Peninsula is profound, as the wealth from these far-off lands—coupled with their products—changed the culinary scene of the Iberian Peninsula forever.

The Spanish are forever linked to the Americas after Christopher Columbus landed in the Caribbean in 1492. In the years that followed this fateful landing, the cuisines of both indigenous Americans and Europeans would be forever changed. Corn, tomatoes, potatoes, squash, beans, and chiles were all introduced into the cuisine of Spain and spread into the rest of Europe as well. A few of those ingredients—in particular, beans, potatoes, and corn—would become important crops and primary food sources for the Spanish in the years to come. Chiles became a significant crop and have remained popular in the cuisine of the Iberian Peninsula, as seen in the use of chili powders and fresh chiles, including the Padron chiles that are prized tapas in Spain and are served fried and sprinkled with salt. There are three typical varieties of chiles powders, or pimentóns, in Spain; the variation depends on how much of the seeds and membranes are included in the blends to yield varying levels of heat in the resulting powders. *Pimentón dulce*, or sweet chili powder, is the mildest, followed by *pimentón agridulce* (a medium powder) and the hottest of the chili powders, which is called *pimentón picante*. The connection between Spain and the Americas will always exist, and the cuisines of both the Iberian Peninsula and the Americas have both been transformed from this connection.

Portugal also became a major influence in the development of the New World after the Spanish returned from the Americas. The Portuguese have had a significant impact on the culture and cuisine of Brazil in South America as well as on parts of the Caribbean. The Portuguese also impacted all European cuisine by finding an alternative route around the tip of Africa to reach the spices of Asia. Prior to the Portuguese discovery, spices were much more expensive for Europeans because they passed through several more hands when crossing the Middle East, and prices increased along the way. This opening up of the market to Indian and other spices helped to make these ingredients more accessible to a greater part of the European population, and the use of these once scarce spices grew in cuisines throughout Europe. These moments in history have proven monumental not only in their impact on the cultures directly involved but also in the development of cuisines all over the world.

Blend of European and Moorish Culture

The unique history of the invasion and rule of the Iberian Peninsula itself plays an important role in the cuisine of the region, as periods of rule by African and Arab peoples made a culinary impact. The Moorish rule of Spain and Portugal that lasted 800 years introduced the people of this region to the foods of North Africa and the Middle East; many of these culinary traditions remain evident today.

The Moors were greatly influenced by Middle Eastern cultures, and many Persian (present-day Iran and surrounding areas) culinary traditions are evident in Spanish cuisine as a result. The combination of meat and fruit in stews, which is still found in some Spanish recipes, conveys this influence, as does the use of cumin, cinnamon, and cloves, which were introduced to the Spanish by the Moors. Cumin is a very common seasoning in Spanish cuisine. Saffron was also introduced to the Spanish by the Moors, and its use is widespread in Spanish cuisine today (including as a notable component of the Spanish dish *paella*, a saffron-colored and flavored rice, meat, and seafood dish). The regular use of almonds and honey can also be attributed to this period of Spanish history, as both of these ingredients were common parts of the Moorish diet and culture.

Once the Moors were expelled from the Iberian Peninsula in 1492, a notable change to the diet was the inclusion of pork; the Catholics who remained in Spain did not have a religious edict to abstain from consuming pork, as the Islamic Moors did. Not only was pork now consumed, its consumption also was used as a means for both declaring one's dedication to the Catholic faith and for exposing any non-Catholics who remained on the peninsula after the Moors left. This is one explanation for the prevalence of pork products in the cuisines of the Iberian Peninsula.

One-Pot Cooking

The nomadic heritage of the Celtic people who were the early inhabitants of the Iberian Peninsula is still evident today in the practice of preparing a one-pot food. Early Celtic tribes would cook available foods over a fire in a large cauldron, and dishes such as paella, *açorda* (Portuguese bread soups with various

other components), *arroz con pollo* (Spanish stewed rice and chicken), and *cocido madrileño* (one-pot meal served in courses with beef, chicken, ham, pork belly, chickpeas, and cabbage with *chorizo* and *morcilla*) are still common today in Portugal and Spain.

SIGNIFICANT SUBREGIONS

For the purpose of this text, the regions have been defined largely along culinary borders rather than political borders. Of course, distinct culinary borders do not actually exist—thus, the following guide should be viewed in general terms. The Iberian Peninsula is located in what historically has been a very significant part of the world, and, as such, many different cultures have called this area home. These cultures have left their imprint on the countries of Spain and Portugal in different areas, resulting in significant regional differences. In addition, there are large geographic and climatic variations within the peninsula that affect each region's cuisine. These regions are organized from west to east and then north to south.

Northern Atlantic and Basque Country

The Northern Atlantic region of Spain includes the Atlantic coast of Spain above Portugal and the north central Basque region bordering the Atlantic and the southwestern corner of France. Included in this region are the areas of Galicia, Asturias, Cantrabria, and Basque Country. The climate in this region is wetter than much of the rest of the country, enabling significant vegetable crops and a productive cattle/dairy industry, which in turn produces some excellent cheeses. The Galicia area has significant influences from the Celts, whereas the Basque region has significant influences from its northern neighbor, France. The Basque Country is home to the very productive Bay of Biscay, which produces significant amounts of shellfish and fish for the local cuisine. The Basque region is also known for its refined sauces and male cooking societies (see "Valencia and the Levante" section). The northern fishermen from this region discovered the abundance of cod and the salting/drying preservation technique that was common to the area of Scandinavia. The salt cod became a significant food source for much of the population, as it was inexpensive and available year round.

Some of the ingredients common to this region include *setas* (wild mushrooms), *pulpo* (octopus), *almejas* (clams), *escupiñas* (little clams), *salmón* (salmon), *calamar* (squid), *merluza* (hake), *bacaloa* (salt cod), *puerco* (pork), fattened liver of ducks or geese (known by its French name, foie gras), papas, *grelos* (turnip greens), frijoles, and *maíz* (corn). Some of the products and recipes unique to this region include *idiazábal* (semisoft sheep's milk cheese), *cabrales* (blue-veined cheese), *fabada asturiana* (pork, blood sausage, and bean stew), *empanadas* (savory filled pies), *bacaloa a la viscaina* (salt cod with chiles), *pulpo a la gallega* (boiled octopus with olive oil and paprika), *pil-pil* (sauce made from salt cod, garlic, and olive oil), and *caldo gallego* (broth with ham, beans, and sausage).

Northeastern Spain: Catalonia and Aragon

This region borders France to the north and the Mediterranean Sea to the east; it encompasses the areas of Catalonia, Navarre, La Rioja, and Aragon.

The area of Catalonia has a mild climate and is surrounded by a harsher terrain and climate, making for fertile land that has been subject to invasion and migration over the years from many cultures, including Roman, Gothic, Arabic, French, and southern Spanish. This region was also the hub of a kingdom that stretched into Italy and has long been a center of the trade routes through Europe and Asia. As a result of these outside influences, this region is probably the most complex in its use of varied ingredients. This area also is known for its combination of fish and meat products in many of the common dishes.

The areas of Aragon, La Rioja, and Navarre are very different in that the climate and geography are much harsher; as such, the cuisine is simpler and traditionally sustaining. These areas are made up of mountain ranges and valleys, which experience frigid winters and hot summers. The vineyards of this region produce many of Spain's good wines, and the land surrounding the vineyards along the River Ebro also produces many fresh vegetables.

Some of the ingredients that are commonly used in the cuisine of this region include *tomates*, *calçots* (spring onions), frijoles, uvas, *bixtos* (special chiles), *espárragos* (asparagus), *rape* (monkfish), *gambas* (shrimp), *níscalo* (wild mushrooms), *cordero* (lamb), calamar, *truchas* (trout), and papas. Some of the specialties and recipes common or unique to this region include *alioli* (olive oil and garlic emulsion), *pa amb tomàquet* (grilled bread rubbed with ripe tomatoes), *calçotada* (special type of spring onion grilled and typically served with romesco sauce), *crema catalana* (custard with caramelized sugar on top), *Camerano* (type of fresh goat's milk cheese), *picada* (paste made from pounded garlic, nuts, bread, olive oil, and a liquid), *samfaina* (summer vegetable sauce or stew), and *migas* (small pieces of olive oil–fried bread).

Balearic Islands

The Balearic Islands off the eastern coast of Spain in the Mediterranean Sea are yet another site of numerous invasions throughout history. Greeks, Romans, Vandals, the Byzantium Empire, Moors, and the Kingdom of Aragon all have controlled the islands over the centuries, and each has left some impression on the cuisine. The cuisine of the islands relies heavily on the sea, because the land is limited in its production of foods; however, many of the everyday foods still come from the land. The cuisine of this region is most similar to the cuisine of Catalonia, as these two regions historically have traded with each other.

Some of the ingredients common to the cuisine in this region include *tomàtigues de ramellet* (local tomatoes), *berenjana* (eggplant), *porc negre* (black pig), *higos* (figs), pimentón, uvas, almendras, *langosta* (lobster), and *sepia* (cuttlefish). Some of the specialty products from this region include *Mahón* (type of sheep's milk cheese), *sobrasada* (pork sausage), *coca* (flatbread with various toppings), *ensaïmada* (spiral-shaped pastry), *pa pages* (compressed fig, anise, and bread cake), *burrida* (fish soup with almonds), and *caldereta de langosta* (lobster stew).

Northern Portugal

This region includes all of Portugal north of the Tagus River, which is a more mountainous and wet climate than the southern region of Portugal. The products are reflective of a cooler climate, and there are fewer Mediterranean ingredients included in the foods here. This region has significant influences from the Celts and possesses similarities to the Galician region of Spain. The climate is favorable for the production of wine, grains, and some vegetables, resulting in a cuisine of sustenance that is often enjoyed with wine and bread.

Some of the ingredients common to this region's cuisine include porco, *cabrito* (young goat), bacalhau, *milho* (corn), trigo, *centeio* (barley), *banha* (lard), *couve galega* (Galician cabbage), *lampreia* (lamprey), *batatas* (potatoes), and *castanha* (Brazil nuts). Some of the significant products and recipes from this region include *bolinhos de bacalhau* (fried salt cod fritters), *chouriço* (chili-spiced sausage), *pão* (bread), *caldo verde* (green soup), *broa* (corn bread), *presunto* (smoked ham), *sopa seca* (layered "dry" soup of meat, vegetables, and bread), and *escabeche* (pickled foods).

Central Spain: Madrid and Extremadura

This is the largest of the regions and includes virtually all of the heartland of the Iberian Peninsula, including the areas of Leon, Castile, Madrid, La Mancha, and Extremadura. This region comprises mostly plains that produce many of the main foods for Spain; sheep rearing, wheat fields, and legumes are common sights throughout. The mountains of the western portion of this region produce one of Spain's most prized culinary products, cured hams, whereas the plains produce the wheat needed to make ham's natural accompaniment, good bread. The capital of Madrid is a melting pot of Spain's culinary traditions, with many regional dishes finding their way onto the menus and tapas found in virtually all bars. The central portion of the country is also known for its many roasted foods, including whole roasted baby pigs and lamb.

Some of the ingredients common to the cuisine of this region include puerco, *harina de trigo* (wheat flour), cordero, *res* (beef), *lentejas* (lentils), *garbanzo* (chickpea), azafrán, and pimentón. Some of the specialty products and recipes from this region include Manchego (hard sheep's milk cheese), *jamón ibérico de bellota* (finest Iberian hams made from native Iberian black pigs that only feed on acorns before slaughter), *jamón ibérico* (cured native Iberian black pig ham), *jamón serrano* (cured mountain ham), and *cocido* (chickpea, pork, and chorizo stew).

Valencia and the Levante

This region is located along the eastern coast of Spain, with the Mediterranean as the eastern border and mountains as the western border. This is a very fertile area that produces many of the vegetables and grains for Spain and abroad, earning the name "Market Garden of Europe." Almost year-round sunshine has made this area not only productive but also a tourist destination. With the centers of Valencia and Murcia surrounded by productive farms and the Mediterranean Sea, the cuisine of this region is based largely on the vegetables and fish found locally. This is also paella country; the paella is traditionally made just by men who cook it over a fire and have developed an excellent sense about how much liquid to add and how to control the heat to end up with an appropriate texture.

Some of the ingredients that are common to the cuisine of this region include naranjas, azúcar, higos, uvas, *chufas* (tiger nuts), almendra, arroz, *trufas* (truffles), *anca de rana* (frog legs), *anguila* (eel), *calamar*, sepia, and *havas* (fava beans). Some of the specialty products and recipes common to this region include *jamón de toro* (cured tuna belly), *horchata* (tiger nut drink), paella (rice dish cooked in a special pan over a fire), *fideuà* (pasta dish with shellfish), *olletas* (bean and meat stew), and *sucs* (fish stew with garlic and almond).

Southern Portugal

This region includes the area south of the Tagus River and is geographically very different from the northern region of Portugal, in that this is not a mountainous region but a fertile valley of rolling hills. As a result of this landscape, the climate is similar to that of the Mediterranean region, and some of the common ingredients to the Mediterranean are common here as well. This region, like southern Spain, was more strongly influenced by the period of Moorish rule than its northern counterpart.

Some of the ingredients common to the cuisine of this region include bacalhau, *tâmaras* (dates), *laranjas* (oranges), *amêndoas* (almonds), *figos* (figs), *azeitonas* (olives), *fava* (fava beans), *capim-santo* (lemongrass), arroz, *borrego* and *cordeiro* (lamb), *pêssegos* (peaches), *pêras* (pears), *mel* (honey), *azeite* (olive oil), and *beldroega* (purslane). Some of the specialty products and recipes common to this region include *Evora* (type of sheep's milk cheese), *Serpa* (type of sheep's milk cheese), *Beja* (type of sheep's milk cheese), *pão* (bread), *açorda* (type of stew), *mousse de chocolate* (Portuguese version of chocolate mousse), *piri-piri* (type of chili and the sauce made from it), and *caldeirada* (stew made from fish, onions, garlic, and tomatoes).

Southern Spain: Andalusia

Located just five miles from northern Africa across the Strait of Gibraltar, this region was the most influenced by the period of Moorish rule. The use of sweets to make sauces for savory dishes and the choice of seasonings are distinctly northern African. This region has a hot climate with mild winters, which results in excellent production of olives and olive oil—in fact, the highest production in Spain. This region also includes the cities of Seville and Jerez; Jerez is well known for its production of sherry. The tradition of taking tapas with drinks and as a snack, which is now common throughout the country, can be traced to Andalusia and more specifically to the period of Moorish influence. One of the most common cooking methods in this region is frying, particularly in the local olive oil.

Some of the ingredients that are common to the cuisine of this region include *fresas* (strawberries), *albaricoques* (apricots), *membrillo* (quince), *melocotón* (peach), *cerezas* (cherries), aceitunas, *aceite de oliva* (olive oil), papas, habas, *anís* (fennel), azafrán, *comino* (cumin), and miel. Some of the specialty products and recipes of this region include *gazpacho* (spiced cold tomato soup), *mojama* (salt-cured tuna loins), *sherry* (fortified wine produced in Jerez), *gazpacho blanco* (cold almond, garlic, and grape soup), migas (fried bread), *pinchitos* (skewered and grilled items), and *pescaito frito* (fried fish).

RECIPES

The following recipes provide an introduction to the cuisine of the Iberian Peninsula. With the popularity of tapas and the likes of restaurants like El Bulli, this region is fast becoming one of the most popular not only in the United States but also in Europe. After exploring the following recipes a deeper understanding of this great cuisine can be achieved by referencing additional sources.

Tortilla Espanola   CENTRAL SPAIN
(SPANISH POTATO OMELET)

INGREDIENTS

3	oz	Olive Oil, pure
2	lbs	Russet Potatoes, peeled and sliced 1/4 inch thick
		Salt and Pepper, to taste
1	Tbsp	Olive Oil, pure
6	oz	Yellow Onions, sliced thin
4	oz	Red Bell Pepper
		Pan Spray, as needed

For Baking the Tortilla

6		Eggs, beaten lightly
2	oz	Ham, diced small
		Onions (see above)
		Red Pepper (see above)
		Salt and Black Pepper, to taste

The Spanish tortilla is nothing like what most people in the United States associate with a tortilla, as it contains no corn or flour. Instead, a tortilla in Spain is essentially a savory cake made from potatoes and eggs and often may include other ingredients (as in this recipe). Spanish tortillas are a common sight in tapas bars or on tapas-style menus.

YIELD: Two 6-inch tortillas

COOKING METHOD (POTATOES): Panfried

COOKING METHOD (ONIONS): Sweating

COOKING METHOD (RED PEPPER): Fire Roasted

COOKING METHOD (FINAL): Baked

PROCEDURE

1. Preheat the oven to 325°F.
2. Heat a sauté pan over medium-high heat; add the olive oil and panfry the potato slices once the oil is hot enough (be sure to panfry until they turn golden brown on both sides).

(continues)

Tortilla Espanola (Spanish tortilla) garnished with roasted red bell peppers

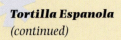

Tortilla Espanola
(continued)

3. Remove the potatoes from the oil (pour the oil into a metal container and save it—it will be used later), and season the potatoes with salt and pepper.

4. In the same pan or a new pan, sweat the yellow onions in the 1 Tbsp of olive oil over a medium flame until they are soft and translucent; remove from heat and set aside.

5. Spray the red bell pepper with the pan spray and fire roast over an open flame until charred on the outside. Cover in plastic and set aside to cool. Once cooled, peel off the burned outer layer and julienne the pepper.

For Baking the Tortilla

1. In a mixing bowl, combine the eggs, diced ham, onions, and roasted bell pepper; mix together, and season with salt and pepper.

2. In two 6-inch nonstick omelet or crepe pans, add 1 Tbsp of the reserved olive oil from panfrying the potatoes in step 3.

3. Layer the potatoes into the nonstick pan by overlapping them in concentric circles, starting at the outside of the pan and working your way in (this will be the top of the tortilla, so you want it to look nice).

4. Pour the egg mixture over the potatoes, dividing it evenly between the two pans. Place pans in the preheated oven and bake until eggs set (approximately 20–25 minutes).

Pa amb Tomàquet   CATALONIA

(BREAD WITH TOMATO AND OLIVE OIL)

INGREDIENTS

1	lb	Country Bread (a baguette can be used if no good-quality country bread is available)
2	lbs	Very Ripe Tomatoes (don't bother to make recipe unless tomatoes are ripe)
6	oz	Extra Virgin Olive Oil
		Kosher Salt, to taste

Rubbing ripe tomato into bread to make the pa amb tomàquet (bread with tomato and olive oil)

This classic is served all over Catalonia, where a special species of tomatoes grows that has an intense flavor and meaty texture, which works perfectly for this dish. Use only very ripe tomatoes—preferably straight from the vine.

YIELD: Approximately 15 portions (3 ounces/portion)

COOKING METHOD: Grilling

PROCEDURE

1. Preheat grill or oven to 400°F (grilling or toasting the bread is optional, but it often helps to break up the tomato).

2. Slice the bread in pieces 1/2 inch thick; if desired, grill or toast the bread until it begins to char slightly and becomes crisp on the exterior.

3. Slice the tomatoes in half and rub the sliced ends on the toasted bread pieces, pressing hard enough to cause the tomato to grate against the bread.

4. Drizzle olive oil over each piece of tomato bread and season with kosher salt.

(**NOTE:** *These are often topped with other ingredients. For example, bread can be topped with serrano ham, grilled vegetables, and cheese; these are called llesques de pa, or "slices of bread."*)

Coca d'spinacs   BALEARIC ISLANDS

(FLATBREAD WITH SPINACH AND PINE NUTS)

INGREDIENTS

For Making the Preferment Dough

1.5	oz	Fresh Compressed Yeast
8	oz	Water (90–100°F)
1	tsp	Sugar, granulated
10	oz	Bread Flour

For Mixing the Dough

		Preferment (see above)
18	oz	Water (90–100°F)
1.5	Tbsp	Salt
4	oz	Extra Virgin Olive Oil
2	lbs	Bread Flour (2 cups of which is used to adjust consistency of dough)

For Preparing the Topping

3	lbs	Spinach, stems removed (if not baby spinach)
2	oz	Extra Virgin Olive Oil
		Salt, to taste
8	oz	Pine Nuts

For Baking Coca

		Bread Flour, as needed
1	oz	Olive Oil
2	ea	1/2 sheet pans

Coca is thought to have been introduced to the Balearic Islands by the Romans during their rule. Coca can be topped with many different ingredients such as sardines, onions, and peppers (or other vegetables), but this recipe uses one of the most common combinations.

YIELD: Two 1/2 sheet pans, which can be cut according to desired size

COOKING METHOD (SPINACH): Blanching Boiling Water

COOKING METHOD (FINAL): Baking

PROCEDURE

1. Preheat the oven to 375°F.

For Making the Preferment Dough

(**NOTE:** *This dough can be made using the straight dough method, although results are more dependable using the preferment method.*)

1. Combine the yeast, warm water, sugar, and flour in a mixing bowl; mix with a dough hook for 5 minutes or until the dough is smooth and elastic.

2. Set the preferment aside in a warm place, and allow it to double in volume and just begin to fall before proceeding to the next step (this will take approximately 1.5 hours; time can vary depending on the temperature held).

For Mixing the Dough

1. Add the water, salt, olive oil, and all but 2 cups of the bread flour to the preferment; begin mixing with the dough hook to form a smooth dough by adding the reserved flour as needed.

(continues)

Coca d'espinacs (flatbread with pine nuts and spinach)

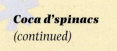

Coca d'spinacs
(continued)

2. Mix the dough until it has developed properly (you should be able to stretch the dough into a thin, see-through sheet with your hands without it tearing).

3. Place the developed dough into the proofbox and allow it to proof until it has doubled in volume (approximately 45 minutes). While proofing, proceed to the next step to have the topping ready.

For Preparing the Topping

1. Bring a pot of salted water, large enough to hold the spinach, to a boil over a high flame.

2. Add spinach to the pot and blanch just long enough to wilt it; remove the spinach from the pot and shock it in an ice bath to cool immediately.

3. Once cooled, remove the spinach from the ice bath and place it in a colander to squeeze out excess moisture (press inside the colander and squeeze to get out excess water—the spinach should be just moist).

4. Toss the blanched spinach with extra virgin olive oil; season well with salt, and set aside.

5. If the pine nuts have not been roasted, roast them in a 300°F oven until they just begin to color; set aside.

For Baking Coca

1. Once the dough has doubled in volume in the proofbox, punch it down, remove it, and place it on a lightly floured workbench.

2. Cut the dough in half; roll out each half into a rectangle the size of the sheet pans.

3. Grease the sheet pans with the olive oil, and place one dough piece on each. Put pans in a preheated 375°F oven and bake for 10 minutes.

4. Remove from the oven and spread the blanched, seasoned spinach evenly over the two dough pieces; return to the oven and bake until the edges are browned and the bottom has set.

5. Remove from the oven and sprinkle the pine nuts over the finished coca.

6. Cut into desired size pieces.

Alioli CATALONIA

(GARLIC OLIVE OIL EMULSION)

INGREDIENTS

1	oz	Garlic Cloves
1/2	tsp	Salt
9	oz	Extra Virgin Olive Oil
		Lemon Juice, to taste

This is the classic recipe for alioli—a contraction of the Catalan words *all* (garlic) and *oli* (oil). Today, this is commonly made with egg yolk, which allows for easier preparation (in a food processor) but has a different texture and taste than the original.

YIELD: 1 cup

SPECIAL METHOD: Emulsion of Olive Oil with Garlic Cloves

(continues)

PROCEDURE

1. Using a mortar and pestle, grind the garlic cloves and salt into a smooth paste (if a mortar and pestle is not available, add one egg yolk and process in a blender).

2. Slowly add the olive oil to the garlic paste—one drop at a time to begin with, then slowly increasing to a slight stream to form a thick paste. The oil must be ground into the paste as it is added.

3. Season with lemon juice and salt, if necessary.

Alioli
(continued)

Bolinhos de Bacalao   PORTUGAL
(SALT COD FRITTERS)

INGREDIENTS

.5	lb	Salt Cod, soaked in multiple changes of cold water overnight and drained
1	lb	Russet Potatoes
1	oz	Olive Oil
5	oz	Yellow Onions, minced
.5	oz	Garlic Cloves, minced
2		Eggs, beaten
1/8	tsp	Cayenne Pepper
1	Tbsp	Cilantro, minced
1	Tbsp	Parsley, minced
		Salt and Pepper, to taste
1	cup	Seasoned Bread Crumbs

YIELD: Approximately 30 (1–1.5 ounces/fritter)

COOKING METHOD (POTATOES): Boiling

COOKING METHOD (SALT COD): Simmering

COOKING METHOD (FINAL FRITTER): Deep Frying

PROCEDURE

1. In a small pot that is large enough to hold the potatoes, bring salted water to a boil and add potatoes to cook until tender. Once they are tender, drain and set aside the potatoes.

2. In a small saucepot, simmer the salt cod in water (just enough to cover the cod) until the salt cod becomes flaky. Drain and set the cod aside.

3. Pass the potatoes through a food mill. Add the salt cod to the potatoes (first picking through the salt cod to remove any bones).

4. In a small sauté pan, heat the olive oil and lightly sauté the onions and garlic until they are tender; add the onions and garlic to the potato/salt cod mixture.

5. Add the beaten egg, cayenne pepper, cilantro, and parsley to the potato/salt cod mixture; fold in to incorporate well.

6. Season with salt and pepper.

7. Separate the salt cod/fritter mixture into 1–1.5-oz pieces, and roll into a ball.

8. Roll the salt cod fritters in the bread crumbs to coat the outside, and deep fry them until golden brown.

Bolinhos de bacalao (salt cod fritters) served with piri-piri (closest to fritters) and alioli sauces

Piri-Piri PORTUGAL
(HOT CHILI SAUCE)

INGREDIENTS

1	lb	Ripe Serrano Chiles (preferably red ripe), seeded and quartered
1	lb	Red Bell Peppers, seeded and cut into 1/2-inch strips (for slightly hotter sauce, substitute Red Fresno Chiles)
4	oz	Red Thai Chiles, fresh, seeded, and cut in half
2	oz	Garlic Clove, minced
4	oz	Salt
12	oz	Sherry Vinegar

This sauce is made with malagueta peppers in Portugal, which are not readily available here in the United States. The recipe has been altered to yield similar results.

YIELD: 3.25 pounds

SPECIAL METHOD: Curing Vegetables

PROCEDURE

1. Combine all of the chiles, bell peppers, and garlic with the salt; toss to coat evenly.
2. Pack into sterilized glass jars, seal, and place aside at room temperature. Allow contents to cure for 2 weeks.
3. Set the jars in a refrigerator and allow the contents to mature for another 2 weeks.
4. Open the jars and blend contents with the sherry vinegar to make a smooth sauce using a blender or food processor. Set aside for at least another day before using.

Calcotada CATALONIA
(GRILLED WHITE STOCKED ONIONS)

INGREDIENTS

16	Spring Onions (or calçots, if available)

This Catalonian specialty is traditionally made with a specific type of green onion that is grown by mounding the soil up around the sides of the onion as it grows (the same method used to grow white asparagus). A suitable substitute would be spring onions or immature torpedo onions.

YIELD: 8 portions (2 onions/portion)

COOKING METHOD: Grilled

PROCEDURE

1. Clean the onions by removing any dead outer leaves and trimming the roots off of the end (do not cut the root tip off, as this helps to hold the onion together during cooking).
2. Place the onions on a very hot grill and allow them to scorch on an open flame.
3. Wrap the scorched onions with foil (traditionally, newspaper was used) and hold for at least 15 minutes to allow the onions to steam and become tender throughout.
4. Serve with salbitxada (see following recipe).

Grilled calcots (spring onions are used in photo) served with salbitxada sauce

Salbitxada CATALONIA

(SPICED GARLIC TOMATO SAUCE)

INGREDIENTS

1.5	oz	Almonds, blanched
2	ea	Thai Chiles (traditionally, bixto would be used), seeds removed and minced
1.5	oz	Garlic Cloves, sliced
.25	tsp	Salt
.75	lb	Tomato, concassée
1	oz	Red Wine Vinegar
4	oz	Extra Virgin Olive Oil
1	Tbsp	Parsley
		Salt and Pepper, to taste

This is the traditional sauce to accompany calçots (it is actually another version of a Romanesco style sauce, but this one is specifically made for calçots).

YIELD: 1 pint

MIXING METHOD: Emulsification

PROCEDURE

1. Using a mortar and pestle, crush the almonds to a powder; add the chiles, garlic, and salt, and continue to crush to form a paste.

2. Transfer that mixture to a blender, and add the tomato concassée and red wine vinegar. While processing those ingredients, slowly add the extra virgin olive oil to form an emulsion.

3. Mix in the parsley, and season with salt and pepper.

Ajotomate LEVANTE

(SPICED TOMATO SALAD)

INGREDIENTS

1	lb	Very Ripe Tomatoes
1.5	oz	Garlic
1/2	tsp	Cumin, whole
1/2	tsp	Salt
2	oz	Red Wine Vinegar
1	tsp	Spanish Paprika
5	oz	Extra Virgin Olive Oil
2.5	lbs	Slicing Tomatoes
		Salt and Pepper, to taste

This simple summer salad is typical of the fertile Levante region, which yields much of the produce for Spain—including many excellent tomatoes

YIELD: 10 portions (6 ounces/portion)

MIXING METHOD (DRESSING): Emulsification

PROCEDURE

1. Using a mortal and pestle, crush the ripe tomato, cumin, garlic, and salt together to form a smooth paste.

2. Add the red wine vinegar and Spanish paprika, and continue to grind to combine all ingredients very well before slowly drizzling in the olive oil to form an emulsion.

3. Once the dressing is made, the slicing tomatoes can be sliced and arranged on plates, topped with the dressing, and seasoned with salt and pepper.

Ajotomate (spiced tomato salad)

Caldo Verde   NORTHERN PORTUGAL
(POTATO AND CABBAGE SOUP)

INGREDIENTS

5	lbs	Russet Potatoes, peeled and cut into large, even pieces
1	lb	Yellow Onion, diced small
1.5	gallons	Water
2	tsp	Salt
2	oz	Extra Virgin Olive Oil
1.5	lbs	Portuguese Cabbage, shredded very fine (this is different from the typical green cabbage found in the United States; you can substitute kale, Swiss chard, or Napa cabbage if the Portuguese variety is unavailable)
		Salt and Freshly Ground Black Pepper, to taste

Like soups found in the Galician area of Spain, just north of this region of Portugal, caldo verde is prized for the cabbage that provides much of its character. Caldo verde is traditionally served with slices of broa, Portuguese corn bread, which is used to soak up extra broth.

YIELD: 20 portions (12 ounces/portion)

COOKING METHOD: Simmering

PROCEDURE

1. Combine the potatoes, onion, water, and salt in an appropriately sized pot, and bring mixture to a simmer over medium-high heat.

2. Turn heat down to simmer the mixture until the potatoes are completely tender (approximately 45 minutes, depending on potato size).

3. Purée the potato/onion mixture to thicken the soup, and add in the olive oil while puréeing to emulsify.

4. Add the cabbage (or substitute) to the now-thickened soup over a medium flame to wilt the cabbage (this should only take a few minutes).

5. Adjust seasoning with salt and fresh black pepper, and serve immediately

NOTE: *This is often accompanied with piri-piri sauce and more extra virgin olive oil.*

Bowl of caldo verde (potato and cabbage soup)

Gazpacho Andaluz ANDALUSIA
(COLD TOMATO SOUP IN THE STYLE OF ANDALUSIA)

INGREDIENTS

For the Croutons

3	oz	Extra Virgin Olive Oil
5	oz	Country Bread, diced into small cubes

For Puréeing the Base

2	slices	(about 2 oz) Country Bread, soaked with 1/2 cup water
1	lb	Cucumbers, peeled and seeded
6	oz	Red Onion
1/2	oz	Garlic Cloves
2	lbs	Ripe Tomatoes, concassée
8	oz	Green Bell Pepper, stem and seeds removed

For the Body and Finishing

		Puréed vegetables (see above)
.75	lb	Cucumber, peeled, seeded, and diced small
6	oz	Red Onion, diced small
3	lbs	Ripe Tomatoes, concasséed and cut small
8	oz	Green Bell Pepper, diced small
3	oz	Red Wine Vinegar
16	oz	Tomato Juice
1	Tbsp	Paprika
5	oz	Extra Virgin Olive Oil
		Salt and Black Pepper, to taste

The original gazpacho was made with water thickened with bread and ground almonds and flavored with garlic. This version came into favor after the introduction of ingredients from the Americas, and it makes for a refreshing soup in the heat of the summer in the hot region of Andalusia.

YIELD: 20 portions (8 ounces/portion)

COOKING METHOD (CROUTONS): Baking

PROCEDURE

For the Croutons

1. Preheat the oven to 325°F.
2. In a mixing bowl, toss the cubed bread pieces with the extra virgin olive oil, and turn out onto a 1/2 sheet pan; place in the preheated oven to bake until golden and crisp (about 8–10 minutes). Remove and set aside to cool.

For Puréeing the Base

1. Place the soaked bread, cucumber, onion, garlic cloves, tomato concassée, and bell peppers to a food processor or blender; purée until smooth.
2. Place the purée in a large mixing bowl.

For the Body and Finishing

1. To the large mixing bowl with the puréed vegetables, add the diced cucumber, red onion, tomato, green bell peppers, red wine vinegar, tomato juice, and paprika; mix very well with a whisk.
2. While mixing with the whisk, slowly pour in the olive oil to emulsify it into the soup base.
3. Adjust seasoning with salt and black pepper. (It is best to let the mixture sit for a couple of hours to allow the flavors to blend.)
4. Transfer to serving bowls and garnish with the croutons.

Bowl of gazpacho andaluz (cold tomato soup) with croutons and sea salt

Açorda de Mariscos   LISBON/SOUTHERN PORTUGAL
(SHELLFISH AND BREAD SOUP)

INGREDIENTS

For Making the Broth

2	lbs	Head-on Shrimp
2	oz	Olive Oil
8	oz	Yellow Onion, diced medium
4	oz	Celery, diced medium
.5	oz	Garlic Cloves, minced
8	oz	Tomato, chopped
6	oz	Dry White Wine
3	qts	Water
2		Bay Leaves
1	tsp	Black Pepper
3	lbs	Hard-Shell Clams, scrubbed clean
12	oz	Dry White Wine
.5	oz	Garlic Cloves, minced
3	lbs	Mussels, debearded and scrubbed clean
		Salt, to taste

Preparing Components for Açorda

2	oz	Extra Virgin Olive Oil
2	lbs	Yellow Onion, sliced
2	oz	Garlic Cloves, sliced
1	Tbsp	Crushed Red Chiles (can use Chili de Arbol or Red Pepper Flakes)
1	tsp	Salt
		Broth (see above; measure broth to ensure there are 3 qts—if not, add water as needed)
		Shrimp (from Making Broth), peeled and deveined
		Salt and Black Pepper, to taste
1.5	lbs	Country Bread, sliced into 1-inch slices and toasted

Assembling the Açorda

12		Large, Hot Bowls
		Toasted Bread (see above)
8	oz	Extra Virgin Olive Oil
		Cooked Clams and Mussels
		Poached Shrimp (see above)

Açorda is one of Portugal's most well-known dishes; many different versions are available, depending on the area and its products. What they all have in common is that they are essentially soups that are simmered and poured over dense country bread and eggs. This version takes advantage of the abundant and high-quality seafood available from the Atlantic.

YIELD: 12 portions (12 ounces/portion)

COOKING METHOD (BROTH): Simmering

COOKING METHOD (SHRIMP): Poaching

COOKING METHOD (BREAD): Toasting

COOKING METHOD (EGGS): Residual Heat Poaching

PROCEDURE

For Making the Broth

1. Remove heads and peel the shrimp, setting the shrimp meat aside for later use (the shrimp meat will need to be deveined as well).

2. In a smaller stockpot, heat the olive oil over a medium flame; once hot, add the shrimp heads, onions, celery, and garlic, and sweat until vegetables are tender and shrimp shells have turned red.

3. Add the chopped tomato and turn heat up to fry slightly in the fat for 2 minutes.

4. Deglaze the pan with the white wine and allow it to reduce au sec (to just about dry).

5. Add the water, bay leaves, and black pepper, and bring the entire mixture up to a simmer; lower the flame to allow contents to lightly poach for 50 minutes.

6. While the shrimp broth is simmering, place a pot large enough to hold the clams on the stove over a medium-high flame. Add the clams, minced garlic, and white wine, and cover tightly to prevent much steam from escaping; steam until clams open (about 5–8 minutes, depending on the size of the clams).

7. Once they are open, remove the clams and add the mussels to the same pot; cover once again and steam the mussels until they open (about 2 minutes).

8. Remove the mussels from the pot and strain the resulting broth into the now-poaching shrimp broth. (Take care to notice whether any sand has been released by the shellfish; if so, it will be on the bottom of the pot. Donít add the sand to the broth!)

9. Once the shrimp shells and heads have poached for 50 minutes to 1 hour and the broth from the clams and mussels has been added, the resulting shellfish broth can be strained through cheesecloth, seasoned with salt, and set aside.

(continues)

Açorda de Mariscos
(continued)

12	Large Eggs
1/2	cup Cilantro, minced
	Piping Hot Broth and Onions (see above)

Preparing Components for Açorda

1. In a large, heavy-bottomed pot (large enough to hold the broth and vegetables), heat the olive oil over a medium-low flame until hot, and then add the sliced onions and garlic; sweat over a medium-low flame until the onions and garlic become very tender and translucent.

2. Once they are tender, add the crushed chiles and salt; mix thoroughly to distribute flavors.

3. Add the broth to the pot, and turn the heat up to bring the mixture to a simmer; lower the flame to adjust broth to a poaching temperature.

4. Poach the shrimp in the broth for 2 minutes, using a strainer so they can be easily removed. Then remove the shrimp and set them aside.

5. Adjust the seasoning of the broth with salt and pepper, if necessary.

6. Turn the heat up to bring the broth to a boil.

7. Toast the sliced country bread in 325°F oven (or under a broiler) until the bread is golden; cut into smaller squares and set aside.

Assembling the Açorda

1. Distribute the toasted bread (drizzled with the extra virgin olive oil), the shellfish, one raw egg, and the cilantro evenly among the hot bowls; ladle the piping-hot broth and vegetables over the ingredients, and serve immediately.

Bowl of açorda de mariscos (shellfish and bread soup)

Paella Valenciana   VALENCIA

(CHICKEN AND SNAILS IN SAFFRON RICE)

INGREDIENTS

For Soaking Beans

1	lb	White Beans
6	cups	Water

For Simmering Beans

		Soaked Beans (see above)
3	cups	Chicken Stock
2	cups	Water
1/4	tsp	Salt

For Making the Paella in the Paellera

6	oz	Olive Oil
5	lbs	Chicken Pieces (legs and thighs work well), seasoned with salt and pepper
1.5	lbs	Onions, sliced thin
1	oz	Garlic, minced
2.5	lbs	Ripe Tomatoes, concassée
1	Tbsp	Spanish Paprika
1.5	tsp	Saffron
1	Tbsp	Fresh Rosemary, minced
2	lbs	Short-Grain Paella Rice
2	tsp	Salt
2	qts	Water

This version of the classic paella includes traditional snails with chicken and is based on recipes that preceded the many variations found today. One thing must remain the same, however, for this dish to truly be considered paella: cooking in a paellera over a direct flame. As a result, this can be a challenging recipe to make.

YIELD: Approximately 15 portions (10 ounces/portion)

COOKING METHOD BEANS: Simmering

SPECIAL COOKING METHOD: Paella Method (Cooking Rice over a Fire)

PROCEDURE

For Soaking and Simmering Beans

(**NOTE:** *Soaking should be done 1 day in advance.*)

1. Soak the dried white beans overnight.
2. Drain the soaking liquid from the beans and combine beans with the chicken stock, water, and salt in a small pot; cook over a medium flame until beans are tender (approximately 1.5 hours).
3. Once tender, strain the beans and set aside to be added to the paella later.

For Making the Paella in the Paellera

(**NOTE:** *This is similar to braising, only paella is never covered.*)

1. Preheat the grill to medium-high heat (if you are using a wood or charcoal-fired grill, let the coals turn white or the flame die down before starting—but make sure the fire is still quite hot).

Paella valenciana (chicken and snails in saffron rice) in traditional paella pan

2. Place the paellera on the grill and add the olive oil to heat until the oil ripples and just begins to smoke; then add the chicken pieces.
3. Turn the chicken pieces in the pan as they color, making sure to brown them well on all sides without burning the bottom of the pan (move the pan to hotter or colder spots on the grill, as needed).
4. Once the chicken has colored well, add the onions and garlic; continue to cook until they become tender.
5. Add the tomato concassée and continue to cook until most of the released liquid is evaporated (about 5–10 minutes).
6. Add the Spanish paprika, saffron, rosemary, rice, salt, and water; let the mixture heat and come to a simmer over the open flame (do not stir or disturb).

(continues)

Paella Valenciana

(continued)

1	lb	Green Beans or Fresh Shelled Fava Beans (if green beans, cut into 1-inch pieces)
		Cooked White Beans (see above)
1/2	Can	Snails (about 40 snails)
		Salt and Freshly Ground Pepper, to taste

7. After 10 minutes, add the green beans (or shelled fava beans), cooked white beans, and snails; allow mixture to cook for another 10 minutes, adding 1/2 cup of water to the pan if it becomes completely dry (if it does not, do not add water).

8. Once the beans and rice are cooked, remove from heat; check and adjust seasoning, as needed. (The paella would traditionally be served out of the pan.)

NOTE: *Because the paella is cooked over an open flame, uncovered, it requires some experience and attention to determine whether or not to add more liquid to obtain properly cooked rice and some caramelization on the bottom of the pan, which is the desired result.*

Bacalao a al Viscaina NORTH ATLANTIC SPAIN

(BASQUE-STYLE SALT COD)

INGREDIENTS

For Poaching the Salt Cod

2	lbs	Salt Cod, soaked in water changed several times over a 2-day period
8	oz	Yellow Onion, sliced
4	oz	Celery, diced small
1/4	bunch	Parsley Stems
2	qts	Water

For Simmering the Potatoes and Leeks

2	oz	Olive Oil
1	lb	Leek Whites, cleaned and sliced thin
.5	oz	Garlic Cloves, minced
3	lbs	Russet Potatoes, peeled and sliced 1/2 inch thick
		Broth from Poaching Salt Cod (remove 1 cup first and set aside for sauce)
2		Bay Leaves
1/4	tsp	Freshly Ground Pepper
		Salt cod (see above)

For Making the Viscaina Sauce

6	oz	Salt Pork, diced small
8	oz	Yellow Onions, sliced thin

The Basques were excellent fishermen and learned about the process of salting and drying cod from northern European cultures. They adopted the salt cod into their cuisine with vigor.

YIELD: 12 portions (approximately 8–9 ounces/portion)

COOKING METHOD (SALT COD): Poaching

COOKING METHOD (POTATOES AND LEEKS): Simmering

PROCEDURE

For Poaching the Salt Cod

1. Be sure to have soaked the salt cod for a minimum of 1 day (2 days is even better), changing the water 3–4 times; otherwise, it will be too salty.

2. Place the drained salt cod (cut into smaller pieces, if necessary), onion, celery, parsley stems, and water in a pot; bring to a simmer and then reduce to a gentle poach.

3. Poach for 15–20 minutes or until cod becomes flaky, and then remove the cod from the broth. Strain the broth through a china cap or cheesecloth to remove onions, stems, and celery, and set the broth aside (it will be used in the next steps).

4. Carefully trim away any pieces of lining on the surface of the cod, and remove any bones from the fillets (depending on what section of the fish your fillet came from, this may be easier or more difficult); try to keep the fillet pieces as whole as possible.

For Simmering the Potatoes and Leeks

1. In a pan large enough to hold the potatoes, leeks, and salt cod, heat the olive oil over a medium-low flame; once hot, add the onions and garlic, and sweat until they are translucent and tender.

(continues)

Bacalao a al Viscaina
(continued)

4	oz	Leek Whites, cleaned and sliced thin
.5	oz	Garlic Cloves
2	Tbsp	Spanish Paprika
1	tsp	Cayenne Pepper
3		Eggs Yolks, hard-boiled
1	cup	Reserved Broth from Poached Salt Cod
1/4	cup	Parsley Leaves
4	oz	Extra Virgin Olive Oil

2. Add sliced potatoes, broth from salt cod (with 1 cup removed), bay leaves, and black pepper; turn the heat up to bring the mixture to a simmer, and simmer mixture until potatoes are just tender.

3. Add the salt cod to the mixture, and turn off the heat.

4. Remove the bay leaves.

For Making the Viscaina Sauce

1. In a medium or large sauté pan, render the salt pork over a low flame until all of the fat has been melted out (this will take approximately 20 minutes; this step can be done during or before cooking the potatoes and leeks).

2. Once rendered, add the yellow onions, leeks, and garlic to the pan; sweat over a medium-low flame until all of the onions and leeks are very tender (control the heat so that you donít caramelize them).

3. Add the paprika and cayenne pepper; continue to cook for 5 more minutes.

4. Transfer this mixture to a blender, and add the egg yolks, reserved cup of broth, and parsley. Blend the mixture to a smooth consistency; with the blender running slowly, pour in olive oil to make an emulsified sauce.

5. Adjust seasoning of sauce with salt and pepper (if sauce is too thick, add water to dilute).

6. Serve the salt cod pieces with potatoes and leeks, and top with the sauce.

Bacalao a al viscaina
(Basque-style salt
cod)

Salsa Romesco CATALONIA
(SPICED GARLIC TOMATO SAUCE)

INGREDIENTS

1	lb	Tomatoes, ripe
1	oz	Olive Oil
1	oz	Almonds, blanched
1	oz	Hazelnuts, blanched
2		Thai Chiles (traditionally, romesco peppers would be used), seeds removed and minced
1	oz	Garlic Cloves, sliced
.25	tsp	Salt
1	oz	Red Wine Vinegar
4	oz	Extra Virgin Olive Oil
1.5	Tbsp	Fresh Mint, minced
		Salt and Pepper, to taste

This well-known sauce is traditionally made with *romesco* peppers, a dried chili from this region (also called *ñora* peppers), and is commonly served to accompany fish and for dipping vegetables. The addition of mint makes this a good version for use in fish dishes; the fish can be panfried and finished with this sauce or roasted in a pan along with this sauce.

YIELD: 1 pint

COOKING METHOD (TOMATO): Roasting

PROCEDURE

1. Preheat the oven to 400°F.
2. Place the ripe tomatoes on a sheet pan and coat them with the olive oil; place them in the preheated oven and roast until they become soft and start to char on the outside.
3. Using a mortar and pestle, crush the almonds and hazelnuts to a powder; add the chiles, garlic, and salt and continue to crush to form a paste.
4. Transfer that mixture to a blender, and add the roasted tomatoes and red wine vinegar. While processing those ingredients, slowly add the extra virgin olive oil to form an emulsion.
5. Add the minced fresh mint to the sauce.
6. Season with salt and pepper.

SUMMARY

The cuisine of the Iberian Peninsula is one of diverse influences, as this peninsula has been both the subject of invasions by other cultures and home to a culture that invaded many other cultures. The Iberian Peninsula is home to the countries of Spain and Portugal and is strategically located at the gate of the Mediterranean Sea, just a handful of miles from the coast of North Africa. Location played an important part in the culinary development of this area; the peninsula was invaded and controlled by the Arab-influenced Moors from the eighth century through the end of the fifteenth century. Many traces of this culture exist in the cuisines of this region, as well as evidence of the inhabitants' quest to regain the land (for example, the prevalence of symbolic foods that Moors would not have eaten because of their Islamic faith).

The cuisines of Spain and Portugal also were greatly influenced by both countries' history of colonialism in other parts of the world—in particular, the Americas and parts of Asia. The cuisines of Spain and Portugal reveal influences from these periods of history, as well as the histories of the indigenous cultures of this area that relied on many stewed and simmered foods still common to this day.

REVIEW QUESTIONS

1. Which culture invaded and ruled the Iberian Peninsula for 800 years? List some influences that this culture had on the foods eaten in Spain and Portugal today.
2. How did the colonization of parts of the Americas change the cuisine of Spain?

3. What was the significance of the Portuguese finding a sea route to India?

4. What cooking methods have been used by the cultures of this region for many centuries?

COMMON TERMS, FOODS, AND INGREDIENTS

The following is a guide to many of the terms commonly encountered when studying Spanish or Portuguese cuisine. The terms are first organized by type of ingredient, followed by terms used to describing cooking methods and recipes. All terms are in Spanish unless followed by a (P), which indicates that they are in Portuguese.

✳ Vegetables, Fruits, and Nuts

aceituna – Olives

albaricoque – Apricots

almendras – Almonds

amêndoa (P) – Almond

anís – Fennel

azafrán – Saffron

azeitonas (P) – Olives

batatas (P) – Potatoes

beldroega (P) – Purslane

berenjena – Eggplant

bixto – Type of chili found in Spain

calçot – Special type of spring onion found in Spain

castanha (P) – Brazil nut

cereza – Cherry

chufa – Tiger nut

couve galega (P) – Galician cabbage

espárragos – Asparagus

espinaca – Spinach

fava (P) – Fava bean

figo (P) – Fig

fresa – Strawberry

frijoles – Beans

grelos – Turnip greens

habas – Fava beans

higos – Figs

laranja (P) – Orange

limónes – Lemons

maíz – Corn

melocotón – Peach

membrillo – Quince

milho (P) – Corn

naranjas – Oranges

níscalo – Type of wild mushroom

ñora – Chili pepper used to make romesco sauce

papas – Potatoes

pêra (P) – Pear

pêssego (P) – Peach

pimientos – Chili peppers

rape – Turnip

romesco – Type of chili pepper used to make romesco sauce in Spain

setas – Wild mushrooms

tâmaras (P) – Dates

tomates – Tomatoes

tomàtigues de ramellet – Tomatoes from the Balearic Islands

truchas – Truffles

uvas – Grapes

✳ Grains and Starches

arroz – Rice

centeio (P) – Barley

garbanzo – Chickpea

harina de trigo – Wheat flour

lentejas – Lentils

trigo – Wheat

✳ Seasonings

azafrán – Saffron

azeite (P) – Olive oil

azúcar – Sugar

capim-santo (P) – Lemongrass

comino – Cumin

mel (P) – Honey

miel – Honey

pimentón – Chili powder

pimentón picante – Hot chili powder

pimentón agridulce – Medium-hot chili powder

pimentón dulce – Sweet chili powder

✳ Fish and Shellfish

almejas – Clams

anca de rana – Frog legs

anguila – Eel

bacalhau (P) – Salt cod

bacaloa – Salt cod

bogavante – European lobster (with claws) caught in the Bay of Biscay

calamar – Squid

escupiñas – Little clams

gambas – Shrimp

lampreia (P) – Lamprey

langosta – Spiny lobster caught in the waters of the Mediterranean

merluza – Hake

pulpo – Octopus

salmón – Salmon

sepia – Cuttlefish

Meats/Poultry

banha (P) – Lard

borrego (P) – Lamb

butifarra blanca – Type of cured sausage from the Catalonia region made from pork and tripe and seasoned with pine nuts

butifarra negra – Another version of the Catalonian sausage made with blood, pork belly, and spices

cabrito (P) – Kid or young goat

chorizo – Mildly spicy cured sausage that is seasoned with paprika; common throughout Spain

chouriço (P) – Cured sausage from Portugal seasoned with paprika and garlic; more garlicky than the Spanish chorizo

cordeiro (P) – Lamb

cordero – Lamb

jamón de toro – Cured beef from the Levante region of Spain

jamón ibérico – Dry cured ham made from the indigenous Iberian black pig, which have the ability to deposit more marbling than non-Iberian pigs

jamón ibérico de bellota – Dry cured ham made from the indigenous Iberian black pigs that increase in weight by 50% after they begin to feed on acorns. These pigs have the highest fat content and make the most prized hams.

jamón serrano – Dry cured mountain ham of non-Iberian pigs; these make up about 90% of the cured hams in Spain

lengua – Tongue, usually beef or veal

linguiça (P) – Pork sausage from Portugal, similar to the chouriço but smaller

morcilla – Blood sausage

pata negra – Black Iberian pig (considered to make the best hams)

porc negre – Black pigs prized for their flavorful meat; this variety has been indigenous to the Balearic Islands for thousands of years

porco (P) – Pork

presunto (P) – Dry cured hams from Portugal that are cured with salt garlic and paprika and then smoked

puerco – Pork

res – Beef

sobrasada – Pork sausage from the Balearic Islands made traditionally from the local black pigs; this sausage is seasoned with chili and is spreadable

Dairy Products

Beja (P) – Fresh rich sheep's milk cheese from Portugal

Cabrales – A mixed milk blue-veined cheese made from cow, sheep, and goat milk from the Asturias region of northern Spain

Camerano – Goat's milk cheese with a sharp taste from northern Spain; usually eaten with honey and fruit for dessert

Castel Branco (P) – Runny sheep's milk cheese from the Viseu area in the northern region of Portugal; this cheese is aged until hard and used as a grating cheese

Evora (P) – Sheep's milk cheese from Portugal; creamy when fresh, and sharp and firm when found matured

Garrotxa – Goat's milk cheese from the Catalunya area with blue mold grown on the exterior, resulting in semisoft, tangy ripened cheese

Ibores – Hard cheese with paprika rubbed on the exterior; from the Extremadura region of south central Spain

Idiazábal – Sheep's milk cheese from the Basque region of Spain that can be found smoked or unsmoked; this is a high-fat cheese with a rich texture and slightly acidic taste

leche – Milk

Mahón – Cow's milk cheese made on the Island of Minorca of the coast of eastern Spain. Mahón can be found in varying stages of maturity, with the younger *semicurado* aged two months, *curado* aged six months, and the brittle *anejo* aged a year. The longer the cheese is aged, the more pronounced the flavor. Commercial versions of Mahón are now common, with much shorter aging periods and thus significantly less character.

Manchego – Hard sheep's milk cheese that is probably the best known of the Spanish cheeses

Mató – Goat curd cheese from the Catalonia region of Spain; this cheese is slightly granular and usually served with fruit as a dessert

Montsec – Hard goat's milk cheese from the Catalonia region of Spain

queijo (P) – Portuguese for "cheese"

queso – Spanish for "cheese"

San Simón – Firm cow's milk cheese from Galicia, partially cured and then smoked over birch wood; has a milder flavor with a slight tang and smoky flavor

Serpa (P) – Ripened sheep's milk cheese from Portugal

✳ National or Regional Dishes/Recipes

açorda (P) – Dish made with leftover bread that is cooked with various ingredients; common throughout Portugal

açorda de mariscos – Shellfish, egg, and bread soup (see recipe)

ajotomate – Tomato salad with cumin dressing

alioli – Emulsion of garlic and extra virgin olive oil with a little salt; the true version of this is made in a mortar and pestle, and the emulsifiers come only from the garlic. This is often made now in a food processor, using egg as the emulsifier.

arroz con pollo – Chicken and rice stew common in Spain

bacaloa a la viscaina – Salt cod preparation from the Basque region of Spain in which the cod is cooked with potatoes, leeks, or onions and spiced with chiles or paprika (see recipe)

bolinhos de bacalhau (P) – Fried salt cod fritters (see recipe)

broa (P) – Cornmeal bread common in northern Portugal

burrida – Mediterranean fish stew with almonds (also the name of fish stew in Italy)

calçotada – Grilled calçots, a type of spring onion, typically served with *salbitxada* sauce (see recipe)

caldereta de langosta – Lobster stew

caldo gallego – Hearty soup made of beans, greens, sausage, beef, or veal; from the Galician region of Spain

caldo verde (P) – Common soup from Portugal made from potatoes and cabbage (see recipe)

coca – Flat sheet bread made from yeast-leaved dough and often topped with various ingredients

coca d'spinacs – Flatbread with spinach from Balearic Islands (see recipe)

cocido – Chickpea, pork, and chorizo stew

cocido gallego – Galician stew of white beans, ham, potatoes, turnip tops, and chorizo

cocido madrilène – The Madrid version of the cocido, or stew, which contains chorizo, cabbage, potatoes, chickpeas, and a variety of meats. This dish is traditionally served in three courses: the first includes the broth, followed by the vegetables and chickpeas and finally the meat.

crema catalana – Dessert from Catalonia made very much like a crème brûlée in France; a custard with a caramelized surface.

croquetas – Thick, cooled béchamel with various other ingredients added, and then breaded and fried; typically served as tapas

empanadas – Pastry pies with various savory fillings; common in northwestern Spain

fabada asturiana – Stew of cabbage, potatoes, beans, ham, and chorizo from the Asturias region of northern Spain

ensaïmada – Spiral-shaped pastry made with lard

fideuà – Paella-like dish from the Valencia region made with pasta instead of rice

frituras de pescados – Fried fish popular in southern Spain, particularly Andalusia

gazpacho – Cold spiced tomato soup; often includes cucumbers, bell peppers, and tomato pieces

gazpacho blanco – White gazpacho made from ground almonds, garlic, and grapes, and also served cold. This was the original gazpacho prior to the arrival of the tomato and chiles from the Americas.

horchata – Drink made from ground dried tiger nuts mixed with lemon and sugar and then filtered

migas – Crispy fried (in olive oil) and salted pieces of bread used to garnish soups and stews or finish sauces. The migas are thought to have originated from the Aragon region in northeastern Spain, although similar recipes are found all over the Iberian Peninsula.

mojama – Salt-cured tuna loins

montaditos – Foods placed on slices of bread or crostini

olletas – Stew dishes from the Valencia region of Spain that may contain many ingredients, including meat, grains, and vegetables

pa amb tomaquat – Crusty country bread rubbed with ripe tomatoes and drizzled with extra virgin olive oil; called *pan con tomate* in Spanish, this is a Catalonian specialty (see recipe)

paella – Classic rice dish with beans, saffron, vegetables, and various meats or seafood. The classic version contains chicken and snails; however, many recipes now use other ingredients. All versions are cooked over an open flame in a paellera, uncovered, making this one of the more challenging dishes to prepare properly. (see recipe)

pa pages – Compressed cakes of figs, anise seed, and bread used to feed the olive field workers of the Balearic Islands.

pescaito frito – Fried fish common in the Andalusia region of Spain

picada – Mixture of bread, almonds, garlic, and onions that is puréed to a paste and used to thicken and finish many soups and other liquids in Spanish cooking

pil-pil – Sauce made in Basque region of Spain from salt cod, olive oil, and garlic

pinchitos – Skewered and grilled meats common to the Andalusia region of Spain

potaje de garbanzos y espinacas – Thick chickpea and spinach soup hailing from the Catalonia region of northeast Spain

pulpo a la gallega – Boiled octopus, sliced and served with olive oil and hot paprika

refogado (P) – Technique of starting a recipe by cooking onions (and sometimes other seasonings) in olive oil until onions are completely tender and golden; this is a very common technique for many of the dishes in Portugal

salbitxada – Traditional sauce to accompany grilled calçots; made of ground almonds, garlic, bitxos, vinegar, and olive oil (see recipe)

salsa romesco – Sauce made from roasted tomatoes with ground almonds, garlic, olive oil, and chili peppers (see recipe)

samfaina – Vegetable mixture of onions, eggplant, sweet peppers, and tomato from the Catalonia region of Spain that is very similar to the ratatouille found in the Provençal region across the border in France

sherry – Fortified wine made in Jerez, Spain, from local grapes; fortified with brandy after fermentation

sofrito – Technique, like the Portuguese refogado, of cooking onions (and sometimes other ingredients) in olive oil until they are broken down and perhaps beginning to color; this technique is used in many Spanish recipes

sopa seca – "Dry soup" common to northern Portugal; made by ladling stock over layers of meats, vegetables, and bread, and baking until the moisture has been absorbed by the ingredients

sucs – Fish stews cooked in paella pans with a sauce made from ground almonds and garlic; found in the Valencia region of Spain

tapas – Small plates of food served in wine bars and now a common aspect of the cuisine throughout the Iberian Peninsula

tortilla Española – Savory potato and egg cake commonly served as a tapa in Spain (see recipe)

zarzuela de marisco – Fisherman's stew made from local shellfish cooked in a flavorful tomato and pepper broth; this dish, from the Catalonia region of Spain, borrows its name from an opera

✳ Equipment

cazuela – Earthenware pot used to cook and serve stews, soups, and beans

comal – Griddle

cuchillo – Knife

paellera – Large, shallow oval or round pan with handles on ends; used to make paella

pinchos – Skewer

plancha – Flat iron pan or griddle used for cooking over a flame

sartén – Frying pan

SECTION 2

CUISINES OF
AFRICA

Not only is African cuisine often overlooked in the United States, the influence that the cuisines of Africa have had on the development of U.S. cuisine is generally underappreciated. Because the brutal history of the slave trade was the means by which this influence was brought to the United States, the Caribbean, and many other parts of the world, a dialogue about Africa's specific contributions to U.S. and other cuisines is often not pursued as it should be. Without a doubt, the contributions of African cooks to the cuisines of the Americas during the years of the slave trade (and after) are as important as the contributions from any European country. When one looks at the cuisine of West Africa, its connection with many foods of the southeastern United States and other regions becomes clear.

Africa is the second largest landmass in the world and is home to many cultures and culinary traditions. The continent is often viewed as four areas in a cultural sense—North Africa, West Africa, East Africa, and South Africa—each with distinct differences from the others. Of these four areas, the one that is recognized the most for the complexity of its cuisine and the uniqueness of its foods is North Africa; as such, this is the section of Africa that is covered in this text. It should be noted that the cuisines of the other three regions are equally important and are thought by many to be the next frontier in culinary arts. It is only because of limited space in this text and lack of resources on these

cuisines that they are not covered in more depth here. The chapters on the Caribbean and South America both discuss the influence of African cuisine on the development of each of those cuisines and are good reference points for beginning to explore West African cuisine.

Although North African cuisine is known for being influenced by Arabs from the east and the native Berber population, as well as for highlighting the diversity and possibilities of a cuisine formed in the Mediterranean climate and heavily influenced by non-European cultures, the other sections of Africa have a history of struggles with sustenance that overshadows their cuisines.

Sub-Saharan African cuisine is notable for the inclusion of a number of key ingredients as well as for being the possible origin of deep frying. Cassava, yams, plantains, corn, and sweet potatoes are all common starchy components of the cuisine of sub-Saharan Africa. Of these, the yam is the only one that is indigenous to Africa. In the United States, varieties of sweet potatoes are often mistakenly labeled "yams," which are rarely found in the states (yams are very large, regularly reaching weights of 30 pounds or more, and are covered with small hair-like roots). Yams and other imported starchy ingredients are often cooked, smashed, and seasoned to yield foo-foo (or fufu), a type of starchy porridge—many variations of which are found in other parts of the world. Some other ingredients that are indigenous to Africa include coffee,

lablab beans, jugo beans, tamarind, sorghum, a number of tubers not found in the United States, okra, melegueta peppers, dates, watermelon, kola nuts (used to make cola beverages), some types of cucumbers, oil palm (used to yield palm oil, an important African cooking oil), and black-eyed beans; many of these still play important roles in the cuisines of Africa. Several of these ingredients—and the methods traditionally used to prepare them—have made their way to other parts of the world, in particular the cuisine of the Americas.

The connection between Africa and the Americas is strong, and many examples of African-inspired or created foods within the Americas are evident in today's cuisines. Africa has had a tragic history of exploitation, and the contributions of Africa to the development of a number of cuisines often has been overlooked or ignored. However, a celebration of the ingenuity of African chefs is long overdue. Much of the modern culinary culture that has developed in the Caribbean, the United States, Brazil and other parts of South America, owe a debt to the African slaves who, in many cases were the original cooks of the cuisines that has developed in parts of these regions. The chapter on North African cuisine is followed by the third section of the text, because the cuisines of the Americas have many ties to the cuisines of Africa (primarily West Africa), and the cuisines of Africa have been greatly impacted by ingredients from the Americas as well.

CHAPTER 11

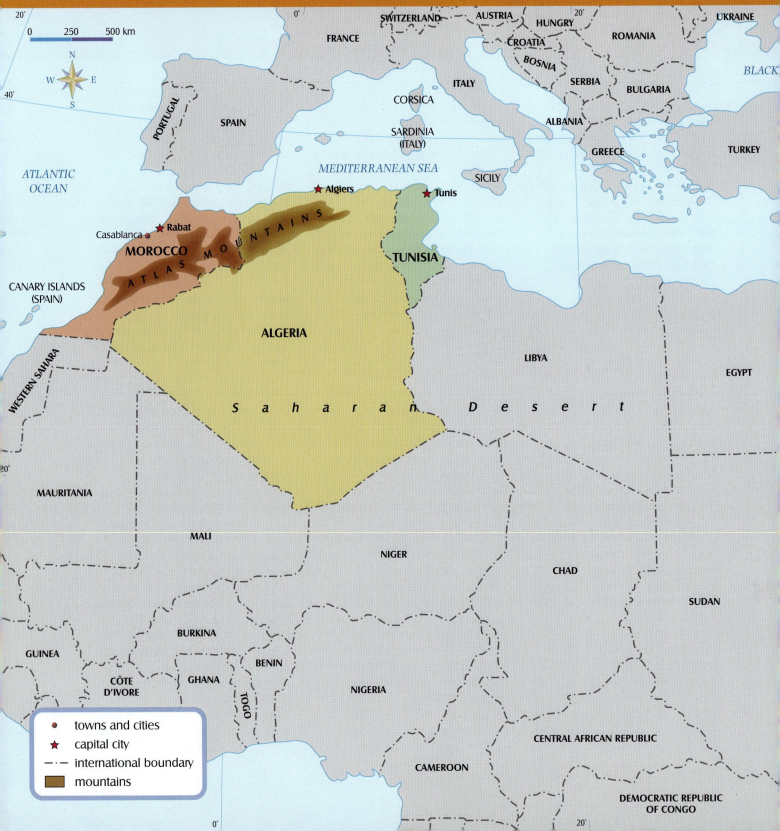

North African Cuisine

OBJECTIVES

Upon completion of this chapter, you will be able to

- explain what makes the cuisines of North Africa unique.
- recognize the common cooking methods used in these traditional cuisines.
- recognize common recipes found in the cuisines of Morocco, Algeria, and Tunisia.
- produce a variety of recipes common to North Africa.
- define the terms listed at the conclusion of the chapter.

INTRODUCTION

North Africa is situated in the middle of a triangle of culinary and cultural influences. With the Arab-dominated Egypt and Middle East to the east, sub-Saharan Africa to the south, and the influences of Europe just miles from the northwestern tip, the cuisine of North Africa is quite varied and very well regarded by all. Because of the similarities of their cuisines, and the influences that have resulted in their development, in this chapter North Africa is considered to be the countries of Morocco, Algeria, and Tunisia. This region is also commonly known as the *Maghreb,* from the Arabic word for "west," and although there are notable differences among the three countries, many similarities bind them together to this day. The other North African countries of Libya and Egypt have storied cuisines of their own that share many traits with those of the Maghreb but will not be examined here for reasons of space—certainly not for lack of culinary artistry.

North Africa is a region of contrasts, with fertile coastlines, arid deserts, mountain ranges, and vast plains; this region is home to a wide variety of conditions that have made the inhabitants of this land experts at maximizing their products to yield a surprisingly rich cuisine.

The cuisine of all of these countries is firmly rooted in the home. The development of restaurants in North Africa is a relatively new aspect, and the general consensus of North Africans is that if you want to experience real North African cuisine, you have to be invited to a family's home to do so. Cooking is done almost exclusively by women, and recipes are passed from mother to daughter with very little in the way of recorded directions or amounts. This has resulted in a culture in which national or regional cuisine is a part of daily life and of the family. North Africans have great pride and respect for their culinary traditions, traits that are always required for a great cuisine.

The cuisine of the Maghreb is reflective of the landscape from which it comes: rich, spicy stews contrast with simple yet refined *couscous;* dry pastries combine with thick, super-sweet syrups; and preserved lemons and olives that remind one of the desert sun mix with fresh produce that suggests lush vegetation. This cuisine has long been considered one of the most interesting mélanges of both ingredients and cultural influences. This chapter examines how this great cuisine came to be.

HISTORIC CULINARY INFLUENCES

North Africa has been a stopping point for a number of cultures that have lent their culinary customs to the development of a unique and highly regarded cuisine. These historical influences have all played a part in today's North African cuisine and are examined in the section that follows.

The Indigenous Berbers

The Berbers are often considered the indigenous people of North Africa—because they have inhabited the region since before written history—although there is evidence that other people lived in the region before the Berbers moved into the area (the original inhabitants are thought to have moved south into sub-Saharan Africa). The Berbers are thought to have emigrated from southwestern Asia sometime around 2000 BC into present-day North Africa (other evidence suggests they migrated from the Middle East as well). These were hunter-gatherers who likely brought with them certain traditions and further developed these traditions in northern Africa. The method of sun-drying and spicing meats in strips (*khlii*) and then preserving them in fat comes from the Berbers, as does roasting whole lambs over a fire on a spit (called *mechoui)*. The Berbers also produced a number of dishes using wheat, fava beans, barley, and dates. At this point in history, the Berbers were nomadic people who subsisted on the edible plants found locally and by hunting game and herding sheep.

The Phoenicians

Phoenician traders began to infiltrate and trade via the Mediterranean beginning in 800 BC, and they introduced a number of new ingredients to the Berbers who inhabited the area. The Phoenicians introduced pomegranates, olives, grapes, lentils, and figs, as well as the cultivation techniques to grow these products. The somewhat nomadic Berbers became more involved in tending fields and developing simple towns while still maintaining their herding ways. This was the first step toward the development of a more dependable agricultural system that would enable a more consistent diet.

The Roman Empire

The Roman Empire expanded into North Africa in 146 BC and ruled the region until the fifth century AD. During this period, the Romans organized the agricultural efforts of North Africa to provide food for the rest of the Roman Empire. Thus, the production of large amounts of wheat and olive oil in North Africa, and the subsequent use of those two ingredients as major components of the local cuisine, began. The vast olive groves in northern Africa today are a testament to the period of Roman influence, as the Romans oversaw the development of irrigation systems to enable these and other crops to be grown in quantity. The Romans' biggest contribution to North African cuisine was probably their influence on the development of these irrigation and farming techniques that allowed for greater production and thus more efficient and plentiful harvests.

The Arabs

In the seventh century AD, Arabs from the Middle East began to invade the area of present-day North Africa following the introduction of Islam. The prophet Mohammed, who is credited with beginning the *Muslim* faith, encouraged the spread of *Islam* to other nations; as a result, Arab armies gained control of North Africa by the end of the seventh century and beginning of the eighth century, following 50 years of resistance on the part of the Berbers. In time, the Berber population converted to Islam, and today the Muslim faith is followed by most North Africans.

The Arabs brought with them spices from their trade with Europe at that time, including black pepper, long pepper, cinnamon, cassia, nutmeg, mace, sesame seeds, and saffron. The Arabs also introduced a method they had learned from the Persians (present-day Iran)—filling thin sheets of dough with flavorful meats and fish—which was incorporated into the North African cuisine in dishes such as *bisteeya* and other filled, flaky savory and sweet pastries.

The Arab influence was one of the most significant on the cuisine of North Africa; religious dietary guidelines became customary, and the culinary traditions of the Arabs became commonplace in the local cuisine. Muslim dietary restrictions, known as *halal* (permissible) and *haram* (impermissible), include the avoidance of pork, improperly slaughtered animals, alcohol, rennet (used to make many cheeses), gelatin, and carnivores (such as birds of prey and cats), and thus these foods are rarely seen in any North African recipes because the majority of the population are of the Muslim faith (cheeses are produced and consumed but not by the rennet method). In addition to the dietary influences of the Muslim faith, the combination of meat and fruit, the use of dried fruits and nuts as sweetmeats, the use of nuts in thickening sauces, and the technique for making thin pastry and honey-soaked pastries all can be attributed to this period of influence from the Arabic peoples.

The Jews

Followers of the Jewish faith have lived in northern Africa throughout recorded history, and the dietary customs of these people are one of the influential factors that have resulted in North African cuisine. As with the Muslim faith, Jewish dietary customs or laws dictate a number of aspects in the diets of followers, including abstinence from pork, shellfish, birds of prey, blood, and improperly slaughtered animals (all are also Muslims dietary restrictions), as well as the practice of not working on Saturday. One of the dishes still found in North African kitchens as a result of this Jewish influence is *dafina*, which is a stew that is cooked from Friday until Saturday and eaten for lunch on Saturday. This stew is typically accompanied by *mahia* (distilled fig and anise liquor) and provides for a hearty lunch on the Sabbath (Saturday). Other Jewish contributions include *tabikha*, a beef and onion stew common among Algerian Jews; *bkaila*, a stew of okra and lamb from Tunisia; and *coclo*, large meatballs made from ground veal or beef, rice, and spices, also from Algeria and often eaten with dafina.

The Moors

The Moors were a people composed of mixed cultures: native Berbers from North Africa, Arabs from the Middle East, and native Spanish and Sicilians, all of whom contributed to a culture that flourished in Spain, Sicily, and North Africa. The influence on North African cuisine that derived from the peoples of this period originated mainly in Spain and continued with their relocation to North Africa.

After the conquest of Spain by the Moors in 711 AD, the Moors developed a sophisticated culture and cuisine in Spain during the centuries that followed before being driven out in 1492 AD. This culture achieved great prominence in the thirteenth and fourteenth centuries and, from the sophisticated culture, a new cuisine evolved. This cuisine is still evident in Spain today and has played a significant role in what has become the cuisine of North Africa—in particular, Moroccan cuisine.

Two separate groups of people were known as the Moors (also often called Saracens): the group that conquered Spain was primarily from Morocco, Algeria, and sub-Saharan Africa, and the group that conquered Sicily was primarily from Algeria and Tunisia. When these groups were expelled from these European countries, they mostly returned to their countries of origin; thus, there is more Spanish influence in Morocco and Algeria, and more Italian influence (Sicilian or southern Italian; see Chapter 4, "Italian Cuisine") in Tunisia and Algeria.

Just as the Moors were being expelled from Spain, the Spanish landed in the Americas and began to bring back ingredients. There was still a significant amount of trade between North Africa and Spain during this time, and many of the ingredients from the Americas made their way into North Africa long before they were introduced into northern and Eastern Europe. Some of the ingredients that were well received and became common in North African cuisine include tomatoes, peppers, potatoes, and chiles.

The Ottoman Empire

The Ottoman Empire stretched into northern Africa during its zenith in the mid-1500s and lasted until the 1800s in both Algeria and Tunisia, leaving an impression on the culture and cuisine of this period. The Ottoman Empire, one of the great empires of history, was based in present-day Turkey, which became a culinary hub with great feasts that drew from the traditions of the lands that the empire controlled.

The cuisine that developed in the Ottoman Empire was a blend of native Turkish cuisine, some European influences (the empire spread into Europe to the west), and—probably most significant—Persian cuisine. The Persians had a very sophisticated and well-respected cuisine at this time in history, highly regarded among the Ottoman rulers, and thus it began to permeate the Ottoman culture. These influences were also transferred into North Africa with the Ottoman armies that conquered both Tunisia and Algeria.

Some of the influences of this period that are still evident in the cuisine today include sweet halvas (sweets made from ground nuts with butter and sugar), baklava and other honey-soaked pastries, as well as other foods made with the thin sheets of pastry known as *briks* and *warka* (attributed to the Ottomans, who learned this from the Persians and introduced it to North Africa). The Ottomans also left their traditions of stuffing foods, such as stuffed vegetables and dolmas (stuffed vine leaves, often grape leaves), as well as their great array of soups known as chorbas. The Ottomans introduced the use of flower essences into the cooking, including the now common use of rose water and orange water in North African cooking.

European Colonialism

In the 1800s, there was increased attention by the European powers on North Africa as a relatively local spot for colonization, and this resulted in the conquest of these areas—principally by the French and Spanish.

Spain controlled the coastal area of Morocco for about 50 years starting in 1904, and this period—along with the lengthier and more significant period of Moorish rule in Spain—resulted in a significant amount of Spanish influence in Morocco, and vice versa.

France colonized parts of all three countries between the early 1800s and mid-1900s before being driven out by the native population. During this period of French rule, many of the tendencies of the French in terms of culinary artistry and cooking in general were adopted by the native populations and are now evident in the cuisine. Some of the influences of French cuisine and culture on the countries of the Maghreb include the increased focus on the presentation of food, the introduction of the classic French mother sauces, and the use of *sachets* (herbs and spices contained in a porous bag).

Other European powers also influenced North African cuisine during periods of brief rule or protectorate, as well as from the period of the Inquisition, during which many people of the Muslim faith left other European countries and relocated to North Africa. One noticeable influence is that of the Italians in Tunisia, where pasta and pasta sauces are common, along with other components of (particularly southern) Italian cuisine. In addition, the British left their mark in the form of the practice of taking tea, which has become a favorite drink in North Africa. Green tea with mint is now one of the most common drinks in Morocco.

UNIQUE COMPONENTS

North African cuisine is regarded by many as one of the most unique and intriguing in the world. Many of these characteristics can be attributed to the North Africa's location, as this area has long been sought by other nations, which has resulted in the introduction of many cultures to the area over the centuries. Those who stayed influenced the native populations, and a new cuisine developed with characteristics that make it distinct from all of its contributors. The following section examines some of the aspects that make this cuisine unique.

Grains, Legumes, Olive Oil, and Herds

The diet of the typical North African is based largely on grains and olive oil combined with legumes and occasional meat from herds of sheep and goats. This is the basis for much of the nourishment of the general population, and the cuisine has developed around these core ingredients.

Wheat is the main grain grown in this region, with a smaller production of millet, sorghum, and rice. The most common use of the grain is in the form of couscous and breads, both of which are primary components in the diets of the Maghreb people. There is also significant production and use of legumes in North African cooking. The main legumes used include chickpeas, fava beans, and lentils. Couscous has a near ritualistic preparation method that requires some attention and deliberate steps that yield a product quite different from what most people in the United States may recognize. Couscous is eaten with *tagines* (a stew-like dish made in an earthenware vessel) and is used to make salads and even sweets. Legumes are also common ingredients in soups, salads, and dishes to accompany meat.

Olives have been grown in this Mediterranean climate for many centuries; after the Roman Empire expanded the production of North African groves, olive oil production has been significant enough to supply the countries with this most Mediterranean of cooking fats. Olive oil is used in North African cooking to deep-fry and sear foods as well as to make dressings and marinades. The fat of the tail from the variety of sheep raised here is also used and prized for the flavor that it provides to dishes.

North Africans have a long tradition and culture as herders, and the consumption of the tended animals has always been a significant part of the cuisine. The main animals that are herded are sheep (lamb and mutton) and goats (goat meat) and, as such, those are the most significant meat sources in the diet. Other protein sources include the prized pigeon (known as squab on restaurant menus in the United States), chicken, and fish. Although vegetables are a significant component of the cuisine of the Maghreb, the tradition of eating vegetables is in fact less pronounced overall than may seem to be the case when looking through North African cookbooks. Much of this part of the world is quite arid; as a result, land with enough water to raise vegetable crops is at a premium. This isn't to say that vegetables are not eaten; they are—particularly in sweet or spicy salads—but vegetables play a smaller role in the typical diet than do starchy foods and meats, poultry, and fish.

Religious Influences: Islam

The vast majority of North Africans are Muslims, the name given to followers of the Islamic faith, and as such they follow the dietary restrictions set forth by the Quran (the written text to which followers of the faith adhere). The Quran lists foods that are considered untouchable (haram) and those that are permitted (halal). Some of the foods excluded from this diet are pork, four-footed animals that catch prey with their mouths, any naturally deceased animals, improperly slaughtered animals (proper slaughter is done by cutting the jugular, carotid artery, and windpipe, and draining the blood), blood, birds of prey, and alcoholic beverages. These items therefore are not customarily found in any of the cuisines in North Africa, unless from another religious minority. Foods that have met the guidelines of the Muslim faith in the United States can be certified halal and labeled as such, similar to the way that kosher foods are labeled.

Muslims also observe periods of fasting that coincide with the Islamic calendar, including a month-long fast during *Ramadan* (the ninth month of the Islamic calendar), six days of the following month (called *Shawwal*), as well as a number of other days during the year. During a fast, followers abstain from eating during daylight hours and eat specific foods such as the thick soup made from lentils and chickpeas (called *harira*). At the end of the fast, feasts are held to celebrate the observance of the fast period. At the end of Ramadan, it is also customary for North Africans to cook lamb if the family has the means to

do so, and spit-roasted lamb and lamb tagines are common at the table on this day of celebration.

These traditions are strongly adhered to in most Muslim families. Because the vast majority of North Africans are Muslim, these are significant components of the cuisine.

Stewing, Steaming, and Baking: The Foundation of Maghreb Cuisine

The most common cooking methods employed in the cuisine of the Maghreb are stewing, steaming, and baking. The many tagine dishes common throughout the region are but one part of the tradition of stewing that has existed here for centuries. Stewed vegetables and the many soups and sauces that provide much of the substance and character of the local diet join the tagines in following this ancient tradition. These stews also provide the flavorful broths and sauces that are used to wet and flavor the couscous and bread that provide the backbone of the cuisine. Traditionally, tagines were named by the types of seasoning that were used in making them; *m'qualli* indicated that the tagine was seasoned with saffron and ginger, and *m'hammer* described a tagine flavored with cumin and paprika. Many variations of tagines that do not fall into these two categories are now common in both North African cooking and in establishments that make foods in this style.

Couscous is a way of life here, and it is ritually steamed to make a product much different from the packaged couscous found in supermarkets across the United States. Couscous is thought to be made correctly only if it has been steamed three times, wetted in between each steaming with cold water, and rubbed with fingers to separate the grains. The couscous used in these countries is not par-cooked, as much of the U.S. version is.

Breads are also a common food in the cuisine of the Maghreb and traditionally were baked in a communal oven shared by the people in a community; people marked their own loaves with symbols to distinguish them from others and gave specific instructions to the baker for the type of loaf they desired. This baking tradition is disappearing from North Africa, as the communal oven is becoming a thing of the past—people either buy bread from a bakery or, more commonly, make it at home. In smaller and more remote villages, this practice still exists, and some of the best breads come from these communal ovens (called *ferrans*).

In addition to the traditions of steaming, stewing, and baking, it is also common in these cuisines for foods to be grilled or cooked on a spit over an open flame. These techniques can be traced back to the nomadic culture and the cooking of animals over a fire, which was common to that period.

Salt-Preserved Lemons and Olives

The salt-preserved lemons called l'hamd mrakad are unique to the cuisine of North Africa, and the salt-preserved (often called oil-cured) olives, which are usually simply called Moroccan olives, are also common. Preserved lemons are used frequently in North African cuisine as spices are used in many other cuisines; being added to tagines, sauces, marinades, and other recipes to give a distinct aroma and a unique sourness that is far more subdued than a fresh lemon's tart taste. The preserved lemons are allowed to break down, which makes the rind softer and mellows the bitterness found in the pith of the lemons—the rind is the part of the lemon primarily used in dishes (some use the pulp too, but many discard it). The lemon used in North Africa is a thin-skinned variety (Meyer lemons are used as substitutes in the United States).

The salted olives of North Africa, which can take well over a month to properly salt-cure, turn into a meaty, salty, and slightly bitter-tasting olive (from an inedible and bitter fresh olive). These olives, often called "oil-cured," have a wrinkled appearance and are usually sold dry, although some are packed in oil. These ingredients are common and unique to the cuisine of the Maghreb, although they are becoming more common in other cuisines as well (other versions of the salt-cured olives are found in Greek and Middle Eastern cuisines, but not as prominently as in Moroccan cuisine). Brine-cured olives are also common and are used to make tagines as well as appetizers. The salt-cured lemons and olives that are a part of North African cuisine provide some of its unique flavor and character.

Spices from the East and West

Eastern spices are very common in the cooking of North Africa, and the use of cumin, coriander, caraway, cinnamon, nutmeg, mace, and peppercorns is an integral part of the cuisine. The spice trade that flowed from India to Europe and the Americas traveled directly through North Africa, and the spices spilled into the soul of North African cooking over the centuries. North African cooks have long been considered some of the most skilled at combining spices and other ingredients in their dishes. The combination of Eastern spices with sweetness (from sugar) is a component unique to this cuisine; savory is often balanced with sweetness, with the deft addition of Eastern spices such as cinnamon and saffron. In addition to Eastern spices, chiles have been broadly included in North African cuisine since their introduction.

Following the Spanish colonization of parts of the Americas and the resulting influx of chiles to Spain, the Western chili became a commonly used ingredient here (Columbus sailed to the Americas in the same year that the Moors were being pushed back into North Africa, and the decades that followed saw many exchanges between Spain and North Africa). The chili has been combined with the spices of the East in many of the North African seasoning combinations.

In Morocco, it is the skilled measure of spices that makes the subtle yet highly aromatic tagines what they are; in Tunisia spices are used with a heavier hand to produce some of the piquant sauces and the famous *harissa* spice paste found throughout North Africa.

Eating and Cooking Customs

Eating customs in this region are very unique and encourage a strong sense of family. First, eating in the Maghreb is a family matter and is done in the home—dining out is a rare occasion reserved for the wealthy—and all members of the family (and any guests) sit on the ground and start the meal by having their hands washed with water to symbolize cleanliness before starting a meal. Eating is done using only the right hand (using the left hand is a sign of uncleanliness), and food is picked up with three fingers unless it is particularly difficult to manage, at which point it is appropriate to use all five fingers (such as when eating couscous). Most foods are served with bread, and the bread is used as a utensil to scoop the food along with the three fingers. The cooking in this region is almost always performed by the women of the house.

Cooking traditions in North Africa have long been passed from mother to daughter, and it is the women who master this great cuisine. There are few written texts on cooking in these regions; instead, cooking methods are learned by females working side by side with their mothers, beginning at a young age. Measuring cups and written directions are a newer addition to the kitchens of North Africa, and most cooks still follow tested instincts to perform what was learned from a young age. Although cookbooks are now written on the cooking of North Africa, many of the best foods are not found in restaurants—those foods can only be produced by women whose families have been making them at home for centuries.

SIGNIFICANT SUBREGIONS

Culturally, North Africa is very different from the rest of Africa. The countries of Morocco, Algeria, and Tunisia—known as the Maghreb—are physically part of the continent of Africa. However, with regard to their culinary customs, they are a continent all their own, with strong influences from the Middle East and other countries of the Mediterranean. These countries do not make up the entire northern part of Africa (Libya and Egypt are also on the northern border with the Mediterranean), but those areas generally are more closely linked to the Middle East and will not be considered in this chapter.

Tunisia

Tunisia is located east of Algeria and is bordered by the Mediterranean Sea to the north and east, and by Libya to the east and south. Tunisia is also located relatively close to the islands of Corsica (under French rule) and Sicily (under Italian rule) and displays the strongest influences from Italy of all the countries examined in this chapter.

Because Tunisia is the country closest to the Middle East, and the one the Arabs and Ottomans conquered first in their drives west, it should be of little surprise that the influences of Middle Eastern (Persian and Arab) and Turkish (Ottoman Empire) cuisines are most pronounced here. The use of the Ottoman and Persian-inspired briks (also spelled *bricks*; thin sheets of dough) is common in Tunisia, as are the many pastries that are made from them as well as sweetmeats. Numerous soups also can be traced to the Ottoman period. Like the other countries of the Maghreb, in Tunisia there is significant use of the spices that the Arabs introduced to the region. One of the most well-known ingredients from Tunisia—used all over North Africa and imported around the world—is the spice paste harissa, which combines the native olive oil, caraway from the East, chiles from the Americas, and garlic. Another spiced product that is strongly associated with the cuisine of Tunisia is *merguez*, a small lamb sausage that is found both fresh and in dried form and is included in a variety of recipes or eaten as a snack or an appetizer. The Tunisians are said to be the fondest of chiles of all the North African countries, and they use them (and, more commonly, harissa) liberally.

There is far less Spanish influence on Tunisia than on Morocco, and the European flavor that is found in the cuisine here is clearly from Italy and France. The close proximity to Italy has played a significant role in the development of the Tunisian cuisine; the island of Sicily and mainland Italy are located directly across the Mediterranean. Pasta is common here, as are red sauces that remind one of the tomato-based sauces so common in southern Italy. There is also a significant Jewish community in Tunisia, because many of their ancestors came from Italy to avoid religious persecution and brought the cooking traditions of Italy with them.

The period of French rule from 1881 to 1956 left its mark here, as evidenced by the use of *sabayon* to make ice cream, as well as the use of baguettes to make fully stuffed sandwiches known as *casse croûte tunisien*.

Algeria

Algeria is the largest of the countries in the Maghreb; it is bordered by Morocco in the northwest and Tunisia along the northeast. Its southern and eastern borders are surrounded by other African countries—Libya to the east; Niger, Mali, and Mauritania in the south; and the Mediterranean Sea to the north. Although Algeria is much larger than Morocco and Tunisia, the majority of the country is part of the Saharan Desert, and the population is concentrated in the northern coastal areas that are not part of the desert.

As with the other countries of the Maghreb, Algeria has experienced a history of occupation, ranging from the Romans to the French in more recent times. Algeria was the westernmost African point of the Ottoman (Turkish) Empire during the height of its power, and as a result Algeria was more influenced by the Turks than was its western neighbor, Morocco. Chorbas (Turkish soups), dolmas (Turkish stuffed leaves), boureks (Turkish stuffed pastries), and Turkish pastries are all common in the cuisine of Algeria. Algeria also shares many of the traditional foods that are found in the other countries of the Maghreb, including many types of couscous, tagines and other stews.

Because this country was under French control for longer than any of the other Maghreb countries (from 1830 to 1962), there are more significant influences from the French here than in the other countries. Algeria was once thought of as another province of France. The French effort to influence the native population has been well documented and is often a subject of controversy among the native population, who generally view that period of their history as a brutal one. Although the presence of the French can clearly be felt, the native population fiercely clung to their traditions and customs, and many of the Arab influences are stronger than any European ones.

Morocco

Morocco is the westernmost country covered in this chapter and is located just miles from the southernmost tip of Europe. Morocco's coastal areas are quite fertile and yield a significant amount of produce that supplies the country with the traditional ingredients that are used in combination with the animals that are herded inland to produce many of the local foods. A number of mountain ranges exist in Morocco and essentially divide the country into different regions. The Atlas ranges, of which there are three sections, divide the southeastern part of the country that is dominated by the desert and leads into the Sahara Desert from the northwestern part of the country that leads to the Atlantic Ocean. The Rif Mountains of northern Morocco divide the coast of the Mediterranean Sea from the inland of northern Morocco. The most fertile and populated area of Morocco is the region south of the Rif range and west of the Atlas ranges and includes the cities of Casablanca, Fés, and Marrakech, as well as the capital, Rabat.

Morocco is well known for its expert use of spices in the traditional cuisine; cinnamon, saffron, cumin, dried ginger, dried turmeric, paprika, chiles, allspice, peppercorns, and caraway are all regular components of this complex cuisine. These spices are often combined with preserved lemons, nuts, olive oil, and dried fruits to yield some of the great Moroccan dishes that make this cuisine so unique.

The Ottoman Empire never conquered Morocco, and thus some of the influences of the empire are less evident in the cuisine found here. However, parts of Morocco were controlled by the Spanish for a period, and significant exchanges between Morocco and Spain have existed over the centuries; as a result, there is a stronger Spanish influence in Morocco than anywhere else in the Maghreb.

This northwestern tip of Africa has been the launching and landing point for invading and invaded peoples for centuries. The well-developed cuisine of the Moors in Spain reached its peak in the fourteenth century, and many of Morocco's great culinary traditions come from this time and place. Leading up to this period—and until the Moors were expelled from Spain—there was a significant amount of cultural and culinary exchange between Morocco and Spain. After the Moors were expelled from Spain in the fifteenth century, the cuisine that had been developed in Spain by the northern African and Spanish peoples found its way into the cooking of Morocco (along with the displaced people). The culture of sophistication and the high regard for fine cooking that were components of Moorish Spain infused themselves into the culture and soul of Moroccan cooking. Many dishes can be traced to this period, including the well-known *bisteeya*, a layered pastry filled with meat and seasonings. In addition to the techniques and traditions that were brought to Morocco from Spain, continued trade between the regions after the expulsion of the Moors at the end of the fifteenth century brought the ingredients of the Americas to North Africa as well. This connection resulted in some of the common dishes found in Morocco, such as the great fish tagines made with *charmoula* (spiced marinade) and cooked with tomatoes and peppers.

Moroccan cuisine is often thought of as the most complex of the cuisines of North Africa, and it certainly has some of the most imaginative tagines, which often include l'hamd mrakad (preserved lemons) and are seasoned with aged *smen* (clarified, flavored, and aged butter) or spices from the East. This cuisine also is highly regarded for the skill and craftsmanship needed to make *seksu* (couscous) and warka (thin pastry sheets) and the many preparations that use these ingredients.

RECIPES

The following recipes provide an introduction to North African cooking by revealing some of the more common and significant preparations used in this cuisine. Many other recipes could be included in this section, of course, and further exploration of this region's cooking style will yield several more that—combined with those included here—make up this fine cuisine.

Harissa TUNISIA ✳

(TUNISIAN SPICE PASTE)

INGREDIENTS

1	Tbsp	Caraway Seeds, whole
2	Tbsp	Coriander Seeds, whole
2	tsp	Cardamom Seeds, whole
1	tsp	Black Peppercorns
2	oz	Small Dried Chiles (such as Chili De Arbol, Thai chilies, etc.)
1	Tbsp	Salt
1	oz	Garlic cloves, chopped
4–6	oz	Olive Oil

This hot paste is used to season many Tunisian dishes, and a version of this would be found in virtually any Tunisian household. This blend is also common in the other North African countries, but the Tunisians have a heavier hand when it comes to seasoning their foods with chiles and spicy condiments like harissa.

YIELD: Approximately 1 cup

COOKING TECHNIQUE: Dry Pan Toasting

PROCEDURE

1. Place all of the whole spices (caraway, coriander, cardamom, and peppercorns) in a sauté pan set over a medium-low flame, and toast them in the dry pan until they begin to become quite fragrant. (By moving the pan around, you can prevent the spices from burning while heightening their flavor when heating the oils they all contain.)

2. Remove the spices from the pan and allow them to cool completely.

3. Place the chiles in the sauté pan and toast over a low flame until they just begin to color and emit a spicy aroma (these often make people cough as they emit their spicy oils).

4. In a spice mill (or coffee grinder), grind the cooled spices into a powder; remove the powder and repeat this procedure with the chiles.

5. Place the salt and garlic in a mortar, and grind to a paste using a pestle.

6. Once the garlic and salt are a paste, add the ground spices and continue to grind to make a thick red/brown paste.

7. Slowly work the olive oil into to the paste—grinding with the pestle all the while—to form a smooth and thick paste.

Mortar and pestle with harissa (Tunisian spice paste), surrounded by the ingredients used to make it (from left: olive oil, garlic cloves, caraway seeds, cardamom mixed with black peppercorns, coriander seeds and dried chile peppers)

Ras-el-Hanout MOROCCO

(SPICE BLEND; LITERAL TRANSLATION IS "HEAD OF THE SHOP OR TOP OF THE SHOP," TO INFER THAT THE SHOPKEEPER SELECTED THE BEST SPICES FOR HIS BLEND)

INGREDIENTS

2	Tbsp	Black Peppercorns, whole
1	Tbsp	Cumin Seeds, whole
1	Tbsp	Coriander Seeds, whole
10	ea	Cardamom Seeds, whole
5		Whole Cloves
1	Tbsp	Ground Ginger
1	Tbsp	Cinnamon
1	tsp	Nutmeg
1	tsp	Cayenne
1	tsp	Turmeric
1	tsp	Salt

This spice blend is used in cooking all across North Africa, but it can vary quite a bit from place to place. This blend traditionally is said to have contained more than 20 spices, although often it is made with far fewer (as in this recipe). The blend will always contain cumin, coriander, ginger, turmeric, cardamom, and nutmeg, and many other spices are added to make a complex mix.

YIELD: 1/2 cup

COOKING TECHNIQUE (WHOLE SPICES): Dry Pan Toasting

PROCEDURE

For Toasting the Whole Spices

1. Combine the black peppercorns, cumin seeds, coriander, and cardamom in a small sauté pan, and set over a medium-low flame. Toast the mixture while moving the spices around constantly.

2. Once the spices become noticeably more fragrant (be careful not to burn them!), turn the heat down and add the whole cloves; cook over medium-low heat for another 1–2 minutes, and then remove from heat and set aside to cool.

3. Once the whole spices have cooled well, transfer them to a spice mill and grind them to a powder.

4. Transfer the freshly ground spices to a bowl, and add in the remaining ingredients; mix very well.

5. Transfer the completed spice mixture to a container with a tight-fitting lid to preserve the fresh flavor.

Tabil TUNISIA

(TUNISIAN SPICE MIX)

INGREDIENTS

3	Tbsp	Coriander Seeds
1	Tbsp	Caraway Seeds
1/2	Tbsp	Cumin Seeds
1/2	Tbsp	Black Peppercorns
2	tsp	Fennel Seeds
2	tsp	Turmeric
1	tsp	Cayenne Pepper, ground (or substitute whole dried chiles and grind fresh)
1	tsp	Salt

Tabil is a common spice mix used for a variety of dishes in Tunisia, including as a flavoring for mirqaz, a spicy lamb sausage.

YIELD: 1/3 cup

COOKING TECHNIQUE: Dry Toasting Whole Spices

PROCEDURE

1. Toast the coriander seeds, caraway seeds, cumin seeds, and black peppercorns in a small sauté pan over a low flame until they become fragrant and give off a slightly sharp aroma; remove the pan from heat.

2. Allow the whole spices time to cool completely, and then transfer them to a spice grinder or another small spice mill and grind them—with the turmeric, cayenne, and salt—into a fine powder.

Smen Morocco

(Aged and Salted Butter)

INGREDIENTS

2	lbs	Unsalted Butter, softened at room temperature
1	cup	Water
2	Tbsp	Fresh Oregano
1	tsp	Dried Thyme
1	oz	Salt

Much like aged cheeses in European cuisine, smen is prized in North African cuisine for its pungent and sharp flavor developed from a gradual breakdown of the fats in butter. This recipe is adapted for the kitchen but also relies on a period of natural aging to yield a unique flavor that lends itself well to tagines and couscous dishes.

YIELD: 1.5 pounds

PRESERVATION TECHNIQUE: Salting and Clarifying

COOKING TECHNIQUE: Slow Evaporation of Water by Low Heat

PROCEDURE

1. Work the water, oregano, and thyme into the butter by kneading it with sanitized hands until all of the water has been worked in and the mixture resembles mashed potatoes.

2. Set this mixture in a colander and allow it to sit at room temperature for 4 hours (or overnight) so the butter can become seasoned.

3. Once the mixture has sat long enough to infuse, transfer it to a pot and melt it over very low heat; clarify it by allowing the heat to slowly evaporate the water (set it over a very low flame and check it after an hour or more to see if it is clarified).

4. Once all of the moisture has been cooked out of the butter, strain it through cheesecloth and allow the butter to set at room temperature.

5. Once the butter solidifies, work the salt into the butter and then pack it into a tightly sealed container; set the container in a cool place for 2 weeks.

6. Store the aged butter in a refrigerator until used (it should keep for months).

NOTE: *In North Africa, this is made by "washing" the butter with herbs and then salting and packing it into tight-fitted earthenware jugs and burying it in the ground. The buried butter is usually left in the ground for a minimum of months to age. The longer the butter is aged, the more prized and pungent it is. Some families bury smen at the birth of their daughter to be dug up on her wedding day as part of the wedding feast.*

L'hamd Mrakad MOROCCO
(PRESERVED LEMONS)

INGREDIENTS

5	lbs	Meyer Lemons, unwaxed, washed, and dried
1.5	cups	Kosher Salt
8	oz	Lemon Juice (preferable from Meyer lemons)
4	oz	Olive Oil

L'hamd mrakad (preserved lemons) packed in a jar; cut lemon on plate displays how salt is used to make this preserve

Preserved lemons are a frequent component of Moroccan cuisine and add a distinct flavor to the dishes to which they are added. Meyer lemons resemble the variety used in Morocco and are the best choice to use for this recipe; if Meyer lemons are not available, choose the thinnest-skinned variety you can find. These will last for months in the refrigerator, so making larger batches should improve efficiency without creating waste.

NOTE: *This is a preservation technique that requires cleanliness throughout the process. It is very important to make sure that the bottling equipment and your hands are clean and sterile!*

YIELD: 3.5 pounds

PRESERVATION TECHNIQUE: Salt Curing

PROCEDURE

1. Thoroughly wash the lemons and dry them with a clean towel. Wash and sterilize your hands.

2. Cut off the ends of the lemons by making a thin slice near the stem and one at the bottom end; discard the ends.

3. In order to maximize the surface area exposed to salt, the lemons are sliced into quarters. While holding the lemon standing on end, cut straight down to within 1/4 inch of cutting it in half (but don't cut it in half!). Then turn the lemon over so the side that you were cutting toward is now on top, rotate it 90°, and make another cut straight down (again, only to 1/4 inch from the end). This will expose the interior of the lemon without separating it.

4. Pack the inside of the lemon with some of the salt, and then press the lemon inside a sterilized mason jar.

5. Continue steps 3 and 4 until there is no open space left in the jars (except for a 1/2 inch or so of air on top).

6. Once the lemons have been packed with salt and placed in jars, top off the jars with any remaining salt or salt that spilled during the packing procedure; add lemon juice so that the lemons are completely covered.

7. Pour a little olive oil on top so that the jars are completely full and no lemon is sticking out of the juice.

8. Put the sterilized lid on the canning jar, and secure it tightly. Set the jars aside at room temperature, and allow them to mature for at least 4 weeks (these can be left for months at room temperature—the salt will prevent the growth of any bacteria. The only thing that can grow is mold; if mold is seen inside the jar, it means the lemons were not packed properly and should be discarded).

9. Once the jars are opened, refrigerate any unused portions and use within a week (it is best to use smaller canning jars so that just what is needed is opened).

10. Discard any jars that bulge or crack during the preservation period; this is very rare but could indicate some contamination of the product.

Beldi wa L'hamd Mrakad MOROCCO
(SALT-CURED OLIVES AND PRESERVED LEMONS)

INGREDIENTS

1 lb	Salt-Cured Olives, pitted (may be called oil-cured olives as well)
3 oz	Preserved Lemon
1 Tbsp	Fresh Oregano, minced
1 tsp	Paprika
3 oz	Extra Virgin Olive Oil
	Salt, to taste (may not be needed, depending on olives)

Salt-cured olives are a favorite snack in Morocco and are often combined with other ingredients to make an appetizer or casual food for a buffet. In this recipe, two unique components of North African cuisine are brought together to make these delicious olives, which are commonly served with bread. For a different variation, omit the preserved lemons and substitute 3 Tbsp of harissa for a spicy olive appetizer.

YIELD: 6 portions (3 ounces/portion)

FLAVORING TECHNIQUE: Infusing

PROCEDURE

1. Combine all of the ingredients together in a nonreactive bowl, and mix to completely combine ingredients.

2. Allow the mixture to infuse by setting it into a refrigerator, covered, for at least two hours before serving (overnight is best).

3. An hour before serving, remove mixture from the refrigerator and spread the olives out onto a serving dish to allow them to come up to room temperature before being eaten.

Harsha (Moroccan flat bread) served with beldi wa l'hamd mrakad (cured olives and preserved lemons)

Beghrir   North Africa

(North African Pancake)

Ingredients

For Making the Batter

.75	lb	Fine Semolina Flour
.25	lb	All-Purpose (A.P.) Flour
1.5	tsp	Salt
1	oz	Fresh Compressed Yeast
1	tsp	Sugar
4	oz	Lukewarm Water
3	cups	Whole Milk
3		Eggs, beaten
2	oz	Vegetable Oil (can substitute Clarified Butter)

For Serving

4	oz	Honey
4	oz	Butter
3	oz	Water

These thin griddle-cooked breads are eaten at breakfast with honey and butter and typically are served with mint tea. The method to make these is similar to making a pancake, but beghrirs are cooked only on one side. The result is a thin cake/bread with a pitted surface. The batter is fermented prior to being made to ensure that the yeast is active, which provides leavening and adds a slight sourness to the batter.

Yield: 24 beghrirs (approximately 2 ounces each)

Cooking Technique: Griddling

Procedure

For Making the Batter

1. Preheat a griddle to 375°F (a pan can be used instead; if so, the beghrir should be cooked over a medium flame).

2. Sift the flours and salt into a mixing bowl large enough to hold all of the ingredients.

3. In a small container, combine the yeast, sugar, and lukewarm water; cover and allow the yeast to bloom (to check the viability of the yeast).

4. In another mixing bowl, combine the bloomed yeast with the milk and eggs, and mix well to combine.

5. Pour 3/4 of the liquid mixture into the flour mixture, and mix with a whisk to combine while slowly working in the remaining liquid to make a smooth batter. (**Note:** Differences in flour composition may result in the need to add more flour or milk; adjust consistency as needed.)

6. Once the batter has been made, allow it to sit—covered with a damp cloth—and ferment for a minimum of 1 hour at room temperature (the batter should get a bit frothy during this time and increase in volume) before cooking.

7. Once the batter has had time to ferment, stir it well and pour 2 oz of the batter onto the greased, preheated griddle; spread it thin with the back of the ladle. Cook batter on one side, until the dough is cooked through and browned on the bottom.

For Serving

1. Heat the butter, water, and honey together in a small saucepan, and allow the mixture to simmer slightly while stirring to thicken.

2. Drizzle the honey/butter mixture over the cooked beghrir, and serve immediately.

Salatat Fool TUNISIA
(FAVA BEAN SALAD WITH PRESERVED LEMON)

INGREDIENTS

For Parboiling the Fava Beans

10	lbs	Fresh Fava Beans in Pods, or 2.5 lbs Fresh Shelled Fava Beans (fresh fava beans in pods will yield approximately 25% of original weight, so 10 lbs of pods will yield about 2.5 lbs of shelled beans)
2	qts	Water
1	Tbsp	Salt

For Stewing the Salad

2	oz	Olive Oil
1	lb	Yellow Onion, sliced thin
8	oz	Red Peppers, diced medium
2	oz	Preserved Lemon Rind, minced (see L'hamd Mrakad recipe, this chapter)
1.5	tsp	Cumin, ground
1/4	tsp	White Pepper, ground
1	tsp	Salt
3	oz	Water
		Fava Beans (see above)
1/4	cup	Fresh Minced Cilantro (about 1/2 bunch)
3	oz	Extra Virgin Olive Oil
		Salt, White Pepper, and Cumin, to taste

Fava beans are a favorite vegetable in Tunisia, as well as in the other countries of the Magrheb. In this recipe, the fresh and tender beans are used to make a very flavorful salad that is best served warm or slightly chilled. Fava beans are a spring vegetable that are indigenous to the Mediterranean. They are enjoyed fresh when in season and used dried (a much more starchy version) in soups and stews.

YIELD: 10 portions (5 ounces/portion)

COOKING TECHNIQUE (FAVA BEANS): Parboiling

COOKING TECHNIQUE (SALAD): Stewing

PROCEDURE

For Parboiling the Fava Beans

1. Prepare the fresh fava beans by removing the beans from the pods (the pods can be saved to make vegetable stock). Look for full pods with medium- to large-size beans (the very large beans are beginning to get starchy and aren't as tender or flavorful, whereas the small beans yield very little and are more labor intensive).

2. Bring the water and salt to a boil in a pot over a high flame.

3. Once the water reaches a boil, add the fava beans and boil for 2 minutes; remove the beans and shock them in an ice bath.

4. Remove the beans from the ice bath once they are cool, and peel the outer membrane off by lifting the outer skin (husk) with your (clean!) thumbnail and squeezing out the two bean pods.

5. Set the cleaned and par-cooked beans aside, and discard the husks.

For Making the Salad

1. In a large sauté pan, heat the olive oil over a medium-low flame until hot; add the onions and red peppers, and sweat over medium-low to low heat until the onions and peppers are very tender but not browned (control heat to ensure they do not get browned).

2. Once the onions and peppers are tender, add the preserved lemon rinds, cumin, white pepper, and salt, and stir to combine well. Cook for a few minutes to allow the flavors to mix.

3. Add the water and the par-cooked fava beans, and turn the heat up to a medium flame to heat the fava beans while mixing with a wooden spoon to combine flavors and ingredients. Cook this mixture for 2 minutes to heat through.

4. Once the beans are heated through, remove them from heat and allow them to cool until just warm to the touch. Add the cilantro and extra virgin olive; adjust seasoning, if necessary.

5. Serve warm or chill slightly to serve.

Salatat Tangiers   Morocco   ✳
(COUSCOUS SALAD IN THE STYLE OF TANGIER)

INGREDIENTS

For Steaming Couscous

1.5	lbs	Couscous, raw (not the packaged par-cooked variety)
2	cups	Ice-Cold Water
7	oz	Extra Virgin Olive Oil
1	cup	Ice-Cold Water
2	Tbsp	Salt

For Blanching Vegetables

1	qt	Water
1	Tbsp	Salt
6	oz	Carrots, diced small
8	oz	Red Bell Pepper, diced small
8	oz	Green Beans, cut into 1/4-inch lengths

For Making Dressing

8	oz	Extra Virgin Olive Oil
4	oz	Lemon Juice
3	oz	Orange Juice
1/4	tsp	Cinnamon
4	oz	Red Onions, diced small
1/4	cup	Packed Parsley Leaves, minced
3	Tbsp	Fresh Mint, minced
4	oz	Currants

Couscous is very commonly used in Morocco and the other North African countries to accompany many of the tagines as well as meat and fish dishes that constitute main courses in the typical diet. Any leftover cooked couscous can be used in a number of ways—for example, in salads (as in this recipe) or desserts.

YIELD: 15 portions (5–6 ounces/portion)

COOKING METHOD (COUSCOUS): Steaming (modified specifically to couscous)

COOKING METHOD (VEGETABLES): Parboiling

MIXING METHOD (DRESSING): Non-emulsified

PROCEDURE

For Steaming Couscous

Follow the directions for steaming couscous on page 287 of this chapter, substituting extra virgin olive oil for butter in the recipe. The couscous can be made specifically for this salad, or extra couscous can be made when preparing other recipes in this chapter (such as the tagine) and saved to make this salad.

For Blanching Vegetables

1. Bring the water and salt to a boil over high heat, and then lower the carrots in a mesh basket into the boiling water; blanch until the carrots are just tender. Once the carrots are tender, remove them from the boiling water and set aside to cool.

(continues)

Plate of two rounds of salatat tangiers (couscous salad), with one round of salatat fool (fava bean salad) shown in center of the couscous salad and along left side of plate

Salatat Tangiers
(continued)

For Mixing Salad

> Cooked Couscous (see above)
> Blanched Carrots, Red Bell Peppers, and Green Beans (see above)
> Dressing (see above)
> Salt and Pepper, to taste

For Garnish

> 6 oz   Roasted Almonds, chopped

2. Using the boiling water, repeat step 1 with the red peppers and green beans so that all vegetables are blanched until just tender; allow them to cool before adding them to the couscous.

For Making Dressing

1. In a mixing bowl, combine all ingredients for the dressing and mix thoroughly.

For Mixing Salad

1. In the mixing bowl that contains the cooled couscous, add the cooled, blanched vegetables and the dressing; mix very well to ensure that the couscous and vegetables are coated with the dressing.

2. Adjust seasoning, if necessary.

3. Garnish completed salad with roasted, chopped almonds.

Warka MOROCCO
(THIN PASTRY)

INGREDIENTS

1.5 lbs	High-Gluten Bread Flour
14 oz	Water
	Water, as needed
2 oz	Clarified Butter

Warka is a unique pastry made by hitting a soft dough against the back of a metal or earthenware pot placed over either a pot of boiling water or a flame. By hitting the soft dough against the pan, a thin layer of dough is left on the pan; this is done repeatedly to yield overlapped circles of dough on the back of the pan that are then lifted off of the pan as a sheet of very thin dough (a well-made warka sheet is thinner than phyllo dough). This dough is used to make a number of North African specialties, including the famous pigeon pie called bisteeya.

YIELD: 100 warkas (may yield more or less, depending on size of pan and skill of maker)

COOKING METHOD: Warka Method (unique method of cooking on back of pan)

PROCEDURE

1. To make the dough, place the bread flour in a mixing bowl and add the 14 oz of water; mix with a dough hook to form smooth dough.

2. Once smooth dough is formed, remove the dough from the mixer and place it in a large mixing bowl.

3. Add more water to the dough as follows: add a couple of tablespoons of water at a time, and work this water into the dough by spreading the dough over the water and then pushing it into the water. As this is done, the dough should be lifted and pulled out of the bowl to elongate it.

4. This addition is continued until the dough begins to resemble a sponge, becoming very soft and elastic. The dough is developed enough when it stretches a least a foot when lifted from the bowl.

5. Once the dough has been developed properly, sprinkle some water over it and cover it with a clean, damp cloth; allow it to rest for 3 hours.

Warka (thin pastry) dough showing the slack consistency

(continues)

Warka
(continued)

Tapping the warka dough on the back of the heated pan to leave a small imprint of the dough on the pan

Removing the warka dough from the pan after repeatedly leaving imprints in a circular pattern to make a sheet of warka pastry

6. To make the warka, bring a pot of water to a boil over high heat on the stove, and place a cake pan (or clean and smooth-bottomed sauté pan) upside down over the boiling water. (You should now have a clean surface to cook the warkas on.)

7. Wipe the outside of the upside-down pan with some of the clarified butter, and then wipe it off (this may need to be done a few times, until the pan gets "seasoned"—you want the warkas to come off of the pan without breaking).

8. Place a container of water by the area where you will be making the warkas, and dip your hand into the water prior to working with the sticky dough.

9. Using one water-dipped hand, break off a piece of the warka dough, about the size of a baseball, and rotate your hand in a circle to form a ball.

10. Turn your hand upside down, moving your fingers inward (and still rotating to keep the dough from sticking to your hand), and begin to allow some of the dough to pass your fingers and tap the upside-down pan over the boiling water (the dough will leave a circular film on the surface of the pan).

11. Continue to tap the pan with the dough, overlapping the previous spot on the pan to make a larger piece of warka.

12. Set the piece of dough down (or, if you are working with a partner, have them do this part) and gently lift the corners of the warka off the upside-down pan as soon as the outer portions of the warka begin to look dry).

13. Continue to work with the dough and tap it against the pan until all of the dough has been made into thin pastry sheets (the first few often do not work, because the pan needs to get "seasoned" before they come off easily).

Bisteeya Bil Hout   MOROCCO ✳

(INDIVIDUAL SEAFOOD PASTRIES/PIES)

INGREDIENTS

For Poaching the Seafood

2	lbs	Lean Fish Fillets (cod, sea bass, flounder, etc.), boneless and skinless
1	lb	Shrimp, peeled and deveined
2	qts	Water
2	Tbsp	Salt
4	oz	Lemon Juice

The classic bisteeya is made with pigeon and seasoned with a lemon egg sauce and almonds, and it is made as a large pastry and served at celebratory feasts. This version uses fish and shellfish and includes the typical heavy dose of fresh parsley and cilantro as part of the seasoning.

YIELD: 15 pastries (4 ounces/pastry)

COOKING METHOD (SEAFOOD): Poaching

COOKING METHOD (PASTRY): Baking

PROCEDURE

For Poaching the Seafood

1. In a small pot, bring the water, salt, and lemon juice to a gentle simmer over a medium flame; add the shrimp to the poaching liquid, and poach until just cooked (about 3–4 minutes).

(continues)

Bisteeya Bil Hout
(continued)

For Making the Filling

	Poached Seafood (see above)
4 oz	Extra Virgin Olive Oil
2 oz	Lemon Juice
1 tsp	Cumin, ground
2 tsp	Paprika
1/4 tsp	Cayenne Pepper
2 tsp	Salt
3 oz	Fresh Parsley, minced (about 1.5 cups)
2 oz	Cilantro, minced (about 1 cup)

For Assembling and Baking the Pastry

15	sheets of warka (if these are not available or made, phyllo can be substituted with good results)
3 oz	Clarified Butter
	Filling (see above)
2	Egg Yolks
2 oz	Water

2. Remove the shrimp as soon as they are cooked, and add the lean fish; poach until the fish just begins to flake apart (time will vary with the thickness of fillets).

3. Remove the fish pieces once they begin flaking, and allow both the shrimp and fish to cool. Flake the fish into smaller pieces (about 1/2 inch each), and cut the shrimp into 1/4-inch pieces.

For Making the Filling

1. Place the flaked fish, cut shrimp, olive oil, lemon juice, spices, salt, and fresh herbs into a mixing bowl; mix thoroughly.

2. Adjust seasoning of filling, if necessary, before proceeding.

For Assembling and Baking the Pastry

1. Preheat the oven to 375°F.

2. Place a sheet of warka on a workbench and brush it with clarified butter.

3. Place 1/2 cup of the seafood filling on the bottom quarter of the warka sheet, leaving an inch of space from the end, and fold the filling and warka directly over to enclose the filling.

4. Fold in the right side of the warka sheet, and roll in the same direction the right side was folded in from (so that you are folding 90° from where you did the first fold).

5. Fold the warka over on itself to enclose the remaining sheet that is exposed.

6. Place the filled pastry, with the last fold down, on a baking sheet.

7. In a small mixing bowl, combine the egg yolk and water; mix thoroughly. Using a pastry brush, brush the surface of the filled pastry.

8. Repeat steps 2 through 7 for the remaining warka sheets.

9. Place the completed pastries into the preheated oven and bake until golden brown and crisp (about 15 minutes); remove and serve right away.

Bisteeya bil hout (stuffed seafood pastry)

Harsha   MOROCCO
(FLATBREAD)

INGREDIENTS

2	tsp	Dried Yeast
2	oz	Whole Milk, lukewarm
6	oz	Salted Butter, softened
1.25	lbs	Semolina, fine ground (you may substitute bread flour, if this is unavailable)
1/2	tsp	Salt
1	Tbsp	Sugar
6	oz	Whole Milk
		Vegetable Oil (as needed), to cook
		Salt, to taste

Flatbreads are very common in North Africa and traditionally are used to scoop up ingredients when eating, much like a utensil would be used in our culture. This recipe uses the fine-ground semolina flour that is commonly used to make breads in North Africa, which may be difficult to obtain; if so, bread flour can be substituted (the liquid in the recipe may need slight adjustment).

YIELD: 6 harsha disks (approximately 6–7 ounces/each)

COOKING TECHNIQUE: Griddling or Panfrying

PROCEDURE

1. Combine the dried yeast and 2 oz of milk, and set aside to allow the yeast to bloom.

2. Rub the softened butter into the fine semolina using clean hands, until the butter is completely incorporated into the flour.

3. Work the remaining ingredients into the flour mixture (add the milk last, and only enough to make a smooth, pliable dough—a different amount may be required if you are using bread flour).

4. Knead the dough by hand or with a dough hook until it is smooth and elastic.

5. Set the dough aside, and allow it to rest for 20 minutes before proceeding.

6. Preheat the griddle (if using one) to 350°F.

7. Divide the dough into 6 even-sized balls, and roll out each of the dough balls to 1/4-inch-thick pieces.

8. If you are using a skillet, heat it over a medium-low flame (if using a griddle, set at 350°F), and add just enough vegetable oil to coat the surface of the pan (or griddle); fry the dough in the oil until it is golden and crisp.

9. Turn the dough over and repeat on the other side (you probably will have to add more oil to allow for even cooking and crispness).

10. Remove from pan and season with salt to taste.

Charmoula NORTH AFRICA
(SPICED MARINADE FOR FISH AND POULTRY)

INGREDIENTS

1	oz	Garlic, minced
3	oz	Preserved Lemon
1/2	tsp	Saffron
1.5	Tbsp	Cumin Seeds, toasted and crushed
1	tsp	Ginger, ground
1	oz	Fresh Red Chili, minced
2	tsp	Salt
6	oz	Extra Virgin Olive Oil
1	lb	Yellow Onions, grated
3	Tbsp	Cilantro, minced
3	Tbsp	Parsley, minced

Charmoula is commonly used to marinate and season fish, as well as lighter meats such as chicken or quail, and is common throughout North Africa. When you marinate with this mixture, be sure to include some of the marinade in the actual cooking of the foods for maximum flavor (fresh marinade often is used as an ingredient in the dish, in which case extra marinade can be made for that purpose). This marinade combined with fish, tomatoes, and peppers would make a traditional Spanish-influenced fish tagine commonly found in Morocco (monkfish are an excellent choice for this preparation).

YIELD: 24 ounces, or enough to marinate 6 pounds of fish or chicken

MIXING TECHNIQUE: Emulsifying Using a Mortar and Pestle

PROCEDURE

1. Using a mortar and pestle, grind together the garlic, preserved lemon (use the whole lemon, including the rind), saffron, toasted cumin seeds, ginger, fresh chiles, and salt until a paste is achieved.

2. Once a paste is achieved, start to slowly add half of the olive oil, alternating with half of the grated onion, to make a thick paste.

3. Remove all of the contents of the mortar and transfer them to a mixing bowl; add the remaining grated onion and fresh herbs, and slowly pour the remaining olive oil into this mixture.

4. Allow the mixture to sit for at least an hour before cooking with it (if it is to be used as a marinade, allow the marinating process to proceed for at least an hour).

5. Use this marinade on lean fish, and cook the fish along with the marinade for maximum flavor.

Couscous NORTH AFRICA
(STEAMED SEMOLINA GRAINS)

INGREDIENTS

1.5	lbs	Couscous, raw (not packaged par-cooked variety)
2	cups	Ice-Cold Water
7	oz	Unsalted Butter
1	cup	Ice-Cold Water
2	Tbsp	Salt

Couscous is a staple of North African cuisine and is frequently eaten with tagines and other stewed foods. It is also used to make a number of sweets and can be mixed with vegetables and other ingredients to make salads. The couscous used in North Africa is not par-cooked, as are many U.S. varieties (often found in boxes) that yield a very different textured product. This recipe is written for raw couscous.

YIELD: 3.5 pounds cooked couscous, or 10 portions (5–6 ounces/portion)

COOKING TECHNIQUE: Steaming

(continues)

Couscous
(continued)

SPECIAL EQUIPMENT

Couscousier, or steamer setup with fine screen or mesh bottom

Couscous cooking in steamer setup (a piece of equipment called a *couscousier* can be used as well)

Rubbing couscous granules together after first addition of water to separate the grains prior to cooking the couscous

Working the butter into the couscous after it has been steamed once

PROCEDURE

1. Set up couscousier for steaming either using water in the bottom or by making a stew in the bottom section (if you are not using a couscousier, set up a steamer).

2. Combine the raw couscous and 2 cups of ice-cold water in a pot, and let them sit for 20 minutes to allow the grains to start to hydrate (the couscous will turn into a solid mass during this process).

3. Turn the couscous out into a large bowl and, using clean hands, rub the granules together until all of the grains separate from one another.

4. Place the separated couscous into the top of the couscousier or steamer setup; steam over the water or the stew cooking in the lower section.

5. Steam the couscous uncovered in the top section for 25 minutes; remove the couscous from the couscousier and turn it out into a large bowl.

6. Divide the butter into two equal portions and the remaining ice water into two equal portions.

7. Sprinkle 4 oz of the ice water (one of the divided portions) over the couscous, and then add half of the salt. Using clean fingers, work 3.5 oz (one of the divided portions) of butter into the couscous grains by rubbing them with your fingers and spreading them simultaneously.

8. Allow the couscous to sit for 15 minutes, and then rub the couscous again to separate the grains; return it to the couscousier or steamer setup, and steam (uncovered) again for 20 minutes.

9. Once the couscous has steamed for the second time, turn it out into a bowl and follow step 7 again: add the ice water, salt, and butter to the couscous, and rub to separate the grains.

10. Once again, allow the couscous to sit for 15 minutes, and then rub to separate the grains before returning it to the steamer.

11. Return the couscous to the steamer for the final steaming, and steam until the couscous is cooked (it should be tender, just past al dente, but not mushy at all).

12. Once the couscous is cooked, remove it from the steamer setup and adjust seasoning, if necessary, with salt and butter.

NOTE: *This may seem like a lot of work when you could just boil packaged couscous, but the results are quite different. Couscous made in this way has a much lighter and more desirable texture and flavor from working the salt and butter into the grain as it cooks. This method is much easier than it sounds and, once you have done it a couple of times, the only adjustment is planning the time needed to make it from start to finish.*

Tagine Lham bil Zitun wa L'hamd Mrakad ✗
(LAMB TAGINE WITH OLIVES AND PRESERVED LEMON)

INGREDIENTS

2	oz	Olive Oil
4	lbs	Lamb Stew Meat, cut into 1-inch cubes and seasoned with salt and pepper
2	lbs	Yellow Onions, diced medium
2	tsp	Saffron
2	tsp	Black Pepper
2	tsp	Salt
2	qts	Water
1	Tbsp	Fresh Oregano, minced
2	Tbsp	Parsley, minced (about 1/2 bunch)
4	oz	Preserved Lemon, seeds removed and sliced 1/4 inch thick
6	oz	Pitted Green Olives
2	Tbsp	Extra Virgin Olive Oil
1	tsp	Fresh Oregano, minced
1	Tbsp	Fresh Parsley, minced
		Salt, to taste

Tagines are one of the most unique and distinct aspects of North African cuisine, and this recipe also includes another unique aspect in its use of salt-preserved lemons. A *tagine* is the name of a conical-shaped earthenware container that is traditionally used to make this type of stew in North Africa. If a tagine is available, use it to make this dish (depending on its size, you may need to scale the recipe to fit)—they lend a certain quality to these stews that cannot be replicated in metal pans. The traditional way to cook this stew is by placing it in the embers of a settling fire and then tending to provide even heat as it cooks, resulting in a rich and flavorful dish.

YIELD: 12 portion (8 ounces/portion)

COOKING METHOD: Stewing

PROCEDURE

1. Heat the olive oil in a large, heavy-bottomed skillet over a medium-high flame, and sear seasoned lamb cubes until they are well caramelized on all sides (taking care not to burn fronds in the pan).
2. Add the onions to the pan, lower the heat, and sweat until onions become soft and translucent.
3. Add saffron, black pepper, and salt to the pan, and continue to cook over a higher flame to bring out the flavors of the spices (about 2–3 minutes).
4. Add the water to the pan, and bring the mixture to a simmer over a medium flame; add oregano and parsley, and simmer uncovered for 1 hour to develop flavor.
5. Add the preserved lemon and olives, and continue to simmer for 15–20 minutes.
6. Finish with extra virgin olive oil, fresh oregano, and parsley, and season with salt.

NOTE: *The resulting tagine is traditionally served with couscous (see preceding recipe).*

Tagine lham bil zitun wa l'hamd mrakad (lamb tagine with olives and preserved lemons), served with couscous in a traditional tagine vessel

Zaalouk MOROCCO
(EGGPLANT AND TOMATO PURÉE)

INGREDIENTS

For Roasting the Eggplant

4	lbs	Eggplant
1.5	qts	Water
4	oz	Lemon Juice

For Stewing the Tomatoes

2	oz	Olive Oil
2	oz	Garlic, minced
1	Tbsp	Paprika
2	tsp	Cumin, ground
1	tsp	Salt
2	lbs	Tomato Concassée

For Making the Zaalouk

		Roasted and Cleaned Eggplant (see above)
		Stewed Tomatoes (see above)
4	oz	Extra Virgin Olive Oil
2	Tbsp	Parsley, minced
3	Tbsp	Cilantro, minced
		Salt, to taste

The eggplant is a favorite vegetable of Moroccan cuisine, and it can be found in a variety of dishes—including this purée, which would be eaten with bread as a starter.

YIELD: 4 pounds, or enough for 16 people as a starter with bread (4 ounces/person)

COOKING TECHNIQUE (EGGPLANT): Roasting

COOKING TECHNIQUE (TOMATO): Stewing

MIXING TECHNIQUE (ZAALOUK): Puréeing or Crushing

PROCEDURE

For Roasting the Eggplant

1. Preheat the oven to 425°F.

2. Pierce each eggplant with a paring knife in ten (or so) spaced-apart spots to prevent it from exploding in the oven.

3. Place the pierced eggplants on a baking sheet covered with aluminum foil, and place the sheet pan in the oven; roast until the eggplants are very tender and shriveled (about 45 minutes).

4. Once the eggplants are tender, remove them from the oven and place them on a cooling rack to cool enough to be handled.

5. Combine the water and lemon juice, and set aside.

6. Once the eggplants have cooled enough to be handled, peel them and place the inner pulp into the water and lemon juice to prevent discoloration; set aside.

For Stewing the Tomatoes

1. In a sauté pan (or a small pot) large enough to hold the tomatoes, heat the olive oil over a medium-low flame.

2. Once the oil has gotten hot, add the minced garlic and spices; gently sweat/fry them until the garlic becomes translucent.

3. Add the tomato concassée, and continue to cook over a medium-low flame until the mixture becomes drier and thick.

4. Reduce the heat to a very low flame, and cook this mixture until the tomatoes are very tender (the length of time will vary with the ripeness of the tomatoes; this usually takes between 15 and 20 minutes).

5. Once the tomatoes are tender, remove them from the heat and set aside to cool.

For Making the Zaalouk

1. Be sure to check that the tomato mixture has cooled to room temperature before making the zaalouk (if it hasn't, it can cool more rapidly in the refrigerator).

(continues)

Zaalouk
(continued)

2. Combine the eggplant pulp and tomato mixture in a food processor (this can be made in a mortar and pestle or mashed with a fork, to yield a more authentic and coarse zaalouk—in which case, the oil is worked into the resulting coarse paste); pulse to make a coarse purée while slowly adding the olive oil.

3. Transfer the mixture to a bowl and fold in the minced herbs; adjust seasoning with salt, if necessary.

Mirqaz (Phonetic Arabic) or Merguez (French)   TUNISIA
(SPICED/DRIED LAMB SAUSAGE)

INGREDIENTS

For Making the Sausage Filling

2	lbs	Lamb Shoulder, heavy connective tissue removed (do not remove fat), very cold, and diced large (or into 1/2-inch strips)
1	lb	Lamb Fat, very cold
1	oz	Garlic Cloves, minced
1.5	tsp	Freshly Ground Fennel Seeds
1.5	Tbsp	Harissa (see recipe, this chapter)
1	tsp	Freshly Ground Black Pepper
1	Tbsp	Salt

For Stuffing the Sausages

12	ft	Lamb Casing (you can substitute 6 ft of hog casing if lamb is unavailable)

Merguez sausages are a well-known specialty of Tunisian cuisine, and they are a flavorful component of many traditional recipes. In North Africa, it is common (in fact, preferred) that these sausages be dried in the sun and then packed in jars with olive oil. Sun drying requires a hot and dry climate and proper facilities to protect the drying sausage from infestation; it is not recommended that this be attempted without a complete understanding of risk factors (botulism and contamination are two significant ones). A similar product can be achieved by piercing the prepared links and oven drying them at a very low temperature (200°F) before packing them in oil.

YIELD: 3 pounds

GRINDING TECHNIQUE: Cold Grinding to Create Emulsified Blend

PROCEDURE

For Making the Sausage Filling

1. Sanitize and prechill all metal grinder parts, including both medium and fine plates.

2. Grind the cold lamb shoulder and fat through a medium grinder plate that has been prechilled, and into a metal bowl set atop another bowl filled with ice.

3. Mix the ground meat with all of the seasoning very well, and then pass the mixture through the smaller plate of the grinder and into the chilled metal bowl.

4. Set this mixture in the refrigerator for at least 1 hour to allow the flavors to infuse.

5. In a small sauté pan over medium heat, cook a small amount of the sausage filling and taste for seasoning; if necessary, adjust seasoning with salt and/or harissa.

For Stuffing the Sausages

1. Rinse the casing under clean water to wash off any salt by placing one end over a clean faucet and gently turning on the water.

(continues)

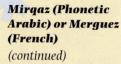

Mirqaz (Phonetic Arabic) or Merguez (French)
(continued)

2. Sanitize the sausage stuffer, and place the sausage mixture inside it; turn the stuffer handle until the sausage reaches the end of the plastic funnel.

3. Place the casing over the end of the plastic funnel by wetting the funnel with water and sliding an open end of the casing over the stuffer; then slide the entire casing length over the plastic funnel, except for the last 6 inches or so, which can be used to tie off the end.

4. Poke a tiny hole in the casing near the tie to release any air in the stuffer and slowly turn the stuffer handle while guiding the casing to form the sausages.

5. Once the sausages are filled they can be used in a variety of ways or cooked by themselves.

Kefta NORTH AFRICA
(SEASONED GROUND BEEF)

INGREDIENTS

For the Seasoned Meat Mixture

2.25	lbs	Ground Lamb or Ground Beef
1	oz	Garlic Cloves
8	oz	Onion, grated
1	Tbsp	Minced Serrano or Jalapeño
1.5	Tbsp	Turmeric
2	Tbsp	Sweet Paprika
1	tsp	Black Pepper
1	Tbsp	Coriander
1	Tbsp	Cumin Seeds
1/2	bunch	Parsley, minced
2	oz	Lemon Juice

For Grilling and Serving

15		Flat Skewers (ideally, you should use skewers with one flat side—these will hold the meat better than thin, round skewers)
8	oz	Salt-Cured Olives
1	lb	Feta Cheese
3/4		Recipe of Couscous, this chapter
1/2	bunch	Parsley, minced

Kefta is used in a number of ways in North African cuisine; for example, it may be formed into cylinders, skewered, and grilled, or formed into balls and cooked in stews. The most common meat used to make kefta in North Africa is lamb, but beef can be used as a substitute.

YIELD: 15 skewers (3 ounces/skewer), or 7.5 portions (2 skewers/portion)

COOKING TECHNIQUE: Grilling

PROCEDURE

For the Seasoned Meat Mixture

1. Combine all of the ingredients in a large mixing bowl, and mix thoroughly using latex gloves or freshly sanitized hands to ensure that all ingredients are well distributed.

2. Set this mixture in the refrigerator to marinate for at least 4 hours (overnight is better).

For Grilling and Serving

(**NOTE:** *Kefta is often cooked on a griddle and could be prepared in that manner if proper skewers are not available.*)

1. Preheat a gas grill or start burning coal/wood for a non-gas grill.

2. Portion the kefta mixture into 15 balls, about 3 oz each, and roll each ball between the palms of two sanitized or glove-covered hands into an elongated cylinder about 4 inches long.

3. Flatten each of these cylinders with your palms, and slide a skewer with a flat side through them (metal flat-sided skewers can be found at ethnic markets).

(continues)

Kefta
(continued)

4. Grill the kefta mixture over very hot coals or the hottest part of a gas grill, turning them as they mark.

5. Once the kefta have been marked on both sides, remove them from the heat and set them in a pan to hold for plating.

6. To serve the kefta, place a mound of couscous on each plate, topped with the feta cheese and cured olives and sprinkled with parsley; place two skewers of grilled kefta on top.

Kefta (seasoned ground lamb) served with couscous, sheep's cheese, and olives

SUMMARY

The cuisine of North Africa is highly regarded because of its uniqueness, and it is often referred to by the Arabic term for "west," *Maghreb*. The cuisine of North Africa has been primarily influenced by the Berber population that existed in this region for centuries, along with strong influences from Arab lands mixed with aspects of southern European cuisines left over from periods of colonial rule.

North African cuisine is noted for its wide use of couscous, lamb, olives, and preserved lemons, and these are all common components of the traditional foods. The most common cooking methods employed in the cuisine include steaming, stewing, and grilling. As in most other Muslim countries, North Africans include flatbreads as a regular part of the meal, and the bread is traditionally used as a utensil to pick up food for eating. North African cuisine is also known for its skillful use of spices; those of both the Mediterranean and Asia are included regularly.

REVIEW QUESTIONS

1. What has been the significance of the Arab influence on North Africa in the development of North African cuisine?

2. What are the most common cooking techniques utilized in North African cooking? Give an example of a North African dish cooked using each technique.

3. Which European countries controlled parts of North Africa, and which were once controlled by North Africa?

4. What is the name of the cooking vessel that has a conical shape and is also the name of the dishes cooked in it?

COMMON TERMS, FOODS, AND INGREDIENTS

The following are some of the more commonly used terms in North African cuisine. Some of the terms are names of ingredients that are central to this cuisine, and others are names of common dishes, equipment, or products used in the local cooking.

✳ Foods/Ingredients

amalou – Paste made from honey, almonds, and olive oil, used as a spread

beghrir (or baghrir) – Spongy pancakes made by street vendors

beldi – Type of olive common to North Africa and often used to make salt-cured olives

bisteeya – Famous dish traditionally consisting of squab, a lemon egg sauce, and sweetened almonds inside thin sheets of warka (thin pastry); this term often is used to describe dishes made with layers of thin pastry filled with meats, fish, etc.

bisteeya bil hout – Version of bisteeya in which seafood is used as the filling and folded between many sheets of thin dough

bkaila – Okra and lamb dish common among the Jews of Tunisia

brik – Type of thin pastry used to make dish of the same name, which is filled with ground lamb, seasonings, and a whole egg, and then panfried

casse croûte tunisien – Tunisian sandwich typically made with a baguette; influenced by the French during the period of their rule

charmoula – Marinade used with fish and poultry to make tagines and other preparations

coclo – Large meatballs made from ground beef or veal with rice and spices

couscous – Small grains of semolina wheat (a hard wheat) made by wetting slightly coarse grounds of the wheat, then coating the grounds in flour and drying them. This results in a grain that is similar in many ways to tiny rounds of pasta that are typically steamed in a particular manner to yield a light-textured grain enjoyed as a regular part of North African diet.

dafina – Stew of Jewish origin that typically contains meat, rice, potatoes, and eggs and is cooked on Friday to be eaten on the holy Saturday

djaj – Chicken

harira – Thick soup made from lentils and chickpeas that is traditionally part of the month-long fasting tradition of the Muslim Ramadan

harissa – Spice paste from Tunisia made from ground chiles, garlic, and spices; used extensively in North Africa as a seasoning

harsha – Flatbread from Morocco

hout – Fish (phonetically also spelled *hut*)

kefta – Spiced and ground lamb

khlii – Sundried and spiced strips of meat

l'hamd mrakad – Preserved lemons made by packing salt into cut whole lemons and aging them in storage containers to yield a softened, salty, and unique lemon preserve that is used as a seasoning for mirqaz *mahia* – Fig and anise liquor traditionally taken on holy Saturdays by Jewish followers

mechoui – Lamb roasted whole on a spit over a fire

merguez – Spiced lamb sausage from Tunisia (also phonetically spelled *mirguez*)

m'hammer – Tagine seasoned with cumin and paprika

m'qualli – Tagine seasoned with saffron and ginger

picholine – Type of small olive common to Morocco (most French picholines are actually grown in Morocco and just packed and labeled in France)

ras-el-hanout – Spice blend commonly used in Moroccan cooking

sabayon – French term for sauce made from egg yolks, sugar, and fortified wine. In this chapter, the term refers to the use of this base in the production of ice cream in Tunisia.

sachet – French term for spices/herbs wrapped in cheesecloth and added to stocks, sauces, or other liquid preparations

salata – Salad

seksu – Berber name for couscous

smen – Aged and spiced clarified butter that is used as a seasoning, especially for couscous

tabikha – Beef and onion stew common among Algerian Jews

tabil – Spice blend commonly used in Tunisian cooking

tagine – Both the name of a type of cooked food and the cooking vessel used to make the food. A tagine is an earthenware dish with a conical shape and a lid making up approximately the top third of the dish, and a flat bottom section that is placed into an oven to cook the contents in a stew-like manner to yield tender dishes also called tagines.

warka (or ourka) – Thin sheets of dough created by slapping soft dough onto a greased pan made especially for this preparation

zaalouk – Moroccan eggplant and tomato purée

zitun – Olive

✳ Cultural Terms/Equipment

couscoussier – Pot and tight-fitting colander combination used to make couscous. The couscous is steamed in the top colander by the food that is cooked in the bottom pot.

ferran – A communal oven used to bake breads; once the ovens cooled from the breads, they were used to make tagines and other stewed or simmered foods. These are much less common in North Africa than they once were but still can be found in smaller villages, where the townspeople can be seen bringing specially marked loaves of breads to the ferran to bake in the manner of their liking.

gedra – The bottom part of a couscousier, where the stew cooks while the couscous steams above

gedra dil trid – Dome-shaped earthenware piece used to stretch the dough to make the pastry for bisteeya; also called *trid*

halal – Foods that are permitted according to the edicts of Islam

haram – Foods that are not permitted according to the edicts of Islam

Islam – Religion that developed in the Middle East and spread to other areas, including North Africa. The religion has a number of dietary restrictions, including the avoidance of pork, shellfish, and fish without scales.

Maghreb – Name for the region of North Africa that includes Morocco, Tunisia, and Algeria. This name derives from the Arabic word for "west."

mashbooh – Foods that are considered questionable, for one reason or another, as to whether they are haram or halal (for example, if lecithin is used in a product, it might not be known whether it derived from a pig or not; thus, it may be considered mashbooh)

Muslim – Follower of the Islamic faith

Ramadan – Month-long fast observed by Muslims; food is avoided during daylight hours, and specific foods are eaten in the evening

Shawwal – Month following Ramadan in the Islamic calendar, during which devoted followers fast for an additional six days

tagine – Clay pot with a conical shape, used to cook stews and bake dishes (or breads) over a fire

tannour – Conical-shaped outdoor clay oven used to bake breads

SECTION 3

CUISINES OF
THE AMERICAS

The Americas are the location of some of the oldest continual cultural cuisines and simultaneously the site of the world's first global fusion cuisines. In parts of Mexico and South America, the cuisine remains strongly linked to how it was 10,000 years ago, whereas in the Caribbean, other sections of South America, and even parts of the United States, foods and techniques from Asia, Africa, the Americas, and Europe have been blended to yield a cuisine that often takes a cultural anthropologist to deconstruct. These aspects make the cuisines of the Americas some of the most promising and exciting in the entire world.

The cuisines of the Americas can in many ways be best explained and described by the cultural groups that have settled in particular areas. This section explores the cuisines of the Caribbean, Mexico, and South America (the cuisines of the United States are well covered by other texts; the regional U.S. variations are a significant feature and are beyond the scope of this text). The cuisines of the three regions covered in this section all have been significantly impacted by Spanish and Native American cultures. Many of the

differences that exist among them can be found in specific Native American cultures from each region. African culture is also featured in the cuisines of the Americas, because the slave trade brought African cooking techniques and foods mainly to the Caribbean and parts of South America (as well as to the United States). The "discovery" of the Americas by Christopher Columbus in 1492 was a watershed moment in culinary history, as the flow of ingredients from the Americas to Europe and Asia—and vice versa—changed the culinary landscape forever.

The Americas have had a tremendous impact on other cuisines; ingredients from the Americas have become common components all over the world. Imagine Irish cuisine without potatoes, Italian cuisine without tomatoes, French desserts without chocolate and vanilla, Thai cuisine without chiles, and Hungarian cuisine without paprika. None of these cuisines would be as they are today had those ingredients not spread from the Americas. Many other ingredients are also indigenous to the Americas, even though

natives of this region often don't realize it. Cashews, pecans, pineapples, many bean varieties (such as black beans, kidney beans, and navy beans), squashes, peanuts, corn, and allspice are ingredients that were once found only in the Americas. All are still used regularly by many cultures, both within the Americas and in other parts of the world. Although examples are widespread of cuisines that use ingredients indigenous to the Americas, the cuisines of the Americas often are more obscure. As can be seen in the following chapters, these cuisines are every bit as enticing as the European cuisines and contain potential that will surely be tapped in the near future by educated chefs in today's market.

Aspiring U.S. chefs should pay close attention to the following chapters, because Latin American food is the fastest growing trend in the United States at the moment. With the Latin American population growing at a faster rate than any other in the United States, this trend is not likely to change.

CHAPTER 12

★ capital city
— region boundary
—·— international boundary

0   250   500 km

MISSISSIPPI ALABAMA GEORGIA
90°   85°
U. S. A.
30°
LOUISIANA

ATLANTIC
OCEAN

FLORIDA

25°

GRAND
BAHAMA   ABACO

ELEUTHERA

THE BAHAMAS (U. K.)

NEW
PROVIDENCE   CAT ISLAND

ANDROS   SAN SALVADOR

GULF
OF
MEXICO

Havana ★

CUBA (SPAIN)

RUM CAY
GREAT   LONG ISLAND
EXUMA   SAMANA CAY
CROOKED ISLAND
LONG CAY   MAYAGUANA
ACKLINS
LITTLE INAGUA

TURKS AND CAICOS
ISLANDS
(U. K.)

CAICOS
ISLANDS   TURK ISLANDS
GREAT INAGUA

ISLA DE LA
JUVENTUD

20°

Yucatan
Peninsula

LITTLE CAYMAN   CAYMAN BRAC
GRAND CAYMAN
CAYMAN
ISLANDS

G R E A T E R   A N T I L L E S

Hispaniola

VIRGIN ISLANDS
(U. S. & U. K.)

ANEGADA

MEXICO

JAMAICA (U. K.)

HAITI
(FRANCE)
Port-au-Prince ★

DOMINICAN
REPUBLIC (SPAIN)

Santo
Domingo

San Juan
★
PUERTO
RICO
(SPAIN)

VIRGIN GORDA
TORTOLA   ANGUILLA
ST. BARTHELEMY
ST. JOHN ST. MARTIN
ST. CROIX   ST. EUSTATIUS
ST. KITTS
NEVIS

BARBUDA

ANTI
BARB
(U. K.)

Kingston   ★

SAINT KITTS AND NEVIS
(U. K.)

ANTIGUA

GUATEMALA

BELIZE

15°

HONDURAS

EL SALVADOR   NICARAGUA

MONTSERRAT
BASSE –TERRE
GUADELOUPE
(FRANCE)

GRA

MARTINIQUE

SAINT LUCIA

CARIBBEAN SEA

SAINT VINCENT
AND THE
GRENADINES
(U. K.)

ST.
B
GREN.
GRENA

10°

COSTA
RICA

CURACAO   BONAIRE

PANAMA

TRINIDAD

VENEZUELA

PACIFIC
OCEAN

5°

COLOMBIA

BRAZIL

0°

ECUADOR

Caribbean Cuisine

OBJECTIVES

Upon completion of this chapter, you will be able to

- identify the major cultures that existed in the Caribbean prior to the arrival of Columbus.
- recognize the ingredients that are indigenous to the Americas.
- discuss the importance of Columbus's voyage to the culture and development of the cuisine in this region.
- discuss the importance of the slave trade in the development of the cuisines of the Caribbean.
- prepare some recipes common to Caribbean cuisine.
- define the terms listed at the conclusion of the chapter.

INTRODUCTION

The Caribbean is home to one of the most significant moments in world culinary history—the landing of Columbus on the island of Hispaniola in 1492—and its cuisine will forever be linked to that day. The period that followed Columbus's landing witnessed a complete overhaul of cuisines all over the world, as ingredients from the Americas reached other parts of the world, and Asian and European ingredients reached the Americas. Out of the Americas came foods like turkey, tomatoes, corn, chiles, potatoes, sweet potatoes, squashes, beans, avocados, pineapples, vanilla, and chocolate. Many of these quickly became common ingredients in both Europe and Asia (chiles and beans), while others took longer to be accepted (tomatoes and potatoes were resisted for decades or more). Conversely, citrus, melons, onions, garlic, cilantro, Asian spices, rice, wheat, domesticated pork, chickens, cows (and thus dairy products), and grapes all were introduced to the cuisines of the Americas. It is hard to think of cuisines on either side of the Atlantic Ocean without each other's products today, but that is exactly what changed. For this reason, the Caribbean will always be known as the birthplace of a dramatic change in foods worldwide.

Just as the Caribbean is known internationally for this influence, it should also be known for its cultural diversity. The Caribbean is a melting pot of peoples and cultures that has developed into a completely new culture, blending influences that have played important roles in the stages of history that led to today.

HISTORIC CULINARY INFLUENCES

The Caribbean has been a hotbed of interest since Columbus first landed there at the end of the fifteenth century. The period of history that followed the European introduction to the Caribbean is pretty well documented by the colonizing countries of Spain, France, England, the Netherlands, Denmark, and Portugal; however, the period that preceded the arrival of the Europeans is a subject of scholarly debate. What is known is that people lived in these islands for thousands of years before the Europeans arrived, and these people had a complex system of procuring their main foods. Any information procured from descriptions of the early days of the European arrival should be examined with the knowledge that the Europeans who wrote them held a decidedly "Western" point of view; their perceptions of how the natives of the Caribbean lived were often warped by this mentality.

Pre-European Contact

The records of this time period aren't in a written format but exist mainly via oral histories, fossil evidence, and other archeological discoveries that provide some detail about the people of the Caribbean (and their diet) prior to the arrival of the Europeans. There were two main societies that existed in the Caribbean when the Europeans arrived—one of which the islands are named after now: the Caribs. The others were the Arawaks (the Caribbean segment of this society was also known as Taino, and smaller tribe segments existed as well). Their heritage is less clear, but there is linguistic evidence that they were related to Native South Americans and came to the Caribbean via present-day Venezuela or Guyana.

These cultures were known to cultivate a number of foods that are thought to have been transported from South America either by the people themselves, or by winds, birds, or other means of natural travel. The foods that were found on the islands at the time of European contact included cassava, squash, corn, beans, potatoes, chiles, and sweet potatoes. Their meals also consisted of a significant amount of local fruits that thrived in this tropical climate, including papaya, guava, mamay, cherimoya, cashew fruit, and pineapple, which—together with the starchy local vegetables—made up the majority of their diet. In addition to the fruits and vegetables, the Arawaks and Caribs also hunted for local animals and were very accomplished fishermen. Many of the common types of seafood in this region today—such as *conch*, crabs, spiny lobsters, oysters, sea bass, *grouper*, *cascadura*, and other shore fish—were also eaten by the natives.

The Europeans who arrived didn't realize that the local people had a much better understanding of the climate and available foods than they did upon arrival, and that much could be learned from these people. The indigenous people of the Caribbean were very accomplished fishermen, developing techniques for catching fish that included spear fishing, mashing (a technique in which bait fish were crushed and added to the water to attract larger fish), trapping, and even poisoning, in which the fishermen would poison the water using a plant that is harmless to humans but would kill or stun the fish. There is even evidence that the islanders used a particular fish called a *remora* (also called a suckerfish)—a parasite that attaches itself to other fish—to catch other fish and turtles by connecting them to a line and then reeling the line back in after the fish had found a prey.

However, the Europeans who arrived noticed few of the talents of these people but instead saw them as a primitive group they had a right to use as laborers and convert into European thinkers. The result was catastrophic and became one of the greatest tragedies in history, as these populations were virtually wiped out (a few native tribes remain in small pockets on a few of the islands today). They left behind traces of their heritage in some words still used today (for example, Aruba, Xaymaca—spoken and spelled "Jamaica"), and in what has become the most American of cooking methods. *Brabacot* was the Arawak (or, more precisely, the Taino faction of the Arawak) term for cooking meats by fire, a term that became the Spanish *barbacoa* and eventually the English barbeque (later abbreviated as BBQ in the United States). The native Arawaks also practiced farming techniques that used what were call *conucos*, mounds of loose earth that grew a variety of food plants. The Europeans thought this farming was very primitive and sought to change the techniques, only to find out years later that this was actually productive in the tropical and sometimes harsh climate of the Caribbean (later on, much was learned about this method that has been utilized in the composting techniques of today).

Another ingenious use of food was the natives' use of the bitter cassava, a poisonous food in its raw state, which was ground to a flour after being squeezed of its juice multiple times. Cassava became a reliable source of starch, and its juice was used as poison for dipping arrows or it was boiled down with seasonings to make *cassareep* (a condiment of sorts; cooking reduces the toxicity of the cassava significantly). Cassareep has been used in the Caribbean to cook and preserve meats, and versions of cassareep stew have been reportedly cooked for years, with constant additions of more ingredients.

The indigenous peoples clearly had a good understanding of their environment and how to yield nourishment from it. Tragically, only small populations of these people remain in the Caribbean, although their traditions live on in many aspects of the Caribbean culture today.

European Colonization

When Columbus landed in the Bahamas in 1492, he set off a deluge of exploration of what is now known as the Caribbean Islands not only by Spanish explorers but by the Dutch, British, French, and Portuguese as well. These newcomers encountered the native peoples of the islands and, using their weapons and numbers, forced the European way of life onto them—including their foods and cooking methods (they also used and adapted many of the ingredients they found in this new world). Some of the ingredients that the Europeans brought to the Caribbean included pork, beef, chickens, onions, garlic, almonds, sugar, citrus, mangoes, coconuts, olives, olive oil, capers, grapes, figs, and wheat, many of which are components of the islands' cuisine today. In addition to these ingredients, the Europeans brought with them many of the methods that are commonly used today. Deep frying, sautéing, and baking or roasting were all introduced to the islands at this time; of these methods, deep frying is perhaps the most commonly associated with modern Caribbean cooking.

The colonization of the islands was perpetrated for a couple different reasons, the most significant being the introduction of plantations and also as ports for distributing supplies and labor to Mexico, South America, and Central America. The formation of plantations is still a dominant feature of the Caribbean today, where sugarcane, tobacco, and coffee have all at one point been the focus of the plantation system. Of these, sugar and sugar plantations were the most significant and, throughout much of the Caribbean, sugar plantations still dominate the landscape. The early efforts by the Europeans to force the native population to work on the plantations turned into one of the great tragedies of history; most of the populations of these islands died during this period from a combination of disease (the natives had never been exposed to the viruses that the Europeans unknowingly carried), poor treatment, conditions forced on them by the invading Europeans, or murder

at their hands. In order to operate the plantations, the European powers (Dutch, French, Spanish, and English) imported slaves to work in them; this would prove to have a significant influence on the development of the Caribbean cuisine.

West Africans

As the European colonizers took hold of the islands of the Caribbean, they developed plantations there to supply goods to their homelands (and also for profit). The Europeans were not happy with the production of the native Caribbean people, whom they enslaved, and most of the natives died shortly after the arrival of the Europeans. As a result, they looked to Africa to supply more slaves to tend to their plantations. The Caribbean would in a short time become the leading production area in the world for sugarcane, rum, and tobacco, and this industry was driven by the importation of slaves from West Africa.

The imported slaves from West Africa brought with them their culinary roots as well as seeds, which would become crops for the newly arriving population. Some of the ingredients that the Africans supplied were black-eyed peas, okra, taro root, sweet potatoes, yams, *ackee*, peanuts, and plantains, and these ingredients combined with those already in use became frequent ingredients of the local Caribbean diet. Ironically, some of these ingredients are indigenous to the Americas, and it was the circle of the slave trade that brought them back and reintroduced them to the local diet after the near extermination of the Caribbean Native Americans. Peanuts and sweet potatoes were introduced to Africa by the Portuguese, and the African slaves subsequently reintroduced them to the Americas. In addition to these starchy foods, the main protein source outside of vegetables was salt cod, which was a major commodity in the area that included the northeastern United States and Europe, supplying what was at that time one of the least expensive forms of preserved meats and seafood.

It is important to understand that, between the 1600s and 1800s, millions of slaves were imported into the Caribbean from Africa; as a result, Africa was one of the dominant cultures to influence Caribbean culinary traditions. Although these slaves didn't have the rights and freedoms of others, their sheer numbers and the fact that they were typically the cooks ensured that African traditions became Caribbean traditions. This is especially true in the areas of Caribbean in which African slaves were concentrated. In Cuba, the

Dominican Republic, and Puerto Rico, there were greater concentrations of Spanish, European indentured servants, Native Americans, and non-African laborers, which resulted in less African influence in these areas. Most of the rest of the Caribbean, however, was heavily influenced by African cookery.

In the areas of the strongest African influence, one common food is *callaloo*, a traditional dish from sub-Saharan Africa that is essentially a stew or soup made with a green leafy vegetable called callaloo (which is often replaced by other greens, such as chard or spinach). *Coocoo* and *foo-foo* are two more common dishes found in these areas, both of which often are eaten with okra; coocoo combines coconut milk and cornmeal, and foo-foo is made from mashed plantains, yams, or cassava, highlighting the importance of these vegetable in African cooking. Another common dish is *dunkanoo*, which is made from grated vegetables that are turned into either a sweet or a savory dough wrapped in banana leaves, and are boiled or steamed to yield something that looks like a tamale (Mexican wrapped corn dough) but is quite different in its usage and taste. Many of these traditions are firmly based in African culinary methods, where foods were often pounded into a dough/paste to be eaten with other ingredients, typically in stewed fashion.

Several of the traditional dishes that reveal the African influence are simpler soups, stews, or mashes that not only tell a story of a connection with Africa but also speak to the ingenuity and perseverance of these proud people who made foods during a period of complete deprivation that are still prized today. The African-influenced dishes of the Caribbean bear an obvious resemblance and spirit to those known as "soul food" in the United States, and the history of slavery surely plays a role in this connection.

East Indians and Chinese Laborers

The historical movements that resulted in the abolition of slavery brought about the next wave of cultural influence in the Caribbean. Following the French revolution at the end of the eighteenth century, the revolts in Haiti began the decline of slavery in the Caribbean. In the middle of the nineteenth century, slavery was abolished in Great Britain, and, as a result, a need for inexpensive labor began the importation of Asians into the Caribbean to work the plantations that the African slaves previously had tended to exclusively. Toward the end of the nineteenth century, Spain also abolished slavery, and Asians were again imported as indentured servants to take the place of African slaves working the plantations. The immigrants looking for an opportunity in a new land brought with them the culinary traditions from their homes, and these traditions were incorporated into the Caribbean diet. Some of the important introductions included rice, spices and spice blends, noodles, ginger, goat as a staple meat, and *roti* (a type of Indian flatbread). All of these influences are still seen in the Caribbean today, as curried dishes, the use of ginger and roti, and the reliance on goat are significant aspects of their current culinary traditions. The most concentrated area of this influence is found on the once British-controlled islands of Trinidad and Tobago, where a large percentage of the population is descended from Asian immigrants.

UNIQUE COMPONENTS

The Caribbean is perhaps the world's most diverse cuisine; the cuisines of Europe, Africa, and Asia have converged in this region of the Americas to evolve into a new cuisine that borrows from all of these areas.

Cultural Melting Pot

The Caribbean is one of the greatest cultural melting pots in the world. Represented in the ethnic makeup of the islands are descendents from all of the European countries that colonized areas of the Caribbean, as well as a large population with African heritage (as a result of the slave trade) and Asian immigrants from India and China. These cultures all intertwined in a foreign land and cooked with new ingredients to yield one of the most exciting cuisines in the world.

The Spanish word *crillo*, meaning "native" or "indigenous," is the origin of the now common term *Creole*, which refers to the blend of cultures and cuisines in this part of the world. It is believed that this term was first meant to describe the mixing of indigenous foods with the techniques of Spain and France, the two major early influences in the Caribbean. This term came to mean more in the ensuing years, as African slaves brought their culinary traditions to the region, and the term is now typically used to describe the cuisine that includes elements of African, European, Asian, and American cuisines.

Although cross-cultural influences exist in many parts of the world, nowhere are they essentially the genesis of the local cuisine except in the Caribbean. The Caribbean is unique in that there are few remnants of the indigenous peoples in the region, and a new cuisine has developed that draws from the cultures that replaced the indigenous culture, while still utilizing many of the indigenous ingredients. Even in the United States, where a similar occurrence has seen segments of the indigenous peoples nearly exterminated or isolated (i.e., the Native American reservation system), the "new" cuisine that has developed mostly comprises imported traditions (Italian cuisine, German cuisine, British cuisine, etc.) that have remained isolated from one another; only recently has a "fusion" of these cuisines occurred—with the exception of the southeastern United States, where a similar Creole culture developed.

Many influences are identifiable in the cuisine of the Caribbean, including Indian roti (flatbread), Spanish *croquettes* (breaded and fried thickened milk with various savory additions), British *pasties* (baked meat-filled dough), French *crème anglaise* (egg-thickened sweet cream), Native American *tamales* (steamed, wrapped corn dough), African *gumbo* (stew with okra), and more; nearly every country contributes in some regard. What is different about these foods is that they often are culturally combined in the Caribbean: the tamales are called *hallacas* and have olives and capers in the stuffing, the roti is served with hot pepper sauce, the gumbo contains tomatoes and cassava, and the crème anglaise is called *coquimol* and is made using coconut milk instead of cream and milk. These are just a few examples of the blending of cultures in the Caribbean that has played a prominent role in the development of the local cuisine. The traditions of the country of origin are often ignored, and an attitude of "whatever works" prevails in the relaxed atmosphere of the Caribbean.

Making Do

The cultural philosophy of the Caribbean is "making do," or surviving using whatever resources are available. This way of thinking is clearly linked to the brutal years of the slave trade, when the majority of the population was severely restricted in its access to foods. Although the Caribbean is a grower's paradise, it certainly wasn't a paradise for those who toiled in the fields and were given only simple and inexpensive foods to eat. Much of the island land was turned into living factories to produce the sugarcane, tobacco, and—to a lesser extent—fruits and coffee that the colonists desired. Slaves were given neither the time nor the means to fish, hunt, or do much else to supple-

ment their diets; as a result, their approach to cooking was to make do with whatever was available. With little means but an apparent unquenchable spirit, these slaves recreated and reinvented the cuisine of their homeland and not only made do but laid the foundation of a new cuisine.

Many of the colonists had slaves cook their meals for them. Because the colonists were used to certain foods from Europe, they expected the slaves to use those same foods in their cooking. However, because most of the slaves came from Africa, they cooked European and New World products with African spices, using African methods, and sometimes even cooking African products using European techniques. This blending of cultures was the beginning of a cuisine that includes multiple cultural backgrounds. The slaves made do at home for their families with the products that were available, and the colonists/slave owners made do without their native homeland chefs; thus, a new blend of cuisines emerged.

The impact on the local culinary culture was to encourage the fusion of products, techniques, and alterations of traditional recipes. As a result, there are many examples in Caribbean cuisine of blended foods, completely new dishes that use whatever ingredients are available, and traditional foods that are altered with new ingredients. This is one of the aspects of Caribbean cuisine that many enjoy, as new interpretations of dishes and ingredients that blur traditional culture lines are part of the norm of the island cuisines.

Tropical Fruits and Nuts

The climate of the Caribbean is tropical, and thus the ingredients that flourish here are different from those in temperate, arid, or arctic climates in other parts of the world. This tropical climate was a significant factor in how the islands were targeted and developed by European nations. The climate not only supported the growth of sugarcane, tobacco, and coffee—the main crops of the colonists' plantation systems—but also many other prized tropical fruits and nuts.

This tropical climate supports the growth of fruits such as papayas, mangoes, ackee, tamarind, guava, avocados, pineapples, *carambola* (also called star fruit), bananas, plantains, and *soursop*, as well as a number of nuts, including coconuts and cashews. Papayas, guava, avocados, pineapples, and cashews are all indigenous to the Caribbean and were common parts of the diet of the native Caribs and Taino; many other tropical fruits (and coconuts) indigenous to Asia were introduced by the Spanish and Portuguese. The inclusion of tropical fruits in the Caribbean diet and cuisine is another unique component of this region.

Barbeque (Brabacot or Barbacoa)

Barbecue, the term so commonly used in the United States to denote foods cooked in the smoke of an open flame, actually derives from a method of Caribbean indigenous cooking. The Arawak people of the Caribbean preserved meats by smoking and cooking them over green wood in a method that they referred to as brabacot (phonetic spelling), which the arriving Spanish translated as *barbacoa*. This was later translated into English as barbeque, or the common abbreviation BBQ. Regardless of the spelling, the root of this term and its association with cooking or preserving foods in the smoke of a fire comes from the Caribbean, where this method is still employed today. One of the most well-known examples of this type of cooking that still exists in the Caribbean is the *jerk* cooking of Jamaica (see the section in this chapter on Jamaica for more information about this method).

Former Colonial Powers

One of the distinct aspects of Caribbean cuisine is how each island was influenced by a former colonial power, and how noticeable the influence is when moving from one island to the next. Language may be the most obvious of the influences left by the European countries that once controlled the islands, but the culture of each island has been affected in many other ways as well. Inherited customs include English tea, French morning coffee and pastry, and stews and soups found in the Spanish-controlled islands. This element of the culture is evident throughout the Caribbean, where the former colonizers left an indelible imprint on the customs of the people (whether the islanders descended from the colonizers or not).

The islands once controlled by the British include Bermuda, the Bahamas, the Virgin Islands, Turks and Caicos, the Cayman Islands, Jamaica, Antigua, Barbuda, Anguilla, Saint Kitts, Nevis, Montserrat, Dominica, Saint Lucia, Saint Vincent, the Grenadine Islands, Barbados, Granada, and Trinidad and Tobago. Some of these islands retain stronger evidence of the British period than others; the British imported a very large number of slaves, and the African and Asian influences often overshadow that of the former colonists. Many slave dishes are dominant culinary features of these islands, and in Trinidad and Tobago, the large number of Indian immigrants had a significant influence on the foods commonly found there. Stews are common throughout these islands, and souse and curry preparations are frequently used.

The islands once controlled by the Spanish include the three biggest islands in the Caribbean: Cuba, Puerto Rico, and the larger section of Hispaniola known as the Dominican Republic (the other part is Haiti, which the French were able to maintain control over during the colonial period). These islands that were once colonies of Spain have the strongest cultural ties to the former colonizer of all of the Caribbean islands. Spain was the first country to come to the Caribbean, and many Spanish people moved into the Caribbean during this period. The vast majority of Spanish people who came to these islands were men, and they often formed families with either Native peoples or, to a greater extent, African slaves. This history resulted in many Spanish customs becoming a strong part of the character of these islands. The Spanish traditions of making stews, frying foods, and rice cookery are all common components of the local cuisines.

The islands that were once controlled by the French include Haiti, Martinique, Guadeloupe, Saint Martin, and Saint Barthélemy. The French influence on these islands is evident in the special shops that sell baguettes and pastry products. These French influences are often offset by African-inspired foods and starches, and mashed foods are common as well.

The islands that the Dutch once controlled include Aruba, Bonaire, Curaçao, and Sint Maarten. The cuisine of these Dutch-influenced islands is notable for its use of Dutch cheeses (such as Gouda) in the cooking, as well as for the Indonesian influences that are a result of the Dutch colonization of part of Indonesia during the time that they controlled these islands.

SIGNIFICANT SUBREGIONS

The Caribbean is generally separated into two main sections geographically: the Greater Antilles, including the four major islands of Cuba, Hispaniola, Puerto Rico, and Jamaica, which together make up 80% of the land mass of the Caribbean; and the Lesser Antilles, a collection of islands that arch from off the coast of Venezuela up toward the Greater Antilles. The Bahamas are also included in this section of the text, as they are culturally and geographically very similar to these sections and are located just north and east of the Greater Antilles.

The Bahamas

A chain of approximately 700 islands makes up the northernmost section of the Caribbean, collectively called the Bahamas—a name meaning "low water" that was given to the area by the first European to land there, Christopher Columbus. Although these islands originally were inhabited by Native Americans, the natives were deported to the island of Hispaniola within a few short decades to work as slaves when the Spanish discovered gold there. Most of the Bahamian heritage today comes from Africa, Spain, France, and Britain. The Bahamas were a British colony during the colonial era, and thus many of the influences here are British, African, or native Arawak.

This region is well known for queen conch, which has been overharvested and is now protected (and farmed). Historically, queen conch has either been eaten raw, similar to ceviche; deep fried, in which case it is known as cracked conch; or minced and turned into fritters or chowder. Other local seafood ingredients include spiny lobsters, land crabs, and tropical fish. In addition to the abundant seafood available on the islands, fresh fruits are plentiful and include the sought-after Eleuthera pineapple as well as other tropical treats such as mangoes, passion fruit, guava, *jujube* (a small, apple like-fruit), and coconuts; all are used in making drinks and can often be found in savory dishes.

As for the dishes that are most common here—besides those that include the conch or other seafood—a number of other components reveal the strong African influence in this region. Grits are a common starch to accompany foods or to be combined with pigeon peas to make that most Caribbean of combinations (typically beans and rice, but in this case the African imported pigeon pea, which arrived in Africa via Asia, takes the part of the pulse). *Souse* is another Bahamian favorite that includes a lime-flavored meat broth with onions, peppers, and celery along with pig's feet or pigs head.

The Bahamas have become a major tourist attraction, and today there are many continental restaurants that cater to tourists, but the soul food of the Bahamas can still be found simmering on the stoves in the islanders' kitchens.

Cuba

Cuba is the largest of the Caribbean islands and is also the largest tropical archipelago in the western hemisphere. This island was home to the Taino Native Americans (a subculture of the Arawaks) prior to the arrival of the Spanish, who turned the island into a major port and shipping point for products of the Americas after their arrival in 1492. Cuba has had a long history of Spanish control, and Spanish is the national language. As with many other parts of the Caribbean, major parts of this island were dedicated to the production of plantation crops of sugarcane and tobacco.

Cuban cuisine differs from other Caribbean cuisines in a number of ways; for example, there is much less use of chiles in Cuba than in other Caribbean areas. Instead, a greater emphasis is placed on herbs and spices for flavor. The Spanish *sofrito* (slow-cooked onions, garlic, tomatoes, peppers, and seasonings) is used, as are garlic, onion, and sometimes cilantro, or another herb not seen much in the United States called *recao*; oregano and cumin are common seasonings as well. Although beans are eaten throughout the Caribbean, in Cuba the black bean is eaten most often. Many varieties of sandwiches are common in Cuba, and their popularity as a street snack is unique to this island. The most common sandwich is made with *pan Cubano* (Cuban bread) and includes roasted pork, ham, cheese, and pickles.

Other common Cuban dishes include *alcaparrado* (a fried banana and taro batter filled with spiced meat), the Spanish-influenced *croquetas* (breaded and fried thick milk dough with various added ingredients), *palomilla* (a thin cut of bottom round marinated in adobe or mojo), *Moros y Cristianos* ("Moors and Christians" is the name given to the combination of black beans and rice that is common in Cuba), *boliche* (beef stuffed with chorizo, a type of spicy pork sausage), and *mojo*, which is used as a marinade and often as a sauce; its chief ingredients are Seville oranges (sour or bitter oranges), garlic, cumin, and olive oil.

This cuisine is gaining in popularity in Miami, where a significant Cuban population yearns to recreate the classics they were raised with. The cuisine of parts of Florida is sometimes called Floribbian because the influence from the Caribbean—and Cuba, in particular—is so evident.

Hispaniola: Haiti and the Dominican Republic

Haiti, the west side of the island of Hispaniola, was controlled by the French from the seventeenth century to the beginning of the nineteenth century. In 1804, slave revolts led to the independence of Haiti, and periods of resulting dictatorships have often plagued the development of this country in the years since. The cuisine of Haiti is a mixture of African and French-inspired dishes. Some dishes show a clear connection with French techniques, such as coquimol (coconut crème anglaise), *boulette* (bread-bound meatballs), and *béchamel* sauce (thickened milk sauce), whereas others are clearly of African descent, such as *pesées* (twice-fried plantains). Many foods probably originated in Haiti, where these cultures collided in a new world and new ingredients became available to both. For example, *sauce ti-malice* (chili-spiced sauce) and *riz et pois colles* (rice with kidney beans) both rely on ingredients from the Americas. Other notable aspects of the cuisine of Haiti include its highly prized mushrooms from the hills, called *djon djon* mushrooms, and its excellent blackberries.

Dominican Republic

As the site of Columbus's arrival in the Caribbean, there has been a strong Spanish influence in the Dominican Republic ever since. The Dominican Republic was also ruled by Haitian dictators for a period after claiming independence from Spain in 1821 before struggling for complete independence 23 years later. The connection with Spanish colonists is clear in Spanish-inspired foods such as the *longaniza sausage*, pastries including *pastelitos* (fried savory pastries), and numerous examples of stewed dishes (*sancocho*, a stew of mixed tubers and meats, is one of the most common). Rice and black beans are also quite common. Rice cookery includes *locrio* (rice cooked with poultry or fish) and *asopao* (rice cooked to a soupy consistency), as well as the *moro* style (rice cooked with beans).

Puerto Rico

Located to the east of the larger island of Hispaniola, Puerto Rico was one of the Spanish-held islands of the Caribbean until 1898, when it was ceded to the United States following the Spanish-American War. There are still significant signs of Spanish influence in the cuisine, and these influences are blended with African and native Taino influences to constitute what is known locally as *cocina criolla*. This blended cuisine is similar to that which is found in Cuba and the Dominican Republic.

Many examples of Spanish-influenced foods exist in the cuisine of Puerto Rico—for example, the use of sofrito to start stews, sauces, and soups, as well as the application of *adobe* (spice rub) to meats for a marinade. The combination of rice and beans in many meals is also very common at Puerto Rican tables, and this also can be attributed to the Spanish period of influence.

Jamaica

Jamaica is located south of Cuba and west of Hispaniola in the Caribbean Sea. This island is well known in the United States for the Rastafarian culture that developed here, and the vegetarian aspect of that culture has a notable influence on the local cuisine. Jamaica was historically one of the major sugar plantations in the Caribbean and had a tumultuous history after the arrival of Europeans and the resulting extermination of the local Arawak people.

After Columbus's arrival in the Caribbean, Spain claimed Jamaica as part of the growing Spanish colonial system and held the island until the seventeenth century, when Britain sent an invasion force that was eventually able to wrest control of the island from the Spanish. Many African slaves that the Spanish had brought to the island—whom the Spanish referred to as the *Maroons*—escaped to the mountains of Jamaica prior to and during the change of power. These people were never brought under British rule; they remained in the remote mountain regions from this point forward, and are still there today. The British ruled the island for the next 200 years, creating one of the biggest plantation economies in the world and serving as the site of major slave revolts during this period. After the abolition of the slave trade in the 1830s, the majority African-imported population of Jamaica slowly and painfully gained power and, eventually, independence from the British. The independent Maroons played a role in this transition.

The jerk method of cooking originated in Jamaica and has grown in popularity, spreading to the rest of the Caribbean and elsewhere. This method was begun by the Maroons, who hybridized a method of preserving meats that they brought with them from Africa. They coated the meats in a spice blend and then cooked them very slowly over wood to yield a highly spiced, moist, and smoky meat. This process was done in Jamaica using the local Scotch bonnet chili pepper; the Spanish introduced garlic, ginger, and spices such as cinnamon and nutmeg to the marinating process, and the meat was cooked over the indigenous pimento wood, the source of allspice. The result is a spicy, flavorful product often imitated by using allspice as a marinade ingredient and cooking meat over a low fire on a grill after the meat has been rubbed with a jerk spice blend.

A number of European-influenced foods complement the primarily African foods that make up the foundation of the cuisine. Stamp and Go (salt cod cakes) and Jamaican patties (spiced beef-filled pastries) both reveal the European influence, whereas the inclusion of cassava, plantains, ackee, and callaloo reveals the strong African influence. The influence of indentured Indian laborers who came to Jamaica in the 1800s is also seen in the cuisine today, as goat and curries are common ingredients in the cuisine as well.

In addition to these outside influences on the cuisine of Jamaica, a number of products have become both local favorites and sought after outside the country as well. Blue Mountain Coffee is a well-known product of Jamaica, and these beans are considered some of the best in the world. Some other notable products include the local marlin and species of jack fish in the surrounding waters, as well as the many tropical fruits such as coconuts, papaya, breadfruit, star fruit, tamarind, and soursop that thrive in this climate.

The Lesser Antilles

This section of the Caribbean is a collection of many islands with a storied history that includes colonization by a number of European powers and the even-tual conversion of these areas to resort destinations. This region is often thought of in terms of which country colonized which islands, because the culture of each island has been largely impacted by these colonizing powers (see the "Unique Components" section for more information). The major colonizing powers in the region included France, Spain, England, and the Netherlands, and their imprints still can be seen on these islands today. As with other parts of the Caribbean, plantations and the slave trade were major influencing factors in this region.

The cuisine of these islands is often a mélange of foods from the various ethnic groups that have populated each island, along with significant representation from Africa and many foods that can be traced back to either the colonial powers or the original inhabitants of these islands, the native Caribs and Arawaks. The islands closest to South America reveal a marked influence from the native South Americans, with dishes such as *hallucas* (wrapped corn dough with various fillings) and *arepas* (masa dough or bread filled with various ingredients) commonly found here.

RECIPES

The following recipes provide an introduction to the cuisines of the Caribbean.

Pan Cubano CUBA
(CUBAN BREAD)

INGREDIENTS

For Making the Starter

1/2 oz	Fresh Compressed Yeast (you can substitute 1/2 oz active dry yeast, if this is unavailable)
8 oz	Water
8 oz	Bread or All-Purpose (A.P.) Flour

For Making the Dough

1 oz	Fresh Compressed Yeast
1 oz	Sugar
24 oz	Room-Temperature Water

In Cuba, sandwiches are a common part of the everyday food that is sold in small shops and by street vendors as well as made in homes all over the country. The Cuban bread traditionally features a ridge down the center that is formed either by making a cut on the surface of the proofed bread, like a baguette, or by laying a string along the center of the bread to leave an indentation. Whatever method is used, the result is bread with great flavor. Cuban sandwiches usually contain roasted pork, ham, cheese, and pickles, sandwiched between a couple of slices of this bread and grilled "*á la plancha*," a technique very similar to making a panini in which the sandwich is placed on a hot griddle with a small amount of fat; it is then weighted to result in a compressed sandwich with a crisp exterior.

YIELD: 5.5 pounds of raw dough, or 4 loaves (approximately 1 pound/loaf)

PREPARATION METHOD: Starter Sponge

MIXING METHOD: Straight Dough Method

COOKING METHOD: Baking

(continues)

Pan Cubano
(continued)

4	oz	Lard (if you want real Cuban bread, don't use a substitute for this)
		Starter (see above)
2.5	lbs	Bread or A.P. Flour + more as needed

For Baking the Bread

4		2-foot-long pieces of dampened Butcher's Twine (traditionally, palmetto leaves were used, but butcher's twine is a good substitute)
2	qts	Water (for creating steam in oven)
		Water (for spraying loaves)

PROCEDURE

For Making the Starter

1. Combine the fresh yeast, water, and flour in a mixing bowl, and mix to combine into a wet dough/paste. Cover with plastic wrap and set aside in a warm place to allow the starter to develop for 2 hours at room temperature.

2. Once the starter has fermented at room temperature for a couple of hours, place the bowl in the refrigerator and allow it to develop further overnight.

3. Once the starter has been allowed to develop, remove it from the refrigerator and allow it to come to room temperature by placing it in a warm place before making the final dough with it. (A cold starter will delay proofing significantly.)

For Making the Dough

1. In a small mixing bowl, combine the fresh compressed yeast, water, and sugar; allow the yeast to bloom for 10 minutes.

2. Once the yeast has bloomed, add the yeast and water solution to a mixing bowl large enough to hold all of the ingredients. (If only smaller mixers are available, it may be best to scale the recipe down to accommodate the mixing capacity.)

3. Add the lard, the starter from the first section, and 3/4 of the flour to the mixing bowl with a dough hook attached; begin to mix the dough at low speed until all of the moisture has been absorbed by the flour and starter.

4. At this point, begin to check the consistency of the dough (the end result needs to be a soft dough that does not stick to the mixing bowl but is pliable and smooth; you can achieve this consistency by adding flour to the mixing bowl, 1/2 cup or so at a time).

5. Once the proper consistency of the dough has been achieved, it needs to be developed properly; this will take different amounts of time, depending on what type/size mixer you are using (approximately 8–15 minutes). The way to determine whether the dough is properly developed is by stopping the machine after mixing for 5 minutes and checking the elasticity of the dough, and then checking every couple of minutes after that until the desired elasticity is achieved. The proper elasticity is achieved when a piece of dough can be stretched thin enough that light can be seen through it without the dough tearing (this is often referred to as the "window").

6. Once the dough has been properly developed, remove it from the mixing bowl and place it in a proofbox (or cover with a damp cloth in a warm place) to proof.

7. Once the dough has doubled in volume, remove it from the proofbox and punch the dough down to force out the trapped gas. Turn the dough out onto a floured workbench for makeup.

8. For making up the dough, divide it into 4 equal pieces (each should weigh approximately 1 lb 6 oz), and form each piece into a loaf shape approximately 14 inches long.

9. Place the formed loaves on a baking sheet, approximately 6 inches apart (they will expand during proofing and baking), and put them

(continues)

Pan Cubano
(continued)

in the proofbox (if no proofbox is available, cover them again with a clean, damp cloth and put them in a warm place) to proof for approximately 40 minutes.

For Baking the Bread

1. Preheat the oven to 400°F.

2. Place an oven-safe pan holding a couple quarts of water in the oven to create steam during the cooking process (this helps create a crisp crust).

3. Remove the proofed dough from the proofbox, and place the wetted butcher's twine down the center of each of the proofed loaves.

4. Spray the outside of the loaves with a little water to dampen them, and then place the loaves in the preheated oven. Bake for 30–35 minutes, or until the loaves are done, spraying the loaves after each 10 minutes in the oven (they should sound hollow when tapped on the bottom and have a nice crisp and browned crust).

5. Remove the bread and allow it to cool by setting it on a wire cooling rack before using.

Sofrito PUERTO RICO
(PUERTO RICAN SEASONING PASTE)

INGREDIENTS

4	oz	Salt Pork, diced small
1/2	oz	Annatto Paste (optional; this will make a redder sofrito and can be left out if sofrito will be used in lightly colored dishes)
4	oz	Ham
1	lb	Onions, sliced thin
1	oz	Garlic Cloves, minced
8	oz	Green Peppers, seeded and diced medium
1	Tbsp	Jalapeño, minced (optional; the use of the sofrito often would determine whether you would want to add spiciness or not)
8	oz	Tomato, concassée
1/4	tsp	Oregano, dried
1	Tbsp	Cilantro, minced
		Salt and Pepper, to taste

The Spanish influence is visible in this preparation, as both the name and the basis of this are of Spanish heritage. However, some Native American ingredients are included in this preparation to make a new version of the Old World starting point to many soups and stews in Spain. This mixture is used also as a starting point for many soups and stews, and it is also used a seasoning by adding it to foods after they are cooked.

YIELD: 1.5 pounds

COOKING METHOD: Slow Braising

PROCEDURE

1. In a heavy-bottomed pot or sauté pan large enough to hold all of the ingredients, add the salt pork and heat over a medium-low flame to slowly render the fat from it.

2. Once the salt pork has rendered, add the annatto paste (if using) and the ham; turn the heat up slightly to sear the ham in the fat that has rendered from the salt pork (try not to color the meat, as a sofrito should not be darkly colored).

3. Once the meat has been seared in the fat, turn the heat down and add the onions, garlic, green peppers, and jalapeño (if using), and cook covered and over a low flame for 30 minutes (set the flame very low to ensure that pan does not get too hot and color the vegetables).

4. After cooking the aromatics covered for 30 minutes, add the tomato concassée and the dried oregano, and continue to cook over

(continues)

Sofrito
(continued)

a low flame until the tomato is completely soft and has mixed into the other ingredients (about 10–15 minutes). Remove the sofrito from the heat.

5. Add the cilantro and adjust the seasoning of the sofrito; it can be used to make other dishes or canned and set aside for later use.

Rendered salt pork with annatto and ham for sofrito; note the lack of dark coloring, as this should be done slowly and not over intense heat

Adding the cilantro to the finished sofrito

Picklese HAITI
(SPICY CABBAGE SALAD)

INGREDIENTS

6		Scotch bonnet peppers, stems and seeds removed and minced (use gloves for this!)
8	oz	Green Cabbage, shredded fine
1	oz	Carrots, shredded fine
2	oz	Yellow Onion, sliced thin
1	oz	Shallots, minced
4		Whole Cloves
1	tsp	Salt
1/2	tsp	Black Peppercorns
3	cups	Vinegar

This spicy condiment is a common Haitian accompaniment to meat and fish dishes, adding some of the island kick that is such a notable component of Caribbean cuisine. The Scotch bonnet is in the same family as the well-known habanero chili that is common in the Yucatan of Mexico, but it is a different pod type (although both are blistering hot, so be careful when handling them!).

YIELD: 1 quart

PRESERVATION METHOD: Acidity

PROCEDURE

1. Combine all ingredients together in jar or another suitable storage container; mix well, making sure that the vegetable ingredients are covered by the vinegar (use a nonreactive utensil to hold the ingredients under the vinegar).

2. Place the jar in the refrigerator and allow contents to develop.

3. Let the flavor develop for at least 2 days before use.

Picklese (Haitian spiced cabbage salad) with very spicy Scotch bonnet peppers (on right) used in making it

Coocoo BARBADOS

(CORNMEAL AND OKRA MASH)

INGREDIENTS

1	lb	Okra, fresh
1	tsp	Salt
1	qt	Cold Water
5	oz	Yellow Onion, diced small
1	oz	Garlic Cloves, minced
2.5	qts	Water
1	Tbsp	Salt
4	oz	Butter
1	lb	Cornmeal

This African-inspired dish is common in many part of the Caribbean, in particular those without a strong Spanish influence. Although corn is indigenous to the Americas and was being grown in the Caribbean by the native Arawaks when Columbus arrived, the African slaves resurrected corn in the Caribbean following the decimation of the native peoples.

YIELD: 3.5 quarts, or 20 portions (5–6 ounces/portion)

COOKING METHOD: Boiling/Simmering

PROCEDURE

1. Cut the okra by first removing the stems end and then cutting the tips off of the tapered ends of the okra pods. Once the ends are removed, cut the okra into 1/4-inch wheels by slicing the pods.

2. In a small pot, combine the cold water, salt, and sliced okra pieces; set aside for 30 minutes to draw off some of the liquid from the okra.

3. After 30 minutes, strain off the liquid the okra has soaked in.

4. In a separate pot large enough to hold all of the ingredients, add the yellow onion, garlic, 2.5 qts of water, salt, butter, and soaked okra; bring this mixture to a boil over high heat.

5. Once the mixture reaches a boil, add the cornmeal, stirring constantly until the mixture thickens into a thick mash.

6. Lower the heat to cook the mixture over low heat for 10 minutes, and then turn it out onto a dish to serve.

Callaloo CARIBBEAN ISLANDS

(CALLALOO LEAF SOUP WITH CRAB)

INGREDIENTS

1	oz	Peanut Oil
2	lbs	Whole Crabs, cleaned and cut into segments to yield claw and body sections (shrimp can be substituted or added as part of crab amount)
6	oz	Salt Pork or Bacon, diced small
4	oz	Celery, diced small
8	oz	Yellow Onion, diced small
1/2	oz	Garlic Cloves, minced

As the most well known of the Caribbean soups, callaloo is found throughout the Caribbean and in many variations.

YIELD: 14 portions (8 ounces/portion)

PROCEDURE

1. In a pot large enough to hold all of the ingredients, add the peanut oil and heat over a medium flame until hot. Add crab sections and sauté until crab shells turn red and brown slightly from the heat, turning frequently to prevent burning and removing from the pot once colored.

2. Once all of the crab has been colored and removed from the pot, set it aside and add the diced salt pork or bacon; panfry over a medium-low flame until the fat has been rendered and it is well caramelized.

(continues)

✳ Callaloo
(continued)

10	oz	Okra, sliced into 1/4-inch rounds
2		Scotch Bonnet Chiles, pricked with a fork (substitute 2 habanero or 4 serrano chiles, if needed)
2	tsp	Fresh Thyme Leaves, minced
2	qts	Water
1	lb	Callaloo Leaves, tough center ribs removed and rolled and cut into 1/2-inch sections (you may substitute dasheen leaves or spinach, if callaloo is unavailable)
2	oz	Lime Juice
		Salt and Freshly Ground Black Pepper, to taste

3. Strain out excess bacon fat, leaving just enough to sweat the vegetables (1–2 Tbsp).

4. Add celery, onions, and garlic; sweat them in the bacon fat until the onions become soft and translucent, taking care not to color the vegetables by controlling the heat as needed.

5. Add the okra, Scotch bonnet chili, thyme, and water; bring mixture to a simmer over a high flame, turning heat down once the mixture reaches a simmer.

6. Add the callaloo leaves to the pot, and gently simmer until the leaves become just tender (this will take about 10–15 minutes). (The soup can be puréed at this point, if desired—just remember to take out the chili before you do so!)

7. Remove the Scotch bonnet chili, and add the crab sections and lime juice. Simmer for an additional 3–4 minutes.

8. Adjust seasoning with salt and pepper.

NOTE: *Callaloo is often served with crabmeat as well, and crabmeat could be added at the end of the cooking process or simply placed on top of the soup as an accompaniment.*

Bowl of callaloo (callaloo leaf soup with crab)

Mojo　Cuba and Other Spanish Islands
(Citrus and Garlic Marinade and Sauce)

INGREDIENTS

3	oz	Garlic Cloves, chopped
2	tsp	Salt
1/2	tsp	Freshly Ground Black Pepper
12	oz	Seville Orange Juice (sour orange; if this is unavailable, substitute 7 oz lime juice mixed with 5 oz orange juice)
4	oz	Yellow Onion, minced
2	tsp	Dried Oregano or 2 Tbsp Minced Fresh Oregano
2	Tbsp	Fresh Flat Leaf Parsley, minced
8	oz	Olive Oil

Mojo is a common marinade and sauce used in Cuba as well as on other islands. It is most commonly used to marinate pork, poultry, and sometimes fish. This is also used as a sauce to be served with cooked meats or cassava.

YIELD: 3 cups

COOKING METHOD: Infusion by Brief Heating

PROCEDURE

1. Using a mortar and pestle, crush the garlic cloves, salt, and pepper together until the mixture resembles a paste.

2. Transfer the garlic paste from the mortar and pestle into a small mixing bowl, and add the orange juice (or lime and orange, if you are not using the Seville orange), yellow onion, oregano, and parsley. Cover and refrigerate for at least a couple of hours before proceeding to the next step.

3. Once the mixture has had time to develop flavor, pour the olive oil into a small pot (large enough to hold all of the ingredients) and heat over a medium-low flame until the oil gets hot (but not very hot; it should heat up to 250–275°F).

4. Once the oil has heated to the proper temperature, add the orange and garlic combination (be careful: the oil will probably splatter a bit as the wet mixture hits it), and then remove the pot from the heat.

5. Allow the mixture to cool for a couple of minutes, and then return the mixture to a low flame and cook for 2–3 minutes to reduce the pungency of the garlic and combine the flavors.

6. Once the mixture has cooked for a few minutes, remove it from the heat and allow it to cool before use; if it is going to be canned, do so while it is still very hot to sterilize the jar.

Picadillo　Cuba
(Stewed Beef or Pork with Tomato, Olives, and Capers)

INGREDIENTS

1	oz	Salt Pork, diced small
1	lb	Ground Beef
2	oz	Ham, diced small
1	Tbsp	Olive Oil
1	tsp	Achiote Paste (also called annatto paste)
6	oz	Yellow Onion, minced

Picadillo is a common component in Cuban cuisine and can be used to make alcapurrias, to accompany a fried egg, or to be served with rice and peas, for example. One of the ingredients for picadillo is rare in the United States and will often need to be substituted with cilantro. It is called roucou and has a distinct taste that somewhat resembles cilantro.

YIELD: 1 quart

COOKING METHOD: Slow Braising

(continues)

Picadillo
(continued)

1	oz	Garlic Cloves, minced
4	oz	Green Peppers, minced
2	Tbsp	Fresh Roucou, minced (substitute cilantro, if this is unavailable)
1/4	tsp	Oregano, dried (or substitute 1 tsp fresh oregano, minced)
2	oz	Spanish Olives, minced
2	Tbsp	Capers, drained
1/2	tsp	Salt
1/4	tsp	Back Pepper
		Salt and Pepper, to taste

PROCEDURE

1. In a heavy-bottomed pan or pot large enough to hold all of the ingredients, add the salt pork and heat over a medium-low flame. Render slowly to extract the fat (this will take about 10–15 minutes).

2. Once the fat has been rendered from the salt pork, turn the heat up; once hot, brown the ground beef in the salt pork fat in batches to ensure that the heat is maintained.

3. Once all of the beef has been browned in the hot fat, turn the heat down to a medium-low flame again, and add the olive oil and the achiote paste; stir well to combine.

4. Add the yellow onion, garlic cloves, green peppers, roucou, and oregano. Cook all of the ingredients together over a low flame for at least 45 minutes, covered (make sure that the flame is low so that the food will not burn or get browned; at this point, the ingredients should simply cook and sweat together).

5. Add the olives and capers once everything has cooked together for the allotted time, and then cook covered for an additional 5 minutes before using.

Alcapurrias   CUBA AND PUERTO RICO
(FRIED PLANTAIN AND TARO DOUGH STUFFED WITH PICADILLO)

INGREDIENTS
For the Dough

3	lbs	Plantains, green
1	gal	Hot Water
1	gal	Salted Water
2	lbs	Taro Root (also called yautia)
3	oz	Olive Oil
1	Tbsp	Achiote Paste (also called annatto)
1	Tbsp	Salt

For Forming and Frying the Alcapurrias

1/2		Picadillo Recipe (this chapter), cooled
		Grated or Puréed Plantain and Taro Mixture (see above), rested and refrigerated overnight
1	oz	Olive Oil
		Aluminum Foil

These fried delights are a marriage of Africa, Europe, and the Americas, combining ingredients, techniques, and tastes from all three places. This recipe requires preparation of the picadillo recipe (also included in this chapter).

YIELD: 25 each (4 ounces/serving)

PREPARATION METHOD (PLANTAIN AND TARO): Grating or Puréeing

COOKING METHOD (ALCAPURRIAS): Deep Frying

PROCEDURE

For Making the Dough

1. Cut off the ends of the green plantains, and then cut them in half, making two shorter-length pieces. Next, make four or five vertical cuts along the length of the plantain pieces, just through the skin and equally spaced, and set the plantains in the hot water; allow them to sit for 20 minutes.

2. After 20 minutes, remove the plantains and peel them by pulling the skin in the opposite direction from the length of the plantain (do not try to peel them like a banana, or pieces will probably break off).

3. Once the plantains have been peeled, put them in a container with the salted water.

4. Peel the taro root, and place the taro pieces into the salted water as well.

5. Finely grate or purée the plantains and taro.

6. In a small saucepan, combine the olive oil and achiote paste; heat over a gentle flame to dissolve and bloom the achiote paste.

(continues)

Alcapurrias
(continued)

7. Combine the achiote oil, salt, grated plantain, and taro in a mixing bowl, and mix well to completely distribute the ingredients.

8. Refrigerate the mixture overnight before using it to make the alcapurrias.

For Forming and Frying the Alcapurrias

1. Preheat the deep fryer to 360°F.

2. Tear off a foot-long piece of aluminum foil, and coat an area (6 in × 6 in) of the torn-off piece with some of the olive oil.

3. Place approximately 3 oz of the batter onto the oiled area, and then spread it out using oiled (and sanitized) fingers or an oiled spatula.

4. Place approximately 1 heaping Tbsp of the picadillo mixture on top of the dough; using the foil, wrap the dough around the filling and seal the ends of the dough to completely envelop the meat mixture.

5. Slide the dough filled with the picadillo into the preheated deep fryer, and fry until the exterior turns golden brown.

6. Remove the fried alcapurrias and allow the excess grease to drip onto a paper towel before serving.

7. Continue steps 3–6 to fry the remaining dough and meat filling to serve.

Peeling green plantains for making alcapurria dough; note that the plantains are being peeled after soaking, and only small sections of the skin are removed at a time

Plantain/taro dough on oiled foil topped with the picadillo for making the alcapurrias

Finished alcapurrias

Cassava Chips JAMAICA

(FRIED CASSAVA CHIPS)

INGREDIENTS

2	lbs	Cassava, peeled
		Salt, to taste
		Vegetable Oil (for deep frying)

Cassava chips and mojo sauce

Cassava has been a regular component in the diet of Caribbean inhabitants for millennia. Following the introduction of deep-frying techniques by the Europeans, the same technique used for potatoes was eventually applied to cassava, as in this recipe.

YIELD: 6 portions (3 ounces/portion)

SLICING METHOD: Electric Slicing

NECESSARY PREPARATION TECHNIQUE: Soaking

COOKING METHOD: Deep Frying

PROCEDURE

1. Preheat deep fryer to 370°F.
2. After peeling the cassava root, slice it in half and then slice each half as thin as possible using an electric slicer (it is best to cut it this way to yield even pieces and to prevent a cut of this very dense root).
3. Place the cassava slices in a container of ice water, and allow the cassava to sit in the ice bath for 30 minutes before using (this is a necessary step to draw out unwanted compounds from the root).
4. Once the cassava has soaked for 30 minutes, strain the cassava chips in a colander and allow any excess water to drain off.
5. Pat the cassava dry using a clean paper towel to ensure that they are not wet prior to being added to the fryer.
6. Deep-fry the cassava chips in the fryer until they become crisp and slightly browned in the hot oil (they will not darken as much as potatoes, so don't only use color as an indicator of doneness; they should be crisp but not very hard).
7. As soon as the cassava chips are removed from the fryer, sprinkle them with salt and serve immediately.

Jerk Rub JAMAICA

(JAMAICAN SEASONING)

INGREDIENTS

2	tsp	Dried Cayenne Pepper
3	Tbsp	Chili Powder
1	Tbsp	Onion Powder
1	Tbsp	Garlic Powder
1	Tbsp	Freshly Ground Black Pepper
1.5	tsp	Ground Cinnamon
1/4	tsp	Ground Cloves
1/2	tsp	Ground Nutmeg
1.5	Tbsp	Salt

Dry jerk rubs are sometimes used instead of marinades on meats or poultry to be grilled.

YIELD: 1/2 cup

PROCEDURE

1. Combine all of the ingredients together in a dry mixing bowl, and toss well to mix.

Jerk Marinade JAMAICA

INGREDIENTS

2	oz	Fresh Red Chiles, chopped
3	oz	Fresh Ginger Root, peeled and chopped
4	oz	Green Onions, chopped (about 2 bunches)
3	oz	Fresh Garlic Cloves, chopped
1	Tbsp	Freshly Ground Black Pepper
2	tsp	Allspice, crushed
2	tsp	Cinnamon, ground
1/2	tsp	Nutmeg
1	cup	Malt Vinegar
1	cup	Soy Sauce
3	oz	Molasses
4	oz	Rum
1.5	Tbsp	Salt

Jerk marinades are complex mixtures of chiles, seasoning, and acids that might also contain any number of other ingredients.

YIELD: 5 cups

PROCEDURE

1. Combine all ingredients in a storage container; using an immersion blender or a food processor, blend until smooth.

Dunkanoo JAMAICA

(SWEET CORN AND COCONUT DUMPLINGS)

INGREDIENTS

3	lbs	Fresh Corn
3	oz	Cornmeal, about 1/2 cup (you may need more, depending on corn moisture content)
4	oz	Brown Sugar
8	oz	Coconut Milk
1	tsp	Cinnamon, ground
1/4	tsp	Dry Ginger

This Jamaican recipe is an adaptation of a dish from Western Africa, assumed to have been introduced to the Caribbean by the West African slaves who were brought to there by European colonists.

YIELD: 30 pieces (2 ounces/piece)

COOKING METHOD: Steaming

PROCEDURE

1. Grate the fresh corn into a large mixing bowl, and add the cornmeal, brown sugar, coconut cream, cinnamon, and ginger; whisk together to form a paste (if it is too thick, add more coconut milk; if it is too thin, add more cornmeal).

Folding raisins into dunkanoo dough (sweet corn and coconut dumplings)

Folding dunkanoo dough into banana leaf; note how the sides are folded in first and then the dough is enclosed before it is secured with butcher's twine

Dunkanoo (sweet corn and coconut dumplings)

(continues)

Dunkanoo
(continued)

4 oz   Raisins (optional)
1 dozen Banana Leaves, cut into
         6-inch squares (you will
         need about 30 squares)

2. Fold in raisins.

3. Bring a small pot of water to a boil, and dip banana leaves into the boiling water briefly to make them pliable.

4. Place 1 ounce of the paste on the bottom third of each banana leaf square.

5. Fold up the small, exposed piece of banana leaf, fold in both sides, and then roll out the remaining flap to fully enclose the paste.

6. The banana leaves can then be secured using butcher's twine and steamed for 45 minutes, or until the dough becomes firm and doesn't stick to the banana leaf.

Beignets de Banane   MARTINIQUE
(FRIED BANANA FRITTERS)

INGREDIENTS

For Marinating the Bananas

2 lbs   Ripe Bananas, diced
         medium
6 oz   Dark Rum
2 oz   Sugar
2 tsp   Vanilla Extract

For Making the Batter

1 lb   A.P. Flour (you may need
         more, depending on
         consistency)
1 oz   Sugar
1.5 tsp Baking Powder
         Banana Mixture (see above)
2   Eggs
8 oz   Milk (you may need more,
         depending on consistency)
1 oz   Unsalted Butter, melted

For Garnishing

4 oz   Caster Sugar (Baker's Sugar)
         or Powdered Sugar (10X)
1 Tbsp   Cinnamon
1 Tbsp   Vanilla Powder (if available)

The French influence in culinary naming and technique can be seen in this recipe; the ingredients are mostly imported from the Caribbean slave trade years (rum, sugar, bananas) combined with a native ingredient (vanilla).

YIELD: Thirty-two 2-ounce fritters
PREPARATION METHOD: Marinating
COOKING METHOD: Deep Frying

PROCEDURE

For Marinating the Bananas

1. Combine the diced bananas, rum, sugar, and vanilla in a mixing bowl; set in the refrigerator and allow the flavors to marinate for at least 1 hour before proceeding to the next step.

For Making the Batter

1. Combine the flour, sugar, and baking powder in a mixing bowl large enough to hold all of the ingredients, and mix to combine; set aside.

2. In a separate bowl, combine the banana mixture from the first section, eggs, milk, and melted butter; mix with a whisk to combine well.

3. Add the wet mixture to the dry mixture, and mix to combine to a relatively smooth paste (do not mix too much, as gluten development is not desired).

For Cooking the Fritters and Garnishing

1. Preheat the deep fryer to 350°F.

2. Using a small ice cream scoop (#40 scoop or smaller), scoop approximately 2 oz of the batter into the preheated fryer; fry the fritters until golden brown, and then remove them to a paper towel to absorb excess oil.

3. Check the consistency of the fritter batter using the one you just fried; adjust if necessary by adding more milk if the batter is too

(continues)

Beignets de Banane
(continued)

thick (the fritters will be overly dense and probably stick to the bottom of the fryer), or more flour if the batter is too thin (the fritter batter will break up into smaller pieces).

4. Combine the caster sugar, cinnamon, and vanilla powder, and put into a dredge (a sifting canister; you can use a fine sifter, if this is unavailable).

5. Once the batter has been properly adjusted, fry the fritters to golden brown and dust them with seasoned sugar.

6. Serve immediately.

Beignets de banane
(fried banana fritters)

SUMMARY

The cuisine of the Caribbean is one of the world's most culturally varied: the dominant represented cultures come from Europe and Africa, and the ingredients come from the Americas and beyond. The slave trade and the period of slave-run plantations were significant factors in the development of the current cuisine, as West African cooks and European colonists developed the framework for these countries' economies as well as their traditional foods. Because this is an island region, tropical fruits and seafood are significant components, as are the plantation products of sugarcane (rum) and later-introduced crops such as coconuts and mangoes. The cuisine of the Caribbean is known for its fusion of cooking methods, ingredients, and traditions—a product of the cultures that combined here and the conditions they were subject to. The specific character of the Caribbean cuisines is often a combination of African influence and whatever colonial power once claimed the island—with native ingredients added—to yield a cuisine that is distinct from one island to the next.

REVIEW QUESTIONS

1. Which European country was the first to establish itself in the Caribbean, and which countries of the Caribbean reflect the most influence from this country today?

2. What is the connection between the Caribbean and the well-known BBQ common to the United States?

3. The jerk method hails from what area of the Caribbean? What about this method makes it different from other cooking methods?

COMMON TERMS, FOODS, AND INGREDIENTS

The Caribbean has a complex history and many influences, and these have had a strong impact on the terminology of the ingredients and dishes that are common to this area. Many of the terms used in this chapter are foreign (mostly West African or Spanish) or not commonly used in the United States. The following guide explains the meanings of these terms and is useful for beginning to understand and decipher words that are common to this region and cuisine.

✴ Ingredients and Foods

accras – Fried savory bean fritters common in Haiti (also spelled *akkra*)

achiote – Dye that is mainly used as a coloring agent in cooking, as it imparts a red/yellow color to foods; also called annato, bijol, or roucou

ackee – Fruit from West African evergreen

adobe – Spice rub used on grilled and roasted meats; often simply made from dried oregano, garlic, salt, and pepper

alcaparrado – Mixture of raisins, capers, and olives of Spanish heritage used in Cuban cuisine

alcapurrias – Fried dough stuffed with spiced meat filling; dough is made from green bananas and taro root, common in Puerto Rico

allaloo – Huge, dark green leaves of taro used in making soups and stews

allspice – Small berry from the pimento tree that is indigenous to the Caribbean; an important seasoning in much of the Caribbean

arepas – Masa corn dough filled with various ingredients and cooked on a flat griddle; these are from the northeastern portion of South America and are also found in various sections of the Caribbean

asopao – Rice cooked and served at a soupy consistency in the Dominican Republic

bacalao – Salt cod; introduced to the Caribbean by the Spanish and became a main component because slave-driven culinary creations required cheap ingredients, and slaves were not afforded time and equipment to fish the rich local waters

barbacoa – Spanish translation of *brabacot*

boliche – Beef stuffed with chorizo sausage (chili-spiced sausage)

bora bean – Long, rope-like green bean added to many vegetable sautés

boulette – Bread-bound meatball found in Haiti

brabacot – Arawak term for a method of preserving foods by smoking and cooking them over green wood fire; origin of the term and cooking method called "barbeque" in the United States

canã de azúcar – Sugarcane; this import from India and Africa (originally from New Guinea) became the major crop in the Caribbean, and its cultivation led to the slave trade in the Americas

carambola – Elongated star-shaped fruit; also commonly called star fruit

carangue – Family of fatty fish common in the Caribbean, including species known locally as cigar fish, big eye, and cavalli jack, to name a few

cascadura – Armored fish that resembles a catfish; found in Trinidad and prized by locals

cassareep – Condiment made from boiling bitter cassava juice with sugar and spices; used in traditional Caribbean cooking. Cassareep has also been used historically as a means of preserving meats by cooking them in this liquid to make a sort of stew that would be continually added to.

conch – Name of a family of large sea snails; the large gigas species is prized in the Caribbean, where it is known for its delicate flesh

congri – Rice cooked with red beans

coocoo – Dish of cornmeal and okra cooked with coconut milk in African-influenced areas of Caribbean

coquimol – Thickened coconut cream made in the same manner as *crème anglaise* but with coconut milk instead of milk or cream

crème anglaise – "English cream" from French influence, who credit this preparation to the English; consists of egg yolks, milk, and sugar (vanilla is often added as well) cooked gently until thickened

croquettes – Breaded and fried thick milk dough/sauce, made essentially like béchamel, that is cooled before breading; various ingredients are added, such as shrimp, chicken, or ham

djon djon – Type of mushroom from the hills of Haiti that is highly prized for its meaty flavor and often added to rice dishes

foo-foo – Traditionally made with mashed yams or cassava, this is also made with plantains in the Caribbean; this dish comes from sub-Saharan West Africa, where the technique of cooking starchy foods until tender and then pounding them into a glutinous mixture has long been part of the culinary tradition

grouper – Type of fish that includes the sea bass that are found in shallow waters and feed on crustaceans and other fish. These types of fish generally have mild, flaky flesh that is highly regarded

guava – Fruit from a shrub or tree of the same name

gumbo – Name of an African-inspired stew that contains okra and other vegetables and meats in spicy broth

hallacas – Caribbean version (also found in South America) of *tamales*, in which the corn dough is filled with beef or pork seasoned with olives and capers and wrapped in banana or plaintain leaves before being boiled or steamed

jerk – Term that describes the cooking technique common in Jamaica, in which foods are marinated or dry rubbed in a spicy mixture and then cooked over a green wood fire

jujube – Small apple-like fruit from Asia

locrio – Rice cooked with meats, poultry, or fish in the Dominican Republic

longaniza sausage – Cured pork sausage flavored with chiles and spices such as cinnamon, anise seed, and garlic; often contains some beef as well and has a semisoft texture. This sausage—which primarily exists on the Spanish-influenced islands of the Caribbean—may be found fresh, in which case it needs to be cooked.

mojo – Sauce/marinade used in Cuban cuisine, made from garlic, onion, bitter orange juice or lime juice, and oil

moro – Rice cooked with vegetables and beans in the Dominican Republic

Moros y Cristianos – Rice and black beans cooked together; named after the Moors and Christians because these two groups once fought for control of the Iberian Peninsula

palomilla – Thin cut of bottom round marinated in adobe or mojo and cooked quickly on a hot griddle or pan

pan Cubano – Cuban bread

pastelitos – Fried savory pastries found on Spanish-influenced islands

pasties – English baked, meat-filled pastries

pecées – Twice-fried plantains found in Haiti (from African influence)

plantain – A banana variety that is higher in starch content and thus often used in preparations as a vegetable; also called *plátano* in Spanish

quingombo – Okra in Spanish-speaking islands, especially Puerto Rico

recao – An herb commonly used in the Caribbean, particularly in the Spanish-influenced areas; used to make the very common *sofrito*. Cilantro is sometimes used as a substitute, although their flavors are different.

remora – Suckerfish

riz et pois colles – Rice and peas; a common preparation in Haiti that reveals the imported influences on the area

roti – A type of Indian flatbread that has become common in some parts of the Caribbean, particularly in Trinidad

sancocho – Stew of mixed tubers and meats found on Spanish-influenced islands of the Caribbean and commonly eaten as part of celebrations

sauce ti-malice – Chili-spiced sauce common in Haiti; often used as a condiment

sofrito – Slow-cooked mixture of onions, garlic, and (often) tomatoes and peppers with seasonings; used to start many soups, sauces, and stew preparations for Spanish-inspired dishes

soursop – Large tropical fruit with a sweet-and-sour taste and a distinct, almost fermented smell

souse – A thick stew commonly made with fish, poultry, pork, or another available protein cooked with onions, cucumbers, peppers, and lime juice

tamale – Corn husk–wrapped corn dough filled with various ingredients and then steamed; from indigenous Native American cuisine

tamarindo – Spanish name for tamarind

tippy tam-bo – Tuber with brown hair-like covered skin and flesh, similar to a water chestnut or Jerusalem artichoke; used in soups and stews. The leaves of the plant are used to wrap foods like tamales.

Cultural Terms

á la plancha – Cooking method in which foods are cooked on a hot griddle

Arawak – One of the indigenous tribes of the Caribbean prior to the arrival of the Europeans

Carib – One of the indigenous tribes that thrived in the Caribbean (*Caribbean* is derived from this tribe's name) prior to the arrival of the Europeans

cocina criolla – Term to describe the cooking of parts of the Caribbean in which native ingredients and techniques have been mixed with European and African techniques and ingredients; see *Creole* and *crillo*

conucos – Mounding technique of farming practiced by the native Arawaks and Caribs in which different types of vegetables were grown together in a mound; this technique is still used in some parts of the Caribbean today

Creole – Term used to describe the native cuisine and culture of the Caribbean. In reference to the cuisine, the term indicates the influence of primarily African and Spanish (and some French) cuisines; many also extend the term to include influences from other cuisines in this region, such as Native American (specifically, Taino and Carib), East Indian, and Chinese.

crillo – Spanish term meaning "native or indigenous" that is the root of the now common term *Creole*

Maroons – Spanish name given to African slaves who escaped to the mountains of Jamaica; these people were believed to have developed the tradition of jerk cooking in the Caribbean

Taino – One of the indigenous tribes of the Caribbean prior to the arrival of the Europeans; part of the Arawak people

CHAPTER 13

120° 115° 110° 105° 100° 95° 90° 85°

N
W   E
S

35°

30°

25°

20°

15°

UNITED STATES

Tijuana

SIERRA SAN PEDRO MARTIR

BAJA CALIFORNIA NORTE

SIERRA DE LA GIGANTA

Baja California

GULF OF CALIFORNIA

BAJA CALIFORNIA SUR

Cabo San Lucas

PACIFIC OCEAN

SONORA

CHIHUAHUA

The North

Rio Grande

Rio Grande

COAHUILA

NUEVO LEON

TAMAULIPAS

SINALOA

DURANGO

SIERRA MADRE OCCIDENTAL

SIERRA MADRE ORIENTAL

M E X I C O

ZACATECAS

The Central Highlands

SAN LUIS POTOSI

NAYARIT

Tequila

Guanajuato

GUANAJUATO

Guadalajara

QUERETARO

HIDALGO

WESTERN JALISCO

EASTERN JALISCO

Morelia

Mexico City

1

3

COLIMA

MICHOACAN

4   5   2

PUEBLA

The Gulf Coast

Veracruz

VERACRUZ

TABASCO

GUERRERO

SIERRA MADRE DEL SUR

OAXACA

Oaxaca

Acapulco

The Southern Pacific Coast

CHIAPAS

GUATEMALA

EL SA

GULF OF MEXICO

Merida

YUCATAN

QUINT

The Yucat Peninsul

CAMPECHE

BEL

1. AGUASCALIENTES
2. MORELIA
3. TLAXCALA
4. ESTATO DE MEXICO
5. DISTITO FEDERAL

Mexican Cuisine

OBJECTIVES

Upon completion of this chapter, you will be able to

- recognize the ingredients that are indigenous to the Americas.
- explain what the diet of the Native Americans included prior to contact with Europeans, and how it changed.
- discuss the impact of colonization on the development of Mexican cuisine.
- prepare some recipes common to Mexican cuisine.
- recognize some of the chiles commonly used in Mexican cuisine.
- define the terms listed at the conclusion of the chapter.

INTRODUCTION

Mexican cuisine is beginning to gain recognition as one of the truly great cuisines of the world, and with good reason. The cuisine is rooted in some of the world's great civilizations and was created by people who were not only experts in astrology but also developed an agricultural system and complex cuisine at a time when much of Europe consisted of nomadic tribes. When the Spanish arrived in Mexico in the early sixteenth century, the cuisine that they found was very complex and grounded in ingredients that they had never seen before. This cuisine has evolved via the addition of Old World ingredients to traditional Mexican cuisine and has become one of the most popular cuisines in countries outside of Mexico. The cuisine the Spanish initially found was based on what has since become known as the *tres hermanas* (three sisters) of *maíz* (corn), *calabaza* (squash), and *frijoles* (beans). These main ingredients of the indigenous cultures—along with chiles and *tomates* (tomatoes)—would forever change the cuisines of many cultures. The indigenous culture was equally changed by the introduction of the ingredients that the Spanish brought with them, including *puerco* (pork), *res* (beef), *citrico* (citrus), *pollo* (chicken), *cebolla* (onion), and *trigo* (wheat). Although this period in history began one of the most horrific times for indigenous peoples of the Americas, it also provided the circumstances that would allow the world to know food as it does today. Mexico was changed by the arrival of the Europeans, but today's Mexican cuisine has a history that dates back thousands of years—unchanged—something that few cuisines in today's world can claim.

The dominant religion in Mexico is Catholicism, and the vast majority of Mexicans are Roman Catholics. In the southern portion of the country, a significant number of indigenous peoples still follow their pagan beliefs (upon which most Native American faith systems were based prior to the arrival of Europeans). Many of the traditional spiritual ceremonies and celebrations have been incorporated into the holidays and culture of the Catholic Church. Like most cultures, the relationship between religious events and the foods associated with them is strong in Mexico.

The period that followed the invasion of the conquistadors resulted in a very rich cuisine that is poorly represented by the fast food and taco stands that serve "Mexican" cuisine in the United States and other parts of the world. Many of the foods found in the United States come from the northern part of Mexico, with little representation of foods from the south (and often a poor representation of the northern cuisine!). A closer look at the diversity and complexity of the culture and its cuisines reveals one of the richest and most enduring cuisines in the world.

HISTORIC CULINARY INFLUENCES

Mexico has been home to a number of great civilizations that are thought to date back potentially as far as 40,000 years, and these civilizations advanced greatly over the centuries, including the cuisine. The native cultures that existed in this area of the Americas did not have a written language, and thus many of the specifics of their history are not known, but we do know that these cultures created and ate many of the foods that are part of the foundation of Mexican cuisine today. The arrival of the Spanish in Mexico in the early sixteenth century began a new chapter for the people and cuisine of this culture, and the following section reviews the culture before the arrival and the major influences since.

Before European Contact

Before Columbus arrived in the Americas, there was a long history of peoples living throughout the region that makes up Mexico today. The northern portion of Mexico was sparsely inhabited by nomadic hunter-gatherers who lived in the harsh, arid climate and survived on what could be found or hunted. A number of developed civilizations existed in the southern portion of present-day Mexico; these were, in many ways, more advanced than European cultures of the time. The original peoples included the Olmecs, Toltecs, Zapotecs, Totonacs, Mayans, and Aztecs, who developed advanced irrigation and the domestication of agricultural products such as maíz, *maguey* (agave), *nopal* (cactus), *mesquite*, calabaza, *cacao* (cocoa beans), chiles, and frijoles.

In addition to these cultivated foods, the people also hunted for local animals such as *venato* (deer), *pavo* (turkey), and *pescado* (fish) from the local waters.

The diet of this period included little in the way of fats, with the exception of occasional meats from hunted foods and more commonly from *aquacate* (avocados), which were prized for their creaminess and used often as sauces would be in other cuisines. The most famous product, and still a favorite today, is *guacamole*—the mixture of avocado, tomato, and chiles (limes and cilantro were to follow later).

These cultures thrived on a mostly vegetarian diet because the availability of significant animal foods was limited. With a foundation of maíz, calabaza, frijoles, tomates, chiles, and other plants, the cultures developed a complex variety of foods, many of which revolved around *nixtamalized* corn (corn treated with an alkali to remove the husk) and the dough called *masa* made from it. The cycle of planting, growing, and harvesting (of corn, in particular) was of great significance and served as the focus of these cultures' spirituality as well as their nutritional well-being. Many of the main dietary components from these civilizations live on today in Mexican foods, including *tortillas* (flat corn dough), *tamales* (steamed corn dough with various fillings), *tlaquetzalli* (chocolate drink), and *sopes* (thick disks of corn dough topped with various ingredients).

The dominant culture of Mexico just prior to the arrival of the Spanish was the Aztecs, who were also called the Mexica (from which the name *Mexico* is derived), and whose culture was centered in the area of what is today Mexico City. The city grew as the Aztec power did, and it was the world's largest city by the time the Spanish arrived in the sixteenth century.

The Arrival of the Spanish

Following the discovery of the Americas by the Europeans, the first people to take root in the region of Mexico were the Spanish. The history of the Spanish colonization of the indigenous peoples and land of Mexico is one of suffering and controversy, but also one of the most profound culinary events of all time. Introduced to the Mexican peoples' diet were puerco, pollo, res, *leche* (milk), *queso* (cheese), *cordero* (lamb), cebolla, *ajo* (garlic), *limones* (lemons), *naranjas* (oranges), cilantro, *zanahorias* (carrots), and *pimienta* (black pepper), which would forever change the culinary culture of the native and immigrating peoples. As large of an impact as these products had on the development of native culinary habits, ingredients and products from the Americas had perhaps an even greater impact on the development of cuisines in Europe, Asia, and beyond.

The Spanish quickly took control of parts of the country as they searched for gold to return to Spain. The Spanish also attempted to convert the native Mexicans to Catholicism and began a system of setting up missions for this purpose. Many of the Spanish who came to Mexico at this time were men, and a new culture was born when many of the men began families with natives. The resulting "mixed" offspring were known as *mestizos*, who are believed to make up the majority of the present population of Mexico. The Spanish influence on the culture is not limited to the genetic aspect; many Spanish techniques and foods are a common part of the current Mexican cuisine.

Spanish culinary influences include the techniques of making cheese, sausage, distillation, stews, the use of fats to sear and sauté foods, and pastry and bread making. All of these aspects are found in numerous examples throughout present Mexican cuisine, including the colorful *pastelitos* (pastries), the prevalence of sausages such as *chorizo* (spiced pork sausage) and *butifarra* (dried pork sausage of Chiapas), the many cheeses (*queso*), and the most Mexican of distilled beverages, *tequila* (distilled from the agave plant).

Brief French Rule

After invading Mexico in 1864, France's Napoleon III installed the Austrian archduke Maximilian and his wife, Carlotta, as the country's emperor and empress. During their brief period of rule, the Austrians introduced the aristocratic lifestyle typical of European royalty at the time. As a result, the French culinary penchant for refined, rich sauces and structured classifications of foods and menus were introduced to the elite members of Mexican society. Although this did not become a major part of the cuisine of Mexico, there are many examples of French and aristocratic traditions in pockets of the country. Some of the notable influences include a number of French baking traditions, ranging from breads such as *bollito* (split-top bread) to crepes (thin pancakes) filled with *cuitlacoche* (prized corn fungus), that are often found on menus.

UNIQUE COMPONENTS

Mexican cuisine is unique in its foundation of indigenous ingredients and techniques that have endured and adapted to the presence of a foreign culture. This section explores some of the components that make Mexican cuisine so distinctive, recognizable, and influential in today's professional kitchen.

Chiles, Chiles, Chiles!

The first thing most people think of when they consider the cuisine of Mexico is the heat provided by its chiles; without a doubt, this is one of the characteristics that influences the cuisine, although it is not only the chiles' heat that is prized. Chiles are indigenous to the Americas, and nowhere are they more utilized to this day than in Mexico, where over a hundred varieties can be found in markets in both fresh and dried forms. Many people assume that chiles are used primarily for the spiciness provided by the *capsaicin* that is found in most chiles in varying levels, but in fact many are used for other characteristics that they provide.

Chiles provide other flavor profiles that make them particularly well suited for dishes now associated with certain regions of Mexico. When it comes to the complex tastes of the *mole* sauces found in the regions of Puebla, Veracruz, and Oaxaca, the many flavor subtleties of this famous creation rest in the specific types of chiles used to make them. *Mole negro*, with its earthy, tobacco flavor and smooth spice, utilizes the chilhuacle negro chili that is found in Oaxaca and nowhere else; *mole poblano* has a smoky flavor and a rich sweetness of dried fruits that comes in large part from the ancho and pasilla chiles. The unique flavors and heat provided by each type of chili are an important part of what makes Mexican cuisine so versatile.

Hundreds of chili varieties are used in Mexican cooking, in both fresh and dried forms. Some of the more common are as follows:

Fresh Chiles

chilaca – Elongated thin and curved chili that is normally used in its dried form, which is called *pasilla*.

habanero – Smaller, squat, very hot chiles from southern Mexico in the Yucatán region. These chiles are typically orange when ripe, although some variants may be closer to red in color; they are most often used in salsa and sauces.

jalapeño – The most common and well known of the Mexican chiles; these are about 3 inches long (sometimes bigger) and are used in making salsas, are pickled and used as a condiment, and are smoked and dried to make the prized *chipotle*.

poblano – Often erroneously called *pasilla* in the United States, these are squat, wide chiles that are used fresh in *chili rellenos* (stuffed chiles) and as filling for *enchiladas* (filled tortillas with chili sauce), among other things. These are milder chiles with thin flesh and a deep, dark green color that makes them easy to differentiate from green bell peppers.

serrano – Smaller chiles with the shape and look of smaller jalapeños, but typically with more heat; these are a common ingredient in salsas.

Dried Chiles

ancho – The dried form of poblano chiles; these are very popular for the earthy and rich aromas they provide when used in dishes. These typically are toasted on a hot *comal* (flat cooking disk) before being used in sauces, soups, and stews, as well as rehydrated and stuffed to make a different version of rellenos. These chiles are very versatile and highly regarded.

cascabel – Called the "rattle bell" because, in its dried form, the seeds rattle within the thin shell of this round, small chili. Cascabels are commonly used in sauces and soups or stews; these come from central Mexico and are most common in this region.

chilhuacle negro and rojo – From the Oaxaca region of southern Mexico, these chiles are an integral part of the mole negro that is found in this region. These chiles are found in two varieties in this region—*negro* (dark) and *rojo* (red)—both of which are short and wide and have a fruity aroma, moderate heat, and deep earthy tobacco notes that make these chiles highly prized.

chili de arbol – Called the "tree" chili, these are typically found dried and are slender and curved, with a high level of capsaicin; mainly used to add heat to dishes.

chiltepin – Very small, hot chiles that are believed to be one of the oldest species and are used in soups, stews, bean dishes, and hot salsas; also sometimes called piquin, or bird pepper, in reference to their sharp bite.

chipotle – Smoked and dried jalapeño chiles; these are often used in cooked salsas and sauces.

pasilla – These elongated and large chiles are dried chilacas; used in making stews and a necessary component in many versions of mole.

The Comal

The cooking utensil of the Native Americans in pre-Columbian Mexico was a flat earthenware disk called a comal. The comal would be heated over a fire to cook numerous ingredients—such as tortillas and sopes—on its surface, or to toast chiles and tomatoes. Today, the disk is typically metal, but the principle remains the same: dry heat cooking without fat. In the majority of European cooking with which Americans are familiar, foods are cooked using fats in a sauté pan, which develops flavors from the caramelization of sugars and the browning reactions, as well as crispness and richness from cooking in the fats. The result is quite different when cooking on a comal: the flavor reactions only come from the components that are put onto the comal, not from oil, and as a result the flavors are typically not as strong but are more true to the food. This provides much of the backbone of Mexican cooking—clean flavors that highlight the specific foods being cooked, with less complexity and interference from oils and other products than are found in many traditional European foods.

Many examples exist of Mexican foods that do use fats as a cooking medium, but this technique was nearly nonexistent prior to the arrival of the Spanish (few animal fats were available, and the refining of vegetable oils was not a part of the Mexican culinary tradition). Crispy *quesadillas* (cheese-filled corn or wheat flatbreads), chili rellenos (chiles filled with cheese and then battered and fried), *chicharron* (pork fat rendered and crisped), and *carnitas* (slow-cooked pork fried in pork fat) all came into being after the arrival of the Spanish in Mexico.

Mestizo Culture

The arrival of the Spanish in Mexico in the sixteenth century began the era of the *mestizo* (a person of mixed Spanish and Native American heritage) culture that is a dominant component of Mexico today. Although the early era of Spanish colonization of present-day Mexico was filled with heart-wrenching tragedies, one cannot argue that the culinary evolution that developed was anything less than revolutionary. The introduction of European goods to the culture of the Native American population resulted in an amazing new cuisine. Pork, cumin, and cilantro, when added to the native tomato, chili, and corn, for example, resulted in numerous dishes that blend these ingredients seamlessly. Mexican culinary arts today are closely associated with the ingredients relied on for millennia by the Native Americans as well as with the ingredients and techniques introduced by the Spanish. It is a testament to the strength of the Native American culture that their traditions were maintained in the centuries following the arrival of the Spanish.

Tortillas (flat corn dough), tamales (masa dough wrapped in corn husk, filled with various fillings, and steamed), enchiladas (filled tortillas topped with chili sauce), mole (complex sauce made with dried chiles, dried fruit, nuts or seeds, and sometimes chocolate), *salsa* (fresh sauce made from tomatoes and chiles), and frijoles were all part of the culinary culture prior to the arrival of the Spanish. These foods remain a distinct part of Mexican culture but now they are typically combined with carnitas, *carne asada* (roasted meat), cheese, cilantro, cumin, and lard—all of which were introduced by the Spanish and blended into the culinary culture so completely that one cannot imagine this cuisine without them. Fusion of culture is a product of history, and nowhere is that more obvious than Mexico.

Corn: The Grain of Life

The indigenous people of Mexico relied on native crops for a major part of their diet, and the ingredients that they relied on most heavily were corn, tomatoes, beans, and squash. Although all of these are still major components of Mexican cuisine, none achieved more importance or reverence in the native culture than corn. The Native Americans discovered that dried corn could be processed with slaked lime to convert the hard kernels to a product called *nixtamal* and then ground into a dough called *masa*, which was used to make tortillas, the basis of many Mexican meals. This dough was also used to make *antijitos* (small appetizers made from masa), tamales, enchiladas, and sopes, as well as other foods that are still common in Mexico today. Corn has become a major grain crop throughout the world, but nowhere is it more revered and appreciated than in Mexico, where it was relied on to sustain the native cultures through periods of scarce supplies for centuries prior to the arrival of the Spanish. Corn is still the focal point of most Mexican meals, typically in the form of tortillas.

In small villages and remote sections of Mexico today, you can still find women processing nixtamal on a saddle-shaped grinding stone called a *metate* to make the daily production of masa dough. The process of making the masa by hand is time consuming and laborious but also yields some of the best masa products when made fresh in this manner. Tortilla production in most of the major cities of Mexico (as in the United States) is handled in factories that produce the perfect stacks of tortillas found in most grocery stores, but many people seek out the small shops to find handmade tortillas made from corn flour (masa harina) or—even better—from nixtamal. Like most things in today's world, the difficulty of making nixtamal is forcing this trade skill to become a novelty, but one worth seeking out when the chance arises.

SIGNIFICANT SUBREGIONS

The regional variations in Mexican cuisine are greatly influenced by the climatic and geographic aspects of each area and the resulting products that are grown or raised there. Another significant factor in the development of regional cuisine is the localization of indigenous peoples and their cultural strengths and culinary traditions. The impact of the Spanish colonial period also varies throughout the country, as the Spanish did not set up many missions or towns in the southernmost area. Each region's proximity to other countries plays a role as well, but not as significantly as in many other regional cuisines. For the purpose of this text, the regions have been defined not along strict state lines but rather by more distinct climatic and cultural lines not found on maps. The following regions are listed west to east and then north to south.

Baja California

This region encompasses the landmass that extends south from the end of California into the Pacific Ocean, including the states of Baja California Norte and Baja California Sur. The region is mostly arid, with the Sierra San Pedro Martir and the Sierra de la Giganta running north to south down the peninsula and providing stark contrasts to the oceans on either side. In the northern section of this region are very fertile valleys that receive enough rain to be productive agricultural areas; this region includes the country's most significant wine-growing area as well as numerous fruit farms and cactus fields. The Baja peninsula is surrounded by water—the Gulf of California on the east and the Pacific Ocean on the west—and, not surprisingly, seafood is abundant in most areas. This area is in fact well known for its seafood, including many varieties of sport fish and abundant shellfish. The southernmost tip of this peninsula is a tourist destination and also contains ports that are used as bases for many fishing expeditions, including those for game fish such as *atun* (tuna), marlin, and *dorado* (mahi mahi). In the border town of Tijuana, a couple of Italian brothers created the now famous *ensalada César* (Caesar salad), which is often thought to have originated in other countries.

The ingredients common to the cuisine of this region include an array of seafood such as *almejas* (clams), *ostiones* (oysters), *mejillón* (mussel), callo (scallop), *callo de hacha* (pinna clam), *calamar* (squid), *opa* (opah), *cazón* (dogfish), and *rabalo* (sea bass), as well as many more, while the fertile valleys of the northern section of Baja yield *uvas* (grapes), aguacate, *fresas* (strawberries), mangoes, *lechuga* (lettuce), maíz, and papaya. The more arid areas are mainly sources of *nopales* (cactus). Some of the dishes and recipes common to this region include ensalada César, *ceviche* (shellfish or fish marinated in citrus and chili), *callo de hacha con aguacate* (scallop-stuffed avocados), and *sopa de almejas* (clam soup).

The North

This large section of Mexico is more rural in general and includes the states of Sonora, Chihuahua, Coahuila, and Nuevo Leon. This region is distinct from most of the rest of Mexico in that it is predominately high desert that yields few products for sustenance. Prior to the arrival of the Spanish, the indigenous culture was nomadic peoples who lived off whatever was available, including roots and insects. Following the arrival of the Spanish and the livestock they brought with them, this became a cattle, crop, and herding region, and the cuisine thus changed to include these products. This region is known for producing excellent cheese and is the primary cattle-rearing and wheat-producing area of Mexico. The cuisine from this region remains simple, as the harsh land prevents much in the way of vegetables and seasonings being grown. There is less influence from the traditional Aztec cuisine in this region, because the Aztecs never conquered the area; those who moved here following the arrival of the Spanish were mostly mestizo or Spanish. Some of the ingredients that are common to the cuisine of this region are *harina de trigo* (wheat flour), res, *chiva* (young goat or kid), jalapeños, tomatoes, cilantro, and frijoles.

Although the cuisine is uncomplicated, this region produces some fine products and recipes that are not only enjoyed here but also sought after in other parts of Mexico, including *queso Chihuahua* (flavorful Mexican cheese), *queso Asadero* (soft, melting Mexican cheese), *cerveza* (beer), *carne seca* (dried beef), *cabrito al pastor* (spit-roasted goat), *tortilla de harina* (flat wheat dough/tortilla), and *frijoles borrachos* (drunken beans).

The Central Pacific Coast

The region of Mexico that borders the Pacific Ocean on the western shores of mainland Mexico includes the states of Sinaloa, Nayarit, Western Jalisco, Colima, and Michoacan. This region boasts excellent seafood and fertile land that produces tropical fruits in abundance, as well as major crops of rice, sugar, and wheat. Manzanillo and Acapulco are significant ports that have historically served as landing areas for goods coming from the Philippines; as a result, there are Filipino influences on some of the area's cuisine. In Western Jalisco, the town of Tequila is famous for its distilled beverage from the local agave tequilana.

Some of the ingredients commonly used in the cuisine of this region are *camarones* (shrimp), maíz, *iguana*, *coco* (coconut), *azúcar* (sugar), *platanos* (plantains), ancho chiles, *jengibre* (ginger), *arroz* (rice), trigo, and mango. Some of the specialty dishes of this region include *menudo* (tripe soup), *ceviche* (fish or shellfish in citrus and chili marinade), tamales, *tortas* (wheat buns with fillings), tequila, *camarones al la diabla* (shrimp in spicy chili sauce), *birria* (stewed goat with chiles), *chilorio* (pork with chili sauce), and *pozole verde* (corn and pork stew with green sauce).

The Central Highlands

The central area of Mexico includes the most states, with Durango, Zacatecas, San Luis Potosi, Eastern Jalisco, Aguascalientes, Guanajuato, Queretaro, Hidalgo, Estato de Mexico, Distito Federal, Tlaxcala, Puebla, and Morelia making up this area. Much of this region comprises fertile plateaus, which produce many of the crops for the country. This region also includes several of the former mining towns where the Spanish found their silver, resulting in well-developed cities with a distinct colonial Spanish feel.

The central states include the major cities of Mexico City, Morelia, Guanajuato, and Guadalajara, and are primarily drier areas with a mild climate and seasonal rains that allow for the growth of crops. These regions contain the largest populations in Mexico and thus help drive the culinary traditions of the country. This is also the region in which much of the revolution against Spanish colonization began, and the holiday that marks the day of independence (September 16) is celebrated here with vigor.

Some of the ingredients that are common to the cuisines of this region are puerco, chiva, cordero, maíz, pavo, agave, fresa, ajo, cebolla, frijoles, and tomates. Because this is a very large region, there are many specialties here. Some of the more common and interesting are *birria* (chili-stewed goat), menudo (tripe and chili), *pozole* (corn and pork stew with garnishments), mole poblano, and numerous *masa antojitos* (appetizers made from corn dough).

The Gulf Coast

This area includes the states of Tamaulipas, Veracruz, and Tabasco and is sandwiched between the Sierra Madre Oriental Mountains in the west and the Gulf of Mexico in the east. This is a mostly fertile coastal area that is probably best known as the place Hernan Cortez and his men made landfall in 1519 and established a port city, just north of present day Veracruz, that would change the world forever. The region retains many traces of Spanish colonization in the ingredients that are grown and used here; a distinct Caribbean influence can also be noted in the cuisine, as Havana was a transfer location for the wealth that left Mexico on its way to Spain. Because of this relationship with the islands of the Caribbean, and the later use of slaves, there are both Spanish and African influences here.

Some of the ingredients common to this region are citrico, pescado, *marisco* (shellfish), *aceite de oliva* (olive oil), *cacahuete* (peanut), *alcaparras* (capers), azúcar, trigo, maíz, tomates, *cacao* (chocolate), *café* (coffee), *vainilla* (vanilla beans), *hoja santa* (leaf of yerba santa), and cilantro. This region is well known for its seafood; some of the common recipes and products from this region are ceviche, *huachinango a la Veracruzana* (snapper cooked in Veracruz style), *pollo encacahuatado* (chicken in peanut sauce), *caldo de mariscos* (shellfish stew), and *salpicón de jaiba* (seasoned and shredded crabmeat).

The Southern Pacific Coast

The states of Guerrero, Oaxaca, and Chiapas make up the southern portion of the pacific coastal section of Mexico. This region is home to both the impressive Sierra Madre del Sur and the beaches of Acapulco. There is a great deal of evidence of the indigenous peoples of Mexico here, including the cuisine. This region was home to the Zapotec, who resisted the Aztec before the arrival of the Spanish and then resisted the Spanish for years; they adhered to their traditions as fiercely as they defended their homeland. The use of chiles, chocolate, Jamaica flowers, masa, and beans is prevalent in the local cuisine. This region

is primarily mountainous, and the climate is warm and mostly dry.

Some of the common ingredients in the cuisine of this region are *frijoles negros* (black beans), *grillos* (grasshoppers), *flor de calabaza* (squash blossoms), *manteca* (lard), *epazote* (a distinct herb sometimes called wormseed in the United States), maíz, tomates, *flor de Jamaica* (hibiscus flowers), *pasilla negro* (dark pasilla chiles), ancho chiles, and the husked relative of the tomato called *tomatillo*. Some of the dishes and recipes that are common to this region are *chapulines* (grasshoppers seasoned with chili and lime), *mole negro* (dark mole), *mole verde* (green mole), *mole rojo* (red mole), and *butifarra* (a type of sausage).

The Yucatán Peninsula

The Yucatán Peninsula includes the states of Campeche, Yucatán, and Quintana Roo, and is distinct geographically in that it juts out into the Gulf of Mexico and toward the Caribbean. Cortez first landed here in 1519, sailing from Cuba, and the great Mayan civilization reached its peak here (and in Chiapas) between 200 and 900 AD. Much of this region is dense tropical forests or flatland, and the climate is very hot. This region is the most unchanged from the times of precontact to present day, as the descendants of the great Mayans still follow many of their customs. There are also strong influences from the Caribbean in this area, because of the proximity to the islands and the interactions with slaves during Spanish rule. The extensive coastline of this region yields a significant amount of seafood in the cuisine as well as tropical ingredients.

Some of the common ingredients in the cuisine of this region are achiote, *platanos* (plantains), *pepitas* (pumpkin seeds), habanero chiles, epazote, frijoles negros, *naranja agria* (bitter orange), pavo, cebolla, and venado. This region also is home to some of the most interesting dishes in Mexico, such as *cochinita pibil* (barbequed pork), *sopa de lima* (lime-infused soup), *papadzules* (tacos topped with pumpkin-seed sauce), *pollo motuleño* (chicken cooked with bitter orange, achiote, and fried plantains) and *poc chuc* (grilled pork with bitter orange).

RECIPES

The following recipes provide a introduction to Mexican cuisine and the ingredients and methods common throughout.

Nixtamal (Maíz para Masa)   CENTRAL AND SOUTHERN MEXICO

(PREPARING CORN FOR TORTILLAS, TAMALES, OR SOPES)

INGREDIENTS

2	lb	Dried White Corn
1	Tbsp	Calcium Oxide
2	qts	Cold Water

Although this is no longer made by nearly every family in Mexico and is often purchased instead, this technique and the resulting dough are perhaps the most Mexican of all foods. The nixtamalization of corn yields a more digestible and nutritious form and gave the native peoples of ancient Mexico a reliable source of food. This recipe yields hominy, or the basis for *masa,* which would traditionally be ground on a flat rock or used whole to make soups and stews, such as today's *pozole.*

YIELD: Approximately 4 pounds

COOKING METHOD: Simmering

PROCEDURE

1. Combine corn and water in a nonreactive pot (not aluminum; pots with a coating over metal are okay) and bring to a simmer.

2. Add the calcium oxide to the simmering water and continue to cook until the husk of the corn kernels becomes loose and papery. (Rub kernels between fingers to test, cleaning hands after testing.) This should take approximately 15 minutes.

3. Remove from heat and set aside to soak overnight.

4. The next day, strain the corn kernels and rub them between your hands under cold running water to remove the skins from the corn. This mixture is now ready to be ground for making masa or used as hominy in its whole form.

Boiling corn before addition of slaked lime (calcium oxide) for making nixtamal (note color)

Boiling Corn after addition of slaked lime (calcium oxide) for making nixtamal (note color)

Rubbing the treated corn kernels together to remove the husks

Tortillas ALL REGIONS

(CORN FLATBREAD)

INGREDIENTS

1	lb	Masa Harina or 1.75 lbs Freshly Made Masa
1	tsp	Salt (optional; traditional version did not contain salt)
		Water, as needed (approximately 2.5 cups for masa harina and very little for the fresh masa)

Tortillas are a main component in Mexican cuisine and are used as both a serving utensil and a basic ingredient in virtually all dishes. Tortillas are traditionally cooked on a comal, a flat-baked clay dish (now often made of metal) set over a wood-burning flame.

YIELD: Approximately 20

COOKING METHOD: Cooking by Direct Contact on Comal or Another Flat, Hot Surface (not sautéing!)

PROCEDURE

1. Preheat the comal or griddle to approximately 375°F.
2. In a mixing bowl, combine the masa and the salt, and mix thoroughly.
3. Add water to the masa in small increments, until the dough is just moist enough to bind to itself (the tendency is to add too much water, in which case the dough will stick to the tortilla press; make sure to add the water slowly and give the masa a chance to absorb it before adding more).
4. Set the dough aside for a minimum of 30 minutes to rest and absorb water.
5. Once the dough has rested, it can be divided into approximately 20 pieces and then pressed on a tortilla press. (While you are pressing the dough, keep the other masa balls covered with a damp cloth to prevent drying out.)
6. Cook the tortillas on the hot comal or griddle until the bottoms become slightly specked with brown spots (about 3 minutes), and then turn and cook them on the other side for an additional 2 minutes. (Once the tortillas are cooked, they should be covered with a damp cloth to keep them from drying out.)

Tamales con Poblano y Queso CENTRAL HIGHLAND REGION

(STEAMED CORN DOUGH IN CORN HUSKS WITH CHILI AND CHEESE)

INGREDIENTS

8	oz	Lard
1/2	tsp	Salt
1	lb	Harina Para Tamales (not masa harina, which has finer texture)

These tamales—traditionally made by hand in Mexico—are quite laborious to make, particularly when the nixtamale and resulting dough are prepared from scratch. With a nearly endless variation of available fillings, tamales may be the most versatile of Mexican foods.

YIELD: Approximately 20

COOKING METHOD (CHILES): Fire Roasted

COOKING METHOD (TAMALES): Steamed

(continues)

*Tamales con
Poblano y Queso*

(continued)

10	oz	Flavorful Chicken Stock (warmed to 80°F)
20–25		Corn Husks, soaked in warm water
10	oz	Salsa Verde
5		Poblano Chiles (about 2 lbs)
1	lb	Queso Oaxaca

PROCEDURE

1. Preheat the steamer.
2. Roast the poblano chiles over a direct flame until they are charred all over, and then place them in a covered container (or in plastic wrap) to steam.
3. Once the chiles are cool enough to handle, peel the charred skin off of the peppers and cut into strips 1/4 inch wide.
4. Cut the cheese into strips approximately 1/4 inch wide and 3 inches long.
5. In a mixer with a whip attachment, combine the lard and salt; beat on high speed until the lard becomes white and doubles in volume.
6. Alternately add harina para tamales and warm broth to the beaten lard—1/4 of total at a time—thoroughly beating them into the lard after each addition.
7. Once all of the harina and broth have been added, place a small ball of the tamale dough into a glass of water. It should float; if it doesn't, beat the mixture further to make it lighter.
8. Once the dough is prepared, set out the soaked corn husks and spread a thin layer of the tamale dough on the widest half (bottom half) of each corn husk (this should require approximately 2 Tbsp of dough/corn husk).
9. Place 1 Tbsp of the salsa verde on the thin layer of tamale dough, and top the salsa with a couple strips of cheese and a few slices of poblano.
10. Fold in both sides of the corn husk, with the pointed end facing away from you, and then fold the pointed end of the husk in half, back toward yourself, to complete the wrapping process. If desired, the husks can be tied with thin strips of corn husk or simply placed in the steamer with the open ends up.
11. Steam the tamales in a commercial steamer for 1 hour, or in a stovetop steamer for 1 hour and 15 minutes.

Tamales con poblano y queso (steamed corn dough in corn husks, filled with poblano chiles and cheese)

Tortillas de Harina NORTE MEXICO
(WHEAT FLOUR FLATBREAD)

INGREDIENTS

1.5	lbs	High-Gluten Flour (Bread Flour) + flour for dusting bench
5	oz	Lard, softened
2	tsp	Salt
		Warm Water, as needed (approximately 12 oz)

Wheat flour tortillas are used mostly in northern Mexico, as the north contains the plains that produce the majority of the country's wheat.

YIELD: 2 pounds of dough, or approximately 20 tortillas (10 inches in diameter)

COOKING METHOD: Cooking by Direct Contact on Comal or Another Flat, Hot Surface (not sautéing!)

PROCEDURE

1. Preheat the griddle to 375°F, and have some clean, damp (not wet) cloths set aside for covering the tortillas as they are cooked to prevent them from drying out.

2. The dough can be made by hand on the bench or in a mixer. If making on the bench, sift the flour onto the bench. If making in a mixer, add the flour to the mixer.

3. Combine the lard and salt, and mix thoroughly.

4. Add the lard to the flour in small pieces, and work it into the flour until the flour resembles coarse meal.

5. Add the water to the flour mixture until a cohesive dough is formed with a smooth, soft texture. Continue to knead the dough until the dough becomes elastic; cover, and allow the dough to rest for 45 minutes.

6. Divide the dough into 20 pieces on the bench, and roll them out into circles using a rolling pin.

7. Place the tortillas on the hot griddle and cook on one side until tortillas puff slightly and brown in spots (less than 1 minute). Turn over and cook tortillas on the second side for another 20–30 seconds, and then remove and cover them with the damp towel.

8. Continue the process with all of the dough pieces.

Salsa Verde CENTRAL HIGHLANDS
(TOMATILLO SAUCE)

INGREDIENTS

4	oz	Red Onion, chopped
.5	oz	Garlic Cloves, chopped
2		Serrano Chiles, chopped (can adjust for varying heat intensity)
1	lb	Tomatillos
2	Tbsp	Cilantro, chopped
		Salt, to taste

This is a very common condiment that is served with tacos, used to make enchiladas, and eaten as a dip for corn chips. The tomatillo is the fruit of a plant not related to tomatoes, although it is sometimes called the green Mexican tomato or husked tomato. The tomatillos need to be dehusked and rinsed to remove the sticky resin from their skin, but they do not need to be skinned to be puréed into smooth salsas.

YIELD: 2 cups

COOKING METHOD: Simmering

(continues)

Salsa Verde
(continued)

PROCEDURE

1. Bring a pot of water large enough to hold all of the ingredients to a boil; add the onions, garlic, and serrano chiles, and simmer for 3 minutes.

2. Add the tomatillos to the pot, and continue to cook until the tomatillos become soft to the touch (about 5 minutes).

3. Strain all of the ingredients and allow them to cool.

4. Place all ingredients in a food processor, and pulse to achieve desired consistency (you may need to add water); add cilantro and season with salt.

Guacamole CENTRAL AND SOUTHERN MEXICO
(SPICED AVOCADO AND CILANTRO CONDIMENT)

INGREDIENTS

2	oz	White Onion, minced
2		Serrano Chiles, minced (use fewer chiles, if you prefer milder)
1/4	cup	Cilantro Leaves, chopped
1/4	tsp	Salt
4		Avocados, seeds and shells removed
1		Tomato, ripe and diced small

This very well-known mixture of avocado, onion, chiles, and cilantro has become a standard in U.S. kitchens. The traditional guacamole is made with a molcajete (mortar and pestle), which results in a far superior product by crushing the chiles and onion, releasing the flavor into the avocados.

YIELD: 2 cups

MIXING METHOD: Grinding in a Molcajete

PROCEDURE

1. Combine onions, chiles, cilantro, and salt in a mortar and pestle, and grind to a paste.

2. Add the avocados to the mortar and pestle, and crush coarsely to create a chunky paste.

3. Mix in tomatoes; adjust seasoning, if necessary.

Guacamole (spiced avocado and cilantro condiment) in a molcajete (traditional bowl)

Salsa Mexicana (Pico de Gallo) MEXICO
(FRESH TOMATO, CHILI, ONION, AND CILANTRO SAUCE)

INGREDIENTS

1	lb	Ripe Tomatoes, diced medium
5	oz	White Onion, diced small
2		Serrano Chiles, minced (adjust to desired spice level; this will be hot)
1/4	cup	Cilantro Leaves, minced
1/4	tsp	Salt (use to adjust taste, which will vary with ripeness of tomatoes)

This versatile condiment, which has become one of the most popular condiments in the United States, is addictive, healthy, and easy to prepare. In some areas of Mexico, this is called pico de gallo, which translates to "beak of the rooster," in reference to its sharp bite.

YIELD: 2.5 cups

PROCEDURE

Combine all prepared ingredients in a nonreactive bowl, and mix thoroughly to blend flavors well. The flavor of this sauce will improve if it is allowed to sit for 30 minutes or so, but it will deteriorate in texture and flavor if it is made too far in advance (anything over 2 hours—and please do not make it a day in advance!).

Chili Rellenos CENTRAL HIGHLANDS
(POBLANO CHILI STUFFED WITH CHEESE)

INGREDIENTS

8		Large Poblano Chiles
1	lb	Quesillo de Oaxaca (if this is unavailable, use Monterey or Pepper Jack cheese), grated
1	cup	Flour
1/2	tsp	Salt
4		Egg Whites
4		Egg Yolks
		Vegetable Oil (enough to measure 1/2 inch in the pan you will be using to panfry the chiles—approximately 2 cups, depending on the pan)

This classic shows how the introduction of cheese to the Mexican diet married wonderfully with the milder poblano chili. The Spanish also introduced the technique of frying foods, and its application in the making of this dish highlights the culinary possibilities that arrived with the Spanish.

YIELD: 8 servings (1 chili/serving)
COOKING METHOD (POBLANO): Fire Roasting
COOKING METHOD (STUFFED AND BATTERED CHILI): Panfrying

PROCEDURE

1. Place the vegetable oil in the pan, and heat over a low flame to preheat the oil (you will want the oil to be 350° for frying later).
2. Roast the chiles over the open flame of the stove burners until they are blackened all over; place them in a container and cover it with plastic wrap right away to steam the chiles.
3. Remove the skins from the chiles by rubbing them with your hands (do not run them under water, which will remove the skin *and* the flavor).
4. Using a sharp knife, make a slit from the stem end of each chili to its tip.
5. Carefully open each chili and, using a paring knife, slice the membrane just above the seed pod to remove the entire seed pod without removing the top of the chili.

(continues)

Chili Rellenos
(continued)

6. Pull out any large vein membranes at the chili segmentation lines.

7. Stuff each of the chiles with 2 oz of the grated Oaxaca cheese.

8. In a small bowl or another appropriate container, sift the flour and salt; mix well.

9. In a mixing bowl with a whip attachment (or in a bowl using a whisk by hand), add the egg whites and whip to soft peaks.

10. While beating, add the egg yolks and salt; beat them into the egg white mixture thoroughly.

11. Turn the heat up under the oil to 350°F (do not try to do this in a deep-fat fryer, because the chiles will stick to the baskets).

12. Dredge the stuffed peppers in the flour (tapping the peppers to remove any excess flour), and then dip the peppers in the egg mixture, coating them completely with the egg mixture prior to setting them in the now-hot oil.

13. Fry the chiles on both sides until slightly golden, and then remove them from the oil and serve immediately.

Chili rellenos (poblano chili stuffed with cheese), shown served with chili sauce

Escalfar Pollo CENTRAL HIGHLANDS

(POACHED CHICKEN)

INGREDIENTS

4	lbs	Whole Bone-in Chicken Breasts, split
2.5	qts	Chicken Stock, cold
1	lb	Onion, sliced
1/2	lb	Carrots, diced medium
2		Jalapeños, sliced
1	tsp	Black Peppercorns, crushed
1	tsp	Salt

Poached chicken is commonly used as a filling for enchiladas, tacos, tostadas, and tortes throughout Mexico. Poaching results in a more tender and juicy product when done properly, and the resulting broth can be used to make soups or sauces.

YIELD: Approximately 2.5 pounds

COOKING METHOD: Poaching

PROCEDURE

1. Place all ingredients in an appropriately sized pot, and bring them to a simmer over a medium-high flame.

2. Lower heat to a medium-low flame to adjust to poaching temperature, and poach until the chicken has reached the proper internal temperature at the thickest part of the breast (this should take approximately 20 minutes after achieving poaching temperature, depending on the thickness of the breasts).

3. Remove the chicken breasts from the poaching liquid and place them in a refrigerator, uncovered, to cool. The resulting broth can be strained and used in other preparations—just be sure to remember that it has had chiles and salt added to it.

4. Once it is cool enough to handle, fabricate the chicken meat off of the bones and set the meat aside to be used in other preparations.

Enchiladas Verde con Pollo CENTRAL HIGHLANDS

(CORN TORTILLAS STUFFED WITH CHICKEN IN GREEN SAUCE)

INGREDIENTS

2	lbs	Poblano Chiles
4	oz	Vegetable Oil
20		Corn Tortillas (5–6 inches in diameter)
4	cups	Salsa Verde (2 x recipe, this chapter)
2	lbs	Poached Chicken, pulled into strips (.8 x recipe, this chapter)
12	oz	Queso Anejo or Cojito, grated

Enchiladas are a common method of eating tortillas with various fillings. Rather than folding the ingredients into a fresh tortilla—as is done when making tacos—enchiladas are fried, dipped in the sauce they will served in, filled, coated with more sauce, and often topped with cheese (as in this recipe).

YIELD: 20 enchiladas (approximately 6 ounces each)

COOKING METHOD (POBLANO): Fire Roasting or Cooking on Comal

PROCEDURE

1. Preheat the oven to 325°F if you want melted cheese on top of the enchiladas.

2. Fire roast the chiles over a flame until they are charred completely black all over, and then set them in a container and cover immediately with plastic wrap to allow them to steam (this can be achieved by cooking the chiles on a hot comal as well). Once cooled, remove

(continues)

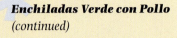

Enchiladas Verde con Pollo
(continued)

the charred skins by brushing them off with your hands (do not run them under water, which will remove skins *and* flavor). Remove the seed pod from each chili and cut them into strips.

3. Heat the vegetable oil in a small sauté pan, until the oil begins to ripple or reaches 350°F. Lightly fry the tortillas in the hot oil by quickly passing one side through the oil, turning them over, and doing the same to the other side (you do not want to make them crisp; just soften them and get a light coating of oil on each one). Once each tortilla has passed through on both sides, place it on a towel to absorb excess oil; continue until they are done.

4. In a separate pan, heat the salsa verde over a low flame until it is just warmed enough to thin slightly.

5. Dip the fried tortillas into the warmed salsa verde, and place them onto a serving dish.

6. Place poached chicken (approximately 1.25 oz) and roasted chili strips (approximately 1 oz) in the center of each tortilla; roll the tortilla around the filling, making sure that the open end of the tortilla is on the bottom of the serving dish. Top the rolled enchiladas with 1 oz of the remaining salsa verde and some of the grated cheese (approximately .5 oz/enchilada).

7. If you desire melted cheese on top of the enchiladas, they can be placed in the preheated oven after being rolled and topped with cheese.

NOTE: *Enchiladas are often served with shredded lettuce, diced onions, refried beans, and sour cream.*

Enchiladas verde con pollo (corn tortillas stuffed with chicken and topped with tomatillo sauce), shown served with rice, beans, lettuce, and tomatoes

Frijoles de la Olla (Black Beans) Southern States
(Pot Beans)

INGREDIENTS

2	lbs	Black Beans or Pinto Beans
2	qts	Water
1	oz	Lard
1/2	lb	Yellow Onions, diced small
1	oz	Garlic Cloves, minced
		Soaked Beans
2.5	qts	Water
1	tsp	Salt
5	sprigs	Epazote (if you are making black beans)
		Salt, to taste

Throughout Mexico, beans regularly follow the main course; the remaining cooked beans are used to make refried beans. Pinto beans are used most often in the northern part of the country, whereas black beans are most common in the south.

YIELD: 4 pounds, or 16 portions (4 ounces/portion)

COOKING METHOD: Simmering

PROCEDURE

1. Combine beans and water in a container, and soak overnight.
2. Drain the water from the soaking beans, and set the beans aside.
3. In a pot large enough to hold all of the ingredients, heat lard until it is rippling in the pan; add the onions and garlic, and sweat until translucent and tender.
4. Add beans, water, and 1 tsp salt to the pot, and bring the entire mixture to a simmer over a medium flame.
5. Simmer beans until they become very tender (approximately 2 hours), and then add the epazote; adjust seasoning with salt.

Arroz a la Mexicana Many Regions
(Rice in the Style of Mexico)

INGREDIENTS

3	cups	Long-Grain Rice
2	oz	Vegetable Oil
5	oz	Yellow Onion, minced
1	oz	Garlic, minced
1	Tbsp	Serrano Chili, minced
12	oz	Tomatoes, diced small
1	tsp	Salt
4.5	cups	Chicken Stock (or vegetable stock)
		Salt, to taste

Although it is not an ingredient indigenous to Mexico, rice has become a regular feature of the Mexican diet, and this recipe is the most common way that it would be prepared. Rice is often cooked plain on the coast and in the southern areas. The method used to make this rice reveals not only the Spanish heritage of this preparation but also the Arab/Persian influence on the Spanish, who brought this method from Spain after it was introduced there by the Moors (Arabic peoples).

YIELD: Approximately 3.75 pounds, or 15 portions (4 ounces/portion)

COOKING METHOD: Persian Cooking of Rice (Cooked in Fat and Then Baked)

PROCEDURE

1. Preheat the oven to 350°F.
2. Rinse the rice in a china cap with cold water until the water runs clear, and then let it stand and drain for 5 minutes.
3. In a 3–4 qt heavy-bottomed pot, heat the oil over a medium flame; add the yellow onion, garlic, and serrano chili, and fry while stirring until the vegetables just begin to color.
4. Add the rice, and continue to fry and stir until the rice begins to turn translucent and brown slightly.

(continues)

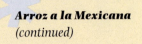

Arroz a la Mexicana
(continued)

5. Add the remaining ingredients, and turn the heat up to bring the mixture to a simmer.

6. Once it is simmering, cover the pot firmly with a lid and foil (if necessary); place the pot in the oven, and bake for 20 minutes (this step can also be done on the stovetop—as it would be done traditionally—but care must be taken to control the heat).

7. Remove the rice from the oven; once it is cool enough to sample, adjust seasoning as needed.

Ensalata Nopalitos   NORTE MEXICO
(CACTUS LEAF SALAD)

INGREDIENTS

For Preparing the Nopales

2	lbs	Nopales (the smaller, the better)
8	oz	Yellow Onion, sliced thin
.5	oz	Garlic Cloves, minced
1		Jalapeño, minced
1/2	tsp	Salt
1	tsp	Mexican Oregano
1	tsp	Baking Soda (or husks from 1 lb of tomatillos)

For Assembling the Salad

		Nopales (see above), diced medium
8	oz	Yellow Onion, shaved very thin (use a mandoline or slicer)
1	tsp	Mexican Oregano
2	Tbsp	Jalapeño, minced
2	Tbsp	Lime Juice
2	oz	Corn Oil (substitute light olive oil, if this is unavailable)
1/2	tsp	Salt
1	lb	Ripe Tomatoes, diced medium
1	cup	Cilantro, chopped (about 1/4 bunch)
2	Ripe	Avocados, sliced thin
8	oz	Queso Fresco, crumbled
		Salt, to taste

Nopales, or cactus pads, have been part of Mexican cuisine for centuries, particularly in the arid north where cactus have long helped produce food and water for the people of this area. Cactus have a bit of a mucilage texture that will thicken soups or stews—much like okra—but this is undesirable in a salad, and thus they need to be rinsed after cooking to remove this.

YIELD: 10 portions (6 ounces/portion)

COOKING METHOD (NOPALES): Simmering

PROCEDURE

For Preparing the Nopales

1. Clean the nopales by taking off the spines (if they aren't removed already) and, using a peeler, peel the tough eyes (the spots where the spines were).

(continues)

Ensalata nopalitos
(cactus leaf salad)

Ensalata Nopalitos
(continued)

2. Place the nopales, onions, garlic, jalapeño, salt, Mexican oregano, and baking soda (or tomatillo husks) in an appropriately sized pan or pot, and cover with water.

3. Simmer the nopales over a medium flame until they become tender (about 20 minutes, depending on the thickness of the nopales).

4. Remove the pan or pot from heat, and then remove the nopales from the water; place the nopales under cold running water to remove the mucilage liquid released. At this point, the nopales are ready to be cut for the salad.

For Assembling the Salad

1. In a bowl, combine the diced nopales, shaved onion, Mexican oregano, jalapeño, lime juice, salt, and corn oil; mix thoroughly and set aside for at least 30 minutes so that ingredients can marinate.

2. When ready for service, toss diced tomato and cilantro with the marinated salad ingredients.

3. Adjust seasoning of salad; plate with a few slices of avocado on the base of each plate, topped with mixed salad, and finished with more avocado slices and crumbled queso fresco.

Sopa de Lima YUCATÁN

(CHICKEN AND LIME SOUP WITH TORTILLAS)

INGREDIENTS

For Making the Broth

(**Note:** If you are also making the poached chicken recipe, substitute the broth from that recipe for the water in this recipe for more flavor.)

1	tsp	Cumin Seeds
1/2	stick	Cinnamon
1	tsp	Black Peppercorns
1/2	tsp	Allspice Berries, whole
2	lbs	Chicken Carcasses, Wings, or Other Bones
2.5	lbs	Chicken Breasts, bone-in (approx 2 unsplit breasts)
.5	lb	Onion, sliced
1	oz	Garlic Cloves, chopped
.25	lb	Limes (preferably Yucatan bitter limes, called *lima agria*, or key limes)
1	gallon	water
2	tsp	Salt

The Yucatán was home to the ancient Mayans, and their reliance on and reverence for corn and tortillas is one of the aspects of their culture that has remained to this day. Following the introduction of citrus by the Spanish, limes made their way into this culture—and are used in this recipe.

YIELD: 12 portions (8 oz/portion) + garnishes

COOKING METHOD (DRIED SPICES): Dry Toasting on Comal or Sauté Pan

COOKING METHOD (BROTH): Poaching

COOKING METHOD (TOMATOES): Charring on Comal or Griddle

COOKING METHOD (CHILI): Charring Over Flame or on Griddle

COOKING METHOD (SOUP): Simmering

PROCEDURE

For Making the Broth

1. Toast the cumin, cinnamon stick, black peppercorns, and allspice berries in a dry sauté pan over a medium-low flame, until the cumin begins to pop and/or the spices begin to release a distinct aroma (be careful not to burn them!).

2. Combine the toasted spices—along with all of the other ingredients—in an appropriately sized pot.

(continues)

❋

Sopa de Lima

(continued)

For Making the Soup

1	lb	Tomatoes
1		Habanero Chili (substitute 2 serranos, if this chili is unavailable)
2		Poblano Chiles
2.5	qts	Chicken Broth (see above)
		Chicken Breast Meat (see above), pulled or diced medium
.5	lb	Limes (preferably Mexican limes or key limes), juiced
		Salt, to taste

For Garnishes

1/2	cup	Cilantro Leaves, chopped
.25	lb	Limes (preferably Mexican limes or key limes), sliced
1	lb	Avocados, diced
8		Corn Tortillas, cut into strips and fried until crisp

3. Bring the whole pot to a simmer over a medium-high flame, and then turn the heat down to a gentle poach; lightly poach for 30 minutes.

4. Remove the chicken breasts from the broth, and set them aside to cool in the refrigerator (uncovered).

5. Continue to simmer the broth for another hour; turn off the heat and strain the broth through cheesecloth.

For Making the Soup

1. On a dry griddle (set to 400°F) or in a dry sauté pan, char the tomatoes until their skin becomes loose and they blacken slightly; set aside.

2. Fire roast the chiles over a flame or on the dry griddle until they are blackened or charred on the exterior; immediately place them in a container and cover them with plastic wrap. Once they have cooled, slide the charred skin off using your hands (wear gloves!).

3. Roughly chop the tomatoes, slice the poblano chiles into strips, and mince the habaneros. Combine all of these with the chicken broth, chicken meat, and lime juice, and bring the entire mixture to a simmer over medium heat.

4. Adjust seasoning with salt.

5. Serve with garnishes on the side.

Bowl of sopa de lima (chicken and lime soup) with garnishes of lime, tortilla chips, and avocado

✳ Pozole JALISCO
(PORK AND HOMINY SOUP)

INGREDIENTS

For Preparing the Corn

2	lbs	Dried Corn for Pozole (large white corn kernels)
3	qts	Cold Water
.5	oz	Calcium Oxide (may be labeled "cal" or "lime")
1	tsp	Salt

For Making the Pozole

4	lbs	Pork Butt, cut into 1.5-inch cubes
2	lbs	Pork Bones
1	lb	Onion, diced medium
1	oz	Garlic Cloves, minced
3	qts	Cold Water
		Prepared Corn (see above)
1	tsp	Salt
		Salt, to taste

For Garnishing the Pozole

8	oz	Radishes, sliced 1/4 inch thick
12	oz	White Onion, diced small
1	lb	Limes, wedged
3	Tbsp	Mexican Oregano
2	Tbsp	Chili de Arbol, powdered (you can substitute cayenne, if this is unavailable)
10	oz	Fried Corn Tortilla Strips

This classic mestizo recipe is very typical of Jalisco and Guerrero, and it highlights the marriage of the Spanish-introduced pork and the native Mexican corn. This can be a soup or an entrée and is served with the traditional garnishes of lime wedges, radishes, diced onion, dried Mexican oregano, chili powder, and corn chips.

YIELD: 15 portions (10 ounces/portion) + garnishes

COOKING METHOD (BOTH CORN AND POZOLE): Simmering

PROCEDURE

For Preparing the Corn

1. In order to shorten the cooking time and cook more evenly, soak the corn in water overnight if possible (as would be done with dried beans).

2. Drain the soaked corn, and combine it with the calcium oxide and water in an appropriately sized pot; bring to a simmer (the corn will change from whitish to yellow in color), and simmer for 20 minutes. Remove from heat.

3. After the corn has cooled enough to handle in the pot (another 20 minutes), strain the corn through a colander; while running cold water over the corn, rub the kernels to remove the slightly slimy husks that have been loosened and deteriorated by the alkali (calcium oxide).

4. Once the husks are off, remove the hard pedicel at the pointed end of the kernels using a paring knife.

5. The corn is now ready to be used in the pozole (this process is the same used to make tortillas or tamales, which would traditionally be ground on a metate but are more commonly made with a grinder now).

For Making the Pozole

1. Combine the cut pork butt, pork bones, onion, garlic, water, prepared corn, and salt in a suitable pot, and bring to a simmer.

2. Reduce heat and slowly simmer until pork is very tender and corn is cooked (approximately 2.5 hours).

For Garnishing the Pozole

1. Serve the pozole on a dish with the garnishes so that guests can add the desired garnishes to their own pozole.

Bowl of pozole (pork with hominy) with garnishes

Mole Poblano   PUEBLA AND OAXACA

(TURKEY WITH CHILI, ONION, CHOCOLATE, AND GROUND SEASONINGS)

INGREDIENTS

4	oz	Ancho Chiles
2	oz	Pasilla Chiles
2	oz	Chili Mulato
4	oz	Peanuts, raw
1.5	lbs	Tomatoes, ripe
10	lbs	Turkey, cleaned (you can substitute 3 whole chickens, if desired)
4	oz	Lard
2	oz	Pumpkins Seeds
1	lb	White Onion, sliced thin
1.5	oz	Garlic Cloves
.5	lb	Tomatillos
6	oz	Raisins
1		Cinnamon Stick
1/2	tsp	Freshly Ground Black Peppercorns
2	qts	Chicken Stock
5	oz	Mexican Chocolate, grated
		Salt, to taste

Mole is one of the more complicated dishes found in Mexican cooking. The name is thought to come from the Nahuatl word *molli*, which refers to a mixture of ingredients ground together. Many variations of mole can be found throughout Mexico (some recipes call for as many as 100 ingredients!), with the most popular ones coming from the Puebla and Oaxaca regions. The following recipe is typical of the Puebla version of this wonderful dish.

YIELD: 10 portions (8 ounces/portion)

COOKING METHOD (DRIED CHILES, PEANUTS, AND TOMATO): Toasting on Comal or Hot Pan

COOKING METHOD (MOLE): Stewing

PROCEDURE

1. Preheat the oven to 325°F.

2. In a dry sauté pan set over a medium-low flame, toast the chiles until they begin to turn fragrant and color slightly (be careful not to burn them!). Turn them so they color on both sides, and then remove the stems and set them aside (leave the seeds in the chiles—just remove the stems).

3. Place the peanuts in the same pan, and toast them until they begin to turn brown; take them out of the pan and set aside.

4. Turn the heat up to a medium-high flame. Once hot, add the tomatoes to the pan and allow the skins to char. Turn them so they char in a few places, and then remove them from the pan and set aside.

5. Fabricate the turkey into legs, thighs, wings, and breasts—cut the breasts into 3 pieces each (you should have a total of 12 pieces)—leaving the bones in and the skin on.

6. Add the lard to a braising pan large enough to hold all of the ingredients, and melt over a medium-high flame until very hot.

7. Season the turkey pieces and sauté them in the lard, turning as necessary, until they are golden brown on all sides; remove them from the pan.

8. Drain excess fat from the pan, leaving about 2 Tbsp, and add the pumpkin seeds; fry them in the fat for 2 minutes, stirring the entire time.

9. Lower the heat, and add the onion and garlic to the pan; sweat until tender and translucent.

10. Add the turkey back to the pan, along with any liquid that may have pooled with sitting; also add the peanuts, tomatoes, chiles, tomatillos, raisins, cinnamon, pepper, and chicken broth (but not the chocolate!).

Mole poblano (turkey cooked in chili/chocolate sauce) served with rice

(continues)

Mole Poblano
(continued)

11. Bring the entire mixture to a simmer, and then cover the pan with foil and a lid. Place the pan in the preheated oven (this step also can be done on the stovetop, which would be more traditional, but it is easier to control heat in the oven). Braise the mixture for 1.5 hours, and then remove.

12. Remove the turkey pieces and the cinnamon stick from the pan (check the deepest part of the turkey to ensure that it has reached the proper internal temperature), and carefully transfer the entire contents of the pan to blender(s); purée to a smooth paste (alternatively, a burr-type shaft blender can be used to process the contents in the pan).

13. Return the sauce to the pan and, over low heat, add the grated chocolate; mix in to melt. If the sauce is too thick, it can be thinned with stock at this point; if it is too thin, it should be reduced to the proper consistency.

14. Check the seasoning of the sauce and adjust, if necessary.

Huachinango a la Veracruzana VERACRUZ
(RED SNAPPER IN THE STYLE OF VERACRUZ)

The use of Spanish ingredients and techniques is perhaps more strongly retained in the cuisine of the Veracruz region than anywhere else in Mexico. This dish includes the use of olives, capers, and olive oil—all ingredients that were not commonly adopted in other regions.

YIELD: 12 portions (7 ounces/portion)

COOKING METHOD: Baking

INGREDIENTS

4	lbs	True Gulf Red Snapper Fillets (true red snapper comes from the Gulf of Mexico—many other fish that are sold as red snapper have a very different flavor and texture; substitute sea bass fillets if red snapper is unavailable)
2	tsp	Salt
3	oz	Lime Juice
1	Tbsp	Serrano Chili, minced
1	oz	Olive Oil
1	lb	Yellow Onions, sliced thin
1	oz	Garlic Cloves, minced
1	Tbsp	Serrano Chili, minced
2	lbs	Tomatoes, diced small
4	oz	Green Spanish Olives, pitted and cut in half
2	Tbsp	Capers, drained
1/2	tsp	Mexican Oregano
1/2	tsp	Freshly Ground Black Pepper
1	oz	Olive Oil
		Salt, to taste

PROCEDURE

1. Preheat the oven to 325°F.

2. Cut the snapper fillets into 12 pieces, approximately 5 oz each. Distribute the salt and lime juice evenly among the fillets, rubbing them in to help penetrate the flesh; cover and set in the refrigerator while you work on the sauce.

3. In a sauté pan large enough to hold all of the ingredients, heat the olive oil over a medium-low flame. Once hot, add the onions and garlic; sweat until they become translucent and very tender.

4. Add the remaining ingredients (except the fish, olive oil, or salt) to the pan, and turn the heat up to bring the mixture to a simmer.

5. Simmer the vegetable mixture for 15 minutes and then add the fish pieces to the pan, making sure to coat each of the pieces with the sauce. Place the pan in the preheated oven.

6. Bake the fish for 10 minutes and then remove; carefully turn the fish over in the pan, using a spatula, again making sure to coat each piece with the sauce. Return the pan to the oven and bake for another 5 minutes.

(continues)

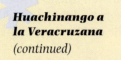

***Huachinango a
la Veracruzana***
(continued)

7. Remove the pan from the oven and check to see if the fish is flaking. If it is, proceed to the next step; if it is not, return the fish to the oven until it just begins to flake.

8. Remove the fish fillets from the pan, and place them in a container while the sauce is finishing.

9. Add the olive oil to the sauce, and check the sauce's seasoning. Pour the sauce over the snapper and serve immediately. (**Note:** This is often served with white rice.)

Huachinago a la Veracruzana (red snapper in the style of Veracruz) served over rice

SUMMARY

Today's Mexican cuisine is the combination of a proud native culture blended with the ingredients and techniques of the Spanish and other influences. Without a doubt, the most prominent stamp on the cuisine of Mexico is that of the native cultures that thrived in this region. The dependence on corn, the use of the comal as a cooking instrument, and the affinity for chiles are all distinct characteristics of Mexican cuisine. The addition of ingredients that flowed from Europe and Asia after the Spanish colonized this region dramatically altered the foods that were eaten here, but clearly the foundation remained. Pork, lard, wheat, cheese, and rice are a few of the ingredients that are regularly used in this cuisine today, and numerous examples of these ingredients exist in the traditional foods of Mexico. The cuisine of Mexico differs by region: wheat, beef, and cheese are more common in the northern parts of the country, whereas more indigenous foods, a dependence on corn, the use of more types of chiles, and the inclusion of other meats (such as goat and lamb) are common in the cooking of the central and southern regions.

REVIEW QUESTIONS

1. What culinary ingredients and techniques were used by the indigenous people of Mexico prior to the arrival of the Europeans?

2. What ingredients were introduced to the cuisine of Mexico following the arrival of the Europeans?

3. How does the cuisine of the northern portion of Mexico differ significantly from that of the southern part of Mexico?

4. What is the traditional Mexican cooking method that utilizes a flat stone or metal disk?

COMMON TERMS, FOODS, AND INGREDIENTS

Mexican cuisine includes numerous terms: some are Spanish in origin, and others are Native American. The following guide provides translations and definitions for some of the terms that may be encountered. (For chili types, refer to "Unique Components" for a listing of different types of fresh and dried chiles.)

✳ Common Ingredients

aceite de oliva – Olive oil

ajo – Garlic

alcaparres – Capers

almejas – Clams

annatto – Seeds (used to make paste or bricks) that add color and a mild musky flavor to foods (called *achiote*)

aquacate – Avocado

arroz – Rice

atun – Tuna

azúcar – Sugar

cacahuete – Peanut

cacao – Cocoa bean

café – Coffee

calabaza – Squash

calamar – Squid

camarones – Shrimp

cazón – Dogfish (essentially small sharks)

cebollas – Onions

cebollas ajo – Garlic

chiva – Young goat (kid)

citrico – Citrus

coco – Coconut

cordero – Lamb

cuitlacoche – Corn fungus (also called huitlacoche) that is prized for its earthy flavor

epazote – Distinct herb sometimes called wormseed in the United States; used in cooking beans and other preparations

flor de calabaza – Squash blossoms

flor de Jamaica – Hibiscus flower

fresa – Strawberry

frijoles – Beans

frijoles negro – Black beans

grillos – Grasshoppers

harina de trigo – Wheat flour

hoja santa – Yerba santa leaf; commonly used in southern Mexican cuisine

iguana – Type of lizard

jengibre – Ginger

lard – Pork fat

leche – Milk

lechuga – Lettuce

lima agria – Bitter lime used in the Yucatán

limones – Lemons

maguey – Agave

maíz – Corn

mariscos – Shellfish

mejillons – Mussels

mesquite – Wood of same name in the United States

naranjas – Oranges

naranjas agria – Bitter oranges

nopal – Cactus

opa – Opah; also called moon fish

ostiones – Oysters

pavo – Turkey

pepitas – Pumpkin seeds

pescado – Fish

pimiento – Black pepper

platanos – Plantains; a member of the banana family, but these are starchier and usually larger than bananas

pollo – Chicken

puerco – Pork

queso – Cheese

rabalo – Sea bass

res – Beef

tomates – Tomatoes

tomatillo – Husk-covered fruit used extensively in Mexican cuisine, particularly in making sauces

trigo – Wheat

uvas – Grapes

vainilla – Vanilla

venado – Venison (deer meat)

zanahorias – Carrots

✳ Common Dishes and Prepared Foods

antijitos – Literally, "little whims" in Spanish; this is the name given to small foods made out of masa dough (corn dough). The name references the great variety of snacks or appetizers that can be made using small amounts of masa dough.

birria – Lamb and chili stew common in the state of Jalisco; the term *birria* translates as "a mess." This stew has many ingredients and often looks like a mess, but it tastes great.

bollito – Split-top bread of French influence

butifarra – Dried pork sausage; a specialty made in the Chiapas region

cabrito al pastor – Spit-roasted goat

caldo – Stew

caldo de mariscos – Shellfish stew

callo de hacha con aquacate – Avocado stuffed with pinna clams

camarones al la diabla – Shrimp in spicy chili sauce

carne asada – Roasted meat

carne seca – Dried beef

carnitas – Pork that has been very slowly cooked until the meat can easily be shredded and then fried before being served

cerveza – Beer

ceviche – Seafood mixed with citrus juice and other seasonings and "cooked" by the acid. Ceviche (or cibiche) is most often found as fresh shellfish with lime, cilantro, and chiles in Mexico.

chapulines – Grasshoppers in the Oaxaca region that are a prized part of the diet when in season. They are often eaten with tortillas, chiles, and lime after being toasted on a comal.

chicharron – Fried pork fat that is eaten as a snack, often with chili sauce and lime juice; common throughout Mexico

chili rellenos – Stuffed chiles dipped in whipped egg whites and fried; the poblano is the most common variety of chili used for this, although others may be used as well

chilorio – Pork and chili stew from the central highland area of Mexico; pork cooked in this manner is often shredded and used in burritos and other preparations

chorizo – Spicy pork sausage that is very common throughout Mexico

cochinita pibil – Barbequed pork wrapped in a banana leaf that is a specialty of the Yucatán region.

enchiladas – Filled tortillas topped with chili sauce

frijoles borrachos – "Drunken" beans; beans are cooked with *mescal* or *tequila* as well as common ingredients, such as pork and onions

guacamole – Sauce traditionally made from crushed avocados, tomatoes, and chiles; today it often includes lime and cilantro as well

huachinango a la Veracruzana – Red snapper cooked in the style of Veracruz; heavily influenced by Spanish culinary techniques and flavors—in this case, olives, capers, and olive oil

maguey – Agave plants; used to make the fermented beverages tequila and mezcal as well as rope

masa – Dough made from corn that has been cooked and cleaned with slaked lime, which removes the tough and difficult-to-digest outer bran of the corn kernel. This dough is used extensively in Mexican cuisine to make everything from tortillas, tamales, and enchiladas to sopes.

menudo – Tripe soup with chili sauce; often includes other ingredients, such as hominy (nixtamalized corn)

mescal – Distilled beverage made from the agave plant; essentially very similar to tequila but not made in the Jalisco region or following the quality standards set by the Mexican government for tequila

mole – Complex dish with numerous variations; typically, a sauce made from dried chiles, dried fruit, seeds and/or nuts, tomatoes, and sometimes chocolate. Some versions of mole include more than 100 ingredients.

mole negro – Mole made with dark chilhuacle negro chiles

mole poblano – Mole made with poblano chiles in the central highlands of Mexico

mole rojo – Mole made with red pasilla chiles

mole verde – Mole made with tomatillos

nixtamal – Dried corn that has been treated with an alkaline (usually slaked lime) to remove the tough outer bran of the corn kernel before the corn is ground to make masa

panuchos – Small tortillas that are fried—resulting in the formation of a pocket that is filled with a black bean paste and a hardboiled egg—refried, and then served with various toppings as a snack. These hail from the Yucatán region of Mexico.

papadzules – Specialty of the Yucatán region; tacos coated in ground pumpkin seed sauce flavored with epazote, filled with chopped cooked eggs, and topped with roasted tomato salsa and pumpkin seed oil.

pepitas – Green pumpkin seeds used in sauces and to make papadzules in the Yucatán

poc chuc – Grilled pork marinated with bitter orange, achiote, and spices and typically served topped with onions; from the Yucatan region

pollo encacahuatado – Chicken in peanut sauce; an African-inspired dish found in Veracruz, a region heavily influenced by the Spanish and the slave period of Spain's colonial rule

pollo motuleño – Chicken marinated and cooked with bitter orange juice, achiote, and fried plantains; from the Yucatán region

pozole – Hearty hominy (calcium oxide–treated corn) and pork stew; commonly found in the Oaxaca and Puebla regions of Mexico

pozole verde – Version of pozole in which the stew contains tomatillos

quesadillas – Panfried tortillas that are folded in half—with various fillings inside—before being cooked

quesillo de Oaxaca – A string cheese from the state of Oaxaca with excellent melting properties and a slight tanginess; these are shaped into small, woven balls from being stretched during processing

queso Asadero – A soft, melting cheese from northern Mexico

queso Chihuahua – A tangy, higher fat cheese made in the Chihuahua region; used to make chili con queso, chili rellenos, and other dishes that require a good melting cheese

queso fresco – Fresh cheese with a crumbly texture and a slightly salty taste; used to make quesadillas, crumble over tacos, and so forth

recados – Spice pastes used in many of the barbeque dishes in the Yucatán region

salpicón de jaiba – Seasoned and shredded crabmeat

salsa – Fresh mixture of tomatoes, cilantro, chiles, onions, and lime juice. Other ingredients may be used (such as tomatillos in salsa verde), and some of the ingredients are cooked first.

sopa – Soup

sopa de almajas – Clam soup common in the Baja region

sopa de lima – Lime-flavored soup; this may contain a variety of other ingredients and is common in the Yucatán region

sopes – Thick rounds of masa dough cooked on a comal with various toppings

tamale – Corn and lard dough wrapped in a corn husk (sometimes wrapped in leaves or other ingredients) and stuffed with various fillings before being steamed

Tequila – The name of both a town and the distilled beverage that is made in the surrounding area of Jalisco in the central Pacific Coast region. The beverage is made from distillation of fermented blue agave juice.

tlaquetzalli – Chocolate drink made by the Aztecs using toasted cocoa beans

tortas – Sandwiches made from hard rolls and various fillings, similar to sandwiches in the United States but the fillings are more likely shredded pork or beef than cold cuts

tortilla – Corn masa dough (traditionally, although it is also made with wheat dough) pressed into thin rounds and cooked on a comal

tortilla de harina – Flatbread made in a manner similar to corn masa tortillas but with a wheat dough

tostadas – Corn tortillas fried and topped or filled with various ingredients

Cultural Terms

capsaicin – Chemical found in chiles in varying levels that causes a burning sensation when eaten. A system of measurement known as the Scoville scale was developed to rate the intensity of the heat from chiles; ratings range from 0 for bell peppers to reportedly over 1 million for naga-bin jolokia chiles grown in India.

comal – Flat cooking stone (now more commonly made of metal), used to cook a variety of traditional Mexican dishes (tortillas, sopes, etc.); also used to char tomatoes and toast dried chiles

mestizo – Term used to describe the people and culture that combine Native American and Spanish heritage

metate – Grinding stone used to turn nixtamal into masa dough in the traditional manner; these rocks are shaped like a horse's saddle and use a pestle-like stone to grind the nixtamal to a paste

olla – Pot; these were traditionally used to cook dried beans

pib – Term used for traditional pits dug to cook foods wrapped in banana leaves in southern Mexico; this term is also sometimes used to describe foods wrapped in banana leaves, as is common in the Yucatán region

CHAPTER 14

GUATEMALA HONDURAS
EL SALVADOR
NICARAGUA
COSTA RICA
PANAMA

CARIBBEAN SEA

CARIBBEAN ISLANDS

NORTH ATLANTIC OCEAN

Caracas
VENEZUELA
Northern and Northwestern
GUIANA HIGHLANDS
Georgetown
Paramaribo SURINAME
Cayenne
FRENCH GUIANA
Bogota
COLOMBIA
GUYANA

Quito
ECUADOR

GALAPAGOS ISLANDS

Amazon River

Amazon River

Amazon River

BRAZIL

PERU
Lima

BOLIVIA
Sucre

BRAZILIAN HIGHLANDS

PACIFIC OCEAN

PARAGUAY
Rio de Janeiro

CHILE
ANDES MOUNTAIN RANGE

ARGENTINA

Asuncion

Southern

Santiago
URUGUAY
Buenos Aires
Montevideo
Pampas

SOUTH ATLANTIC OCEAN

N
W   E
S

0   250   500 km

FALKLAND ISLANDS

SOUTH GEORGIA ISLA

- towns and cities
★ capital city
-·- international boundary
▨ mountains

South American Cuisine

OBJECTIVES

Upon completion of this chapter, you will be able to

- identify the countries that constitute South America.
- discuss the components of South American cuisine that make it unique.
- discuss the impact of colonization and the slave trade on the development of the cuisine of South America.
- identify which European countries have played significant roles in the development of South American cuisine.
- prepare some recipes common to South American cuisine.
- define the terms listed at the conclusion of the chapter.

INTRODUCTION

South American cuisine, like the cuisines of the rest of the Americas, is a complex collusion of cultures and ingredients. The continent comprises the countries of Colombia, Venezuela, Guyana, Suriname, French Guiana, Ecuador, Peru, Brazil, Chile, Bolivia, Paraguay, Argentina, and Uruguay. Although there were many different indigenous cultures in South America, the Incas are known to have possessed a sophisticated culture and culinary traditions prior to the arrival of the European conquistadors. The Spanish and—to a lesser degree—other European nations introduced the Christian faith to the Native Americans (often forcefully) upon their arrival in South America. As a result, the vast majority of South Americans are Roman Catholics, although many pagan festivals and rituals have been maintained or incorporated into the typical Roman Catholic practices. The Europeans also introduced many new ingredients and techniques that began a transformation of the local cuisine that is still evolving today.

South America is a huge continent that stretches nearly 5,000 miles from top to bottom. The northern portion of the continent is mostly tropical, and much of it is covered in dense rain forests, although significant sections of fertile highland also exist. The vast Brazilian highlands stretch south and east from the Amazon forest and are one of the richest agricultural areas of the world. The western portion of the continent is dominated by the Andes mountain range, which runs the entire length of the continent—from Venezuela in the north to Chile in the south. The northwestern section of the Andes is extensively irrigated and populated with descendants of the *Quechua*, who still cultivate the potatoes, chiles, quinoa, and corn that have sustained them for millennia. The coastal area has significant stretches of desert along the central and southern shores of the Pacific; inland, there is a fertile, temperate central valley in Chile and rivers that descend from the western slopes of the Andes. The southeastern portion of the country comprises mostly vast grasslands that stretch east of the Andes in Argentina, as well as significant stretches of inhospitable barren desert or scrublands. As a result of the climatic conditions, this area has become a major cattle and grazing region.

South America encompasses a huge area that is very dynamic in its geography, culture, history, and—not surprisingly—cuisines. The following chapter provides an entry into this complexity by looking at some of the major factors that have influenced the development of this exquisite cuisine.

HISTORIC CULINARY INFLUENCES

South American cultures have endured a tragic history of conquest and enslavement at the hands of the European nations that exploited its native peoples, but the current cultures have emerged with a culinary tradition that is both unique and impressive. In the years preceding the arrival of Europeans, a complex culture with advanced culinary traditions had evolved in South America; in many places, these traditions have changed little. In other areas, a blended cuisine developed from the introduction of new ingredients and techniques. The following guide covers the major influences on what are known today as the cuisines of South America.

Incas/Quechua/Other Native Americans

A number of cultures existed in South America prior to the arrival of the Europeans, and some of these cultures were in many ways more advanced that any other cultures in the world. Of these cultures, the most impressive (and largest) were the Quechua people of the Andes and the vast and advanced Inca Empire, whose influence stretched from Ecuador to Chile and east to Argentina. These cultures were masters of cultivating plant food and had extensive irrigation and storage systems that sustained tens of millions of people prior to contact. Before the arrival of the Europeans, these cultures had developed complicated irrigation and cultivating techniques that took advantage of the varied climatic conditions throughout the different elevations of the Andes. Decades before the arrival of Europeans in South America, the Inca had developed scientific agricultural areas in the Andes to better understand what crops to grow and where, using techniques that rival laboratories today. Their main crops would soon

spread throughout the world, once European explorers discovered this continent.

Some of the ingredients that appeared regularly in the diet at this time were *papas* (potatoes), *chuño* (freeze-dried potatoes), *papas seca* (dried potatoes), *maíz* (corn), *aji* (chiles), *plátanos* (plantains), *aquacate* (avocado), *zapallo* (a large variety of winter squash), *calabaza* (squash), *frijoles* (beans), *quinua* (quinoa), *oca* (a type of tuber), *yucca* (cassava), *tomate* (tomato), and *tamarillo* (sometimes called the tree tomato), to name a few. Meat was not a major part of the diet at this time, but *cuy* (guinea pigs), *charqui* (dried llama or alpaca meat), and various shellfish and fish were eaten. Most of the cooking was done over an open fire, in hides filled with water and heated with rocks from a fire, or by burying food in a pit (called *pachamanca* in Peru). The flow of these ingredients into Europe and Asia would forever change the cuisines of those continents' cultures. While many of these ingredients began to be included in the cuisines of Europe and Asia after their discovery in Mexico and the Caribbean, it should be noted that potatoes came from South America; the potato has had a major impact on other cuisines since its acceptance in Europe (see Chapters 6–8, in particular).

Spanish Conquistadors

The Spanish discovered the Americas in an attempt to find a shorter route to Asia and later became obsessed with finding gold in the New World. As a result of the many stories of gold discovery in the Americas, a wave of Spanish explorers descended on South America and forcefully took control of many parts of the continent. As this occurred, Native American women were required to cook food for the initially male invaders. In this way, the native women learned new cooking techniques from the Spanish and also influenced the Spanish palate with their own culinary traditions. The Spanish brought with them many of the foods to which they were accustomed, and thus these foods became crops or domesticated animals on this new continent. These early encounters saw the beginning of the *mestizo* ("mixed"; also called *Creole* or *crillo*) cuisine that is still developing today.

The flow of ingredients from the Americas to Europe, and vice versa, had a tremendous effect on the development of the newly emerging South American cuisine. Some of the ingredients incorporated into this new cuisine were *trigo* (wheat), *arroz* (rice), *cebolla* (onion), *ajo* (garlic), *lima* (lime), *limón* (lemon), *naranja* (orange), *coco* (coconut), *uvas* (grapes), *alloza* or *almendra* (almond), *carne de res* (beef), *puerco* (pork), *azúcar* (sugar), *pimienta negra* (black pepper), *pimienta blanca* (white pepper), and *queso* (cheese). These ingredients were embraced by the Native American and mestizo populations of South America, and are found dispersed throughout the cuisine today. In addition to ingredients, the Spanish also introduced a number of methods and techniques that have been important aspects in the development of South American cuisine.

Because the Spanish quickly became the ruling class, the adoption of the methods and recipes to which they were accustomed occurred at a rapid rate. These new methods and recipes were taught to the native cooks, who incorporated them into their own cuisine and adapted them to their ingredients. The significant culinary introductions included the slow sweating of aromatics in oil (such as *soffrito*), *saltear* (sautéing), *freir* (frying), cheese making, and techniques to produce *vinagre* (vinegar), *helados* (ice cream), and *manteca* (rendered pork fat), which were used in the development of this emerging mestizo or Creole cuisine. The manteca was an important introduction in that it was used in new cooking methods to make, for example, soffrito, saltear, and freir. The introduction of vinagre and uvas led to the *escabeches* (preserved fish or vegetables in vinegar) that now are common throughout South America; queso is also a main ingredient in many preparations.

Portuguese Explorers and Plantations

The Portuguese had a very similar influence on South American cuisine; in fact, any of the influences attributed to the Spanish may actually have come from the Portuguese. Historical records are not very clear, except that the Portuguese were the main force behind the introduction of West African slaves to South America. The Portuguese also introduced their ingredients and techniques to the Native *Tupi* who lived in the area now known as Brazil. The Portuguese were more interested in developing plantations and another trade post than finding the gold the Spanish were looking for. As a result, the Portuguese played a more significant role in the development of the cuisine in Brazil; they looked to establish crops and lay down roots more than the Spanish did in the other parts of South America.

Some of the significant introductions attributed to the Portuguese include the dishes *caldo verde* (soup made from potatoes and cabbage), *broa* (cornmeal bread), *flan* (custard with caramel on the bottom),

cozido (stew with vegetables), and *bacalhau* (salt cod), to name a few. Both the Spanish and the Portuguese brought many of the ingredients from the Old World to the Americas.

West African Slaves

As the American colonies developed into agricultural centers for the European powers, the need for cheap labor increased, and these nations turned to the slave trade in Africa to meet their needs. The West African slaves were forcefully removed from their homeland and shipped on boats to South America to work in sugar plantations and other agricultural crops, mainly in the areas of today's Brazil, Venezuela, and Colombia. The arriving West Africans found their new surroundings similar to their homeland, and, because African women often would carry seeds tied into their hair, they were able to establish many of their homeland crops—including *couve* (collard greens), *inhame* (taro root), *quiabo* (okra), coco, *pimento malagueta* (malagueta pepper), *dendê* (palm oil), and *fradinho* (black-eyed peas). As a result of this history and the subsequent population of West African descendants, there are strong ties to African cooking intertwined in the current cuisine of Brazil. Cuisine with clear African influence is called *cozinha baiana*, or Bahian cuisine, so named because incoming slaves were brought to the Bahian area at the port of Salvador in Brazil.

UNIQUE COMPONENTS

South American cuisine is beginning to be recognized as one of the great fusion cuisines in the world, as well as a region of many great indigenous contributions. South American products have been introduced to many other parts of the world, but in their native home they are found in great variety and are used in ways that many have never seen. To many people, South American cuisine is both exotic and yet somehow familiar; surely in time, the cuisines of this continent will become more familiar as people become exposed to it.

Maiz, Aji, and Papa (Corn, Chili, and Potato)

The crops of the South American mountain regions include corn, chiles, and potatoes, and all three play significant roles in the culture and cuisine of South America. Corn is depended on in South America—much like it is in Mexico—in most of the highland areas and in many of the valleys. It is used to make the dough called *masa*, which can also be found in Mexico, although it is not as universally depended on in South America. Although corn is certainly one of the major ingredients of South American cuisine, the other two familiar components—potatoes and chiles—differentiate the cuisine of South America from that of Mexico more clearly.

These two ingredients, which are indigenous to South America, are familiar to us all; however, the species of these ingredients that we know so well have adapted to our own environment and are different from the many varieties found in South America. *Aji* (chiles) and papas are both native to South America (particularly in the Andes, with regard to the potato); chiles can be found throughout most of northern and western South America. These two ingredients are regular components in traditional South American cookery and are used in a large variety of recipes.

Prior to the arrival of Europeans in South America, the dominant culture of the western portion of the continent belonged to the Inca Empire, and the cuisine of the Incas was in many ways similar to that of the Mayans and Aztecs in Mexico (see Chapter 13, "Mexican Cuisine"): there was little in the way of fats, and fewer meats than are common in these places today. One difference between the Mayan, Aztec, and Incan diets, however, was the prevalence and importance of potatoes in the diet of the Incas.

Chiles

Similar to the traditional cuisine of Mexico, chiles are a major component of South American cuisine, particularly in the northern portion of the continent; however, the varieties of chiles used in South American cuisine often differ from those used in Mexico. There are many varieties of chiles (not common to the United States) that are used regularly in South American cooking. Some of the most common types of chiles are as follows:

aji amarillo – Very common chili in Peru and Bolivia, where they are used to make sauces served as condiments for many foods. These are elongated, stubby, finger-shaped yellow chiles (they resemble a large yellow jalapeño) that are very hot.

aji cacho de cabra – Chilean chili; these long, thin chiles turn red when ripe and are very hot. They are used locally to make hot pepper sauces.

aji chivato – Very small, round chili from Colombia, used to make fresh salsas. These are extremely hot chiles.

aji colorado – Chili found and used in Peruvian cuisine, often used dried (called aji panca). These elongated chilis turn deep red to burgundy colored when ripe; they are very similar to the aji amarillo in size and shape but are not as spicy, with a thicker skin and a somewhat fruity flavor. These chiles are also sometimes called aji especial, and the only chili used more often in Peruvian cuisine is the aji amarillo.

aji mirasol – Dried version of aji amarillo (sometimes aji amarillo is called mirasol)

aji panca – Dried form of aji colorado

aji verde – Light-green chili found in Chile, with a thicker skin similar to a Fresno chili (also called wax peppers) in heat and texture; used to make condiment sauces in Chile. These chiles are short and squat but still elongated, averaging 3 inches in length.

aribibi – Chili indigenous to Peru that is very small and elongated; these are very hot and used mainly to make fresh salsas (also called aji limo)

habanero – Thought to have originated in the Amazon basin, this is one of the hottest chiles available. Habaneros are bell shaped and orange to red in color, and they have a thin skin.

pimenta de cheiro – Small, round chili found in Brazil, with yellow flesh and mild heat

pimenta de cheirosa – Small, round green chili found in Brazil

rocoto – A common chili of the Andes; these are quite large, sometimes as large as a bell pepper, and have a thick flesh similar to bell peppers. These are usually very hot peppers and can be found in different colors, such as yellow, brown, orange, or red.

Potatoes and Other Tubers

Many varieties of potatoes and other tubers are found only in the Andes or valleys of South America, and these varieties have been a major component in the diet of native South Americans throughout their culture. All potatoes originally came from South America, but many have been bred to have the characteristics that we are familiar with in the common russet, Red Bliss, and Yukon Gold varieties that are found in U.S. markets as well as sweet potatoes. The Purple Peruvian and fingerling varieties are the most common "new" potatoes that have been introduced into U.S. markets, but there are literally hundreds of varieties still grown in South America that never make their way to U.S. stores. Some of these different tubers are as follows:

arracacha – Common in the valleys of Bolivia and Colombia, these tubers are used in soups as well as desserts. These are also used as commercial thickeners in Brazil.

mashwa – Cultivated throughout the Andes, this potato variety is often left out to frost overnight and eaten with honey or sugar syrup; also used in stews or roasted and eaten.

oca – This tuber variety is used in soups and stews and is often sun-dried; may also be dried and ground to flour to be used as a thickener. Oca range from slightly sweet to slightly sour in flavor and have a bumpy exterior with varied colors.

ococuri (or choquepito) – Commonly called the "bitter potato" in English, this potato is grown in the Andes, where the climatic conditions enable the production of chuno and tunta, two types of freeze-dried potatoes. Both chuno and tunta are naturally freeze-dried potatoes that are common to the cultures that live high in the Andes, because they can be stored and thus helped to sustain these cultures for centuries.

papa amarilla – Yellow variant of common waxy potatoes found in the United States; these are the traditional potato used to make the Peruvian dish called *causa*.

papa huayro – Purple skinned-variety of potato found in Peru.

ullucu – This variety is cultivated for its tuber as well as its leaves, and it is found in many areas of the Andes. One classic South American dish called *chupe* is often made with ullucu, meat, cheese, and eggs. The ullucu also is found in a dish called aji de papalisa (potatoes are also called lisa or papalisa), in which the potatoes are combined with chiles. Ullucu look like waxy, long, colorful potatoes and have a crisp texture (that remains after cooking), a smooth consistency, and a slightly nutty flavor.

Native versus Mestizo or African

The cultures of South America are often quite different in strongly native regions—such as in many of the high country areas of the Andes and the dense jungle of the Amazon—than they are in the cities, where much of the population if often mestizo, a mixture of European and native peoples, or in the northern and eastern areas of South America, where African influences are strong.

In the native areas, much of the culinary culture is similar to what it was prior to the arrival of the Spanish and Portuguese: many exotic ingredients are still eaten, and a much greater emphasis is placed on sustenance than on experimentation or art. In the Andes, the potato and bitter potato still reign supreme and are consumed in both fresh and freeze-dried (for preservation) forms. Cuy (guinea pig) is a regular protein that is still enjoyed in the Andean region, as is llama meat, which can be air-dried to yield *charqui*. The diet differs in the lower elevations and the valleys, with corn (some varieties of which are also grown in the Andes) serving as the major ingredient of the native diet, along with *manioc* or *yucca* (cassava) in the tropical regions. Corn is typically used to make masa, which appears in a great variety of preparations. Chiles also are a common flavoring component in the native regions, and they are often used in sauces or added to soups and stews. The native cultures of South America are still strong and play a major role in the character of the cuisine; the arrival of the Spanish and Portuguese in many cases had little effect on the more remote people of this continent.

In the mestizo regions of South America, the cuisine retains a strong sense of the Native American traditions and foods from the mountains, valleys, and tropics, but often in combination with European ingredients and methods. The urban areas of many South American countries are where mixed heritages and the influences from each are likely to be the basis of much of the cuisine that is found. The introduction of cheeses, meats (such as pork, beef, and sheep), and other European and Asian crops brought by the colonists or imported slaves resulted in an influx of new foods to the diet. Large sections of the highland plains of Brazil, Venezuela, Argentina, and Uruguay are now dedicated to cattle ranching, yielding one of the more European of foods—beef—as well as significant yields of another European mainstay, wheat. The blending of the products from Europe and the products that were cultivated in South America for centuries prior to the arrival of Europeans on this continent is a major component of the cuisine that has developed.

The African influence on the cuisine of South America is mostly concentrated in the countries of Venezuela, Colombia, and Brazil, where West African foods are common components to the cuisine. Some important African introductions to South American cuisine are coconut, actually from Asia but brought to South America from Africa, where it had previously been introduced; *atare* or *pimento malagueta*, which is not a pepper at all but a spicy seed; quiabo (okra); and dendê (palm oil), which provides a red/yellow color and rich flavor to foods cooked in this fat. These ingredients are particularly common in Brazil, because the Portuguese who colonized Brazil brought many slaves from West Africa to work in the plantation fields, and these people brought the foods of home with them.

SIGNIFICANT SUBREGIONS

For the purpose of this text, South America can be roughly divided into four regions based on the similarities of the cuisines within these regions. The cuisines within these regions are similar for a variety of reasons, with some of the biggest factors including the availability of local ingredients, geography and climate, colonial history, the history of slavery, and the degree to which native traditions have been retained. The following guide is organized from west to east and then north to south.

North and Northwest: Colombia, Venezuela, Guyana, Suriname, French Guiana, Ecuador, and Peru

The cuisines of the northern reaches of the continent are the most reflective of the cuisine of the native peoples prior to contact with the Europeans. Many examples exist of influences from European countries that colonized or settled here, but those influences still rest on a backbone of native traditions. The reliance on potatoes, cassava, beans, and corn is still the basis of the cuisines throughout this region. The region is defined largely by the culture that has developed in a land of mountains and tropical forests, and it has a history of cultivating crops at various altitudes to yield a wide variety of produce used in the local cuisine. It was in this region that the great Inca Empire thrived just before the Spanish arrived, and that the Inca had developed agricultural experiments and testing methods that rival those used by scientists today. The Inca had a deep understanding of the crops of the Andes, and the people who live in these sections today reflect this tradition.

In contrast to the people of the Andes, those who live in the western coastal areas are subject to a very arid climate for the most part and have long relied on the ocean for seafood and on crops that are grown along the shores of the rivers that run down from the Andes. Most of the European influence and culture is felt in the coastal areas. There is substantially more rainfall on the eastern side of the Andes, and it is this tropical area that many people think of when picturing South America. Many of the tropical regions are in northern Brazil (see next section), but this region also contains a large area of tropical climate. Here, much of the land is inaccessible because it is so densely grown, and most of the communities live off of the river water that snakes through the rain forest. In these regions, cassava is the main food source, and the people also rely on fishing the rivers and hunting throughout parts of the jungles. Many tropical fruits and nuts are common in this part of South America, as well as plantains, avocados, papaya, cashews, and coconuts.

In the northern part of this area, in the countries of Venezuela and Colombia, are sections of hills and grasslands that are a significant source of cattle and other grazing animals for the more European populations of these two countries. Both countries have significant mestizo populations, who influence the cuisines.

This part of the continent is dominated by the Andes, which run from the top of South America in Venezuela and Colombia, down the western coast through Ecuador, Peru, and Chile. Much of the northern and eastern portion of this region is part of the vast tropical forests of South America, and is thus productive when accessible and home to tropical produce. The mountainous areas that follow the Andes down the western portion of the country are home to the complicated cultivating communities that have learned to plant particular plants in certain locations/elevations to yield the crops that have sustained these people for millennia. All of these areas have felt the impact of the Spanish colonization and emerged a unique and proud culture whose cuisine is often overlooked in the United Stated but surely won't remain that way.

Some of the common ingredients used in the cuisine of this region are papas, arroz, manioc (or yuca), maíz, frijoles, calabaza, quinua, aguacate, coco, plátano, carne de res, puerco, cuy, pollo, *camarón* (shrimp), *huachinango* (snapper), *pulpo* (octopus), *calamar* (squid), and *lenguado* (sole or flounder). Some of the common products and recipes from this region include *causa* (layered potato "cake"), *anticuchos* (skewered and grilled foods), *ceviche* (seafood mixed with onion and lime), *chupe* (fish stew/chowder), *chicharrón* (fried pork skin), *tamales* (filled corn dough wrapped in corn husk), *escabeche* (vinegar-preserved foods), *tiradito* (thinly sliced and seasoned raw fish), *arepa* (corn dough disks, often filled with other ingredients), *tacu tacu* (filled rice and bean "loaf"), *picarones* (fried pumpkin donuts), pachamanca (foods cooked buried in a pit), and *papas a la huancaina* (potatoes with spicy cheese sauce).

Brazil

The cuisine of Brazil draws from many cultures and has resulted in one of the most dynamic cuisines in the world. While Spain and Portugal secured colonies throughout the world in the sixteenth century, a plea was made to the pope to decide who had rights to what lands, and the resulting decision created a line of demarcation that split the continent of South America in half—roughly separating present-day Brazil from the rest of South America and giving the rights to the area of Brazil to Portugal, and the other portion of the continent to Spain. As a result, Brazil became a colony of Portugal; the drive from the Portuguese to create plantations of sugarcane and other crops for export to Europe, and the subsequent introduction of slaves from West Africa to work the field, helped a triangle of cuisines converge and blend to create a new cuisine. This new cuisine draws on ingredients and techniques native to South America, Portuguese ingredients, and a number of ingredients and techniques brought with the West African slaves. Brazil is a very large country. Parts of the northwest are covered by the dense Amazon rain forests, and fertile highlands known as Planalto Central (Brazilian Highlands) and Pampas cover the eastern and southern regions. The majority of people live in the eastern and southern portions of the country, where the highlands are the source of the world's highest production of *cana de açúcar* (sugarcane), *mamão* (papaya), *mandioca* (cassava), and *laranga* (orange). This abundance, coupled with the diversity of influences, has created a most interesting cuisine that unfortunately is also one of the most obscure in the United States.

Some of the common ingredients used in the cuisine of Brazil are *bacalhau* (salt cod), quiabo, pimento malagueta, mandioca, coco, *carne de boi* (beef), *feijão* (beans), *feijão preto* (black beans), arroz, dendê, *amendoim* (peanuts), bananas, and *caju* (cashews). Some of the common products and recipes from this region include *cozido* (meat and vegetable stew), *feijoada* (stew of black beans and smoked meats), *carne seca* (dried beef), *farofas* (cassava meal browned in butter), *piraos* (cassava flour porridge), *vatapá* (thick sauce made from dried shrimp, peanuts, cashews, coconut, and palm oil), *couve à mineira* (collard greens with onions and garlic), *pudim flan* (pudding or custard with caramel base), and *broa* (cornbread).

Chile

Chile is unique in both its climate and geographical elements, as well as in the settlement of a large number of German immigrants in the country along with mestizos (Spanish and native Auracanian). Chile is dominated by the Andes, which compose a border along the length of the Chile to the east. Chile is also home to the driest region in the world, with a very arid coastline to the west. In between the huge Andes range and the ocean is a valley with a temperate climate, and this is where the majority of the crops are grown. The Andes are very steep in this part of South America and thus are not cultivated as much as in the north; as a result, there is more reliance on the products of the temperate valley and the sea. Chile has a large industry that supplies seafood to the population.

Some of the ingredients common in the cuisine of the coastal portion of this region include uvas, *congrios* (conger eels), *erizos* (sea urchins), *mejillónes* (mussels), *ostra* (oyster), *macha* (razor clam), *aji cacho de cabra* (local red chiles), camarón, and carne de res. In the Andes Mountains, the diet is more likely to include grains such as *avena* (oats), trigo, and quinoa or the long-held main ingredients of maíz and papas, *topinambur* (sunchoke or Jerusalem artichokes), and *lenteja* (lentils). Some of the products and recipes common to this region include *chupe* (fish chowder), *curantos* (shellfish or meat stew with potatoes), *sopaipillas* (small fried pastries eaten with syrup), *empanadas* (fried filled pastry), *pastel de choclo* (fresh corn pie), *pebre* (sauce made from herbs, onions, and chiles), and *cazuelas* (soup with meat, potatoes, and corn).

South: Argentina, Bolivia, Uruguay, and Paraguay

The southern third of the continent has a cuisine that mostly resembles that of the European peoples who settled in this region—primarily Spanish, Italian, and German, with smaller groups of French, Swiss, and

Eastern European residents. This area includes the largest percentage of immigrants, and these immigrants have all left an imprint on the cuisine. Bolivia is the one country within this section that still has a large population that lives as the people did prior to the arrival of the European; Bolivia has many high-altitude populations, as is the case in Peru, Ecuador, and Chile.

This region includes the countries of Argentina, Bolivia, Uruguay, and Paraguay and is known for the local *gauchos* (cowboys) who tend the large herds of cattle that fill the grassy plains in the heartland of Argentina. This area is mostly temperate in climate, and the main agricultural product is the field of feed for the large cattle (and, in Uruguay, sheep industries). Many of the gauchos who settled this area have either Spanish or mestizo heritage, while the more urban areas have significant populations of Italian or German immigrants. Much of this area is also suitable for growing wheat and thus serves as the main wheat-growing region of South America. In Bolivia, the Andes again dominate the landscape, and the culture and diet of Bolivians have many similarities to those of the northern countries that include the Andes within their borders.

Some of the ingredients common to the cuisine of this region are trigo, carne de res, *carnero* (mutton), *borrego* (lamb), maíz, uvas, *manzana* (apple), *pera* (pear), *melocotón* (peach), *cereza* (cherry), calabasa, papas, topinambur, fresas, and bananas. Some of the products and recipes common to this region include quesos, *flan* (custard), empanadas (fried filled pastries), *matambre* (rolled and stuffed beef), *asado* (fire-charred meats served with fries and chimichurri), *salteñas* (juicy meat-filled pastries) *alfajores* (cookies filled with *dulce de leche*), *humitas* (corn dough with fillings and wrapped in corn husk), *polenta* (cornmeal porridge), *carbonada* (meat and vegetable stew), and *maté* (a drink made from *yerba maté*).

RECIPES

The following collection of recipes provides an introduction to the cuisines of South America and the influences that have played a role in the great diversity of recipes common throughout the continent.

Pasta de Aji Amarillo PERU
(YELLOW PERUVIAN CHILI PASTE)

INGREDIENTS

2	qts	Water
1.5	tsp	Salt
1	lb	Aji Amarillo, stemmed and seeded
2	oz	Sugar
3	oz	White Wine Vinegar
1	tsp	Salt
2	oz	Vegetable Oil

Aji amarillos are long, finger-shaped chiles with yellow/orange skin that are very common in Peruvian cooking. These are available from specialty suppliers of South American ingredients. This recipe can be used to make a paste out of any type of chili.

YIELD: Approximately 1 pound/1 pint

COOKING METHOD: Simmering

PROCEDURE

1. Combine water, salt, and chiles in a small pot, and bring to a boil over high heat; turn down to a gentle simmer.

2. Gently simmer the chiles until they are very soft (about 20–30 minutes), and then strain.

3. Place the strained chiles—along with the sugar, vinegar, and salt—in a blender. With the blender running slowly, add the oil to form a smooth paste.

4. Press the resulting paste through a sieve to remove any pieces of skin.

Anticuchos con Salsa Criolla PERU

(SKEWERED MARINATED BEEF WITH ONION SALSA)

INGREDIENTS

For Making the Marinade

2	oz	Aji Chiles, seeds removed and minced (if these are unavailable, use serrano)
.5	oz	Dried Chili de Arbol, crushed (substitute another hot, dried red chili, if necessary)
.5	oz	Achiote
2	tsp	Cumin Seeds
3	oz	Olive Oil
1	oz	Garlic Cloves, minced
6	oz	Red Wine Vinegar
1.5	tsp	Salt
1	tsp	Freshly Ground Black Pepper

For Making the Salsa

1	lb	Yellow Onions, cut in half and shaved very thin
2	oz	Aji Chiles, seeds removed and chopped (if these are unavailable, use serrano)
1/4	cup	Cilantro, minced (about 1/4 bunch)
2	oz	Lemon Juice
1/2	tsp	Salt

For Making the Skewers

3	lbs	Beef (tri-tip, hanging tender, or another suitable cut for grilling), cut into 1-inch cubes and marinated for a minimum of 3 hours
20		Skewers, soaked in water (or use metal skewers)

This recipe is an adaptation of the ancient Peruvian recipe for anticuchos that was commonly used prior to the Europeans' arrival. The recipe at that time would have used llama (specifically, the heart; this can be made using beef heart instead)—and would have been seasoned with chiles and achiote. This recipe is also common in Bolivia, but potatoes are included on the skewers in the Bolivian version, and it is typically eaten with a peanut sauce.

YIELD: 20 skewers (2.5 ounces/skewer) + dipping sauce

COOKING METHOD: Grilling

PROCEDURE

For Making the Marinade

1. Combine all ingredients in a mixing bowl, and mix thoroughly; set aside.
2. First cut any connective tissue from the beef, and then combine the beef with the marinade, mixing thoroughly; place the mixture in a nonreactive dish and refrigerate it for at least 3 hours before use (overnight is fine).

For Making the Salsa

1. Be sure to shave the onion very thin, using either a slicer or a mandoline, and then combine the onion with all of the other ingredients; mix thoroughly.
2. Allow salsa to develop for at least 1 hour before use.

(continues)

Antichuchos con salsa criolla (skewered beef with onion salsa)

Anticuchos con Salsa Criolla
(continued)

For Making the Skewers

1. Preheat the grill and soak the skewers in water (if using wooden skewers).

2. Place the marinated beef cubes onto the skewers, and grill the meat to desired doneness.

3. Serve with the salsa as a condiment.

Causa de Camarones   PERU
(LAYERED POTATO "CAKE" WITH SHRIMP)

INGREDIENTS

For Making the Potato Base

2	gal	Water
2	Tbsp	Salt
2	lbs	Purple Peruvian Potatoes, peeled (if these are unavailable, use all Yukon Gold)
2	lbs	Yukon Gold Potatoes, peeled
4	oz	Extra Virgin Olive Oil (traditionally just vegetable oil)
2	oz	Fresh Lime Juice
2	oz	Aji Amarillo Paste (see recipe, this chapter)
2	tsp	Salt
1/2	tsp	White Pepper
		Salt and Pepper, to taste

For Making the Filling and Garnish

3		Avocados, pits removed and sliced 1/4 inch thick
40		Shrimp (26/30), peeled, deveined (from the inside, not back), and poached
8	oz	Red Onion, minced
4		Eggs, hard-boiled
12	oz	Queso Panela, crumbled
2	Tbsp	Cilantro, minced

This is not a cake in the sense of the dessert we are used to in the United States, but rather a savory, layered creation that makes for a beautiful presentation of color as well as a unique use of potatoes. Causa is an ancient Peruvian creation that has adapted to the introduction of new ingredients by incorporating some as fillings. Causa is made with a yellow variety of potato not available in the United States, but the Purple Peruvian or Yukon Gold can be substituted.

YIELD: 20 portions (5 ounces/portion) as an appetizer; fewer if used as an entrée

COOKING METHOD: Boiling

PROCEDURE

For Making the Potato Base

1. Add 1 qt of water, 1 Tbsp of salt, and each of the potato types to each of two separate pots; bring to a boil over a high flame.

2. Once the potatoes are tender throughout, strain them through a colander and allow any excess water to drain and steam off for 5 minutes.

3. While they are still hot, press the cooked potatoes through a food mill or a sieve to yield lump-free, smooth potatoes, making sure to keep the two types of potatoes separate.

4. In a small mixing bowl, combine 1/2 of the extra virgin olive oil, all of the lime juice, and all of the aji paste (this mixture will be used with the yellow potatoes; the purple potatoes will only be seasoned with 1/2 of the oil and salt and pepper).

5. Add all of the chili/lime mixture to the yellow potatoes and 1/2 of the olive oil, salt, and pepper to each of the types of mashed potatoes, mixing them in with a whisk to yield a smooth potato mixture (this should be done while the potatoes are still hot/quite warm, so have all ingredients ready for this step).

6. Taste the potato mixtures and season, if necessary, with salt and pepper.

7. Transfer each of the potato mixtures to a pastry bag with a round tip.

(continues)

Causa de Camarones
(continued)

Piping the Yukon potato layer to assemble the causa de camarones (layer potato "cake" with shrimp)

Adding the shrimp layer on top of the piped purple potatoes to make the causa

A finished plate of causa de camarones

For Assembling the Causa

1. To assemble into individual portions, gather 20 small shaped molds and coat the insides with a very thin layer of vegetable oil or pan spray. To assemble into a larger portion, a springform cake pan works well for molding a circle, which can then be cut into wedges (also coat the inside of the springform pan with vegetable oil or pan spray before starting).

2. If you are using the individual molds, place the molds on a sheet pan covered in plastic wrap, and pipe a single, solid layer of the Yukon potato mixture onto the sheet pan and inside the mold. If you are using the springform pan, place it directly on the serving platter and assemble there. (As you add the remaining ingredients, remember that it is only the outside of the container you are filling that will be visible [unless you are making this in the large cake form and then cutting for serving], and thus you want the ingredients in the layers up against the outside container so they are visible when unmolded.)

3. Place the avocado slices on top of the Yukon mixture, pressing down slightly to keep compact and keeping them at the edge of the small molds (if using small molds).

4. Next, pipe a solid layer of the purple potato mixture—twice as thick as the first Yukon potato layer—on top of the avocado.

5. On top of the purple potato mixture, place pieces of the poached shrimp with the uncut back facing the very edge of the mold; add some of the minced red onion to make it an even layer. Compress slightly to keep everything tight in the mold.

6. Next, pipe another layer of the Yukon potato mixture on top of the shrimp, and spread flat with a metal spatula dipped in water.

7. Cover the top of the causa with plastic wrap, and refrigerate it until completely cool (about 1 hour; the process up to this point can be done a day ahead of serving).

For Garnishing the Causa

1. Release the causa from the springform pan, if you are making the larger presentation. If you are using the individual molds, carefully remove each causa by pressing on the top of it and sliding the mold off of the mold; then transfer each causa to a serving plate using a metal spatula.

2. Once the causa has been released and is on the plate to be served, it can be garnished with the hard-boiled eggs (chopped or wedged, if desired), queso panela, and cilantro.

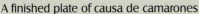

Masa de Arepa   COLOMBIA AND VENEZUELA

(CORNBREAD DOUGH)

INGREDIENTS

1	lb	Arepa Flour (also labeled masarepa, harina precocida, or masa al instante; not the same as masa harina)
1.5	tsp	Salt
4	cups	Warm Water (you may need to adjust the amount, so have more ready if needed)

Arepas were a common corn preparation of the Native Americans of Colombia and Venezuela and are still a very common snack in these countries. The process of making the dough is basically the same as making the nixtamal used in Mexico for tortillas—only in this case the dough is thicker and would be cooked on a flagstone slab, often with some fat rubbed on the surface. Today, many arepas are made with flour created from processed corn (again using the same process used to make masa harina, except this is cooked), which has been cooked and then dried.

YIELD: 3 pounds

PROCEDURE

1. In a large mixing bowl, combine the flour and salt; mix thoroughly. Add the warm water to the flour, and work with clean hands to form a smooth, soft dough.

2. If the dough is too dry, it will crack around the edges when pressed into a disk. If it feels too dry at this point, wet your hands in more warm water and continue to knead the dough—occasionally dipping your hands in the water—until the dough no longer cracks when pressed into a disk. This basic arepa dough is ready to be used to make any type of arepa desired.

Arepas Rellenas Con Carne   VENEZUELA

(CORN DOUGH STUFFED WITH MEAT)

INGREDIENTS

1	Tbsp	Vegetable Oil
1	tsp	Achiote Paste
5	oz	Yellow Onion, minced
4	oz	Green Pepper, minced
.5	oz	Garlic Cloves, minced
1/2	tsp	Cumin, ground
1/4	tsp	Freshly Ground Black Pepper
1	lb	Ground Beef (or pork, or a combination of both)
1	lb	Tomatoes, chopped
1	tsp	Salt
1	oz	Capers, drained and rinsed
		Arepas Dough (from preceding recipe)
		Salt and Pepper, to taste

In this arepa recipe, the corn dough is stuffed with a Spanish-influenced beef mixture that is stewed with a soffrito mixture and capers to yield a flavorful combination of the very Native American arepa dough and Spanish stewed meat.

YIELD: 18 arepas (4 ounces/each)

COOKING METHOD (ACHIOTE): Frying

COOKING METHOD (AROMATIC VEGETABLES): Soffrito—Slow Sweating in Fat

COOKING METHOD (BEEF): Stewing

COOKING METHOD (AREPAS): Griddling

PROCEDURE

For Cooking the Stuffing

1. Heat a small, heavy-bottomed pot, and add the vegetable oil and achiote paste; fry for 30 seconds to heighten the aroma and develop color in the oil.

2. Add the onions, green peppers, and garlic; turn the heat down to slowly sweat and tenderize the vegetables in the fat.

(continues)

Arepas Rellenas Con Carne
(continued)

3. Once the vegetables are very soft, add the cumin and black pepper; turn the heat up to fry the spices with the fat and vegetables for 2–3 minutes.

4. Add the ground beef—leaving the flame high—and continue to cook over high heat until the meat begins to brown.

5. Once the meat has begun to brown, add the tomatoes, salt, and capers; turn the heat down to bring the mixture to a gentle simmer.

6. Gently simmer the mixture for 30 minutes, and adjust seasoning.

7. Once seasoned, set aside; keep mixture warm while you cook the arepas.

For Cooking the Arepas

1. Preheat a griddle to 325°F and coat the surface with a thin layer of oil.

2. Flatten pieces of the arepas dough into circles approximately 3 inches in diameter and 3/4 inch thick; cook on the hot griddle (or a comal) with very little fat added to the griddle prior to cooking.

3. Turn the arepas every couple of minutes until a light brown crust forms on the exterior (they should take at least 10 minutes to cook; if they are cooking more quickly, your griddle is too hot!).

4. Once the arepas are cooked, cut them in half. If the centers are doughy, scoop them out and ladle some of the meat sauce into each one. Return the tops, and serve.

Arepas con carne (corn dough stuffed with meat)

Carbonada   URUGUAY
(STEWED BEEF WITH SQUASH AND PEARS)

INGREDIENTS

1	oz	Vegetable Oil
12	oz	Yellow Onion, sliced thin
8	oz	Green Pepper, diced medium
1	oz	Garlic, minced
.5	oz	Serrano Chili, minced
3	lbs	Beef Stew Meat, cut into 1-inch cubes
1/2	tsp	Freshly Ground Black Pepper
2	tsp	Salt
1/2	tsp	Dried Oregano
1	qt	Veal Stock
1.5	lbs	Tomato Concassée, chopped fine
1	Tbsp	Fresh Thyme, minced
6	oz	Corn Kernels
6	oz	Butternut Squash, diced medium
8	oz	Red Bliss Potatoes, diced medium
8	oz	Sweet Potatoes, diced medium
8	oz	Bartlett Pears, diced medium
		Salt and Black Pepper, to taste

This recipe is an obvious example of the European influence on South American cuisine, with some added twists from local ingredients. In the eastern/central and southern sections of South America, much of the population comprises immigrants from Europe, and the cuisine reflects this.

YIELD: 15 portions (7 ounces/portion)

COOKING METHOD (AROMATIC VEGETABLES): Soffrito—Slow Sweating in Fat

COOKING METHOD (FINAL): Stewing

PROCEDURE

1. In a pot large enough to hold all of the ingredients, heat the vegetable oil over a medium-low flame until hot; add the onions, green peppers, garlic, and serrano chiles, and sweat until vegetables are completely soft (approximately 10–15 minutes).

2. Once the vegetables are tender, add the stew meat and turn heat up to dry out the pan. Just begin to color the meat.

3. Once the meat begins to color, add the salt, dried oregano, stock, and tomato concassée, and bring the entire mixture to a simmer over a medium-high flame.

4. Once the mixture comes to a simmer, reduce the heat to low to gently simmer the mixture for 1.5 hours.

5. After the mixture has simmered for 1.5 hours, add the thyme, corn, butternut squash, potatoes, and sweet potatoes; simmer until the potatoes are tender (about 15–20 minutes).

6. Once the potatoes are tender, add the diced pears; adjust seasoning with salt and pepper, if necessary.

7. Serve with white rice.

Chimichurri   ARGENTINA
(ARGENTINE PARSLEY SAUCE)

INGREDIENTS

6	oz	Red Wine Vinegar
1	oz	Garlic Cloves, minced
2	Tbsp	Fresh Oregano, minced (or 2 tsp dried)
2		small Dried Red Chiles, minced (such as chili de arbol or japones)
2	bunches	Italian Parsley, stems removed (approximately 1.5 cups packed leaves), minced
4	oz	Extra Virgin Olive Oil
1	tsp	Salt

Chimichurri is commonly served with Argentinean grilled meats, as well as with other dishes.

YIELD: 1 pint

PROCEDURE

1. Combine all ingredients in a mixing bowl, and mix thoroughly.

2. Allow mixture to sit for at least 2 hours before using. (Alternatively, this can be made as an emulsified sauce in a blender by placing all of the ingredients except the olive oil in the blender, and slowly pouring in the olive oil as the blender is running.)

✳ Matambre ARGENTINA

(MATAMBRE STEAK STUFFED WITH SEASONED VEGETABLE AND EGGS)

INGREDIENTS

For Marinating the Steak

3	lbs	Matambre Steak (an Argentinean cut of beef or veal; you can substitute flank steak or tri-tip, if necessary)
2	oz	Red Wine Vinegar
1	oz	Garlic Cloves, minced
1.5	Tbsp	Fresh Oregano, minced
1/2	tsp	Crushed Red Chiles
1	tsp	Salt
1/4	tsp	Freshly Ground Black Pepper
4	oz	Vegetable Oil

For Sautéing the Spinach

1	lb	Spinach, cleaned and stems removed (if large)
1	oz	Olive Oil

For Stuffing and Rolling the Matambre

1/4	bunch	Parsley, minced
1/2	tsp	Crushed Dried Red Chili
1/4	tsp	Salt
		Freshly Ground Black Pepper, to taste
4	oz	Parmesan Cheese, grated
1	lb	Red Pepper, fire roasted, peeled, seeded, and cut into strips 1/2 inch wide
4		Eggs, hard-boiled, peeled, and chopped
		Spinach (see above)

For Braising the Matambre

		Marinated Beef (see above)
		Stuffing (see above)
2	oz	Olive Oil
1.5	qts	Veal Stock
		Salt and Pepper, to taste

This well-known Argentinean classic is most commonly served chilled as an appetizer or as a component in a buffet, where it would be served with chimichurri.

YIELD: 16 portions (6 ounces/portion)

COOKING METHOD (SPINACH): Sautéing

COOKING METHOD (MATAMBRE): Braising

PROCEDURE

For Marinating the Steak

1. Trim the meat of any noticeable connective tissue and heavy fat, but leave any fat that is 1/4 inch thick or less.

2. If you are not using matambre, butterfly the meat so the steak is approximately 1/2–3/4 inch thick throughout.

3. In a small mixing bowl, combine the remaining ingredients and mix thoroughly.

4. Coat the meat with the marinade and place it in a nonreactive container; refrigerate it for a minimum of 3 hours before proceeding (marinating overnight is fine).

For Sautéing the Spinach

1. In a large sauté pan, sauté the spinach in the olive oil until the spinach just wilts, tossing as you cook to move the uncooked spinach around the hot pan. Once all of the spinach has wilted, set it aside to cool.

For Stuffing and Rolling the Matambre

1. Remove the marinated beef from the refrigerator, and place it on a clean cutting board with the grain going in an east/west direction from where you are standing.

2. Season the surface of the meat by coating it with the parsley, crushed red chili, salt, and black pepper.

3. Distribute the Parmesan cheese over the surface, leaving an inch-wide border across the top and bottom of the steak without cheese.

4. Arrange the red pepper strips, chopped eggs, and sautéed spinach in rows—going east to west with the grain of the meat—spread out so they cover the area that was previously covered by the cheese (press the rows down a bit to spread them out).

5. Roll the meat away from you to form a log, rolling up the different fillings as you do so.

6. Secure the steak with butcher's twine at one end; using the looping technique used to truss a stuffed roast, secure the entire length of the stuffed meat.

For Braising the Matambre

1. Preheat the oven to 375°F.

2. Heat a braising pan over a medium-high flame, and add the olive oil.

(continues)

Matambre
(continued)

Flattened and marinated steak with fillings for making the matambre

3. Once the pan is hot, add the stuffed roast and sear it on all sides until it is nicely browned.

4. Once the roast is browned on all sides, add the veal stock and rub the pan with a wooden spoon to dissolve any browned spots.

5. Cover the pan with a tight-fitting lid, and place it in the preheated oven; cook to desired doneness (approximately 25–30 minutes for rare meat). (Note that matambre is often eaten cool as part of a buffet or as an appetizer, served with chimichurri and salads.)

6. If serving hot, remove the meat from the pan and set it aside to rest before carving. While the meat is resting, place a pan with the sauce leftover from braising back on the stovetop, and season it with salt and pepper (you can also thicken the mixture slightly with slurry, if desired). This sauce can be served with the meat.

7. If serving cold, remove the meat from the pan and allow it to cool at room temperature for 45 minutes before placing it in an appropriate container for storage. While the meat is cooling, place the leftover sauce from braising back on the stovetop and reduce it to a very flavorful liquid (until about 1.5 cups are left). Season with salt and pepper, if necessary, and pour this over the meat prior to refrigeration.

Matambre (stuffed steak) with chimichurri sauce (Argentine parsley sauce)

Vatapá BRAZIL

(SPICED SHRIMP AND COCONUT STEW)

INGREDIENTS

1	oz	Dendê (also called palm oil; if this is unavailable, use vegetable oil or annatto oil)
12	oz	Yellow Onion, sliced thin
1	oz	Garlic, minced
3	oz	Green Onions, sliced thin (about 1 bunch)
2	oz	Ginger Root, grated
1	oz	Manzano Chili, minced (substitute 2 oz serrano, if this is unavailable)
8	oz	Green Bell Pepper, sliced thin
1	lb	Tomato Concassée, chopped fine
1/2	tsp	Salt
1/2	bunch	Cilantro
2	oz	Dried Shrimp, peeled and ground
28	oz	Coconut Milk
6	oz	Peanuts, roasted and ground
2	oz	Lime Juice
1	cup	Day-Old Bread, soaked in 1 cup of water and puréed
2	lbs	Shrimp (26/30), peeled and deveined
1/4	bunch	Cilantro, minced
		Salt and Black Pepper, to taste

This is a classic example of the blending of cultures that is common throughout much of the South American cuisine. With its influences and ingredients coming from Africa (dendé, dried shrimp, and coconuts), Portugal (bread, onions, and garlic), and native South America (tomatoes, chiles, and peanuts), vatapá displays the wealth of several cuisines.

YIELD: 5 pounds, or 15 portions (5 ounces/portion)
COOKING METHOD (AROMATIC VEGETABLES AND SEASONINGS): Refogado—Slow Sweating in Fat
COOKING METHOD (FINAL): Stewing/Simmering

PROCEDURE

1. Heat a pot large enough to hold all of the ingredients over a medium-low flame, and add the dendê.
2. Once the dendê is hot, add the onion, garlic, green onion, ginger, chili, and bell pepper; sweat the ingredients over a medium-low flame until they are very soft (approximately 15–20 minutes).
3. Add the tomato to the pot; turn the heat up to stew the liquid from the tomato for 5 minutes, or until the pan begins to appear dry again.
4. Add the cilantro, salt, and ground shrimp, and stir very well to combine.
5. Add the coconut milk, and remove mixture from heat.
6. Transfer the mixture to a blender, and blend until smooth; return the mixture to the pot.
7. Bring the mixture to a gentle simmer over a medium flame, and stir in the ground peanuts, lime juice, and soaked and puréed bread; allow these to cook while stirring to thicken (if the vatapá gets too thick, add water to thin it).
8. Once the vatapá begins to thicken, add the shrimp and continue to stir while the shrimp cooks (about 3 minutes).
9. Remove from heat; season with fresh cilantro, salt, and pepper.
10. Serve over rice.

Vatapá (spiced shrimp and coconut stew), shown served over rice

Cuscuz de Tapioca BRAZIL
(TAPIOCA AND COCONUT CAKE)

INGREDIENTS

12	oz	Milk
10	oz	Unsweetened Coconut Milk
5	oz	Brown Sugar
1/4	tsp	Salt
7	oz	Fresh Coconut, grated
10	oz	Par-Cooked Tapioca
3	oz	Sweetened Shredded Coconut

Tapioca, which comes from the cassava (called yuca, manioc, mandioca, or aipín in South America), is the South American version of cassava most commonly encountered in the United States. Here it is combined with coconut from West Africa to make a typically Brazilian recipe.

YIELD: 10 portions (3.5 ounces/portion)

COOKING METHOD: Simmering

PROCEDURE

1. Add the milk, unsweetened coconut milk, sugar, and salt to a small saucepan; heat over a medium flame, stirring until the mixture comes to a gentle simmer (the sugar should have dissolved by this point; if not, simmer gently until it does).

2. Add the grated coconut and tapioca to the simmering mixture, stirring well; remove from heat, and continue to stir until the mixture becomes thick.

3. Spray a 9-inch cake pan, a 9-inch round metal ring on a sheet pan, or a 9-inch springform pan lightly with pan spray. Pour the tapioca/coconut mixture into the pan, and allow it to cool at room temperature before placing it in the refrigerator overnight.

4. Remove from the mold and top with sweetened coconut.

Cuscuz de tapioca
(tapioca and
coconut cake)

Chucula ECUADOR
(PLANTAIN MILKSHAKE)

INGREDIENTS

1	lb	Very Ripe Plantains (black), sliced 1/4 inch thick
1		Cinnamon Stick
1	qt	Water
2	oz	Brown Sugar
8	oz	Ice
16	fl oz	Milk
1/2	tsp	Vanilla Extract

This recipe is for a very common—and refreshing—drink found in the Andes, particularly Ecuador. In Ecuador, plantains are used to make sweet drinks such as this one, and also as a starch in stews or to accompany other dishes.

YIELD: 4 portions (10 ounces/portion)

COOKING METHOD: Boiling

PROCEDURE

1. Place the plantains, cinnamon stick, water, and brown sugar in a small saucepot, and bring the mixture to a boil; continue to boil until the plantain is falling apart (about 10–15 minutes).

2. Remove the mixture from heat, and remove the cinnamon stick from the mixture. If there is a lot of water in the pot, remove the plantains and reduce the liquid to 1/2 cup.

3. Place the plantains, reduced liquid, ice, milk, and vanilla extract in a blender, and blend until smooth.

SUMMARY

The cuisine of South America is one of mixed cultures; the Native American culture provides much of the influence in the northern part of the continent, whereas the European culture is more prevalent in the southern part of the continent. The Native American component of this cuisine includes many of the classic techniques that have been used for centuries in this culture, such as making corn dough called masa to be combined with other ingredients. Native South American cuisine also uses potatoes and chiles extensively, and many varieties of both are utilized often in typical preparations.

REVIEW QUESTIONS

1. Which countries of South America were colonized by Spain? Which were colonized by Portugal?

2. Where did the Incas live in South America, and what were some of the foods that they were known to eat before any Europeans arrived?

3. What area of South America is tropical? What are some foods that would be found in this area that would not be found in the Andes or coastal areas?

COMMON TERMS, FOODS, AND INGREDIENTS

The cuisine of South America is full of recipes and ingredients that are unknown to many people. The following guide lists some of the more common terms. Most of the terms are Spanish; those that are Portuguese (from Brazil) are indicated with a (P).

Ingredients and Foods

acajú – Native name of cashew in South American tropics

achiote – Annatto seeds; also called bija, bijol, and onoto

aguacate – Avocado

aji – General term for chili pepper; usually referred to by specific type—mirasol, habanero, etc. For more information on individual chili types of South America, refer to the list in the "Unique Components" section of the chapter.

aji amarillo – Yellow chili pepper that is very common in Peruvian cuisine

aji dulce – Mild paprika; also called aji de color

ajo – Garlic

alloza – Almond; also called *almendra*

amendoim (P) – Peanut

arroz – Rice

atare – Malegueta pepper (see pimenta malegueta)

avena – Oat

azúcar – Sugar

bacalhua (P) – Salt cod

batata – Sweet potato; also called camote, cumar, monato, nanqui, or patata dulce

borrego – Lamb

cajú (P) – Cashew fruit

calabasa – Pumpkin or squash; general term for this group of vegetables

calamar – Squid

camarón – Shrimp

cana de açucar (P) – Sugarcane

cancha – Popping corn; different from well-known popcorn in that it is larger and doesn't actually explode

carne de boi (P) – Beef

carne de res – Beef

carnero – Mutton

cebolla – Onion

cereza – Cherry

choclo – Fresh corn; also called coronta, tuzas, and mazorca de maíz tierno

chuño – Freeze-dried potato; a method of preservation that has been part of the Andean way of life for many centuries

coco – Coconut

congrios – Conger eels

couve (P) – Collard greens

cuy – South American guinea pig

dendê (P) – Palm nut oil; this oil is orange in color, distinctly flavored, and comes from a variety of African palm

erizos de mar – Sea urchins

farinha de mandioca (P) – Cassava flour

feijãos (P) – Beans

feijãos preto (P) – Black beans

fradinho (P) – Black-eyed peas

fresas – Strawberries

fríjol – Bean

fríjol de manteca – Lima bean

fríjol negro – Black bean

huachinango – Snapper

inhame (P) – Yam

jitomate – Tomato; also called tomate rojo, tomatl, and xitomatl

laranga (P) – Orange

lenguado – Sole or flounder

lenteja – Lentil

lima – Lime

limón – Lemon

macha – Razor clam

maíz – Corn; also called chalo, choclo, elote, jojote, and abatí

maíz jora – Dried, sprouted, and fermented corn used to make beverages

maíz morado – Dried purple corn from Peru used to make drinks and desserts

mamão (P) – Papaya

mandioca (P) – Cassava

manioc – Cassava; type of tuber common in the tropical area of South America

manteca – Pork fat, lard

manzana – Apple

maranon – Cashew

mejillón – Mussel

melocotón – Peach

naranja – Orange

oca – Type of tuber similar to the potato, with a range of colors and tastes (from sweet to slightly sour or tangy)

ostra – Oyster

papas – Potatoes (for more information on potato type in South America, see the list in the "Unique Components" section)

papa morada – Purple potato

papa negra – Black potato

papa seca – Freeze-dried cooked potato

pera – Pear

pimento malagueta (P) – Malagueta pepper; not actually related to the pepper, this is a pungent seed from Africa that is common in African-influenced areas of South America (especially Brazil)

pimienta blanca – White pepper

pimienta de Jamaica – Allspice

pimienta negro – Black pepper

pirarucú – Large freshwater fish found in waters of Amazon Basin and once a significant food source in Brazil. These fish are threatened today but still are caught weighing over 200 lbs.

plátano – Plantain

pollo – Chicken

puerco – Pork

pulpo – Octopus

queso – Cheese

quiabo (P) – Okra

quinua – Quinoa; also called chancas, dalma, trigo inca, and jupa

tamarillo – Fruit shaped like an egg and sometimes called a tree tomato

tomate – Tomato

topinambur – Sunchoke or Jerusalem artichoke

trigo – Wheat

uvas – Grapes

yuca – Another name for manioc or cassava, a type of tuber

zapallo – Large squash with green skin and orange-colored flesh that is common in northern South America

Argentina

alfajores – Cookies with dulce de leche filling; common throughout South America, particularly in the southern countries

arroz con pollo – Chicken and rice casserole with eggs and vegetables

asado – Various cuts of meat cooked over coals and usually served with chimichurri marinade, french fries, and salad

carbonada – Beef stew with rice, potatoes, sweet potatoes, corn, squash, apples, and pears

chimichurri – Sauce made from fresh herbs, vinegar, chili, and onions or garlic to be served with grilled meats

chuchoca – Corn cooked on hot embers

dulce de leche – Caramelized milk, often made with sweetened condensed milk, simply boiled in an unopened can in water until caramelized (takes about four hours)

empanadas – Fried filled pastries

empanada de humita – Pastry filled with corn, onion, cheese, and flour

flan – Custard

humitas en chala – Steamed cornmeal dough or ground fresh corn with various fillings wrapped in a corn husk; also the name for ground and spiced fresh corn

locro – Stewed corn, white beans, beef, sausage, and squash

matambre – Rolled, stuffed beef with hard-boiled eggs and vegetables; often served as a starter or on platters cold

maté (or yerba maté) – Strong drink made from yerba maté and drunk with a bombilla (metal straw); this is a highly caffeinated drink commonly used by the *gauchos* (cowboys) working in the pastures

ñoquis – Gnocchi or potato dumplings served with marinara or another tomato sauce

polenta – Cornmeal mush that borrows its name from the Italian polenta dish

puchero – Beef, chicken, bacon, sausage, corn, peppers, tomatoes, onions, cabbage, sweet potatoes, and squash casserole; may also include beans

puchero de gallina – Braised chicken, sausage, corn, potatoes, and squash

Bolivia

carne de sol – Grilled, salted meat served with beans, rice, and vegetables

chairo – Lamb soup with potatoes, vegetables, chuños, and ají

chuño – Freeze-dried potato made in the Andes for millennia

empanadas – Fried pastries with various fillings

humitas – Ground fresh corn steamed in corn leaves

pique a lo macho – Chopped beef with onions and vegetables

pukacapas – Spicy cheese pastries; similar to empanadas but these are baked

sajta de pollo – Chicken in hot sauce with chuños and vegetables

salteñas – Meat and vegetable pastries; similar to empanadas but these are baked, and the filling is wetter than is typical of empanadas

silpancho – Beef prepared schnitzel style

tamale – Steamed cornmeal dough with various fillings

Chile

arroz con pollo – Braised chicken and rice; common throughout South America

cazuela – Soup with meat or chicken, potato, corn, and squash or other vegetables; influence comes from Italy

chicha – National drink of Chile that is made from fermented corn; also found in other parts of South America

chupe – Chowder-like fish soup

curantos – Baked stew/casserole made with alternating layers of meats, sausages, potatoes, and cabbage (and sometimes other ingredients); reflects some of the German influence in Chile. Often, this preparation is also found along the coast, where it is made with shellfish instead of meat.

empanadas – Meat or other fillings wrapped in dough and fried

escabeche de pescado – Pickled fish; very common throughout the Pacific coast of South America

lomo a lo pobre – Fried beef with eggs, onions, and french fries

pastel de choclo – Fresh corn pie with meat, vegetables, chicken, olives, and hard-boiled eggs

pebre – Sauce made from fresh herbs (cilantro and parsley are common) onions, chiles, lemon, and olive oil to be served with grilled meats (similar to chimichurri in Argentina)

sopaipillas – Fried dough dipped in various syrups

✳ Colombia

ajiaco – Chicken soup with potatoes, corn, and capers

bandeja paisa – Dish of ground beef, chorizo, beans, fried plantains, fried egg, chicharrón, and avocado

chicharrón – Fried pork fat eaten as a snack

cuy – Grilled guinea pig

hallacas – Steamed cornmeal dough with various fillings; also called bolos or tamales

hormiga culona – Fried ants; unique to Santander

lechona – Baked pig stuffed with meat, rice, and peas

masa – Dough made from dried corn treated with alkali

✳ Ecuador

caldo (or sopa) – Soup; many varieties are available, especially in markets

churrasco – Beef, fried eggs, vegetables, fried potatoes, avocado, rice, and tomato

cuy – Grilled guinea pig

lechón – Roasted suckling pig

llapingachos – Potato and cheese pancake; often served with small bits of meat

locro – Soup with potatoes, corn, and avocado

masa – Dough made from corn treated with alkali

parrilla – Mixed meat, barbequed in Argentine style

picarones – Squash or sweet potato dough, fried and served with (often spiced) syrup

tamales – Steamed cornmeal dough with various fillings; also called quimbolitos or hallacas

tortillas de maíz – Corn pancakes

✳ Paraguay

bori-bori – Chicken soup with cornmeal dumplings

chipa – Manioc (cassava) bread with egg and cheese

chipa soo – Cornbread with meat filling

mazamorroa – Corn mush

mbaipy-he-é – Dessert of corn, milk, and molasses

mbaipy-so-ó – Corn pudding with chunks of meat

parrillada – Various cuts of meat cooked over coals (as in Argentina)

sooyo sopy – Soup with ground meat, served with rice or noodles

✳ Peru

anticucho de corazón – Skewered and grilled beef hearts; other variations are common, using different ingredients

causa – Potatoes cooked, puréed, and layered with various ingredients, including peppers, hard-boiled eggs, olives, sweet potatoes, lettuce, and cheese; often served with onion sauce

ceviche – Cold, raw seafood marinated in lime juice, peppers, and onions; served with cold potatoes and sweet potatoes

chichi – Fermented corn beverage common throughout much of South America

choclo con queso – Corn on the cob with melted cheese

chorros a la criolla – Steamed mussels cooled and topped with onion and corn salsa

chupe – Chowder-like fish soup; common to Peru, Ecuador, and Chile

chupe de camarones – Shrimp stew

cuy – Guinea pig; typically wood-fire roasted

escabeche – Preserved fish or vegetables in vinegar

locro – Soup with potatoes, corn, and avocado

lomo saltado – Fried chopped steak with onions, tomatoes, potatoes, and rice

pachamanca – Meat, potatoes, and vegetables all cooked in an "oven" formed by burning the foods with very hot volcanic rocks. This is a national favorite in Peru.

palta a la jardinera – Avocado stuffed with cold vegetables or salad

papas a la huancaina – Potatoes with a spicy cheese sauce

picarone – Fried pumpkin dough eaten as a snack; very similar to a donut but made from pumpkin dough

rocoto relleno – Green peppers stuffed with beef and vegetables

tacu tacu – Dish of rice and beans wrapped around various fillings; this national style was said to have been invented by an African slave in Peru. This dish is usually made with leftover cooked beans and rice and is prepared on a griddle.

tamales – Ground corn stuffed with meat or cheese, and then steamed in a leaf or corn husk; also called juanes or chapanas

tiradito – A relative of ceviche, this preparation is also made with raw fish, but the fish is cut into thin strips and flattened—and not mixed with onions—and is often served topped with condiments and other seasonings (whereas ceviche is mixed with onions, lime juice, and chiles)

✳ Uruguay

cazuela – Soup made with either seafood or tripe

chivito – Steak sandwich with lettuce, bacon, tomato, and cheese; the larger version is called chivito al plato

olympicos – Club sandwich with bacon, lettuce, and parrilla (Argentinean-style grilled meats)

puchero – Beef, vegetables, chicken, bacon, beans, and sausages

✳ Venezuela

arepas – Corn flatbread, either served plain at meals or filled with meat, cheese, or fish and eaten as a snack from an arepera

bollos – Steamed corn dough with various fillings; also called cachapas

cachapa – Fresh corn pancake, like a tortilla, served with cheese and/or ham

cachito – Hot bread roll stuffed with ham

hallaca – Meat, vegetables, and olive stuffing in corn dough; steamed in plantain leaves

mondongo – Tripe cooked in bouillon with vegetables, corn, and potatoes

muchacho – Roast loin of beef in sauce

pabellón – Shredded beef, rice, beans, and fried plantains

sancocho – Fish stew with vegetables

✳ Brazil

acaraje – Fried mashed bean balls stuffed with vatapá sauce

bolo – Cake; often made from cassava flour

broa – Cornmeal bread common in northern Portugal

caldo de peixe – Coconut soup with fish

caldo verde – Common soup from Portugal made from potatoes and cabbage

camarão con coco – Shrimp in coconut sauce

carne de sol – Grilled, salted meat served with beans, rice, and vegetables

carne seca – Air-dried and salted beef (similar to jerky)

caruru – Mixture of okra, shrimp, vegetables, and peppers made into a sauce for fish

couve à mineira – Collard greens cooked with onions and garlic

cozido – Stew with many vegetables (usually contains yuca, cabbage, corn, and green plantains)

farofas – Cassava meal browned in butter

feijoada – Meat stew served with rice and beans

flan – Custard with caramel on the bottom

mocueca – Seafood sauce/stew made with coconut milk and cooked in a clay pot

pato no tucupi – Roast duck with tucupi sauce made from manioc and vegetables

peixe a delícia – Broiled or grilled fish served with bananas and coconut milk

piraos – Cassava flour porridge

pudim flan – Custard with caramel base

refogado – Technique of starting a recipe by cooking onions—and sometimes other seasonings, such as garlic—in olive oil until onions are completely tender and golden. This is a very common start to many of the dishes in Brazil.

sopa de feijão preto – Brazilian black bean soup

tucupi – Sauce made from extracted cassava juice; used in the northern part of Brazil

tutu á mineira – Bean, bacon, and manioc sauce served with cabbage

vatapá – Seafood served with manioc sauce (or sometimes bread), nuts, dried shrimp, coconut, and dendé oil

✳ Cultural Terms and Techniques

cozinha baiano (P) – Cuisine of the Bahia region of Brazil that is considered to be the most creative and influential in the country, mostly because of the influence of the African immigrants (from the slave trade via Portugal) who lent techniques and ingredients to the development of this cuisine.

Creole – Term used to describe the mixed indigenous and European culture, and the cuisine that has developed since these cultures have come together

crillo – Spanish term for "native," which is the root word of the now common term *Creole* that has come to mean the blended culture of South America

escabeche – Preserved in vinegar; a common technique in Spanish-influenced areas

freir – Fried

gauchos – Name of the cowboys who work cattle on the ranches of South America's Pampas region

helado – Ice cream; technique introduced by the Spanish

Inca – Great empire of South America that was centered in the Andes and had developed very complex agricultural systems before the arrival of the Spanish

mestizo – Person of mixed ancestry—both native South American and European (primarily Spanish)

pachamanca – Foods buried with hot volcanic rocks and cooked by the trapped heat

Quechua – Native Andean people of Bolivia and Peru

refogado (P) – Portuguese term for *soffrito*

saltear – Sautéed

soffrito – Technique of slow sweating of aromatic vegetables and other seasonings to start many preparations, including sauces, soups, and stews; this is a Spanish technique that has been adopted in many parts of South America

Tupi – Native culture of Brazil that the Portuguese first encountered

vinagre – Vinegar; the process of making this was introduced to South America by the Spanish

SECTION 4

CUISINES OF
ASIA

Asian cuisines diverge the most from the typical cuisines of the United States and often are the most enlightening and inspiring for chefs who don't come from an Asian background.

Asian cuisine is very diverse and includes the vastly different areas of Southeast Asia (Thailand, Vietnam, Cambodia, etc.), India, Kazakhstan, Mongolia, China, and Japan, as well as parts of Russia. The Middle East is also typically included in the political map of Asia, but it was included in the first section of this text because of its importance to the development of European cuisine. Russia is also covered in the European and Middle Eastern section of the text; Russia is located in both Asia and Europe, and a large part of the Russian population (and thus the traditions) lives in the European section. Some areas—such as Mongolia—are not covered in this text, mainly due to a lack of space. This section begins with India and then moves eastward, ending in Japan.

Asian cuisine is a new frontier for many people in the United States, and many are intimidated by the wide variety of ingredients with which they may not be familiar. Quite often, the only reason "foreign" foods are not widely enjoyed outside of

their own culture is simply because of a lack of exposure. All humans learn to crave foods based on exposure to their aromas; in the absence of preconceived notions, all of us would eat the same foods that other cultures eat. When an uninitiated person is first exposed to fish sauce or shrimp paste, his or her initial reaction is typically disgust. But if you don't tell people that phat thai contains fish sauce, or that a red curry with coconut sauce contains shrimp paste, most will not flinch as they enjoy either of these Thai dishes. We are all physiologically the same, and this becomes apparent in many cases—most strongly in our enjoyment of cuisines. One of the first lessons for all aspiring chefs is that they should "learn" to like everything; in the process of acquiring this habit, most will find that they do, actually, like everything.

Although the regions covered in this chapter are highly varied and diverse, a number of generalities are also notable across the cuisines of Asia. Rice is the most common starchy ingredient eaten throughout this region. The one area covered in this section with significant subregions that don't rely on rice as the main component is the Indian subcontinent: in the northern areas

of India and Pakistan, wheat is much more common than rice. The Asian continent also has many indigenous ingredients that are not common in other parts of the world, and these constitute a major part of many of these cuisines. Many ingredients that are common in other parts of the world also are indigenous to Asia, although this is surprising to some. Common ingredients that are originally from Asia include citrus, mangoes, coconuts, bananas and plantains, sugar, rice, tea, cilantro, black and white peppercorns, nutmeg, lentils, lemongrass, ginger, eggplant, peaches, apricots, apples, and cucumbers (to name a few that are commonly used in the United States today).

The cuisines of Asia provide the typical U.S. culinarian with a rich array of flavors, techniques, and styles that enliven the senses and provoke many possibilities for fusion cuisine. Before one can understand the applications of ingredients outside of a familiar context, it is best to learn the applications of these ingredients in the context of their native homes. This section provides a glimpse into the wonders of Asian cuisines and flavors, and hopefully will inspire further study of this great arena of the culinary arts.

CHAPTER 15

Legend:
- towns and cities
- ★ capital city
- river
- region boundary
- sub-region boundary
- international boundary
- mountains

0   250   500 km

TURKMENISTAN

TAJIKISTAN

AFGHANISTAN

IRAN

CHINA

★ Islamabad

PAKISTAN

Indus

Karachi

JAMMU AND
KASHMIR

HIMACHAL
PRADESH

PUNJAB

UTTARAKHAND

HARYANA

★ New Delhi

Northern India/Nepal

UTTAR PRADESH

HIMALAYAN MOUNTAINS

NEPAL

★ Kathmandu

SIKKIM

BHUTAN

ARUNACHAL
PRADESH

ASSAM

NAGALAND

MEGHALAYA

MANIPUR

RAJASTHAN

INDIA

Ganges

BIHAR

Ganges

BANGLADESH

*Eastern India/
Bangladesh*

MIZORAM

BURMA
(MYANMA

Western India

GUJARAT

MADHYA PRADESH

CHATTISGARH

JHARKHAND

WEST
BENGAL

★ Dhaka

TRIPURA

Calcutta

ORISSA

MAHARASHTRA

WESTERN GHAT MOUNTAINS

EASTERN GHAT MOUNTAINS

Bhubaneswar

ARABIAN
SEA

Mumbai
(Bombay)

ANDHRA
PRADESH

BAY
OF
BENGAL

GOA

**Southern India/
Sri Lanka**

KARNATAKA

Chennai
(Madras)

KERALA

TAMIL NADU

LAKSHADWEEP
(INDIA)

ANDAMAN AND
NICOBAR ISLANDS
(INDIA)

ANDAM
SEA

SRI
LANKA

Colombo ★

MALDIVES

INDIAN OCEAN

Cuisines of the Indian Subcontinent

OBJECTIVES

Upon completion of this chapter, you will be able to

- identify countries of the Indian subcontinent.
- explain important aspects of Indian culture that affect the cuisine.
- explain the effect the spice trade had on Indian cuisine.
- discuss what makes the cuisine of the Indian subcontinent unique.
- recognize Indian cooking techniques.
- produce some recipes common to the Indian subcontinent.
- define the terms listed at the conclusion of the chapter.

INTRODUCTION

The Indian subcontinent includes the countries of Pakistan, India, Nepal, Bhutan, Bangladesh, and Sri Lanka and covers a vast area ranging from high mountain ranges to tropical valleys, vast deserts, and terraced foothills. The northeastern part of this subcontinent is dominated by the Himalayan mountain range, while the northwestern portion is home to the vast Thar Desert and—further west, in Pakistan—the Indus River. The eastern section is home to the great Ganges River and Delta and forms a fertile wetland throughout much of Bangladesh. Moving south, to where this great landmass stretches into the Indian Ocean, one can find great croplands and two rising sections of land known as the Western Ghats and Eastern Ghats. Much of the southern portion of the subcontinent is tropical—including the island of Sri Lanka, which lies of the southeastern coast of India. The subcontinent is also home to more than one-fifth of the world's population, with nearly all ethnic groups on Earth represented in some capacity somewhere in this area. Not surprisingly, this makes for complex cuisines with a number of influences.

One important influence on the cuisines is the different religions that are followed. The dominant religion in India is Hinduism, and many of its followers practice vegetarianism. Another culinary practice of Hindus is the reverence of the cow—and the subsequent abstinence from eating any beef—something that is rare in most parts of India. In Pakistan, the dominant religion is Islam, and the culinary practices of Muslims include the avoidance of pork. Bhutan is a Buddhist country, and thus followers generally abstain from eating animal products. The majority of the Bangladeshi population is Muslim, and the majority of the Sri Lankan population is Buddhist, although it is common for meat and fish to be eaten in Sri Lanka. The subcontinent is also home to devout followers of Jainism, a religion that includes what are regarded as the strictest vegetarian edicts of all religions; Christianity (with its associated fasting periods) and Sikhism are also significant religions in this region.

There are several misconceptions regarding the food of this region, as many people associate the yellow curry powder and mango chutney found in supermarkets with these cuisines. Although one would be correct to associate dry spice blends with Indian cuisine, the variety is far more diverse than generic curry powder, and mango chutney is but one example of the flavorful condiments from these diverse cuisines. This area is home to diverse cultural and ethnical populations that have come to the subcontinent from different areas throughout history. Some distinct differences are noticeable when moving from north to south: the northern area has been significantly influenced by Aryan peoples and the period of Moghul rule, whereas the south was influenced by earlier inhabitants of Dravidian heritage, Indonesia, and—to a lesser extent—European countries that once used this area as a port for trading goods.

A number of cultural aspects of the Indian people can help to understand their cuisine. One important aspect that influences the cuisine is the belief that certain foods are pure, and that by eating them one becomes pure. Some of the ingredients thought to be pure include water, ghee, curds, and milk; adding these items to food is believed to purify it and, thus, oneself.

Alternately, pollution is considered a way to destroy the purity of food. Food can be polluted by going bad (molding, for example), by being touched by hands during the cooking process (thus, food is not sampled during cooking), and by being placed on an unclean surface. Because of the latter method, it is very common in some parts of India for people to eat their food off of a leaf, which is pure and can be discarded once eating is finished. In addition, much of the population adheres to a belief in the need for balance in life, including their food; foods are considered either "hot" (exciting) or "cool" (calming), and these need to be balanced.

These are just a few aspects that play a role in this great cuisine, which has provided much of the world with inspiration in the use of spices that we all take for granted. The following sections explore more aspects in greater depth.

HISTORIC CULINARY INFLUENCES

The Indian subcontinent has been the focus of many other cultures for centuries, because the spices found there were much sought after for the cuisines of Asians, Arabs, and Europeans. As a result, Indian cuisine has impacted the Old World, and the cuisines of the trading countries have influenced Indian cuisine in return. The following sections examine these impacts more closely.

Ancient India

The original inhabitants of India are thought to have migrated from the Middle East or Northeastern Africa to present-day India; they were nomadic people who subsisted on any available foods that could be gathered or hunted and had been in southern India for centuries before others started coming to this area. These earliest known inhabitants of the Indian subcontinent were of Munda and Dravidian lineage. It is believed that these people began a settled existence in areas of southern India, including what is considered the world's largest city at this time (around 2500 BC). This people grew many of the same crops that are common in this section of India today, including *chaawal* (rice), *gehun* (wheat), *karakkan* (millet), *channa* (chickpea), *masoor dal* (red lentil), *til* (sesame), *am* (mango), and *rai* (mustard). In addition to the crops grown, the Dravidian peoples also herded goats and sheep and used water buffalo for working the fields and cattle for *dhoodh* (milk) production. Some of this lineage has links to populations in Southeast Asia and Indonesia, and most descendents are found in southern India today.

In the second millennium BC, there was an influx of Aryan people into northern India. Aryans came from the region of present-day Iran and Turkey, and they brought with them the cattle that were a big part of their diet. As these people evolved, they began to raise cattle and tend many of the same crops as the Dravidians, as well as some they brought with them, including other varieties of *dal* (legumes), various *tindora* and *meetha-toray* (gourds), and roots such as the *kamel* (lotus root), They also took advantage of the indigenous products, such as mangoes, mustard, and sesame. Seasoning was achieved through the use of *asefoetida* (a gum resin from roots of the giant fennel variety), *adrak* (ginger root), *huldi* (turmeric), *methi* (fenugreek), *mirch* (peppercorns), *imli* (tamarind), and *elaichi* (cardamom).

As these people settled into the area, so did their use of the cattle. Fertile cows were depended on to provide *ghee* (clarified butter), *paneer* (cheese), and dhoodh, all of which were important components of the Aryan diet. It is believed that the cow became a sacred symbol and eventually a deity because a fertile cow could provide far more nutrition via the dairy it produced than it could by being slaughtered for meat; in addition, there were a limited number of cows. Eventually, the cattle were protected from slaughter by religious laws and edict, and this reverence persists in India today. The agricultural systems and the reliance on grain and other starchy foods as mainstays of the diet were influences that remain a dominant feature of the cuisine today.

Hinduism and Buddhism

Hinduism is one of the oldest religions and is believed to have developed on the Indian subcontinent thousands of years before the birth of Christ. Hinduism was once the dominant religion throughout much of southern Asia and is now centralized in India. During the development of Hinduism, the reverence for the cow and products derived from the cow (ghee, for example) became a significant feature of the culture of India. In the sixth century BC, Siddhartha Gautama began what would develop into the religion of Buddhism in India. One of the beliefs of this developing religion was that all living beings were integral parts of a harmonious world and, as such, should not be harmed. This belief stretched the previous Hindu belief of the diet to include no animal products derived from harming any animal (yielding milk from a cow is not believed to harm the cow, for example). Followers of this Buddhist religion and lifestyle thus became vegetarians.

In 300 BC, the Indian Empire was ruled by Ashoka, who became disturbed by all of the violence that he saw surrounding the expansion of the Indian Empire and the "invading" outside forces. The emperor converted to Buddhism and extolled its virtues to his countrymen. He also issued a series of edicts that forbade the killing of living beings. This began what would become a dominant aspect of Hinduism in India, as parts of the population became largely vegetarian. Prior to this, many people were vegetarians by necessity, but now it became a symbol of purity and faith and thus moved into the upper social realm. Buddhism did not supplant Hinduism as the major religion but did influence the attitude of the population regarding taking the life of animals, and thus impacted the cuisine in this way.

In addition, another religion called Jainism developed around the same time that Buddhism began, and even more was expected of its strict followers to ensure that they did not harm animals. People who follow the edicts of Jainism go so far as to abstain from actions that may result in harm to microorganisms. Although both Buddhism and Jainism are still practiced in India, they are minority religions. Many people on the Indian subcontinent do eat meat, but a significant number do not (estimates range from 20 to 35 percent of the population being completely vegetarian) or eat a diet with little meat; this can largely be attributed to the influences of Buddhism and Jainism.

Persian/Arabic Influences

Early in the history of the subcontinent, the area was an important trade route between Asians as far east as China and the inhabitants of the Middle East (especially Persians and Arabs), and this trade route resulted in the transfer of ingredients and ideas from east to west, and vice versa. Some of the significant culinary introductions to India from this trade route included new types of dals, *saag* (spinach), *badam* (almond), *jeera* (cumin seed), *bindi* (okra, originally from Africa), and *ruh gulab* (rosewater), all of which would find their way into the cuisines found in the subcontinent. These influences also included religious aspects; the Islamic religion made its way to the Indian subcontinent in the eleventh and twelfth centuries. With the introduction of Islam came the dietary customs of this faith, most notably the acceptance of eating certain animals, such as lamb and goat, and the exclusion of pork.

Moghul Empire

From the dawn of the second millennium to approximately the fifteenth century, Muslim peoples from the areas of present-day Turkey, Afghanistan, and other parts of central Asia descended on northern India and introduced new religious and cultural practices to the subcontinent. One of the more significant introductions at this time was religious in nature, as these people were primarily Muslim (followers of the Islamic faith). The influence of Islam on the diet included the eating of meats such as goat, lamb, and chicken, as well as the introduction of fast periods as part of the Islamic calendar. The Moghul rule of much of India that began in the period would play an important role in the development of the "high" cuisine of India.

This is often considered a great period in the history of the Indian subcontinent; the Moghul Empire ruled a vast land (extending outside the subcontinent), and many of the area's impressive architectural achievements were completed in the late sixteenth century and early seventeenth century. One important legacy of this period was the great feasts that included many of the foods cooked with spices in sauces (generically called *curries* by Westerners), dals (spiced and wet legume preparations), rice dishes, sweet confections, and chutneys (highly flavored fruit and herb condiments) that are main components of Indian cuisine today. This was a time of prosperity, and thus the cuisine flourished.

European Spice Traders

European tastes for the spices of India created pressure to find less expensive methods of obtaining them than trading with the Arabic merchants who controlled the routes between India and Europe. This pressure eventually led seafaring nations to discover routes to India and a direct source of the spices. The first nation to make this contact was Portugal, which established a colony at Goa on the southwestern shores of India in 1510. The effects of this colonization are still visible in Goa today, as there is a sizable Christian presence and many in this area eat pork.

After the other European powers saw the profits that the Portuguese were reaping from their access to the Indian spices, they too began looking to establish colonies in India; as a result, Dutch, French, British, and Danish trading posts were soon in place. As it turned out, the most significant culinary influences from this European incursion into India were not from Europe at all but rather from the recently "discovered" Americas. The Portuguese introduced the *psi hui* (chili) to India, and it was quickly adopted as a major seasoning in the local cuisines. Other important introductions from the Americas via the European traders included *aloo* (potato), *kaju* (cashew), *rajma* (kidney bean), and *lal mirch* and *hari mirch* (varieties of green and red chiles).

British Colonial Period

Following the discovery of the spice route around Africa to reach India, the British Empire looked to enter into this trade and eventually established colonies on both the western shore (present-day Bombay) and eastern shore (present-day Calcutta) of India in the seventeenth century. After a period of struggle with the fading Moghul Empire and other European interests, Britain gained control of most of present-day India and began to colonize the country in earnest. This period of struggle and tragedy lasted until the middle of the twentieth century, when independence finally was won for the subcontinent, resulting in the countries of Hindu India and Islamic Pakistan. This period of influence is surprisingly unremarkable with regard to the effect on local cuisine. Perhaps the most notable effects were the introduction of tea, the most common beverage in India today (besides water), and the British love for what they referred to as curry. The Tamil (dialect of southern India) name for a dish with a spiced sauce sounds much like the English spelling for this food, and thus to the English this name came to represent the spice blend used to make it, which they called curry. Although most prepared foods are known by individual names, in India the term *curry* means a food cooked with spices and typically in a sauce; the yellow spice blend called "curry" that is found in stores in the United States is a poor representation of the use of spices in India.

The use of silverware was also introduced to India during this period; however, its use has never fully taken hold in India, where it is believed that for food to taste its best it must be eaten with the bare hand; the cleaning of hands prior to eating is an unspoken expectation and custom.

UNIQUE COMPONENTS

The cuisines of the Indian subcontinent are quite different from many other cuisines in a number of ways—the prevalence of vegetarian foods and the use of spices being two of the most obvious differences. The following section explores these and other components that distinguish these great cuisines.

Hinduism and the Resulting Vegetarianism

The major religion of India is Hinduism, and strict followers of this religion observe a vegetarian diet; even followers who are not as strict still follow many of the dietary tenets that are part of this belief system. According to the tenets of Hinduism, certain foods are sacred, some are purifying, others are responsible for upsetting the balance of the mind and body, and still others are simply harmful. The most notable food that is considered sacred in Hinduism is beef—cows are seen as godlike beings that are to be revered and certainly not slaughtered. As a result, it is very rare to encounter an authentic Indian recipe that lists beef as an ingredient. Other foods are seen as purifying to the person who consumes them. Purifying foods include water and ghee (a type of clarified butter), both of which are commonly used in cooking and eating.

Ingredients are categorized within this faith as falling into one of three groups that indicates each ingredient's effect on the mind/body balance or overall health. Much like the Chinese philosophy of a balance of yin and yang (see Chapter 17, "Chinese Cuisine"), Hindus believe in maintaining balance through diet; this is achieved partly by including certain foods in the regular diet and minimizing or avoiding others. The three food categories are: sattvic foods, which are thought to help promote health and calmness of the mind; rajasic foods, which are thought to excite the body and make the mind restless, and are eaten in moderation; and tamasic foods, which are thought to be harmful to both the mind and the body and are avoided by close followers of this faith. The following lists provide examples of the types of foods that would be included in the three groups:

Sattvic Foods: cereal grains, legumes, soft cheeses, nuts, seeds, milk, ghee, honey, herbal teas, fresh fruit, fresh vegetables, and breads

Rajasic Foods: spices (particularly heavy use), chiles, coffee, tea, eggs, chocolate, dried cheeses, sour cream, aged yogurt, unripe fruit, garlic, and jaggary (raw form of sugar)

Tamasic Foods: meats, non-scaly fish, alcohol, tobacco, strongly fermented foods, vinegar, stale or overripe foods, heavy use of onions or garlic (and overeating in general)

This core belief in the proper way of eating and living goes to the very center of how the typical Indian diet developed as part of this culture. Other parts of the Indian subcontinent are not dominated by this religion, and thus the cuisines of these areas often differ from the rest of the subcontinent. For example, the main religion in Pakistan is Islam, and thus the dietary edicts of Islam are more prevalent there (see Chapter 1, "Middle Eastern Cuisine," for more on Islamic dietary habits).

Legumes

Legumes are very popular and varied in the cuisine of the Indian subcontinent, and they are highly regarded as a healthy food by both nutritionists and religious scholars. In India, legumes are typically cooked from a dried form after being skinned, split, and turned into a sort of mash or stew known as a dal (also the name of the dried split legume). Dals often contain a number of the spices that are also a signature part of Indian cuisine. Some of the most common legumes eaten in this area are as follows:

arhar dal – These are often called beluga lentils because, when cooked, they become shinny and glisten like beluga caviar; black in color and round

bengal gram (or kaala channa) – Black chickpeas; these are typically found whole and are used in many preparations similar to common chickpeas. They are particularly common in southern and western Indian food.

channa dal – Made from smaller species of related chickpea, these are the most common dal food in Indian cuisine, and their sweet and nutty flavor is highly prized. Because these are high in indigestible soluble fibers that can cause flatulence, they are often cooked with *asafoetida* to counter this effect.

chowli dal – Skinned and split black-eyed peas

masoor dal – Orange-colored split lentils

mattar – Green peas, fresh or dried

moath – Small brown bean

moong dal – Mung beans that have been split and skinned; these are yellow colored, flat, and quick to cook

toor – Grey-colored whole lentil that hides a yellow color beneath its outer skin

toor dal – Split and skinned toor lentils; these are yellow in color and have a nutty flavor. They can be ground into flour and used as a thickener in dishes.

urad – Whole small black bean with a creamy white interior; the skins provide a strong, earthy flavor

urad dal – Split and skinned (or sometimes sold with the dark skin still on to retain its strong flavor) creamy white bean; without skin, these are mildly flavored

val dal – Split and skinned lablab bean; these are yellow and larger than the other beans in this list

All of the listed legumes are included in the diets in particular parts of India. When combined with grains and vegetables, these legumes provide the protein needed to nourish India's many vegetarians.

Spices

The prevalence of spices and the variety of their uses is one of the hallmarks of the cuisine of the Indian subcontinent. Dried spice blends are a common component of Indian cuisine, and numerous blends are used in the preparation of many traditional foods. A spice blend is called *masala* in India, and some examples of common blends are *garam masala, tikka masala, tandoori masala,* and *vindaloo masala.* Cinnamon, cardamom, black pepper, cumin, coriander, nutmeg, mace, fennel seeds, black mustard seeds, asafoetida, fenugreek, ginger, nigella seeds, dried chiles, turmeric, cloves, and dried mango are all used either to make spice blends or individually for their particular characteristics. It is also common for spice pastes to be made in southern India, much like in Southeast Asia (see Chapter 16 for more on Southeast Asian blends). Fresh ingredients are often used in the south to make the "wet" spice blends that flavor many of the foods in these regions.

The blending of these spices is an art form in of itself, and it is not uncommon for an Indian spice blender to be faithfully followed by families or individuals for years to provide a particular guarded blend for customers. Many families also blend their own spices, and the number and variation of these blends is staggering. Garam masala is one of the early spice blends, and a recipe for it is given in this chapter although even garam masala's spice combination varies often, depending on who is asked and how traditional their beliefs are. An important point of clarification that often arises on this subject is the term curry and its English meaning versus its Indian meaning. Curry's English meaning is simply a spice blend with a large amount of turmeric added to provide the yellow color that is often associated with foods of this name. The word *curry* actually derives from the Tamil (an ancient language spoken in southern India) word *kari,* which can be loosely translated as a food with a spiced sauce to be eaten with rice. The English standardized the spice blend and referred to it as curry, while in reality many different blends would be called a kari in southern India. Incidentally, the term curry or kari is now quite common in southern India, but it is rarely used in the north, where *masala* is most commonly used to describe spice blends.

The cuisine of the Indian subcontinent is widely regarded as one of the most complex in its uses of spices, and it is no wonder that chefs look to this cuisine to learn more about spices and their applications.

SIGNIFICANT SUBREGIONS

The Indian subcontinent is a very large area that includes the high, frozen peaks of the Himalayas as well as tropical Sri Lanka; thus, the cuisine varies considerably from one region to another. Climate,

religious practices, and proximity to the ocean all play large roles in the variation of the regional cuisines.

The majority of Indian cuisine found in the United States is representative of the cuisine of northern India, and thus many of the continent's other styles and traditional dishes are not well known. The following guide covers the major regions of the subcontinent and is organized from west to east and then north to south.

Pakistan

The major religion in Pakistan is Islam, and this plays a significant role in the cuisine of this country, which includes more meat and bears many similarities to Middle Eastern cuisine. Because Islam is the major religion, pork is not eaten by the vast majority of the population here, but other meats are viewed as premium products. Pakistan is a mountainous country with ranges on the western border and a fertile valley running from north to south that is fed by the Indus River. Large pasturelands also support herds of sheep and goats in the ranges that border Afghanistan and the south. The cuisine of Pakistan has been influenced by both Persia and India; many current Pakistanis immigrated to Pakistan when India was partitioned into Muslim Pakistan and Hindu India following its independence from Britain in 1947. The use of tandoors is common in Pakistan, particularly in the northern Punjab area.

Some of the common ingredients used in Pakistan are *gosht* (lamb and goat), *yakni* (mutton), *murgh* (chicken), *gayka* (beef), gehun, *piyas* (onions), dal, bindi, and chaawal. Some of the regional dishes and recipes that are common in Pakistan include *rotis* (flatbreads), *pulao* (Persian-inspired rice dishes, often with nuts and dried fruits), *biryani* (layered meat and rice dishes), *halvas* (sweets made from semolina and nuts), and *naan* (flatbread traditionally cooked in a tandoor oven).

Western India

The western portion of India includes significant stretches of desert, and the cuisine of this region is centered on the grains of barley, wheat, corn, and millet. This area includes the provinces of Rajasthan, Gujarat, and Maharashtra, as well as the major cities Bombay and Goa. The foods of the coastal areas of this region differ from those of the inland dramatically; they are much more likely to include fish or meats and often rely on coconut milk mixed with spices for their strong character. Inland is an area of a simpler (mostly vegetarian) cuisine that includes many types of breads made from wheat and other grains, or even dals that are eaten along with the milk of the herds and the local vegetables. In the mountainous portion of this area, a major feature is the grazing herds of sheep, goats, and camels, and the use of dairy products from these animals is common. On part of the coastal area is Goa, which was a Portuguese colony even during the period of British rule. A significant number of Christians live in this area, and some of the influences from the Portuguese are evident in the use of vinegar and onions and the inclusion of pork. The cuisine of Goa also frequently includes *nariyal* (coconut), rice, and the abundant seafood that is found off the coast of this city. The cuisine of Bombay also is connected to the ocean, and it is here that the prized "Bombay duck"—which is actually a fish—is found and prized. One of the features of the cuisine of Bombay is the influence of the Parsi (from Persian Iran) population who lived here following their migration in the thirteenth century. The Parsi brought their tradition of cooking rice dishes, the use of lamb as a common meat, and the spices of Persia, including *dhania* (coriander) and *jeera* (cumin).

Northern India/Nepal

The northern portions of India and Nepal are prime rice-growing areas, and the foothills of the geographically dominant Himalayas and Ganges River basin make up a large part of this region. Although rice is a staple in this region, and is used to make pulau and biryani, it is overshadowed by the vast wheat production that is used to make such well-known foods as naan and *chapatis*. This area includes the provinces of Himachal Pradesh, Punjab, Kashmir, Uttar Pradesh, and Madhya Pradesh in India, as well as the country Nepal and the major city Delhi. This region has many culinary influences from the history of rule by Persians and Turks, including the extensive use of fruits and nuts in many dishes. This is also the area of India in which the Punjab *tandoor* originated, and the cooking of foods in this oven is not only common here but has spread to other parts of India as well.

Eastern India/Bangladesh

This eastern region includes the provinces of Bihar, Assam, Bengal, and Orissa in India, as well as the country Bangladesh and the major cities Calcutta and Bhubaneshwar. This region is significantly influenced by the predominance of water and waterways that intersect the area. Fish is a common ingredient in much of the cooking here and is often combined with different spice blends to make dishes with a spicy sauce (often called curries). Rice is grown in many parts of this area, and it is a regular component in the local cuisine. In addition to the many fish and rice preparations, this is the region of India where sweet preparations—including *sandesh* (sweetened cheese with nuts and seasoned with cardamom)—are most well known.

The climate of this region is tropical, and yearly monsoons bring significant flooding and frequent displacement, particularly in Bangladesh. Many types of root vegetables are grown here, with *aloo* (potatoes) and *jamikand* (yams) commonly found in curries and other dishes. Common spices include rai and its oil, and *posto* (poppy seeds) and chutneys are frequently used condiments.

Southern India/Sri Lanka

This region encompasses the southernmost provinces of Karnataka, Andhra Pradesh, Kerala, and Tamil Nadu in India, as well as the island country Sri Lanka. Climate and religion play important roles in the cuisines of these areas: the tropical climate supports the growth of many ingredients uncommon in the northern areas, and religious customs influence what—if any—meats are eaten. This region is home to many tropical fruits and vegetables that are combined with rice, dals, and Indian spices to make the local cuisine. This cuisine is often considered the spiciest of the subcontinent; the liberal use of chiles provides much of the heat, particularly in Sri Lanka. This region is also largely vegetarian; a vast majority of the population in the Indian provinces are devout Hindus, and the majority of Sri Lanka's people are devout Buddhists. This region experienced much less influence from the Moghul period of rule.

Two common vegetables of this region are *brinja* (eggplant) and *karela* (bitter gourd), which are commonly seasoned with spices such as *methi* (fenugreek), *elaichi* (cardamom), *meetha neem* (curry leaves), and *hari mirch* (red chiles); often these are mixed with milk extracted from coconuts. In addition, lentils are commonly mixed with vegetables to make the common *sambar* (vegetables and lentils in spicy sauce) found in southern India. In the coastal areas, it is not uncommon for people to eat seafood (again, most of the inland residents are vegetarians); *jinga* (shrimp) is commonly found on the coastal menu. For seasonings, *imli* (tamarind) is used to add tartness to foods, and coconuts add richness.

Southern India and Sri Lanka are notorious for their use of chiles to make some of the spicier foods found on the subcontinent, and these regions are also well regarded for the artful combination of vegetables and seasonings, the creamy coconut milk-sauced preparations, and the coastal fish dishes.

RECIPES

The following recipes provide an introduction to the cuisine of the Indian subcontinent. The recipes for spice blends are presented first—because they form the backbone of the cuisines—followed by other regional and national specialties.

Garam Masala   NORTHERN INDIA
(INDIAN DRY SPICE BLEND)

INGREDIENTS

For Toasting Whole Spices

2	Tbsp	Whole Black Peppercorns
4	Tbsp	Cumin Seeds
2	Tbsp	Fennel Seeds
3	Tbsp	Coriander Seeds
1.5	tsp	Whole Cloves
2		Small Dried Chiles (you can use chili de arbol or another small dried chili, or substitute 1 tsp red chili flakes; if using the red pepper flakes, put them in the pan for only 30 seconds)
1		Whole Cinnamon Stick

For Grinding Toasted Spices with Additional Ingredients

		Toasted Spice Mixture (see above)
4		Bay Leaves
1	Tbsp	Ground Cardamom (whole can be used and added to the toasted spices)
2	tsp	Ground Mace

Toasting spices in a pan for garam masala (Indian dry spice blend)

Garam masala is one of the common spice blends used to season many Indian dishes. Spices and their blends are a cornerstone of Indian cuisine and are often misunderstood in the United States, where curry powder is often thought of as a spice or a standard mixture. In reality, curry powder is a spice blend, and there are as many versions of curry powder as there are merchants in India. Traditional garam masala would be made using only hot or warming spices, which include black peppercorns, black cardamom, nutmeg, mace, cinnamon, cloves, and bay leaves (although many variations are common in India). The following recipe for garam masala is typical of a merchant style, but keep in mind that variations abound, and the blending of spices for specific uses is one of the many arts of Indian cuisine.

YIELD: Approximately 1 cup

COOKING METHOD: Dry Pan Toasting

PROCEDURE

1. Combine the whole spices, except for the chiles and cinnamon; smell them to become familiar with their muted (at this point) aromatic quality.

2. Place the whole spices (except for the chiles and cinnamon) in a small sauté pan over a medium-low flame, and heat the spices to begin to toast them. Keep the spices moving in the pan to ensure that they do not get burned. Continue to toast the spices until they just begin to get fragrant (remember what they smelled like at the beginning?).

3. Once the whole spices have just begun to get fragrant, add the chiles and cinnamon to the pan; continue to move all of the spices over the medium-low flame until the chiles just start to color (the whole spices may begin to color slightly as well, but they should not turn black—except for those that were black to begin with).

4. Remove the pan from the heat, and transfer the spices to another container to ensure that they do not burn in the hot pan.

5. Once cool, place them in a spice grinder (or a coffee grinder) with the other ground spices and bay leaves; grind everything into powder.

6. Keep spices in a well-sealed container to reduce flavor loss if they won't be used within a couple of days.

Bafat SOUTHERN INDIA

(MULTIUSE SPICE BLEND FROM SOUTHERN INDIA)

INGREDIENTS

For Toasting the Spices

1	Tbsp	Whole Cardamom (if only ground is available, use 1.5 Tbsp and add along with other ground spices)
1	Tbsp	Black Pepper
1/2	tsp	Whole Cloves
1	tsp	Fenugreek Seeds
1	tsp	Fennel Seeds
3	Tbsp	Cumin Seeds
2	Tbsp	Mustard Seeds
3	Tbsp	Coriander Seeds
1	oz	Dried Red Chili (such as chili de arbol or japones) or Cayenne Powder

For Grinding the Spices

2	Tbsp	Turmeric, ground
2	tsp	Ginger, ground
1	tsp	Cinnamon, ground
2	Tbsp	Kosher Salt

This is the Indian version of the curry powder that most Americans are familiar with, but when made fresh this actually delivers what the store-bought version promises. This blend can be used in the place of curry powder in recipes and is a good overall general-use blend. I have included salt in this recipe, but it can be omitted if desired. Note that this blend has considerably more kick and flavor than the curry powder you're probably used to, so start out by using ¼ of what is called for in recipes that use this ingredient.

YIELD: 1.25 cups

COOKING METHOD: Dry Pan Toasting

PROCEDURE

For Toasting the Spices

1. Combine the whole cardamom, black pepper, cloves, fenugreek, and fennel together in a container, and smell them to become familiar with their muted aroma (at this point). Place them in a sauté pan over a medium-low flame to toast them; keep them moving to prevent scorching.

2. Toast the whole spices for 3–4 minutes over this flame (they should not begin to color but should start to become more fragrant).

3. Add the whole cumin seeds, mustard, and coriander to the pan, and continue to toast all of the spices together—while moving them—until you begin to notice some of them becoming darker (not burning, just browning).

4. Once you notice the color changing, add the chiles and cook for another 2 minutes over the medium-low flame; remove from heat.

5. Once the spice blend cools, grind all of the whole spices with the ground spices and then place them in a well-sealed container to preserve the flavor until used.

Sambar Masal SOUTHERN INDIA

(SOUTH INDIAN SPICE BLEND)

INGREDIENTS

1	Tbsp	Vegetable Oil
1/2	Tbsp	Black Peppercorns
1/2	Tbsp	Fenugreek Seeds

This spice blend is typical of southern India and is used to make the vegetable/legume dishes of the south known as *sambars*.

YIELD: 3/4 cup

COOKING METHOD: Pan Toasting

(continues)

Sambar Masal
(continued)

1	Tbsp	Moong Dal
1	Tbsp	Urad Dal
1/2	Tbsp	Cumin Seeds
1/4	cup	Coriander Seeds
1	Tbsp	Mustard Seeds
3	Tbsp	Crushed Dried Chiles (such as chili de arbol or japones; about 6 each)
1/2	tsp	Asafoetida
15		Curry Leaves
1	tsp	Salt

PROCEDURE

1. In a sauté pan, heat the oil over medium heat; once the oil is hot, add the peppercorns, fenugreek, moong dal, and urad dal. Cook, stirring constantly, for 2–3 minutes.

2. Add the coriander seeds, mustard, and cumin, and continue cooking and stirring for an additional 3–4 minutes (at which point the spices should start to become fragrant).

3. Add the chiles and asafoetida, and continue to cook and stir until the chiles begin to change color.

4. Once the chiles begin to change color, add the curry leaves and continue to cook and stir for an additional 2 minutes. Remove the pan from heat, and transfer the contents to another container to cool.

5. Once cool, purée all of the ingredients in a spice grinder and store them in a well-sealed container.

Pol Sambol   SRI LANKA
(COCONUT SAMBOL)

INGREDIENTS

2	oz	Fresh Red Chiles (such as cayenne or ripe serrano), stems removed and chopped (you can substitute .5 oz dried chiles, if necessary, with stems and seeds removed)
.5	oz	Garlic Cloves, chopped
2	oz	Shallots, chopped
1	tsp	Salt
1	tsp	Black Peppercorns, crushed
1	tsp	Sugar
6	oz	Fresh Coconut, grated
2	oz	Lime Juice
2	oz	Vegetable Oil (optional; this will make the sambol smoother)

Sambols are pastes made of fresh chiles and onions or shallots combined with other ingredients and served with breads or other foods as a condiment. This version is typical of Sri Lanka in that it has significant heat (as long as the chiles do!) and adds coconut to make a flavorful blend.

YIELD: 1.5 cups

COOKING METHOD: Blending/Puréeing

PROCEDURE

1. In a mortar, combine the chiles, garlic, shallots, salt, and black pepper; crush with the pestle until the mixture resembles coarse paste.

2. Add the sugar and grated coconut, and continue to grind together until a coarse paste consistency is achieved.

3. Transfer the mixture to a blender and add lime juice. With the blender running, slowly pour in the vegetable oil to make a smoother paste (if you are not adding oil, simply add the lime juice after step 2 to finish).

Raita INDIAN SUBCONTINENT
(YOGURT RELISH)

INGREDIENTS:

2	cups	Yogurt, plain (see Chapter 2, "Greek Cuisine," for recipe)
1	tsp	Cumin, ground
1	lb	Cucumber, peeled and diced small
8	oz	Tomato, seeded and diced small
1	oz	Green Chili, seeded and minced (you can use jalapeño, serrano, etc.)
1/4	cup	Packed Mint Leaves, chopped
1/2	tsp	Salt

Yogurt is a favorite condiment in the subcontinent and is often combined with seasonings for different dishes. Making yogurt has long been a way to preserve milk yielded from cows, and yogurt is commonly used in preparations such as this raita, as well as in sauces. This recipe produces a very refreshing and cooling condiment that perfectly complements spicy dishes.

YIELD: 4 cups

COOKING METHOD: Mixing and Infusing

PROCEDURE

1. Combine all ingredients in a mixing bowl, and whisk them together to combine thoroughly.

2. Check seasoning and adjust, if necessary. Refrigerate mixture and allow infusing for at least 30 minutes before use.

Ghee NORTHERN INDIA/PAKISTAN
(CLARIFIED AND CARAMELIZED BUTTER)

INGREDIENTS

2	lbs	Unsalted Butter

Ghee is the preferred fat to cook with in much of northern India and Pakistan, and it is easy to make. The butter found in India has a different taste than the butter found in the United States, but this recipe yields a flavorful product that substitutes well for purchased ghee.

YIELD: 1.5 pounds

COOKING METHOD: Modified Simmering

PROCEDURE

1. Place the butter in a small, heavy-bottomed pot, and melt it gently over a low flame.

2. Once the butter has melted, turn the heat up to a medium-low flame, which should bring the mixture to a simmer (the water in the butter will settle to the bottom and steam out through the fat).

3. Milk solids will gather at the surface of the mixture; as they do, push them back into the solution as it simmers to form a somewhat white-looking liquid (it should slightly resemble cream).

4. Continue step 3 until all of the water has evaporated (you will know this has happened when the mixture becomes a clear butter color).

5. Once the water has evaporated, turn the heat down and slowly allow the milk solids to caramelize and settle to the bottom of the pot.

6. Remove the pot from heat and allow it to cool slightly before pouring the ghee off of the caramelized solids on the bottom of the pot.

(continues)

Ghee
(continued)

Melted butter simmering to make ghee (clarified and caramelized butter); note the whitish color of the butter from the emulsion maintained by slow simmering

Finished ghee; note the caramelized specks on the bottom of the pan

Basmati   NORTHERN INDIA

(STEAMED BASMATI RICE)

INGREDIENTS

3 cups Basmati Rice, rinsed in cold water and drained well

4 cups Cold Water

The most common types of rice on the Indian subcontinent are long grain, and one of the most prized is the very fragrant basmati rice from the Himalayan foothills. Rice is cooked in different ways, depending on who is cooking it and what they intend to do with it: it might be boiled/ steamed, as in this recipe, or cooked in ample boiling water (like pasta) or a rice cooker.

YIELD: 6 cups cooked

COOKING METHOD: Boiling/Steaming

Bands of basmati rice and tok dal (red lentils with tamarind and lime) topped with pol sambal (coconut spice paste) and limes

PROCEDURE

1. After rinsing the rice with cold water, place it in a colander to drain off excess water.

2. Combine the rice with the water in a small pot, and allow it to soak for at least 45 minutes before cooking it (this allows the rice to start to absorb water, and it will cook more evenly and quickly as a result).

3. Place the pot on the stove and bring the mixture to a boil over high heat; once it comes to a boil, reduce the heat to a low flame and cover the pot with a very tight-fitting lid (use foil crimped on the rim of the pot if you don't have a good lid).

4. Cook covered and over a very low flame (the lid should not be forced off by steam) for 12 minutes; turn the heat off but leave the lid on.

5. Leave the pot covered for another 10 minutes, off of the heat (this will allow the steam to finish cooking the rice), and then uncover and fluff with a fork.

Tok Dal EASTERN INDIA/BANGLADESH

(RED LENTIL WITH TAMARIND AND LIME)

INGREDIENTS

For Cooking the Lentils

1	lb	Red Lentils (also called masoor dal)
2.5	qts	Water

For Making the Tarka

4	oz	Vegetable Oil
2	tsp	Cumin, ground
1	tsp	Coriander, ground
1.5	tsp	Turmeric, ground
1/2	tsp	Fennel Seeds, ground
1	tsp	Cayenne Pepper, ground (or another ground chili)
1	oz	Garlic Cloves, minced
10	oz	Yellow Onion, sliced very thin
2	tsp	Salt

For Final Seasoning and Garnish

1	oz	Tamarind Pulp, soaked in 1/2 cup hot water and pressed through a sieve
2	oz	Lime Juice
1/2	bunch	Cilantro, leaves chopped
		Salt, to taste
2		Limes, cut into 8 wedges each

This recipe, for one of the many types of dals that might be found in India, includes the red lentils common in India and the sour tamarind that is used in many parts of India and Bangladesh.

YIELD: 3 pounds, or 8 portions (6 ounces/portion)

COOKING METHOD: Simmering and Tarka

PROCEDURE

For Cooking the Lentils

1. Place the lentils and water in an appropriately sized pot, and bring the mixture to a boil over high heat.

2. Once the mixture has come to a boil, reduce the heat to simmer gently and skim any foam that rises to the top.

3. Simmer the lentils until they just become tender (about 15–18 minutes); remove them from the heat and set aside to add the tarka and seasonings.

For Making the Tarka

1. Add the oil to a heavy-bottomed sauté pan, and heat over a medium flame until hot.

2. Add the ground spices to the hot oil, and sauté/stir fry for a minute to release the flavor of the spices.

3. Add the minced garlic and sliced onions to the pan; lower the heat to sweat the onions and garlic until they are tender and translucent (about 10 minutes).

4. Once they are tender and translucent, add the salt and transfer the entire mixture to the cooked lentils; stir in.

For Final Seasoning and Garnish

1. After adding the tarka to the lentils, add the tamarind liquid that has been pressed through a sieve (to remove any seeds or skin) along with the lime juice and half of the chopped cilantro.

2. Taste the red lentils and adjust seasoning with salt, if necessary. Garnish with the lime wedges and cilantro.

Chane ki Dal Laukiwali   WESTERN INDIA
(YELLOW SPLIT PEAS WITH SPICED TOMATO AND ZUCCHINI)

INGREDIENTS

For Cooking the Yellow Split Peas

1	qt	Water
1	lb	Yellow Split Peas (called toovar dal in India)
2	tsp	Ground Turmeric
1	tsp	Salt

For Making the Tarka and Sautéing the Vegetables

2	oz	Ghee (see recipe, this chapter, if necessary)
1	tsp	Cumin Seeds
1	tsp	Fennel Seeds
1/2	tsp	Coriander Seeds
2		Small Dried Red Chiles (such as chili de arbol or japonese, or substitute 1 tsp red pepper flakes)
.5	oz	Garlic Cloves, minced
1	oz	Ginger, minced
8	oz	Yellow Onion, diced small
8	oz	Zucchini, diced medium
10	oz	Tomato Concassée or Canned Diced Tomato
1	Tbsp	Garam Masala (see recipe, this chapter)
1	oz	Lemon Juice
1/4	cup	Packed Chopped Fresh Cilantro (about 1/4 to 1/3 bunch)
		Salt, to taste

This is another example of the use of the tarka method of toasting spices and then adding them to cooked ingredients, which is a common way to season foods in India.

YIELD: 10 portions (5–6 ounces/portion)

COOKING METHOD (SPLIT PEAS): Simmering

COOKING METHOD (SPICES): Tarka

COOKING METHOD (VEGETABLES): Sautéing

PROCEDURE

For Cooking the Yellow Split Peas

1. Combine the water, yellow split peas, turmeric, and salt in a small pot, and bring to a boil over a medium-high flame.

2. Once the split pea mixture has come to a boil, lower the heat to a gentle simmer and cover to cook the peas until they are tender (about 20–25 minutes). (Add more water to the pot if the peas become uncovered at any time during this process.)

3. Once the peas are tender, remove them from the heat and set the pot aside until the vegetables and seasoning are done (these can be prepared as the split peas are cooking).

For Making the Tarka and Sautéing the Vegetables

1. In a heavy-bottomed pan large enough to hold the vegetables and the split peas, heat the ghee over a medium flame until it is hot; add the whole spice seeds to make the tarka.

2. Once the spice seeds have become fragrant, add the whole dried chiles; stir the spices and chiles in the ghee to prevent burning, and cook in fat for 1–2 minutes to infuse the oil.

3. Add the minced garlic cloves and ginger; continue to stir to quickly sauté the seasonings. Add the onion, lower the heat, and sweat the onion until tender.

4. Once the onion becomes tender, turn the heat back up and add the zucchini; sauté the zucchini until it just begins to brown (about 4–5 minutes).

5. Once the zucchini begins to color, add the tomato and garam masala; bring the entire mixture to a simmer over a medium-high flame, and simmer for 5 minutes.

6. Once the mixture has simmered for 5 minutes, add the cooked yellow split peas to the pot and stir them into the seasoned vegetable mixture. Bring the entire mixture to a gentle simmer over low heat.

7. Once hot, add the lemon juice and cilantro. Season with salt, if necessary, and serve.

Chane ki dal laukiwali (yellow split peas) served with chapatis (Indian flatbread)

Masala Murgh NORTHERN INDIA

(MARINATED BRAISED CHICKEN IN SPICED TOMATO/YOGURT SAUCE)

INGREDIENTS

For Marinating the Chicken

4	lbs	Boneless/Skinless Chicken Breasts or Thighs
1/2	Tbsp	Salt
1/2	tsp	Freshly Ground Black Pepper
1	Tbsp	Garam Masala (see recipe, this chapter)
1	tsp	Cumin Seeds, ground
1	tsp	Fennel Seeds, ground
2	oz	Lemon Juice
1/2	oz	Garlic Cloves, minced
1	oz	Fresh Ginger, minced

For Making the Tarka

4	oz	Vegetable Oil
1	tsp	Cardamom, whole
1/4	tsp	Fennel Seeds, whole
1/2	tsp	Cumin Seeds, whole
1	tsp	Garam Masala

For Braising the Chicken

		Tarka Oil (see above)
		Marinated Chicken (see above)
1/2	cup	Chickpea Flour (substitute all-purpose flour or cornstarch, if this is unavailable)
1/2	cup	Almonds, raw and ground fine in spice mill
1	lb	Yellow Onion, diced small
2	lbs	Tomato Concassée or Canned Diced Tomato
1	pt	Chicken Stock or Water
1	pt	Drained Yogurt (you will need about 1.5 pts to yield 1 pt drained)
		Salt, to taste

This recipe, from northern India, is seen often in the United States. Masala murgh combines some of the classic seasonings and techniques used in India with something from the Americas—tomatoes are a significant part of this recipe's sauce.

YIELD: 20 portions (7 ounces/portion)

COOKING METHOD (SPICES): Tarka

COOKING METHOD (CHICKEN): Braising

PROCEDURE

For Marinating the Chicken

(**NOTE:** *This can be done up to a day ahead of time.*)

1. Combine all ingredients in a nonreactive container, and mix thoroughly; cover and store in the refrigerator.

2. Allow mixture to marinate in the refrigerator for at least 1 hour before use.

For Making the Tarka

1. Heat the vegetable oil in a small sauté pan over a medium flame; when hot, add the whole cardamom and stir in pan for 2–3 minutes.

2. Add the whole fennel seeds and cumin seeds to the pan, and continue to stir-fry in the oil until all of the seeds begin to become aromatic (be careful not to scorch them—lower the heat if the oil gets too hot).

(continues)

Masala murgh (marinated and braised chicken in tomato/yogurt sauce) served with basmati rice and aloo paratha (potato-filled flatbread)

Masala Murgh
(continued)

3. Once the spices become aromatic, remove them from the oil with a slotted spoon, leaving the oil behind in the pan.

4. Place the toasted spices in a paper towel to remove any excess grease, and transfer the whole spices to a spice grinder; once cool, grind them to a powder.

5. Return the spices to the pan with the oil, and add the garam masala; cook over a medium-low flame to toast the spices together.

6. Strain 2 oz of the resulting oil into a large sauté pan.

For Braising the Chicken

1. Preheat the oven to 325°F.

2. Heat the large sauté pan with the tarka oil over a medium-high flame; once hot, add the marinated chicken to the pan (after lightly coating chicken in chickpea flour).

3. Sauté the chicken in the oil until golden and then remove it from the pan (use more of the tarka oil, if necessary, to brown all of the chicken).

4. Once all of the chicken has been sautéed, add 1 oz of the tarka oil to the pan and add the ground almond (if all of the tarka oil has been used to sauté the chicken, use additional vegetable oil).

5. Briefly cook the ground almond in the fat (1–2 minutes), and then add the yellow onion, the spices, and any remaining oil from making the tarka.

6. Turn the heat down to low, and slowly sweat the onions until they are tender and translucent.

7. Once the onions are cooked, add the tomato concassée and chicken stock. Return the chicken to the pan.

8. Cover the pan and place it in the preheated oven; allow to cook until chicken is done (about 20 minutes, depending on size).

9. Remove the pan from the oven and place it on the stove. Swirl the yogurt into the sauce.

10. If the sauce is too thin, reduce it gently over a low flame.

11. Adjust seasoning with salt. Serve with naan or chapatis.

Chapatis   ALL OF SUBCONTINENT
(INDIAN FLATBREAD)

INGREDIENTS

2	tsp	Salt
1	lb	(16 oz) Warm Water

Often called rotis in Pakistan and northern India, this style of bread is very common throughout the subcontinent.

YIELD: 12 chapatis (3 ounces/each)

MIXING METHOD: Straight Dough Method

COOKING METHOD: Griddling/Panfrying

(continues)

Chapatis
(continued)

1.25	lbs	Atta Flour (substitute 1 lb all-purpose flour and .25 lb whole wheat flour, if this is unavailable); more will be needed for rolling the dough, and perhaps more for the dough itself
2	oz	Ghee

PROCEDURE

1. Preheat the griddle to 375°F (or a large sauté pan can be used).
2. Combine the salt and water, and mix to dissolve the salt.
3. Add the flour to the mixing bowl of a mixer with a dough hook; with the machine running, add all of the water/salt mixture.
4. Once the dough has formed, check its consistency. If it sticks to the mixing bowl, add a little more flour (it should be soft but not sticky).
5. Mix the dough until it becomes smooth and stretches easily without tearing (about 10–12 minutes for most machines).
6. Once it has developed well, remove the dough from the mixer, cover it with a clean cloth, and allow it to rest for 30 minutes.
7. Once the dough has rested, divide it into about 12 pieces; using a rolling pin, roll out these pieces on a workbench until they are approximately 1/4 inch thick.
8. Once the dough has been rolled out, place it on the preheated griddle (after adding a small amount of ghee to the griddle).
9. Cook on one side for 1 minute, and the turn over and cook on the second side for 2 minutes; turn back to first side.
10. Allow the dough to cook until done, which often can be determined when air bubbles form in the dough as it cooks through (this is a good characteristic of chapatis, so don't pop the air bubbles!).
11. Once done, remove from the griddle and serve.

Aloo Paratha WESTERN INDIA
(POTATO-FILLED FLATBREAD)

INGREDIENTS

For Cooking the Potatoes

1.5	lbs	Russet Potatoes
2	qts	Water
1	Tbsp	Salt
2	Tbsp	Ghee (see recipe, this chapter)
1/2	tsp	Coriander Seeds, whole
1	tsp	Mustard Seeds, whole
.5	oz	Garlic, minced
6	oz	Yellow Onion, grated
1	oz	Fresh Green Chili (such as serrano or jalapeño), minced
2	tsp	Turmeric, ground
1/4	tsp	Freshly Ground Black Pepper
1.5	tsp	Salt

For Mixing the Dough

2	tsp	Salt
16	oz	Warm Water

One of the many types of bread found in Western India and Pakistan, this version included a spiced potato that is rolled into the paratha to yield moist dough that makes a nice appetizer or accompaniment to an entrée.

YIELD: 12 portions (6 ounces/portion)

COOKING METHOD (POTATOES): Boiling

COOKING METHOD (FILLING): Modified Sautéing

MIXING METHOD (DOUGH): Straight Dough

COOKING METHOD (PARATHAS): Griddle Frying/Panfrying

PROCEDURE

For Cooking the Potatoes

1. Preheat the oven to 325°F.
2. Combine the potatoes, water, and salt in a small pot, and bring to a boil over high heat. Boil the potatoes until they just become tender.
3. Once cooked, drain the water and set the potatoes aside to cool until they can be handled, at which time they can be peeled. Once peeled and cooled, cut the potatoes into 1/4-inch slices.

(continues)

Aloo Paratha
(continued)

1.25 lbs	Atta Flour (substitute 1 lb all-purpose flour and .25 lb whole wheat flour, if this is unavailable); more will be needed for rolling the dough, and perhaps more for the dough itself
3 oz	Ghee

For Griddle Frying/Panfrying the Paratha

4 oz	Ghee
	Rolled Filled Dough and Potatoes (see above)
	Salt, to taste

4. Place the potatoes in the preheated oven for 5 minutes to dry them out slightly.

5. In a sauté pan large enough to hold the potatoes, add the ghee and heat over a medium-low flame.

6. Once the ghee is hot, add the coriander seeds and lightly fry in fat for 2 minutes.

7. Add the mustard seeds, and continue to cook over a medium-low flame until the seeds begin to pop.

8. Once the mustard seeds have begun to pop, add the minced garlic, grated onion (and its liquid), and minced chili; continue to cook over a medium-low flame until all of the vegetables are very tender.

9. Once the vegetables are tender, add the turmeric and black pepper, and turn the heat up to a medium-high flame. Cook over high heat for 3–4 minutes.

10. Add the potatoes and salt, and mix well with all of the ingredients. Don't worry if you break up the potatoes (you're going to crush them later, anyway!).

For Mixing the Dough

1. Combine the salt and water, and mix thoroughly to dissolve the water.

2. Add the flour to the mixing bowl of a mixer with a dough hook; with the machine running, add all of the water/salt mixture.

3. Once the dough has formed, check its consistency. If it sticks to the mixing bowl, add a little more flour until it forms a soft dough.

4. Mix the dough until it becomes smooth and stretches easily without tearing (about 10–12 minutes for most machines).

5. Once it has developed well, remove the dough from the mixer, cover it with a clean cloth, and allow it to rest for 30 minutes.

6. Once the dough has rested, divide it into about 12 pieces; using a rolling pin, roll out these pieces on a workbench until they are approximately 1/4 inch thick.

7. To assemble the parathas, place 2 oz of the cooled potato mixture on one half of each of the 12 pieces of dough. Fold the uncovered half on top of the potato-covered half, and seal the edges by pressing them with a fork.

8. Roll out the half-moon-shaped filled dough with a rolling pin until it is slightly thicker than it was before you added the filling.

9. Fold the dough over again, in half, and roll out the dough until it is close to its original 1/4 inch thickness (some of the potato mixture may squeeze out during this process, which is normal).

10. Once the dough has been rolled twice, it is ready to be cooked.

For Griddle Frying/Panfrying the Parathas

1. If you are using a griddle, preheat it to 375°F. Otherwise, preheat a large, flat sauté pan over a medium flame.

2. Place enough ghee on the griddle or sauté pan to coat the cooking area well, and then add as many dough pieces as will fit without dropping the temperature much. Cook on one side until golden brown.

(continues)

Aloo Paratha
(continued)

3. Turn the parathas over, and cook on the second side until both sides are golden and the dough is cooked through.

4. Remove parathas from the griddle or pan, and season with salt.

5. Repeat steps 2–4 until all of the dough has been cooked.

Gosht Pulao   PAKISTAN/NORTHWESTERN INDIA
(SPICED STEWED LAMB AND BASMATI)

INGREDIENTS

For Soaking the Rice

| 1.5 | lbs | Basmati Rice |
| 2 | qts | Water |

For Marinating the Lamb

3	lbs	Lamb Stew Meat, cleaned of connective tissue
1	Tbsp	Salt
2	tsp	Freshly Ground Black Pepper
2	tsp	Cumin, ground
1	tsp	Cayenne Pepper
1.5	tsp	Turmeric, ground

For Making the Stew

4	oz	Ghee (see recipe, this chapter)
1		Cinnamon Stick
1	Tbsp	Cardamom, whole (about a dozen)
1/2	tsp	Cloves, whole (about a dozen)
1.5	lbs	Yellow Onion, sliced thin
2	oz	Garlic Cloves, minced or grated
2	oz	Ginger, minced or grated
1/4	tsp	Nutmeg, ground
1/2	tsp	Freshly Ground Black Pepper
1	Tbsp	Coriander, ground
		Marinated Lamb (see above)
1	lb	Diced Tomatoes (concassée if tomatoes are ripe, or canned if tomatoes are not)
3		Bay Leaves
		Basmati Rice (see above), drained
1	qt	Water
		Salt and Pepper, to taste
1/2	bunch	Cilantro, chopped (for garnish)

Puloas have a clear Moghul (via Persia) influence and are found in what was once a stronghold of the Moghul Empire. The use of cardamom, cinnamon, and cloves is a hallmark of this cuisine and can be found in this recipe.

YIELD: 20 portions (7 ounces/portion)

COOKING METHOD: Stewing

PROCEDURE

For Soaking the Rice

1. Rinse rice in a china cap under cool running water until the water runs clear.

2. Transfer rice to a mixing bowl or another container large enough to hold the rice and water. Combine the rice with 2 qts of water, and allow the rice to soak for at least 1 hour before proceeding with the recipe. (This step is important for the rice to cook properly; if it is skipped, this recipe will not have enough liquid.)

For Marinating the Lamb

1. Combine the lamb and all of the spices in a mixing bowl, and mix thoroughly to coat the lamb evenly with the seasoning.

2. Place the lamb in the refrigerator, and allow it to marinate for 1 hour before proceeding.

For Making the Stew

1. Preheat the oven to 300°F.

2. In an appropriately sized heavy-bottomed pot, heat the ghee over a medium flame; add the cinnamon stick, cardamom, and cloves, and stir to "toast" the spices and draw out flavor for 1 minute.

3. Add the sliced onions, garlic, and ginger; lower the heat and sweat the ingredients until the onions are very tender and translucent (approximately 15–20 minutes).

4. Add the dry ground spices, and turn the heat up to a medium-high flame. Continue to cook until the pot begins to look dry and the spices are very fragrant.

5. Add the marinated lamb to the pot, and turn the heat up to a high flame. Continually stir to brown the lamb while making sure not to burn the bottom of the pot.

(continues)

*

Gosht Pulao
(continued)

6. Once the lamb is caramelized, add the diced tomatoes, bay leaves, soaked rice, and water; bring the entire mixture to a simmer.

7. Once the mixture comes to a boil, cover the pot with aluminum foil, making sure to crimp the ends to prevent moisture from leaving the pot; place a lid on top of the pot to hold the foil in place.

8. Place the covered pot in the preheated oven, and bake for 1 hour.

9. Remove from the oven and check seasoning; serve.

Gosht pulao (spiced stewed lamb with basmati rice)

* **Am Kulfi**   NORTHERN INDIA

(INDIAN MANGO ICE CREAM)

INGREDIENTS

3	cups	Condensed Milk
2	cups	Whole Milk
1	tsp	Cardamom, ground
2	oz	Sugar, granulated or superfine
3	oz	Pistachios, ground (optional)
2	cups	Sweetened Condensed Milk
1.5	lbs	Mango Purée (preferably fresh ripe mangoes or, if those are unavailable, frozen mangoes)

Ice cream in India is thought to have originated from the Moghuls of central Asia and was being made in India as early as 1590 for the Moghul emperor Akbar. Traditionally, it is made by placing the mixture in conical earthenware containers that are sealed with dough and packed into ice-filled containers. The result is somewhat granular but delicious!

YIELD: 2.5 quarts

COOKING METHOD: Poaching/Infusing

FREEZING METHOD: Set Freezing or Alternative Method of Turned Freezing

PROCEDURE

1. In a small saucepan, combine the condensed milk, whole milk, ground cardamom, sugar, and pistachios; bring mixture to a gentle simmer over a low flame.

2. Once simmering gently, continue to cook over a very low flame for 5 minutes to infuse flavors into the mixture.

3. Remove the pan from the heat, and allow it to cool completely by stirring over an ice bath to prevent the formation of a film.

4. Once cooled, add the sweetened condensed milk and mango purée.

(continues)

Am Kulfi
(continued)

5. Taste the mixture for mango flavor, which should be pronounced; if it isn't, add more mango (the ripeness of the mangoes will affect this).

6. Place the mixture in a metal container and store in the freezer until solidified.

    An alternate method is to place it in an ice cream–making machine and freeze according to instructions, which will result in a smoother ice cream that is more similar to the European style commonly found in the United States.

Am kulfi (mango ice cream)

SUMMARY

The cuisine of the Indian subcontinent is one of spices and vegetarianism, and it includes a wide variety of starchy ingredients that are commonly combined with vegetables and legumes. The Indian subcontinent includes India, the Muslim country Pakistan, Nepal, Bangladesh, and Sri Lanka. These countries share the common use of spices in everyday cooking but vary notably in the level of spice used and also in the typical foods eaten. Indian cuisine is known for its many vegetables and starches, partly because so many residents are vegetarians as a result of their Hindu, Buddhist, or Jain religious beliefs. When animal foods are eaten, it is most often fish, goat, lamb, or poultry; the cow is considered sacred in India, so beef is not eaten. Butter is highly prized, however, because it is considered a purifying food. Butter is most commonly processed into a clarified form called ghee that is often used as a cooking fat. The toasting of spices in oil or ghee—and adding this seasoning to cooked foods—is one of the unique characteristics of this cuisine, as are the many types of flatbreads that are common throughout this region.

REVIEW QUESTIONS

1. What is the dominant religion in India, and how does the religion influence the dietary habits of the population?

2. Which part of the subcontinent is known for using a lot of chiles and making the food quite spicy?

3. In which part of India did the tandoor oven originate?

4. What Indian word is the root of the term *curry*, and how has this name changed in meaning over time?

COMMON TERMS, FOODS, AND INGREDIENTS

The cuisine of the Indian subcontinent is an ancient cuisine with many traditional foods and recipes. For additional information regarding legumes and pulses, see the "Unique Components" section of this chapter. The following guide will help to navigate the terms that are encountered when learning about this cuisine.

✳ Ingredients and Foods

adrak – Ginger root

aloo – Potato

am – Mango

am choor – Green mango powder; sour powder used to add tartness to dishes (also called khatai)

asafoetida – Dried sap of large fennel-like plant common to Indian subcontinent; used extensively in the cuisine, especially in dals and bean dishes that are broken down by components in the asafoetida that aid in digestion. This has a very pungent smell that mellows when cooked and should be used sparingly.

badam – Almond

basmati – Fragrant rice with elongated thin grains; grown in the Himalayan foothills

besan – Chickpea flour (also called gram flour)

bindi – Okra

brinja – Eggplant

chaawal – Rice (uncooked)

channa – Chickpea

dal – Split pulses or legumes (lentils, beans, peas, etc.)

dhania – Coriander (called cilantro when the leaves are used)

dhoodh – Milk

elaichi – Cardamom

gayka – Beef (only common in non-Hindu areas such as Pakistan)

ghee – Clarified and caramelized butter, made by caramelizing the milk solids during the clarification process

gehun – Wheat

gosht – Lamb or goat (sometimes used as the word *meat* would be used in the United States)

gur – Jaggary; unrefined sugar

hari mirch – Red chiles

hing – Asefoetida

huldi – Turmeric

imli – Tamarind

jamikand – Yam

jeera – Cumin seeds

kaju – Cashew

kamel – Lotus root

karakkan – Millet

karela – Bitter gourd

lal mirch – Green chiles

masala – Spice mixture

    chaat masala – Tart spice blend made from green mango powder, cumin, black salt, asafoetida, black pepper, ginger, chili, and sometimes pomegranate powder (anardana) and mint

    dhansak masala – Spice blend common in the western coastal region of India, where Persian peoples landed and influenced the cuisine. This blend would typically contain cinnamon, cardamom, cloves, cumin, black pepper, coriander, nutmeg, star anise, fenugreek leaves, ginger, and chiles

    garam masala – Common spice blend of northern India that contains coriander, cumin, black pepper, cardamom, cloves, cinnamon, nutmeg, bay leaves, and often a small amount of chili and fennel seeds

    tandoori masala – Common spice blend of Punjab made of cumin, coriander, cloves, turmeric, cinnamon, cayenne, mace, and ginger, and usually colored with red food coloring

    tikka masala – Tikka actually means "little pieces," but the marinated and skewered pieces of meat made in this fashion have come to refer to foods coated with a typical spice mix that includes garam masala, cumin, and coriander and often is served with yogurt and tomato sauce

    vindaloo masala – This type of spice mixture is a wet blend and is heavily influenced by the Portuguese, who once colonized the area of Goa in southwestern India. This paste would typically contain vinegar, garlic, chiles, and various additional spices.

masoor dal – Red-orange lentil

mattar – Green peas (often called English peas)

meetha neem – Curry leaves; unrelated to the term *curry* or to spice blends, these are leaves from a plant that provide a musky, slightly bitter and aromatic quality to foods

meetha-toray – Sponge gourd

methi – Fenugreek

mirch – Peppercorns

murgh – Chicken

nariyal – Coconuts

paneer – Cow's milk cheese common in India

piyas – Onion

posto – Poppy seeds

psi hui – Cayenne chili introduced by the Portuguese

ria – Mustard seeds

rajma – Kidney beans

rosematta – Red rice grown in southern India

ruh gulab – Rosewater

saag – Spinach

sambhar – Dried spice mixture made from mustard, cumin, fenugreek, black peppercorns, coriander, curry leaves, turmeric, chiles, and asafoetida; common in southern India *til* – Sesame

tindora – Small squash that resembles a cucumber

yakni – Mutton

✳ Common Prepared Foods

achar – Pickled vegetables

biryanis – Rice and meat dishes common throughout the subcontinent, which are made by layering partially cooked rice and marinated (and sometimes cooked) meats, and then cooking them together in a sealed earthenware vessel over a flame until done. These are usually made on festive occasions and are considered the pinnacle of rice cookery in the cuisines of the subcontinent.

chapati – Flat, round bread made from wheat flour and cooked in oil or ghee on a tava (flat griddle-like pan); common in the northern part of the Indian subcontinent

chhana – Curds made from boiled milk with a souring agent; used in Bengali sweets

chutney – Relish made from various ingredients; often sweet and spicy

curry – Generic English term for foods with a spiced sauce from the period in which the British colonized India. The term is thought to have derived from the Tamil *kari*, which denoted a dish made with black pepper and which would typically have a spicy sauce. Curry powder is an English invention and has little in common with the many spice blends in India (most are called *masala* in India).

dahi – Yogurt

dal – General term for cooked dishes with pulses or legumes

dosa – Thin flatbread made from rice and lentil flour; also called dosai

ghee – Clarified and caramelized butter, made by caramelizing the milk solids in butter as it is clarified.

halvas – Sweets made from various grains, fruits or vegetables, sugar, milk or cream, ghee, and often spices; very common snacks or offerings on the Indian subcontinent. Halvas are often made from semolina wheat.

idlis – Steamed rice bread

kachoris – Deep-fried breads with various fillings

kari – Tamil name for "sauce"; probably the source of the term *curry*. This term is used to describe a spice sauce in which meat or vegetables are cooked (or the generic yellow spice powder found in stores).

kichiri – Dish of lentils and rice

koya – Reduced milk used to make many of the sweet preparations in India

kulcha – Wheat bread common in Hyderabad

kulfi – Indian ice cream (pistachio, mango, and vanilla are traditional flavors) made from condensed milk (called *koya* in India)

laddos – Sweets made from chickpea flour and sugar, and coated with sesame seeds

naan – Leavened flatbread cooked inside a tandoori oven; this bread is common in the northern region of India

paneer – Pressed curd cheese

paratha – Flatbread that often includes other ingredients by having them rolled into the dough and then cooked on a tava (flat griddle-like pan) with ghee

pulao – Rice dish of Persian influence made by coating and cooking the rice in ghee before it is cooked in a broth or other liquid. Pulao is often mixed with nuts and seasoned with spices.

puri – Deep-fried unleavened bread

raita – Yogurt-based sauce served as a condiment that may contain many types of seasonings, such as cucumber and mint

roti – Flat, unleavened bread made from atta wheat flour and cooked on a tava (flat griddle-like pan)

sambar – Southern Indian dish traditionally made with toovar dal and vegetables, and seasoned with tamarind

sambol – Condiment made from fresh chiles, onions, and other flavorful ingredients

samosa – Meat- or vegetable-filled fried dough, usually highly seasoned and often served with chutney

sandesh – Bengali sweet made from paneer that is sweetened and flavored with cardamom and mixed with nuts

shingara – Bengali name for vegetable-filled samosa

✳ Cooking Terms and Equipment

baghar – Term for toasting spices in ghee to heighten their flavor (also called *tarka*)

balchao – Pickling

batta – Stone pounding tool used for sil batta (like a mortar and pestle)

dum – Slow-cooking or braising foods in a sealed pot; this was traditionally done in pots whose lids were sealed with dough to prevent moisture from escaping

sil – Large stone with a bowl shape; used to pound foods to a paste (such as when making spice pastes) using a batta (a stone pounding tool)

tandoor – Clay oven used in northern India and Pakistan to cook naan and other foods

tarka – Term that describes the toasting of spices in ghee or oil before starting a dish, or to be added to a dish after it is done (also called *baghar*)

tava – Flat griddle-like pan used to cook many of the flatbreads common throughout the subcontinent

tikka – Literally translates to "small pieces"; used to describe foods that are cut up, marinated, skewered, and grilled, or baked in a tandoori

CHAPTER 16

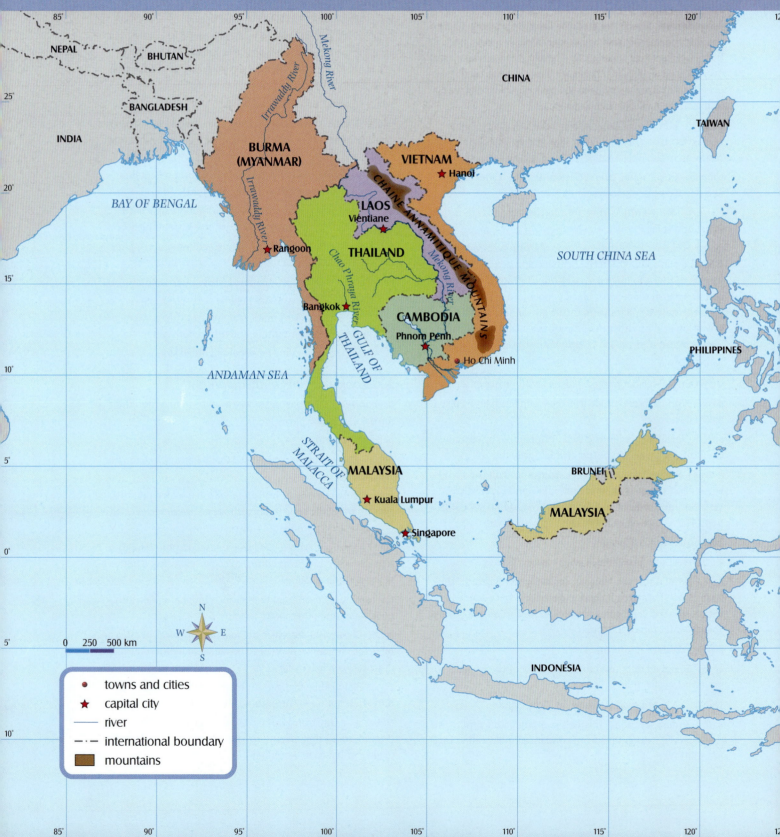

Southeast Asian Cuisine

OBJECTIVES

Upon completion of this chapter, you will be able to

- identify the countries that constitute Southeast Asia.
- identify ingredients that are indigenous to Southeast Asia.
- discuss what makes Southeast Asian cuisine unique.
- prepare some recipes common to Southeast Asia.
- list some of the major ingredients that are the foundation of Southeast Asian cuisine.
- define the terms listed at the conclusion of the chapter.

INTRODUCTION

Southeast Asia encompasses the countries of Burma (also called Myanmar), Laos, Vietnam, Thailand, Cambodia, and part of Malaysia, which make up the mainland of the southern part of Asia, separating the Bay of Bengal and the South China Sea. These countries are home to a rich culinary tradition that is known for its flavorful and healthy characteristics. For Americans, the most well known of these cuisines is probably Thai cuisine, which has become quite popular since the Vietnam War, after which many Thai and Vietnamese people immigrated to the United States. Although the other cuisines are less known, they will seem familiar to anyone who patronizes Thai or Vietnamese restaurants in the United States.

Much of Southeast Asia has a tropical climate and thus is home to many tropical crops. The river systems throughout the countries are vital to the livelihood of much of the population, who rely on the rivers to supply water to the vast rice paddies found in nearly all of the valleys as well as aiding travel via boat. Southeast Asia is home to the largest exporter of rice in Thailand and has access to the rich waters of the Gulf of Thailand, the South China Sea, and the Bay of Bengal. Not surprisingly, fish and sea products play a major role in the cuisines of most of the countries encompassed by this area.

The people of Southeast Asia have immigrated to this area from a variety of other regions, with the largest groups from China, the islands of Indonesia, and India. Many of the eastern and central populations can trace their heritage back to China, because periods of historic unrest or brutal leadership drove ethnic groups and families from western China into Southeast Asia. Many groups also came from the islands of Indonesia and moved primarily into Malaysia, southern Thailand, and Cambodia. The northwest (particularly Burma) experienced significant influence from India, as well as a long history of immigration from the Mongols, of whom many Burmese are descendants.

The countries in Southeast Asia have experienced their fair share of conflicts and external influences throughout their history. Some of the significant influences were periods of rule by the Chinese in some parts of Southeast Asia, the effects of trade routes going through much of Southeast Asia, and the colonization of all of the countries but Thailand by European powers. Throughout these periods of unrest, the people and the cultures have adapted and thrived, creating what has become one of the most sought-after cuisines in the world.

SIGNIFICANT CULINARY INFLUENCES

The cuisines of Southeast Asia are unique among the cuisines of the world for their reliance on highly flavored aromatic ingredients in making many of the common foods to accompany rice. Although the cuisine is unique, its influences are also quite evident and can be traced mainly to India and China (along with some influences from the periods of European domination in this region in more recent times). These influences are examined in the following section.

Early Peoples and Traditions

A number of ethnic groups are thought to have been the early inhabitants of the Southeast Asian region, including Mon (in present-day Burma), Thai (throughout all of present day Southeast Asia, especially Laos and Thailand), Khmer (present-day Cambodia), and Hmong (hills of Southeast Asia), as well as Malay (present-day Malaysia) and Han (China and throughout present-day Southeast Asia). The diets of these groups featured numerous differences, because they lived in different areas, but they also had some similarities. One similarity was the reliance on rice as the main component of their diet, something that has persisted in this area to this day. Many also made a sauce out of *nam pla* (fermented fish) or a paste out of fermented shrimp; both of these preparations still exist in the cuisine of Southeast Asia today. In addition to the rice and sauces, these early people also were known to use galangal, lemongrass, limes, and coconuts in their cooking—all ingredients that provide much of the character of Southeast Asian food.

Chinese

Over the centuries, the Chinese have migrated into the countries of Southeast Asia and have brought with them their customs and cooking habits. Many of the ethnic groups of Southeast Asia can be traced back to parts of southern China and, not surprisingly, numerous techniques and common cooking habits are evident in both cultures. Stir-frying and steaming are common techniques in much of Southeast Asia and most likely were part of the customs of those who migrated from China to this area. In addition, the techniques of making pickled foods, rice noodles, and wheat noodles are also believed to have been introduced to the Southeast Asian region by the Chinese. Other important introductions from China include soy sauce, star anise, fermented bean sauce, bean curd, the wok (Malaysia and Thailand), and chopsticks (Thailand and Vietnam).

Indian

It is believed that areas of Southeast Asia were at times either part of the Indian Empire or under the rule of the leaders of India; as a result, a number of Indian methods and techniques are found in much of Southeast Asia's cuisine. The areas of Southeast Asia that have been most affected by the Indian influence are those more easily accessed from the west. Indian spices flowed into this region and became a major part of the cuisine of this area as a result of the trade and interaction between the people of India and Southeast Asia. Some of the Indian spices and vegetables that are common in Southeast Asian cuisine include tamarind, turmeric, ginger, gourds, onions, and garlic. One of India's major contributions to the cuisine of Southeast Asia was the practice of making spice blends—in particular, wet spice blends—that are often referred to as *curries* by Westerners. In many parts of Southeast Asia, the freshly made spice blends lend much of the aromatic flavor to the dishes that make them so distinct. Although many of the ingredients used to make these dishes may not come from India, such as galangal and kaffir lime, the technique for making and using them does. The isolated areas of Laos and parts of Vietnam are less influenced by Indian techniques and the use of spice blends is less prevalent in the cooking.

Portuguese

The Portuguese traders of the sixteenth century set up posts in Malaysia and Indonesia to the south, and the flow of ingredients from Europe and eventually the Americas thus increased. As in other parts of the world, the introduction of foods from the Americas changed the cuisine of this region forever. Chiles were quickly adopted and are now one of the dominant seasonings throughout much of Southeast Asia. Other important crop foods from the Americas that were introduced by the Portuguese include corn, beans, peanuts, cashews, papaya, cassava, tomatoes, and potatoes. Many of these have become major crops throughout Southeast Asia: papayas are commonly used in salads, peanuts are used for oil or making sauces (and to give crunch and flavor to salads), beans are a common vegetable, cassava is used to make flour, and tomatoes are added to stews and salads. Of all of the foods introduced at this time, the chili is most significant, because it provides a distinct characteristic to the cuisines of Southeast Asia, particularly Malaysia and Thailand. Chiles are prized for their fiery heat and cooling effect on the body.

French Colonization

The French sought to gain a foothold in the spice trade and with other traded goods from Asia that began in earnest with the Portuguese in the sixteenth century. After repeated failed attempts to establish a colony in Southeast Asia, the French were successful in the late nineteenth century and eventually gained control of present-day Laos, Cambodia, and Vietnam. There are remnants of the French colonial period in all of these areas, although the culinary influences are mostly minimal, with Vietnam being the most heavily influences of the three countries. In Vietnam, sandwiches are common and are made with baguettes that reveal the French influence; the famous northern Vietnamese soup called *pho* is also believed to be strongly influenced by the French penchant for making stocks. The French introduced coffee into Southeast Asia, and this has also been adapted into the culture of the Vietnamese. Although the French influence isn't a major part of the cuisine of Southeast Asia, it does provide another unique layer.

UNIQUE COMPONENTS

The cuisines of Southeast Asia are unique for their aromatic qualities, their expert use of fresh ingredients, and their choice of dishes to complement rice, which provides the basis of nourishment in the diet. Southeast Asian cuisines are currently experiencing great popularity in the United States. Thai and

Vietnamese restaurants are common in most cities, and the foods that are attracting people highlight some of the components that make these cuisines so popular. The following section examines some of the aspects that make these cuisines stand out.

Rice

Rice is a basis of the diet throughout Southeast Asia and in the daily lives of the many ethnic groups found in this part of the world. Although the methods used to cook rice may differ, and in some cases the types of rice used may vary, the reliance on rice as the basis of a meal remains constant throughout much of this region. Most of the countries of Southeast Asia utilize the longer grains of rice, with the exception of Laos and parts of northern Thailand, where short-grain sticky rice is used regularly. This likely explains why Laotian food differs from the other cuisines; Laotian food is often drier and includes little sauce (otherwise, it would be difficult to eat, because hands are often used to eat the rice and it would fall apart if not for the sticky rice). In much of Southeast Asia rice is cooked by the absorption method and most often is cooked plain and unseasoned, to be served with other flavorful foods. Foods with flavorful sauces complement the rice perfectly. Rice cooked by the absorption method is fluffy and readily takes on the flavors of sauces.

Rice is also consumed in the form of rice noodles, which are very common throughout this region. Broths filled with rice noodles and surrounded by garnishments and condiments are a regular dish in many parts of Southeast Asia. In Vietnam, pho (pronounced "pha") is the daily fare for most of the population; in Thailand and Cambodia, the same type of preparation is made but with different names, and there are numerous examples of stir-fry dishes and salads made with rice noodles. Rice is a fundamental part of Southeast Asian cuisines, and any discussion of the traditional foods of this region should start with rice.

Lemongrass, Ginger, Kaffir Lime Leaves, Coconuts, and Other Flavor Powerhouses

The cuisines of Southeast Asia are very distinctive in large part because of the aromatic ingredients that are a central part of the cooking. Similar to the way garlic and basil provide a distinct Italian flavor to foods, the use of lemongrass, ginger, *kaffir lime* leaves, fish sauce, and other highly aromatic components in the cooking of Southeast Asia makes it easily identifiable and distinct.

Lemongrass has a distinct aroma reminiscent of lemon/citrus that it lends to soups, stews, and curries and that cannot be duplicated. Ginger and *galangal* (also called *kha* or *laos*) are other intensely fragrant ingredients that are commonly used in many of the same types of applications as lemongrass. All are very woody and will not soften from cooking; they are best used in a sachet—minced or microplained very fine—or, in the case of lemongrass, smashed with a mallet and then removed before serving. In traditional Southeast Asian cooking, lemongrass, ginger, and galangal are all typically sliced thin and used as whole slices in soups and stews. Americans are often surprised to find hard pieces in their soups and stews; thus, processing these ingredients differently may be the best approach (however, leaving these ingredients in soups and stews helps to release more of their flavors into the foods). These aromatics are also used in the curry pastes made by crushing these ingredients (along with others).

Kaffir lime leaves are another distinct aromatic ingredient used in Southeast Asian cookery. These are also commonly added to soups and stews and sometimes ground into curry pastes. Kaffir lime is a specific variety of citrus that is indigenous to Southeast Asia and is now being grown in the United States as well (where fresh leaves are available in Asian specialty stores).

Because Southeast Asia is a tropical region, a number of tropical crops are used extensively in the cuisines. Coconuts, for example, are used for their coconut milk, which provides a rich character to many of the typical curries and soups found in this region.

Balance of Flavors and Aromas

One constant in the cuisine of Southeast Asia is the use of many highly flavored components that have strong flavor character and often can dominate a dish (such as those discussed in the previous section). Although these ingredients are highly aromatic and flavorful, the chefs and population in general of these countries are experts at balancing these aspects in recipes. A dish that is created well will have a balance of sour, sweet, salty, bitter, spicy,

and aromatic qualities to it. These aspects are regularly found if one looks more closely at the ingredients that are common throughout the region. Chiles, ginger, garlic, and peppercorns all provide spicy characteristics to the foods they are used in; limes and tamarind are commonly used to provide the sour component; sweetness comes from coconut milk, palm sugar, and *jaggary* (unrefined sugar); the salty character is found in fish sauce; and bitterness is provided by the many greens and herbs that are used. Add to this the aromatic qualities of kaffir lime leaves, lemongrass, ginger, and galangal, and you have a complex composition that—when blended properly—creates the magic that is instantly recognizable as a dish from this region of the world. This balance is something that is achieved through tasting one's way to a properly seasoned food, knowing which ingredients provides which aspect, and adjusting the final product with whatever is needed to bring the whole food into the desired harmony. Although this may sound daunting, it is precisely the skill that every chef needs to master if he or she wants to cook great food every time; ingredients don't remain static, and the ability to recognize and adjust a recipe to bring about the proper balance of flavors should be the goal of anyone who creates great food.

Curry Pastes

One of the components that distinguishes the cuisines of Southeast Asia is the many pastes that are common here, particularly in Thailand. These pastes are called curry pastes here in the United States and can be made from a variety of ingredients and differ strongly from the curries of the Indian subcontinent in that they contain more fresh ingredients and significantly fewer dried spices. The word *curry* is Indian in origin; it was derived from a Tamil (Indian language) word that described spiced foods served with rice. The term is now widely used to describe the spiced foods as well as the pastes used to make them in Southeast Asian cuisine. In Thailand, the word *gaeng* (phonetic spelling) is used for curry and, like the Tamil use of the word, refers to a sauce served with food.

Most of the curries in Southeast Asian cuisine use either a water base or a coconut milk base for the liquid part of the sauce. The ingredients used in these sauces are quite varied and include some of the more fragrant flavors available. Some common components of the curry pastes are lemongrass, red or green chiles, shallots, ginger, galangal, shrimp paste, kaffir lime leaves, coriander root (the roots of the cilantro plant), and other dried spices. These ingredients are combined in various quantities; adding or omitting these or other ingredients yields a diverse collection of highly flavored pastes that are used to make the sauces of this region.

Some of the more common pastes are as follows:

gaeng kiew wahn – Green curry paste; this paste is made from unripe chiles, which provide much of the green color, and may also include herbs as part of the blend. This curry is often used with poultry dishes.

gaeng leuang – Yellow curry paste; this paste contains turmeric, which gives it a rich yellow color. It is usually used with poultry.

gaeng mussaman – Mussaman curry paste; influenced by India, this paste contains dried coriander and cumin as part of the blend and typically adds lemongrass and garlic or shallots, as well as some chiles.

gaeng panang – Panang curry paste; roasted and ground peanuts are added to this paste.

gaeng peht – Red curry paste; this paste uses either dried or fresh red, ripe chiles along with galangal and lemongrass. It is used in a variety of coconut milk–based dishes.

gaeng som – Orange curry paste; this has a higher proportion of shrimp and is typically used in seafood dishes.

Although these are Thai curry pastes, the same styles are found in other sections of Southeast Asia, where they are known by different names but often follow very similar techniques and use similar ingredients. This type of sauce making is certainly one of the strong characteristics of the cuisines of Southeast Asia, and it is one of the reasons for the growing popularity of this region's culinary traditions.

SIGNIFICANT SUBREGIONS

The cuisines of Southeast Asia all share a generally familiar theme but feature important variances from one location to the next, largely due to the history of the indigenous groups, colonization history, and geographic and agricultural differences. The following guide explores these variations, as well as the ingredients used in the each of the countries that make up Southeast Asia. The guide is organized from west to east and then from north to south.

Burma (Myanmar)

Burma is bordered by India to the northwest, China to the northeast, Laos and Thailand to the southeast, and the Bay of Bengal to the southwest. Burma has a central valley that is surrounded by very rugged highlands, and the climate throughout is tropical (with monsoon seasons that differ in the southwest and northeast). The original inhabitants of Burma immigrated from present-day Mongolia and China and were descendants of the Mon peoples. In addition to these original inhabitants, people from the Khan armies (China), Tibet, Southeast Asia, and India have become significant ethnic groups. The major religion of Burma is Buddhism, with a small but significant amount of Christian as well.

Burma is a major producer of rice, and the fertile central valley—fed by the Irrawaddy River—produces the long-grain varieties that are commonly used in Burma. Burma was the world's leading rice producer until relatively recently, because political turmoil has impacted the country's economy. The Burmese are unique in that they cook their rice with salt, which most other Southeast Asians do not.

Burma has been an independent country since 1948, when it won its independence from England and officially changed its name to Myanmar in 1989 (although it is still commonly called Burma). The English influenced this region to some degree during their colonization of India and Burma, although not as significantly as in India. Some of the ingredients that are commonly used in the Burmese kitchen are cilantro, garlic, ginger, chili, water spinach, turmeric, cumin, coriander seed, cinnamon, coconut milk, fish sauce, long-grain rice, legumes and fish. The cuisine of Burma reflects the trading relationship that has existed between Burma and India for centuries; as a result, there are many examples of foods similar to those found in India, particularly eastern India (see Chapter 15, "Cuisines of the Indian Subcontinent," for more information). Although the cuisine of Burma is clearly influenced by Indian cuisine, it is more similar to the other cuisines of Southeast Asia: rice is the main ingredient and is often served with foods cooked in spiced sauces. Fish and shellfish are also common in the cuisine and are found on the tables of those who do not practice a strict interpretation of Buddhism.

Laos

Laos is a landlocked country that is mainly bordered by Vietnam to the east and Thailand to the west. It is also bordered by China to the north and Cambodia to the south. Laos may be landlocked, but its people and cuisine are dependent on the water—in this case, the Mekong River that runs through the lowlands of the country. Most of the population of Laos lives near the banks of the Mekong. Because this is a poor country, the culinary traditions are primarily based on subsistence, with rice, vegetables, and freshwater fish appearing regularly in the everyday meals. Like the other countries in Southeast Asia, the climate is tropical and the waterways are vital for both food and transportation.

The majority of Laotians are Buddhist, although a significant portion of the population lives in the dense forests and hills that surround the lowlands as part of tribes that have no affiliation to the major religions. Although many are Buddhist, much of the Laotian population eats pork when it is available, as well as fish and vegetables.

Laos was part of the Khmer Empire (the main population was centered in Cambodia) prior to an influx of Lao people from China in the thirteenth century. In more recent years, Laos was ruled by the Siamese (Thai) prior to a period of colonization by the French as part of Indochina. There are many similarities between Laotian cuisine and Thai cuisine, as well as numerous examples of French influence, such as baguettes, dressed salads, and cakes.

The preferred rice in Laos is short-grain glutinous rice that is steamed in bamboo baskets to yield very sticky rice, which is used as a utensil to eat the food accompanying it. The sticky rice that is found at nearly every meal is normally served with vegetables and (most often) freshwater fish, if a protein is eaten. The most common seasonings used are fish sauce, galangal or ginger, lemongrass, chiles, Thai basil, mint, and cilantro.

Some of the ingredients common to this country's cuisine are *nam pa* (fish sauce), *padek* (fermented fish pieces), *khao niao* (sticky rice), *khao khoua* (roasted rice), *ped* (duck), *sommu* (spiced pickled pork sausage),

hua khar (galangal), *bai si khai* (lemongrass), *mark karm* (tamarind), and *rau ngo* (cilantro), to name just a few.

Laotian cuisine has many foods in common with neighboring Thailand; although the food is less spicy than typical Thai creations, it is still common to see many curries that resemble those of Thailand. Some of the other prepared foods found here include *kaeng jeuud kalampi* (pork and cabbage soup with egg), *kaeng som pa* (fish soup seasoned with lemongrass, fish sauce, lime juice, and cilantro), *kalee ped* (curried duck with potatoes), *kai yad sai* (braised chicken stuffed with chiles, cilantro, shallots, and garlic), and *laap* (a well-known salad made from pounded meat or fish seasoned with mint, lime juice, fish sauce, and chiles, and topped with roasted rice powder).

Vietnam

Vietnam is a long country situated north to south along the South China Sea; its northern neighbor is China, and Laos and Cambodia border it to the west. The original inhabitants of Vietnam came from China, which occupied and ruled over this area until the tenth century. As a result, there are numerous examples of China's influence on the cuisine, including the use of hoisin sauce and oyster sauce and seasonings like star anise and cloves. Some of the traits leftover from this time include the use of chopsticks to eat as well as the preponderance of stir-fried foods. Although Vietnamese cuisine often reveals Chinese influences, it is also quite distinct in a number of ways. There is little fat used in Vietnamese cooking, most vegetables are eaten raw, and fish sauce is the major condiment used (rather than soy sauce). Vietnam also has been greatly influenced by its period of French occupation—beginning in the late sixteenth century, followed by eventual rule from 1883 to 1954, when Vietnam was a French protectorate—and the daily sight of baguettes in the streets and pâté in the restaurants attests to this period.

Most Vietnamese do not affiliate themselves with any religion. Of those who do, about half are Buddhists; the next largest group is Christians.

Vietnam is blessed with fertile land and a long coast with plentiful seafood. The northern part of the country is colder and has a smaller variety of produce available than the warmer, southern portion of the country. Both areas are bordered by the sea, and thus seafood plays a central role across all of Vietnam. Vietnamese cuisine is often divided into three sections: the north, where living is more difficult and the food often is used for subsistence; the central portion of the country, which has a history of a more sophisticated cuisine; and the south, which has the most diverse cultural influences and access to ingredients. The majority of the people spend their days working outside, and markets and street vendors are a big part of the daily scene in Vietnam. The street vendors sell snack foods that the public are always eager to sample. Many foods are wrapped in banana leaves, formed into cakes, or used as fillings for thin pancakes similar to crepes (from the French influence) and sold by vendors.

The Vietnamese prefer long-grain rice; it is cooked without salt and instead is seasoned by the sauces that accompany it. Much of the cooking at home in Vietnam is done over a fire, whether it is grilling foods or cooking in a wok that is heated by the fire. Most foods are served with fresh ingredients that can be added to the dish by the person eating at his or her will. It is very common for foods to be assembled at the table so that those eating it also take part in making it.

Some of the ingredients (besides rice) that are common to this country's cuisine include *nuoc mam* (fish sauce), *bac ha* (mint), *banh trang* (rice paper or wrapper), *ca de* (Japanese eggplant), *dau dua* (long beans), *gia* (bean sprout), *ca rot* (carrot), *cu cai trang* (daikon radish), *dau phong* (peanut), *gung* (ginger root), chanh vo xanh (lime), *rau muong* (water spinach), and *ngo gai* (saw leaf; a type of herb). The specialty products and recipes from this country include many examples of street food such as *banh* (savory or sweet cakes or buns, often filled with other ingredients), *pho* (broth with rice noodles and various ingredients), and *cha gio* (fried spring rolls). In addition to the many street foods, the meals created at home center around steamed rice and likely include a number of dishes chosen from the freshest ingredients found at the market that day (unlike kitchens in the United States, most Vietnamese homes have no refrigerator and thus the people shop daily for food). A typical meal to accompany the rice would include a meat or fish dish with a flavorful sauce, as well as a couple of preparations with vegetables (often including some that are uncooked), and all served with rice and dipping sauces (always *nouc cham*).

Thailand

Thailand is a country shaped like an elephant head; it encompasses much of the heart of mainland Southeast Asia and stretches down toward the islands of Malaysia and the Gulf of Thailand. Thailand is bordered by Burma to the north and west, Laos and Cambodia to the east, and Malaysia to the south. The vast majority of Thai residents are Buddhists, and all Thai men spend a period of time in one of the many monasteries through the country. Although it is a predominantly Buddhist country, vegetarianism is not a major dietary pattern in Thailand. The original inhabitants of present-day Thailand are thought to have migrated from China during the rule of the Mongols; as a result, Chinese culinary customs are apparent in Thailand. Thailand has never come under the control of a European power, although the colonization of countries surrounding it has influenced the cuisine and eating habits of the Thai people.

A number of culinary practices show the influence of Chinese ancestral roots, such as the use of a wok and the context of the five flavors (salty, sour, bitter, sweet, and spicy). Indian influence can be found as well, particularly in the curries, but—like Vietnam—Thai cuisine differs from these other cuisines in many ways. Thai cuisine is considered the spiciest in Southeast Asia, and the spiciness often comes from the pastes that are commonly used to make the many curries found in this country. In addition, the cuisine of Thailand differs from those of the other countries thanks to a long tradition of restaurants in Thailand. Although other countries have restaurants today, in Thailand restaurants have been part of the everyday life for decades, and this has pushed Thai cuisine to a higher level when it comes to variations and presentations of the foods that are made here. As with all of the other Southeast Asian countries, rice is the focal point of all meals, and foods are generally served all at once—family style—to be chosen by guests as desired to accompany their rice.

Rice cookery in Thailand differs greatly in the north, where short-grain glutinous rice is steamed in bamboo baskets and often used as a utensil for eating. In the south, long-grain rice is boiled and then steamed until done, and thus cooked by the absorption method.

Some of the ingredients common to this country's cuisine are *khao hom ma-ree* (jasmine rice), *khao kate* (basmati rice), *kwaytiow* (rice noodles), *makheua muang* (eggplant), *prik kii noo* (Thai chiles), *naw mai* (bamboo shoots), *ga lum phee* (cabbage), *puck whan* (water spinach), *ma-kham* (tamarind), *magroot* (kaffir lime), *gape* (shrimp paste), *nahm ga-ti* (coconut milk), *nam pla* (fish sauce), *takrai* (lemongrass), and *kha* (galangal). Specialty products and recipes include *miang khum* (lettuce with chiles, peanuts, limes, and sauce), *phat thai* (noodle dish with savory sweet-and-sour sauce), *tom kha gai* (aromatic soup with chicken and coconut milk), *som thum* (green papaya salad with lime and chili dressing); *gaeng kiew wahn* (green curry paste), *gaeng leuang* (yellow curry paste), and *gaeng peht* (red curry paste) are used extensively to make the many examples of curry dishes that are typical of a meal found in Thai restaurants.

Cambodia

Cambodia is located in the southern part of the mainland. It is bordered to the west and south by southern Vietnam, to the north by Laos and Thailand, and it sits on the shores of the Gulf of Thailand. Cambodia has a tumultuous history, having been ruled by Indian, Khmer, Thai, Vietnamese, and French populations prior to gaining independence in 1953, when the French rule of Indochina ended. The Khmer Rouge eventually regained power, with horrific results: between 1975 and 1979, approximately 30 percent of the Cambodian population was killed. All of these periods have left their impact on Cambodia, and there are clear examples of Indian, Thai, Vietnamese, and French influences in the cuisine. Like neighboring southern Thailand, the rice eaten here daily is the long-grain variety, and fish sauce, coconut milk, chiles, lemongrass, and galangal are common flavoring ingredients.

Malaysia

Malaysia makes up the southernmost portion of mainland Southeast Asia and is included within the area of islands known as Indonesia. The people who settled this area are mostly ethnic Malay (who can trace their lineage back to China or Taiwan), Chinese, or Indian/Pakistani, with smaller Thai and Javanese (from Indonesia) populations as well. As a result of this ethnic diversity, it is not surprising that the cuisine of Malaysia reflects many cultures.

This region is predominantly Muslim, and the next largest religious population is Hindu; as such, the cuisine reflects the foods that are accepted by these faiths. Muslims do not eat pork and Hindus do not eat beef, so the dominant protein eaten here is fish. Vegetables and rice are daily components of the Malaysian diet. The climate here is tropical, and the terrain includes coastal plains that rise to dense forests and mountains to the north. The cuisine shows strong influences from both China and India, because both of these areas have been involved in trade with the people of the coastal areas of Indonesia and mainland Southeast Asia and have left their imprint on the foods that are eaten here. Soy sauce, spice blends, and tamarind are a few of the ingredients from China and India that are common in the cuisine.

Some of the ingredients in this country's cuisine that reflect the Chinese influence are *kicap* (soy sauce), *daging* (meat), *babi* (pork; commonly eaten by nonreligious peoples), *sos tarim* (oyster sauce), *sos plam* (plum sauce), hoisin sauce, and spices like star anise and cloves used to make *serbuk rempah* (five-spice powder). In addition, the Indian influence is evident in the dry spice blends called *rempah*, the use of *asam jawa* and *minyak sapi* (ghee), and *baji sawi* (mustard seeds). These influences, combined with the more common Southeast Asian ingredients of *blacan* (shrimp paste), *kelapa* (coconut), *budu* (fish sauce), *daun* (fresh herbs), *pandan* (screwpine), *santan* (coconut milk), and *serai* (lemongrass), hint at the complexity that is found as one moves south toward Indonesia. Specialty products and recipes from this country include *sambals* (chili pastes), *nasi goreng* (fried rice), *rendang* (meat cooked with coconut milk and spiced until dry), *satays* (skewered and grilled or griddled meats), and *ketupat* (rice dumpling), as well as a number of Indian-inspired foods such as many of the flatbreads found in India (roti, naan, etc.) and Thai-inspired curries with coconut milk.

RECIPES

The following recipes provide an overview of some of the many foods that are found in Southeast Asian cuisine.

Gaeng Leuang THAILAND

(YELLOW CURRY PASTE)

INGREDIENTS

1	Tbsp	Coriander Seeds
1	tsp	Cumin Seeds
1/2	oz	Dried Red Thai Chiles
4	oz	Lemongrass Stalks, chopped (weigh after removing the dead outer blades, top 1/3, and root end)
2	oz	Ginger
1	Tbsp	Salt
2	oz	Shallots, minced
1	oz	Garlic Cloves, minced
1	Tbsp	Dried Turmeric, ground
2	tsp	Shrimp Paste

This is one of the curries regularly eaten in Thailand; it is influenced by nearby India and the use of spices in the dry curries there.

YIELD: 2 cups

PREPARATION METHOD: Grinding in Mortar and Pestle

PROCEDURE

1. In a dry sauté pan set over a medium-low flame, toast the coriander and cumin (while moving the pan around to prevent them from burning) until the spices become noticeably more fragrant and darken slightly.

2. Place the toasted spices in a spice grinder (or a coffee grinder), along with the dried chiles, and grind to a powder; set the powder aside.

3. Using a large mortar and pestle, crush the lemongrass and ginger together to form a rough paste.

4. Add the salt to the mortar, and continue grinding to work in the salt.

5. Add the shallots and garlic to the mortar, and grind all of the ingredients together to form a paste (it will not be completely smooth, like something made in a food processor).

6. Remove the mixture from the mortar. Mix the shrimp paste, turmeric, and ground spices from step 2 into the curry to finish.

Three curry pastes; from top to bottom: gaeng leuang (yellow curry), gaeng peht (red curry), and gaeng kiew wahn (green curry)

Gaeng Peht   THAILAND
(RED CURRY PASTE)

INGREDIENTS

2	Tbsp	Coriander Seeds
1	tsp	Cumin Seeds
1	tsp	Whole Black Peppercorns
2	oz	Dried Red Thai Chiles
4	oz	Lemongrass Stalks, chopped (weigh after removing the dead outer blades, top 1/3, and root end)
2	oz	Cilantro Roots, cleaned (if unavailable, substitute 1/4 bunch whole cilantro)
2	oz	Galangal, chopped (if unavailable, substitute ginger)
1	Tbsp	Kaffir Lime Leaves, minced
1	Tbsp	Salt
2	oz	Shallots, minced
1/2	oz	Garlic Cloves, minced
2	tsp	Shrimp Paste

Another of the regular curry pastes used in Thai cuisine, this one relies on the developed taste of ripe chiles for some of its complexity.

YIELD: 2 cups

PREPARATION METHOD: Grinding in Mortar and Pestle

PROCEDURE

1. In a dry sauté pan set over a medium-low flame, toast the coriander, cumin, and black peppercorns (while moving the pan around to prevent them from burning) until the spices become noticeably more fragrant and darken slightly.

2. Place the toasted spices in a spice grinder (or a coffee grinder), along with the dried chiles, and grind to a powder; set the powder aside.

3. Using a large mortar and pestle, crush the lemongrass, cilantro roots, galangal, and kaffir lime leaves together to form a rough paste.

4. Add the salt to the mortar, and continue grinding to work in the salt.

5. Add the shallots and garlic to the mortar, and grind all of the ingredients together to form a paste (it will not be completely smooth, like something made in a food processor).

6. Remove the mixture from the mortar. Mix the shrimp paste, spice, and chili powder into the curry to finish.

Gaeng Kiew Wahn   THAILAND
(GREEN CURRY PASTE)

INGREDIENTS

2	Tbsp	Coriander Seeds
1	tsp	Cumin Seeds
1	tsp	Whole Black Peppercorns
4	oz	Lemongrass Stalks, chopped (weigh after removing the dead outer blades, top 1/3, and root end)
2	oz	Cilantro Roots, cleaned (if unavailable, substitute 1/4 bunch whole cilantro)
2	oz	Galangal, chopped (if unavailable, substitute ginger)
1	Tbsp	Kaffir Lime Leaves, minced
1	Tbsp	Salt
2	oz	Shallots, minced

Although many people think that red curry is the hottest of the Thai curry pastes, green curry is usually the spiciest. It is green because it is made with unripe chiles—they may be unripe, but they're still hot!

YIELD: 2.5 cups

PREPARATION METHOD: Grinding in Mortar and Pestle

PROCEDURE

1. In a dry sauté pan set over a medium-low flame, toast the coriander, cumin, and black peppercorns (while moving the pan around to prevent them from burning) until the spices become noticeably more fragrant and darken slightly.

2. Place the toasted spices in a spice grinder (or a coffee grinder) and grind to a powder; set the powder aside.

3. Using a large mortar and pestle, crush the lemongrass, cilantro roots, galangal, and kaffir lime leaves together to form a rough paste.

(continues)

Gaeng Kiew Wahn
(continued)

1/2 oz	Garlic Cloves, minced
4 oz	Green Thai Chiles, chopped
2 tsp	Shrimp Paste

4. Add the salt to the mortar, and continue grinding to work in the salt.

5. Add the shallots, garlic, and green chiles to the mortar, and grind all of the ingredients together to form a paste (it will not be completely smooth, like something made in a food processor).

6. Remove the mixture from the mortar. Mix the shrimp paste and dried spice powder into the curry to finish.

Gaeng Ped Hoi Mang Phu THAILAND
(THAI MUSSELS WITH COCONUT RED CURRY SAUCE)

INGREDIENTS

14 oz	Coconut Milk
2 oz	Lime Juice
1 oz	Red Curry Paste (see recipe, this chapter)
1 oz	Galangal, minced (if unavailable, substitute ginger)
1 Tbsp	Thai Fish Sauce
1 Tbsp	Palm Sugar (if unavailable, substitute brown sugar)
3 lbs	Mussels, debearded and scrubbed
1/2 cup	Cilantro, minced (about 1/4 bunch)
	Salt, to taste
2	Limes, cut into wedges

This is a good representation of a coconut curry that would be served with rice in Thailand. Although in Thailand this may be made with a variety of ingredients other than mussels, the mussels work well to highlight how seafood can be paired with a strong but balanced sauce such as this.

YIELD: 8 portions (8 ounces/portion, including mussel shells; appetizer size)
COOKING METHOD (SAUCE): Simmering
COOKING METHOD (MUSSELS): Steaming

PROCEDURE

1. In a pot large enough to hold all of the mussels, combine the coconut milk, lime juice, red curry paste, galangal, fish sauce, and palm sugar; heat over a medium-low flame to bring the mixture to a gentle simmer.

2. Allow the mixture to simmer for 10 minutes to develop flavor.

3. Add the mussels to the pot, and cover; turn heat up to boil/steam mussels (this should only take a couple of minutes).

4. As soon as the mussels have opened, remove them from the heat. Add the cilantro and season with salt.

5. Serve with garnish of lime wedges.

Bowl of gaeng ped hoi mang phu (mussels with coconut curry sauce)

Tom Kha Gai   THAILAND
(THAI COCONUT CHICKEN SOUP)

INGREDIENTS

2	oz	Vegetable Oil
1	lb	Yellow Onion, diced medium
1	lb	Red Bell Peppers, diced medium
12	oz	Mushrooms, quartered
3	qts	Light Chicken Stock (or 2 qts + 1 qt water, if dense stock)
10		Kaffir Lime Leaves
5		Lemongrass Stalks (about 8 oz before trimming), wilted blades removed, cut into 12-inch sections, smashed with a mallet, and tied together with butcher's twine
5	oz	Galangal (if unavailable, substitute ginger), peeled and sliced thin
4	oz	Fish Sauce
3	oz	Lemon Juice
2	Tbsp	Dried Thai Chiles, minced
1.5	lbs	Chicken Breast, diced medium
16	fl oz	Coconut Milk

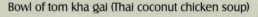

One of the classic Thai soups served in virtually every Thai restaurant, tom kha gai is full of flavor and quite addictive.

YIELD: 1 gallon

COOKING METHOD: Simmering

PROCEDURE

1. Heat an appropriately sized pot over a medium flame; add oil, and sweat the onions, bell peppers, and mushrooms until soft.

2. Add all of the remaining ingredients—except the chicken and coconut milk—and gently simmer for 1–1.5 hours to develop flavor.

3. Add the chicken breast and coconut milk, and bring the mixture back to a light simmer. Continue to simmer until the chicken is cooked (5 minutes).

4. Check seasoning and adjust with salt; serve.

Bowl of tom kha gai (Thai coconut chicken soup)

Nam Jim Tua THAILAND
(SPICY/SWEET CUCUMBER RELISH)

INGREDIENTS

10	oz	Rice Wine Vinegar
6	oz	Palm Sugar
1	oz	Tamarind Paste
2	tsp	Salt
1/2	oz	Thai Chiles, minced (if unavailable, substitute 2 oz jalapeño)
3	oz	Shallots, shaved
1	lb	English Cucumber, peeled and seeded and then sliced thin
1/4	cup	packed Cilantro Leaves, minced

This is a very common condiment used in Thailand to accompany satays and deep-fried foods. Pickled foods are quite common in Southeast Asia because they can be preserved in the humid climate. Pickled foods also provide a refreshing break from many of the spicy foods eaten here.

YIELD: 1 pound

PREPARATION METHOD: Pickling with Vinegar

PROCEDURE

1. In a small saucepan, combine the rice wine vinegar, palm sugar, tamarind paste, salt, and chiles. Heat over a low flame until the sugar is dissolved into the vinegar.

2. Once the sugar has dissolved into the vinegar, remove the pan from heat and allow the contents to cool completely before proceeding to the next step.

3. Combine the cooled sugar/vinegar mixture with the shaved shallots, sliced cucumber, and cilantro; mix thoroughly.

4. Set mixture in the refrigerator for at least 45 minutes before use (it will keep in the refrigerator for 4–5 days).

Phat Thai
(THAI FRIED NOODLE WITH SHRIMP)

INGREDIENTS

1	lb	Rice Noodles, thin (sen lek)
1/2	tsp	Ground Thai Chili
2	oz	Palm Sugar
1.5	oz	Fish Sauce
2	oz	Chicken Stock
1.5	oz	Lime Juice
2	oz	Peanut Oil
1/2	oz	Garlic Cloves, minced
1	oz	Shallots, minced
4	oz	Chicken Breast, cut into 1/4-inch strips
8	oz	Shrimp (16–20), peeled and deveined
2		Large Eggs
4	oz	Firm Tofu, cut into 1/4-inch strips
4	oz	Bean Sprouts

This is without a doubt the most common Thai recipe found in the United States, although it may be spelled differently on menus (it is often called pad thai). In Thailand, street vendors make phat thai to order in woks and gain loyal customers if they make it well.

YIELD: 6 portions (8 ounces/portion)

COOKING METHOD: Stir Frying

PROCEDURE

1. Soften the rice noodles by soaking them in 1 gallon of hot water for at least 15 minutes before starting the recipe.

2. Combine the ground Thai chili, palm sugar, fish sauce, chicken stock, and lime juice in a small mixing bowl; mix and set aside.

3. In a wok or large sauté pan, heat peanut oil over a high flame. Add the garlic and shallots once the oil is very hot (and be prepared to add the next ingredients almost immediately).

4. As soon as the garlic and shallots start to color (this will happen almost instantly), add the slices of chicken. Stir to fry them in the oil until the chicken is almost cooked (about 1–2 minutes).

(continues)

Phat Thai
(continued)

2 oz   Unsalted Roasted Peanuts, crushed coarsely
1   Lime, cut into wedges for garnish
3 oz   Green Cabbage, sliced very thin

5. Add the shrimp and stir-fry for 30 seconds; add the egg, while mixing constantly to cook.

6. Once the egg is cooked, add the tofu and soaked rice noodles. Toss everything to mix the ingredients and break the egg into smaller pieces.

7. Add the combined liquids and continue to toss all of the ingredients together, scraping the sides of the pan to pull off any bits that may have gotten stuck.

8. Add the bean sprouts to the pan, and toss to mix. Transfer the contents to serving dishes, and garnish with lime wedges and sliced cabbage.

Phat thai (Thai fried noodle with shrimp)

Som Thum   THAILAND

(GREEN PAPAYA SALAD)

INGREDIENTS

10 oz   Green Papaya (unripened), peeled and cut julienne
2   Limes, juiced
1   Thai Chili, minced (add more, if you desire more spice)
2 Tbsp Ginger, minced

This salad is found in Thailand as well as in other Southeast Asian countries. It combines the sweetness of palm sugar, the tartness of limes, and the heat of chiles to make a very flavorful salad. Ingredients from the Americas—chiles, peanuts, tomatoes, and papayas—are all featured in this recipe.

YIELD: 4 portions (4 ounces/portion)

PREPARATION METHOD: Marinating of Fruit with Savory Ingredients

(continues)

Som Thum
(continued)

2	tsp	Palm Sugar
1	Tbsp	Peanut Oil
1/8	tsp	Salt
3	oz	Cherry Tomatoes, cut in half
2	Tbsp	Cilantro, minced
2	oz	Peanuts, roasted and crushed

PROCEDURE

1. Combine the papaya, lime juice, chiles, ginger, palm sugar, peanut oil, and salt in a mixing bowl, and mix thoroughly to coat the papaya with dressing. Allow the mixture to sit at room temperature for 30 minutes to 1 hour to "marinate" the papaya.

2. Add cherry tomatoes and cilantro to the above mixture, and mix just before serving.

3. Top salad with crushed peanuts.

Som thum (green papaya salad)

Pho Bo VIETNAM
(RICE NOODLES IN BROTH WITH GARNISHES)

INGREDIENTS

For Making the Broth

6	oz	Ginger
2	lbs	Onions
1		Thai Chili
8		Star Anise
5		Cloves
1	tsp	Black Peppercorns
5	lbs	Oxtails
2	lbs	Beef Chuck
2	oz	Fish Sauce
2	oz	Sugar
2	gal	Water
1	Tbsp	Salt

For Assembling the Pho

1	lb	Thin Rice Noodles (bun or pho)
2	qts	Hot Water

This is a very popular dish, served in areas of the United States in which there are Vietnamese or other Southeast Asian populations. There are many variations of the broth and noodle combination, but the garnishes virtually always stay the same.

YIELD: 15 portions (12 ounces/portion)

COOKING METHOD (ONIONS, GINGER, AND CHILES): Charring over High Heat

COOKING METHOD (DRY SPICES): Dry Toasting

COOKING METHOD (BROTH): Simmering

PROCEDURE

1. Either directly over a flame or on a grill, char the onion, ginger, and Thai chili until blackened on their surfaces. Once all of the onion, ginger, and chiles have been blackened, peel off the outer skin (that has been charred) and discard; chop the remaining sections into 1/2-inch pieces, and set aside.

2. In a small sauté pan, toast the star anise, cloves, and peppercorns over a medium-low flame to heighten the flavor (be careful not to burn them!). Once done, set aside.

(continues)

Bowl of pho bo (rice noodles in broth) with garnishes

Pho Bo
(continued)

8	oz	Lean Beef, frozen and then sliced paper thin
		Broth (see above)

For the Garnish

8	oz	Yellow Onion, shaved
1/2	bunch	Scallions, sliced thin on a bias
1	bunch	Thai Basil
1/2	bunch	Cilantro
2		Limes, wedged
2	oz	Thai Chiles, minced

3. Place the oxtails and beef in a stockpot large enough to hold them. Cover them with water and bring to a boil.

4. Once the water has come to a boil, turn the heat off and remove the meat from the pot; discard the liquid.

5. Place the blanched oxtails and beef, toasted spices, fire-roasted onion, chili, ginger, fish sauce, sugar, and water in a stockpot, and bring to a simmer over a medium-high flame.

6. Once the mixture reaches a simmer, skim the film developing on the surface and turn the heat to a gentle simmer.

7. After the broth has gently simmered for 1.5 hours, remove the beef chuck and set it aside to cool.

8. Once the chuck has cooled, slice it thin and set aside.

9. After the broth has gently simmered for a total of 2 hours, place the dried rice noodles in a container with 2 qts of hot water to hydrate.

10. After the broth has gently simmered for a total of 2.5 hours, strain the broth and keep it hot.

11. To serve, place a small pile of the hydrated rice noodles in a bowl, along with a couple slices of the beef chuck, and top with a couple slices of paper-thin raw beef; ladle 8 oz of broth over this.

12. Serve with a small amount of each of the garnishes, to be added to the soup by the diner at his or her discretion.

Nuoc Cham VIETNAM
(TABLE SAUCE)

INGREDIENTS

4	fl oz	Lime Juice, fresh
4	fl oz	Water
1	fl oz	Rice Wine Vinegar
3	fl oz	Fish Sauce (good quality)
1	oz	Sugar
1	Tbsp	Garlic Cloves, minced
2	Tbsp	Thai Chili, minced
1/4	tsp	Salt

This condiment is used in Vietnam like salt and pepper are used in the United States. It can be found on every table and is used to season almost anything.

YIELD: 1.5 cups

PREPARATION METHOD: Infusing Flavors

PROCEDURE

1. Combine all ingredients in a mixing bowl or a storage container with a tight-fitting lid, and mix thoroughly.

2. Set in the refrigerator for at least 2 hours before use.

Goi Cuon   VIETNAM AND CAMBODIA
(RICE WRAP WITH SHRIMP)

INGREDIENTS

2	qts	Water
1	Tbsp	Salt
15		Skewers (approximately 6 inches or longer)
1.25	lbs	Shrimp (26–30) (30 shrimp are needed for 30 wraps)
8	oz	Rice Noodles, thin (sen lek)
8	oz	Dau Chua (see recipe, this chapter)
6	oz	Bean Sprouts
1	bunch	Scallions, cut into 3-inch sections
4	oz	Cucumber, peeled, seeded, and sliced julienne
1/2	bunch	Fresh Mint
1/2	bunch	Fresh Cilantro
5		Thai Chiles, minced (optional)
30		Rice Paper Wrappers (8 inches in diameter)

This is a very healthy recipe that uses only fresh ingredients, cooked shrimp, and noodles. This would typically be served with nuoc cham.

YIELD: 30 wraps (approximately 3 ounces/wrap)

COOKING METHOD (SHRIMP): Poaching

PREPARATION METHOD (RICE NOODLES AND RICE PAPER): Absorbing/Hydrating

PROCEDURE

1. Place the water and salt in a pot that will allow room for the skewers, and set over a medium flame to bring to a poaching temperature.

2. Skewer the shrimp by running the skewer right under the shell on the leg side of the shrimp, all the way out through the tail; place two shrimp on each skewer.

3. Poach the shrimp in the salted water until they just turn pink (about 2–3 minutes); remove them and set aside to cool.

4. Once all of the shrimp have been poached, bring the water to a boil over high heat; pour the water into a container with the rice noodles, and set aside.

5. Once the shrimp have cooled, peel and devein them. Then cut them in half the long way, and place them in a container.

6. Drain the noodles and cut them into 4-inch lengths; set them in a container.

7. Chop the fresh herbs coarsely and mix them with the chiles (if you are using chiles). Set these in a container and place it near your work area.

8. Organize your work area by placing all of the fillings in containers near your cutting board.

9. Place a container that is large enough to immerse the rice paper in near your work area, and fill it halfway with warm water.

10. To assemble, place the rice paper in the warm water and allow it to soften (this will happen within a minute); remove the rice paper and place it on a clean, damp cloth on your work surface.

11. Put about 20 pieces of the rice noodle on the rice paper wrap, along with approximately 1 Tbsp of the dau chua, a couple pieces of scallion, a couple pieces of cucumber, and approximately 1 Tbsp of the herb/chili mixture.

12. Roll the wrap partially by folding up the bottom section and folding in both sides; then fold the wrap over.

13. Place two pieces of the shrimp (that were cut in half) on the remaining flap of unwrapped rice paper, and then fold over the last of the wrap to seal it.

14. Once wrapped, cut the roll in half on a bias and serve it with dipping sauce (you can use peanut sauce or nuoc cham)

Goi Ga VIETNAM
(CHICKEN AND CABBAGE SALAD)

INGREDIENTS

For Making the Dressing

5	oz	Lime Juice
3	oz	Fish Sauce
3	oz	Palm Sugar, granulated
1	oz	Garlic Cloves, minced
5		Thai Chiles, minced (if unavailable, substitute 2 serrano chiles)
1	tsp	Salt
4	oz	Peanut Oil

For Making the Salad

3	lbs	Green Cabbage or Napa Cabbage, shredded thin
2	lbs	Poached Chicken, torn into shreds
8	oz	Carrots, cut julienne
8	oz	Cucumber, peeled, seeded, and cut julienne
1	bunch	(about 3/4 cup packed leaves) Mint, chiffonade
1/2	bunch	(about 1/4 cup packed leaves) Cilantro, minced
		Dressing (see above), as needed
8	oz	Dry Roasted Peanuts, crushed

Salads are a common part of the diet of Southeast Asians, but the salads are often different from what most of us might imagine. It is very common to dress all sorts of foods with a highly flavored mixture that contains sweet, sour, salty, and spicy tastes. The dressing used in this salad could be adapted to many other salads as well.

YIELD: 20 portions (6 ounces/portion)

PREPARATION METHOD: Infusing Flavor for Dressing

PROCEDURE

For Making the Dressing

1. In a small bowl, combine all of the ingredients for the dressing—except the peanut oil—and whisk together to combine well.
2. Whisk in the peanut oil, and set the dressing aside to allow it to infuse.

For Making the Salad

1. Combine all of the ingredients—except the dressing and peanuts—in a mixing bowl, and mix thoroughly.
2. Dress the salad with just enough dressing to coat all of the ingredients just before serving, and then place on a plate topped with the roasted and crushed peanuts.

Goi ga (chicken and cabbage salad)

Miang Kham   LAOS AND NORTHERN THAILAND

(LETTUCE SNACK WITH SPICED FILLING)

INGREDIENTS

For Making the Sauce

1	oz	Shallots, minced
1	oz	Galangal, grated
5	oz	Palm Sugar
1	tsp	Thai Chili, minced
1	Tbsp	Fish Sauce
2	oz	Coconut, grated
1	tsp	Shrimp Paste
2	oz	Lime Juice, freshly squeezed
1	Tbsp	Tamarind Paste
4	oz	Water (you may need to adjust amount for consistency, depending on how dry the ingredients are)

For Prepping and Assembling

2	heads	Butter Lettuce, cleaned, spun dry, and then torn into pieces about 3 inches in diameter
2		Limes, cut into small wedges (with peel left on)
4	oz	Dry Roasted Peanuts, unsalted and crushed coarsely
1	oz	Thai Chiles (or 2 jalapeño or serrano chiles), minced
4	oz	Coconut, grated
1	oz	Dried Shrimp, chopped
1/4	bunch	Cilantro, chopped

This appetizer is packed with flavor and makes an excellent buffet starter; it can be completely assembled and refrigerated beforehand, and simply unwrapped and served when needed. In Laos or Thailand, this would be eaten as a snack and the wrapping may be any number of leafy greens.

YIELD: 20 appetizers (2 ounces each)

PREPARATIONS METHOD: Making Emulsified Sauce

PROCEDURE

For Making the Sauce

1. Combine all of the ingredients—except the water—in a food processor. With the processor running, add water until the mixture has a runny but still slightly viscous consistency.

2. Set the mixture aside while prepping ingredients for filling.

For Prepping and Assembling

1. Once the lettuce has been cleaned, spun dry, and torn into 3-inch pieces, set it in a container next to your work area.

2. In a small mixing bowl, combine the remaining ingredients; toss gently to mix thoroughly.

3. To assemble, place a few pieces of the lettuce on top of one another. Top them with approximately 1 oz (about 2 Tbsp) of the coconut/peanut/chili mixture, followed by approximately 1 Tbsp of the sauce.

Miang kham (lettuce appetizer with spiced filling)

Poat Dot CAMBODIA

(GRILLED FRESH CORN WITH SWEET ONION OIL)

INGREDIENTS

10	ears	Fresh Yellow or White Corn, husks removed
2	Tbsp	Vegetable Oil (for brushing the corn)
2	oz	Fish Sauce (good quality, such as Three Crabs or Tiparos)
2	oz	Palm Sugar
3	oz	Water
1/2	bunch	Green Onions, minced (about 8 onions)
1		Small Thai Chili, minced (optional)
1.5	tsp	Salt
2	oz	Vegetable Oil

This common Cambodian street food combines corn from the Americas with the fish sauce and palm sugar used throughout Southeast Asia.

YIELD: 10 portions (1 ear of corn/portion)

PROCEDURE

1. Preheat the grill.

2. Lightly coat the corn with the 2 Tbsp of oil, and cook on the cooler part of the grill; turn the corn frequently to yield a lightly caramelized surface (about 8–10 minutes, turning often). Once the corn is done, remove it from the grill and set it aside (keep it warm, if the next step is not yet completed).

3. In a small pot or saucepan, combine the fish sauce, palm sugar, water, green onions, Thai chili (if you are using it), and salt. Over a very low flame, heat for 5 minutes to infuse flavors and dissolve sugar and salt (you should have nearly the same amount of liquid left at the end by keeping the flame very low; if not, add more water).

4. In a separate saucepot large enough to hold the infusing sauce and the 2 oz of oil, add the oil and heat over a medium flame until hot. Add the onion/fish sauce mixture (be careful—it will spit a bit of oil at first), and cook together until the mixture becomes slightly thick (about 3 minutes); remove from heat.

5. Once the sauce is ready, coat the corn with the sauce by pouring it over the cobs or brushing it on with a pastry brush; serve immediately.

SUMMARY

The cuisines of Southeast Asia are some of the most intensely flavored in the world, and these cuisines blend techniques from China, India, and other regions with native ingredients and traditions to make unique rice-based cuisines of their own. Southeast Asia is primarily a tropical region, which allows for the growing of many fruits and vegetables that require warmer climates. Rice is the main ingredient throughout Southeast Asia, and the most common type is long grain cooked by the absorption method. Rice is also processed into dough to make dried noodles and sheets for use in different applications. Built around this foundation of rice are many very flavorful preparations that often rely on curry pastes for their flavor. Coconut milk is also used as a cooking liquid with the curry pastes, resulting in foods that are rich and full of flavor.

REVIEW QUESTIONS

1. What is the climate of Southeast Asia, and how does this impact the availability of ingredients?

2. Describe a curry of Southeast Asia, and list some of the typical ingredients that might be found in one.

3. What type of rice is most commonly eaten in Southeast Asia? In which country is this not the case?

4. What other forms of rice are commonly used in the cuisine of Southeast Asia?

COMMON TERMS, FOODS, AND INGREDIENTS

Southeast Asian cuisines have experienced tremendous growth in the United States in recent years, and this trend doesn't appear to be slowing. As a result, it is important for students to be familiar with some of the foods and ingredients that constitute the backbone of these cuisines. The following guide explains some of the more commonly used terms (for information on Thai curries, see the list in the "Unique Components" section of this chapter).

✳ Foods and Ingredients from Specific Countries

Laos

bai si khai – Lemongrass

hua khar – Galangal

kaeng jeuud kalampi – Pork and cabbage soup with egg

kaeng som pa – Fish soup with lemongrass, lime juice, fish sauce, and cilantro

kai yad sai – Braised chicken stuffed with chiles, shallots, garlic, and cilantro

kalee ped – Curried duck with potatoes

khao khoua – Roasted rice powder

khao niao – Sticky rice

laap – Salad made from pounded meat or fish seasoned with mint, lime juice, fish sauce, and chiles and topped with toasted rice powder

mark karm – Tamarind

miang kham – Snack common in Laos and northern Thailand in which chiles, limes, peanuts, and coconut are wrapped in a leaf and eaten with a sweet sauce

nam pa – Fish sauce

padek – Fermented fish and fish sauce with pieces of the fish still in it. This is commonly used to season other foods, with the fermented fish pieces often pounded and added to dishes.

ped – Duck

rau ngo – Cilantro

sommu – Spicy pickled pork sausage

Malaysia

asam jawa – Tamarind

babi – Pork

baji sawi – Mustard seed

blancan – Shrimp paste

budu – Fish sauce

daging – Meat

daun – Fresh herbs (leaves)

kelapa – Coconut

ketupat – Rice wrapped in palm leaves and steamed or boiled to yield a dense rice dumpling

kicap – Soy sauce

kicap manis – Thick, sweet soy sauce

minyah sapi – Ghee (clarified butter)

nasi goreng – Fried rice

pandan – Screwpine (a distinct seasoning)

rempah – Spice paste or spice blend

rendang – Meat curry made by cooking spiced meat with coconut milk until the liquid from the coconut milk is virtually gone

sambal – Chili paste

santan – Coconut milk

satay – Skewered and grilled or griddled meats served as a snack by street vendors

serbuk rempah – Five-spice powder

seria – Lemongrass

sos plam – Plum sauce

sos tarim – Oyster sauce

Thailand

ba mii – Wheat noodle

ga lum phee – Cabbage

gape – Shrimp paste

kha – Galangal

khanom jiin – Rice noodle made from forcing dough through a sieve

khao – Rice

khao hom ma-ree – Jasmine rice

khao kate – Basmati rice

khing – Ginger

kuaytiaw – Flat rice noodle

kwaytiow – Rice noodle

magroot – Kaffir lime

ma kham – Tamarind

makheua muang – Eggplant

miang khum – Snack made from wrapping chopped limes, peanuts, coconut, and chiles in lettuce leaves with sweet sauce

nahm go fi – Coconut milk

nam jim tua – Pickled and spiced cucumber

nam pla – Fish sauce

naw mai – Bamboo shoot

phat Thai – Also called pad Thai; dish of rice noodles with bean sprouts, green onions, and fried egg with sweet-and-sour sauce

prik – Chili

prik kii noo – Thai chili

puck whan – Water spinach

som thum – Green papaya salad seasoned with chiles, lime, and fish sauce

takrai – Lemongrass

tom kha gai – Chicken soup with coconut milk, galangal, lemongrass, fish sauce, and vegetables in flavorful broth

Vietnam

bac ha – Mint

bang trang – Rice paper or rice wrapper

ca de – Japanese eggplant

ca rot – Carrot

chanh vo xanh – Lime

cu cai trang – Daikon radish

dau dua – Long beans; also called yard-long beans

dau hao – Oyster sauce

ga – Chicken

gao – Rice

gia – Bean sprout

goi cuon – Rice wrap with shrimp

goi ga – Chicken and cabbage salad

gung – Ginger root

ngo gai – Saw leaf (a type of herb)

nuoc cham – Condiment sauce made from fish sauce, lime juice, chiles, and garlic

nuoc mam – Fish sauce

ot – Chili pepper

pho – Flavorful broth served with noodles and various other ingredients

pho bo – Beef pho with noodles and garnishes

rau muong – Water spinach (not related to spinach but used in a similar manner)

toi – Garlic

xi dau – Soy sauce

✳ Southeast Asian Ingredients Found in the United States

galangal – Rhizome related to ginger, with similar uses and aroma, but with a slightly stronger flavor and lighter-colored skin; can be found in the produce section of Asian specialty stores

ginger – Rhizome commonly found in supermarkets; has an aromatic quality and a fibrous interior. Ginger can be used as a substitute for galangal; it has a slightly different flavor but works well when galangal is unavailable.

kaffir lime – Type of citrus found in Southeast Asia, the leaves of which are often used in cooking. The leaves are very aromatic and contribute their distinct aroma to many dishes; these can be found in the produce section of Asian specialty stores

lesser ginger – The name often listed on packages of fresh turmeric

nam pla – Fish sauce; many varieties are available and may be found under different names (such as nouc mam)

CHAPTER 17

Map Legend

- ● towns and cities
- ★ capital city
- — river
- — region boundary
- — sub-region boundary
- —·— international boundary
- ▨ mountains

N
W · E
S

0   250   500 km

RUSSIA

KAZAKHSTAN

MONGOLIA

KYRGYZSTAN

TAJIKISTAN

PAKISTAN

C H I N A

HEILONGJIANG
● Shanshi

JILAN

LIAONING

NORTH
KOREA

SEA
OF
JAPAN

Beijing ★

HOPEI

GULF OF
BO HAI

SOUTH
KOREA

Huang He River

Northeastern
Region

SHANTUNG

YELLOW
SEA

XIZANG
(TIBET)

PLATEAU OF TIBET

HONON

JIANGSU

ANHUI

Yangtze River

HIMALAYAN MOUNTAINS

NEPAL

BHUTAN

SICHUAN
Chengtu ●

SICHUAN
PENDI
● Chungking

Yangtze River

Western Inland
Region

HUNAN

Eastern Central
Region

● Shanghai

CHEKIANG

EAST
CHINA
SEA

KWEICHOW

FUKIEN

● Foochow

PACIFIC
OCEAN

BANGLADESH

INDIA

YUNNAN

Southern
Region

GUANGDONG
● Canton

TAIWAN

BURMA
(MYANMAR)

GUANGXI

Macao ● ● Hong Kong

VIETNAM

LAOS

GULF
OF
TONGKING

BAY
OF
BENGAL

THAILAND

SOUTH
CHINA
SEA

PHILIPPINES

Chinese Cuisine

OBJECTIVES

Upon completion of this chapter, you will be able to

- explain what makes Chinese cuisine unique.
- discuss the influence Chinese cuisine has had on other Asian cuisines.
- recognize the common cooking methods used in Chinese cuisine.
- recognize the recipes commonly found in Chinese cuisine.
- produce a variety of recipes common to Chinese cuisine.
- define the terms listed at the conclusion of the chapter.

INTRODUCTION

When the introductory greeting in a culture translates to "Have you eaten yet?" you know you are in a country that values cuisine. The Chinese are indeed a cuisine-focused culture and have one of the oldest civilized, continuous cultures in the world—one that places emphasis on the importance of what is eaten. Chinese philosophers, royalty, and even those in the medical profession have all turned their attention to the types of foods being eaten, the techniques used, and the quality of the foods and ingredients in their analysis of a healthy population. Food is intricately intertwined with one's personal well-being in the minds of most Chinese-born people, a mentality that cannot be overstated with regard to Chinese cuisine.

China's written records go back nearly 5,000 years, to a time when the Chinese were already cultivating crops, diverting water, and fermenting grains. Over the centuries, the Chinese developed a complicated and impressive repertoire of culinary artistry that has now influenced many other cultures throughout the world. The following chapter examines some of this amazing cuisine by exploring the regions of China, the influences on the cuisine's development, and the elements that make Chinese cuisine different from others.

Chinese cuisine can be intimidating to the Western cook because of the many unfamiliar ingredients, the seemingly complex methods employed, and the sheer volume of recipes. Although it is certainly understandable to feel a bit overwhelmed by this cuisine, cooks should not avoid it—embracing Chinese cuisine opens the palate, the senses, and the mind to flavors and techniques that are simply too good and have too much potential to be overlooked.

This chapter should be considered only an introduction because, in reality, this cuisine is much more deep, varied, and complex than can ever be conveyed in a single chapter.

HISTORIC CULINARY INFLUENCES

China is often thought of in terms of the influences its culture has had on other cuisines; although this is certainly true, China's cuisine has also been influenced by others. The following section reviews some of the more significant influences on Chinese cuisine.

Early Chinese Culture

China is home to one of the oldest settled civilizations in the world, one that has made significant advances in the areas of agriculture, food preservation, and early cooking that rival those of the Middle East and the Americas (and greatly influenced other Asian communities). The Chinese have cultivated rice, millet, sorghum, and other crops for many millennia, and they established the sophisticated preservation techniques of salting and fermenting many vegetables, seafood, and grains to preserve them. Many of these techniques are still part of the Chinese culinary repertoire, and sauces (soy sauce, oyster sauce, black bean sauce, etc.) and other condiments often are produced using these methods today.

Some of the ingredients that were cultivated and eaten in early China include mung bean sprouts, water chestnuts, bean sprouts, bamboo shoots, lotus root, soybeans, rice, millet, and sorghum. In addition to these crops, the people of early Chinese civilization also hunted pigs and fished for many species of fish that are still found in the waters of the Pacific Ocean and in the rivers and streams of China. The strong legacy of the people and food of China had an early beginning, and this long history has resulted in a remarkably diverse cuisine.

Influences from India

During the early periods of trading via the Silk Road (from 200 BC onward), which enabled trading between the East and West, a number of foods, preparation methods, and religious influences flowed into China from India. Buddhism as a Chinese religion can be traced to this time period and provided one of the most significant influences on Chinese cuisine: the belief in the sanctity of all living animals, and thus vegetarianism. Although Buddhism is no longer followed by rulers of a Chinese dynasty, the traditions remain, particularly in western China. Some ingredients and methods that India is thought to have introduced to the Chinese are sugarcane, coriander, and the tradition of blending dry spices, which was probably the impetus for the Chinese five-spice powder.

Persian Influences

Another early influence on Chinese cuisine came from the culture that took root in what is now known as the Middle East, the Persian Empire. The beginning of what became known as the Silk Road is attributed to a Chinese general named Zhang Qian, who marked this route; this eventually brought several products and methods to the northern Chinese from India, the Middle East, and beyond. From the Middle East came eggplant, spinach, figs, sugar beets, pomegranates, garlic, walnuts, sesame seeds, and oil. General Qian also introduce the mill, which was used to grind the northern grains and eventually led to the ability to make noodles and other preparations using flour.

Mongols

Invading tribes from Mongolia ruled part of present-day northern China in the thirteenth century AD and introduced more of a focus on meat, particularly lamb and mutton. This influence is still seen, mostly in the northern inland parts of China, although the Mongols did set up posts in other areas as well—notably in the area that is discussed in this chapter as the western region (south of Sichuan). The techniques that were introduced by the Mongols and are still seen in some parts of China include grilling over open flames on skewers (as with kebabs) and the production of fermented milk products. It should be noted that most of these influences are confined to populations with heritages that can be traced to the nomadic Mongolian peoples. Many of these practices were specifically avoided by the main Chinese population, who viewed the Mongols unfavorably after having been invaded and ruled by Mongol peoples for a period.

European Colonists and Traders

During the age of exploration and colonization by the European powers in the beginning of the sixteenth century, China was introduced to the Western world directly rather than through the spice trade. This period saw a number of European powers set up trade ports in China and resulted in the flow of more ingredients and techniques from Europe. The most important of these, with respect to impact on China, came from America.

The Portuguese arrived and set up a port in the southern city of Macao in 1514, and they soon introduced the ingredients of the Americas to China. Chiles were introduced at this point, originally on the coast (in Macao, where the Portuguese set up their trading post). Most likely as a result of the region's culinary styles and habits, chiles never caught on in the southern region of China, but they did in Sichuan. Sichuan cuisine already had a tradition of using pungent ingredients like ginger and the numbing Sichuan pepper, so the inclusion of chiles was a natural one. A number of other ingredients from the Americas that were introduced by the Portuguese or other European traders also became very important in various regions of China, including sweet potatoes, potatoes, corn, and tomatoes. Some of these European influences have had a long history in China; the Portuguese only recently relinquished authority of this area to China, just as the British recently left Hong Kong.

Outward Influences

It is hard to examine the influences on Chinese cuisine without mentioning the profound effect that Chinese cuisine has had on other cultures. Consider some of the traditions that are believed to have started in China:

1. Irrigation and Cultivation of Rice: Rice is one of the most common grains in the world (along with wheat and corn) and is the major energy source for virtually all southern Asian countries.

2. Noodle Making: The making of dough that was pulled thin and dried (and later cooked) is believed to have originated in China. Marco Polo visited eastern China and is thought to have brought this technique back to Italy, and much of the tradition of pasta making in Italy evolved from this introduction (there is also evidence that pasta was already being made in Italy prior to Marco Polo's trek, but clearly the technique was developed in China earlier than anywhere else in the world).

3. Soy Products: Soy sauce, bean curd, tofu, and black bean sauce/paste (actually fermented soy beans) all originated in China and spread into Japan, Korea, and other cultures.

4. Preservation: Many preservation techniques were developed in China and spread to surrounding communities. The process of fermenting grain (originally millet and sorghum) to yield a preserved liquid; the process of pickling first with salt and then with vinegar; the process of refrigeration by cutting large blocks of ice and storing them in huge holes in

the ground, along with food; and the drying of fish all were introduced by the Chinese to others.

Although China has certainly adopted techniques and foods from other parts of the world, Chinese cuisine clearly has had a large outward impact on the development of world cuisines. Not only has the cuisine of China influenced the countries that surround it, such as Korea, Japan, all of Southeast Asia, Mongolia, and Russia, but through these countries it has also seen its culinary techniques and ingredients spread to most other parts of the world.

UNIQUE COMPONENTS

Chinese cuisine is often misunderstood in the United States, because the exposure to Chinese cuisine is often limited to restaurants that have adapted local ingredients and customs to the foods of China. Chinese cuisine is far more varied and venturesome, and typically contains far less meat than its versions in the United States. The following guide explores some of the aspects of Chinese cuisine that make it different from others of the world.

Chinese Philosophy and Food

Food is more closely associated with health in China than in many other parts of the world, particularly in contrast to Western philosophy in this area. Whereas the typical American who feels ill immediately thinks about medicine or seeing a doctor, in China someone who feels ill immediately thinks about diet or seeing an herbalist. Traditional Chinese medicine is often food, and included in the education of an individual growing up in China are the principles of yin and yang, and the proper balance of these fundamental components of life in the daily diet. It cannot be overstated how ingrained this idea is in the Chinese food culture, and thus in the cuisine of the typical Chinese person.

The following are foods that are considered yin, yang, or neutral:

Yin Foods – Almond, apple, asparagus, bamboo, banana, barley, bean curd, bean sprout, beer, broccoli, cabbage, celery, clam, corn, crab, cucumber, duck, eel, fish, grape, honey, ice cream, lemon, mussel, orange, oyster, peppermint tea, pineapple, salt, shrimp, spinach, strawberry, soy bean, white sugar, tofu, tomato, water, watercress

Yang Foods – Beef, black pepper, brown sugar, butter, cheese, chicken liver and fat, chiles, chocolate, coffee, egg, smoked fish, garlic, glutinous rice, ginger, green pepper, goose, ham, kidney bean, leek, onion, peanut butter, roasted peanut, potato, rabbit, turkey, walnut, whiskey, and wine

Neutral Foods – Bread, carrot, cauliflower, cherry, lean chicken meat, date, milk, peach, pea, pigeon (squab), plum, raisin, brown rice, and steamed white rice

Food is not viewed primarily as a source of pleasure and satisfaction, as it is in the United States (although it has these attributes in China as well). It is viewed first and foremost as a component of a balanced well-being that should be attended to in order to ensure that the balance is maintained. With this focus on food and its connection to one's well-being, it should not be surprising that the Chinese place a great deal of importance on the balance of these components in their diets. This philosophy has many similarities to the Indian or Hindu philosophy of balance in the diet; as in India, the diet of the Chinese has evolved to both nourish and provide a balance.

Efficiency

No other traditional cuisine can claim the efficiency of Chinese cuisine, which as a rule utilizes every part of a food source and each as quickly as possible, and in the most fuel-efficient manner. The Chinese have become masters of efficiency over the centuries, because it has the world's largest population (about 2 billion people) and a relatively small amount of arable (farmable) land (10%, compared to nearly 20% in the United States). The terraced hillsides that are found throughout the country are one example of such efficiency, as is the centuries-old practice of sowing multiple crops in one year (rice in much of southern China, and rotating crops of wheat, millet, and sorghum in the north).

Not only do the Chinese cultivate virtually every available piece of land; they are also well known for their willingness to eat a wide variety of foods. Many plants and animals that are not considered food sources in the United States and even in Europe are not only eaten but often are considered delicacies in China. Snakes, turtles, small birds, insects, larvae, various fungi other than mushrooms, nests of certain birds, shark fins, nearly every nonpoisonous

indigenous plant, and similar edibles are often prized in China. The cuisine served in U.S. Chinese restaurants does not even begin to cover the diversity of foods that are part of the typical diet in China. Many of these foods would likely be shunned by the typical American, but many more that might be enjoyed aren't readily available because of a lack of local production or the difficulty of transporting them.

The methods used to prepare these foods are often quite efficient; the traditional methods of cookery in China are limited by fuel sources that typically are organic (dried manure and wood or other dried plant material). Preparing foods by quickly stir frying or steaming are common in Chinese cookery, and these enable the efficient use of a heat source, which can then be extinguished for later use (as opposed to methods that cook for a long time and use more energy in the process).

The high utilization of available products and the methods of cooking those products quickly allow the Chinese to employ efficient cookery. As a result of the recent strengthening of the Chinese economy, some changes in the Chinese diet are taking place. Many people in China can now afford to purchase stoves and other cooking equipment, which could result in changes to Chinese cookery in the future.

Cooking Methods

The methods used in Chinese cuisine differ in a number of ways from those used in Western and even many Eastern cuisines. There are said to be more than 40 cooking methods in Sichuan, with many of these employing multiple individual methods as steps. The seemingly greater quantities of cooking methods taught in Chinese cuisine often comprise either these combined methods or specific differences in the steps of a particular method. For example, if a sauce is added when stir frying and is allowed to reduce until it is almost dry, this is considered a different cooking method from an identical recipe that is made without reducing the sauce but thickening it with a starch. In this way, the methods used in Chinese cuisine are often more precise than many that are learned in Western culinary arts. Much of this precision can be attributed to a more developed culinary vocabulary than is common in the cuisines of European influence. The unique methods employed in Chinese cuisine include *chao* (stir frying), *hong shao* (red cooking), and many combination methods.

Chao, or stir frying, is a technique developed in China that is often compared to sautéing, but in reality it differs in some important ways. Stir frying requires the constant motion of food; sautéing typically is done with periods of constant contact with the pan. Stir frying requires that the food be cut into small pieces, but this is not always the case with sautéing. Stir frying is often begun using strong aromatics such as ginger, garlic, or chiles; when sautéing, these types of ingredients may be added *after* the main ingredients, such as chicken or pork. Stir frying is ideally executed at heats higher than sautéing and results in vegetables being cooked less.

Combination cooking methods are common in Chinese cuisine—in particular, boiling, deep frying, or steaming, followed by another method. The technique of deep frying and then stir frying is a common combination method that can be seen in a couple of the recipes in this chapter. The cooking method called hong shao, or red cooking, is also unique in that it relies on some specific ingredients (soy sauce, rice wine, sugar, and aromatics) to break down and simultaneously glaze the foods that are cooked. (Again, there is a recipe that employs this method in this chapter.) The refinement of the cooking methods is certainly one of the reasons that Chinese cuisine is as varied and well respected as it is.

Fan: The Focal Point of the Meal

One aspect of Chinese cuisine that is often hard for those raised in a European-based culture to grasp is the focus that is placed on side dishes. In the United States, as well as in most European cultures, the focus of a meal is the meat, which would be considered the main entrée; in China, the focal point is the starch (the generic term is *fan*). *Ch'in fan* translates roughly as "to have a meal" or "to eat rice" (or another cooked grain), and this Chinese saying sums up their approach to food. The accompaniments to the starch, or fan, might include meat, sauces, and vegetables, but the rice is the main component. The mentality toward food and eating is quite different in China— the idea of eating large amounts of a specific food, such as someone eating a steak, would be viewed as selfish and insulting to others. Food is meant to be eaten communally, and each person is to enjoy a small amount of the accompaniments to the rice, noodles, or other starch. Thus, everyone is expected to be conservative with regard to the amount of accompaniments they eat.

It should be noted that China has suffered through some of the worst natural disasters in history, including horrible famines; it is a country with a long history of control by imperial dynasties; it has a population of more than 1 billion people; and it has developed a communist system that focuses on community, not the individual. As a result of these factors (and others), food is primarily a source of health and nourishment, and everything that comes with that nourishment (i.e., rice, noodles, and dumplings) is seen as a luxury to be enjoyed to the fullest.

SIGNIFICANT SUBREGIONS

China is a large country, slightly larger in size than the United States, and some distinct regional variations can be found in cuisines throughout the land. Although Chinese cuisine could certainly be reviewed using in-depth analysis, it is commonly perceived—in a regional sense—as four main areas of distinct cuisines. The following guide examines these four regions to help provide an overall picture of the variations that, when brought together, compose this wonderful cuisine. The regions are presented from north to south and then from east to west.

Northeastern Region: Hopei/Shangtung/ Shanshi/Honon/Jilan and Liaoning Provinces (Major City: Peking/Beijing)

The cuisine of the northeastern region of China is quite different from what many Americans may think of as Chinese cuisine. This is a cold and mostly arid region that has traditionally been a producer and consumer of wheat, millet, and sorghum—and not of rice, probably the first ingredient people think of as Chinese. Other cold crops, such as potatoes, cabbage, and onions, are also significant in this region and are used extensively in the local cooking (often flavored with garlic). Although rice is certainly not uncommon in this region, the other grains are much more common still, and significant amounts of wheat-based dishes remain the main sources of starch in this region today. Noodles, dumplings, steamed buns, pancakes, and even some varieties of breads are common to this region because of its historic reliance on these grains.

Although this region lies right on the ocean, and the Yellow River slices through it, fishing is not nearly as significant as it is in the more southerly areas. The little seafood or fish that is eaten is most often the giant shrimp from the Gulf of Bohai and carp from the Yellow River. Meat is the protein eaten most often in this region, and the famous Peking duck is but one technique used to prepare the abundant poultry found here. The most common cooking methods in this region are roasting, steaming, and preparing soups and stews.

The Mongols descended from the north and ruled this part of China, leaving their imprint on the culinary habits of the local peoples. In this region, one is more likely to be served lamb, mutton, and the hot pot, all results of the periods of rule by their northerly neighbors.

Beijing (formerly known as Peking) has been the capital of China since the 1300s, and as such has had a long culinary history as the home of imperial cuisine, or what is often referred to as court cuisine. Generally, this cuisine was dramatically different from what the local people would enjoy; it often was very elaborate and included many foods found in other parts of China that were brought in especially for those in the ruling dynasty. As a result, the cuisine of this region is a mix of peasant foods—upon which the majority of the population relies—and the court cuisine and regional cuisine found in the capital.

Eastern Central Region: Kiangsu/Anhui/Chekiang/Fukien Provinces (Major Cities: Shanghai and Foochow)

The eastern region's major geological feature is water. Whether it takes the form of marshes, rivers, ponds, or the Yellow Sea (Huang Hai), water is both a lifeline and a curse in this region. This region is mostly flat and drains the highlands of western China through various rivers, including the mighty Yangtze River. Most of the agricultural products of this region depend on a good supply of water, and floods historically have brought misery to this region—often in the form of failed crops. This region includes the major city port of Shanghai.

The reliance on foods yielded from water has resulted in a nickname for this area—"the land of fish and rice"—and these two foods often form the backbone of the local cuisine. Another central component of the local cuisine is made in the region: *shao-xing* (rice wine) is used extensively in marinades, sauces, and even to finish some dishes.

In contrast to the cuisine of the northern region, this region's cuisine features rice instead of wheat or millet, and rice is in fact central to nearly every meal. Often rice is combined with some of the local seafood or used in a hong shao dish, a cooking method that is believed to have originated here. Some of the fine seafood that might be found here includes four gilled carp, catfish, shrimp, hairy crab, and other crabs, and these are often included in some of the region's soups. The most common meat eaten here is pork, such as in the preparation of *shi ji tau* ("lion's head"; large pork meatballs), and pork fat is often used as a cooking fat; chicken and duck are also commonly used.

The cooking of this region includes many uses of rice dough, including the well-known *wor tip* (pot sticker) that has become common in the United States, as well as *xiaolongbao* (soupy pork-filled steamed buns), which have devout followers throughout Shanghai, where they are eaten with a ginger-infused vinegar. Many of the dishes from this region tend to be sweeter than in other parts of China, such as those that are red cooked and other dishes that include rock sugar. A number of sweet pastries are common to this region as well, including many that are steamed and a few that are fried.

Southern Region: Guangdong/Guangxi Provinces (Major Cities: Canton and Hong Kong)

The southern region of China is semitropical and very fertile, resulting in a distinctly different cuisine from that of the more northern areas. The cuisine of the south is praised all over China, as this is the home of many of the country's great culinary traditions and dishes.

Southern China lies on the South China Sea and, at its most southerly point, the Gulf of Tonkin, both areas with abundant sea life that is a big part of the local cuisine. Because this area has a tropical climate, many ingredients can be grown here, and the variety and quality of produce are unmatched anywhere else in China.

The cooking style of this region is often less intrusive than in other regions, and stir frying and steaming are the most common methods used. In the south, the cooks and chefs tend to cook the foods less, so that vegetables are crunchy and meats and fish retain their inherent tenderness and moisture. Perhaps the most common element of the south's cuisine that is gaining popularity in the United States is dim sum. With the dizzying array of *bao* (steamed wheat buns), *gok* (dumplings), *cheung fun* (steamed rice rolls), and *go* (fried cakes) that is eaten as part of the dim sum tradition, it is no wonder that its popularity is spreading.

This is the region that had the most interaction with the Europeans when the first direct contact occurred between Europe and China, and as such many of the products of the New World were introduced (mostly by the Portuguese) to Chinese cuisine here. The inclusion of chiles, tomatoes, corn, peanuts, potatoes, and sweet potatoes in the Chinese diet all began in this region. Perhaps the Portuguese knew that they had landed among people who were willing to try new foods when they arrived in Macao, as this is the land of variety. There is a saying in this land—if it walks with its spine facing the heavens, it's edible—and the people of this region eat just about everything but other humans, and it turns out they know how to cook everything as well.

Some of the ingredients that are particularly common in this region are tiger prawns, pork, and citrus; seasonings include oyster sauce, scallions, ginger, garlic, soy sauce, and fermented soybeans. The climate is conducive to growing many fruits and vegetables, such as coconut, lychees, papaya, mangoes, and oranges, all of which are found in the local cuisine.

Western Inland Region: Hunan/Kweichow/Sichuan/Yunnan Provinces (Major Cities: Chengtu and Chungking)

The cuisine of the western region is dominated by that of the valley of Sichuan, the land of spice. Sichuan is located in western China in what can only be described as a hidden valley among towering mountain ranges. The Sichuan area is surrounded by hills and mountains, with the Plateau of Tibet bordering the western portion, the Qin Ling Mountains to the north, and the uplands of the Yun Gui Gaoyuan bordering the south and east. This geography has made Sichuan a humid and fertile valley that has provided a long history of crop cultivation and the crops' subsequent inclusion in the local cuisine. Some of the crops that are particularly important to the local cuisine include rice, the well-known Sichuan pepper (no relation to the black or white pepper), ginger, bamboo shoots, soybeans, mushrooms from the surrounding mountains, water spinach, pork, mandarins, and now chiles.

Sichuan is one of the schools of Chinese cuisine that is most common in the United States (the other is Canton). The cuisine is well known for its liberal use of spices; although that is a significant component of the local cuisine, it certainly isn't the only one. Sichuan cuisine is also known throughout China for its vegetarian dishes, use of tofu, and many cooking techniques. In China, Sichuan cuisine is appreciated for its complexity of flavors, with many components typically included in a single dish: sweet and sour; spicy and sour; sweet, spicy, and sour. All of these combinations and more can be found in Sichuan's cuisine.

Combined cooking methods are used often here. It is very common to see vegetables first deep-fried and then stir-fried with a sauce, or to first deep-fry pieces of meat before braising it. These methods provide richness to the final recipe as well as different textures and intense flavors that identify the cuisine.

The region's reputation for spicy food is well earned. In years past, the spiciness came from Sichuan peppers, ginger, and betel nuts; then, black and white peppercorns were introduced from India (other Indian influences include Buddhism and thus vegetarianism). Finally, in the nineteenth century, chiles were adopted after being introduced by the Portuguese along the southeastern coast in the sixteenth century. Chiles quickly became a significant ingredient in this land of humidity, because they provided some of the same cooling effect as the previous sources of heat, and they grew abundantly in the local climate. Interestingly, chiles are known as *hai jiao* in Sichuan, which means "sea peppers"—their point of origin from the Chinese perspective.

The western region comprises many ethnicities, because this region has been home to a number of cultures over the centuries, many of which are still represented in significant numbers here, including descendants of Thai, Vietnamese, Mongolian, Hakka (originally from northern China), and Burmese peoples, to name a few. All of these cultures have contributed to the development of the local cuisine.

Some dishes that hail from this region are *gong bao* (kung pao chicken), *tang cu li ji* (sweet and sour pork), *gan bian si ji dou* (spicy stir-fried green beans), and *suan la rou si tang* (hot and sour soup).

RECIPES

The following recipes provide an introduction to Chinese cuisine by revealing commonly used ingredients and some of the unique methods employed in the Chinese kitchen. Hopefully this introduction inspires a closer look at this varied and complex cuisine (many texts explore this in greater depth, some of which are listed in the References section of this book).

Fan CHINA
(PLAIN COOKED RICE)

INGREDIENTS

3 cups Long-Grain Rice (soak the rice for the directed time, or the water amount will not be correct)

3 cups Water

As the main ingredient of Chinese cuisine, rice has been a symbol of food and eating for centuries. Rice is commonly eaten at each meal and is thought to be a neutral component of any meal, thus helping to provide balance to one's diet.

YIELD: About 6–7 cups, or 8–10 portions (.75 cup/portion)

COOKING METHOD: Boiling/Steaming

PROCEDURE

1. Rinse the rice by placing it in a pot filled with cold water and rubbing the grains between your fingers.

2. Discard the cold water and repeat this procedure one or two more times, until the water is almost clear when it is emptied from the pot.

3. Once the grains have been rinsed, place the rice in the pot and cover it with cool water; allow the rice to rest for 45 minutes (it will absorb some water during this period, so this must be done for the water ratio to be correct. Also be sure that the rice is covered by a couple inches of water, as the rice will swell a bit).

4. Once the rice has soaked for 45 minutes, remove it from the pot and place it in a strainer to drain out the water it soaked in.

5. Transfer the drained rice to a pot, and add 3 cups of water.

6. Turn the heat to a high flame and bring the mixture to a boil, uncovered (do not leave it, because it will need to be covered as soon as it reaches a boil).

7. Once it boils, turn the heat down to a low flame and cover the pot tightly with a lid (if a tight-fitting lid is not available, use foil and place a lid on top of the foil to hold it down).

8. Cook the rice over a low flame for 5 minutes (you should not see water coming out of the pot—if you do, the heat is too high). Turn the heat off and allow the pot to sit for another 10 minutes (to allow the rice to finish by steaming).

9. Remove the lid and fluff the rice using a fork or chopsticks; serve immediately, or cover tightly with plastic wrap if you are not serving right away.

Rinsing and rubbing rice for making fan (steamed rice)

Soaking rice for making fan

Cooked fan; note the pockets on the surface of this properly cooked rice

Yangzhou Chau Fan EASTERN CHINA
(STIR-FRIED RICE IN THE STYLE OF YANGZHOU)

INGREDIENTS

4	oz	Lard (you can substitute peanut oil, if desired)
6	oz	Shrimp, peeled, deveined, and cut into 1/4-inch pieces
5		Large Eggs, beaten
1/4	tsp	Salt
1	oz	Soy Sauce
2	oz	Rice Wine
1	oz	Oyster Sauce
1	Tbsp	Sesame Oil
1	tsp	Sugar
1	tsp	Salt
1	oz	Fresh Ginger, minced
1/2	oz	Garlic Cloves, minced
6	oz	Cantonese Roasted Pork (called Char Sui—you can substitute another roasted pork, if this is unavailable; the char sui recipe is included in this chapter, if needed)
1		recipe of Cooked Rice (called Fan; see recipe, this chapter), cooled to room temperature
1	bunch	Scallions, sliced thin on a bias

Fried rice is one of the well-known preparations in Chinese cooking, and many variations exist. This recipe is in the style of Yangzhou. Depending on the size and thickness of your wok, this recipe may be best prepared by dividing it in half and making it in two batches to ensure that the ingredients are stir-fried and do not stick to the bottom of the wok.

YIELD: 15 portions (5 ounces/portion)

COOKING METHOD: Stir Frying

PROCEDURE

1. Place a wok over a wok ring on a burner and turn the heat to a high flame; add 1/2 of the lard to the wok.

2. Once the lard just begins to wisp smoke, add the shrimp and stir-fry for about 30 seconds or until all of the shrimp pieces turn pink. Remove the wok from heat; remove the shrimp and set them aside.

3. Pour off any excess fat in the wok, set it aside, and return the wok to the heat.

4. Combine the beaten eggs and the salt; once the wok is hot, add the eggs and quickly stir-fry them until they are just cooked. Once again, remove them from the wok and set them aside. Cut the eggs into small strips.

5. Combine the soy sauce, rice wine, oyster sauce, sesame oil, salt, and sugar, and set aside.

6. Return the wok to the wok circle, and add the remaining lard to the wok; place over a high flame to heat.

7. Once the wok begins to release wisps of smoke again, add the ginger and stir-fry for 5 seconds. Next, add the garlic; stir-fry for 5 seconds before adding the pork.

8. Once the pork has stir-fried for a minute or so, add the shrimp, the rice, the cut eggs, and the sauce, all while stir frying to keep the ingredients from sticking to the bottom.

9. Add the scallions and any lard that was poured off from stir frying the shrimp; serve immediately.

Yangzhou chau fan (stir-fried rice)

Qiang Huang Qua   WESTERN CHINA

(SPICY CUCUMBER)

INGREDIENTS

1.5	lb	Cucumbers, peeled, deseeded, and cut into batonnet pieces
1.5	Tbsp	Salt
1	oz	Peanut Oil
10		Dried Red Chiles (about 2 inches in length), stems and seeds removed, and cut in half
2	tsp	Sichuan Peppercorns, crushed with the back of a cleaver
1.5	oz	Sesame Oil

This recipe—a great example of the simplicity and efficiency of using a wok—takes just seconds once the ingredients are prepared, and it packs the punch of those most Sichuan of flavors: chiles and Sichuan peppers. This dish is most definitely fiery, so if a tamer taste is desired, reduce the amount of chiles and Sichuan peppers in the recipe.

YIELD: 6 portions (4 ounces/portion)

COOKING METHOD: Stir Frying

PROCEDURE

1. Combine the cucumber slices and the salt, tossing the two together in a mixing bowl to combine well; set the cucumber aside to allow the salt to draw out moisture for 30 minutes.

2. Once the cucumber has sat for 30 minutes, transfer it to a colander and rinse the cucumber off with cold water; pat dry with a clean cloth or paper towels.

3. Once the cucumber is dry, add the peanut oil to a wok and set over a high flame to heat.

4. Once the oil is hot (the oil should just begin to release wisps of smoke), add the chiles and Sichuan peppers. Remove the wok from the heat immediately, while simultaneously moving the chiles and Sichuan peppers around in the wok.

5. Add the cucumber slices to the pan, and toss to coat them well with the chiles and oil.

6. Transfer the seasoned cucumbers to a container and allow them to cool completely before adding the sesame oil; serve.

Bang Bang Ji Si   WESTERN CHINA

(CHICKEN WITH BANG BANG SAUCE)

INGREDIENTS

For Making the Sauce

1/4	cup	Sesame Seeds, white
2	oz	Soy Sauce
1.5	oz	Sugar
2	oz	Black Chinese Vinegar (Chinkiang)
1	tsp	Sichuan Peppers, ground
1	oz	Sesame Oil
2	oz	Chili Oil

For Assembling the Plates

2	lbs	Cooked Chicken Breast, cooled, smashed with the side of a cleaver, and pulled into strips

This dish is from Leshan, a town in the Sichuan region that is well known for its quality chicken. This dish is said to have received its name from cooks who used a wooden instrument (called a *bang*) to smash the back of a cleaver over the cooked chicken meat to break the fibers so that the chicken would shred easily (which is how this dish is traditionally served). The sauce can be made ahead of time as a great way to utilize leftover cooked chicken.

YIELD: 8 portions (6 ounces/portion)

COOKING METHOD: None (the chicken should be precooked)

PROCEDURE

For Making the Sauce

1. Using a medium-size sauté pan or wok, set the pan over a low flame and dry toast the sesame seeds until they turn brown and become fragrant.

(continues)

2. Using a mortar and pestle, crush the toasted sesame seeds into a paste, and then set them aside.

3. In a mixing bowl, combine the soy sauce, black vinegar, and Sichuan peppers, and mix to combine; add the ground sesame paste while stirring constantly.

4. Once the sesame paste has been added, slowly drizzle in the oils, whisking all the while to form an emulsified dressing.

5. Set the dressing aside to prepare to assemble the plates.

For Assembling the Plates

1. Place approximately 4 oz of the shredded chicken meat on each plate, and top it with a small amount of the sliced scallions.

2. Pour 1.5 oz of the dressing over the scallions and chicken, and garnish with the black sesame seeds or toasted white sesame seeds.

*** Bang Bang Ji Si**
(continued)

2 bunches Scallions, the white parts cut into 2-inch sections, split in quarters lengthwise (use the green part in other recipes)
Dressing (see above)
2 Tbsp Sesame Seeds, black or toasted white

Bang bang ji si (bang bang chicken), with rice in the center of the plate and qiang huang qua (spicy cucumber) on both ends of the plate

Wor Tip EASTERN CHINA/SHANGHAI
(POT STICKERS)

INGREDIENTS
For Blanching the Bok Choy

8 oz Bok Choy
1.5 qts water
2 tsp Salt

These Chinese dumplings are well known in the United States, yet these are simply one example from a family of filled-dough dumplings that are found throughout China. The dough used to make these is now widely available frozen, although it is often made with eggs, which the traditional dough did not contain. There are a few varieties of eggless wonton skins, or the dough can be made fresh.

YIELD: Forty 1-oz pot stickers + sauce
COOKING METHOD (BOK CHOY): Blanching by Boiling
COOKING METHOD (POT STICKERS): Quick Braising

(continues)

For Making the Filling

1	lb	Lean Ground Pork
2		Egg Whites, whipped until just frothy
2	oz	Soy Sauce
1	oz	Rice Wine (Shao-Hsing, if available)
2	tsp	Sugar
1	oz	Sesame Oil
1	oz	Ginger, minced
1/2	bunch	Scallions, minced
		Prepared Bok Choy (see above), diced small

For Filling the Pot Stickers

		Filling (see above)
40		Pot Sticker Wrappers (these can also be made using All-Purpose [A.P.] Flour and cold water to make a stiff dough that is then rolled into thin rounds; you would need approximately 2.5 cups of flour and 1 cup or more of cold water to form a smooth dough to use, if desired)
1	cup	Cold Water
		Corn Starch, if needed

For Cooking the Pot Stickers

6	oz	Peanut Oil
2.5	qts	Chicken Stock
4	oz	Soy Sauce
4	oz	Carrots, cut brunoise
4	oz	Celery, cut brunoise

PROCEDURE

For Blanching the Bok Choy

1. In a small pot, combine the water and salt; place the pot over a high flame and bring contents to a boil.
2. Once the water reaches a boil, add the bok choy stems and blanch until just tender; remove the stems and shock them in an ice bath.
3. Once the stems are blanched, add the leaves and blanch until just wilted (this will happen very quickly, within 30 seconds or so, so be attentive). Once the leaves are wilted, add them to the ice water to shock as well.
4. Remove all of the bok choy from the ice bath, and pat it dry with a clean paper towel.
5. Dice all of the bok choy into small pieces, mincing the leaves.
6. Transfer the cut bok choy to a clean, dry cloth, and wring out any excess moisture; set aside for the filling.

For Making the Filling

1. In a mixing bowl, combine the ground pork and the whipped egg whites; mix well to combine.
2. Slowly work in the soy sauce, rice wine, and sugar using clean, sanitized hands or a fork; then drizzle in the sesame oil, working it in with your hands or a fork.
3. Once the liquids have been added to the filling, the minced ginger, scallions, and prepared bok choy can be folded into the mixture. The mixture is ready to be used to fill the dough.

For Filling the Pot Stickers

1. Prepare to make the pot stickers by placing the cold water (and the pot sticker skins and filling) in a container near your work area, and work with one skin at a time.
2. Place 1/2 tablespoon of the filling in the center of the pot sticker skin, and wet the edges of the skin with a little bit of the cold water (using either clean, sanitized fingers or a pastry brush). Fold over the skin to form a semicircle with the dough, enclosing the filling inside the center of the dough/skin (be sure not to trap pockets of air inside the pot sticker when doing this, or they may burst when cooked).
3. Once the pot sticker is folded over, firmly press together the edges of the skins that overlap (using clean, sanitary fingers). Press the two pieces of dough together and seal them.
4. Repeat steps 2 and 3 to fill all of the pot stickers, sealing each one as you go and setting them on a sheet tray lined with parchment paper to be ready for cooking (if they will not be made immediately after prepping, it is a good idea to dust them with corn starch to prevent them from sticking to the paper or tray).

For Cooking the Pot Stickers

(**NOTE:** *This step will be need to be done in 8–10 batches for best results; the following procedure uses 8 steps, so just reduce the amount of stock, etc., in each batch if you will be using more steps.*)

1. Add 1.5 Tbsp of peanut oil to a medium- to large-size sauté pan, and heat over a medium-high flame on the stove.

(continues)

2. Once the oil gets hot (it should ripple and just begin to smoke), add 5 pot stickers to the pan and sauté them until they become golden on the bottom side (they will release from the pan as soon as they are golden, so if they stick, wait!). Add 10 oz of chicken stock to the pan.

3. Next, add 1 Tbsp soy sauce, 1/2 oz carrots, and 1/2 oz celery; simmer the pot stickers in the stock for approximately 3 minutes, or until the stock reduces by 25%. Turn out the pot stickers to a dish to serve immediately.

4. Repeat steps 2 and 3 seven more times to cook all of the pot stickers.

NOTE: *These are often simply sautéed and finished with water and then served with a dipping sauce made by combining equal portions of soy sauce and rice wine vinegar topped with scallions and chili oil and diluted to taste with chicken stock.*

Wor tip (pot stickers)

Far Jiu Fun   Western/Sichuan
(Sichuan Peppercorn Paste)

INGREDIENTS

.5	oz	Sichuan Peppercorns
2	oz	Ginger, peeled and minced
1	tsp	Salt
3	oz	Green Onions (about 1 bunch), sliced thin

In Sichuan, this paste is commonly used to make sauces and marinades, especially for the many dishes that translate as "fish flavored." This fish flavor comes from the sauce, which in fact contains no fish but rather a combination of other ingredients that are said to have a similar aroma. Typically, this paste is one of those ingredients.

YIELD: 5 ounces, or about 1/2 cup

PREPARATION METHOD: Crushing in Mortar and Pestle

PROCEDURE

1. Combine peppercorns, ginger, and salt in a mortar, and crush to a rough paste with a pestle.

2. Add green onions, and continue to grind with the pestle until a smooth paste is formed.

Gan Bian Si Ji Dou   WESTERN CHINA/SICHUAN

(SPICY STIR-FRIED GREEN BEANS)

INGREDIENTS

For Blanching the Green Beans

6	cups	Peanut Oil
2	lbs	Fresh Green Beans, ends snipped

For Stir Frying the Green Beans

1	Tbsp	Cornstarch
3	oz	Water, cold
2	Tbsp	Dark Soy Sauce
2	tsp	Rice Wine Vinegar
2	oz	Chinese Rice Wine (called Shao-Hsing or Shao-Xing)
2	tsp	Sugar
1.5	oz	Peanut Oil
2	Tbsp	Ginger, minced
2	Tbsp	Garlic, minced
		Green Beans (see above)
2	Tbsp	Fresh Red Chili, minced (such as Tabasco or cayenne chili)
1	Tbsp	Sesame Oil

One unique method commonly used in Chinese cooking is to deep-fry ingredients first and then to finish cooking them using another technique. This is often done in braised and stir-fried dishes, such as this example from the Sichuan region.

YIELD: 8 portions (4 ounces/portion)

COOKING METHOD (BLANCHING GREEN BEANS): Deep Frying

COOKING METHOD (FINAL COOKING): Stir Frying

PROCEDURE

For Blanching the Green Beans

1. Add the peanut oil to a wok and heat over a medium-high flame until the oil just starts to release wisps of white smoke.

2. As soon as the smoke appears, drop 1/2 of the cleaned green beans into the oil; blanch for 1–2 minutes, or until the beans just start to soften.

3. Once the beans begin to soften, remove them with a wire basket or strainer, and set them aside to drain.

4. Repeat steps 2 and 3 with the second batch of beans, once again straining them when they are tender. When finished, carefully transfer the hot oil from the wok into a suitable container.

For Stir Frying the Green Beans

1. Combine the cornstarch and cold water to make a slurry, and then add the dark soy sauce, rice wine vinegar, rice wine, and sugar; mix well to combine, and set this aside for the sauce.

2. In the now empty wok, add the peanut oil and heat over a high flame until wisps of white smoke start to rise from the pan.

3. As soon as the pan starts to smoke, add the ginger and garlic; stir-fry these ingredients for about 10 seconds before adding the blanched green beans to the pan.

4. Once the green beans have been added, add the minced chiles; continue to stir- fry these ingredients for another 30 seconds.

5. Once the green beans and chiles have been stir-fried for 30 seconds, add the sauce mixture from step 1.

6. Continue to cook over high heat until the sauce starts to thicken slightly, and then remove it from the heat (this will happen quickly); drizzle in the sesame oil while tossing the ingredients in the wok together.

7. Turn out the prepared green beans to a platter, and serve at once.

Gan bian si ji dou (spicy stir-fried green beans)

Chun Chuan P'i NORTHEASTERN REGION

(SPRING ROLL WRAPPERS)

INGREDIENTS

1	lb	Unbleached Flour, sifted
1/2	tsp	Salt
14	oz	Water

These wrappers are commonly used to make both cooked and uncooked savory stuffed pastries in various parts of China. This variety is made with a technique that resembles that used in North Africa to make what are known as warka or brik wrappers; very soft dough is pressed into a hot pan and then immediately removed to leave a thin film behind, which then cooks to make the wrapper.

YIELD: Twenty to twenty-five 6–7-inch wrappers

COOKING METHOD: Unique Method to Make Thin Wrappers

PROCEDURE

1. Add the sifted flour and salt to a mixer with a dough hook attachment, and mix to combine.

2. Add 1 cup of the water to the mixer; with the mixer on low, slowly add the remaining water.

3. Continue to mix on a low speed until the dough becomes smooth, very soft, and elastic (this will take about 12 minutes or so).

4. Once the dough has mixed properly, remove it from the mixer and place it in a suitable container. Set it in the refrigerator and allow it to become cold and firmer (this will take a couple of hours).

5. Heat a dry 10-inch sauté pan (not a nonstick pan!) or griddle to 375°F (use a surface thermometer or laser thermometer to measure this; it is very important that the temperature be correct. If the pan is too cool, the dough will form too thick a film. If the pan is too hot, it will sear and not stick at all).

6. Remove the dough from the refrigerator and gather about a third of it (return the rest to the refrigerator until you are ready to make more) with one clean, sanitized hand. While rolling your hand around to keep the dough from running, quickly press some of the dough into the preheated pan, making sure it touches the entire bottom of the pan (or a circle with a 6–7-inch diameter, if you are using a griddle), and then pull the dough away to leave a thin film on the very bottom of the pan.

7. The dough film should dry on the edges in a matter of seconds. When this occurs, remove the dough with your free hand and place it on a dry plate or another container.

8. Continue to cook the dough film pieces as described in the previous steps until either all of the dough is cooked off or the dough starts to become too soft to handle (as it warms up, it will become thinner and may need to be returned to the refrigerator).

9. After completing the first batch of wrappers, wipe the pan with a clean, dry cloth to remove any particles that have stuck to the pan.

10. Once you are done with the first dough piece, gather another third of the dough and continue the process until all the dough has been cooked off.

Hong Shao Roa   EASTERN CHINA
(PORK BELLY IN RED COOKED STYLE)

INGREDIENTS

For Par-Cooking the Pork

4	lbs	Pork Belly, skinless
2	gal	Water

For Marinating the Pork

1	cup	Chinese Rice Wine (called Shaoxing Jiu; you can substitute Japanese, if this is unavailable)
4	oz	Ginger, peeled and sliced into thin circles
1	oz	Garlic, minced
1	tsp	Salt

For Cooking the Pork

2	oz	Peanut Oil
2		Whole Star Anise
1		Cinnamon Stick
4	oz	Ginger, peeled and sliced into thin circles
2	bunches	Scallions, cut into 3-inch lengths
6	oz	Chinese Rice Wine
6	oz	Mushroom-Flavored Dark Soy Sauce
1	tsp	Salt
20	oz	Water
4	oz	Sugar
		Salt or Soy Sauce, to taste

The hong shao (Mandarin name) cooking style is found in a number of places in Chinese cuisine, but it is believed to have originated in the Shanghai region and is still most popular there today. This style of cooking is very similar to braising except it sometimes is done without any searing at the beginning. The term *red* that is used to describe this method doesn't apply to the color but rather to the spirit of the color as the Chinese perceive it—indicating luck or, in this case, a method that is favorable.

YIELD: 12 portions

COOKING METHOD: Red Cooking, or Hong Shao

PROCEDURE

For Par-Cooking the Pork

1. Cut the pork belly into strips approximately 1.5 inches wide.
2. Cut the pork belly strips into 1.5-inch cubes.
3. Combine the water and pork belly pieces in a pot, and place the pot over a high flame; bring to a boil.
4. Once the pot reaches a boil, turn the heat down and simmer the pork pieces for 5 minutes; remove them from the heat and strain out the pork belly. Set aside to cool.

For Marinating the Pork

1. In a mixing bowl, combine the cooled pork belly pieces and the rice wine, ginger slices, garlic, and salt; mix well and transfer to an appropriate container to cover and refrigerate overnight.
2. Allow the pork to marinate for at least 4 hours (for best results, marinate overnight).

For Cooking the Pork

1. Place a pan by your work area to hold ingredients as they are being sautéed, and be sure to have a wooden spoon or another stirrer on hand to move the foods in the pan.
2. Using either a large, flat-bottomed stir-fry pan or a large sauté pan, place the pan over a high flame (you may want to use two pans to ensure that everything will fit); add 2 Tbsp of the peanut oil.
3. Once the peanut oil gets hot, add 1 piece of star anise and the cinnamon stick; stir-fry for 20 seconds or so. Add 1/2 of the sliced ginger and scallion pieces, and stir-fry for another 30 seconds, moving everything in the pan the whole time.
4. At this point, add 1/2 of the marinated pork belly (leave the ginger pieces in the marinade and discard when finished) and continue to stir-fry all of the ingredients for another minute or so. Remove everything from the pan and set it in the holding pan mentioned in step 1.

(continues)

Hong Shao Roa
(continued)

5. Repeat steps 2 through 4 with the remaining ingredients. Once the pork belly has been added and stir-fried, add the rice wine and the wine left over from the marinade to the pan, and cook down until the pan is dry.

6. Add the pork to the pan, along with the other ingredients that were set aside in the holding pan. Next, add the mushroom-flavored soy sauce, salt, and water, and reduce the heat to a low flame.

7. Allow the mixture to settle at an easy simmer, and then cover and gently simmer for an hour.

8. Once the pork has simmered for an hour, check to see if the meat is tender by taking out a piece of pork and trying it. It should be very tender and not tough; if it is tough, return the cover and continue to cook until the pork is tender.

9. Once the pork is tender, add the sugar and turn the heat up to simmer the mixture until the sauce thickens slightly.

10. Adjust seasoning, if necessary, and serve with plain rice.

Hong shao roa (red cooked pork) served with with steamed bok choy and fan

Char Sui SOUTHERN CHINA/CANTON
(ROASTED PORK IN CANTONESE STYLE)

INGREDIENTS

4	lbs	Boneless Pork Butt, slice into 1.5-inch pieces
2	oz	Hoisin Sauce
6	oz	Soy Sauce
4	oz	Sugar
4	oz	Chinese Rice Wine (called Shaoxing Jiu)
1	oz	Garlic Cloves, minced
1/4	tsp	Red Food Coloring

For Glazing the Cooked Pork

4	oz	Honey

Char sui is a traditional dish from China that is common in the United States. This well-known pork preparation is often used to make steamed dumplings (see recipe that follows); it is also used in rice dishes or simply eaten on its own with rice.

YIELD: 12 portions (5 ounces/portion)

PREPARATION METHOD: Marinating (Overnight, or a minimum of 4 hours)

COOKING METHOD: Roasting

PROCEDURE

1. Combine all of the ingredients and place them in a container that will ensure that the marinade covers the pork pieces.

2. Marinate the pork for a minimum of 4 hours (overnight, if possible).

3. Preheat the oven to 400°F.

4. Remove the pork pieces from the marinade (do not discard), place them on a roasting rack, and place the rack inside a roasting pan.

5. Pour a cup of water in the bottom of the roasting pan.

6. Roast the pork for 10 minutes and then baste the pork with some of the marinade.

7. Return the pork to the oven, and roast it for 15 additional minutes before basting with marinade again. This time, check to make sure that there is still some water in the bottom of the roasting pan; as it gets low, add more water (1/2 cup at a time) to ensure that a sauce will be left at the end.

8. Continue to roast and baste every 10–15 minutes, always checking the water level, until the pork has developed a nicely crisped skin and is cooked throughout (about 75–90 minutes total).

9. Remove the pork from the oven and set it aside to rest. While it is resting, strain the pan drippings and sauce from the roasting pan, and degrease the surface using a small ladle.

10. Once the pork has rested for 10 minutes or so, brush the pork pieces with the honey and slice them into smaller strips; serve with some of the pan drippings and plain rice.

Glazing the char sui (roasted pork)

NOTE: *Leftovers can be used to make char siu bao and yangzhou chau fan.*

Char Sui Bao SOUTHERN CHINA/CANTON
(ROASTED PORK BUNS)

INGREDIENTS

For Making the Bun Dough

1	oz	Fresh Compressed Yeast
1	oz	Sugar
3	cups	Water
2	lbs	Cake Flour + more as needed (for consistency of dough and for dusting)
2	tsp	Baking Powder
3	oz	Lard

For Making the Stuffing

2	tsp	Corn Starch
2	oz	Rice Wine (Shaoxing), cool
1	oz	Vegetable Oil
1	bunch	Scallions, sliced thin on a bias
1/2		recipe of Char Sui (see recipe, this chapter), chopped fine
2	oz	Light Soy Sauce
2	oz	Oyster Sauce
1	oz	Hoisin Sauce

For Forming and Steaming the Buns

		Dough (see above)
		Cooled Pork Filling (see above)
30		small pieces of Parchment Paper

Canton and Hong Kong are home to the now well-known tradition of dim sum that has become quite common in the United States. Char siu bao is one of the steamed buns offered at dim sum restaurants in both China and the United States.

YIELD: 30 buns (2–3 ounces/bun)

MIXING METHOD (DOUGH): Straight Dough Method

COOKING METHOD: Steaming

PROCEDURE

For Making the Bun Dough

1. Combine the yeast, sugar, and water in a mixing bowl, and whisk ingredients together to combine well; set bowl aside, and cover it with a clean, damp towel for 5 minutes.

2. After 5 minutes, check to see if the yeast is active by looking for foam on top or a distinct yeasty smell. If either is evident, proceed to the next step. If not, give yeast another 5 minutes, after which it should have become active. If not, discard it and start over with fresh yeast.

3. Once the yeast has been determined to be active, add the other ingredients to a mixer with a paddle attachment; mix on low speed until a dough is formed, adding more flour if necessary to form a smooth, soft dough that doesn't stick to the inside of the mixing bowl when mixing.

4. Mix the dough until it becomes smooth and elastic, and then transfer it from the mixing bowl to a suitable container. Cover it with plastic wrap and place it in a proofbox; allow the dough to double in volume (this will take approximately 45 minutes).

5. Once the dough has doubled in volume, remove it from the proofbox. After removing the plastic wrap, punch the dough down and turn it out onto a floured work surface.

6. Divide the dough into 30 pieces, and knead each one briefly until it is smooth and no air bubbles are evident, at which time the dough is ready to be used to make the filled buns (cover the dough pieces with plastic wrap until they are filled).

For Making the Stuffing

1. Combine the cornstarch and cool rice wine; stir to dissolve the cornstarch, and then set aside for later use.

2. In a wok, heat the vegetable oil over a high flame until the oil just starts to smoke. Add the scallions to the wok and stir-fry briefly (20 seconds); immediately add the finely chopped pork to the wok, all while moving the ingredients around in the wok.

3. Continue to cook the pork in the wok for approximately 2 minutes, or long enough for it to get hot. Then add the remaining ingredients, including the cornstarch/rice wine mixture from step 1.

(continues)

Char Sui Bao
(continued)

4. Continue to cook all of the ingredients in the wok until the liquid begins to thicken. Take the wok off of the heat, and transfer the mixture to a metal container to allow the filling to cool.

5. Set the filling in a refrigerator to cool before using it to make the stuffed buns.

For Forming and Steaming the Buns

1. Prepare the steamer setup: use either a bamboo steamer on top of a wok (the traditional method) or a commercial or stovetop steamer setup.

2. To form the buns, take one piece of the dough and flatten it in the palm of your clean, sanitized hand. Place a couple of tablespoons of the pork filling in the center of the dough, and close your fingers to form the dough around the pork filling, pinching off the top of the dough as you do so.

3. Place the formed pork-filled bun on a piece of parchment paper, and place the bun with the paper on one of the steamer trays.

4. Continue steps 2 and 3 with the remaining pieces of dough and pork filling until all of the pork buns have been formed and are set inside steamer trays (but are not touching one another; it may be necessary to cook the pork buns in batches if they do not fit in your steamer setup all at once).

5. Place the steamer trays with the pork buns in the steamer setup, and steam over high heat for about 12 minutes or until the buns are cooked throughout.

6. Remove the buns from the steamer when done, and serve immediately.

Har Cheung Fun SOUTHERN CHINA
(SHRIMP-FILLED STEAMED RICE ROLLS)

INGREDIENTS

For Marinating the Shrimp

1.5	lbs	Shrimp, peeled and deveined (about 2 lbs unpeeled)
3	oz	Rice Wine (Chinese Rice Wine; called Shao-Xing or Shao Hsing)
1	oz	Ginger, minced
2	oz	Light Soy Sauce

Rice and seafood are central components of the cuisine in the south, and rice-wrapped and steamed dishes are common in Cantonese cooking. This recipe utilizes these two in a simple preparation that highlights the quality of the shrimp.

YIELD: 24 portions (4 ounces/portion)

MIXING METHOD (RICE DOUGH): Boiling Liquid

COOKING METHOD: Steaming

PROCEDURE

For Marinating the Shrimp

1. Combine the peeled and deveined shrimp with the rice wine, ginger, and soy sauce, and allow marinating for 30–60 minutes.

(continues)

★

Har Cheung Fun
(continued)

For Making the Rice Dough

1	lb	Rice Flour
4	oz	Tapioca Starch (sometimes called cassava or tapioca flour)
28	oz	Boiling Water (boil more than 28 oz and measure just before adding)
4	oz +	Tapioca Starch (you may need more when rolling out)

For Making and Serving the Rolls

		Rice Dough (see above)
		Marinated Shrimp (see above)
4	oz	Soy Sauce
4	oz	Peanut Oil
1	bunch	Scallions, sliced very thin on a bias

For Making the Rice Dough

(**NOTE:** *You can use rice wrapper instead, but this yields a better texture.*)

1. In a mixing bowl, combine the rice flour with the first 4 oz of tapioca starch, and mix well to combine.

2. Add the boiling water (measuring the water just before adding), and mix together using a wooden spoon to form a smooth dough (this can also be made in a mixer with a paddle attachment).

3. Cover the dough with plastic wrap or a clean, damp towel, and set it aside to rest for 15 minutes before proceeding to the next step.

4. Once the dough has rested and cooled, divide it into 24 equal portions (about 2 oz each). Roll each portion into an 1/8-inch-thick sheet or circle (using the additional tapioca starch to dust the workbench to prevent sticking), and stack the rolled rice dough pieces between pieces of divider paper and a very light dusting of the tapioca starch.

For Making and Serving the Rolls

1. Set up a steamer arrangement and start preheating the water (make sure the steamer can hold whatever size plates you are going to steam the rolls on).

2. To form each roll, place about an ounce of the marinated shrimp in the center of the rice dough sheet, and fold the dough over the shrimp from both sides to wrap the shrimp completely in dough.

(continues)

Har cheung fun (shrimp-filled steamed rice rolls)

Har Cheung Fun
(continued)

3. Place each shrimp roll on a plate (use a heatproof plate only; this will be placed in a steamer) with the seam created from folding on the bottom (against the plate).

4. Continue steps 2 and 3 to roll all of the shrimp. Make sure that, as they are placed on the plates, the rolls are not overlapping or touching one another so they will cook evenly.

5. When you are ready to cook the rolls, place them inside the steamer setup and steam for 8–10 minutes to cook them throughout (the shrimp should be pink, and the dough should become firm). Serve with 1 tsp of soy sauce and 1 tsp of peanut oil drizzled over each roll on a serving plate, topped with the green onion slivers.

Har Yeun   SOUTHERN CHINA

(SHRIMP BALLS)

INGREDIENTS

For Making the Mixture

1	lb	Tiger Shrimp (any size), peeled and deveined (remember to save the shells—they can be used in many applications, such as shrimp broth, shrimp butter, etc.)
1	Tbsp	Soy Sauce
1	Tbsp	Rice Wine
2	tsp	Oyster Sauce
2		Egg Whites
1	tsp	Sugar
1	Tbsp	Peanut Oil
2	Tbsp	Cilantro, minced
1	bunch	Scallions, green section and roots removed, and minced finely
2	qts	Cold Water

For Cooking the Shrimp Balls

1	gal	Water
2	Tbsp	Salt

These shrimp balls are a common component of the varied cuisines of southern China; they are included in Cantonese cuisine recipes and are eaten by Hakka and Chiu Chow populations in the south. The mixture is sometimes used to fill dumplings (as in Cantonese dim sum), and the balls are also cooked and eaten with dipping sauces or used in soups.

YIELD: 1.25 pounds of mixture, or 25–30 shrimp balls (.75 ounce/ball)

MIXING METHOD: Protein Emulsion from Hand Chopping/Mixing

COOKING METHOD: Boiling

PROCEDURE

For Making the Mixture

1. Cut the shrimp into small pieces (approximately 1/4 inch in diameter).

2. Place the cut pieces of shrimp on a large cutting board. Using either a chef's knife or a cleaver, mince/chop the shrimp pieces into a paste (this will take a little time and require a lot of chopping, but it is important to do this by hand).

3. Once the shrimp mixture is beginning to look like a paste, start to drizzle in the soy sauce, rice wine, and oyster sauce while continuing to chop and fold the mixture (watch your fingers, and be sure to keep the liquids in the shrimp mixture and don't allow them to drain away).

4. Once all of the liquids have been added, add the egg whites to a mixing bowl and whip them until they become foamy and light (not so much that they become soft peaks, but enough that they trap a good amount of air).

(continues)

Har Yeun
(continued)

5. Transfer the shrimp mixture to the bowl with the whipped egg whites, and gently mix the two together while adding the sugar; slowly drizzle in the oil.

6. Once all of the oil has been added, fold in the minced scallions and cilantro.

7. Once the mixture is done, the balls can be formed. To do this, you will need a clean workstation, clean and sanitized hands, the shrimp mixture, cold water, a clean spoon, and a container to hold the finished balls.

8. Dip both hands in the cold water so they are wet.

9. Dip the spoon in the cold water and scoop out a small amount of the shrimp mixture. Using your wet hands, form a small ball of the shrimp mixture (about an inch in diameter) and transfer it to the container (it is a good idea to put a little water in the container as well, to help keep the balls from sticking together).

10. Continue to form the shrimp mixture until all of it has been used up.

For Cooking the Shrimp Balls

1. Place the water and salt in a pot on the stove; heat over a high flame, and bring the water to a boil.

2. Once the water reaches a boil, add the shrimp balls to the pot; cook for 3 minutes once the pot returns to a boil.

3. Immediately remove the pot from the heat, and remove the shrimp balls gently using a slotted spoon or a wire basket. If you are not serving them immediately, place the shrimp balls in cold water to prevent them from overcooking, and reheat them when ready to serve.

NOTE: *This recipe describes how to cook the shrimp mixture, but it can also be used as a filling for dumplings or cooked and served in soups.*

SUMMARY

Chinese cuisine is one of the most varied in the world, and the typical diet is linked with the Chinese philosophy of balance. Although Chinese cuisine has been influenced by other cultures—with India, the Persian Empire, and European traders having the most significant impact—it has had an even more important influence on the development of other cuisines outside its borders. The cuisines of China are often viewed regionally, with the major cuisine centers being Beijing in the north, Shanghai in the center and east, Sichuan in the west, and Canton in the south. Whereas Chinese cuisine centers on rice, wheat is more common in much of the northern country, and the accompaniments to the main starches are almost as numerous as the nearly 2 billion inhabitants of this culinary superpower. Beyond the daily rice or other grain intake, the Chinese diet is extremely varied; these adventurous and efficient people have included in their diet seemingly everything that is edible in the country.

REVIEW QUESTIONS

1. Chinese philosophy is entwined with the dietary habits of the country; discuss this connection—in particular, the yin and yang association of foods.

2. The cuisine of northern China differs significantly from that of southern China. What are some of the distinctions between these areas?

3. The cooking methods employed in Chinese cuisine are varied and utilize techniques not commonly found in European cuisines. What are some of the methods that make Chinese cuisine unique?

COMMON TERMS, FOODS, AND INGREDIENTS

Some of the terms used in this chapter are phonetic spellings of common Chinese terms that are used in the culinary arena. Because these are phonetic spellings, they may be spelled a little differently in other sources, but they should prove helpful for understanding Chinese cooking.

✳ Common Ingredients

Sauces and Other Prepared Ingredients

chao tian jiao – Small red chili that is commonly dried and used in Chinese cooking, especially in Sichuan cuisine

dou ban jiang – Chili paste made from fermented chiles and fava beans; this can be found in various stages of maturity and is commonly used in Sichuan cooking

dou chi – Fermented black beans; actually green soybeans that have been fermented and often have ginger, chiles, and rice wine added to the mixture

dou fu ru – Fermented bean curd

er jin tiao – Chili type used to make dou ban jiang

hong you – Chili oil

lao zao – Fermented glutinous rice wine

oyster sauce – Sauce from Guangdong in southern China

✳ Common Recipes and Ingredients

bao – Steamed wheat bun

bao zi – Filled steamed bun

char siu – Cantonese roasted pork, typically made with red food coloring to dye the meat red

char siu bao – Roast pork-filled steamed buns, made with leftover char siu

cheung fun – Steamed rice roll

chiao-tzu – Pot stickers in the style of Beijing (translates to "little dumplings")

congee – Rice porridge-like dish with various toppings

fan – Rice

gan bian si ji dou – Spicy stir-fried green beans

gan hai jiao – Dried chiles

go – Fried cake

goh – Dumpling

gong bao – Called kung pao in the United States, this is typically made with chicken that is stir-fried with chiles, vegetables, and peanuts

hong shao gai – Red cooked chicken

hong shao rou – Red cooked pork belly

hong shao yu – Red cooked fish

jiaozi – Dumplings

mantou – Steamed bun

shao-xing – Chinese rice wine (very different from Japanese rice wine)

shi ji tau – "Lion's head"; large pork meatballs braised with bok choy

suan la rou si tang – Hot and sour soup

tang cu li ji – Sweet and sour pork

wor tip – Pot stickers in the style of Shanghai (said to be their place of origin)

xiaolongbao – Steamed dumpling from the southern region, filled with a gelatinous seasoned pork mixture that becomes soup-like when cooked, resulting in a steamed bun with liquid filling

✳ Cooking Methods and Equipment

Methods

ban – To toss prepared foods in a sauce

chao – Stir frying

chao xiang – Stir frying in infused oils

chui – Technique of using the back of a cleaver to pummel or mash a product; often done to meats to tenderize them

gan bian – Deep frying

hong shao – Cooking method known as "red" cooking that relies on soy sauce, rice wine, sugar, and aromatics, which are used to slowly simmer or braise the desired meat, poultry, or fish. This method is common to the Shanghai region.

kao – Roasting

ma wei – Marinating

pao – Brining/brined

shao – Method of bringing food and a seasoned liquid to a boil, and then lowering heat to gently poach/simmer the food until it is tender and the liquid has thickened

shu zi bei – Roll-cut technique for cutting long vegetables (such as carrots), in which the vegetable is rolled a quarter turn after each cut to yield relatively even-sized cuts

zheng – Steaming

Equipment

cai dao – Chinese cleaver

cai dun – Cutting board; typically a slice of tree trunk that has been treated with salt and oil. The best boards are made from dense trees such as honey locust, ginkgo, and Chinese olive.

chao guo – Wok; these are typically made of iron and must be properly seasoned and thoroughly dried after each use, or they will rust

dian fan guo – Rice cooker

kuai zi – Long chopsticks used for cooking

piao zi – Wok ladle

shao ji – Bamboo basket

zhao li – Wire mesh strainer with a bamboo handle

zheng long – Steamer

zhu shua – Wok brush made of bamboo bristles

✳ Cultural

yang – Forces of light; associated with the exterior of the body, the gallbladder, stomach, intestines, and bladder. Symptoms of problems within these areas are thought to be caused by an excess of yang, and relief may be sought by including more yin foods in one's diet. Also a term used to describe a part of Chinese philosophy that separates foods based on their inherent effect on the human body; effects are described either as hot and warming, with associations with energy and fire, or as cold and cooling, with associations with calming and ice.

yin – Forces of dark; associated with the heart, liver, spleen, kidneys, and lungs. Symptoms of problems within these areas are thought to be caused by an excess of yin, and relief may be sought through an increase in yang foods.

CHAPTER 18

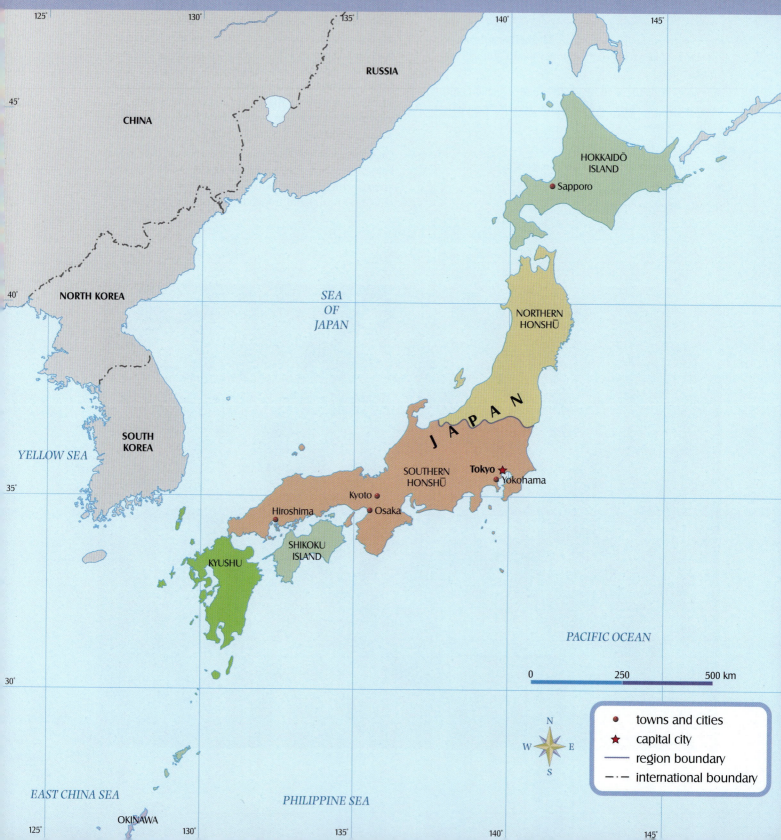

125°   130°   135°   140°   145°

45°

RUSSIA

CHINA

HOKKAIDŌ
ISLAND

● Sapporo

40°

NORTH KOREA

SEA
OF
JAPAN

NORTHERN
HONSHŪ

J A P A N

YELLOW SEA

SOUTH
KOREA

SOUTHERN
HONSHŪ

Tokyo ★

● Yokohama

35°

Kyoto ●

Hiroshima ●

● Osaka

SHIKOKU
ISLAND

KYUSHU

PACIFIC OCEAN

0   250   500 km

30°

N
W   E
S

● towns and cities
★ capital city
—— region boundary
–·–·– international boundary

EAST CHINA SEA

PHILIPPINE SEA

OKINAWA

125°   130°   135°   140°   145°

Japanese Cuisine

OBJECTIVES

Upon completion of this chapter, you will be able to

- discuss what makes Japanese cuisine unique from others.
- identify the major religion of Japan.
- discuss the importance of the tea ceremony in Japanese culture and how it has played a role in the development of Japanese cuisine.
- discuss the importance of rice in Japanese cuisine.
- prepare some of the recipes that are common in Japan.
- define the terms listed at the conclusion of the chapter.

INTRODUCTION

Japanese cuisine is unique in a number of ways, and if only one word were to be used to describe the difference, it would be *natural*. Many cuisines focus on seasonal ingredients but none to the extent of Japanese cuisine, in which ingredients are altered little to highlight their natural characteristics, and the entire event of eating is centered around seasons. Whether it is the color of china chosen, the color of the ornaments on the table, the method by which the ingredients are presented, or the traditional ingredients that symbolize a particular season, the Japanese take eating to another level in connecting it with nature.

The presentation of food in Japan is very important, and the Japanese are responsible for a great deal of the techniques and expertise that have spread to restaurant kitchens with regard to garnishes and elaborate presentations. The beauty of sushi is well known to most Americans, but many don't realize that most Japanese dishes are presented in attractive ways and in small pieces (nearly everything is eaten with chopsticks). The majority of dishes are presented simply and beautifully, and each item is usually presented separately, including sauces. This style of eating allows each person to control how much sauce, wasabi, or other accompaniment he or she would like to add to the food. In addition to this focus on presentation and separation of each component, all meals typically include rice.

Japan now produces more rice than it consumes, but this wasn't the case just 50 years ago when rice was not always available to the lower-income population. Rice is a daily ingredient for virtually all Japanese; in fact, the word for cooked rice (*gohan*) actually translates to "meal." The importance of this grain in Japan's daily life cannot be overstated.

Historically, Japan has been significantly influenced by Korea and China, but Japan also went through an extended period of isolation that enabled the country's cuisine to develop largely internally. As a result of this period, during which most of the country ate a vegetarian diet focused on simplicity and harmony with nature, the cuisine is significantly different from those of its neighboring countries. Only relatively recently has the general population of Japan begun to eat meat dishes; the diet is still primarily based on seafood, vegetables, and rice.

Although Japanese cuisine is first and foremost a rice-based cuisine, to a typical Westerner the impressive difference is the array of seafood that is available and utilized. On a typical day in Japanese markets, nearly 3,000 kinds of seafood products move from the seas to the kitchens. This variety, along with the Japanese expertise with foods that come from the sea, is what is usually most impressive to the Western chef.

HISTORIC CULINARY INFLUENCES

The most substantial outside influences on Japanese cuisine are without a doubt from neighbors China and Korea, with both philosophical and religious ideas crossing the seas and playing significant roles in its development. One of the most important aspects of influence is the religious one. The ideals of the native beliefs of the Shinto religion were combined with the beliefs of Buddhism coming from China and Korea, and resulted in a culinary belief about the sacredness of animals, which were originally excluded for the most part from the Japanese diet. Another very important transfer of ideas regarded the cultivation of rice, and a diet based mainly on rice, vegetables, and seafood became the norm in Japan.

In more recent times, Japan also was influenced by European nations during their period of exploration, including the introduction of the same ingredients that were spreading across Europe from the Americas. This period was followed by a nearly three-century-long period of isolation that may have had nearly as much impact on the development of the current Japanese cuisine as any other influence.

Early Culture

The early cultures of Japan developed into mostly settled civilizations as techniques in agriculture and food production enabled these people to do so. A number of cultures have lived on the islands that today constitute Japan; some of the most prominent are the Ainu people of the island of Hokkaidō, the Ryukyuan of the southern islands of Japan, and what are now commonly referred to as the Yamato people, who form the majority of the population of present-day Japan and

who lived on the island of what is today called Honshū. These early peoples relied on the products of the sea as well as what was cultivated on the islands. Although not much is known about the culinary habits of these people, we do know that they learned about cultivating rice from mainland Asia (probably China) and that the Yamato people followed a religion that revered nature and the natural. This religion is known as *Shinto,* and it is believed that the religion's reverence for the natural world is largely responsible for Japan's focus on maintaining foods in their natural state to highlight their qualities. The tea ceremony and its focus on nature, seasonality, and nature as art also is believed to be related to the Shinto religion.

China and Korea

Many of the foods that are fundamental to Japanese cuisine were introduced to Japan by China and Korea. The most important of these introductions formed the basis of modern Japanese cuisine, much as it did for the last three millennia: the introduction and cultivation of rice (uncooked rice is called *kome*) allowed for the development of civilization in Japan.

The introduction of ingredients and cultivation techniques from China and Korea played an important role in developing the emerging Japanese cuisine, but the introduction of Buddhism from China may have had a bigger impact in the long run. As part of the religious principles of Buddhism, killing animals was mostly forbidden, and thus the availability and social acceptance of meats waned. Buddhism has been largely accepted in Japan, where this respect for other living beings coincides with the Shinto beliefs in the importance of nature and the natural. Together, Shinto and Buddhism are the most common religions among the Japanese today—more than 90% of the population declare themselves followers of one or both. With this focus on vegetables and grains as the main sources of nutrition, the cuisine of Japan has become one of the world's healthiest. Although it has become much more common in today's Japan for people to consume meat products, the basis of the cuisine remains rice, noodles, vegetables, and seafood. These components still define Japanese cuisine today.

Portugal and European Contact

In the sixteenth century, Portuguese explorers and traders were the first Europeans to make contact with the Japanese, and they quickly introduced new ingredients and techniques to the country's cuisine. One of the most significant introductions at this time was the method of battering and deep frying foods, which developed into the current tempura cooking style. The Portuguese deep-fried cod with a light batter, a method that was adapted and altered over time. This was a significant change from typical Japanese cooking methods at this time, as very little fat was used prior to this introduction.

The Portuguese were not the only European nation to come in contact with Japan during this very important period of history; some other significant influences included Holland, Spain, and England. These traders brought their religions as well as new ingredients from Europe and, perhaps more significantly, the New World. During this period, Japan was introduced to *jaga-imo* (potatoes), *satsuma-imo* (sweet potatoes), *pīman* (chiles), and *tōmorokoshi* (corn).

Isolation

Following European contact with Japan and the resulting religious influence felt in the country, the new rulers of Japan started what became a nearly 300-year period of isolation, from 1600 to 1868. Although this period did not result in significant influence from outside sources, it did result in a maturation of Japanese cuisine at a time when many cuisines were changing. During this period, Japanese cuisine developed much of the refinement that characterizes it today.

Shortly before this period began, Sen-No-Rikkyu formalized the etiquette and procedure of formal tea ceremonies, which became more popular and elaborate. The focus on proper colors, arrangements, and dishes seen in tea ceremonies also began to apply to food and its seasonality. These traditions continued to be refined throughout this period and are a fundamental part of current Japanese customs in their approach to food and drink.

UNIQUE COMPONENTS

Japanese cuisine differs significantly from the perception that most Americans may have, courtesy of the sushi and tempura that are commonly found in U.S. restaurants; the forms these foods currently take developed relatively recently (in the case of sushi) and essentially are a European import (in the case of tempura). Much of the traditional Japanese cuisine is based on cookery of vegetables and seafood in dishes that most Americans have never seen. It is not just the products that make Japanese cuisine different from many others, but also the philosophy of food's role in daily life—as we shall see.

Tea Ceremony and Presentation

The tea ceremony developed over several centuries following the introduction of tea to Japan from China. Partly because of this ritual, performed by the upper class, an appreciation and reverence for the natural was heightened in Japan. Buddhism teaches an appreciation for nature, and the natural state of one's environment has been a part of Japanese culture for centuries; this focus only grew with the development of the tea ceremony in Japan. The objective of the tea ceremony is for a host to create an atmosphere of beauty and comfort for his/her guests, attend to their needs, and thus allow those in attendance to marvel at what the natural world offers. In terms of the culinary aspects of the tea ceremony, foods and their presentation are carefully chosen, and this focus is one of the components that are currently found in many aspects of Japanese cuisine.

Kaiseki is the light meal served with a traditional Japanese tea ceremony, and the foods chosen would be seasonal vegetables, cooked to highlight their specific qualities and presented in a manner that accentuates their beauty. This focus on the qualities of an ingredient, on the presentation of the item, and on cooking an item to highlight its intrinsic characteristics is a hallmark of Japanese cuisine. The tea ceremony may have been the vehicle that introduced this philosophy of cooking to the Japanese, but it is evident now in other aspects of the cuisine as well. Sushi is a fine example of this philosophy; many traditionalists believe that sushi is its best simply as seasoned rice and raw fish with a small amount of soy sauce and wasabi, undistracted by mayonnaise-based sauces, avocado, cream cheese, or other ingredients that have been added to sushi in recent years.

Another common tradition in Japanese cuisine highlights the natural beauty of ingredients by presenting foods without masking them with other ingredients and using elaborate garnishes to mimic their natural components. Again, the tea ceremony and the foods eaten as part of this tradition increased the focus on this aspect of the cuisine. Japanese cuisine has long been appreciated for the complex garnish work used to display foods, as well as the retention of natural flavors and appearances by limiting alterations when cooking and presenting foods. Japanese presentation is unique in both the craftsmanship and skill displayed by the garniture as well as the tendency to keep ingredients separate and unmasked. In Japanese presentation, the components of a presented dish will often be keep separate in order to ensure that each part is notable in the presentation.

Although most people in modern Japan do not practice the tea ceremony in all of its ritualized form, the impact of its philosophy on the aesthetics of food presentation and order has been significant. Food presentation has been one of Japan's defining culinary features for many years, and this aspect of the cuisine helps set it apart from others.

Seaweed

Seaweed is a central part of Japanese cuisine, and it is used in many aspects of traditional foods. Because it is an island nation, Japan has long looked to the sea for sustenance, and the wealth of algae growths that are found in the waters surrounding this nation were recognized for their high nutritional quality early in Japan's history. Several types of seaweed are used regularly in the cuisine, ranging from kelp types to very small seaweeds, with the most common usage being a dried form for use after reconstitution.

Kombu is a type of dried seaweed that resembles kelp and is used to make *dashi* (seaweed stock), which is used in many Japanese dishes—ranging from a base for soups and sauces to a cooking liquid for vegetables. *Wakame* is a type of seaweed used to make miso soups or salads. *Nori* is a dried sheet of small seaweed that is grown on nets in the Pacific; most would recognize it as the outer wrapper used to make sushi rolls. *Kanten* (also called *agar agar*) is extracted from a type of seaweed and used much like gelatin is in the United States, because it will thicken a liquid when cooled. *Hijiki* is used to make simple dashi-based soups as well as in stir-fry dishes and salads. *Arame* is brown seaweed used to make salads and cooked with vegetables. Of these, kombu is the most significant, because dashi stock is used extensively in Japanese cooking. Dashi provides the foundation for many Japanese foods, much the way meat and vegetable stocks do for many European dishes. Although kombu plays a central role in the cuisine, all of these varieties are common components and provide a unique texture, taste, and nutritional benefit to the typical diet.

Seafood, Rice, and Vegetables

Japan historically has subsisted off of the bounty from the ocean or the fields. Rice is a daily ingredient in the diet, and the typical meal revolves around it. The thought of eating without rice is simply not part of the Japanese culture—a meal is thought to consist of rice with other food. This is one aspect of Japanese cuisine that is often difficult for Westerners to grasp, as it is not very common in many Western cultures (especially the United States) to eat a single food on such a consistent basis. The rice varieties that form the backbone of Japanese cuisine are short grain: the non-glutinous varieties (*uruchi mai*) are used for most preparations, such as gohan and *su-meshi* (vinegar rice for sushi), and the glutinous varieties—also called *mochi gome* (sweet rice)—are used mostly for sweet preparations or savory *mochi* (glutinous rice dough that may be grilled).

In addition to rice, the typical Japanese meal is likely to include vegetables as well, and many are eaten after being steamed or pickled. Soybeans are a main vegetable that highlights the ingenuity of the Japanese in creating food products, because soybeans are used to produce tofu, tempeh, soy sauce, miso, soy nuts, and, in their fresh form, *edamame*. As previously mentioned, seaweeds are also a significant part of the traditional cuisine, and both soy and seaweed products are common components of a Japanese meal (along with rice, of course).

The Japanese dependence on plant foods is linked to their early religious beliefs. The major religion of Japan is Buddhism, which includes a belief that living animals should be treated with care and never harmed. In centuries past, this belief meant that strict followers of the religion (including monks) would not eat meat or even seafood but only plant foods. In time, the restrictions were relaxed to allow for the inclusion of seafood, as it was believed that fish and shellfish were not part of the same animal group as land animals. This inclusion of seafood led to a significant cultural focus on harvesting products of the sea. The Japanese developed a sophisticated fishing culture and learned to farm sea products such as seaweed. This focus on products of the sea, rice, and vegetables became a regular part of the culinary culture.

In Japan today, fundamental Buddhists still follow the vegetarian diet of ancient times, but a large part of population now eats a significant amount of seafood as well as a number of meat sources.

Specialists

When dining out, the Japanese appreciate and look for those who can prepare a particular style of food well, which has resulted in a profusion of specialty shops across Japan. Whether one is looking for *sushi* (vinegar-seasoned rice with various toppings), *ramen* (noodle soups), *tempura* (battered and fried foods), *sembei* (rice cakes), *soba* (noodles made with buckwheat flour), *yakitori* (grilled chicken skewers), *unagi* (dishes made with freshwater eel), or *tonkatsu* (breaded and deep-fried pork cutlets), there are shops that are specifically dedicated to these items. In Japan, a shop that makes one item is highly regarded, and many will stand in line to get their yakitori, soba, or another specific item from these specialized shops.

SIGNIFICANT SUBREGIONS

Japan is made up of a chain of almost 4,000 islands that stretch for more than 1,500 miles through the Pacific Ocean and off the coast of mainland Asia. Four main islands constitute the main part of Japan: Hokkaidō, Honshū, Shikoku, and Kyūshū. The vast majority of Japanese people live on these islands. Honshū is the largest and includes the cities of Tokyo, Yokohama, Osaka, Hiroshima, and Kyoto.

Japanese cuisine does not have the stark regional variations and contrasts that many other cuisines do; however, specialties can be found within the regions, as well as significant differences between local ingredients. The principles of simplicity, seasonality, and presentation are found throughout the country and probably can be attributed to factors such as religion and historic periods. Much of the continuity of Japanese cuisine can be attributed to the significant period of isolation and nationalism that Japan experienced, resulting in more of a national cuisine than a regional one. Unlike countries like Italy, which historically has had its political boundaries changed and many different ethnic groups living in different regions, Japan has experienced a more homogenous history.

Although sushi can be found in all regions of Japan, and the practice of eating *miso* soup in the morning is a national tradition, there are still variations that exist depending on what region is being examined. The following guide focuses on some of the specialties and variations found across the regions, but any differences should be examined in the context of a primarily familiar tone throughout the country. The principles of following seasons, bringing nature into the kitchen, and appreciating simplicity and authenticity run throughout all of the regions as a basis for the cuisine. The following regions are organized from north to south.

Hokkaidō Island

The northernmost of Japan's islands is also the most sparsely inhabited and coldest, and thus has a more simple cuisine than much of the rest of the country. This region is well known for the quality salmon found in the many rivers than run from the mountains of the island; it is also the source of much of the limited cattle and dairy products produced in Japan. This region has harsh, cold winters and short summers, and as such it has long been dependent on the fertile cold waters that surround it for sustenance. It was once home to the Ainu people, and small populations still can be found among sections of the island. The Ainu lived off of the local ingredients and contributed the technique of cooking a variety of ingredients in a large pot over a fire that evolved into today's *nabemono* (hotpot dish), of which this region has many versions. The most common and prized result of this style of cooking is the *ishikari-nabe* (salmon, tofu, and miso hotpot), which may contain many local ingredients but includes salmon, miso, and tofu in most versions.

This region is heavily dependent on the products of the ocean; many of the prized products are caught in the waters off of this island and include *sake* (salmon), *kani* (crab), *tara* (Pacific cod), *kaki* (oyster), *masu* (pink salmon), *ika* (squid), and the *konbu* (kelp) that is used to make *dashi* (seaweek stock) all across the country. This region is also one of the prime ranching areas of Japan and produces some of the best *hitsuji* (lamb) and *gyūnikū* (beef), which are featured on many local menus.

Because this is the most northern section of Japan, the climate is not conducive to growing rice; rather, crops of *komugi* (wheat), *tōmorokoshi* (corn), and jaga-imo (potatoes) are often found here. In addition to the many different nabe (hotpots) that are a significant part of this region's cuisine, other specialty products and recipes include many examples of noodles and noodle dishes such as *ramen* (thin wheat noodles), *ika-sōmen* (squid with wheat flour noodles), and noodle soups made by adding *udon* or other noodles to the broth that remains after making a nabe or *shabu shabu* (thinly sliced meats served with simmered broth). Other local specialties include *jingisukan* (barbequed lamb or mutton and vegetables), *tako-shabu* (octopus hotpot), *ruibe* (frozen salmon sliced paper thin and served with soy dipping sauce), and rice dishes such as *kani-meshi* (rice with crab) and *ika meshi* (rice with squid).

Northern Honshū

The northern portion of the main island of Japan is less populated than the southern part of the island and is also the main rice-producing area. This is a more rural area with significant agricultural production. This region is mostly mountainous and colder than the southern reaches, and as such the cuisine is heartier and heavily based on soups. The region also has a rich tradition of fishing and plentiful seafood from the cold waters that surround it. Because this is a colder region, soups are a common part of the local cuisine; many examples of soups and noodle dishes can be found here.

Some of the ingredients that are common in the local cuisine of this region include kome, *hotategai* (scallops), *awabi* (abalone), tara, *uni* (sea urchin), kaki, *miso* (fermented soybean paste), soba, and *goma* (sesame seeds). Using these ingredients—as well as others that are common throughout Japan—many of the local foods are created in the traditional methods of Japanese cookery, including simmering, steaming, and stewing. Soups such as *fuka-hire* (shark's fin soup), *ichigoni* (abalone and sea urchin soup), and *jappa-juri* (cod and miso soup) are all common in this region, and soba noodles are commonly eaten cold as *wanko-soba*. In addition to its soba noodles, this region is also known for producing excellent *o-sake* (rice wine), which is enjoyed with many of the fine products of the sea from the cold northern waters.

Southern Honshū

This region includes many of the major cities of Japan, including Tokyo, Osaka, Kyoto, and Hiroshima, and is thus home to the majority of the population. Because this is a very populated area, there is less space dedicated to agriculture, and the region relies on other areas for many of its products. The major cities are home to virtually every type of eating establishment found in Japan, from *sushi-ya* (sushi specialty restaurant), *teppanyaki* (restaurant specializing in griddle-cooked foods), *tempura* (restaurant specializing in batter-fried foods), or *men-dokoro* (restaurant specializing in noodle dishes) to *nabemono-ryōri-ya* (restaurant specializing in hotpot foods) and *shabu-shabu* (restaurant specializing in thinly sliced meats cooked tableside); these establishments carry on the traditions of Japanese cuisine from all over the country. Variation is the overall theme of the cuisine of this region, with most styles found throughout the country readily available in these cities.

Shikoku Island

This island features fertile soil and abundant seafood surrounding its shores. Like most other sections of Japan, seafood is the main component of this region, but it is also known for products made from locally grown wheat as well (the region does not get enough regular rainfall to support much rice production). The island also produces citrus and Asian pears in significant quantities for the rest of Japan.

This region is a large producer of a number of tree crops, including *mikan* (mandarin oranges), a unique type of citrus called *yuzu*, and *nashi* (Asian pears), all of which are common components in the local cuisine when in season. In addition, this region is known for its excellent wheat noodles, including udon and the fine wheat noodles called sōmen. The local waters yield an excellent seaweed called *wakame* as well as the ever important *katsuo* (bonito), which is dried to make dashi (seaweed and bonito stock) or cooked fresh in preparations such as *katsuo no tataki* (bonito cooked quickly on a grill). Other notable sea products include *tai* (sea bream), *iwashi* (sardines), and the river crabs called *magani*. Some of the specialty recipes from this region include *kake-udon* (wheat noodles in broth), *tai-meshi* (rice with sea bream), *ponzu* (sauce made from yuzu juice, soy sauce, mirin, rice vinegar, and dashi), and *oshinuki-zushi* (pressed sushi with mackerel).

Kyūshū

Kyūshū is the southernmost of the large islands and, as such, has a subtropical climate that is home to many fruits and other ingredients that are not able to grow in the colder north. This island is subject to periodic typhoons, which have been known to wipe out the rice crops and have resulted in the inclusion of other main foods in the event of such an occurrence. The cuisine here, as in the other regions of Japan, is dependent on the fruits of the sea complemented by rice or noodles.

On the northern end of this island are the Ariake tidelands, which yield a number of prized species such as *hamaguri* (clams), kani, and nori. Other ingredients used in the local cuisine of this region are *fugu* (blowfish), sweetfish from the rivers called *ayu*, yellow wheat noodles called *ramen*, satsuma-imo, *biwa* (loquats), and *renkon* (lotus root), as well as numerous *sakana* (fish) and *kai* (shellfish) from the local waters. Some of the specialty products and recipes from this region include *tonkotsu* (caramelized pork; unlike the breaded cutlets in other parts of

Japan), ramen, and *basashi* (thinly sliced raw horse-meat served with soy sauce).

Okinawa

This southernmost island of Japan covered in this chapter has the most tropical and unstable climate, as well as significant historical influences from Southeast Asia and Portugal. The island is subject to typhoons, which can devastate local crops and have resulted in an affinity for tubers (such as sweet potatoes) and a reliance on products from the sea. Okinawa was once an independent island that traded extensively not only with China and Korea—as did mainland Japan—but also with Southeast Asia and, later, Portuguese traders. As a result of these influences, a number of dishes commonly found in this part of Japan bear a resemblance to Southeast Asian and European cuisine. This region is the most distant in terms of techniques and influences from those of the previously discussed main islands of Japan. The food of Okinawa tends to be more aggressive and heavily spiced than what is found in the larger islands of Japan and also reveals influences from China and Southeast Asia.

Some of the ingredients common to this region are beni imo, *shima-dōfu* (dense soybean cake), *goya* (bitter melon), *nabera* (winter melon), *butaniku* (pork), *hiijaa* (goat), *unjanaba* (water spinach), ika, and seaweed called *hijiki* and *mozuku*. Influences from cultures other than the main islands of Japan are evident in some of the local dishes, such as *andagi* (Okinawan doughnuts), *chanpuru* (stir-fried dishes), *rafute* (pork stewed with soy sauce, miso, and ginger), and *jimami dufu* (peanut tofu).

RECIPES

The following recipes provide some insight into Japanese cuisine. When making these recipes, remember that Japanese cuisine is strongly defined by seasonality and the purity of ingredients. Thus, these dishes will highlight high-quality ingredients or, conversely, expose poor-quality ingredients.

Ichiban Dashi JAPAN
(STRONGER SEAWEED STOCK)

INGREDIENTS

1	gal	Water
4	oz	Konbu
1/4	cup	Katsuo-Bushi

This main component of Japanese cooking is used to cook vegetables and make soups, and it is the base of many sauces as well. Without it, the overall taste of Japanese cuisine cannot be fully appreciated. The konbu and bonito can be reserved to make a second stock called niban dashi that has a more subtle flavor.

YIELD: 3.5 quarts

COOKING METHOD: Boiling and Infusing

Dashi (seaweed stock) in a bowl with the ingredients used to make it: kombu (dried kelp) and bonito flakes in front of the bowl

PROCEDURE

1. Place the konbu and water in an appropriately sized pot, and set aside for 1 hour.

2. Place the pot over a medium-high flame and heat mixture just to a boil. Remove the pot from heat once it has reached a boil. Remove the konbu, reserving it to use in a second dashi. (If you are not making a second dashi, leave the konbu in the pot until the end.)

3. Add the katsuo-bushi to the pot, and set the pot aside for 45 minutes (without stirring).

4. Strain off the resulting broth, saving the katsuo-bushi for the second dashi (if you are making it); the dashi is ready for use.

Niban Dashi JAPAN
(LIGHTER SEAWEED STOCK)

INGREDIENTS

1	gal	Water
		Reserved Konbu and Katsuo-Bushi (from first dashi)
1/4	cup	Katsuo-Bushi

This version of dashi is commonly made with the strained konbu and bonito as a way to be more efficient, and to prepare a lighter stock for desired applications (poaching light vegetables, for example).

YIELD: 3 quarts

COOKING METHOD: Simmering

PROCEDURE

1. Place the reserved konbu and katsuo-bushi and the water in an appropriately sized pot, and bring the mixture to a boil; once a boil is reached, reduce the heat to a light simmer.

2. Simmer over a low flame until reduced by approximately 20% (about 30 minutes).

3. Add the katsuo-bushi to the pot, and set the pot aside for 30 minutes (without stirring).

4. Strain off the resulting broth, and the dashi is ready for use.

Ponzu Sauce SOUTHERN ISLANDS
(CITRUS SOY SAUCE)

INGREDIENTS

1	oz	Cornstarch
3	oz	Cold Water
3	oz	Rice Wine Vinegar
3	oz	Mirin
4	oz	Yuzu Juice
6	oz	Soy Sauce
8	oz	Dashi

This sauce is very commonly used as both a condiment and a component of other sauces.

YIELD: 3 cups

COOKING METHOD: Simmering

PROCEDURE

1. Dissolve the cornstarch in cold water, and combine the resulting slurry with all of the other ingredients.

2. Place the mixture in an appropriately sized pot over a medium-low flame, and bring the mixture to a simmer. Simmer for 5 minutes and then remove from heat. The ponzu is ready for use.

Teriyaki Sauce JAPAN
(SWEETENED SOY/RICE WINE SAUCE)

INGREDIENTS

8	fl oz	Soy Sauce
6	fl oz	Sake
6	fl oz	Mirin
4	oz	Sugar

This basic teriyaki recipe can be used for a wide variety of dishes—for example, as a marinade or to make dipping sauces or glazes. The word *teriyaki* translates as glazed "teri" and grilled or griddled "yaki"; traditionally, this term would be used to describe foods that were glazed by applying the ingredients listed in this recipe during the last part of the grilling or griddling process. Teriyaki sauce is often used in ways that do not adhere to its original meaning, but perhaps it is best to use the term just as it was intended.

YIELD: 3 cups

PREPARATION METHOD: Dissolving Sugar into Liquid Base

PROCEDURE

1. Combine all of the ingredients in an appropriately sized pot. Heat over a low flame until the sugar is dissolved, and then remove from heat and cool for use.

2. If you are using this as a glaze, the sauce can slowly be reduced until it thickens slightly (so it is thick enough to coat the back of a spoon) and then brushed on foods as they are finishing on the grill or griddle.

Su-Meshi JAPAN (ORIGINALLY TOKYO ON HONSHŪ)
(VINEGARED SHORT-GRAIN RICE)

INGREDIENTS

1.5	lbs	Sushi Rice (short-grain rice, often labeled "sweet rice")
36	fl oz	Water
4	oz	Rice Wine Vinegar
3	oz	Sugar
2	tsp	Salt

The short-grain rice most commonly used in Japan, combined with a sweetened rice wine vinegar mixture, forms the base of all sushi styles. For the rice to be made correctly, it is important to follow the steps just as described; the rice's texture and stickiness result from the addition of the vinegar mixture to the hot rice.

YIELD: 3.5 pounds

COOKING METHOD (RICE): Absorbing

PREPARATION METHOD (VINEGAR SOLUTION): Dissolving Sugar and Salt in Liquid Base

PROCEDURE

1. Rinse the sushi rice under cold running water in a china cap or chinois until the water runs clear; then set it aside to allow any excess water to drain off.

2. If you are using a rice cooker, add the rice and water to the rice cooker and follow the cooker's directions. If you are using the stove, place the rice and water in a pot with a very good lid (if you do not have a tight-fitting lid, use aluminum foil and a lid or pan to ensure that too much steam does not escape), and bring to a boil over high heat.

(continues)

Su-Meshi
(continued)

Su-Meshi (vinegar rice) being mixed; the vinegar solution should be "cut" into the rice to prevent crushing the cooked rice grains

3. Once the rice comes to a boil, turn the heat down to a low flame and cover the pot very tightly to prevent loss of moisture during cooking.

4. Cook over a low flame for 8–10 minutes (8 minutes if the rice is shallow in the pot, 10 minutes if it is deep in the pot); turn the flame off and leave the rice covered tightly.

5. Allow the rice to sit and steam for another 10–15 minutes; then the rice is ready to make su-meshi.

6. In a small saucepan, heat the rice wine vinegar, sugar, and salt over a low flame to dissolve the sugar and salt.

7. Transfer the hot cooked rice to a large bowl (this is traditionally done in a large wooden bowl called an ohitsu); this step must be done while the rice is still hot, because the glaze formed on the rice is dependent on the vinegar's evaporation.

8. Using a rice paddle or a wide wooden spoon, simultaneously "cut" the rice and slowly drizzle in the rice wine vinegar solution. (In Japan, someone would assist with this step by fanning as the vinegar is added, aiding its evaporation.)

9. Once all of the vinegar solution had been incorporated, the rice should be very sticky and glossy. Once it cools to room temperature, the rice is ready to be used to make sushi.

NOTE: *Su-meshi should be used the day it is made and should not be refrigerated, because the texture will change significantly.*

Nigiri Tokyo (Southern Honshū)
(Hand-Formed Vinegared Rice with Toppings)

Ingredients

.5		Recipe of Su-Meshi (see recipe, this chapter)
1	lb	Various Sushi-Grade Fish or Shellfish, sliced into 1/4-inch-thick pieces (approximately 1 inch × 2 inch)
2	Tbsp	Wasabi Powder, hydrated with water to form paste
1	sheet	Nori (optional), cut into 1/4-inch strips (4 inches long)
1	gal	Container of Hot Water
4	oz	Pickled Ginger (Gari)
2	Tbsp	Wasabi Powder, hydrated with water to form paste
6	oz	Soy Sauce

Sushi as it is primarily known today began as nigiri in Tokyo, when a street vendor placed raw fish on small, compact balls of rice that could be eaten out of hand. This style of sushi has become very common in Japan as well as everywhere else sushi is popular.

Yield: Approximately 25 pieces

Preparation Method: Forming Hand-Rolled Sushi

Procedure

1. Place the hot water next to the cutting board and dip clean hands in it, as needed, to ensure that the rice doesn't stick to your fingers.

2. Place a golf-ball-size amount of su-meshi in the palm of one hand; use the middle finger and index finger of the other hand to compress it while also cupping your hand to form a compressed, football-shaped rice ball.

3. Using the index finger of the hand not holding the rice, place a small amount of wasabi paste on one side of the rice ball.

(continues)

Nigiri
(continued)

4. Place a piece of sliced fish or shellfish on the su meshi, covering the wasabi paste.

5. If you are using the nori, place the strips around the center of the nigiri roll; serve nigiri with the pickled ginger, a small amount of wasabi paste, and soy sauce as accompaniments.

Maki-Mono TOKYO (SOUTHERN HONSHŪ)

(VINEGARED RICE AND FILLINGS ROLLED IN ROASTED SEAWEED)

INGREDIENTS

1		Recipe of Su-Meshi (see recipe, this chapter)
10	sheets	Nori
1		Cucumber, peeled. seeded, and cut into 1/4-inch strips (6 inches long)
1		Avocado, seeded and sliced into 1/4-inch strips
10		Green Onions (about 1 bunch)
1	lb	Various Fish and Shellfish for fillings (such as crabmeat, shrimp, salmon, tuna, etc.
6	oz	Pickled Ginger
1	oz	Wasabi Powder, hydrated to form paste
20	fl oz	Soy Sauce

Rolled sushi is probably one of the most recognizable Japanese preparations for most people in the United States, where sushi restaurants have become extremely popular. This recipe makes a traditional roll, in which the chosen seafood items are placed in the center of the rice. It is very common in the United States for the fish to be compressed onto the exterior of the rolls as well, to show the vivid colors of the chosen seafood items.

YIELD: 10 sushi rolls, or about 60 pieces

PREPARATION METHOD: Rolling Nori-Wrapped Sushi

PROCEDURE

1. Place a nori sheet onto a bamboo sushi mat on a clean work surface, and place a gallon-size container of hot water next to your work area.

2. Dip clean hands in the hot water, take a handful of rice, and press it onto the nori sheet. Continue to press rice onto the sheet until all but 1.5 inches of nori sheet opposite you, and .5 inch of nori sheet closest to you, is covered with 1/4 inch of rice.

3. Place the desired filling in the center of the nori sheet on top of the compressed rice (don't put too much filling inside the roll, or it will

Preparing to roll the sushi; a bamboo sushi mat is shown with nori covered with rice, and tuna and avocado ready to be included

The sushi roll just before it is rolled and compressed, notice how the fillings (avocado and tuna in this case) are placed on top and in the center of the nori covered with rice (always have a bowl of water handy as well to dip hands into before touching the rice)

(continues)

Maki-Mono
(continued)

be overfilled; if everything is cut into 1/4-inch strips. you should be able to add 4–5 different items).

4. To roll the sushi, hold the corners of the nori sheet and the bamboo sheet with your thumb and index finger; using your middle and ring finger, hold the filling in place while bringing the nori roll closest to you up and over, to the end of the compressed rice on the side farthest from you.

5. Once you have begun to make the roll, remove the bamboo mat from the top of the sushi and roll out the remaining nori sheet.

6. Move the sushi roll to the center of the sushi mat; roll with the mat again and compress with your hands to tightly pack contents.

7. Once the sushi roll has been formed, cut it by dipping a clean, sharp knife in hot water between each cut to prevent sticking and tearing of the roll.

8. Serve the cut rolls with pickled ginger, wasabi paste, and soy sauce.

A plate of sushi with nigiri topped with tuna on the bottom of the plate with wasabi paste on either side of the three pieces and soy sauce in the sauce boat next to the nigiri as well as two styles of rolled sushi across the top of the plate with pickled ginger in the center of the plate

The rolled and compressed sushi roll, notice how the chef is drawing the bottom part of the bamboo mat that has been rolled over and is away from him in toward himself. This compresses the roll into the cylinder shape so that it is not "flattened" on the end.

The cut roll of Maki Mono; this would traditionally be served with grated wasabi root, pickled ginger, and soy sauce

Naganegi no Soba HONSHŪ AND HOKKAIDŌ ISLANDS

(CHILLED BUCKWHEAT NOODLES WITH LEEKS AND DIPPING SAUCE)

INGREDIENTS

For the Dipping Sauce

2	Tbsp	Yuzu Juice
4	oz	Soy Sauce
3	oz	Mirin Rice Wine
16	oz	Ichiban Dashi

For the Soba Noodles

2	gal	Water, in a large pot on high flame
1	pt	Cold Water
1	lb	Soba Noodles
6	oz	Leek Whites, sliced julienne
2	Tbsp	Wasabi Powder, hydrated with water to form paste

Soba noodles are one of the common noodle types enjoyed in many parts of Japan. One aspect of Japanese cuisine that can be difficult for Westerners to grasp is the use of cold pasta. Although pasta may be eaten cold in pasta salad, this preparation is quite different: in this dish, pasta is dipped in a seasoned sauce after being topped with an onion called *naganegi* (often simply called *negi*), which is similar to a leek.

YIELD: 8 portions (4 ounces/portion)

COOKING METHOD: Modified Boiling (shocking with cool water)

PROCEDURE

For the Dipping Sauce

1. Combine the yuzu juice, soy sauce, mirin, and dashi in a ming bowl; mix thoroughly, and set in the refrigerator.

For the Soba Noodles

1. Bring the 2 gal of water to a boil in a large pot, and then add the soba noodles, mixing with a spoon as they are added to keep them from sticking together.

2. Once the water returns to a boil after the addition of the soba noodles, add the cold water to the pot to cool the cooking liquid (this will enable more even cooking of the noodles throughout, and is very different from the typical Western method of cooking pasta). Continue to cook over a high flame until the soba noodles are just cooked (al dente); remove from heat and drain the noodles in a colander.

3. Run cold water over the noodles to chill them, and then allow any excess water to drain off of the noodles.

4. To serve, curl 1/8 of the cooked soba noodles on a plate, top with leeks, place a small mound of wasabi paste next to the roll, and serve with a small dish of dipping sauce.

Tempura Kyūshū

(Battered and Fried Fish and Vegetables)

INGREDIENTS

For Deep Frying the Ingredients

1	qt	Vegetable Oil
4	fl oz	Sesame Oil

For the Dipping Sauce

10	fl oz	Ichiban Dashi
4	fl oz	Mirin
5	fl oz	Soy Sauce
5	oz	Daikon Radish, grated

For the Batter

2		Eggs
1	cup	Ice-Cold Water
1	cup	All-Purpose (A.P.) Flour
1/2	cup	Corn Starch

Tempura is an example of both foreign influence and local adaptation, as this style of cooking was introduced by Portuguese traders and then refined by Japanese chefs. The main difference between tempura and Western-style deep-fried foods is the lightness of the batter coating and the lack of greasy oil left on the foods. The consistency of the batter, the quality of the oil, and a proper frying temperature all are important factors in yielding this quality.

YIELD: 10 portions (8 ounces/portion)

COOKING METHOD: Deep Frying

PROCEDURE

1. Place the oils in a small pot, leaving at least 2 inches of open space below the rim of the pot, and preheat over a medium-low flame. (Make sure not to overheat the oil, because it will break down; the oil needs to be between 345°F and 360°F for best results.)

(continues)

Plate of tempura fried fish and vegetables with dipping sauce. Notice the flaky texture of the fried batter on the exterior, a result of keeping batter very cold just before use

Tempura
(continued)

Ingredients to be Battered and Fried

(Note: Different items can be included, substituted, or omitted.)

10		Large Shrimp (if using 16–20, approximately 9–10 oz), peeled and deveined
1.5	lbs	Lean Fish Fillets (such as sole, snapper, or sea bass), cut into strips 1.5 inches wide
10		Large Mushrooms (about 8 oz)
1		Lotus Root (about 8 oz), peeled and sliced 1/4 inch thick, and held in vinegar water
2		Red Peppers (about 1 lb), seeded and cut into 1-inch strips
1	lb	Japanese Eggplant (about 3 eggplants or 1 globe eggplant)
2	tsp	Salt

2. To make the dipping sauce, combine all of the ingredients (except the daikon radish) in a small saucepan, and bring them to a simmer over a medium-low flame. Once simmering, remove them from heat and add the grated daikon. Set this aside to be served with the tempura.

3. To make the batter, beat eggs with a whisk in a mixing bowl to lighten; add cold water and whisk again to combine. (Once the batter is made, it should be used quickly—the texture will change if it sits for very long.)

4. Sift flour and cornstarch together, and sift again to add to the egg and water mixture, mixing lightly and quickly with the liquids to produce a light tempura batter (do not overmix; it is fine if some lumps remain in the mixture).

5. The shrimp and fish can be threaded on skewers for dipping, or tongs can be used (if the shrimp are skewered, they will stay straight rather than curl as they cook).

6. Once the oil temperature has reached the desired range, the ingredients can be dipped into the tempura batter and fried until they just begin to brown; at this point, they should be removed and placed on absorbent paper towels, and then served with a small bowl of the dipping sauce. (Be sure to fry only a small amount at a time so the oil temperature does not drop too much.)

Miso Shiru JAPAN

(SEAWEED BROTH WITH FERMENTED SOYBEAN PASTE)

INGREDIENTS

3	qts	Ichiban Dashi (see recipe, this chapter)
12	oz	Miso (the type will affect the amount of salt in the recipe and may require adjustments of dashi or salt at the end)
8	oz	Fresh Shiitake or Nameko Mushrooms (or 3 oz Dried Shiitake)
1	lb	Tofu, diced medium
3	oz	Green Onions, sliced on a bias 1/4 inch thick (about 1 bunch)

This is a very common soup that is traditionally eaten in the morning all across Japan. Western-style breakfasts are becoming more common in Japan, but miso shiru remains the typical morning meal.

YIELD: 3.5 quarts, or 14 portions (8 fluid ounces/portion)

COOKING METHOD: Simmering

PROCEDURE

1. Hydrate the miso using 2 cups of the dashi; mix together with a whisk in a pot large enough to hold all of the ingredients.

2. Add the remaining dashi and the shiitake mushrooms, and bring the mixture to a simmer over a medium-low flame.

3. After simmering the mixture for 15 minutes, add the tofu and simmer for an additional 5 minutes. Add the green onions, and serve.

Sake No Miso   HOKKAIDŌ ISLAND
(SALMON MARINATED WITH MISO)

INGREDIENTS

1	lb	White Miso Paste
5	fl oz	Mirin
5	fl oz	Sake
4	oz	Soy Sauce
2	oz	Ponzu Sauce (you can substitute yuzu juice)
4	lbs	Boneless Salmon Fillet, cut into 10 portions (approximately 6 oz each)

The salmon of Hokkaidō are prized for their clean taste; in this recipe, the rich salmon is paired with miso, which is made from salted and fermented soybeans. The slightly salty miso enhances the flavor of the salmon and yields a very flavorful and moist salmon fillet.

YIELD: Approximately 10 portions

COOKING METHOD: Roasting

PROCEDURE

1. Combine the miso, mirin, sake, soy sauce, and ponzu sauce in a mixing bowl, and mix thoroughly.
2. Coat the salmon fillets with the miso marinade, cover, and refrigerate for at least 6 hours (and no more than 1 day).
3. Preheat the oven to 350°F.
4. Remove the salmon from the marinade and wipe off any excess. Place the salmon fillet in the oven and roast for 10–15 minutes, or until fillets are not quite cooked all the way through; remove and serve.

Plate of sake no miso (salmon marinated with miso) shown served with steamed short grain rice and steamed bok choy

Ichigo Daifuku HONSHŪ

(RICE FLOUR PASTRY WITH SWEET BEANS AND STRAWBERRY)

INGREDIENTS

For Making the Azuki Paste and Stuffed Balls

20	oz	Azuki Beans (about 3 cups), dry
1.5	qts	Water
		Soaked Beans (see above)
2	qts	Water
1	tsp	Salt
3	cups	Water
8	oz	Sugar
30		Small Strawberries (equivalent to approximately 1 lb; if they are not already the size of a quarter, cut them into that size and you will need less)

For Making the Rice Dough and Wrapping

20	oz	Water
11	oz	Mochiko Powder
11	oz	Sugar
11	oz	Cornstarch

This is an adaptation of the very common mochi sweets found throughout Japan. Mochi is commonly wrapped around a sweet adzuki bean paste; in this recipe, strawberries are included in the very center.

YIELD: 30 (approximately 2 ounces each)

COOKING METHOD (AZUKI BEANS): Gentle Simmering

COOKING METHOD (RICE DOUGH): Boiling

PROCEDURE

For Making the Azuki Paste and Stuffed Balls

(**NOTE:** *This part of the procedure should be started a day in advance.*)

1. Combine the azuki beans and the 1.5 qts of water, and soak overnight (or for 1 day).

2. Drain the water from the soaking azuki beans, rinse them, and combine the azuki beans with the 2 qts of water and salt. Bring to a boil over high heat on the stove.

3. Once the beans come to a boil, turn the flame down and allow the beans to cook gently over lower heat until they just begin to get soft throughout (about 40 minutes).

4. Once the beans are soft throughout, pour off any liquid still remaining in the pot, and add the 3 cups of water and the sugar. Return to heat and cook until the beans are very tender, paying attention to ensure that the pot does not go dry during this process.

5. Once the beans are very tender, take them off of the heat and mash them using a wooden spoon or a potato masher (at this

(continues)

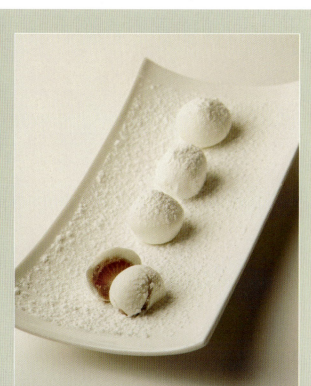

Ichigo daifuku shown with one cut in half to reveal the sweet bean paste and strawberry that is contained within the sweet pastry. This Japanese style of sweet has become a popular way of making rice dough wrapped ice cream called mochi (also the name of other preparations similar to the one shown here)

Ichigo Daifuku
(continued)

point, a couple different styles of balls can be made: a more refined one, in which the beans are passed through a sieve, or a more rustic one, in which the tougher exterior of the beans is left in the paste).

6. If you are making the smoother paste, pass the mashed beans through a fine sieve; if not, proceed to the next step.

7. Return the bean purée to the pot, and cook out any remaining moisture until the beans become quite thick and form a smooth paste.

8. Set the bean purée aside and cover it with a damp cloth; allow the bean purée to cool.

9. Once the purée has cooled, divide it into 30 pieces. After flattening them with your hand, place a strawberry in the center of each and form the bean purée around each strawberry (or piece of strawberry).

10. Once completed, set all of the bean and strawberry balls aside until the dough is ready (keep them covered with a damp cloth to prevent them from drying out).

For Making the Rice Dough and Wrapping

1. In a small pot, bring the water to a boil and then stir in the rice flour (mochiko flour); mix continuously with a wooden spoon to make a smooth, thick dough (approximately 2–4 minutes). As the mixture thickens, lower the heat to prevent burning the bottom.

2. Once the flour and water have thickened, begin to add the sugar (while stirring constantly over a low flame—it will take some effort to work in the sugar).

3. Continue to add the sugar slowly until all of it has combined completely with the dough (it will get gluey and pull away from the pan, somewhat like making choux paste).

4. Once all of the sugar has been added, remove the pan from the heat and bring it to the work area.

5. Place a sheet pan or half sheet pan in the work area and coat it with the cornstarch.

6. Pour the rice dough out onto the sheet pan, on top of the cornstarch, and press the dough out until it is 1/4 inch thick.

7. Once the dough has been flattened to 1/4 inch, cut out circular pieces (approximately three inches in diameter—you can use a dough cutter or pastry mold to do this). With the surface still coated in cornstarch, place a ball of the azuki paste wrapped around the strawberry in the center of the dough, and pull/pinch the dough up to the top of the ball; seal by pinching the dough together.

8. You will end up with an ichigo daifuku ball that has one slightly rough-looking end (where you pinched it together); roll it using lightly coated (and clean!) cornstarch hands, and place it—sealed side down—on a tray.

9. Continue steps 7 and 8 until all of the azuki balls have been wrapped; once cooled, enjoy!

SUMMARY

Japanese cuisine stands alone among the world's cuisines in a number of areas, including dependency of seafood, artful presentations, and unique food preparations. Seafood is a major part of the cuisine in most areas of Japan, and many products of the sea that are not common in other cuisines are regularly used here. In Japan, an emphasis is placed on seasonal products, and this focus can be seen in the way food is presented—with a distinct appreciation for the identification of seasonal cues. The tea ceremony is one example of the pride and respect that the Japanese have for practice and skill, and this has influenced the cuisine as well. The Japanese also appreciate culinary specialists, and shops that specialize in just one area of the cuisine are common. The cuisine is noted for its use of seaweed and seaweed stock, as well as for retention of each individual ingredient's characteristics. Like many Asian cuisines, Japanese cuisine is built around rice; the preferred rice in Japan is short-grain varieties that are either non-glutinous or glutinous, depending on the preparation.

REVIEW QUESTIONS

1. What is the significance of the seasons in the cuisine of Japan, and how does it relate to the tea ceremony?

2. What types of rice are used in Japanese cuisine, and what are the primary uses of each?

3. What is dashi, and why is it important in Japanese cuisine?

COMMON TERMS, FOODS, AND INGREDIENTS

Japanese cuisine has become very popular in recent years (sushi, in particular), but many people are uninitiated to the other wonderful foods that come from this region. This guide provides some of the more common terms one might encounter when venturing beyond the world of sushi (as well as many terms that are important for understanding and making sushi). It contains specific sections on sushi terms, soy products, seaweed types, and mushrooms, as well as common ingredients, prepared foods, and cultural terms.

✳ *Common Ingredients*

Japanese cuisine is likely to include many of the following ingredients.

Grains, Vegetables, Meats, and Fish

awabi – Abalone

ayu – Sweetfish species from rivers

azuki – Red bean

biwa – Loquat

butaniku – Pork

daikon – Large white radish

fugu – Blowfish

goma – Sesame seed

goya – Bitter melon

gyūnikū – Beef

hamaguri – Clam

hiijaa – Goat

hitsuji – Lamb

hotategai – Scallop

ika – Squid

jaga-imo – Potato

kaki – Oyster

kani – Crab

kome – Uncooked rice

komugi – Wheat

magani – River crab

masu – Pink salmon

mochi gomé – Glutinous short-grain rice variety, often called sweet rice in the United States

naganegi – Leek-like onion

nashi – Asian pear

nebera – Winter melon

piman – Chiles

renkon – Lotus root

sake – Salmon

satsuma-imo – Sweet potato

soba – Buckwheat (or buckwheat noodles)

tai – Snapper or bream

tara – Pacific cod

tōgarashi – Type of chili used and prized in Japan

tōmorokoshi – Corn

unagi – Freshwater eel that is roasted and glazed for use in a variety of dishes *uni* – Sea urchin

unjanaba – Water spinach

uruchi mai – Non-glutinous short-grain rice variety that is most commonly used in Japanese cuisine

wasabi – Pungent root that is ground and served with sushi; fresh wasabi is very rare and expensive in both the United States and Japan

Soy Products

edamame – Fresh soya beans

edo miso – Lightly salty red miso

haku miso – Sweet white miso made with a high proportion of rice malt

hatchō miso – Miso made with only soybeans; a rich source of protein

kome miso – Paste made from salted, fermented rice and soybeans that is aged to develop its characteristic flavor

mugi miso – Paste made from salted, fermented wheat, barley, soybeans, and rice

shima-dōfu – Dense soybean cake from Okinawa region

tofu – Made from coagulated soya bean "milk," which is made from boiling and crushing soya beans. There are various types of tofu, with differences mostly in texture and quality.

yuba – Dried soya bean skin made from the film that forms on the surface of soya milk during tofu production

Mushrooms (Kinoko)

enokitake – Wild mushroom grows in clusters on specific trees; the wild mushrooms are shorter and darker than the more commonly cultivated enokitake which are grown in clusters with long stems and very small caps. Often simply called *enoki*.

maitake – Japanese "dancing" mushroom with whitish/grey thin caps used in soups or in broiled dishes

matsutake – Very popular mushroom in Japan that is considered a sign of autumn; these have medium-sized brown caps and large, meaty stems. The flavor is distinct and also delicate and cannot be cooked too long or it will be lost. These are very expensive and rare in Japan and only eaten fresh.

nameko – Small orange mushroom with a gelatinous texture that is found mostly canned in brine. These are used in miso soup and as a flavoring in side dishes.

shiitake – Most common mushroom of Japanese cuisine (also very common in Chinese cuisine); these are used especially in soups and vegetable dishes but often found in other preparations a swell. Shiitake have a firm texture and an earthy flavor that is retained in drying.

shimeji – Popular Japanese mushroom with small brown caps that grow in clusters; these have a firm texture, similar to the shiitake, but a very mild aroma (oyster mushrooms are sometimes used as a substitute).

Seaweed (Kaisō)

agar-agar – Common name of the U.S. product made from kanten seaweed; similar to gelatin in its properties (thickens liquids upon cooling)

arame – Brown seaweed that is dried and chopped; often added to rice

asa – Soft seaweed found growing on reefs and used in soups

hijiki – Black, bland seaweed often cooked with vegetables or tofu for its high vitamin and mineral content

kanten – Fern-like seaweed used to make agar-agar, which is used as a thickening agent similar to the way gelatin is used in Western cultures

konbu – Giant kelp used to make dashi and also in other preparations; usually used dried but is sometimes shaved fresh

mozuku – Surface seaweed with a soft texture; used in soups and with vegetables

nori – Thin, dried seaweed sheets used to make rolled sushi

wakame – Variety of seaweed used commonly in soups and as a salad

Sushi Terms

chirashi – Scattered sushi made by placing ingredients on top of the sushi rice

fukusa-zushi – Thin egg omelet-wrapped sushi

futo maki – Thick-rolled sushi

gari – Pickled ginger

gunkan-maki – "Warship roll" (named because of its shape); rolled sushi topped with ingredients that are difficult to put inside a roll (such as urchin)

hangiri – Shallow wooden bowl made out of cypress and used to mix the cooked short-grain rice and vinegar solution to make sushi rice

hoso maki – Thin-rolled sushi

maki-mono – Rolled sushi; this style usually is made with nori, but other ingredients are used to encase the rice and fillings

makisu – Bamboo mat used to make sushi rolls

nakiri bocho – Rectangular-shaped knife used to cut vegetables

nigiri – Hand-formed sushi with various sashimi toppings

oshi-zushi – Compressed sushi; rice and other ingredients are compressed together in a rectangular box. This style dates back to the origin of sushi, when fish were packed with rice to preserve them by fermentation of the rice.

sashimi bocho – Long, thin knife used to cut fish for sushi

shamoji – Wooden spoon with a wide, flat end used to "cut" and mix the sushi rice as the vinegar solution is added in the hangiri

su – Rice vinegar

su-meshi – Vinegared rice

tamago-yaki – Omelet

uchiwa – Fan used to cool the rice and assist in evaporation of vinegar while mixing in the hangiri

uramaki – Inside-out sushi roll, in which the nori is encased by rice instead of the other way around

Specialty Products and Recipes

an – Sweet paste made from azuki beans and sugar

andagi – Fried doughnut common in Okinawa (from Portuguese influence)

chanpuru – Stir-fried dishes common in Okinawa region

dashi – Seaweed stock made from kombu and bonito flakes; used extensively in Japanese cuisine in soups, sauces, and other preparations. Ichiban dashi is the name of the initial (and stronger) stock that is often strained and the konbu and bonito reused to make the niban dashi (second dashi), which is weaker in aroma and taste.

dengaku – Skewered and grilled vegetables and other ingredients with miso glaze/marinade

dofu – Another name for tofu

ekiben – Station lunchbox (bento) for which each region has its own variations; these are sold at the train stations and usually highlight local ingredients

fuka-hire – Shark's fin soup

ichigo daifuku – Mochi balls stuffed with sweet azuki bean paste and strawberries

ichigoni – Abalone and sea urchin soup

ika meshi – Rice with squid

ika sōmen – Squid with wheat flour noodle

ishikari-nabe – Specialty of the Hokkaidō region; salmon cooked with potatoes, tofu, miso, and vegetables

jappa-jiru – Cod soup with daikon and miso; from the northern portion of the main island

jimami dofu – Tofu made from ground peanuts gelled with potato starch

jingisukan – Dish named after Genghis Khan, the Mongolian leader; made from cooked mutton or lamb with vegetables and seasonings

kake-udon – Hot udon noodles served in hot broth; common in Shikoku

kaki-soba – Soba noodles served in a broth with garnishes

kani meshi – Rice with crab

katsuo no tataki – Bonito braised over hot coals

kushiage – Skewered, breaded, and fried foods

men-dokoro – Eating establishment that specializes in noodle dishes

mirin – Sweet rice wine

miso – Salted and fermented soybeans. There are many versions of miso (see section on soy products).

mochi – Rice cake made from a particular variety of short-grain rice; often sweet

mochiko – Brand name of rice flour made from glutinous rice

mori-soba – Soba noodles served chilled with dipping sauce, wasabi, and garnishes

nabemono – Hot pot common throughout Japan, in which select ingredients are provided so the guest can select what (and how much) is added to his or her broth

nabemono-ryōri-ya – Eating establishment that specializes in the nabemono hot pots common throughout Japan

nigiri-zushi – Hand-formed sushi with various toppings

obentô – Boxed lunch popular throughout the country; these signified solidarity and support during the early part of World War II and have been popular ever since

o-sake – Rice wine or sake; not to be confused with sake (salmon)

oshinuki-zushi – Pressed style of sushi with mackerel

ponzu – Sauce made from yuzu juice, soy sauce, mirin (sweet rice wine), rice vinegar, and dashi (seaweed stock)

rafute – Pork stewed with miso, soy sauce, and ginger

rāmen – Yellow wheat noodle served in broth, with every imaginable ingredient potentially added to this dish

rāmen-ya – Eating establishment that specializes in rāmen

ruibe – Freshly frozen salmon sashimi, sliced paper thin and served still frozen to be eaten with a spicy soy sauce dip

sanuki udon – Very thin noodles from the island of Shikoku

sashimi – Raw seafood or, less commonly, meat

shabu-shabu – Thinly sliced meat/fish (usually beef) dipped into a hot pot (broth) and served with dipping sauces

shinko – Shredded pickled cabbage

soba – Buckwheat noodles

somen – Thin wheat flour noodles

sumibi-yaki – Mochi rice balls mixed with potato and sesame and grilled over coals

sunomono – Foods pickled in vinegar

sushi – Short-grain rice with sweetened (or sometimes not sweetened) and vinegared rice with various toppings

sushi-ya – Eating establishment that specializes in sushi

tai meshi – Rice with sea bream

tako-shabu – Hotpot (seasoned broth kept simmering) served with thinly sliced octopus

tempura – Deep-fried foods in light batter

teppanyaki – Foods cooked on a hot plate in front of customers

teriyaki – Foods cooked with soy sauce, mirin, and sugar; usually grilled

tonkatsu – Breaded and deep-fried pork cutlets (usually pork tenderloin)

tonkotsu ramen – Rāmen with rich pork broth; common in Kyūsū

udon – Medium-thickness wheat flour noodles

wanko soba – Soba noodles served cold

yakitori – Skewered chicken that is grilled and often served in specialty shops dedicated to grilled foods

✳ *Cultural Terms*

Ainu – Indigenous people of the northern island of Hokkaidō

Buddhism – Religion followed by many in Japan that developed in India, spread into China, and was introduced to Japan by the Chinese. Part of the belief system includes striving not to harm other living animals; thus, many Buddhists are vegetarians.

kaiseki – Formal coursed meal derived from the foods served as a part of the tea ceremony. This style of dining and menu creation is highly focused on the seasonality of the foods as well as their presentation.

Ryukyuan – Indigenous people of the southern islands of Japan

Shinto – Ancient Japanese religion; followers believe in the sacredness and cycles of nature. It is widely held that this belief system is one of the major reasons such a premium is placed on seasonal foods and the preservation of foods' natural qualities.

washoku – Translates as "harmony of food," a philosophy and way of cooking in Japan that recognized the relationship between nourishment and all aspects of food in attaining it

APPENDIX
MEASUREMENTS, CONVERSIONS, AND EQUIVALENTS

CALCULATION FORMULA SHEET

Basic Math Rules and Symbols

+ Addition	− Subtraction
× Multiplication	/ Division

When performing mathematical problems, you always do any multiplication and division BEFORE addition and subtraction UNLESS the addition and/or subtraction are in parentheses. For example, $2 + 2 \times 8 = 18$, but $(2 + 2) \times 8 = 32$.

In division, you are dealing with fractions such as 3/8, in which 3 is the **numerator** and 8 is the **denominator.** If you were to put that fraction into your calculator, it would tell you that it $= 0.375$, so 3/8 and 0.375 are equivalent: 0.375 is the decimal form equivalent of the fraction 3/8.

Measuring

In a professional kitchen, you will typically use two different methods to measure your ingredients: weight and volume.

Conversions Between Different Weight Measures	
Weight	Measured in pounds (lb), ounces (oz), grams (g), or kilograms (kg)
1 kg	= 2.205 lbs
1 oz	= 28.35 g
1 lb	= 16 oz

Conversions Between Different Volume Measures	
Volume	Measured in liters (l), teaspoons (tsp), Tablespoons (Tbsp), cups, pints, quarts (qt), and gallons (gal)
1 l	= 1.05625 qts
5 ml	= 1 tsp
3 tsp	= 1 Tbsp
16 Tbsp	= 1 cup
2 cups	= 1 pint
2 pints	= 1 qt
4 qts	= 1 gal

Weight to Volume/Volume to Weight

Converting from weight to volume is one of the most common mistakes made in the kitchen, because it is only valid for the common units in relation to water, or a liquid composed primarily of water (for example, vinegar or soy sauce). If you used these conversions for olive oil, for example, you would be off slightly from the original amount. If you used these conversions for flour, you would be *way* off!

Common Conversions Between Weight and Volume (for Water!)	
2 Tbsp (water)	= 1 oz (water)
1 cup (water)	= 8 oz (water)
1 pint (water)	= 16 oz (water)
2 cups (water)	= 1 lb (water)
1 qt (water)	= 32 oz (water)
1 gal (water)	= 128 oz (water)
1 gal (water)	= 8 lbs (water)

Conversion Factors (CF)

Conversion factors are used to change the size of a recipe to yield the amount of a product you need.

Formula:	**New Yield/Old Yield = Conversion Factor**
	If your recipe yields 25 portions, and you want to make this recipe for 4 people, what would your conversion factor be?
	New Yield = the number of portions or amount you want = 4
	Old Yield = the number of portions or amount the recipe makes = 25
	Conversion Factor = 4/25 = 0.16
	Therefore, you would multiply all of the ingredients in the recipe by 0.16.

Yield Percentage (Yield Factors [YF]) and Edible Portions (EP)

Many of the items purchased for kitchens will have some amount of them discarded (waste); if some part of the product is thrown out, you need to calculate the actual cost of your edible portion (EP), or you may need to calculate this loss (or gain, in some cases—for example, dry pasta or dry rice) so that you order enough product.

Formulas:	**Yield Factor (YF) = Edible Portion (EP)/As Purchased Amount (AP)**
	As Purchased Price (AP)/Yield Factor (YF) = Edible Portion (EP) Cost
	To make things easier to conceptualize, the Yield Factor (YF) is often represented as a percentage (yield percentage). Just remember to use the Yield Factor in the equations in it's decimal form when performing these calculations. (So, 70% = .70, because most people can visualize 70% of a product better than they can visualize .7 of a product, but we need to use the .7 when performing equations).

COMMON CONVERSIONS AND EQUIVALENTS

U.S. System

Mass	measures how much an item weighs
1 lb	= 16 ounces (mass-mass)
Volume	**measures how much space an item occupies**
3 teaspoons	= 1 Tablespoon
2 Tablespoons	= 1/8 cup
4 Tablespoons	= 1/4 cup
8 Tablespoons	= 1/2 cup
16 Tablespoons	= 1 cup
2 cups	= 1 pint
2 pints	= 1 quart
4 quarts	= 1 gallon
2 gallons	= 1 peck
4 pecks	= 1 bushel

Volume to Mass (Based on the mass of WATER specifically)—these units should only be used to measure liquids very similar to water (vinegar, juices, most oils, etc.; if you use these to measure other liquids—such as molasses, honey, or a heavy syrup—you will most likely be off significantly from their actual weights or volumes).

2 Tablespoons	= 1 ounce of **water**
1 cup	= 8 ounces of **water**
1 pint	= 16 ounces of **water**
1 quart	= 32 ounces of **water**
1 gallon	= 128 ounces of **water**
Temperature	Degrees Fahrenheit

Metric System

Mass	Grams
1000 grams	= 1 kilogram (kg)
Volume	Liter
1/1000 liters	= 1 milliliter (ml)
Volume to Mass	(As with the U.S. system, this is based on water.)
1 liter	= 1 kilogram of **water**
Temperature	Degrees Celsius

U.S. System to Metric System

Use the following guide to convert from the U.S. system to the metric system, or vice versa. (Note: You can also move from the "To Get" unit to the "Multiply" unit by dividing by the number instead of multiplying.)

Multiply	By	To Get
ounces	28.35	grams (mass-mass)
grams	0.0353	ounces (mass-mass)
pounds	0.4536	kilograms (mass-mass)
kilograms	2.205	pounds (mass-mass)
quarts	0.946	liters (volume-volume)
liters	1.0567	quarts (volume-volume)
cups	0.2365	liters (volume-volume)
liters	4.23	cups (volume-volume)
gallons	3.785	liters (volume-volume)
liters	33.8	fluid ounces of WATER (volume-mass)

Quick U.S. to Metric Guide (rounded to closest whole number)

U.S. System	Metric System	
1/4 oz	7 grams	(mass-mass)
1/2 oz	14 grams	(mass-mass)
1 oz	28 grams	(mass-mass)
4 oz	113 grams	(mass-mass)
8 oz	227 grams	(mass-mass)
16 oz	454 grams	(mass-mass)
1 teaspoon	5 ml	(volume-volume)
1 Tablespoon	15 ml	(volume-volume)
2 Tablespoons (1 fl oz of water)	30 ml	(volume-volume)
1 cup	240 ml	(volume-volume)
1 pint	480 ml	(volume-volume)
1 qt	960 ml	(volume-volume)

Equivalents

Ingredient	Volume	Weight	Each	Weight
Dried Grains and Legumes				
Beans, Azuki	1 cup	7 oz		
Beans, Black	1 cup	6.9 oz		
Beans, Cannellini	1 cup	6.5 oz		
Beans, Pinto	1 cup	6.5 oz		
Beans, Sm. White	1 cup	7 oz		
Black-Eyed Peas	1 cup	6.25 oz		
Bulgur	1 cup	6.5 oz		
Cornmeal	1 cup	6 oz		
Lentils, Brown	1 cup	7 oz		
Lentils, Red	1 cup	7 oz		
Mushroom, Oyster, Dried	1 cup	0.5 oz		
Oats, Rolled	1 cup	3.5 oz		
Panko	1 cup	1.75 oz		
Pearl Barley	1 cup	6.9 oz		
Peas, Green Split	1 cup	7.5 oz		
Polenta	1 cup	6.5 oz		
Quinoa	1 cup	6.5 oz		
Rice, Jasmine	1 cup	7 oz		
Rice, Long Grain	1 cup	6.75 oz		
Rice, Med. Grain	1 cup	7 oz		
Rice, Sushi	1 cup	7.25 oz		
Rolled Oats	1 cup	3.25 oz		
Split Peas	1 cup	7.25 oz		
Sun-Dried Tomato	1 cup	3 oz		
Wild Rice	1 cup	6.5 oz		
Fruit				
Apple 88 ct			1	7 oz
Banana			1	5.25 oz
Kiwi			1	2.5 oz
Lemon			1	4 oz
Lime			1	3 oz
Orange			1	7.5 oz
Peach (Large)			1	10.25 oz
Pear, Bartlett			1	6 oz
Tomato			1	5 oz
Zucchini			1	6.5 oz

(continues)

(continued)

Ingredient	Volume	Weight	Each	Weight
Strawberries			1 ct	1 lb
Cranberries, Dried	1 cup	4.75 oz		
Raisins	1 cup	5.25 oz		
Blueberries (Frozen)	1 cup	5 oz		
Vegetables				
Broccoli (Small), whole piece			1	8.5 oz
Cabbage (Green)			1	2.5–3 lb
Carrot			1	5.25 oz
Celery			1 (Bunch)	1 lb 11 oz
Garlic			1 (Whole)	2 oz
Garlic, Cloves			6 cloves	1 oz
Jalapeño			1	1 oz
Leek (Large)			1	15 oz
Lemongrass			1	1.8 oz
Onion, Yellow (Med.)			1	11 oz
Onion, Green			1 (Bunch)	3.25 oz
Pasilla Chili			1	5.5 oz
Pepper, Bell			1	8 oz
Potato, Yukon (Med.)			1	5.5 oz
Potato, Red Bliss B			1	3.5 oz
Potato, Russet			1	7 oz
Shallot			1	1.75 oz
Bakery (Flour, Nuts, etc.)				
High-Gluten Flour	1 cup	4.75 oz		
Medium-Gluten Flour	1 cup	4.6 oz		
A.P. Flour	1 cup	4.5 oz		
Pastry Flour	1 cup	4.25 oz		
Cake Flour	1 cup	4.25 oz		
Whole Wheat Flour	1 cup	4.25 oz		
Rye Flour	1 cup	3.6 oz		
Bran	1 cup	1.75 oz		
8-Grain Meal	1 cup	5.5 oz		
Sugar	1 cup	7 oz		
Confectioners' Sugar (Unsifted)	1 cup	4.25 oz		
Brown Sugar (Light), Packed	1 cup	8.5 oz		
Walnuts (Chopped)	1 cup	4 oz		
Walnuts (Halves & Pieces)	1 cup	4 oz		
Pecans (Pieces)	1 cup	4 oz		
Almonds (Sliced)	1 cup	3.25 oz		

(continues)

(continued)

Ingredient	Volume	Weight	Each	Weight
Almonds (Whole)	1 cup	5 oz		
Chocolate Chips	1 cup	6.25 oz		
Cocoa Powder	1 cup	3.25 oz		
Coconut	1 cup	3.75 oz		
Corn Syrup	1 cup	11.75 oz		
Dark Corn Syrup	1 cup	11.4 oz		
Honey	1 cup	11.5 oz		
Molasses	1 cup	11.5 oz		
Peanut Butter (Creamy)	1 cup	9.25 oz		
Pumpkin Puree	1 cup	8.5 oz		
Pancake Syrup	1 cup	11 oz		
Sour Cream	1 cup	8.75 oz		
Cornstarch	1 cup	4 oz		
Baking Powder, Soda	1 tsp	0.17 oz		
Salt	1 tsp	0.2 oz		
Cinnamon	1 tsp	0.06 oz		
Ground Spices	1 tsp	0.07 oz		

REFERENCES

a

Achaya, K. (1998). *A historical dictionary of Indian food.* New Delhi: Oxford University Press.

Adam, H. (1967). *The International Wine and Food Society's guide to German cookery.* New York: Bonanza Books.

Algar, A. (1991). *Classic Turkish cooking.* New York: Harper Perennial.

Alford, J., & Duguid, N. (2005). *Mangoes and curry leaves.* New York: Artisan Books.

Allen, D. (1995). *Irish traditional cooking.* London: Kyle Books.

Anderson, E. (1988). *The food of China.* New Haven, CT: Yale University Press.

Anderson, J., & Würz, H. (1993). *The new German cookbook.* New York: HarperCollins.

Andoh, E. (2005). *Washoku: Recipes from the Japanese home kitchen.* Berkeley, CA: Ten Speed Press.

b

Barber, K. (2004). *The Japanese kitchen.* Lanham, MD: Kyle Books.

Barer-Stein, T. (1999). *You eat what you are: People, culture and food traditions.* New York: Firefly Books.

Batmanglij, N. (2001). *New food of life: Ancient Persian and modern Iranian cooking and ceremonies.* Washington, DC: Mage.

Bhumichitr, V. (1988). *The taste of Thailand.* New York: Macmillan.

Bladholm, L. (2000). *The Indian grocery store demystified.* New York: St. Martin's Griffin.

Blake, A., & Crewe, Q. (1978). *Great chefs of France.* London: Marshall Editions Limited.

Bremzen, A., & Welchman, J. (1990). *Please to the table: The Russian cookbook.* New York: Workman.

Brobeck, F., & Kjellberg, M. (1948). *Scandinavian cookery for Americans.* New York: Grosset & Dunlap.

Brown, D. (1968). *The cooking of Scandinavia.* New York: Time-Life Books.

Bsisu, M. (2005). *The Arab table: Recipes and culinary traditions.* New York: William Morrow and Company.

c

Caramitti, M. (2006). *Russia: A menu guide for travelers.* Rome: Gremese.

Chandra, S., & Chandra, S. (2001). *Cuisines of India.* New York: HarperCollins.

Claiborne, C., & Franey, P. (1978). *Foods of the world: Classic French cooking.* Alexandria, VA: Time-Life Books.

Connery, C. (1992). *In an Irish country kitchen.* New York: Simon & Schuster.

Cost, B. (1988). *Asian ingredients: A guide to foodstuffs of China, Japan, Korea, Thailand, and Vietnam.* New York: William Morrow and Company.

d

Dalby, A. (2000). *Dangerous tastes: The story of spices.* Berkeley: University of California Press.

David, E. (1970). *French provincial cooking.* New York: Penguin Books.

Davidson, A. (1999). *The Penguin companion to food.* New York: Penguin Books.

DeWitt, D. (1999). *The chili pepper encyclopedia.* New York: William Morrow and Company.

DeWitt, D., & Pais, A. (1994). *A world of curries.* New York: Little, Brown and Company.

Ditter, M., & Römer, J. (2000). *Culinaria: European specialties.* Cologne, Germany: Könemann.

Divina, F., & Divina, M. (2004). *Foods of the Americas.* Berkeley, CA: Ten Speed Press.

Dunlop, F. (2001). *Land of plenty: A treasure of authentic Sichuan cooking.* New York: W. W. Norton and Company.

f

Fallon, S., & Rothschild, M. (2000). *World food: France.* Victoria, Australia: Lonely Planet.

Fisher, M. F. K. (1968). *Foods of the world: The cooking of provincial France.* New York: Time-Life Books.

Fukuoka, Y. (2003). *Sushi.* London: Salamander Books.

g

Gerbino, V., & Kayal, P. (2003). *A taste of Syria.* New York: Hippocrene Books.

Grey, W. (1965). *Caribbean cookery.* London: Collins.

Grigson, J. (1984). *The world atlas of food.* New York: Exeter Books.

h

Hahn, E. (1968). *Foods of the world: The cooking of China.* New York: Time-Life Books.

Harris, J. (1991). *Skyjuice and flying fish: Traditional Caribbean cooking.* New York: Fireside Books.

Hekmat, F. (1994). *The art of Persian cooking.* New York: Hippocrene Books.

Houston, L. (2005). *Food culture in the Caribbean.* Westport, CT: Greenwood Press.

Hughes, H. (1999). *Germany's regional recipes.* Iowa City, IA: Penfield Press.

Hyman, G. (1995). *The new cooking of Britain and Ireland.* New York: John Wiley & Sons.

j

Jaffrey, M. (2003). *From curries to kebabs.* New York: Clarkson Potter.

Johnson, M. (1999). *Irish heritage cookbook.* San Francisco: Chronicle Books.

Jue, J. (2000). *Savoring Southeast Asia.* New York: Time-Life Books.

k

Kazuko, E. (2005). *The complete book of Japanese cooking.* London: Hermes House.

Kennedy, D. (1972). *The cuisines of Mexico.* New York: Harper & Row.

Kennedy, D. (2003). *From my Mexican kitchen: Techniques and ingredients.* New York: Clarkson Potter.

Keys, J. (1966). *Japanese cuisine: A culinary tour.* Rutland, VT: Charles Tuttle.

Kijac, M. (2003). *The South American table.* Boston: The Harvard Common Press.

Kittler, P., & Sucher, K. (2001). *Food and culture* (3rd ed.). Belmont, CA: Wadsworth/Thomson Learning.

Klepper, N. (1997). *Taste of Romania: Its cookery and glimpses of its history, folklore, art, literature and poetry.* New York: Hippocrene Books.

Kochilas, D. (2001). *The glorious foods of Greece.* New York: HarperCollins.

Kramarz, I. (1972). *The Balkan cookbook.* New York: Crown.

Kropotkin, A. (1993). *The best of Russian cooking.* New York: Hippocrene Books.

l

Lang, G. (1971). *The cuisine of Hungary.* New York: Atheneum.

Lin, F. (1975). *Florence Lin's Chinese regional cookbook.* New York: Hawthorn Books.

Lo, K. (1979). *Chinese provincial cooking.* London: Elm Tree Books.

Luard, E. (2002). *The Latin American kitchen.* San Diego, CA: Laurel Glen.

Luard, E. (2005). *The food of Spain and Portugal.* London: Kyle Books.

m

Mack, G., & Surina, A. (2005). *Food culture in Russia and central Asia.* Westport, CT: Greenwood Press.

Masui, C., & Masui, K. (2004). *Sushi secrets.* London: Hachette Illustrated.

Matsui, K., & Yamada T. (1996). *French cheeses.* New York: Dorling Kindersley.

Mazouz, M. (2004). *The Momo cookbook: A gastronomic journey through North Africa.* London: Simon & Schuster.

Millon K., & Millon, M. (1982). *The wine and food of Europe: An illustrated guide.* Seacaucus, NJ: Chartwell Books.

Morse, K. (1996). *North Africa: The vegetarian table.* San Francisco: Chronicle Books.

n

Nelson, K. (1973). *The Eastern European cookbook.* Chicago, IL: Henry Regnery Company.

Nelson, K. (2001). *All along the Rhine: Recipes, wines and lore from Germany, France, Switzerland, Austria, Liechtenstein, and Holland.* New York: Hippocrene Books.

Newman, J. (2004). *Food culture in China.* Westport, CT: Greenwood Press.

o

Ojakangas, B. (1964). *The Finnish cookbook.* New York: Crown.

Ojakangas, B. (1999). *The great Scandinavian baking book.* Minneapolis: University of Minnesota Press.

Omae, K., & Tachibana, Y. (1995). *The book of sushi.* New York: Kodansha International.

Ortiz, E. (1973). *The complete book of Caribbean cooking.* New York: M. Evans and Company.

p

Panjabi, C. (1995). *The great curries of India.* New York: Simon & Schuster.

Papashvily, H., & Papashvily, G. (1969). *Foods of the world: Russian cooking.* New York: Time-Life Books.

Parkinson, R. (1999). *Culinaria: The Caribbean—A culinary discovery.* Köln: Könemann.

Peterson, D., & Peterson, J. (2000). *Eat smart in Poland: How to decipher the menu, know the market foods, and embark on a tasting adventure.* Madison, WI: Ginkgo Press.

Peterson, J. (2002). *Glorious French food.* Hoboken, NJ: John Wiley & Sons.

r

Richie, D. (1992). *A taste of Japan.* New York: Kodansha International.

Roden, C. (1996). *The book of Jewish food: An odyssey from Samarkand and Vilna to the present day.* New York: Penguin Books.

Roden, C. (2006). *Arabesque.* New York: Alfred A. Knopf.

Rojas-Lombardi, F. (1991). *The art of South American cooking.* New York: HarperCollins.

s

Salloum, H., & Peters, J. (2004). *From the lands of figs and olives.* New York: Interlink.

Samuelsson, M. (2003). *Aquavit.* New York: Houghton Mifflin.

Sen, C. (2004). *Food culture in India.* Westport, CT: Greenwood Press.

Sharfenberg, H. (1980). *The cuisines of Germany: Regional specialties and traditional home cooking.* New York: Poseidon Press.

Shulman, M. (2002). *The food lover's atlas of the world.* Buffalo, NY: Firefly Books.

Sodsook, V. (1995). *True Thai.* New York: William Morrow and Company.

Sonnenfeld, A. (1996). *Food: A culinary history.* New York: Columbia University Press.

Spang, R. (2000). *The invention of the restaurant: Paris and modern gastronomic culture.* Cambridge, MA: Harvard University Press.

Stewart, K. (1997). *The hungry traveler: Germany.* Kansas City, MO: Andrews McMeel.

t

Tannahill, R. (1988). *Food in history.* New York: Three Rivers Press.

Toomre, J. (1992). *Classic Russian cooking: Elena Molokhovets' A gift to young housewives.* Indianapolis: Indiana University Press.

Trang, C. (2003). *Essentials of Asian cuisine: Fundamentals and favorite recipes.* New York: Simon & Schuster.

Trotter, C. (2004). *The Scottish kitchen.* London: Aurum Press Limited.

u

Uvezian, S. (2001). *The cuisine of Armenia* (3rd ed.). Northbrook, IL: The Siamanto Press.

V

Van Wyk, B. (2005). *Food plants of the world: An illustrated guide.* Portland, OR: Timber Press.

Volokh, A. (1983). *The art of Russian cuisine.* New York: Collier Books/Macmillan.

W

Willan, A. (1981). *French regional cooking.* New York: William Morrow and Company.

Wolfert, P. (2005). *The cooking of southwest France* (Rev. ed.). Hoboken, NJ: John Wiley & Sons.

y

Yin-Fei Lo, E. (1999). *The Chinese kitchen.* New York: William Morrow and Company.

z

Zaslavsky, N. (1995). *A cook's tour of Mexico: Authentic recipes from the country's best open-air markets, city fondas, and home kitchens.* New York: St. Martin's Griffin.

Zibart, E. (2001). *The ethnic food lover's companion: Understanding the cuisines of the world.* Birmingham, AL: Menasha Ridge Press.

Zubaida, S., & Tapper, R. (2000). *A taste of thyme: Culinary cultures of the Middle East.* New York: Tauris Parke Paperbacks.

GLOSSARY

a

abbacchio Young lamb. (Italy)

abbrustolito Cooked over an open flame. (Italy)

acajú Native name of cashew in South American tropics. (South America)

acaraje Fried mashed bean balls stuffed with vatapá sauce. (Brazil)

acciuga Anchovy. (Italy)

accras Fried savory bean fritters common in Haiti (also spelled *akkras*). (Caribbean)

aceite de oliva Olive oil. (Mexico)

aceituna Olives. (Iberian Peninsula)

aceto balsamico Balsamic vinegar. (Italy)

achar Pickled vegetables. (Indian subcontinent)

achiote (Caribbean) Dye that is mainly used as a coloring agent in cooking, as it imparts a red/yellow color to foods; also called annatto, bijol, or roucou.

   (South America) Annatto seeds; also called bija, bijol, and onoto.

acini di pepe One of the smallest pastas; resembles peppercorns and is typically used in light broths. (Italy)

ackee Fruit from West African evergreen. (Caribbean)

açorda Dish made with leftover bread that is cooked with various ingredients; common throughout Portugal. (Iberian Peninsula)

açorda de mariscos Shellfish, egg, and bread soup. (Iberian Peninsula)

adobe Spice rub used on grilled and roasted meats; often simply made from dried oregano, garlic, salt, and pepper. (Caribbean)

adrak Ginger root. (Indian subcontinent)

affogato Poached. (Italy)

affumicato Smoked. (Italy)

agar-agar Common name of the U.S. product made from kanten seaweed; similar to gelatin in its properties (thickens liquids upon cooling). (Japan)

aglio Garlic. (Italy)

agneau Lamb. (France)

agnello Lamb. (Italy)

agnolotti Half-moon shaped stuffed pastas formed by folding a circular piece of dough in half over a small amount of stuffing. These typically include cheese and/or vegetable fillings. (Italy)

agooryets Cucumbers. (Russia)

aguacate Avocado. (South America)

ai ferri Grilled or barbecued. (Italy)

Ainu Indigenous people of the northern island of Hokkaidō. (Japan)

aioli Emulsion made from garlic and olive oil, often with the addition of eggs (much like mayonnaise). (France)

aji General term for chili pepper; usually referred to by specific type—mirasol, habanero, etc. (South America)

ajiaco Chicken soup with potatoes, corn, and capers. (Colombia)

aji amarillo Yellow chili pepper that is very common in Peruvian cuisine. (South America)

aji cacho de cabra Chilean chili; these long, thin chiles turn red when ripe and are very hot. They are used locally to make hot pepper sauces. (South America)

aji chivato Very small, round chili from Colombia, used to make fresh salsas. These are extremely hot chiles. (South America)

aji colorado Chili found and used in Peruvian cuisine, often used dried (called aji panca). These elongated chiles turn deep red to burgundy colored when ripe; they are very similar to the aji amarillo in size and shape but are not as spicy, with a thicker skin and a somewhat fruity flavor. These chiles are also sometimes called aji especial, and the only chili used more often in Peruvian cuisine is the aji amarillo. (South America)

aji dulce Mild paprika; also called aji de color. (South America)

ajika Fiery red chili sauce from Georgia region. (Russia)

aji mirasol Dried version of aji amarillo (sometimes aji amarillo is called mirasol). (South America)

aji panca Dried form of aji colorado. (South America)

aji verde Light-green chili found in Chile, with a thicker skin similar to a Fresno chili (also called wax peppers) in heat and texture; used to make condiment sauces in Chile. These chiles are short and squat but still elongated, averaging 3 inches in length. (South America)

ajo Garlic. (Mexico/South America)

ajotomate Tomato salad with cumin dressing. (Iberian Peninsula)

à la carbonnade Cooked with beer, mustard, and onions. (France)

à la plancha Cooking method in which foods are cooked on a hot griddle. (Caribbean)

albaricoque   Apricots. (Iberian Peninsula)

alcaparrado   Mixture of raisins, capers, and olives of Spanish heritage used in Cuban cuisine. (Caribbean)

alcaparres   Capers. (Mexico)

alcapurrias   Fried dough stuffed with spiced meat filling; dough is made from green bananas and taro root, common in Puerto Rico. (Caribbean)

al dente   "To the tooth"; denoting the degree to which something is cooked. (Italy)

alfajores   Cookies with dulce de leche filling; common throughout South America, particularly in the southern countries. (Argentina)

al forno   Baked. (Italy)

aligot   Mashed potatoes flavored with cheese and garlic; from the south central mountain region. (France)

alioli   Emulsion of garlic and extra virgin olive oil with a little salt; the true version of this is made in a mortar and pestle, and the emulsifiers come only from the garlic. This is often made now in a food processor, using egg as the emulsifier. (Iberian Peninsula)

al vapore   Steamed. (Italy)

alla graticola   Broiled; usually refers to seafood cooked in this way. (Italy)

alla griglia   Grilled. (Italy)

allaloo   Huge, dark green leaves of taro used in making soups and stews. (Caribbean)

allo spiedo   Broiled on a spit; usually refers to meats. (Italy)

alloza   Almond; also called *almendra*. (South America)

allspice   Small berry from the pimento tree that is indigenous to the Caribbean; an important seasoning in much of the Caribbean. (Caribbean)

almejas   Clams. (Iberian Peninsula/Mexico)

almendras   Almonds. (Iberian Peninsula)

aloo   Potato. (Indian subcontinent)

alya   Rendered lamb fat taken from the tail. (Arabic-speaking countries)

am   Mango. (Indian subcontinent)

amalou   Paste made from honey almonds and olive oil, used as a spread. (North Africa)

ambar-boo   Amber-scented, long-grain rice that is very highly prized and comes from the northern region of Iran. (Persia/Iran)

am choor   Green mango powder; sour powder used to add tartness to dishes (also called khatai). (Indian subcontinent)

amêndoa   Almond. (Iberian Peninsula)

amendoim   Peanut. (South America)

amfissa   Brine-cured, rounder black olive. (Greece)

an   Sweet paste made from azuki beans and sugar. (Japan)

anca de rana   Frog legs. (Iberian Peninsula)

ancho   The dried form of poblano chiles; these are very popular for the earthy and rich aromas they provide when used in dishes. These typically are toasted on a hot *comal* (flat cooking disk) before being used in sauces, soups, and stews, as well as rehydrated and stuffed to make a different version of rellenos. These chiles are very versatile and highly regarded. (Mexico)

andagi   Fried doughnut common in Okinawa (from Portuguese influence). (Japan)

andouillettes de mâcon   Small, smoked pork sausage from Burgundy region. (France)

anguila   Eel. (Iberian Peninsula)

anguilla   Eel. (Italy)

anguille   Eel. (France)

anís   Fennel. (Iberian Peninsula)

anka   Duck. (Scandinavia)

annatto   Seeds (used to make paste or bricks) that add color and a mild musky flavor to foods (called *achiote*). (Mexico)

anolini   Half-moon–shaped stuffed pasta from the Emilia-Romagna region; traditionally served in a broth. (Italy)

anthotiro   Sheep's or goat's milk cheese made from whey; it is typically soft, with characteristics similar to ricotta. (Greece)

anticucho de corazón   Skewered and grilled beef hearts; other variations are common, using different ingredients. (Peru)

antijitos   Literally, "little whims" in Spanish; this is the name given to small foods made out of masa dough (corn dough). The name references the great variety of snacks or appetizers that can be made using small amounts of masa dough. (Mexico)

apfel   Apple. (Germany)

apfelmus   Applesauce. (Germany)

apfelstrudel   Apple strudel (apple-filled thin pastry). (Germany)

äppelkaka   Applecake. (Sweden)

apprenti   Cook apprentice in brigade system. (France)

aquacate   Avocado. (Mexico)

arame   Brown seaweed that is dried and chopped; often added to rice. (Japan)

arancia   Orange. (Italy)

arancini   Fried rice balls filled with various filling. (Italy)

Arawak   One of the indigenous tribes of the Caribbean prior to the arrival of the Europeans. (Caribbean)

arborio   Short-grain rice commonly used to make risotto. (Italy)

Arbroath smokies   Small haddock that are cleaned, salted, and then tied into pairs by the tail and smoked over a fire of oak or silver birch chips. (Scotland)

ardalena   Made from the milk of water buffalos, this cheese is highly prized for its flavor and its excellent grating and cooking properties. (Romania)

ardi gasna   Basque name for sheep's milk cheeses. (France)

arepas   (Venezuela) Corn flatbread, either served plain at meals or filled with meat, cheese, or fish and eaten as a snack from an arepera.

(Caribbean) Masa corn dough filled with various ingredients and cooked on a flat griddle; these are from the northeastern portion of South America and are also found in various sections of the Caribbean.

arhar dal   These are often called beluga lentils because, when cooked, they become shiny and glisten like beluga caviar; black in color and round. (Indian subcontinent)

aribibi Chili indigenous to Peru that is very small and elongated; these are very hot and used mainly to make fresh salsas (also called aji limo). (South America)

arrista alla fiorentina Tuscan/Florentine roasted pork with rosemary and garlic. (Italy)

arrosto Roasted. (Italy)

arroz Rice. (Iberian Peninsula/Mexico/South America)

arroz con pollo (Argentina) Chicken and rice casserole with eggs and vegetables.

    (Chile) Braised chicken and rice; common throughout South America.

    (Iberian Peninsula) Chicken and rice stew common in Spain.

artichaut Artichoke. (France)

artichauts de blanc Artichokes cooked to remain white (cooked in a blanc). (France)

ärtsoppa Yellow split pea soup; a common part of the winter diet in Sweden. (Sweden)

asa Soft seaweed found growing on reefs and used in soups. (Japan)

asado Various cuts of meat cooked over coals and usually served with chimichurri marinade, french fries, and salad. (Argentina)

asafoetida Dried sap of large fennel-like plant common to Indian subcontinent; used extensively in the cuisine, especially in dals and bean dishes that are broken down by components in the asafoetida that aid in digestion. This has a very pungent smell that mellows when cooked and should be used sparingly. (Indian subcontinent)

asam jawa Tamarind. (Malaysia)

Asiago A high-fat cow's milk cheese from the Veneto region that is aged (to sharpen the flavor) and formed in large wheels. (Italy)

asopao Rice cooked and served at a soupy consistency in the Dominican Republic. (Caribbean)

asparagi Asparagus. (Italy)

asparagi alla parmigiano Asparagus topped with Parmesan cheese and then broiled. (Italy)

asperges Asparagus. (France)

aspic Gelatin set consommé and used to glaze cold charcuterie products. (France)

atare Malegueta pepper (see pimenta malegueta). (South America)

atun Tuna. (Mexico)

au sec Nearly dry; a term used to describe the amount of reduction in a liquid just before the pan dries. (France)

avena Oat. (South America)

avgolemono Lemon sauce common in Greek cuisine; also the name of a soup prepared in the same manner. (Greece)

avyos Oats. (Russia)

awabi Abalone. (Japan)

ayu Sweetfish species from rivers. (Japan)

azafrán Saffron. (Iberian Peninsula)

azeite Olive oil. (Iberian Peninsula)

azeitonas Olives. (Iberian Peninsula)

azúcar Sugar. (Iberian Peninsula/Mexico/South America)

azuki Red bean. (Japan)

b

baba ghanoush Puréed eggplant seasoned with garlic, olive oil, and lemon juice. This is a common appetizer served with bread. (Arabic-speaking countries/Turkey)

babi Pork. (Malaysia)

babka Rich yeast cake with almonds and raisins, traditionally eaten for Easter celebration. (Poland)

bacalao (Caribbean) Salt cod; introduced to the Caribbean by the Spanish and became a main component because slave-driven culinary creations required cheap ingredients, and slaves were not afforded time and equipment to fish the rich local waters.

    (Iberian Peninsula) Salt cod.

bacalhau Salt cod. (Iberian Peninsula/South America)

bacaloa a la viscaina Salt cod preparation from the Basque region of Spain in which the cod is cooked with potatoes, leeks, or onions and spiced with chiles or paprika. (Iberian Peninsula)

baccala Dried salted cod. (Italy)

baccelli Fresh fava beans. (Italy)

bac ha Mint. (Vietnam)

badam Almond. (Indian subcontinent)

baghar Term for toasting spices in ghee to heighten their flavor (also called *tarka*). (Indian subcontinent)

bagna caôda* or *bagna cauda Sauce of olive oil, butter, garlic, and anchovies gently melted together; often served with raw vegetables to dip in the sauce. (Italy)

baharat Spice blend (many versions). (Arabic-speaking countries)

bai si khai Lemongrass. (Laos)

baji sawi Mustard seed. (Malaysia)

bakalar Salt cod. (Croatia)

baklava (Arabic-speaking countries) Pastry made of layers of thin sheets of buttered dough, coated with ground nuts and seasonings, and then baked. It is then coated with a sweet syrup that usually contains honey, lemon, and rose or orange water. The origin of this well-known pastry is not clear; it has a long history in Iran, Turkey, Greece, and the Arab countries in the Middle East.

    (Greece) Pastry made from layering and buttering phyllo dough with nuts, spices, and sugar, and then topping with a flavored honey syrup after baking.

    (Balkans) Layered phyllo, nut, and honey sweet of Middle Eastern origin (introduced by the Ottomans).

balaton Firm cow's milk cheese with small holes and mild flavor. This cheese is loaf shaped and used in a variety of manners, from a table cheese to inclusion in recipes as a melting cheese. (Hungary)

balchao Pickling. (Indian subcontinent)

ballotine Boned, stuffed, and rolled poultry, often served hot. (France)

ba mii Wheat noodle. (Thailand)

ban To toss prepared foods in a sauce. (China)

bandeja paisa Dish of ground beef, chorizo, beans, fried plantains, fried egg, chicharrón, and avocado. (Colombia)

bang trang Rice paper or rice wrapper. (Vietnam)

banha Lard. (Iberian Peninsula)

bao Steamed wheat bun. (China)

bao zi Filled steamed bun. (China)

bara brith Spiced fruit bread. (Wales)

barátfüle Pasta filled with plum jam. (Hungary)

barbacoa Spanish translation of *brabacot*. (Caribbean)

barbari Persian flatbread. (Persia/Iran)

barmbrack Spice and fruit bread commonly eaten on Halloween. (Ireland)

barszcz Beet soup. (Poland)

basilico Basil. (Italy)

basmati (Middle East) Aromatic long-grain rice from India, often used to replace aromatic rice of Iranian cuisine. (Indian subcontinent) Fragrant rice with elongated thin grains; grown in the Himalayan foothills.

basterma Dried, spiced beef. (Armenia)

bastible Heavy iron pot with three legs used to bake and roast foods over a fire. (British Isles)

batata (South America) Sweet potato; also called camote, cumar, monato, nanqui, or patata dulce. (Iberian Peninsula) Potato.

batta Stone pounding tool used for sil batta (like a mortar and pestle). (Indian subcontinent)

battawa Egyptian flatbread, typically highly seasoned with fenugreek. (Arabic-speaking countries)

bayerische crème Bavarian cream, a thickened vanilla-flavored custard mixture often served with fruits or flavored with liqueurs. (Germany)

bazha Walnut sauce from Georgia region. (Russia)

beeren Berries. (Germany)

beghrir (or baghrir) Spongy pancakes made by street vendors. (North Africa)

Beja Fresh rich sheep's milk cheese from Portugal. (Iberian Peninsula)

beldi Type of olive common to North Africa and often used to make salt-cured olives. (North Africa)

beldroega Purslane. (Iberian Peninsula)

bel paese A rich cow's milk cheese made to imitate the French Port Salut; this cheese is from the Lombardy region. (Italy)

beluga Considered the best of the sturgeon caviars, this comes from the largest species of the Caspian sturgeon and features larger (usually black, but sometimes lighter in color, ranging to gray) eggs. (Russia)

belyashi Tartar dish of fried dough with minced meat and onion filling. (Russia)

bengal gram (or kaala channa) Black chickpeas; these are typically found whole and are used in many preparations similar to common chickpeas. They are particularly common in southern and western Indian food. (Indian subcontinent)

berenjena Eggplant. (Iberian Peninsula)

besan Chickpea flour (also called gram flour). (Indian subcontinent)

betterave Beet. (France)

bier Beer. (Germany)

bigos Dish of sauerkraut and various meats and sausage stewed with onions, often mushrooms, and sometimes prunes to yield a highly flavored stew. (Poland)

binden To thicken a soup or sauce with a starch. (Germany)

bindi Okra. (Indian subcontinent)

birnen Pears. (Germany)

birnen, boden, und speck Hamburg dish of pears, beans, and bacon. (Germany)

birria Lamb and chili stew common in the state of Jalisco; the term *birria* translates as "a mess." This stew has many ingredients and often looks like a mess, but it tastes great. (Mexico)

biryanis Rice and meat dishes common throughout the subcontinent, which are made by layering partially cooked rice and marinated (and sometimes cooked) meats, and then cooking them together in a sealed earthenware vessel over a flame until done. These are usually made on festive occasions and are considered the pinnacle of rice cookery in the cuisines of the subcontinent. (Indian subcontinent)

bisteeya Famous dish traditionally consisting of squab, a lemon egg sauce, and sweetened almonds inside thin sheets of warka (thin pastry); this term often is used to describe dishes made with layers of thin pastry filled with meats, fish, etc. (North Africa)

bisteeya bil hout Version of bisteeya in which seafood is used as the filling and folded between many sheets of thin dough. (North Africa)

bitki Highly seasoned small meatballs common on a zakuski table. (Russia)

biwa Loquat. (Japan)

bixto Type of chili found in Spain. (Iberian Peninsula)

bkaila Okra and lamb dish common among the Jews of Tunisia. (North Africa)

black pudding Made from pig's blood and pork fat, this is a common accompaniment to the English breakfast. (England)

blanc Method of cooking or blanching white vegetables in water to which an acid and flour have been added; preserves the color of the vegetables. (France)

blancan Shrimp paste. (Malaysia)

blanchieren To blanch in boiling water. (Germany)

blé Wheat. (France)

Bleu d'Auvergne Rich, creamy, and pungent blue-veined cheese from the south central mountain region. (France)

blinchiki Thin, pancake-like crepe served as dessert. (Russia)

blinis Small, thin pancakes that are eaten with either sweet or savory fillings. (Finland)

bliny Buckwheat pancake or crêpe. (Russia)

boereg Stuffed pastry; these are found throughout Turkish- and Greek-influenced areas under various names that are often phonetically similar to the term *borek*. (Armenia)

bœuf Beef. (France)

bogavante European lobster (with claws) caught in the Bay of Biscay. (Iberian Peninsula)

bográs gulyás Beef gulyas (stew). (Hungary)

boliche Beef stuffed with chorizo sausage (chili-spiced sausage). (Caribbean)

bolinhos de bacalhau   Fried salt cod fritters. (Iberian Peninsula)

bollito   (Italy) Boiled.
(Mexico) Split-top bread of French influence.

bollito misto   Mixed boiled meats typically containing sausages, tongue, beef, veal, chicken and calf's head, combined with vegetables to make a very rich and flavorful meal, traditionally found in the Piedmont area. (Italy)

bollos   Steamed corn dough with various fillings; also called cachapas. (Venezuela)

bora bean   Long, rope-like green bean added to many vegetable sautés. (Caribbean)

(à la) bordelaise   made in the style of Bordeaux; most often means that a dish includes a wine sauce that has been flavored with shallots, thyme, and stock or marrow. (France)

borek   Small, stuffed savory pastries in the shape of a cigar, made from phyllo-type doughs; typically filled with cheese and often other ingredients. (Turkey)

bori-bori   Chicken soup with cornmeal dumplings. (Paraguay)

borrego   Lamb. (Iberian Peninsula/South America)

borsch   Beet soup. (Finland)

borscht   Beet soup brought from Eastern Europe and Russia. (Israel/Russia)

bottarga   Dried, compressed roe of the grey mullet eaten as an antipasto with olive oil and lemon. (Italy)

boucher   Butcher in brigade system. (France)

boudin   A type of blood sausage found in the Aosta Valley (as well as France) that is made from pig's blood and a mixture of boiled potatoes and bacon. (Italy)

bouillabaisse   Fisherman's stew from the southern Mediterranean region, colored and flavored with saffron. (France)

boulanger   Baker in brigade system. (France)

boulette   Bread-bound meatball found in Haiti. (Caribbean)

(à la) bourguignonne   In the style of Burgundy, typically denoting that a dish is cooked with red wine and includes mushrooms, onions, and bacon. (France)

boxty   Potato griddle cake made from grated potatoes cooked on a flat iron pan. (Ireland)

brabacot   Arawak term for a method of preserving foods by smoking and cooking them over green wood fire; origin of the term and cooking method called "barbeque" in the United States. (Caribbean)

brânz   Rich and salty brine-cured sheep's milk cheese found in various stages of maturity and used in a variety of ways. (Romania)

branzino   Sea bass. (Italy)

brasato   Braised. (Italy)

braten   To braise. (Germany)

bresaola   Meat made from beef that has been salted and spiced and wrapped in netting prior to being dry aged. (Italy)

bresi   Cured and smoked beef. (France)

briami   Baked, seasoned vegetable mixture topped with feta cheese. (Greece)

brigade system   Kitchen organizational system created by Escoffier; designed after a military system in which the chef is the general, and organized in a way to make the staff as efficient as possible. (France)

brik   Type of thin pastry used to make dish of the same name, which is filled with ground lamb, seasonings, and a whole egg, and then panfried. (North Africa)

brinja   Eggplant. (Indian subcontinent)

broa   Cornmeal bread common in northern Portugal. (Iberian Peninsula/Brazil)

brochet   Pike. (France)

brød   Bread. (Denmark)

brodetto   Fish soup common throughout the Adriatic Sea region. (Italy)

brot   Bread. (Germany)

bubble and squeak   Dish of leftover roast beef cooked with cabbage and onions; today, this dish commonly incorporates leftover cooked mashed potatoes as well. (England)

bucatini   Long, thin tubular pasta traditionally used with sauces containing pancetta. (Italy)

buccellato   Tuscan cake flavored with grappa, anise, citrus peel, and raisins; probably originated in Sicily. (Italy)

buerre   Butter. (France)

bukek   Croatian name for borek (see boereg). (Croatia)

bublichki   Bread in the form of a ring. (Russia)

Buddhism   Religion followed by many in Japan that developed in India, spread into China, and was introduced to Japan by the Chinese. Part of the belief system includes striving not to harm other living animals; thus, many Buddhists are vegetarians. (Japan)

budu   Fish sauce. (Malaysia)

bulghur   Cooked and cracked wheat common in the Balkan region. (Balkans)

buninca   Rich pudding set with eggs that may contain meat or vegetables. (Romania)

burghul   Bulgur wheat. (Arabic-speaking countries)

burrata   Soft cow's milk cheese made in a laborious process that includes stuffing cooked curd and cream into strings of cheese to form a balloon-shaped cheese that is traditionally wrapped in leeks and develops a unique flavor with a creamy texture. This is a very perishable cheese that only lasts a day or so. (Italy)

burrida   (Italy) Ligurian fish soup made with cuttlefish or squid, shrimp, and other fish stewed with onions, mushrooms, tomatoes, anchovies, wine, pine nuts, and extra virgin olive oil.
(Iberian Peninsula) Mediterranean fish stew with almonds.

burro   Butter. (Italy)

butaniku   Pork. (Japan)

butifarra   Dried pork sausage; a specialty made in the Chiapas region. (Mexico)

butifarra blanca   Type of cured sausage from the Catalonia region made from pork and tripe and seasoned with pine nuts. (Iberian Peninsula)

butifarra negra   Another version of the Catalonian sausage made with blood, pork belly, and spices. (Iberian Peninsula)

(à la) cabonnade   Term describing a dish cooked with beer, onions, and often mustard; from the north. (France)

C

Cabrales   A mixed milk blue-veined cheese made from cow, sheep, and goat milk from the Asturias region of northern Spain. (Iberian Peninsula)

cabrito   Kid or young goat. (Iberian Peninsula)

cabrito al pastor   Spit-roasted goat. (Mexico)

cacahuete   Peanut. (Mexico)

cacao   Cocoa bean. (Mexico)

cacciatorino   Hunter's salami; salami made of half pork and half beef with pork fat, black pepper, garlic, and other spices that are aged for at least a month. This traditionally was made to be taken and eaten on trips (hence, the term *hunter*). (Italy)

cacciucco   Fishermen's stew of Livorno (in Tuscany region). (Italy)

cachapa   Fresh corn pancake, like a tortilla, served with cheese and/or ham. (Venezuela)

cachito   Hot bread roll stuffed with ham. (Venezuela)

caciocavallo   A semisoft cow's milk cheese common in southern Italy, versatile in its use depending on its age. When young, it is eaten as a table cheese; after aging for months, it will be used as a grating cheese. (Italy)

caciotta   Cheese that may be made with cow's, ewe's, or goat's milk, or a mixture of milks. It is a small, flat cheese that weighs less than 2 pounds and is very common in central Italy. (Italy)

ca de   Japanese eggplant. (Vietnam)

Caerphilly   Well-known Welsh cow's milk cheese with moist texture and mild flavor; this cheese is used in cooking and often eaten with bread. (Wales)

café   Coffee. (Mexico)

caffe   Coffee. (Italy)

cai dao   Chinese cleaver. (China)

cai dun   Cutting board; typically a slice of tree trunk that has been treated with salt and oil. The best boards are made from dense trees such as honey locust, ginkgo, and Chinese olive. (China)

cajú   Cashew fruit. (South America)

calabasa   Pumpkin or squash; general term for this group of vegetables. (South America)

calabaza   Squash. (Mexico)

calamar   Squid. (Iberian Peninsula/Mexico/South America)

calamari   Squid. (Italy)

calçot   Special type of spring onion found in Spain. (Iberian Peninsula)

calçotada   Grilled calçots, a type of spring onion, typically served with *salbitxada* sauce. (Iberian Peninsula)

caldereta de langosta   Lobster stew. (Iberian Peninsula)

caldo   (Ecuador) Soup (also called sopa); many varieties are available, especially in markets. (Mexico) Stew.

caldo de mariscos   Shellfish stew. (Mexico)

caldo de peixe   Coconut soup with fish. (Brazil)

caldo gallego   Hearty soup made of beans, greens, sausage, beef, or veal; from the Galacian region of Spain. (Iberian Peninsula)

caldo verde   Common soup from Portugal made from potatoes and cabbage. (Iberian Peninsula/Brazil)

callo de hacha con aguacate   Avocado stuffed with pinna clams (Mexico)

caltaboşi   Type of sausage made with pork and liver. (Romania)

calvados   Apple brandy from Normandy region. (France)

calzone   Stuffed dough filled with various fillings and baked; this is essentially a pizza that has been folded to enclose the toppings before baking. (Italy)

camarão con coco   Shrimp in coconut sauce. (Brazil)

camarónes   Shrimp. (Mexico and South America)

camarónes a la diabla   Shrimp in spicy chili sauce. (Mexico)

Camembert   Rich cow's milk cheese produced originally in village of same name in Normandy. (France)

Camerano   Goat's milk cheese with a sharp taste from northern Spain; usually eaten with honey and fruit for dessert. (Iberian Peninsula)

cana de açucar   Sugarcane. (South America)

canã de azúcar   Sugarcane; this import from India and Africa (originally from New Guinea) became the major crop in the Caribbean, and its cultivation led to the slave trade in the Americas. (Caribbean)

cancha   Popping corn; different from well-known popcorn in that it is larger and doesn't actually explode. (South America)

candele   Long and large tubular pastas that are traditional for meat sauces. (Italy)

canederli   Dumplings. (Italy)

canestrato   Uncooked hard ripened ewe's milk cheese. (Italy)

cannelloni   Large, tube-shaped pastas that typically include thick meat fillings and are baked after being smothered with sauce and sometimes cheese. These are made by cutting rectangles of pasta sheets, piping the filling along the entire center of the length, and then rolling the pasta sheets around the filling—ending up with a filled pasta "log." (Italy)

cannoli   Fried pastry dough filled with sweetened ricotta cheese and other ingredients. (Italy)

Cantal   Cow's milk cheese found in varying stages of maturity (and thus with a stronger taste in longer-aged selections) from the southern central mountains. (France)

capellini   Very thin ribbon pasta best used with broth-based or sieved sauces that cling to this delicate pasta. (Italy)

capim-santo   Lemongrass. (Iberian Peninsula)

capocolla   Cured pork shoulder seasoned with either hot or sweet peppers (sold as hot or sweet capocolla). (Italy)

caponata   Eggplant cooked in sweet-and-sour sauce from Sicily. (Italy)

cappelletti   Pasta shaped like a kerchief that is made by filling a 2-inch square piece of dough, folding the dough in half to cover the filling by putting the points of opposite corners together to form a triangle, and then pulling the two other ends together to cover the filled section of the dough. These are typically filled with meat or cheese. (Italy)

capperi Caper. (Italy)

caprese Fresh tomato and water buffalo mozzarella (called "fresh mozzarella" in the United States) salad topped with basil and extra virgin olive oil. (Italy)

capretto Young goat. (Italy)

capriolo Venison. (Italy)

capsaicin Chemical found in chiles in varying levels that causes a burning sensation when eaten. A system of measurement known as the Scoville scale was developed to rate the intensity of the heat from chiles; ratings range from 0 for bell peppers to reportedly over 1 million for naga-bin jolokia chiles grown in India. (Mexico)

carambola Elongated star-shaped fruit; also commonly called star fruit. (Caribbean)

caramelle Filled pastas that are shaped like a wrapped candy and traditionally would be filled with a sweet filling, such as pumpkin or winter squash. These are made by filling lengths of rectangular pasta with intermittent small amounts of the sweet filling, cutting in between the fillings, and rolling the filling with the pasta (leaving approximately 3/4 of an inch of unfilled dough on each end of the filled sections). The free ends are then twisted like a candy wrapper, and the resulting filled pastas are often cooked and served with a light butter sauce. (Italy)

carangue Family of fatty fish common in the Caribbean, including species known locally as cigar fish, big eye, and cavalli jack, to name a few. (Caribbean)

carbonada Beef stew with rice, potatoes, sweet potatoes, corn, squash, apples, and pears. (Argentina)

carbonara Cooked with sauce made from cured pork jowl or pancetta, eggs, and Parmesan cheese; popular way of cooking pasta, for example, spaghetti alla carbonara. (Italy)

carciofi Globe artichokes. (Italy)

cardi Cardoons. (Italy)

Carême, Marie-Antoine Famous French chef credited with developing mother sauces, inventing the wedding cake, and refining the cuisine of his day. (France)

Carib One of the indigenous tribes that thrived in the Caribbean (*Caribbean* is derived from this tribe's name) prior to the arrival of the Europeans. (Caribbean)

carnaroli Prized short-grain rice used to make risotto. (Italy)

carne asada Roasted meat. (Mexico)

carne de boi Beef (Portuguese term). (South America)

carne de res Beef. (South America)

carne de sol Grilled, salted meat served with beans, rice, and vegetables. (Bolivia/Brazil)

carnero Mutton. (South America)

carne seca (Brazil) Air-dried and salted beef (similar to jerky).
(Mexico) Dried beef.

carnitas Pork that has been very slowly cooked until the meat can easily be shredded and then fried before being served. (Mexico)

ca rot Carrot. (Vietnam)

carotte Carrot. (France)

carpaccio Thinly sliced beef topped with sliced mushrooms and traditionally served with a sauce made from parsley, capers, anchovies, olive oil, and vinegar. (Italy)

cartoccio Wrapped in parchment or foil and baked. (Italy)

caruru Mixture of okra, shrimp, vegetables, and peppers made into a sauce for fish. (Brazil)

cascabel Called the "rattle bell" because, in its dried form, the seeds rattle within the thin shell of this round, small chili. Cascabels are commonly used in sauces and soups or stews; these come from central Mexico and are most common in this region. (Mexico)

cascadura Armored fish that resembles a catfish; found in Trinidad and prized by locals. (Caribbean)

cassareep Condiment made from boiling bitter cassava juice with sugar and spices; used in traditional Caribbean cooking. Cassareep has also been used historically as a means of preserving meats by cooking them in this liquid to make a sort of stew that would be continually added to. (Caribbean)

cassata Sweet, rich cake made with dried fruit and almond paste. (Italy)

casse croûte tunisien Tunisian sandwich typically made with a baguette; influenced by the French during the period of their rule. (North Africa)

cassoulet Dish of stewed beans and various meats; from the southwest region. (France)

castagne Chestnut. (Italy)

castagnoccio Flatbread made from chestnut flour. (Italy)

castanha Brazil nut. (Iberian Peninsula)

Castel Branco Runny sheep's milk cheese from the Viseu area in the northern region of Portugal; this cheese is aged until hard and used as a grating cheese. (Iberian Peninsula)

castelmagno A very highly regarded semisoft cow's milk cheese from the Piedmont region, which, when mature, develops a blue-veined mold. (Italy)

casumarzu Essentially a pecorino that has had maggots added to it during its maturation, to impart a particular flavor to the cheese. (Italy)

catalogna Type of chicory sometimes called Italian dandelion. (Italy)

causa Potatoes cooked, puréed, and layered with various ingredients, including peppers, hardboiled eggs, olives, sweet potatoes, lettuce, and cheese; often served with onion sauce. (Peru)

cavolfiore Cauliflower. (Italy)

cavolo Cabbage. (Italy)

cavolo nero Tuscan cabbage. (Italy)

cawl Welsh stew made from lamb and leeks. (Wales)

cazón Dogfish (essentially small sharks). (Mexico)

cazuela (Iberian Peninsula) Earthenware pot used to cook and serve stews, soups, and beans.
(Chile) Soup with meat or chicken, potato, corn, and squash or other vegetables; influence comes from Italy.
(Uruguay) Soup made with either seafood or tripe.

cebollas Onions. (Mexico/South America)

cebollas ajo Garlic. (Mexico)

centeio Barley. (Iberian Peninsula)

cereza Cherry. (Iberian Peninsula/South America)

cernia Grouper. (Italy)

cerveza Beer. (Mexico)

ceviche (Mexico) Seafood mixed with citrus juice and other seasonings and "cooked" by the acid. Ceviche (or cibiche) is most often found as fresh shellfish with lime, cilantro, and chiles in Mexico.

(Peru) Cold, raw seafood marinated in lime juice, peppers, and onions; served with cold potatoes and sweet potatoes.

chaat masala   Tart spice blend made from green mango powder, cumin, black salt, asafoetida, black pepper, ginger, chili, and sometimes pomegranate powder (anardana) and mint. (Indian subcontinent)

chaawal   Rice (uncooked). (Indian subcontinent).

chai   Tea. (Russia)

chairo   Lamb soup with potatoes, vegetables, chuños, and ají. (Bolivia)

champ   Mashed potatoes and spring onions. (Ireland)

Champagne   Name of region and of sparkling wine from same region in northern France. (France)

champignon   General term for mushroom. (France)

champignon de Paris   Button mushroom. (France)

chanh vo xanh   Lime. (Vietnam)

channa   Chickpea. (Indian subcontinent)

channa dal   Made from smaller species of related chickpea, these are the most common dal food in Indian cuisine, and their sweet and nutty flavor is highly prized. Because these are high in indigestible soluble fibers that can cause flatulence, they are often cooked with *asafoetida* to counter this effect. (Indian subcontinent)

chanpuru   Stir-fried dishes common in Okinawa region. (Japan)

chao   Stir frying. (China)

chao guo   Wok; these are typically made of iron and must be properly seasoned and thoroughly dried after each use, or they will rust. (China)

chao tian jiao   Small red chili that is commonly dried and used in Chinese cooking, especially in Sichuan cuisine. (China)

chao xiang   Stir frying in infused oils. (China)

chapati   Flat, round bread made from wheat flour and cooked in oil or ghee on a tava (flat griddle-like pan); common in the northern part of the Indian subcontinent. (Indian subcontinent)

chapulines   Grasshoppers in the Oaxaca region that are a prized part of the diet when in season. They are often eaten with tortillas, chiles, and lime after being toasted on a comal. (Mexico)

charcuterie   General term for foods made from force-meats and other preservation techniques, such as sausages, pâtés, ballotines, galantines, mousselines, and terrines. (France)

charlotte russe   Dessert made of sweetened and congealed mousse inside a ring of ladyfinger cookies. (Russia)

charmoula   Marinade used with fish and poultry to make tagines and other preparations. (North Africa)

Charollais   Breed of cattle prized for flavorful and tender meat. (France)

char siu   Cantonese roasted pork, typically made with red food coloring to dye the meat red. (China)

char siu bao   Roast pork-filled steamed buns, made with leftover char siu. (China)

chiao-tzu   Pot stickers in the style of Beijing (translates to "little dumplings"). (China)

châtaigne   Chestnut. (France)

chaudiere   Rustic fisherman's stew from northern part of the country. (France)

chebureki   Fried pastry with mutton or lamb and onion filling; of Crimean Tartar origin. (Russia)

cheddar   Semifirm cow's milk cheese with varying levels of sharp flavor, depending on the amount of aging. (England)

chef de cuisine   Kitchen chef in the brigade system who would oversee the daily operation of the staff and food production. (France)

chef de partie   Senior chef in the brigade system. (France)

chelou   Persian style of cooking rice in which a portion of cooked rice is mixed with eggs or sometimes yogurt, placed on the bottom of a pan and covered with more cooked rice, and then baked with clarified butter to yield a crusted bottom that is served on top of or along with the finished rice dish. (Persia/Iran)

cheung fun   Steamed rice roll. (China)

chèvre   Goat cheese. (France)

chhana   Curds made from boiled milk with a souring agent; used in Bengali sweets. (Indian subcontinent)

chicha   National drink of Chile that is made from fermented corn; also found in other parts of South America. (Chile)

chicharrón   (Mexico) Fried pork fat that is eaten as a snack, often with chili sauce and lime juice; common throughout Mexico.

(Colombia) Fried pork fat eaten as a snack.

chichi   Fermented corn beverage common throughout much of South America. (Peru)

chilaca   Elongated thin and curved chili that is normally dried and used in its dried form, which is called *pasilla*. (Mexico)

chilhuacle negro   From the Oaxaca region of southern Mexico, these chiles are an integral part of the mole negro that is found in this region. (Mexico)

chili de arbol   Called the "tree" chili, these are typically found dried and are slender and curved, with a high level of capsaicin; mainly used to add heat to dishes. (Mexico)

chili rellenos   Stuffed chiles dipped in whipped egg whites and fried; the poblano is the most common variety of chili used for this, although others may be used as well. (Mexico)

chilorio   Pork and chili stew from the central highland area of Mexico; pork cooked in this manner is often shredded and used in burritos and other preparations. (Mexico)

chiltepin   Very small, hot chiles that are believed to be one of the oldest species and are used in soups, stews, bean dishes, and hot salsas; also sometimes called piquin, or bird pepper, in reference to their sharp bite. (Mexico)

chimichurri Sauce made from fresh herbs, vinegar, chili, and onions or garlic to be served with grilled meats. (Argentina)

chipa Manioc bread with egg and cheese. (Paraguay)

chipa soo Cornbread with meat filling. (Paraguay)

chipotle Smoked and dried jalapeño chiles; these are often used in cooked salsas and sauces. (Mexico)

chirashi Scattered sushi made by placing ingredients on top of the sushi rice. (Japan)

chiryeshnya Cherry. (Russia)

chiva Young goat (kid). (Mexico)

chivito Steak sandwich with lettuce, bacon, tomato, and cheese; the larger version is called chivito al plato. (Uruguay)

choclo Fresh corn; also called coronta, tuzas, and mazorca de maíz tierno. (South America)

choclo con queso Corn on the cob with melted cheese. (Peru)

chorba Soup. (Turkey)

chorizo (Iberian Peninsula) Mildly spicy cured sausage that is seasoned with paprika; common throughout Spain.
(Mexico) Spicy pork sausage that is very common throughout Mexico.

chorros a la criolla Steamed mussels cooled and topped with onion and corn salsa. (Peru)

chou Cabbage. (France)

choucroute Sauerkraut; fermented (soured) cabbage. (France)

choufleur Cauliflower. (France)

chouriço Cured sausage from Portugal seasoned with paprika and garlic; more garlicky than the Spanish chorizo. (Iberian Peninsula)

chowli dal Skinned and split black-eyed peas. (Indian subcontinent)

chuchoca Corn cooked on hot embers. (Argentina)

chufa Tiger nut. (Iberian Peninsula)

chui Technique of using the back of a cleaver to pummel or mash a product; often done to meats to tenderize them. (China)

chuño (South America) Freeze-dried potato; a method of preservation that has been part of the Andean way of life for many centuries

chupe Chowder-like fish soup. (Chile/Ecuador/Peru)

chupe de camarones Shrimp stew. (Peru)

churrasco Beef, fried eggs, vegetables, fried potatoes, avocado, rice, and tomato. (Ecuador)

chutney Relish made from various ingredients; often sweet and spicy. (Indian subcontinent)

cidre Fermented juice of pears or apples. (France)

cime di rapa Turnip greens. (Italy)

ciorbă Tangy soup. (Romania)

cipolle Onions. (Italy)

citrico Citrus. (Mexico)

citron Citrus fruit. (Italy)

ciuppin Ligurian fish stew with tomatoes, garlic, and white wine; the cioppino of San Francisco is a version of this stew. (Italy)

clafouti Baked custard typically made with cherries; from the south central mountain region. (France)

clafouti aux myrtilles Clafouti with blueberries. (France)

clătite Thin pancake or crepe. (Romania)

coca Flat sheet bread made from yeast-leavened dough and often topped with various ingredients. (Iberian Peninsula)

coca d'spinacs Flatbread with spinach from Balearic Islands. (Iberian Peninsula)

cochinita pibil Barbequed pork wrapped in a banana leaf that is a specialty of the Yucatán region. (Mexico)

cocido Chickpea, pork, and chorizo stew. (Iberian Peninsula)

cocido gallego Galician stew of white beans, ham, potatoes, turnip tops, and chorizo. (Iberian Peninsula)

cocido madrilène The Madrid version of the cocido, or stew, which contains chorizo, cabbage, potatoes, chickpeas, and a variety of meats. This dish is traditionally served in three courses: the first includes the broth, followed by the vegetables and chickpeas and finally the meat. (Iberian Peninsula)

cocina criolla Term to describe the cooking of parts of the Caribbean in which native ingredients and techniques have been mixed with European and African techniques and ingredients; see Creole and crillo. (Caribbean)

coclo Large meatballs made from ground beef or veal with rice and spices. (North Africa)

coco Coconut. (Mexico/South America)

colcannon Dish of mashed potatoes with cabbage or kale. (Ireland)

comal (Iberian Peninsula) Griddle.
(Mexico) Flat cooking stone (now more commonly made of metal), used to cook a variety of traditional Mexican dishes (tortillas, sopes, etc.); also used to char tomatoes and toast dried chiles.

communard Cook who prepared the food for the staff in brigade system. (France)

Comté Excellent melting cheese from the Jura region; made from cow's milk and formed into very large wheels, often used in making fondue. (France)

conch Name of a family of large sea snails; the large gigas species is prized in the Caribbean, where it is known for its delicate flesh. (Caribbean)

conchigliette Small, seashell-shaped pasta that is well suited for broth-based soups containing small vegetables or legumes. (Italy)

conchiglioni Very large, shell-shaped pastas meant to be cooked and then stuffed and baked. (Italy)

confit General term used to describe a preserve; most often used to describe duck, goose, or pork cooked and preserved in their own fat. (France)

confit de canard Duck legs cooked and preserved in their own fat. (France)

congee Rice porridge-like dish with various toppings. (China)

congri Rice cooked with red beans. (Caribbean)

congrios Conger eels. (South America)

coniglio Rabbit. (Italy)

coniglio in porchetta Rabbit cooked in manner of Tuscan roast pig (see *porchetta*). (Italy)

consommé Clarified flavorful stocks garnished with various ingredients and cuts. (France)

conucos Mounding technique of farming practiced by the native Arawaks and Caribs in which different types of vegetables were grown together in a mound; this technique is still used in some parts of the Caribbean today. (Caribbean)

coocoo Dish of cornmeal and okra cooked with coconut milk in African-influenced areas of Caribbean. (Caribbean)

coppa Also known as *capocollo*, this a pork neck that is marinated in stages with wine, salt, and seasoning, and then is encased before being aged. (Italy)

coppa al ginepro A specialty type of coppa that is rubbed with juniper berries during the aging process to impart its special flavor. (Italy)

coq au vin Cockerel stewed in red wine. (France)

coquille Saint Jacques Scallop. (France)

coquimol Thickened coconut cream made in the same manner as *crème anglaise* but with coconut milk instead of milk or cream. (Caribbean)

cordeiro Lamb. (Iberian Peninsula)

cordero Lamb. (Iberian Peninsula/Mexico)

Cornish pasty Pastry filled with meat, vegetables, and sometimes sweets that was traditionally taken to work for a carry-out meal. (England)

Cotswold Type of Gloucester cheese made from cow's milk with a sharp flavor and a semifirm texture; usually flavored with chives and colored orange/yellow. (England)

couscous Small grains of semolina wheat (a hard wheat) made by wetting slightly coarse grounds of the wheat, then coating the grounds in flour and drying them. This results in a grain that is similar in many ways to tiny rounds of pasta that are typically steamed in a particular manner to yield a light-textured grain enjoyed as a regular part of North African diet. (North Africa)

couscoussier Pot and tight-fitting colander combination used to make couscous. The couscous is steamed in the top colander by the food that is cooked in the bottom pot. (North Africa)

couve Collard greens. (South America)

couve à mineira Collard greens cooked with onions and garlic. (Brazil)

couve galega Galician cabbage. (Iberian Peninsula)

cozido Stew with many vegetables (usually contains yuca, cabbage, corn, and green plantains). (Brazil)

cozinha baiano Cuisine of the Bahia region of Brazil that is considered to be the most creative and influential in the country, mostly because of the influence of the African immigrants (from the slave trade via Portugal) who lent techniques and ingredients to the development of this cuisine. (South America)

cozza Mussels. (Italy)

crauti Sauerkraut. (Italy)

crema al limone Lemon cream used in sweet preparations. (Italy)

crema catalana Dessert from Catalonia made very much like a crème brûlée in France; a custard with a caramelized surface. (Iberian Peninsula)

crème Cream. (France)

crème anglaise "English cream" from French influence, who credit this preparation to the English; consists of egg yolks, milk, and sugar (vanilla is often added as well) cooked gently until thickened. (Caribbean)

crème de cassis Liqueur made from black currants. (France)

crempogs Buttermilk pancakes. (Wales)

Creole (Caribbean) Term used to describe the native cuisine and culture of the Caribbean. In reference to the cuisine, the term indicates the influence of primarily African and Spanish (and some French) cuisines; many also extend the term to include influences from other cuisines in this region, such as Native American (specifically, Taino and Carib), East Indian, and Chinese.

(South America) Term used to describe the mixed indigenous and European culture, and the cuisine that has developed since these cultures have come together.

crème fraîche Clotted, soured cream. (France)

crêpe Thin, delicate pancake, often used in sweet preparations by wrapping these around fillings or layering with other ingredients. (France)

crillo Spanish term meaning "native or indigenous" that is the root of the now common term *Creole*. (Caribbean/South America)

croquetas (Iberian Peninsula) Thick, cooled béchamel with various other ingredients added, and then breaded and fried; typically served as tapas.

(Caribbean) Breaded and fried thick milk dough/sauce, made essentially like béchamel, that is cooled before breading; various ingredients are added, such as shrimp, chicken, or ham.

crostini Sliced and toasted bread topped with various ingredients. (Italy)

croustade Rustic pastry wrapped around various sweet fillings; from southwestern region. Also a term that describes an edible container used to hold other foods. (France)

cu cai trang Daikon radish. (Vietnam)

cuchillo Knife. (Iberian Peninsula)

cuitlacoche Corn fungus (also called huitlacoche) that is prized for its earthy flavor. (Mexico)

culatello Cured rump of pork; this is a specialty of the Parma area of Emilia-Romagna. (Italy)

Cullen skink Chowder made of finnan haddock. (Scotland)

curantos Baked stew/casserole made with alternating layers of meats, sausages, potatoes, and cabbage (and sometimes other ingredients); reflects some of the German influence in Chile. Often, this preparation is also found along the coast, where it is made with shellfish instead of meat. (Chile)

curries Generic name used to describe Indian-influenced spice dishes that contain some of the typical Indian spice blends commonly referred to as "curry" by the British (although not by the Indians; in India, a *kari* is the name of a vegetable dish in Southern India that contains spices and coconut milk). (England)

curry (Sweden) Generic name for spice blends of Indian origin used in the cuisine of Sweden and other Scandinavian countries.

(Indian subcontinent) Generic English term for foods with a spiced sauce from the period in which the British colonized India. The term is thought to have derived from the Tamil *kari*, which denoted a dish that was made with black pepper and would typically have a spicy sauce. Curry powder is an English invention and has little in common with the many spice blends in India (most are called *masala* in India).

cuy Guinea pig. (South America)

d

dafina Stew of Jewish origin that typically contains meat, rice, potatoes, and eggs and is cooked on Friday to be eaten on the holy Saturday. (North Africa)

dahi Yogurt. (Indian subcontinent)

daikon Large white radish. (Japan)

daging Meat. (Malaysia)

dal Split pulses (lentils, beans, peas, etc.); also the general term for cooked dishes with pulses. (Indian subcontinent)

dämpfen To steam (sometimes called *dünsten*). (Germany)

Danbo Nutty-flavored semisoft cow's milk cheese that is a very common household cheese in Denmark. (Denmark)

darbari Prized long-grain rice from Iran. (Persia/Iran)

dashi Seaweed stock made from kombu and bonito flakes; used extensively in Japanese cuisine in soups, sauces, and other preparations. Ichiban Dashi is the name of the initial (and stronger) stock, which is often strained and the konbu and bonito re-used to make a niban dashi (second dashi), which is weaker in aroma and strength. (Japan)

dau dua Long beans; also called yard-long beans. (Vietnam)

dau hao Oyster sauce. (Vietnam)

daun Fresh herbs (leaves). (Malaysia)

dendê Palm nut oil; this oil is orange in color, distinctly flavored, and comes from a variety of African palm. (South America)

dengaku Skewered and grilled vegetables and other ingredients with miso glaze/marinade. (Japan)

dentice Delicate Mediterranean fish; sometimes called "dentex" in the United States. (Italy)

derelye Filled pasta. (Hungary)

dfina One-pot stew (to be eaten on the Sabbath) common to the Sephardi Jews. (Israel)

dhania Coriander (called *cilantro* when the leaves are used). (Indian subcontinent)

dhansak masala Spice blend common in the western coastal region of India, where Persian peoples landed and influenced the cuisine. This blend would typically contain cinnamon, cardamom, cloves, cumin, black pepper, coriander, nutmeg, star anise, fenugreek leaves, ginger, and chiles. (Indian subcontinent)

dhoodh Milk. (Indian subcontinent)

dian fan guo Rice cooker. (China)

dibs Concentrated grape juice. (Arabic-speaking countries)

dibs rim'an Pomegranate syrup (often called pomegranate molasses). (Arabic-speaking countries)

Dijon City in central France in which wine mustard is produced under the same name. (France)

dill Herb; has same name in the United States. (Sweden)

djaj Chicken. (North Africa)

djon djon Type of mushroom from the hills of Haiti that is highly prized for its meaty flavor and often added to rice dishes. (Caribbean)

dofu Another name for tofu. (Japan)

dolmas Stuffed vegetables. Turkey: Stuffed foods; a typical dolma is grape leaves stuffed with seasoned rice and lamb. (Armenia)

donbeh Rendered fat of fat-tailed sheep used as cooking fat, traditionally in Persian cuisine. (Persia/Iran)

dosa Thin flatbread made from rice and lentil flour; also called dosai. (Indian subcontinent)

dou ban jiang Chili paste made from fermented chiles and fava beans; this can be found in various stages of maturity and is commonly used in Sichuan cooking. (China)

double Gloucester Whole milk cheese from the Gloucester area of England with a creamy texture and a full flavor. (England)

dou chi Fermented black beans; actually green soybeans that have been fermented and often have ginger, chiles, and rice wine added to the mixture. (China)

dou fu ru Fermented bean curd. (China)

dry pastas Dried pastas are a part of southern Italian cuisine; this part of Italy experienced a large growth in the manufacturing of dried pastas in the eighteenth and nineteenth centuries. Dried pasta was much cheaper to make than fresh pasta, and it contains no egg. (Italy)

dulce de leche Caramelized milk, often made with sweetened condensed milk, simply boiled in an unopened can in water until caramelized (takes about four hours). (Argentina)

dum Slow-cooking or braising foods in a sealed pot; this was traditionally done in pots whose lids were sealed with dough to prevent moisture from escaping. (Indian subcontinent)

dünsten (or pochieren) To poach (also may mean to steam, depending on usage). (Germany)

duxelle Ground mushrooms and shallots cooked in butter and finished with herbs (and sometimes cream). (France)

e

edamame Fresh soya beans. (Japan)

edo miso Lightly salty red miso. (Japan)

eintopf Stews or casseroles with a variety of ingredients to make a one-pot meal; also a term used to indicate the stewing method. (Germany)

ekiben Station lunchbox (bento) for which each region has its own variations; these are sold at the train stations and usually highlight local ingredients. (Japan)

elaichi Cardamom. (Indian subcontinent)

elies neratzates Olives cured and then steeped in bitter orange juice. (Greece)

empanada de humita Pastry filled with corn, onion, cheese, and flour. (Argentina)

empanadas Spanish term for pastry pies with various savory fillings that are typically fried; common in northwestern Spain, Mexico, and South America. (Iberian Peninsula, Argentina, Bolivia, Chile and Mexico)

enchiladas Filled tortillas topped with chili sauce. (Mexico)

endive Belgian endive. (France)

enokitake Wild mushroom grows in clusters on specific trees; the wild mushrooms are shorter and darker than the more commonly cultivated enokitake which are grown in clusters with long stems and very small caps. Often simply called *enoki*. (Japan)

ensaïmada Spiral-shaped pastry made with lard. (Iberian Peninsula)

entremetier Entrée cook in the brigade system. (France)

epazote Distinct herb sometimes called wormseed in the United States; used in cooking beans and other preparations. (Mexico)

epoisses Strong cheeses from Burgundy region; both rich and salty. (France)

erbe aromatiche Aromatic herbs. (Italy)

erizos de mar Sea urchins. (South America)

er jin tiao Chili type used to make dou ban jiang. (China)

escabeche (Peru) Preserved fish or vegetables in vinegar. (South America) Preserved in vinegar; a common technique in Spanish-influenced areas.

escabeche de pescado Pickled fish; very common throughout the Pacific coast of South America. (Chile)

escargot Broiled snails stuffed with garlic and herb butter. (France)

Escoffier, Georges Auguste Famous French chef credited with developing the brigade system for organizing a large kitchen operation and with refining the cuisine of his day. (France)

escupiñas Little clams. (Iberian Peninsula)

espárragos Asparagus. (Iberian Peninsula)

espinaca Spinach. (Iberian Peninsula)

etli beber dolmasi Stuffed green peppers. (Turkey)

Evora Sheep's milk cheese from Portugal; creamy when fresh, and sharp and firm when found matured. (Iberian Peninsula)

f

fabada asturiana Stew of cabbage, potatoes, beans, ham, and chorizo from the Asturias region of northern Spain. (Iberian Peninsula)

fagiano Pheasant. (Italy)

fagioli Beans. (Italy)

falafel Seasoned fava bean or chickpea purée that is deep fried; common in Arab-influenced Middle Eastern countries. (Arabic-speaking countries/Israel)

falukorv Smooth boiled sausage made with a mixture of beef or veal with pork; these are lightly smoked for a milder flavor. (Sweden)

fan Rice. (China)

fänkål Fennel. (Sweden)

farcito Stuffed. (Italy)

farinha de mandioca Cassava flour. (South America)

fårkött Mutton. (Scandinavia)

farls Individual soda breads that are traditionally eaten with Irish Fry or sliced in half to hold eggs, bacon, or sausage between the layers (think of a breakfast sandwich—these are the originals). Also a name given to foods that are cut into wedges; for example, potato farls would be wedged cuts of potato. (Ireland)

farofas Cassava meal browned in butter. (Brazil)

farro A type of wheat variety that is typically cooked and eaten as whole grain. (Italy)

fava Fava bean. (Iberian Peninsula)

fava santorinis Yellow split pea purée. (Greece)

favata Pork and bean stew with fennel and cabbage of Sardinia. (Italy)

fegatini Chicken liver spread often served with crostini. (Italy)

fegatino Pork liver sausage from Marche. (Italy)

feijãos Beans. (South America)

feijãos preto Black beans. (South America)

feijoada Meat stew served with rice and beans. (Brazil)

ferran A communal oven used to bake breads; once the ovens cooled from the breads, they were used to make tagines and other stewed or simmered foods. These are much less common in North Africa than they once were but still can be found in smaller villages, where the townspeople can be seen bringing specially marked loaves of breads to the ferran to bake in the manner of their liking. (North Africa)

feta The best known of the Greek cheeses, made from either sheep's or goat's milk; it is typically stored in brine. (Greece)

fettuccine Thicker ribbon pasta, meant to be used with thicker, cream-based sauces or other sauces of similar consistency. (Italy)

fideuà Paella-like dish from the Valencia region made with pasta instead of rice. (Iberian Peninsula)

figo Fig. (Italy/Iberian Peninsula)

finnan haddock Cured and smoked haddock made in Findon; this is well known and sought after all over the world. (Scotland)

finocchiella Fennel seeds. (Italy)

finocchio Fennel. (Italy)

finocchiona Anise-flavored salami made of finely ground pork and pork fat seasoned with fennel seeds. (Italy)

fisch Fish. (Germany)

fish and chips Battered and fried fish (usually cod or other lean whitefish) and fried potatoes. (England)

fiskefarse Fish forcemeat, often shaped like a meatball and poached. (Norway)

fiskepudding Similar to fish forcemeat, but it might be a little softer and formed in a casserole. (Norway) *fiskesuppe*   Fish soup; many varieties are common in Norway, including several that are similar to chowders. (Norway)

flan   (Argentina) Custard.
(Brazil) Custard with caramel on the bottom.

fleisch   Meat. (Germany)

flomaria   Pasta type that is either thin like a string or slightly flattened like linguini. (Greece)

flor de calabaza   Squash blossoms. (Mexico)

flor de jamaica   Hibiscus flower. (Mexico)

focaccia   Yeast-leavened bread made in Liguria; flattened like a pizza (but usually square) and topped with olive oil, salt, and sometimes onions or olives. (Italy)

fogas   Fish found only in Lake Balaton in Hungary, and a relative of the salmon; these have white flesh and are very flavorful. (Hungary)

fogolar   Open hearth. (Italy)

foie gras (de canard, de oie)   Fattened liver (of duck, of goose). (France)

fondue   Melted; term is used to describe melted cheese used for dipping other ingredients. (France)

fonduta   Melted cheese dip. (Italy)

fontina   Rich cow's milk cheese from the Val D'Aosta region, with excellent melting qualities and flavor. (Italy)

foo-foo   Traditionally made with mashed yams or cassava, this is also made with plantains in the Caribbean; this dish comes from sub-Saharan West Africa, where the technique of cooking starchy foods until tender and then pounding them into a glutinous mixture has long been part of the culinary tradition. (Caribbean)

fool   Mixture of sweetened fruit and cream. (Ireland)

fool akhdar   Fresh fava beans. (Arabic-speaking countries)

fool misri   Small, dried brown fava beans. (Arabic-speaking countries)

fool mudammas   Mashed and spiced fava beans. (Arabic-speaking countries)

forelle   Trout. (Germany)

fradinho   Black-eyed peas. (South America)

Frankfurter grüne sosse   Green sauce in the style of Frankfurter; this sauce is made by crushing fresh herbs and mixing them with mayonnaise and sour cream to yield a highly flavored sauce that is served with potatoes or other bland foods. (Germany)

freir   Fried. (South America)

fresa   Strawberry. (Iberian Peninsula/Mexico/South America)

fresh pastas   Fresh pastas are made with egg as well as wheat and water. These yield a more delicate product, as they do not have the strength that dried, eggless pastas have. Fresh pastas can also be flavored and will deliver flavor better than would a dried pasta made without egg (dried, eggless pastas are often colored and said to be flavored, but the most notable part is the color). (Italy)

frico   Cheese fritter. (Italy)

fríjol de manteca   Lima bean. (South America)

frijoles   Beans. (Iberian Peninsula/Mexico/South America)

frijoles borrachos   "Drunken" beans; beans are cooked with mescal or tequila as well as common ingredients, such as pork and onions. (Mexico)

frijoles negro   Black beans. (Mexico)

fríjol negro   Black bean. (South America)

fritto   Fried. (Italy)

frituras de pescados   Fried fish popular in southern Spain, particularly Andalusia. (Iberian Peninsula)

fruit de mer   "Fruits of the sea"; seafood. (France)

Fry Up   Name of traditional breakfast throughout much of the UK; this would typically consist of eggs and bacon, which may be accompanied by many other items, such as sausages, ham, blood sausage, bubble and squeak, tomatoes, fry bread, and mushrooms. (England)

fugu   Blowfish. (Japan)

fuka-hire   Shark's fin soup. (Japan)

fukusa-zushi   Thin egg omelet-wrapped sushi. (Japan)

funghi   Mushrooms. (Italy)

fusilli   Corkscrew-shaped pastas that are meant to hold meat-based sauces inside the curls of the pasta. (Italy)

futo maki   Thick-rolled sushi. (Japan)

g

ga   Chicken. (Vietnam)

gaeng kiew wahn   Green curry paste; this paste is made from unripe chiles, which provide much of the green color, and may also include herbs as part of the blend. This curry is often used with poultry dishes. (Thailand)

gaeng leuang   Yellow curry paste; this paste contains turmeric, which gives it a rich yellow color. It is usually used with poultry. (Thailand)

gaeng mussaman   Mussaman curry paste; influenced by India, this paste contains dried coriander and cumin as part of the blend and typically adds lemongrass and garlic or shallots, as well as some chiles. (Thailand)

gaeng panang   Panang curry paste; roasted and ground peanuts are added to this paste. (Thailand)

gaeng peht   Red curry paste; this paste uses either dried or fresh red, ripe chiles along with galangal and lemongrass. It is used in a variety of coconut milk–based dishes. (Thailand)

gaeng som   Orange curry paste; this has a higher proportion of shrimp and is typically used in seafood dishes. (Thailand)

galangal   Rhizome related to ginger, with similar uses and aroma, but with a slightly stronger flavor and lighter-colored skin; can be found in the produce section of Asian specialty stores. (Southeast Asia)

galantine   Boned, stuffed, or rolled poultry (typically) cooked and then chilled and served cold with aspic glaze. (France)

galette   Round, thin cake or savory pancake. (France)

galettes au jambon, au fromage et a l'oeuf   Buckwheat pancake filled with ham, eggs, and cheese. (France)

ga lum phee   Cabbage. (Thailand)

gambas   Shrimp. (Iberian Peninsula)

gan bian   Deep frying. (China)

gan bian si ji dou   Spicy stir-fried green beans. (China)

gan hai jiao   Dried chiles. (China)

gao   Rice. (Vietnam)

gape   Shrimp paste. (Thailand)

garam masala   (Indian subcontinent) Common spice blend of northern India that contains coriander, cumin, black pepper, cardamom, cloves, cinnamon, nutmeg, bay leaves, and often a small amount of chili and fennel seeds.
(Sweden) "Warm" spice blend of India common in Scandinavian cooking.

garbanzo beans   Another name for chickpeas. (Greece/Iberian Peninsula)

garde manger   Pantry supervisor in the brigade system. (France)

gari   Vinegared ginger. (Japan)

garo   Walnut and garlic sauce with coriander; from the Georgia region. (Russia)

Garrotxa   Goat's milk cheese from the Catalunya area with blue mold grown on the exterior, resulting in semisoft, tangy ripened cheese. (Iberian Peninsula)

gås   Goose. (Scandinavia)

gauchos   Name of the cowboys who work cattle on the ranches of South America's Pampas region. (South America)

gayka   Beef (only common in non-Hindu areas such as Pakistan). (Indian subcontinent)

gazpacho   Cold spiced tomato soup; often includes cucumbers, bell peppers, and tomato pieces. (Iberian Peninsula)

gazpacho blanco   White gazpacho made from ground almonds, garlic, and grapes, and also served cold. This was the original gazpacho prior to the arrival of the tomato and chiles from the Americas. (Iberian Peninsula)

gaufres   Waffles. (France)

gebäck   Chef. (Germany)

gedra   The bottom part of a couscousier, where the stew cooks while the couscous steams above. (North Africa)

gedra dil trid   Dome-shaped earthenware piece used to stretch the dough to make the pastry for bisteeya; also called *trid*. (North Africa)

gedünstetes kraut   Braised cabbage. (Poland)

gefilte fish   Poached fish forcemeat or dumpling common to the cooking of Ashkenazi Jews. (Israel)

gehun   Wheat. (Indian subcontinent)

gelato   Frozen sweetened and often flavored milk; similar to ice cream but traditionally lighter and with less air incorporated during the freezing process. (Italy)

geräuchert   Smoked. (Germany)

geschmort   Braised; also called *braten*. (Germany)

gesotten   Simmered. (Germany)

ghee   Clarified and caramelized butter, made by caramelizing the milk solids during the clarification process. (Indian subcontinent)

gia   Bean sprout. (Vietnam)

ginger   Rhizome commonly found in supermarkets; it has an aromatic quality and a fibrous interior. Ginger can be used as a substitute for galangal; it has a slightly different flavor but works well when galangal is unavailable. (Southeast Asia)

gnocchi   Small dumplings made from a variety of different ingredients including potatoes (gnocchi di patate), corn (gnocchi di polenta), and wheat (gnocchi di semolina). (Italy)

go   Fried cake. (China)

goh   Dumpling, also spelled gao or gow. (China)

goi cuon   Rice wrap with shrimp. (Vietnam)

goi ga   Chicken and cabbage salad. (Vietnam)

golabki   Stuffed cabbage rolls filled with various items, ranging from grains and mushrooms to seasoned meat mixtures and sauerkraut, and typically served with sour cream. (Poland)

goma   Sesame seed. (Japan)

gong bao   Called kung pao in the United States, this is typically made with chicken that is stir fried with chiles, vegetables, and peanuts. (China)

Gorgonzola   Famous blue-veined cow's milk cheese from the outskirts of Milan. This is a rich cheese with piquant flavor due to the growth of mold that forms naturally within the cheese as it ages in caves. (Italy)

gosht   Lamb or goat (sometimes used as the word *meat* would be used in the United States). (Indian subcontinent)

goulash   (Italy) Spiced stew of Hungarian origin common in northeastern Italy as a result of Austrian influence in the area.
(Israel) Spiced stew of Eastern European heritage, common among Israeli populations whose families once lived in this region.

gournay   Soft, rich cow's milk cheese from Normandy region used to make Boursin cheese when blended with various herbs and spices. (France)

goya   Bitter melon. (Japan)

grana   Term for hard, aged cheeses with granular textures, such as Parmesan. Also the name of some of the lesser-known cheeses made in the same style as Parmesan, such as grana padano from the Po Valley regions of northern Italy. (Italy)

granita   Slushy sweetened and flavored ice. (Italy)

grano   Wheat. (Italy)

granoturco   Corn. (Italy)

grappa   Distilled grape pomace made from the remnants of grapes after they have been processed for wine. (Italy)

grassini   Thin breadsticks, which originated in Turin, served as a snack all over Italy. (Italy)

grasso   Fat; general term for fat and oils. (Italy)

gratin   Browned crust formed on top of foods from intense heat from above or a very hot oven. (France)

graviera   Hard cheese made from cow's milk, similar in texture and flavor to Swiss cheese. (Greece)

gravlax   Salmon fillet cured in a salt/sugar/dill mixture. The name *gravlax* ("grave salmon") comes from the ancient method of preparing this, in which the salmon would be buried and allowed to ferment. (Sweden)

gravlaxsås Sauce to accompany gravlax, typically made with mustard and dill. (Sweden)

grelos Turnip greens. (Iberian Peninsula)

gremolata Mixture of lemon zest, garlic, and parsley used to season foods. (Italy)

griby Mushroom. (Russia)

griddle Flat cast-iron cooking surface used to make the many examples of quick drop breads and seared foods found in the cuisines of the British Isles. (British Isles)

grillos Grasshoppers. (Mexico)

gros Bourgogne Large snails from the Burgundy region. (France)

gross pieces Name given to elaborate decorations used in classical French banquet or court cuisine; rarely created today. (France)

grouper Type of fish that includes the sea bass that are found in shallow waters and feed on crustaceans and other fish. These types of fish generally have mild, flaky flesh that is highly regarded. (Caribbean)

guacamole Sauce traditionally made from crushed avocados, tomatoes, and chiles; today it often includes lime and cilantro as well. (Mexico)

guérande Prized sea salt from Brittany's coast. (France)

găluşcă Dumpling. (Romania)

guiveciu de ciuperci Braised mushrooms in sour cream sauce. (Romania)

gulyas Goulash, stews, and soups of meats and vegetables cooked in heavily spiced broth (typically spiced with paprika). (Hungary)

gumbo Name of an African-inspired stew that contains okra and other vegetables and meats in spicy broth. (Caribbean)

gung Ginger root. (Vietnam)

gunkan–maki "Warship roll" (named because of its shape); rolled sushi topped with ingredients that are difficult to put inside a roll (such as urchin). (Japan)

gur Jaggary; unrefined sugar. (Indian subcontinent)

gyūnikū Beef. (Japan)

h

haba (Arabic-speaking countries) Large, dried split fava bean.

(Iberian Peninsula) Fava bean.

habanero Smaller, squat, very hot chiles from southern Mexico in the Yucatán region. These chilies are typically orange when ripe, although some variants may be closer to red in color; they are most often used in salsa and sauces. (Mexico)

(South America) Thought to have originated in the Amazon basin, this is one of the hottest chiles available. Habaneros are bell shaped and orange to red in color, and they have a thin skin.

hackepeter Chopped raw pork, highly seasoned and served on a roll. (Germany)

haggis Traditional boiled meat "pudding" made from filling the stomach lining of a sheep with seasoned and ground offal and suet bound with oatmeal. (Scotland)

haku miso Sweet white miso made with a high proportion of rice malt. (Japan)

halal Foods that are permitted to be eaten according to the laws of Islam. (Arabic-speaking countries)

halászlé Fish stew spiced with sweet and spicy paprikas. (Hungary)

halkidika Brine-cured, large green olive. (Greece)

hallaca (Venezuela) Meat, vegetables, and olive stuffing in corn dough; steamed in plantain leaves.

(Caribbean) Caribbean version (also found in South America) of *tamales*, in which the corn dough is filled with beef or pork seasoned with olives and capers and wrapped in banana or plaintain leaves before being boiled or steamed.

(Colombia) Steamed cornmeal dough with various fillings; also called bolos or tamales.

haloumi Firm sheep's or goat's milk cheese with a very high protein content, which allows it to hold its shape when heated and enables it to be grilled. (Greece)

halva Middle Eastern sweet bar made by cooking sesame seeds with honey and dried fruits or nuts (introduced by the Ottomans). (Balkans)

halvas Sweet, dense cakes seasoned with various ingredients and eaten as a snack or dessert. These are made from cooking thickened, sweetened mixtures and then pouring them to let them set before cutting into smaller pieces; called halawah or halawa in some parts of the Middle East. (Arabic-speaking countries)

halwas Sweets made from various fruits or vegetables, sugar, milk or cream, ghee, and often spices; very common snacks or offerings on the Indian subcontinent. Halwas are often made from semolina wheat. (Indian subcontinent)

hamaguri Clam. (Japan)

hangiri Shallow wooden bowl made out of cypress and used to mix the cooked short-grain rice and vinegar solution to make sushi rice. (Japan)

haram Foods that are prohibited according to the laws of Islam. (Arabic-speaking countries)

hari mirch Red chiles. (Indian subcontinent)

harina de trigo Wheat flour. (Iberian Peninsula/ Mexico)

harira Thick soup made from lentils and chickpeas that is traditionally part of the month-long fasting tradition of the Muslim Ramadan. (North Africa)

harissa Spice paste from Tunisia made from ground chiles, garlic, and spices; used extensively in North Africa as a seasoning. (North Africa)

harsha Flatbread from Morocco. (North Africa)

hasen Hare. (Germany)

hashwa Lamb and rice. (Arabic-speaking countries)

hatchō miso Miso made with only soybeans; a rich source of protein. (Japan)

haute cuisine High cuisine or grand cuisine that developed in the French hotels and is now referred to as classical French cuisine. (France)

Havarti Semisoft cow's milk cheese with a buttery-sweet taste; may or may not be flavored with ingredients such as dill or caraway seeds. (Denmark)

havre   Oats. (Scandinavia)

hearth   Low fireplace found in homes throughout the British Isles, used for heating the home and for cooking. (British Isles)

helado   Ice cream; technique introduced by the Spanish. (South America)

hering   Herring. (Germany)

heringsstippe   Herring and apple salad. (Germany)

herrgårdskorv   Rich smoked pork sausage. (Sweden)

higos   Figs. (Iberian Peninsula)

hiijaa   Goat. (Japan)

hijiki   Black, bland seaweed often cooked with vegetables or tofu for its high vitamin and mineral content. (Japan)

hilopittes   Egg noodles, either long and thin or square. (Greece)

Himmel und Erde   "Heaven and Earth"; dish of mashed potatoes and cooked apples topped with panfried blood sausage and sautéed onion rings. (Germany)

hing   Asefoetida. (Indian subcontinent)

hitsuji   Lamb. (Japan)

hjell   Special drying racks common in western Norway to make the air-dried cod called stockfisk or tørrfisk. (Norway)

hjortron   Cloudberry. (Sweden)

hoja santa   Yerba santa leaf; commonly used in southern Mexican cuisine. (Mexico)

homard   Lobster. (France)

hong shao   Cooking method known as "red" cooking that relies on soy sauce, rice wine, sugar, and aromatics, which are used to slowly simmer or braise the desired meat, poultry, or fish. This method is common to the Shanghai region. (China)

hong shao gai   Red cooked chicken. (China)

hong shao rou   Red cooked pork belly. (China)

hong shao yu   Red cooked fish. (China)

hong you   Chili oil. (China)

honig   Honey. (Germany)

horchata   Drink made from ground dried tiger nuts mixed with lemon and sugar and then filtered. (Iberian Peninsula)

hormiga culona   Fried ants; unique to Santander. (Colombia)

horta   Wild greens. (Greece)

hoso maki   Thin-rolled sushi. (Japan)

hotategai   Scallop

hourmades   Dried, wrinkled black olives from the Aegean Islands off of the coast of Turkey. (Greece)

hout   Fish (phonetically also spelled *hut*). (North Africa)

hua khar   Galangal. (Laos)

huachinango   Snapper. (South America)

huachinango a la Veracruzana   Red snapper cooked in the style of Veracruz; heavily influenced by Spanish culinary techniques and flavors—in this case, olives, capers, and olive oil. (Mexico)

huiles de cepes   Oil infused with cepes (wild mushrooms). (France)

huitre   Oyster. (France)

huldi   Turmeric. (Indian subcontinent)

humintas   Ground fresh corn steamed in corn leaves. (Bolivia)

humitas en chala   Steamed cornmeal dough or ground fresh corn with various fillings wrapped in a corn husk (see *tamales*); also the name for ground and spiced fresh corn. (Argentina)

hummus   (Israel) Chickpea purée seasoned with tahini, lemon juice, and garlic.
      (Balkans) Chickpea purée seasoned with lemon, olive oil, garlic, and often tahini (sesame seed purée).

hummus bi tahini   Cooked and puréed chickpeas seasoned with olive oil, garlic, lemon juice, and tahini. (Greece)

hushållsost   Semihard cow's milk cheese with good melting qualities and a mild, somewhat sour taste. (Sweden)

i

iablaka   Apple. (Russia)

Ibores   Hard cheese with paprika rubbed on the exterior; from the Extremadura region of south central Spain. (Iberian Peninsula)

ichigo daifuku   Mochi balls stuffed with sweet azuki bean paste and strawberries. (Japan)

ichigoni   Abalone and sea urchin soup. (Japan)

ichmyen   Barley. (Russia)

Idiazábal   Sheep's milk cheese from the Basque region of Spain that can be found smoked or unsmoked; this is a high-fat cheese with a rich texture and slightly acidic taste. (Iberian Peninsula)

idlis   Steamed rice bread. (Indian subcontinent)

iguana   Type of lizard. (Mexico)

ika   Squid. (Japan)

ika meshi   Rice with squid. (Japan)

ika sōmen   Squid with wheat flour noodle. (Japan)

ikra   Caviar. (Russia)

imam bayaldi   Eggplant stuffed with tomato. (Turkey)

imli   Tamarind. (Indian subcontinent)

Inca   Great empire of South America that was centered in the Andes and had developed very complex agricultural systems before the arrival of the Spanish. (South America)

incapriata   Vegetable dish of puréed dried fava beans and boiled chicory, served together with olive oil. (Italy)

inhame   Yam. (South America)

inlagd sill   Pickled herring. (Sweden)

innereien   Innards/offal from animals. (Germany)

insalata   Salad. (Italy)

insalata di arance   Orange salad. (Italy)

insalata di mare   Seafood salad. (Italy)

Irish Fry   Traditional breakfast; this would usually consist of bacon, sausage, black pudding, eggs, and potato cakes or farls. (Ireland)

Irish stew   Stew made traditionally by layering lamb or mutton with vegetables (now often with potatoes) and then covered with water and cooked over a fire in a bastible for a couple hours, or until everything is very tender. (Ireland)

ishikari-nabe Specialty of the Hokkaidō region; salmon cooked with potatoes, tofu, miso, and vegetables. (Japan)

Islam Religion that developed in the Middle East and spread to other areas, including North Africa. The religion has a number of dietary restrictions, including the avoidance of pork, shellfish, and fish without scales. (North Africa)

j

jaga-imo Potato. (Japan)

jalapeño The most common and well known of the Mexican chiles; these are about 3 inches long (sometimes bigger) and are used in making salsas, are pickled and used as a condiment, and are smoked and dried to make the prized *chipotle.* (Mexico)

jambon Smoked ham. (France)

jambon de Bayonne Prized hams of Basque area in southwest region. (France)

jamikand Yam. (Indian subcontinent)

jamón de toro Cured beef from the Levante region of Spain (Iberian Peninsula)

jamón ibérico Dry cured ham made from the indigenous Iberian black pig, which have the ability to deposit more marbling than non-Iberian pigs. (Iberian Peninsula)

jamón ibérico de bellota Dry cured ham made from the indigenous Iberian black pigs that increase in weight by 50% after they begin to feed on acorns. These pigs have the highest fat content and make the most prized hams. (Iberian Peninsula)

jamón serrano Dry cured ham of non-Iberian pigs; these make up about 90% of the cured hams in Spain. (Iberian Peninsula)

Janssons frestelse Jansson's temptation; a dish of herring, potatoes, and onions that are cooked with cream and butter and commonly served either as part of a smorgasbord or as a late-night snack. (Sweden)

jappa-jiru Cod soup with daikon and miso; from the northern portion of the main island. (Japan)

jeera Cumin seeds. (Indian subcontinent)

jengibre Ginger. (Mexico)

jerk Term that describes the cooking technique common in Jamaica, in which foods are marinated or dry rubbed in a spicy mixture and then cooked over a green wood fire. (Caribbean)

jiaozi Dumplings. (China)

jimami dofu Tofu made from ground peanuts gelled with potato starch. (Japan)

jingisukan Dish named after Genghis Khan, the Mongolian leader; made from cooked mutton or lamb with vegetables and seasonings. (Japan)

jitomate Tomato; also called tomate rojo, tomatl, and xitomatl. (South America)

jota Bean and barley stew. (Italy)

jujube Small, apple-like fruit from Asia. (Caribbean)

k

kachoris Deep-fried breads with various fillings. (Indian subcontinent)

kaeng jeuud kalampi Pork and cabbage soup with egg. (Laos)

kaeng kai sai hed Chicken soup with mushrooms. (Southeast Asia)

kaeng som pa Fish soup with lemongrass, lime juice, fish sauce, and cilantro. (Laos)

kaffir lime Type of citrus found in Southeast Asia, the leaves of which are often used in cooking. The leaves are very aromatic and contribute their distinct aroma to many dishes; these can be found in the produce section of Asian specialty stores. (Southeast Asia)

kaiseki Formal coursed meal derived from the foods served as a part of the tea ceremony. This style of dining and menu creation is highly focused on the seasonality of the foods as well as their presentation. (Japan)

kai yad sai Braised chicken stuffed with chiles, shallots, garlic, and cilantro. (Laos)

kaju Cashew. (Indian subcontinent)

kake-udon Hot udon noodles served in hot broth; common in Shikoku. (Japan)

kaki Oyster. (Japan)

kaki-soba Soba noodles served in a broth with garnishes. (Japan)

kål Cabbage. (Scandinavia)

kalamata Brine-cured, elongated black olive. (Greece)

kalb Veal. (Germany)

kalbsrolle Stuffed rolled veal breast. (Germany)

kalee ped Curried duck with potatoes. (Laos)

kamel Lotus root. (Indian subcontinent)

kanach Sheep's cheese ripened with mold from Armenia, similar in method and characteristics to Roquefort. (Armenia)

kani Crab. (Japan)

kani meshi Rice with crab. (Japan)

kanten Fern-like seaweed used to make agar-agar, which is used as a thickening agent similar to the way gelatin is used in Western cultures. (Japan)

kao Roasting. (China)

káposzta Cabbage or sauerkraut. (Hungary)

karakkan Millet. (Indian subcontinent)

karela Bitter gourd. (Indian subcontinent)

kari Tamil name for "sauce"; probably the source of the term *curry.* This term is used to describe a spice sauce in which meat or vegetables are cooked (or the generic yellow spice powder found in stores). (Indian subcontinent)

karjalanpaisti Karelian stew. (Finland)

kartoffelklösse Name for potato dumpling in northern Germany. (Germany)

kartoffelknödel Name for potato dumpling in southern Germany. (Germany)

kartoffelpfannkuchen Potato pancake; also called *kartoffelpuffer.* (Germany)

kartoffelpuffer Potato dumpling. (Germany)

kartoffels Potatoes. (Germany)

kartoffelsalat Potato salad. (Germany)

kartoffelsalat mit speck Potato salad with bacon. (Germany)

kasha Cooked grains, often simply boiled and served with butter. (Russia)

kashrut   Jewish dietary laws or edicts that govern acceptable foods, unacceptable foods, or combinations of foods to be followed by those of the Jewish faith. (Israel)

kasseri   Semi-hard sheep's milk cheese. (Greece)

kasza   Groats made from various grains. (Poland)

katsuo no tataki   Bonito braised over hot coals. (Japan)

kazi   Dried horsemeat sausage. (Russia)

kebabs   Skewered and grilled meats; versions range from simple marinated lamb pieces to kofte or other seasoned ground meats. (Turkey)

kefalograviera   Hard grating cheese, typically made from the milk of goats, sheep, or a combination of the two. (Greece)

kefalotyri   Salty, tangy hard cheese made from sheep's or goat's milk. (Greece)

kefta   Spiced and ground lamb. (North Africa)

keftedes   Seasoned lamb meatballs. (Greece)

kelapa   Coconut. (Malaysia)

ketupat   Rice wrapped in palm leaves and steamed or boiled to yield a dense rice dumpling. (Malaysia)

kha   Galangal. (Thailand)

khalvas   Middle Eastern–inspired sweets traditionally made from sesame paste (called *halvas* in the Middle East). (Russia)

khanom jiin   Rice noodle made from forcing dough through a sieve. (Thailand)

khao   Rice. (Thailand)

khao hom ma-ree   Jasmine rice. (Thailand)

khao kate   Basmati rice. (Thailand)

khao khoua   Roasted rice powder. (Laos)

khao niao   Sticky rice. (Laos)

kharouf   Lamb. (Arabic-speaking countries)

khing   Ginger. (Thailand)

khlii   Sundried and spiced strips of meat. (North Africa)

kibbeh   Pounded lamb and burghul, seasoned with spices, olive oil, and often onions; served raw or used to make a number of cooked dishes from the raw form, including fried balls stuffed with various ingredients. (Arabic-speaking countries)

kicap   Soy sauce. (Malaysia)

kicap manis   Thick, sweet soy sauce. (Malaysia)

kichiri   Dish of lentils and rice. (Indian subcontinent)

kielbasa   Polish sausage. (Poland)

kig ha farz   Breton stew made with beef, salt pork, potatoes, onions, garlic, and leeks, stewed with a sack of buckwheat porridge and eaten together when finished. (France)

kinza   Coriander or cilantro. (Russia)

kippers   Smoked herring. (Scotland)

kirch   Cherry brandy. (France)

kizil   Tart cherry found in the Caucus area of Russia. (Russia)

klippfisk   Salted and air-dried cod (unlike stockfisk, which is just air dried). (Norway)

klöss   Dumpling (more common name in northern Germany). (Germany)

knaap kuung   Shrimp, lemongrass, shallots, chiles, and green onions, chopped and wrapped in banana leaves and then cooked over a grill. (Southeast Asia)

knaap pa   Fish with lemongrass, chiles, shallots, and fish sauce, baked wrapped in banana skins or leaves. (Southeast Asia)

kneten   To knead. (Germany)

knish   Thin pancake filled with savory foods (typically fish or cheese), from Russian influence. (Israel)

knödel   Dumpling. (Germany)

kofte   Ground and seasoned meat shaped into a ball; these may be added to stews or soups, or skewered and grilled to make a kebab. (Turkey)

kolbasa   Cured and often smoked pork sausage (similar to Polish kielbasa). (Russia)

koldamer   Cow's milk cheese with small holes and excellent melting qualities. (Poland)

kombu   Dried seaweed, similar to kelp, which is used to make stock called dashi. (Japan)

kome   Uncooked rice. (Japan)

kome miso   Paste made from salted, fermented rice and soybeans that is aged to develop its characteristic flavor. (Japan)

komugi   Wheat. (Japan)

konbu   Giant kelp used to make dashi and also in other preparations; usually used dried but is sometimes shaved fresh. (Japan)

konditori   Bakeries. (Denmark)

korn   Barley. (Scandinavia)

korv   Swedish sausage; made with potatoes and ground meats. (Sweden)

kosher   Designation given to foods that have been deemed "fit for use" according to the laws or edicts of kashruth. (Israel)

koteleti po Kievski   Chicken Kiev; a classic preparation of chicken that is stuffed with a seasoned butter and then breaded before being panfried. (Russia)

kotlety   Ground meat patty. (Russia)

kotlety pozharsky   Breaded chicken cutlets. (Russia)

kotmis garo   Grilled chicken with walnut/garlic sauce; from Georgia. (Russia)

köttbullar   Swedish meatballs. (Sweden)

koumiss   Fermented mare's milk common in the northern Asian portion of Russia. (Russia)

koya   Reduced milk used to make many of the sweet preparations in India. (Indian subcontinent)

kräftor   Crayfish. (Sweden)

kraut   Cabbage. (Germany)

kritharakia   Greek pasta shaped like a rice grain that traditionally were made from barley but now are often made from wheat; commonly called orzo in the United States. (Greece)

krumkake   Delicate cone-shaped cookie. (Norway/Denmark)

kuai zi   Long chopsticks used for cooking. (China)

kuaytiaw   Flat rice noodle. (Thailand)

kuchen   Cake. (Germany)

kulcha   Wheat bread common in Hyderabad. (Indian subcontinent)

kulfi   Indian ice cream (pistachio, mango, and vanilla are traditional flavors). (Indian subcontinent)

kulich   Traditional Russian Easter bread. (Russia)

kurdiuk Fat-tailed sheep of central Asia, prized for the cooking fat yielded from their tails. (Russia)

kushiage Skewered, breaded, and fried foods. (Japan)

kvashinaya kapusta Fermented cabbage (sauerkraut). (Russia)

kwaytiow Rice noodle. (Thailand)

l

laap Salad made from pounded meat or fish seasoned with mint, lime juice, fish sauce, and chiles and topped with toasted rice powder. (Laos)

laddos Sweets made from chickpea flour and sugar, and coated with sesame seeds. (Indian subcontinent)

ladotiri Hard cheese matured in oil. (Greece)

lal mirch Green chiles. (Indian subcontinent)

lampreia Lamprey. (Iberian Peninsula)

langosta Spiny lobster caught in the waters of the Mediterranean. (Iberian Peninsula)

laos Name for *galangal* in Indonesia and Malaysia. (Southeast Asia)

lao zao Fermented glutinous rice wine. (China)

lapsha Noodles. (Russia)

laranga Orange. (South America)

laranja Orange. (Iberian Peninsula)

lard Pork fat. (Mexico)

lardons Bacon. (France)

lasagna This well-known variety is made in both fresh and dried forms and is one of the largest sheet pastas and ribbon pastas made. Lasagna typically is layered with sauces and other ingredients to make the familiar baked casserole recipes that are common in the United States as well as Italy. (Italy)

latkes Thin potato pancakes, popular during the holiday of Chanukah. (Israel)

lavash Thin, yeast-leavened bread cooked on the inside wall of a clay or earthenware oven and traditionally used to scoop food when eating. (Persia/Iran)

laverbread A dish made of cooked laver, a type of seaweed, which is rolled in oats and panfried. (Wales)

La Varenne, François Pierre Author of the book *Le Cuisinier François* that has been identified as one of the turning points in the development of French cuisine. (France)

lax Salmon. (Sweden)

lax med potatis Salmon and potato salad. (Sweden)

leberknödel Liver dumplings. (Habsburg Empire)

lebkuchen Gingerbread. (Germany)

leche Milk. (Iberian Peninsula/Mexico)

lechón Roasted suckling pig. (Ecuador)

lechona Baked pig stuffed with meat, rice, and peas. (Colombia)

lechuga Lettuce. (Mexico)

lefse Potato and flour flatbread commonly often used to wrap other ingredients to eat. (Norway)

légumier Cook responsible for cooking the vegetables in the brigade system. (France)

lengua Tongue, usually beef or veal. (Iberian Peninsula)

lenguado Sole or flounder. (South America)

lentejas Lentils. (Iberian Peninsula/South America)

lenticcha Lentils. (Italy)

lentilles vertes du Puy Prized green lentils from the south central region. (France)

lesco Either a sauce or a salad made from slowly stewed onions, green peppers, and tomatoes (and often spiced with paprika). (Hungary)

lesser ginger The name often listed on packages of fresh turmeric. (Southeast Asia)

l'hamd mrakad Preserved lemons made by packing salt into cut whole lemons and aging them in storage containers to yield a softened, salty, and unique lemon preserve that is used as a seasoning for mirqaz. (North Africa)

lima Lime. (South America)

lima agria Bitter lime used in the Yucatán. (Mexico)

limone Lemon. (Italy)

limónes Lemons. (Iberian Peninsula/Mexico/South America)

(à la) limousine In the style of Limousin; typically denotes that a dish is served with braised red cabbage and chestnuts. (France)

limu omani Dried limes (also called *loumi*). (Persia/Iran)

lingon Lingonberry. (Sweden)

lingua Tongue (from veal or pork). (Italy)

linguiça Pork sausage from Portugal, similar to the chouriço but smaller. (Iberian Peninsula)

linguine Medium-thickness ribbon pasta meant to be used with butter or olive oil sauces or with pesto sauce. (Italy)

linsensuppe Lentil soup. (Germany)

liptauer A blended cheese made from a mixture of sheep's and cow's milk, with a distinct flavor that combines very well with the spiciness of Hungarian food. (Hungary)

livarot Strong, ripened cow's milk cheese from Normandy. (France)

llapingachos Potato and cheese pancake; often served with small bits of meat. (Ecuador)

locro (Argentina) Stewed corn, white beans, beef, sausage, and squash.
(Ecuador/Peru) Soup with potatoes, corn, and avocado.

lök Onion. (Scandinavia)

lombo di maiale ripieno Roasted pork loin stuffed with salumi. (Italy)

lomo a lo pobre Fried beef with eggs, onions, and french fries. (Chile)

lomo saltado Fried chopped steak with onions, tomatoes, potatoes, and rice. (Peru)

longaniza sausage Cured pork sausage flavored with chiles and spices such as cinnamon, anise seed, and garlic; often contains some beef as well and has a semisoft texture. This sausage—which primarily exists on the Spanish-influenced islands of the Caribbean—may be found fresh, in which case it needs to be cooked. (Caribbean)

look Onion. (Russia)

louquenkas Garlic-flavored sausage from the southwest region. (France)

louza Cured pork loin made by salting and washing the loins followed by a spice rub and air drying; some types are also soaked in wine and given a spice rub before being smoked over burning grape vines. (Greece)

lutefisk Air-dried cod treated with lye and rehydrated to form a sort of fish paste; this has long been a part of the Scandinavian diet. (Norway)

m

macaroon Meringue flavored with almond. (France)

maccheroni alla chittara Fresh ribbon pasta made by pressing a sheet of pasta through a metal stringed tool (called a chittara) that resembles the stringed section of a guitar and slices the sheet into strips of width determined by the amount of space between the metal strings. (Italy)

macha Razor clam. (South America)

mâche Corn lettuce or lamb's lettuce. (France)

madeleine Scalloped, shell-shaped cake with lemon flavor. (France)

magani River crab. (Japan)

Maghreb French name for the region of North Africa that includes Morocco, Tunisia, and Algeria. This name derives from the Arabic word for "west." (North Africa)

magroot Kaffir lime. (Thailand)

maguey Agave plants; used to make the fermented beverages tequila and mezcal as well as rope. (Mexico)

mahia Fig and anise liquor traditionally taken on holy Saturdays by Jewish followers. (North Africa)

Mahón Cow's milk cheese made on the Island of Minorca of the coast of eastern Spain. Mahón can be found in varying stages of maturity, with the younger *semicurado* aged two months, the *curado* aged six months, and the brittle *anejo* aged a year. The longer the cheese is aged, the more pronounced the flavor. Commercial versions of Mahón are now common, with much shorter aging periods and thus significantly less character. (Iberian Peninsula)

maiale Pork. (Italy)

maitake Japanese "dancing" mushroom with whitish/grey thin caps used in soups or in broiled dishes. (Japan)

maíz (South America) Corn; also called chalo, choclo, elote, jojote, and abatí.

  (Iberian Peninsula/Mexico). Corn.

maíz cau Another name for *choclero.* (South America)

maíz jora Dried, sprouted, and fermented corn used to make beverages. (South America)

maíz morado Dried purple corn from Peru used to make drinks and desserts. (South America)

ma kham Tamarind. (Thailand)

makheua muang Eggplant. (Thailand)

maki-mono Rolled sushi; this style usually is made with nori, but other ingredients are used to encase the rice and fillings. (Japan)

makisu Bamboo mat used to make sushi rolls. (Japan)

malloreddus Small gnocchi made from semolina and colored and flavored with saffron. (Italy)

malossol Lightly salted; the most prized caviars are this type, where the eggs are fresher from not being salted as heavily as some lower grades. Beluga, osetra, and sevruga all can be found in this form. (Russia)

mamão Papaya. (South America)

mămăligă Polenta. (Romania)

Manchego Hard sheep's milk cheese that is probably the best known of the Spanish cheeses. (Iberian Peninsula)

mandioca Cassava (Portuguese term). (South America)

mandorla Almond. (Italy)

manioc Cassava; type of tuber common in the tropical area of South America. (South America)

manouri Mild, soft sheep's milk cheese. (Greece)

manteca Pork fat, lard. (South America)

manti (Turkey) Oval-shaped pasta with an open pouch, filled with various stuffing (usually ground lamb) and poached in broth.

  (Russia) Filled steamed dumpling, or a dumpling baked in a tomato broth, typically filled with spiced ground lamb mixture; from Central Asia.

mantou Steamed bun. (China)

manzana Apple. (South America)

manzo Young ox. (Italy)

maonias Brine-cured black olive. (Greece)

maranon Cashew. (South America)

marc Type of distillate made from the fermentation of leftover skins or grapes from wine making. (France)

marinieren To marinate. (Germany)

marinovannye griby Marinated mushrooms. (Russia)

mariscos Shellfish. (Mexico)

mark karm Tamarind. (Laos)

Maroons Spanish name given to African slaves who escaped to the mountains of Jamaica; these people were believed to have developed the tradition of jerk cooking in the Caribbean. (Caribbean)

Marsala Fortified wine produced in Sicily. (Italy)

marzapane Almond paste made from almond, sugar and eggs; called "marzipan" in the United States. (Italy)

masa (Mexico) Dough made from corn that has been cooked and cleaned with slaked lime, which removes the tough and difficult-to-digest outer bran of the corn kernel. This dough is used extensively in Mexican cuisine to make everything from tortillas, tamales, and enchiladas to sopes.

  (Colombia/Ecuador) Dough made from dried corn treated with alkali.

masala (England) Name of Indian-inspired dish of meat (often chicken) cooked in a spiced tomato/yogurt sauce and usually served with rice.

  (Indian subcontinent) Spice mixture.

mascarpone A very rich cream cheese made originally in the Lombardy region. (Italy)

mashbooh Foods that are considered questionable, for one reason or another, as to whether they are haram or halal (for example, if lecithin is used in a product, it might not be known whether it derived from a pig or not; thus, it may be considered mashbooh). (North Africa)

maslo Butter. (Russia)

masoor dal Red-orange lentils. (Indian subcontinent)

massepain   Almond paste (marzipan). (France)

masu   Pink salmon. (Japan)

matafans   Cornmeal pancake. (France)

matambre   Rolled, stuffed beef with hardboiled eggs and vegetables; often served as a starter or on platters cold. (Argentina)

maté (or yerba maté)   Strong drink made from yerba maté and drunk with a bombilla (metal straw); this is a highly caffeinated drink commonly used by the gauchos working in the pastures. (Argentina)

Mató   Goat curd cheese from the Catalonia region of Spain; this cheese is slightly granular and usually served with fruit as a dessert. (Iberian Peninsula)

matsutake   Very popular mushroom in Japan that is considered a sign of autumn; these have medium-sized brown caps and large, meaty stems. The flavor is distinct and also delicate and cannot be cooked too long or it will be lost. These are very expensive and rare in Japan and only eaten fresh. (Japan)

mattar   Green peas (often called English peas). (Indian subcontinent)

matzoh   Unleavened bread eaten during Passover. (Israel)

maultaschen   Filled pasta of the Swabian region of Germany that is formed like ravioli or rolled like strudel. (Germany)

ma wei   Marinating. (China)

mazamorroa   Corn mush. (Paraguay)

mazurkas   Flat cakes topped with various ingredients. (Poland)

mbaipy-he-é   Dessert of corn, milk, and molasses. (Paraguay)

mbaipy-so-ó   Corn pudding with chunks of meat. (Paraguay)

mechoui   Lamb roasted whole on a spit over a fire. (North Africa)

medivnik   Honey walnut cake. (Russia)

meetha neem   Curry leaves; unrelated to the term *curry* or to spice blends, these are leaves from a plant that provide a musky, slightly bitter and aromatic quality to foods. (Indian subcontinent)

meetha-toray   Sponge gourd. (Indian subcontinent)

mejillons   Mussels. (Mexico/South America)

mel   Honey. (Iberian Peninsula)

mela   Apple. (Italy)

melanzana   Eggplant. (Italy)

meleg tészták   Hot, sweet noodle dishes. (Hungary)

melocotón   Peach. (Iberian Peninsula/South America)

membrillo   Quince (Iberian Peninsula)

men-dokoro   Eating establishment that specializes in noodle dishes. (Japan)

menudo   Tripe soup with chili sauce; often includes other ingredients, such as hominy (nixtamalized corn). (Mexico)

merguez   Spiced lamb sausage from Tunisia (also phonetically spelled *mirguez*). (North Africa)

meringue   Stiffly whipped egg white and sugar. (France)

merlu   Hake. (France)

merluza   Hake. (Iberian Peninsula)

mescal   Distilled beverage made from the agave plant; essentially very similar to tequila but not made in the Jalisco region or following the quality standards set by the Mexican government for tequila. (Mexico)

mesquite   Wood of same name in the United States. (Mexico)

mestizo   (Mexico) Term used to describe the people and culture that combine Native American and Spanish heritage.

(South America) Person of mixed ancestry—both native South American and European (primarily Spanish).

metate   Grinding stone used to turn nixtamal into masa dough in the traditional manner; these rocks are shaped like a horse's saddle and use a pestle-like stone to grind the nixtamal to a paste. (Mexico)

methi   Fenugreek. (Indian subcontinent)

(en) meurette   Dish served in the style of Burgundy; that is, served with red wine sauce. (France)

meze   (Greece) Small snacks or bite-size portions of food, typically served with alcohol.

(Balkans) Appetizer foods served in style similar to Spanish tapas.

mezzaluna   Small, half-moon–shaped, filled pastas that are typically served with a cream sauce and may have a wide variety of fillings, including meats, cheeses, and vegetables. These are made just like agnolotti, only the circular pieces of dough are smaller and there is less filling. (Italy)

mezze   A number of flavorful foods served prior to a meal or sometimes as a meal. This style of eating is similar to the tapas style in Spain, in which several foods are eaten in small quantities. (Turkey)

m'hammer   Tagine seasoned with cumin and paprika. (North Africa)

miang kham   Snack common in Laos and northern Thailand in which chiles, limes, peanuts, and coconut are wrapped in a leaf and eaten with a sweet sauce. (Laos and Thailand)

miel   Honey. (France/Iberian Peninsula)

migas   Crispy fried (in olive oil) and salted pieces of bread used to garnish soups and stews or finish sauces. The migas are thought to have originated from the Aragon region in northeastern Spain, although similar recipes are found all over the Iberian Peninsula. (Iberian Peninsula)

milho   Corn. (Iberian Peninsula)

minyah sapi   Ghee (clarified butter). (Malaysia)

mirch   Peppercorns. (Indian subcontinent)

mirin   Sweet rice wine. (Japan)

miso   Salted and fermented soybeans. (Japan)

mitzithra   Semi-soft sheep's milk cheese with crumbly texture, made from whey. (Greece)

moath   Small brown bean. (Indian subcontinent)

mocette   Traditionally made from ibex meat (but no longer made from ibex because they are threatened), this is now made from goat or chamois meat. Mocette is a specialty of the Aosta Valley in northern Italy, and it is made by brining the meat prior to its being hung to air-dry and age. (Italy)

mochi   Rice cake made from a particular variety of short-grain rice; often sweet. (Japan)

mochi gomé   Glutinous short-grain rice variety, often called sweet rice in the United States. (Japan)

Mochiko   Brand name of rice flour made from glutinous rice. (Japan)

mocueca   Seafood sauce/stew made with coconut milk and cooked in a clay pot. (Brazil)

mojama   Salt-cured tuna loins. (Iberian Peninsula)

mojo   Sauce/marinade used in Cuban cuisine, made from garlic, onion, bitter orange juice or lime juice, and oil. (Caribbean)

mole   Complex dish with numerous variations; typically, a sauce made from dried chiles, dried fruit, seeds and/or nuts, tomatoes, and sometimes chocolate. Some versions of mole include more than 100 ingredients. (Mexico)

mole negro   Mole made with dark chilhuacle negro chiles. (Mexico)

mole poblano   Mole made with poblano chiles in the central highlands of Mexico. (Mexico)

mole rojo   Mole made with red pasilla chiles. (Mexico)

mole verde   Mole made with tomatillos. (Mexico)

mondongo   Tripe cooked in bouillon with vegetables, corn, and potatoes. (Venezuela)

montaditos   Foods placed on slices of bread or crostini. (Iberian Peninsula)

montasio   Semisoft or ripened hard cheese with small holes and sweet-to-piquant flavor, depending on its age. (Italy)

montebianco   Chestnuts cooked in milk and puréed and seasoned with sugar, vanilla, rum, and cocoa, and then topped with whipped cream. (Italy)

Montsec   Hard goat's milk cheese from the Catalonia region of Spain. (Iberian Peninsula)

moong dal   Mung beans that have been split and skinned; these are yellow colored, flat, and quick to cook. (Indian subcontinent)

mørbrad med svedsker og aebler   Pork loin stuffed with prunes and apples. (Denmark)

morcilla   Blood sausage. (Iberian Peninsula)

morille   Morel. (France)

mori-soba   Soba noodles served chilled with dipping sauce, wasabi, and garnishes. (Japan)

moro   Rice cooked with vegetables or beans in the Dominican Republic. (Caribbean)

Moros y Cristianos   Rice and black beans cooked together; named after the Moors and Christians because these two groups once fought for control of the Iberian Peninsula. (Caribbean)

mortadella   Made from very finely ground beef and/or pork and pork fat, and seasoned with pepper, coriander, pistachios, and wine, this meat is packed into either a pig's or cow's bladder and cooked very slowly. Mortadella typically also has pieces of lard mixed into the forcemeat and is perishable, so it is kept in a cooler. (Italy)

morue   Salt cod. (France)

moule   Mussel. (France)

moussaka   Baked dish made from layered eggplant with white sauce, meat sauce, and cheese. (Greece)

mousse   Light and air-filled food made from folding in whipped cream and/or egg whites. (France)

mousseline   Lightened preparation from addition of whipped heavy cream or egg whites; term commonly used to describe forcemeats with cream that provides the fat for the emulsion. (France)

mousseline de saumon aux poireau   Salmon mousseline with creamed leeks. (France)

mozuku   Surface seaweed with a soft texture; used in soups and with vegetables. (Japan)

mozzarella   Originally the name of a fresh, soft cheese made from water buffalo's milk with a mild taste and excellent melting quality. This was a common cheese of southern Italy used in many familiar dishes, such as pizza and caprese. This name is now used to describe not only the original cheese but also the semisoft cow's milk cheese made in a similar manner as the original that also has good melting properties. (Italy)

m'qualli   Tagine seasoned with saffron and ginger. (North Africa)

muchacho   Roast loin of beef in sauce. (Venezuela)

mugi miso   Paste made from salted, fermented wheat, barley, soybeans, and rice. (Japan)

muhammara   Seasoned walnut paste common in Lebanon. (Arabic-speaking countries)

muikku   Tiny relative of the salmon, usually cooked whole because its bones disintegrate during cooking. (Finland)

murgh   Chicken. (Indian subcontinent)

musaca   Eggplant dish of Greek/Turkish influence (called *moussaka* in Greece). (Romania)

Muslim   Follower of the Islamic faith. (North Africa)

n

naan   Leavened bread cooked inside a tandoori oven; this bread is common in the northern region of India. (Indian subcontinent)

nabemono   Hot pot common throughout Japan, in which select ingredients are provided so the guest can select what (and how much) is added to his or her broth. (Japan)

nabemono-ryōri-ya   Eating establishment that specializes in the nabemono hot pots common throughout Japan. (Japan)

nahm go fi   Coconut milk. (Thailand)

nakiri bocho   Rectangular-shaped knife used to cut vegetables. (Japan)

nameko   Small orange mushroom with a gelatinous texture that is found mostly canned in brine. These are used in miso soup and as a flavoring in side dishes. (Japan)

nam jim tua   Pickled and spiced cucumber. (Thailand)

nam pa   Fish sauce. (Laos)

nam pla   Fish sauce. (Thailand)

naganegi   Leek-like onion. (Japan)

nappe Term that describes the proper consistency of a sauce so that it will coat the food it is intended to be served with yet be thin enough to flow naturally; often described as the thickness required to coat and cling to the back of a spoon. (France)

naranjas Oranges. (Iberian Peninsula/Mexico/South America)

naranjas agria Bitter oranges. (Mexico)

nariyal Coconut. (Indian subcontinent)

nashi Asian pear. (Japan)

nasi goreng Fried rice. (Malaysia)

naw mai Bamboo shoot. (Thailand)

nebera Winter melon. (Japan)

Neufchâtel Creamy cow's milk cheese from Normandy region; typically heart shaped. (France)

ngo gai Saw leaf (a type of herb). (Vietnam)

niakbouri Dill. (Russia)

niederrheinische leberwurst Country-style liver sausage from lower Rhineland region of Germany. (Germany)

nigiri Hand-formed sushi with various sashimi toppings. (Japan)

nigiri-zushi Hand-formed sushi with various toppings. (Japan)

níscalo Type of wild mushroom. (Iberian Peninsula)

nixtamal Dried corn that has been treated with an alkaline (usually slaked lime) to remove the tough outer bran of the corn kernel before the corn is ground to make masa. (Mexico)

nocciola Hazelnut. (Italy)

noce Walnut. (Italy)

noix Walnut. (France)

non Flatbread. (Russia)

nopal Cactus. (Mexico)

ñoquis Gnocchi or potato dumplings served with marinara or another tomato sauce. (Argentina)

ñora Chili pepper used to make romesco sauce. (Iberian Peninsula)

nori Thin, dried seaweed sheets used to make rolled sushi. (Japan)

nouilles Noodles. (France)

nouvelle Young; this term has been used to describe the emergence of a lighter cooking style that focused more on quality ingredients and less on heavy sauces. This style has grown in popularity within the last century in France and beyond. (France)

nudeln Noodle. (Germany)

nuoc cham Condiment sauce made from fish sauce, lime juice, chiles, and garlic. (Vietnam)

nuoc mam Fish sauce. (Vietnam)

O

obentô Boxed lunch popular throughout the country; these signified solidarity and support during the early part of World War II and have been popular ever since. (Japan)

oca (Italy) Goose.
(South America) Type of tuber similar to the potato, with a range of colors and tastes (from sweet to slightly sour or tangy).

ogórki kiszone Brine-pickled cucumbers. (Poland)

oie Goose. (France)

oignons Onions. (France)

olio d'oliva Olive oil. (Italy)

oliva Olive. (Italy)

olive alla ascolana Olives stuffed with seasoned meat and cheese. (Italy)

olla Pot; these were traditionally used to cook dried beans. (Mexico)

olletas Stew dishes from the Valencia region of Spain that may contain many ingredients, including meat, grains, and vegetables. (Iberian Peninsula)

olympicos Club sandwich with bacon, lettuce, and parrilla (Argentinean-style grilled meats). (Uruguay)

opa Opah; also called moon fish. (Mexico)

orecchiette Pasta shaped like little ears; meant to be cooked with thicker, vegetable-based sauces. (Italy)

origano Oregano. (Italy)

orw sod kai Chicken stew with eggplant, mushrooms, lemongrass, galangal, chiles, and cilantro. (Southeast Asia)

orzo Italian name for kritharakia, rice-shaped pasta (Greece/Italy)

o-sake Rice wine or sake; not to be confused with sake (salmon). (Japan)

osetra Smaller sturgeon (and smaller caviar) than the prized beluga. (Russia)

oshinuki-zushi Pressed style of sushi with mackerel. (Japan)

oshi-zushi Compressed sushi; rice and other ingredients are compressed together in a rectangular box. This style dates back to the origin of sushi, when fish were packed with rice to preserve them by fermentation of the rice. (Japan)

osso bucco Braised veal shanks. (Italy)

ostiones Oysters. (Mexico)

ostra Oyster. (South America)

ot Chili pepper. (Vietnam)

ouzo Anise-flavored distilled beverage. (Greece)

oyster sauce Sauce from Guangdong in southern China. (China)

p

pa amb tomaquat Crusty country bread rubbed with ripe tomatoes and drizzled with extra virgin olive oil; called *pan con tomate* in Spanish, this is a Catalonian specialty. (Iberian Peninsula)

pabellón Shredded beef, rice, beans, and fried plantains. (Venezuela)

pachamanca Meat, potatoes, and vegetables all cooked in an "oven" formed by burning the foods with very hot volcanic rocks. This is a national favorite in Peru. (Peru/South America)

padek Fermented fish and fish sauce with pieces of the fish still in it. This is commonly used to season other foods, with the fermented fish pieces often pounded and added to dishes. (Laos)

paella Classic rice dish with beans, saffron, vegetables, and various meats or seafood. The classic version contains chicken and snails; however, many recipes now use other ingredients. All versions are cooked over an open flame in a paellera, uncovered, making this one of the more challenging dishes to prepare properly. (Iberian Peninsula)

paellera Large, shallow oval or round pan with handles on ends; used to make paella. (Iberian Peninsula)

pain d'espices Ginger-spiced bread from the north. (France)

palacsinta Thin pancake. (Hungary)

pålæg Sandwich toppings for the open-face sandwiches that are common in Denmark. (Denmark)

palomilla Thin cut of bottom round marinated in adobe or mojo and cooked quickly on a hot griddle or pan. (Caribbean)

palourde Clam. (France)

palov Rice dish that originated from the influence of the Persian and Ottoman empires in parts of Russia and former states in the Central Asian region. (Russia)

palta a la jardinera Avocado stuffed with cold vegetables or salad. (Peru)

pancetta This common product is often found in the United States, as it is very versatile and can be used in sauces or on its own after being rendered. Pancetta is the cured belly from pork, which is then rolled to yield something that looks quite different from bacon (bacon is also smoked, but pancetta is just cured), even though it is made from the same cut. (Italy)

pancetta steccata An uncommon but interesting specialty of the Aosta Valley, pancetta steccata is a type of pancetta (cured pork belly) that is sewn to itself and pressed between two pieces of juniper wood for two months for its dry aging. (Italy)

pan Cubano Cuban bread. (Caribbean)

pandan Screwpine (a distinct seasoning). (Malaysia)

pane carasau Thin, crisp bread of Sardinia. (Italy)

paneer Pressed curd cheese. (Indian subcontinent)

panforte Christmas fruit and spice cake. (Italy)

panieren To coat with bread crumbs or another starch. (Germany)

pannetone Rich cake from Milan with golden raisins and citrus peels. (Italy)

panuchos Small tortillas that are fried—resulting in the formation of a pocket that is filled with a black bean paste and a hardboiled egg—refried, and then served with various toppings as a snack. These hail from the Yucatán region of Mexico. (Mexico)

panzenella Bread and tomato salad common in central Italy. (Italy)

pao Brining/brined. (China)

papadzules Specialty of the Yucatán region; tacos coated in ground pumpkin seed sauce flavored with epazote, filled with chopped cooked eggs, and topped with roasted tomato salsa and pumpkin seed oil. (Mexico)

pa pages Compressed cakes of figs, anise seed, and bread used to feed the olive field workers of the Balearic Islands. (Iberian Peninsula)

papa morada Purple potato. (South America)

papa negra Black potato. (South America)

papas Potatoes. (Iberian Peninsula/South America)

papas a la huancaina Potatoes with a spicy cheese sauce. (Peru)

papa seca Freeze-dried cooked potato. (South America)

pappardelle Thick pasta ribbons, approximately 3/4–1 inch in width, which traditionally have fluted edges. Pappardelle is typically served with thick and hearty sauces that this larger pasta can support. (Italy)

papperdelle alla cacciatore Thick, fresh ribbon pasta with sausage. (Italy)

paprikas Chiles. Also refers to stews made with meats or poultry in rich paprika-based sauce; similar to goulash (*gulyas*) but thicker and cooked with sour cream to yield thick, rich stew. (Hungary)

paratha Flatbread that often includes other ingredients by having them rolled into the dough and then cooked on a tava (flat griddle-like pan) with ghee. (Indian subcontinent)

pareve Foods that are considered neutral under the guidelines of kashruth and thus can be eaten with either dairy products or meat. These foods are considered to be inherently kosher and thus fit for consumption. (Israel)

Parmesan Famous sharp, dry aged cow's milk cheese from the Emilia-Romagna region of Italy. The large wheels go through a long maturation process (18 months to 2 years) to produce this fine grana-style cheese. This is the most well-known cheese of Italy, with the parmigiano-reggiano being one of the most highly regarded. (Italy)

Parmesan di melazane Fried eggplant layered with tomato sauce and cheese, and then baked; called "eggplant Parmesan" in the United States. (Italy)

parrilla Mixed meat, barbequed in Argentine style. (Ecuador)

parrillada Various cuts of meat cooked over coals (as in Argentina). (Paraguay)

pasha Cheesecake. (Finland)

pashtet Similar to a pâté, cooked meat is seasoned, pushed through a sieve, and encrusted in a pastry before being baked and cooled; served cold. (Russia)

pasilla These elongated and large chiles are dried chilacas; used in making stews and a necessary component in many versions of mole (Mexico)

paskha Cheese spread shaped like a pyramid and eaten as part of the Easter celebration. (Russia)

pasta e fagioli Pasta and beans made with cannellini beans, pasta, and typically a tomato-based sauce. (Italy)

pasta fresca Fresh egg pasta. (Italy)

pasta reale Marzipan paste shaped and colored like fruit; a Sicilian specialty. (Italy)

pastel de choclo Fresh corn pie with meat, vegetables, chicken, olives, and hardboiled eggs. (Chile)

pastelitos Fried savory pastries found on Spanish-influenced islands. (Caribbean)

pasties (England) Pastry filled with savory ingredients and baked; a traditional preparation thought to have originated in Cornwall, one of the Celtic regions of the United Kingdom.

(Wales) Savory pastries filled with meat or seafood and eaten out of hand.

(Caribbean) English baked, meat-filled pastries.

pata negra Black Iberian pig (considered to make the best hams). (Iberian Peninsula)

patata Potato. (Italy)

patates psites Roasted potatoes with lemon and oregano. (Greece)

pâté Potted meat; typically made with smooth forcemeat with a significant portion of fat incorporated into the preserve, making this a rich and flavorful food. (France)

pâté de foie gras Potted forcemeat made with fattened goose or duck liver. (France)

pâtissier Pastry cook in brigade system. (France)

pato no tucupi Roast duck with tucupi sauce made from manioc and vegetables. (Brazil)

payo Turkey. (Mexico)

pebre Sauce made from fresh herbs (cilantro and parsley are common), onions, chiles, lemon, and olive oil to be served with grilled meats (similar to chimichurri in Argentina). (Chile)

pecées Twice-fried plantains found in Haiti (from African influence). (Caribbean)

pecorino A sheep's milk cheese usually aged and used as a grating cheese; when served young and softer, it is called pecorino da tavola. There are many versions of this cheese in Italy, which vary depending on which region they are made in. Some of the more highly regarded versions include pecorino romano, originally made outside the city of Rome, and fiore sardo from Sardinia. (Italy)

ped Duck. (Laos)

ped tom khathi Duck and coconut soup with galangal and garlic. (Southeast Asia)

peixe a delícia Broiled or grilled fish served with bananas and coconut milk. (Brazil)

pel'meni Noodle dumpling from Siberia, typical filled with a mixture of ground meats. (Russia)

penne rigate Short, ridged tubular pasta shapes that are meant to cling to olive oil-based sauces. Penne are cut on a bias and thus have a quill shape. (Italy)

peperonata Stewed onion, tomatoes, and peppers with olive oil. (Italy)

peperoncini Chili peppers. (Italy)

peperoncino Chiles. (Italy)

peperone Bell peppers. (Italy)

pepitas Green pumpkin seeds used in sauces and to make papadzules in the Yucatán. (Mexico)

pepperkakor Crispy, thin gingersnaps. (Sweden)

pera Pear. (South America)

pêra Pear. (Iberian Peninsula)

Pernod Anise-flavored liqueur. (France)

Pesach Passover; during this holy period, followers are to avoid all leavened products (thus, the importance of matzoh). (Israel)

pescado Fish. (Mexico)

pescaito frito Fried fish common in the Andalusia region of Spain. (Iberian Peninsula)

pesce Fish. (Italy)

pesce spada Swordfish. (Italy)

pesées Twice-fried plantains. (Haiti - Caribbean)

pêssego Peach. (Iberian Peninsula)

pesto Blend of basil, garlic, pine nuts, Parmesan cheese, and olive oil; traditionally made using a mortar and pestle. (Italy)

pesto alla Genovese Paste made from basil, garlic, pine nuts, Parmesan, and pecorino cheeses and olive oil. (Italy)

petit pois English pea. (France)

pfannen Pan. (Germany)

pfannengerichte Panfried. (Germany)

phat Thai Also called pad Thai; dish of rice noodles with bean sprouts, green onions, and fried egg with sweet-and-sour sauce. (Thailand)

pho Flavorful broth served with noodles and various other ingredients. (Vietnam)

pho bo Beef pho with noodles and garnishes. (Vietnam)

phyllo Thin dough common to both Greek and Middle Eastern cuisines; the literal translation is "leaf," as this dough is compared to thin leaves. (Greece)

piao zi Wok ladle. (China)

pib Term used for traditional pits dug to cook foods wrapped in banana leaves in southern Mexico; this term is also sometimes used to describe foods wrapped in banana leaves, as is common in the Yucatán region. (Mexico)

picada Mixture of bread, almonds, garlic, and onions that is puréed to a paste and used to thicken and finish many soups and other liquids in Spanish cooking. (Iberian Peninsula)

picarone Fried pumpkin dough eaten as a snack; very similar to a donut but made from pumpkin dough. (Peru)

picarones Squash or sweet potato dough, fried and served with (often spiced) syrup. (Ecuador)

pichelsteiner eintopf Meat and vegetable stew common throughout Germany. (Germany)

picholine Type of small olive common to Morocco (most French picholines are actually grown in Morocco and just packed and labeled in France). (North Africa)

pie Often refers to a savory-filled pastry crust (as in the other countries of the British Isles). (Wales)

pierogi Stuffed noodle dough, similar to ravioli (Italy) or *variniki* (Ukraine), and typically filled with sauerkraut, potato mixture, mushrooms, cheese, or a combination of these. (Poland)

piirakka Pasties or savory filled pies. (Finland)

pilaf (Romania) Rice cooked in pilaf style from Turkish influence.

(Turkey) Rice cooked first in fat, along with onions, and then finished with liquid.

pilav Rice dished cooked in Ottoman (Turkish) style. (Balkans)

pil-pil Sauce made in Basque region of Spain from salt cod, olive oil, and garlic. (Iberian Peninsula)

pilze Mushrooms. (Germany)

piman   Chiles. (Japan)

pimenta de cheiro   Small, round chili found in Brazil, with yellow flesh and mild heat. (South America)

pimenta de cheirosa   Small, round green chili found in Brazil. (South America)

pimento malagueta   Malagueta pepper; not actually related to the pepper, this is a pungent seed from Africa that is common in African-influenced areas of South America (especially Brazil). (South America)

pimentón   Chili powder. (Iberian Peninsula)

pimentón agridulce   Medium-hot chili powder. (Iberian Peninsula)

pimentón dulce   Sweet chili powder. (Iberian Peninsula)

pimentón picante   Hot chili powder. (Iberian Peninsula)

pimienta blanca   White pepper. (South America)

pimienta de Jamaica   Allspice. (South America)

pimienta negro   Black pepper. (South America)

pimiento   Black pepper. (Mexico)

pimientos   Chili peppers. (Iberian Peninsula)

pinchitos   Skewered and grilled meats common to the Andalusia region of Spain. (Iberian Peninsula)

pinchos   Skewered and grilled tapas items; also the term used for the skewer itself. (Iberian Peninsula)

pinoli   Pine nut. (Italy)

pique a lo macho   Chopped beef with onions and vegetables. (Bolivia)

pirog   Savory pie. (Russia)

pirozhki   Stuffed yeast dough with savory filling; usually fried or baked. (Russia)

pisella alla fiorentina   Florentine-style spring peas with pancetta. (Italy)

piselli   Peas. (Italy)

pissaladière   Flatbread topped with onions, capers, and anchovies; from the southern Mediterranean region. (France)

pistou   Paste made of basil, garlic, and olive oil; from the southern Mediterranean region. (France)

pita   (Greece) Flatbread baked at very high temperatures, which causes it to puff and have a pocket in the center (also spelled "pitta").
  (Balkans) Name given to phyllo dough in Balkan area.

piyas   Onions. (Indian subcontinent)

pizza   Flat dough topped with tomato sauce and cheese and various other topping and then baked. (Italy)

pizza margarita   Pizza with fresh tomato, basil, and mozzarella cheese. (Italy)

pizzoccheri   Pasta made from buckwheat that has the appearance of a whole-grain pasta product (in that it is brown in color). This is a specialty of the Lombardy area and is traditionally served with potatoes and cabbage and topped with cheese. (Italy)

plăcinte   Savory pies. (Romania)

plancha   Flat iron pan or griddle used for cooking over a flame. (Iberian Peninsula)

plantain   A banana variety that is higher in starch content and thus often used in preparations as a vegetable; also called *plátano* in Spanish. (Caribbean)

plátano   Plantain. (Mexico/South America)

pleeta   Traditional Russian furnace/stove used to both heat the home and cook the food. (Russia)

plie   Plaice; fish in the flounder family caught in the English Channel. (France)

poblano   Often erroneously called *pasilla* in the United States, these are squat, wide chiles that are used fresh in *chili rellenos* (stuffed chiles) and as filling for *enchiladas* (filled tortillas with chili sauce), among other things. These are milder chiles with thin flesh and a deep, dark green color that makes them easy to differentiate from green bell peppers. (Mexico)

poc chuc   Grilled pork marinated with bitter orange, achiote, and spices and typically served topped with onions; from the Yucatán region. (Mexico)

Point, Fernand   Chef with a philosophy of not wavering from using the very best products, handling them the best way, and cooking them to highlight their qualities, not to mask them. He also trained a number of other chefs who have themselves gone on to become highly regarded. (France)

poire   Pear. (France)

poireau   Leek. (France)

poissonnier   Fish cook in the brigade system. (France)

pökelfische   Pickled herring. (Germany)

polenta   (Italy) Coarse ground, dried corn used to make a porridge-like dish common throughout northern Italy.
  (Balkans) Italian cornmeal porridge common in the Balkan region.
  (Argentina) Cornmeal mush that borrows its name from the Italian polenta dish.

polenta burro   Polenta with butter. (Italy)

polenta cunsa   Polenta layered with cheese and mushrooms. (Italy)

polipetti   Small octopus. (Italy)

pollo   Chicken. (Mexico/South America)

pollo encacahuatado   Chicken in peanut sauce; an African-inspired dish found in Veracruz, a region heavily influenced by the Spanish and the slave period of Spain's colonial rule. (Mexico)

pollo motuleño   Chicken marinated and cooked with bitter orange juice, achiote, and fried plantains; from the Yucatán region. (Mexico)

polou   Any of a number of Persian rice dishes that are served with other ingredients. (Persia/Iran)

polpo   Octopus. (Italy)

pomme   Apple. (France)

pomme de terre   Potato. (France)

pomodoro   Tomatoes. (Italy)

ponzu   Sauce made from yuzu juice, soy sauce, mirin (sweet rice wine), rice vinegar, and dashi (seaweed stock). (Japan)

porc   Pork. (France)

porceddu   Spit-roasted piglet cooked over juniper and olive wood; a specialty of Sardinia. (Italy)

porchetta   Small pig roasted in a wood-fired oven and typically stuffed with peppers, garlic, rosemary, and fennel. (Italy)

porc negre   Black pigs prized for their flavorful meat; this variety has been indigenous to the Balearic Islands for thousands of years. (Iberian Peninsula)

porco   Pork. (Iberian Peninsula)

pörkölt   Thick, spiced stew made in similar style as goulash (*gulyas*) but with less liquid. (Hungary)

porridge   Made by cooking oatmeal with milk or water and added seasonings to yield a thick, cooked starch. (British Isles)

posto   Poppy seed. (Indian subcontinent)

potager   Soup cook in the brigade system. (France)

potaje de garbanzos y espinacas   Thick chickpea and spinach soup hailing from the Catalonia region of northeast Spain. (Iberian Peninsula)

poulet   Chicken. (France)

poulet sauté a la normande   Sautéed chicken in the style of Normandy. (France)

pozole   Hearty hominy (calcium oxide–treated corn) and pork stew; commonly found in the Oaxaca and Puebla regions of Mexico. (Mexico)

pozole verde   Version of pozole in which the stew contains tomatillos. (Mexico)

presunto   Dry cured hams from Portugal that are cured with salt garlic and paprika and then smoked. (Iberian Peninsula)

prik   Chili. (Thailand)

prik kii noo   Thai chili. (Thailand)

provatura   Soft buffalo's milk cheese that is shaped in small balls and eaten fresh. (Italy)

prosciutto   Made from salted and aged pork legs, this Italian specialty has gained particular attention in the United States. The pork legs are salted for a period of about 2 weeks and then dry-aged in well-ventilated areas after the exposed cut surface has been sealed with pork fat. The aging process for the fine prosciuttos made in the Parma area and in the San Daniele area of Fruili takes at least a year. (Italy)

provolone   Cows milk cheese with creamy texture; excellent for melting. (Italy)

prune   Plum. (France)

psari   Fish. (Greece)

psarolia   Cured fish found on some of the islands; fish is salted and sundried for preservation. This is used in making some fish keftedes (chopped fish patties). (Greece)

psi hui   Cayenne chili introduced by the Portuguese. (Indian subcontinent)

puchero   (Argentina) Beef, chicken, bacon, sausage, corn, peppers, tomatoes, onions, cabbage, sweet potatoes, and squash casserole; may also include beans. (Uruguay) Beef, vegetables, chicken, bacon, beans, and sausages.

puchero de gallina   Braised chicken, sausage, corn, potatoes, and squash. (Argentina)

puck whan   Water spinach. (Thailand)

pudim flan   Custard with caramel base. (Brazil)

puerco   Pork. (Iberian Peninsula/Mexico/South America)

pukacapas   Spicy cheese pasties; similar to empanadas but these are baked. (Bolivia)

pulao   Rice dish of Persian influence made by coating and cooking the rice in ghee before it is cooked in a broth or other liquid. Pulao is often mixed with nuts and seasoned with spices. (Indian subcontinent)

pulpo   Octopus. (Iberian Peninsula/South America)

pulpo a la gallega   Boiled octopus, sliced and served with olive oil and hot paprika. (Iberian Peninsula)

pumpernickel   Bread made from rye from the Westphalia region of Germany. (Germany)

puntarelle   Chicory. (Italy)

puri   Deep-fried unleavened bread. (Indian subcontinent)

puttanesca   Tomato sauce with black olives, capers, anchovies, and garlic. (Italy)

q

qawrama   Preserved lamb fat. (Arabic-speaking countries)

quaglie   Quail. (Italy)

Quechua   Native Andean people of Bolivia and Peru. (South America)

queijo   Portuguese for "cheese." (Iberian Peninsula)

quenelle   Dumpling; typically formed into three-sided shape using two spoons. (France)

quesadillas   Panfried tortillas that are folded in half—with various fillings inside—before being cooked. (Mexico)

quesillo de Oaxaca   A string cheese from the state of Oaxaca with excellent melting properties and a slight tanginess; these are shaped into small, woven balls from being stretched during processing. (Mexico)

queso   Spanish for "cheese." (Iberian Peninsula/Mexico/South America)

queso Asadero   A soft, melting cheese from northern Mexico. (Mexico)

queso Chihuahua   A tangy, higher fat cheese made in the Chihuahua region; used to make chili con queso, chili rellenos, and other dishes that require a good melting cheese. (Mexico)

queso fresco   Fresh cheese with a crumbly texture and a slightly salty taste; used to make quesadillas, crumble over tacos, and so forth. (Mexico)

quiabo   Okra. (South America)

quiche   Pastry shell with savory custard filling. (France)

quiche Lorraine   Quiche made with bacon. (France)

quingombo   Okra in Spanish-speaking islands, especially Puerto Rico. (Caribbean)

quinua   Quinoa; also called chancas, dalma, trigo inca, and jupa. (South America)

r

rabalo   Sea bass. (Mexico)

raclette   Dish of boiled potatoes with melted raclette cheese. (France)

radicchio   Lettuce with red leaves and a slightly bitter taste; common in northern Italy as one of three species: the round radicchio *variegato* (most common in the United States), the elongated radicchio *trevisano*, and the white-based radicchio *di chioggia*. (Italy)

raffolait   Thickened, caramelized milk. (France)

rafute   Pork stewed with miso, soy sauce, and ginger. (Japan)

råg   Rye. (Scandinavia)

ragoût   Stewed. (France)

rågsiktlimpör   Spiced rye bread. (Sweden)

ragu   Tomato meat sauce. (Italy)

ragu alla Bolognese   Traditional meat sauce of Bologna that is served with fresh pasta from the region (Emilia-Romagna). (Italy)

ragusano   Made in Sicily, this is a used as a table cheese when younger and then grated when it has matured and dried further. It is a sweeter cheese when young that develops a sharpness from aging. (Italy)

raita   Yogurt-based sauce served as a condiment that may contain many types of seasonings, such as cucumber and mint. (Indian subcontinent)

rajma   Kidney beans. (Indian subcontinent)

Ramadan   Month-long fast observed by Muslims; food is avoided during daylight hours, and specific foods are eaten in the evening. (North Africa)

rāmen   Yellow wheat noodle served in broth, with every imaginable ingredient potentially added to this dish. (Japan)

rāmen-ya   Eating establishment that specializes in rāmen. (Japan)

rana pescatrice   Monkfish. (Italy)

rape   Turnip. (Iberian Peninsula)

ras-el-hanout   Spice blend commonly used in Moroccan cooking. (North Africa)

rassol'nik   Soup made with sorrel, brined cucumber, and various other vegetables and topped with chopped kidney. (Russia)

ratatouille   Stewed vegetable recipe from the southern Mediterranean region; made with zucchini, tomatoes, eggplant, onions, peppers, and garlic. (France)

rau muong   Water spinach (not related to spinach but used in a similar manner. (Vietnam)

rau ngo   Cilantro. (Laos)

ravioli   These are made by laying double sheets of pasta, one on top of the other, with fillings placed in between the two sheets. Ravioli are often made using forms that cut the dough with fluted edges, and they are cut into squares to maximize yield. (Italy)

rebani   Opal basil. (Russia)

recados   Spice pastes used in many of the barbeque dishes in the Yucatán region. (Mexico)

recao   An herb commonly used in the Caribbean, particularly in the Spanish-influenced areas; used to make the very common *sofrito*. Cilantro is sometimes used as a substitute, although their flavors are different. (Caribbean)

refogado   Technique of starting a recipe by cooking onions (and sometimes other seasonings) in olive oil until onions are completely tender and golden; this is a very common technique for many of the dishes in Portugal. (Iberian Peninsula/Brazil)

rekesaus   Shrimp sauce commonly served with fish or fish forcemeats. (Norway)

remora   Suckerfish. (Caribbean)

rempah   Spice paste or spice blend. (Malaysia)

rendang   Meat curry made by cooking spiced meat with coconut milk until the liquid from the coconut milk is virtually gone. (Malaysia)

renkon   Lotus root. (Japan)

renkött   Reindeer. (Scandinavia)

res   Beef. (Iberian Peninsula/Mexico)

restaurant   Translates as "restorative"; this was originally a place to eat a simple bite that would provide the fuel needed to get home for the real food. It evolved into what we know it as today: a place to go to enjoy some of the best food, made by professionals. (France)

rete   Caul fat (from pork). (Italy)

rétes   Hungarian name for strudels. (Hungary)

rheinischer sauerbraten   Marinated and braised beef in the style of the Rhineland. The meat is marinated in wine and vinegar and then braised and served with the sour sauce, to which raisins have been added for sweetness. (Germany)

ria   Mustard seed. (Indian subcontinent)

ribbon fresh pastas   Like dried pastas, there are many versions of ribbon-shaped fresh pastas, and once again many of the differences have to do with the thickness of the lengths of pasta that are made. Many of the dried forms of pasta are mimicked with fresh pasta, but fresh egg pasta is not as sturdy as dried eggless pasta, and applications of the pasta should be considered before deciding which shape to use, and whether the pasta should he fresh or dried. (Italy)

ribbon pastas   Ribbon pastas are typically meant to be served tossed with a simple sauce that clings well to the noodles. (Italy)

ricotta   Mostly made in southern Italy, this cheese is made from whey that remains from other cheese making (*ricotto* means "twice cooked"). Most ricotta is used as a fresh cheese, although in the marches it is salted and preserved between aromatic leaves, and it is also made into ricotta *salada* (a salted, preserved ricotta). (Italy)

rideeska   Radish. (Russia)

rigatoni   Ridged and short tubular pasta shapes that are cut square on the ends; these are meant for meat-based sauces and are also used in baked pasta dishes. (Italy)

rindsfleisch   Beef. (Germany)

rindsfleisch tartare   Steak tartare. (Germany)

rindsrouladen   Rolled and stuffed beef cutlet cooked with gravy. (Germany)

ripieno   Stuffed. (Italy)

risi   Pasta shaped like a grain of rice. (Italy)

risi e bisi   Rice and peas. (Italy)

riso   Rice. (Italy)

risotto   Short-grain rice cooked while adding liquid slowly and stirring, which results in a creamy rice dish. (Italy)

risotto alla Milanese   Risotto cooked with saffron to yield creamy, yellow/orange rice. (Italy)

riz et pois colles   Rice and peas; a common preparation in Haiti that reveals the imported influences on the area. (Caribbean)

rocoto   A common chili of the Andes; these are quite large, sometimes as large as a bell pepper, and have a thick flesh similar to bell peppers. These are usually very hot peppers and can be found in different colors, such as yellow, brown, orange, or red. (South America)

rocoto relleno   Green peppers stuffed with beef and vegetables. (Peru)

rödbeta   Beet. (Scandinavia)

roget sill   Smoked herring. (Sweden)

roka   Arugula. (Greece)

romesco   Type of chili pepper used to make romesco sauce in Spain. (Iberian Peninsula)

Roquefort   Strong blue-veined sheep's milk cheese produced in southern France. (France)

rosematta   Red rice grown in southern India. (Indian subcontinent)

rosette de Lyon   Salami-like forcemeat from Lyon in the central eastern region. (France)

roti   (Caribbean) A type of Indian flatbread that has become common in some parts of the Caribbean, particularly in Trinidad
   (Indian subcontinent) Flat, unleavened bread made from atta wheat flour and cooked on a tava (flat griddle-like pan)

rôti   Roast. (France)

rotisserie   Rotating oven or spit oven. (France)

rôtisseur   Grill or rotisserie cook in the brigade system. (France)

rotkohl mit äpfeln   Braised red cabbage and apples. (Germany)

rouladen   Rolled stuffed meat, usually filled with bacon and mustard or sauerkraut. (Germany)

roux   Equal parts by weight clarified butter and flour (though often slightly more flour), cooked to varying degrees and used as a thickener. (France)

rucola   Arugula. (Italy)

rugbrød   Rye bread. (Denmark)

ruh gulab   Rosewater. (Indian subcontinent)

ruibe   Freshly frozen salmon sashimi, sliced paper thin and served still frozen to be eaten with a spicy soy sauce dip. (Japan)

ruisleip   Sour rye bread. (Finland)

ryepa   Turnip. (Russia)

Ryukyuan   Indigenous people of the southern islands of Japan. (Japan)

S

saag   Spinach. (Indian subcontinent)

sabayon   French term for sauce made from egg yolks, sugar, and fortified wine. (North Africa)

sabodet   Strong pork sausage made from the head and skin of the pig and typically served hot. (France)

sachertorte   Chocolate torte. (Germany)

sachet   French term for spices/herbs wrapped in cheesecloth and added to stocks, sauces, or other liquid preparations. (North Africa)

sadri   Long-grain rice from Iran that is very similar to basmati from India (may actually be a basmati variety brought to Iran from India long ago). (Persia/Iran)

Saint-Nectaire   Rich, semihard cow's milk cheese from the south central mountain region. (France)

Saint-Pierre   John Dory. (France)

sajta de pollo   Chicken in hot sauce with chuños and vegetables. (Bolivia)

sake   Salmon. (Japan)

salame di milano   Salami from the Lombardy area consisting of equal parts pork, beef, and pork fat. (Italy)

salame di varza   Traditional salami from the Lombardy area made with coarsely ground lean pork, pork fat, and seasoned with white wine. (Italy)

salame napolentano   Salami flavored with chili peppers made from dried ground peperoncino (chiles), lean pork, and pork fat. This salami has a distinctive red hue from chiles and is quite thin. (Italy)

salata   Salad. (North Africa)

salat oliv'ye   Salad made with potatoes, peas, carrots, onions, pickles, and chicken, bound with mayonnaise. (Russia)

salbitxada   Traditional sauce to accompany grilled calcots made of ground almonds, garlic, bitxos, vinegar, and olive oil. (Iberian Peninsula)

sale   Salt. (Italy)

salmón   Salmon. (Iberian Peninsula)

salpicón de jaiba   Seasoned and shredded crabmeat. (Mexico)

salsa   Fresh mixture of tomatoes, cilantro, chiles, onions, and lime juice. Other ingredients may be used (such as tomatillos in salsa verde), and some of the ingredients are cooked first. (Mexico)

salsa di noci   Walnut sauce. (Italy)

salsa per carpaccio   Sauce to be served with carpaccio (thin sliced beef) made from an emulsification of capers, cornichons, and anchovies with vinegar and oil. (Italy)

salsa romesco   Sauce made from roasted tomatoes with ground almonds, garlic, olive oil, and chili peppers. (Iberian Peninsula)

salsa verde   Green sauce made from parsley, extra virgin olive oil, and good quality vinegar; often has bread, capers, garlic, onion, and anchovy added to it. This sauce hails from the Lombardy region. (Italy)

saltear   Sautéed. (South America)

salteñas   Meat and vegetable pastries; similar to empanadas but these are baked, and the filling is wetter than is typical of empanadas. (Bolivia)

saltimbocca   Thin pieces of veal, chicken, or pork sautéed and topped with prosciutto and sage; typically made with a Marsala sauce. (Italy)

salumi   Meat products. (Italy)

salvia   Sage. (Italy)

sambal   Chili paste. (Malaysia)

sambar   Southern Indian dish traditionally made with toovar dal and vegetables, and seasoned with tamarind. (Indian subcontinent)

sambhar   Dried spice mixture made from mustard, cumin, fenugreek, black peppercorns, coriander, curry leaves, turmeric, chiles, and asafoetida; common in southern India. (Indian subcontinent)

sambol   Condiment made from fresh chiles, onions, and other flavorful ingredients. (Indian subcontinent).

samfaina   Vegetable mixture of onions, eggplant, sweet peppers, and tomato from the Catalonia region of Spain that is very similar to the ratatouille found in the Provençal region across the border in France. (Iberian Peninsula)

samosa Meat- or vegetable-filled fried dough, usually highly seasoned and often served with chutney. (Indian subcontinent)

samovar Tea kettle used to make tea on the stove and keep it hot. (Russia)

Samso Often called the "cheddar of Denmark," this is a ripened cow's milk cheese that improves and sharpens with age. (Denmark)

sancocho (Caribbean) Stew of mixed tubers and meats found on Spanish-influenced islands of the Caribbean and commonly eaten as part of celebrations.
(Venezuela) Fish stew with vegetables.

sandesh Bengali sweet made from paneer that is sweetened and flavored with cardamom and mixed with nuts. (Indian subcontinent)

San Simón Firm cow's milk cheese from Galicia, partially cured and then smoked over birch wood; has a milder flavor with a slight tang and smoky flavor. (Iberian Peninsula)

santan Coconut milk. (Malaysia)

sanuki udon Very thin noodles from the island of Shikoku. (Japan)

sarago Sea bream. (Italy)

sarda or sardina Sardine. (Italy)

sarma Stuffed sauerkraut, typically filled with rice and seasoned ground meat (usually beef, veal, or pork). (Croatia)

sarmale Stuffed vegetables, common in Romanian cuisine. (Romania)

sartén Frying pan. (Iberian Peninsula)

sashimi Raw seafood or, less commonly, meat. (Japan)

sashimi bocho Long, thin knife used to cut fish for sushi. (Japan)

satay Skewered and grilled or griddled meats served as a snack by street vendors. (Malaysia)

satsivi Turkey with walnut sauce. (Russia)

satsuma-imo Sweet potato. (Japan)

sauce mignonette Vinegar infused with coarse black pepper and shallots, used as an accompaniment to oysters on the half shell. (France)

sauce ti-malice Chili-spiced sauce common in Haiti; often used as a condiment. (Caribbean)

saucier Cook responsible for making the sauces in the brigade system. (France)

saucisse de Morteau Smoked plump pork sausage. (France)

saucisson Sausage. (France)

sauerbraten Marinated and braised sour beef. (Germany)

sauerkraut (Poland) Fermented and preserved cabbage.
(Germany) Fermented and soured cabbage.

saumon Salmon. (France)

saure crème Sour cream. (Germany)

sauté To cook quickly in a hot pan with little fat. (France)

sauté de ris de veau Sautéed veal sweetbreads (thymus glands). (France)

scaloppini al limone Sautéed thin slices of meat or poultry in lemon sauce. (Italy)

scaloppini alla Marsala Thin slices of meat or poultry sautéed and cooked with Marsala wine sauce. (Italy)

scamorza Pear-shaped cow's milk curd cheese with mild flavor; these are sometimes smoked to yield a slightly colored rind and light, smoky flavor. (Italy)

scampi Saltwater crustacean resembling small lobsters with claws (not a type of shrimp, which is often incorrectly called *scampi*). (Italy)

schiacciata Tuscan yeast-leavened bread rolled flat and seasoned with salt and olive oil (often rosemary and sage, as well); similar to focaccia of Liguria. (Italy)

schnapps (France) Fruit distillate.
(Germany) Distillate of fruit or grain common in southern Germany; often made from the fruit of the local orchards.

schwäbischer kartoffelsalat Swabian-style potato salad; this salad includes mustard and herbs, indicative of the French influence in the region. (Germany)

Schwarzwälder Kirschtorte Black Forest cake. (Germany)

schwein Pork. (Germany)

schweinshaxen Braised pork knuckles. (Germany)

schwenken To sauté. (Germany)

seksu Berber name for couscous. (North Africa)

senap Mustard. (Sweden)

sepia Cuttlefish. (Iberian Peninsula)

seppia Cuttlefish. (Italy)

serbuk rempah Five-spice powder. (Malaysia)

seria Lemongrass. (Malaysia)

sernik Cheesecake. (Poland)

Serpa Ripened sheep's milk cheese from Portugal. (Iberian Peninsula)

serrano Smaller chiles with the shape and look of smaller jalapeños, but typically with more heat; these are a common ingredient in salsas. (Mexico)

setas Wild mushrooms. (Iberian Peninsula)

sevruga Smallest of the sturgeon; this yields the smallest caviar. (Russia)

shabu-shabu Thinly sliced meat/fish (usually beef) dipped into a hot pot and served with dipping sauces. (Japan)

shaffron False saffron made from marigold flower petals. (Russia)

shamoji Wooden spoon with a wide, flat end used to "cut" and mix the sushi rice as the vinegar solution is added in the hangiri. (Japan)

shao Method of bringing food and a seasoned liquid to a boil, and then lowering heat to gently poach/simmer the food until it is tender and the liquid has thickened. (China)

shao ji Bamboo basket. (China)

shao-xing Chinese rice wine (very different from Japanese rice wine). (China)

shaped pastas Pastas shaped either to imitate something else or to help hold specific sauces or foods. (Italy)

sharbat Sherbet; frozen fruit juices; these have been enjoyed in the Middle East for centuries, with the tradition thought to have originated in the northern mountainous region of present-day Iran. (Persia/Iran)

shashlyk Sis kebab (Russian name for Turkish skewered and grilled meats). (Russia)

Shawwal Month following Ramadan in the Islamic calendar, during which devoted followers fast for an additional six days. (North Africa)

shchi Cabbage soup. (Russia)

shepherd's pie A dish consisting of minced, cooked mutton or lamb and onions covered with mashed potatoes and baked until golden. (England)

sherbet Same meaning as English name (which comes from the Turkish name); believed to have been incorporated into the cuisine from the influence of Persian cuisine on the Ottoman Empire. (Turkey)

sherry Fortified wine made in Jerez, Spain, from local grapes; fortified with brandy after fermentation. (Iberian Peninsula)

shiitake Most common mushroom of Japanese cuisine (also very common in Chinese cuisine); these are used especially in soups and vegetable dishes but often found in other preparations as well. Shiitake have a firm texture and an earthy flavor that is retained in drying. (Japan)

shi ji tau "Lion's head"; large pork meatballs braised with bok choy. (China)

shima-dōfu Dense soybean cake from Okinawa region. (Japan)

shimeji Popular Japanese mushroom with small brown caps that grow in clusters; these have a firm texture, similar to the shiitake, but a very mild aroma (oyster mushrooms are sometimes used as a substitute). (Japan)

shingara Bengali name for vegetable-filled samosa. (Indian subcontinent)

shinko Shredded pickled cabbage. (Japan)

Shinto Ancient Japanese religion; followers believe in the sacredness and cycles of nature. It is widely held that this belief system is one of the major reasons such a premium is placed on seasonal foods and the preservation of foods' natural qualities. (Japan)

shoyo Soy sauce. (Japan)

shu zi bei Roll-cut technique for cutting long vegetables (such as carrots), in which the vegetable is rolled a quarter turn after each cut to yield relatively even-sized cuts. (China)

sil Large stone with a bowl shape; used to pound foods to a paste (such as when making spice pastes) using a batta (a stone pounding tool). (Indian subcontinent)

sill Herring. (Sweden)

sillsallad Herring salad with sour cream dressing. (Sweden)

silpancho Beef prepared schnitzel style. (Bolivia)

silyotka Herring. (Russia)

sis kebabi Skewered and grilled meats, typically lamb or mutton. (Turkey)

skinken Ham from central Germany. (Germany)

skogshare Arctic hare. (Scandinavia)

sloke Type of seaweed used in traditional Celtic cuisine. (Ireland)

smen Aged and spiced clarified butter that is used as a seasoning, especially for couscous. (North Africa)

smetana Sour cream. (Russia)

smørdampete nypoteter Buttered new potatoes. (Norway)

smörgåsbord Elaborate table of cold and hot items that is eaten buffet style and was common to Sweden and other parts of Scandinavia; this is still found on a limited basis at specialty restaurants. (Sweden)

smörgåsgurka Sweet pickled cucumbers. (Sweden)

smørrebrød Butter and bread sandwich served open-faced with various ingredients. (Denmark)

soba Buckwheat (or buckwheat noodles). (Japan)

sobrasada Pork sausage from the Balearic Islands made traditionally from the local black pigs; this sausage is seasoned with chili. (Iberian Peninsula)

sofrito Technique, like the Portuguese refogado, of cooking onions (and often other ingredients such as garlic, tomatoes, and peppers) in olive oil until they are broken down and perhaps beginning to color; this technique is used in many Spanish recipes. (Iberian Peninsula, South America, Caribbean)

sogliola Sole. (Italy)

solionye ogurtsy Brined cucumbers. (Russia)

somen Thin wheat flour noodles. (Japan)

sommu Spicy pickled pork sausage. (Laos)

som thum Green papaya salad seasoned with chiles, lime, and fish sauce. (Thailand)

sooyo sopy Soup with ground meat, served with rice or noodles. (Paraguay)

sopa Soup. (Mexico)

sopa de almejas Clam soup common in the Baja region. (Mexico)

sopa de feijão preto Brazilian black bean soup. (Brazil)

sopa de lima Lime-flavored soup; this may contain a variety of other ingredients and is common in the Yucatán region. (Mexico)

sopaipillas Fried dough dipped in various syrups. (Chile)

sopa seca "Dry soup" common to northern Portugal; made by ladling stock over layers of meats, vegetables, and bread, and baking until the moisture has been absorbed by the ingredients. (Iberian Peninsula)

sopes Thick rounds of masa dough cooked on a comal with various toppings. (Mexico)

soppressa Made from pork shoulder or legs, this is made in much the same way as the coppa, but it is aged longer (because it is larger). This meat is a specialty of the Veneto area. (Italy)

sorbeto Frozen and sweetened mixtures made without dairy. (Italy)

sos plam Plum sauce. (Malaysia)

sos tarim Oyster sauce. (Malaysia)

soup pastas Soup pastas are used in all varieties or soups, from simple light broths to heavier thick soups, with the pasta selected typically from smallest for light broths to somewhat larger for thicker soups. (Italy)

soursop Large tropical fruit with a sweet-and-sour taste and a distinct, almost fermented smell. (Caribbean)

sous chef de cuisine   Deputy kitchen chef who is in charge of the kitchen in the brigade system when the chef de cuisine is not present. (France)

souse   A thick stew commonly made with fish, poultry, pork, or another available protein cooked with onions, cucumbers, peppers, and lime juice. (Caribbean)

souvlakia   Skewered and grilled lamb. (Greece)

spaetzle   "Little sparrows"; name given to tiny dumplings. (Germany)

spaghetti   Smaller ribbon pasta used traditionally with lighter tomato sauces and olive oil–based sauces. (Italy)

spaghetti alla carbonara   Thin ribbon pasta with carbonara sauce (see *carbonara*). (Italy)

spaghetti alla puttanesca   Thin ribbon pasta with puttanesca sauce (see *puttanesca*). (Italy)

spanakopita   Savory pies wrapped in phyllo and typically baked. (Greece)

spargel   Asparagus. (Germany)

spätzle   "Little sparrows"; name given to tiny dumplings of Swabia; name also could have derived from the Italian *spezzato*, which means "pieces cut into strips," an accurate description of the traditional way of making spätzle. (Germany)

specie   Spice. (Italy)

speck   (Italy) Made with pork leg that has been cured and marinated with spices and juniper berries prior to being smoked over burning juniper wood, this specialty is produced in the northern Adige area.
  (Germany) Cured and smoked pork belly (very similar to bacon).

speckknödeln   Bacon dumplings. (Habsburg Empire)

spelding   Wind-dried and cured whiting. (Scotland)

spezie   Spice. (Italy)

spiekekorv   Slightly sour fermented and dried pork sausage similar to a salami. (Sweden)

spinaci   Spinach. (Italy)

sqonn   Gaelic name for dropped-batter breads; now known as scones. (Scotland/Ireland)

steinhäger   Juniper berry–flavored distillate from Steinhägen; similar to gin in the United States. (Germany)

sterlet   Rare golden-colored sturgeon caviar. (Russia)

Stilton   Blue-veined cow's milk cheese prized for its creamy texture and rich flavor. (England)

stoccafisso   Dried cod. (Italy)

stockfische   Salt cod. (Germany)

stokkfisk   Air-dried cod; also called tørrfisk (differs from klippfisk in not being salted). (Norway)

stroganoff   Meat stew that is thickened and flavored with sour cream. (Finland)

strudel   (Italy) Filled pastry made from paper-thin sheets of dough that are filled with various fillings before being baked; this technique is the result of Austrian influences in northeastern Italy.
  (Germany) Thin dough wrapped around various fillings and baked in loaf form.

strutto   Rendered pork fat. (Italy)

stuffed pastas   Stuffed fresh pastas are common in a number of regions of Italy and vary less with regard to how they will hold sauces than with what they are filled or their desired size and appearance. (Italy)

su   Rice vinegar. (Japan)

suan la rou si tang   Hot and sour soup. (China)

sucs   Fish stews cooked in paella pans with a sauce made from ground almonds and garlic; found in the Valencia region of Spain. (Iberian Peninsula)

sultanas   Golden raisins. (Italy)

su-meshi   Vinegared rice. (Japan)

sumibi-yaki   Mochi rice balls mixed with potato and sesame and grilled over coals. (Japan)

sunomono   Foods pickled in vinegar. (Japan)

suppe   Soup. (Germany)

surströmming   Soured Baltic herring; this spread is made by fermenting the Baltic herring until it has become quite soft and pungent. It is considered a delicacy in Sweden. (Sweden)

sushi   Short-grain rice with sweetened (or sometimes not sweetened) and vinegared rice with various toppings. (Japan)

sushi-ya   Eating establishment that specializes in sushi. (Japan)

sveciaost   Semifirm cow's milk cheese with irregular holes, a creamy texture, and a light yellow color. (Sweden)

svyokla   Beets. (Russia)

syltede rødbeder   Pickled beets. (Denmarl)

syomga   Atlantic salmon. (Russia)

t

ta'amia   Spiced fava bean or chickpea fritters (also called falafel). (Arabic-speaking countries)

tabaka   Roasted, butterflied, and pressed chicken from Georgia. (Russia)

tabbouleh   Salad of chopped herbs and bulgur, seasoned with lemon juice and olive oil. (Arabic-speaking countries)

tabikha   Beef and onion stew common among Algerian Jews. (North Africa)

tabil   Spice blend commonly used in Tunisian cooking. (North Africa)

tacu tacu   Dish of rice and beans wrapped around various fillings; this national style was said to have been invented by an African slave in Peru. This dish is usually made with leftover cooked beans and rice. (Peru)

tagine   Both the name of a type of cooked food and the cooking vessel used to make the food. A tagine is an earthenware dish with a conical shape and a lid making up approximately the top third of the dish, and a flat bottom section that is placed into an oven to cook the contents in a stew-like manner to yield tender dishes also called tagines. (North Africa)

tagliatelle   Fresh ribbon pasta traditionally made in the Emilia-Romagna region and served with Bolognese sauce. (Italy)

tahini   (Arabic-speaking countries/Greece) Sesame seed paste.
  (Balkans) Sesame seed purée.

tai   Snapper or bream. (Japan)

tai meshi   Rice with sea bream. (Japan)

Taino One of the indigenous tribes of the Caribbean prior to the arrival of the Europeans; part of the Arawak people. (Caribbean)

tako-shabu Hotpot (seasoned broth kept simmering) served with thinly sliced octopus. (Japan)

takrai Lemongrass. (Thailand)

tamago-yaki Omelet. (Japan)

tamale (Mexico) Corn and lard dough wrapped in a corn husk (sometimes wrapped in leaves or other ingredients) and stuffed with various fillings before being steamed.

(Caribbean) Corn husk–wrapped corn dough filled with various ingredients and then steamed; from indigenous Native American cuisine.

(South America) Steamed cornmeal dough with various fillings.

tâmaras Dates. (Iberian Peninsula)

tamarillo Fruit shaped like an egg and sometimes called a tree tomato. (South America)

tamarindo Spanish name for tamarind. (Caribbean)

tandoor Clay oven used in northern India and Pakistan to cook naan and other foods. (Indian subcontinent)

tandoori masala Common spice blend of Punjab made of cumin, coriander, cloves, turmeric, cinnamon, cayenne, mace, and ginger, and usually colored with red food coloring. (Indian subcontinent)

tang cu li ji Sweet and sour pork. (China)

tannour Conical-shaped outdoor clay oven used to bake breads. (North Africa)

tapas Small plates of food served in wine bars and now a common aspect of the cuisine throughout the Iberian Peninsula. (Iberian Peninsula)

tapenade Paste made of olives, capers, garlic, and olive oil; from the southern Mediterranean region. (France)

tara Pacific cod. (Japan)

tarantello Fish "sausage" made from cured and spiced tuna belly packed into casing. (Italy)

taratoor Sauce made from tahini seasoned with lemon juice and garlic. (Arabic-speaking countries)

tarhonya "Egg barley" made from forming dough with flour and eggs and rubbing between hands to produce little balls of pasta, which are then dried and stored to be used to cook and accompany dishes. This method is an ancient Magyar tradition that has been performed for centuries, much like the tradition of making couscous in North Africa. (Hungary)

tarka Term that describes the toasting of spices in ghee or oil before starting a dish, or to be added to a dish after it is done (also called *baghar*). (Indian subcontinent)

tartufi Truffles. (Italy)

tava Flat griddle-like pan used to cook many of the flatbreads common throughout the subcontinent. (Indian subcontinent).

telemea Sheep's milk cheese that is brine-cured much like feta. This cheese is used mostly in salads, or it is eaten along with other ingredients, such as olives, or by itself as a snack. (Romania)

teliatina po-Orlovski Veal Prince Orlov; a French-influenced preparation of mushroom purée layered between veal loin slices, topped with a béchamel sauce, and then browned under the broiler. (Russia)

tempura Deep-fried foods in light batter. (Japan)

teppanyaki Foods cooked on a hot plate in front of customers. (Japan)

Tequila The name of both a town and the distilled beverage that is made in the surrounding area of Jalisco in the central Pacific Coast region. The beverage is made from distillation of fermented blue agave juice. (Mexico)

teriyaki Foods cooked with soy sauce, mirin, and sugar; usually grilled. (Japan)

terrine Rectangular-shaped mold used to pack and serve cold preparations. (France)

terrine de ris de veau aux champignon Veal terrine with sweetbreads and mushrooms. (France)

tésztáks Dumplings. (Hungary)

thassos throumba Salt-cured black olive. (Greece)

tikka Literally translates to "small pieces"; used to describe foods that are cut up, marinated, skewered, and grilled or baked in a tandoori. (Indian subcontinent).

tikka masala Marinated and skewered pieces of meat made in this fashion have come to refer to foods coated with a typical spice mix that includes garam masala, cumin, and coriander and often is served with yogurt and tomato sauce. (Indian subcontinent)

tikooschii Currants. (Russia)

til Sesame. (Indian subcontinent)

tindora Small squash that resembles a cucumber. (Indian subcontinent)

tippy tam-bo Tuber with brown hair-like covered skin and flesh, similar to a water chestnut or Jerusalem artichoke; used in soups and stews. The leaves of the plant are used to wrap foods like tamales. (Caribbean)

tiradito A relative of ceviche, this preparation is also made with raw fish, but the fish is cut into thin strips and flattened—and not mixed with onions—and is often served topped with condiments and other seasonings (whereas ceviche is mixed with onions, lime juice, and chiles). (Peru)

tiramisu Espresso-soaked sponge cake (ladyfingers) layered with sweetened mascarpone cream and topped with shaved chocolate or powdered cocoa; literally, "pick me up." (Italy)

titvash Home-cured pickles. (Armenia)

tkemali Type of tart plum used in Georgian cuisine, especially for making sauces. (Russia)

tlaquetzalli Chocolate drink made by the Aztecs using toasted cocoa beans. (Mexico)

tofu Made from coagulated soya bean "milk," which is made from boiling and crushing soya beans. There are various types of tofu, with differences mostly in texture and quality. (Japan)

tōgarashi Type of chili used and prized in Japan. (Japan)

toi Garlic. (Vietnam)

tokány Another stew variant that resembles goulash (*gulyas*), but the meats used in this preparation are cut into strips, and fewer onions and seasonings are used. (Hungary)

töltött káposzta   Stuffed cabbage filled with seasoned ground pork and rice. (Hungary)

tomates   Tomatoes. (Iberian Peninsula/Mexico/South America)

tomàtigues de ramellet   Tomatoes from the Balearic Islands. (Iberian Peninsula)

tomatillo   Husk-covered fruit used extensively in Mexican cuisine, particularly in making sauces. (Mexico)

tomini   A goat's milk cheese that is preserved in pepper; a specialty of the Piedmont region. (Italy)

tom kha gai   Chicken soup with coconut milk, galangal, lemongrass, fish sauce, and vegetables in flavorful broth. (Thailand)

tomme de Savoie   Mild, excellent melting cow's milk cheese from the Savoy region. (France)

tōmorokoshi   Corn. (Japan)

tonkatsu   Breaded and deep-fried pork cutlets (usually pork tenderloin). (Japan)

tonkotsu rāmen   Ramen with rich pork broth; common in Kyūshū. (Japan)

tonno   Tuna. (Italy)

toor   Grey-colored whole lentil that hides a yellow color beneath its outer skin. (Indian subcontinent)

toor dal   Split and skinned toor lentils; these are yellow in color and have a nutty flavor. They can be ground into flour and used as a thickener in dishes. (Indian subcontinent)

topinambur   Sunchoke or Jerusalem artichoke. (South America)

töpfe   Pot. (Germany)

tørrfisk   Air-dried cod; also called stokkfisk. (Norway)

torshi limu   Pickled limes. (Persia/Iran)

torshis   Pickled vegetables. (Persia/Iran)

torsk   Cod. (Norway)

tortáks   Tortes. (Hungary)

torta pasqualina   Easter pie made with layered dough filled with sliced artichokes, swiss chard, cheese, and eggs. (Italy)

tortas   Sandwiches made from hard rolls and various fillings, similar to sandwiches in the United States but the fillings are more likely shredded pork or beef than cold cuts. (Mexico)

tortelli de zucca   Pasta filled with zucca squash (similar to pumpkin) found in Piedmont region. (Italy)

tortellini   Small, triangular-shaped stuffed pasta that has its thin edges folded back and sealed to yield a shape resembling a hat and typically filled with cheese (these are also made dried). (Italy)

tortes   Sweet, moist cakes and tarts. (Germany)

tortilla   Corn masa dough (traditionally, although it is also made with wheat dough) pressed into thin rounds and cooked on a comal. (Mexico)

tortilla de harina   Flatbread made in a manner similar to corn masa tortillas but with a wheat dough. (Mexico)

tortilla Española   Savory potato and egg cake commonly served as a tapa in Spain. (Iberian Peninsula)

tortillas de maíz   Corn pancakes. (Ecuador)

tostadas   Corn tortillas fried and topped or filled with various ingredients. (Mexico)

trenette   Thin ribbon pasta, similar to linguini from the Liguria region; this is the traditional pasta to serve with Liguria pesto sauce. (Italy)

trigo   Wheat. (Iberian Peninsula/Mexico/South America)

trota   Trout. (Italy)

truchas   Truffles. (Iberian Peninsula)

truffle   Name of tuber-shaped aromatic fungus prized in France; also called *truffle* in the United States. (France)

truite   Trout. (France)

tsitseli   Chiles. (Russia)

tsitsila   Chicken. (Russia)

tubetti   Short, tube-shaped pasta used in thicker soups such as thick minestrones. (Italy)

tubular pastas   Tubular pastas have the advantage of holding sauces (and potentially other foods) inside a tube; these grew in popularity after the invention of cast dies that were used to extract this dried form of eggless pasta. (Italy)

tucupi   Sauce made from extracted cassava juice; used in the northern part of Brazil. (Brazil)

Tupi   Native culture of Brazil that the Portuguese first encountered. (South America)

tutu á mineira   Bean, bacon, and manioc sauce served with cabbage. (Brazil)

tvorog   Fresh cheese similar to cottage cheese. (Russia)

Tybo   Similar to the Samso cheese that it is modeled after, this variety is often flavored with caraway seeds. (Denmark)

tzatziki   Yogurt cucumber sauce seasoned with garlic. (Greece)

U

überkrusten   To brown the top surface of a dish using a broiler or salamander (often called *gratin* in the United States). (Germany)

uchiwa   Fan used to cool the rice and assist in evaporation of vinegar while mixing in the hangiri. (Japan)

udon   Medium-thickness wheat flour noodles. (Japan)

ukha   Fish soup, typically made with freshwater fish. (Russia)

unagi   Freshwater eel that is roasted and glazed for use in a variety of dishes. (Japan)

uni   Sea urchin. (Japan)

unjanaba   Water spinach. (Japan)

unterheben   To fold in an ingredient to another base. (Germany)

uova   Eggs. (Italy)

urad   Whole small black bean with a creamy white interior; the skins provide a strong, earthy flavor. (Indian subcontinent)

urad dal   Split and skinned (or sometimes sold with the dark skin still on to retain its strong flavor) creamy white bean; without skin, these are mildly flavored. (Indian subcontinent)

uramaki   Inside-out sushi roll, in which the nori is encased by rice instead of the other way around. (Japan)

uruchi mai   Non-glutinous short-grain rice variety that is most commonly used in Japanese cuisine. (Japan)

utskho suneli   Spice used in Georgian cuisine that is similar to fenugreek. (Russia)

uvas   Grapes. (Italy/Iberian Peninsula/Mexico/South America)

V

vainilla   Vanilla. (Mexico)

val dal   Split and skinned lablab bean. (Indian subcontinent)

vareniki   Ukrainian stuffed noodles filled with various mixtures that include sauerkraut, cheese, and potatoes, or sweet fillings such as cherries. Savory versions are typically served with sour cream, and sweet versions are served with confectioners' sugar or crème fraîche. (Russia)

Västerbottenost   Highly prized hard aged cow's milk cheese from Västerbotten with a granular texture; aged for a minimum of one year. (Sweden)

vatapá   Seafood served with manioc sauce (or sometimes bread), nuts, dried shrimp, coconut, and dendé oil. (Brazil)

venado   Venison (deer meat). (Mexico)

ventricina   Pork salami from the Puglia region flavored with peperoncino, fennel, and orange zest. (Italy)

verdure   vegetables. (Italy)

verjuice   Juice of unripened grapes. (Middle East)

vetchina   Smoked pork, ham, or other cut. (Russia)

vinagre   Vinegar; the process of making this was introduced to South America by the Spanish. (South America)

vincigrassi   Liguria baked pasta with prosciutto, mushrooms, and sweetbreads. (Italy)

vindaloo masala   This type of spice mixture is a wet blend and is heavily influenced by the Portuguese, who once colonized the area of Goa in southwestern India. This paste would typically contain vinegar, garlic, chiles, and various additional spices. (Indian subcontinent)

vinegret   Salad of potatoes, pickled cucumbers, beets, carrots, and onions, dressed with an oil and vinegar dressing. (Russia)

vitello   Veal. (Italy)

vitellone   Beef slaughtered between 14 and 16 months of age. (Italy)

vongola   Clam. (Italy)

W

wakame   Variety of seaweed used commonly in soups and as a salad. (Japan)

wammerl   Pickled pork belly. (Germany)

wanko soba   Soba noodles served cold. (Japan)

warka (or ourka)   Thin sheets of dough created by slapping soft dough onto a greased pan made especially for this preparation. (North Africa)

wasabi   Pungent root that is ground and served with sushi; fresh wasabi is very rare and expensive in both the United States and Japan. (Japan)

washoku   Translates as "harmony of food," a philosophy and way of cooking in Japan that recognized the relationship between nourishment and all aspects of food in attaining it. (Japan)

Welsh rarebit   A dish of cheese sauce served over or with toast; also called Welsh rabbit. (Wales)

wienerbrød   (Denmark) Vienna bread; the name given to Danish pastries and the method of layering butter between sheets of dough. This food came to Denmark from Viennese pastry chefs/bakers who worked in the country during a bakers' strike in the 1800s. This product was much loved, and Danish bakers are said to have improved on the Viennese techniques over the years.

(Germany) Literal translation is Vienna bread, but these are known as Danish pastries in the United States.

Wiener schnitzel   Breaded and panfried veal cutlet. (Germany)

wildbret   Venison. (Germany)

wor tip   Pot stickers in the style of Shanghai (said to be their place of origin). (China)

wurst   Sausage. (Germany)

X

xiaolongbao   Steamed dumpling from the southern region, filled with a gelatinous seasoned pork mixture that becomes soup-like when cooked, resulting in a steamed bun with liquid filling. (China)

xi dau   Soy sauce. (Vietnam)

y

yagada   Berry. (Russia)

yakitori   Skewered chicken that is grilled and often served in specialty shops dedicated to grilled foods. (Japan)

yakni   Mutton. (Indian subcontinent)

yang   Forces of light; associated with the exterior of the body, the gallbladder, stomach, intestines, and bladder. Symptoms of problems within these areas are thought to be caused by an excess of yang, and relief may be sought by including more yin foods in one's diet. Also a term used to describe a part of Chinese philosophy that separates foods based on their inherent effect on the human body; effects are described either as hot and warming, with associations with energy and fire, or as cold and cooling, with associations with calming and ice. (China)

yin   Forces of dark; associated with the heart, liver, spleen, kidneys, and lungs. Symptoms of problems within these areas are thought to be caused by an excess of yin, and relief may be sought through an increase in yang foods. (China)

Yorkshire pudding   Savory pudding made from a batter and cooked in the drippings of a roast beef, for which it is the traditional accompaniment. (England)

yuba   Dried soya bean skin made from the film that forms on the surface of soya milk during tofu production. (Japan)

yuca   Another name for manioc or cassava, a type of tuber. (South America)

Z

zaalouk   Moroccan eggplant and tomato purée. (North Africa)

za'atar   Spice blend commonly eaten with Arab bread and olive oil; made from sumac, sesame seeds, oregano, and thyme. (Arabic-speaking countries)

zabaglione   Rich dessert sauce made from whipping egg yolks, sugar, and Marsala wine together over a double boiler until it gets thick and frothy. (Italy)

zacuscă   Spreads made from eggplant, roasted peppers, and spices; served with bread (sometimes made with beans instead of eggplant, and may include other ingredients such as tomato and onion). (Romania)

zakuski   Small bites; appetizers set out to be eaten prior to the beginning of a meal. (Russia)

zalivnoe   Jellied meats, poultry, or fish. (Russia)

zanahorias   Carrots. (Mexico)

zapallo   Large squash with green skin and orange-colored flesh that is common in northern South America. (South America)

zarzuela de marisco   Fisherman's stew made from local shellfish cooked in a flavorful tomato and pepper broth; this dish, from the Catalonia region of Spain, borrows its name from a type of opera. (Iberian Peninsula)

zayats   Hare. (Russia)

zhao li   Wire mesh strainer with a bamboo handle. (China)

zharkoe   Stew made from slow-simmered roasted meats with potatoes and other vegetables. (Russia)

zheng   Steaming. (China)

zheng long   Steamer. (China)

zhug   Spiced relish used for seasoning; made with garlic, cumin, fenugreek, chiles, and coriander. (Israel)

zhu shua   Wok brush made of bamboo bristles. (China)

zitun   Olive. (North Africa)

zoupes   Wrinkled, black, salt-cured olives found on the Dodecanese Islands. (Greece)

zucca   Gourd squash. (Italy)

zupa   Soup. (Poland)

zuppa di pane   Bread soup flavored with meat broth and garlic, and often topped with cheese. (Italy)

zwiebels   Onions. (Germany)

RECIPE INDEX

SUBJECT INDEX